Nien Cheng

KT-161-883

Nien Cheng was born in Peking in 1915. After studying at the London School of Economics in 1935-8, she married a Chinese diplomat, and from 1941 to 1948 they lived in Canberra, Australia. Following the Communist Revolution her husband became general manager of Shell in Shanghai until his death of cancer in 1957. She herself then became Shell's Adviser to Management from 1957 to 1966. Nien Cheng left China in 1980. She lives in Washington D.C.

Further reviews of *Life and Death in Shanghai*

'Brilliant; not only the most intelligent and unsparing memoir to date of the Chinese Revolution, but also the most daring and complex revelation of Chinese character'
Roxane Witke

'Nien Cheng's moving first-hand account of the nightmare of China's Cultural Revolution depicts the extremes of human nature. At one pole stands her own courageous determination not only to survive, but to do so with her integrity uncompromised . . . When eventually released following the Chou-En-lai-Nixon detente, to her jailors' astonishment she refused to leave prison unless they gave her an apology . . . Nobody reading this book can fail to wonder if they would have a quarter of the author's courage.'
BEN WHITAKER, *Sunday Times*

'Excellent . . . her book is a record of fighting back, of maintaining her dignity, and of refusing to capitulate . . . the best [memoir] I have read. . . . Mrs Cheng's book is so valuable. It is much more than a memoir. It is the history of the Cultural Revolution, charting the rise and fall of the Red Guards, the senility and death of Mao, the power struggle of the Gang of Four.'
PAUL THEROUX, *Literary Review*

'The most powerful account yet of the Cultural Revolution . . . Cheng's book, describing life ruled by the vacuous quotations of the Little Red book and Marxist fundamentalism, will be the classic of the era. She writes clearly and well, and her account echoes Kafka and Solzhenitsyn.'
EWEN MACASKILL, *Scotsman*

'From the lower depths of the Cultural Revolution comes a song of defiance, sanity and courage behind bars.'
NIGEL WADE, *Daily Telegraph*

Further reviews overleaf

'Her life shows that one person can make a difference. Mrs Cheng stood up against Mao Tse-tung's battalions, and she won. Nothing can reveal to us how this one woman found the courage to act on the knowledge that how a person lives is more important than for how long, but one can rejoice that the principle remains true.'

BARBARA AMIEL, *The Times*

'Being innocent, Mrs Cheng refused to confess. On a human level, the greatest interest of her memoir lies in the account of her resistance to psychological and physical pressures that would have broken most people . . . *Life and Death in Shanghai* is an absorbing story of resourcefulness and courage . . . it also provides fascinating insights into thought reform in Mao's China.'   J. M. COETZEE, *New York Times Book Review*

'At the heart of this book is not the darkness of this cell, but the light of Nien Cheng's mind. And it is a place of breathtaking clarity and conviction . . . Far from depressing, it is almost exhilarating to witness her mind do battle.'   CHRISTOPHER LEHMANN-HAUPT, *New York Times*

'Shanghai's recent past comes violently to life in one woman's excellently written account of her arrest and subsequent surveillance during the Cultural Revolution . . . Nien Cheng's progress through prison to eventual rehabilitation makes absorbing reading as it chronicles the behaviour of the Shanghai bureaucracy, wriggling to escape responsibility for her unjust fate and that of thousands more.'

COLINA MCDOUGALL, *Financial Times*

'Nien Cheng is a survivor of the worst excesses of China's Cultural Revolution, and has written a remarkable account of her ordeals. In doing so she has also produced a totally fascinating history of revolutionary politics during those terrifying years which began with the Red Guards' rise to power in 1966 . . . She writes extremely well throughout the book, but never more impressively than during her descriptions of the many disciplines, mental and physical, that allowed her to keep her sanity and a glimmer of hope alive through those long years of solitary confinement . . . The story of Nien's life in Shanghai during the turbulent years following her release from detention is as engrossing and full of enlightening detail as the rest of her account . . . One quarter of the world's population lives in China, and Nien Cheng's book provides an all too rare opportunity to understand more about their recent past and their place in the world today. It is a magnificent achievement and deserves a wide readership.'   ALANNAH HOPKIN, *Irish Times*

NIEN CHENG

Life and Death in Shanghai

Flamingo
An Imprint of HarperCollinsPublishers

Flamingo
An Imprint of HarperCollins*Publishers*
77–85 Fulham Palace Road,
Hammersmith, London W6 8JB

Published by Flamingo 1995
9 8 7 6 5 4

Previously published in paperback by Grafton 1987
Reprinted 9 times

First published in Great Britain by
Grafton 1986

Copyright © Nien Cheng 1986

The Author asserts the moral right to
be identified as the author of this work

Author photograph by Tom Victor

ISBN 0 00 654861 X

Set in Baskerville

Printed and bound in Great Britain by
Caledonian International Book Manufacturing Ltd, Glasgow,G64

To Meiping

Contents

PART I

The Wind of Revolution

CHAPTER 1

Witch-hunt

THE PAST IS FOREVER with me and I remember it all. I now move back in time and space to a hot summer's night in July 1966, to the study of my old home in Shanghai. My daughter was asleep in her bedroom, the servants had gone to their quarters, and I was alone in my study. I hear again the slow whirling of the ceiling fan overhead; I see the white carnations drooping in the heat in the white Chien Lung vase on my desk. In front of my eyes were the bookshelves lining the walls filled with English and Chinese titles. The shaded reading lamp left half the room in shadows, but the gleam of silk brocade of the red cushions on the white sofa stood out vividly.

An English friend, a frequent visitor to my home in Shanghai, once called it 'an oasis of comfort and elegance in the midst of the city's drabness'. Indeed, my house was not a mansion, and by western standards, it was modest. But I had spent time and thought to make it a home and a haven for my daughter and myself so that we could continue to enjoy good taste while the rest of the city was being taken over by proletarian realism.

Not many private people in Shanghai lived as we did, seventeen years after the Communist Party took over China. In the city of ten million, perhaps only a dozen or so families managed to preserve their old lifestyle: maintaining their original homes and employing a staff of servants. The Party did not decree how the people should live. In fact, in 1949, when the Communist Army entered Shanghai, we were forbidden to discharge our domestic staff to aggravate the unemployment problem. But the political campaigns that periodically convulsed the country rendered many formerly wealthy people poor. When they became victims, they were forced to pay large fines or had their income drastically reduced. And many industrialists were relocated inland with their families when their factories were removed from Shanghai. I did not voluntarily change my way of life not only because I had the means to maintain my standard of living but also because the Shanghai Municipal Government treated me with courtesy and consideration through its United Front Organization. However, my daughter and I lived quietly with circumspection. Believing the

Communist Revolution a historical inevitability for China, we were prepared to go along with it.

The reason I am so often carried back to those few hours before midnight on 3 July 1966 is not only because I look back upon my old life with my daughter with nostalgia but mainly because they were the last few hours of normal life I was to enjoy for many years. The heat lay like a heavy weight on the city even at night. No breeze came through the open windows. My face and arms were damp with perspiration and my blouse was clammy on my back as I bent over the newspapers spread on my desk reading the articles of vehement denunciation that always preceded action at the beginning of a political movement. The propaganda effort was supposed to create a suitable atmosphere of tension and to mobilize the public. Often careful reading of those articles, written by activists selected by Party officials, yielded hints as to the purpose of the movement and its possible victims. Because I had never been involved in a political movement before, I had no premonition of impending personal disaster. But as was always the case, the violent language used in the propaganda articles made me uneasy.

My servant Lao Chao had left a thermos of iced tea for me on a tray on the coffee table. As I drank the refreshing tea, my eyes strayed to a photograph of my late husband. Nearly nine years had passed since he died but the void his death left in my heart remained. I always felt abandoned and alone whenever I was uneasy about the political situation, as I felt the need for his support.

I had met my husband when he was working for his Ph D degree in London in 1935. After we were married and returned to Chungking, China's wartime capital, in 1939, he became a diplomatic officer of the Kuomintang Government. In 1949, when the Communist Army entered Shanghai, he was director of the Shanghai office of the Ministry of Foreign Affairs of the Kuomintang Government. When the Communist representative, Chang Han-fu, took over his office, Chang invited him to remain with the new government during the transitional period as foreign affairs adviser to the newly appointed Mayor of Shanghai, Marshal Chen Yi. In the following year, he was allowed to leave the People's Government and accept the offer from Shell International Petroleum Company to become the general manager of its Shanghai office. Shell was one of the few British firms of international standing – such as the Imperial Chemical Industries, Hong Kong Shanghai Banking Corporation and Jardines – that tried to maintain an office in Shanghai. Because Shell was the only major oil company in the world wishing to remain in mainland China, the Party officials who favoured trade with the West treated the company and ourselves with courtesy.

In 1957, my husband died of cancer. A British general manager was appointed to succeed him. I was asked by Shell to become his assistant with the title of adviser to management. I worked in that capacity until 1966.

Successive British general managers depended on me to steer the company clear of the many pitfalls that often surrounded a capitalist enterprise maintaining an office in Maoist China. It was up to me to find ways to resolve the problems we had to face without either sacrificing the dignity of Shell or causing the Chinese officials to lose face. My job was to manage the staff, act as liaison between the general manager and the Shell Labour Union, analysing the union demands and working out compromises. I drafted the more important correspondence the company had with the Chinese government agencies which had to be in the Chinese language. Whenever the general manager went on home leave or to Peking for talks with Chinese government corporations, I acted as general manager. I thought myself fortunate to have a job I could do well and enjoyed the distinction of being the only woman in Shanghai occupying a senior position in a company of world renown.

In the spring of 1966, Shell closed its Shanghai office after negotiating with a Chinese government agency which signed an 'Assets Against Liability Agreement' with the company. We handed over our assets in China and the Chinese government agency took over our staff with the commitment to give them employment and provide retirement pensions. As a member of management, I was not included in the agreement; its scope was limited to our staff who belonged to the Shell Labour Union, a branch of the Shanghai Labour Union, which is a government organization for the control of industrial and office workers.

When the agreement was signed, my daughter, a young actress of the Shanghai Film Studio, was performing with her unit in North China. I thought I would make a trip to Hong Kong when she came back. But while I was waiting for her return, the Cultural Revolution was launched. My daughter's group was hastily summoned back to Shanghai by the Film Studio to enable its members to take part in the Cultural Revolution. Since I knew that during a political movement government officials were reluctant to make decisions and that work in government departments generally slowed down, if not came to a complete standstill, I decided not to apply for a travel permit to Hong

Kong and risk a refusal. A refusal would go into the personal dossier
which the police kept on everyone. It might make future application
difficult. So I remained in Shanghai, believing the Cultural Revolution
would last no longer than a year, the usual length of time for a political
campaign.

The tea cooled me somewhat. I got up to go into my bedroom next
door, had a shower and lay down on my bed. In spite of the heat, I
dropped off to sleep. The next thing I knew was that Chen Mah, my
maid, was gently pushing me to wake me up.

I looked at the clock on my bedside table. It was only half past six,
but sunlight was already on the awning outside the windows and the
temperature in the room was rising.

'Chi and another man from your old office have come to see you,'
Chen Mah said.

'What do they want?' I asked her drowsily.

'They didn't say. But they behaved in a very unusual manner. They
marched straight into the living room and sat down on the sofa instead
of waiting in the hall as they used to do before the office closed,' Chen
Mah said.

'Who is the other man?' I asked her as I headed for the bathroom.
Chi, I knew, was the Vice-Chairman of our office branch of the
Shanghai Labour Union. I had often conducted negotiations with him
as it was part of my job. He had seemed a nice man: reasonable and
conciliatory.

'I don't know his name. He hasn't been here before. I think he may
be one of the guards,' Chen Mah said. 'He's tall and thin.'

From Chen Mah's description, I thought the man was one of the
activists of the Shell Union. We had no Party members. From the way
the few activists in the Union behaved, I knew they were encouraged to
act as watchdogs in our office for the Shanghai Labour Union. Since I
had no direct contact with the activists who were mostly guards or
cleaners, I learned of their activities mainly from the department
heads.

There was a knock on the door. Lao Chao, my manservant, handed
Chen Mah a tray and said through the half-open door, 'They say the
mistress must hurry.'

'All right, Lao Chao,' I said. 'Tell them I'll be down presently. Give
them a cold drink and some cigarettes.'

I did not hurry. I wanted time to think and be ready to cope with
whatever was coming. The visit of these two men at this early hour of
the morning was unusual. However, in China, whenever one had to

attend a meeting to hear a lecture or political indoctrination, one was seldom told in advance. The officials assumed that everybody should drop everything whenever called upon to do so. I wondered whether these two men had come to ask me to join one of their political indoctrination lectures. I knew the Shanghai Labour Union was organizing classes for the ex-staff of Shell so that they could be prepared for their assignment to work with lower pay in government organizations.

While I ate toast and drank my tea, I reviewed the events leading to the closure of the office of Shell and re-examined my own behaviour throughout the negotiations between the company and the Chinese government agency. Although I had accompanied the general manager to all the sessions, I had not taken part in any of the discussions. It was my job only to observe and advise the general manager afterwards when we returned to our office. I decided that if I were asked questions concerning Shell I could always procrastinate by offering to write to London for information.

I put on a white cotton shirt, a pair of grey slacks and black sandals, the clothes Chinese women wore in public places to avoid being conspicuous. When I walked downstairs I thought those who sent the men to call on me so early in the morning probably hoped to disconcert me. I walked slowly, deliberately creating the impression of composure.

When I entered the living room, I saw that both men were sprawled on the sofa with a glass of orange squash untouched on the table in front of each of them. When he saw me, Chi stood up from force of habit but when he saw that the activist remained seated, he went red in the face with embarrassment and hastily sat down again. It was a calculated gesture of discourtesy on the part of the other man to remain seated when I entered the room. In 1949, not long after the Communist Army entered Shanghai, the new policeman in charge of the area in which I lived had made the first of his periodical unannounced visits to our house. He brushed past Lao Chao at the front door, marched straight into the living room where I was and spat on the carpet. That was the first time I saw a declaration of power made in a gesture of rudeness. Since then, I had come to realize that the junior officers of the Party often used the exaggerated gesture of rudeness to cover up their feeling of inferiority.

I ignored Chi's confusion and the other man's rudeness, sat down on an upright chair and calmly asked them, 'Why have you come to see me so early in the morning?'

'We have come to fetch you to a meeting,' Chi said.

'You have been so slow that we will probably be late,' the other man added and stood up.

'What's the meeting about?' I asked. 'Who has organized it? Who has sent you to ask me to participate?'

'There's no need to ask so many questions. We would not be here if we did not have authority. All the former members of Shell have to attend this meeting. It's very important,' the activist said. In a tone of exasperation, he added, 'Don't you know the Great Proletarian Cultural Revolution has started?'

'What has a Cultural Revolution got to do with us? We worked for a commercial firm, not a cultural establishment,' I said.

'Chairman Mao has said that everybody in China must take part in the Cultural Revolution,' Chi said.

They both said rather impatiently, 'We are late. We must leave at once.'

Chi also stood up. I looked at the carriage clock on the mantelpiece; it was a quarter past eight.

Chen Mah was waiting in the hall with my handbag and a navy blue silk parasol. As I took them from her I smiled but she did not smile back. She was staring at me anxiously, obviously worried.

'I'll be back for lunch,' I tried to reassure her.

She merely nodded.

Lao Chao was there standing beside the open front gate. He also looked anxious, but said nothing, simply closing the gate behind us.

The apprehension of my servants was completely understandable. We all knew that during the seventeen years of Mao Tze-tung's rule innumerable people had left their homes during political campaigns and had never come back.

There were few people in the streets but the bus was crowded with solemn-looking passengers. It took a circuitous route so that we did not get to our destination until after nine o'clock.

A number of young men and women were gathered in front of the technical school where the meeting was to be held. When they caught sight of us approaching from the bus stop, a few ran into the building shouting, 'They have come! They have come!'

A man came out and said to my escorts irritably, 'Why have you been so long? The meeting was called for eight o'clock.'

The two men turned their heads in my direction and said, 'Ask her!' before hurrying into the building.

This man now said to me, 'Come this way.' I followed him into the meeting room.

The large room was already packed with people. Among those seated on narrow wooden benches in front of the assembly I saw Shell's physician and other senior members of the staff. The drivers, guards, liftmen, cleaners and clerks sat behind them among a large number of young people who were probably the students of the school. Quite a number stood in the aisles and in the space at the back of the hall. Hot sun streamed into the stifling room through bare windows, but very few people were using their fans. The atmosphere in the room was tense and expectant.

Although we had worked in the same office and seen one another daily for almost nine years, not one of the senior staff greeted me or showed any sign of recognition when I brushed past them to take up the seat allocated to me in the second row. Most of the men averted their glances; the few whose gaze met mine looked deeply troubled.

I wondered what these men had been through in the months since Shell had closed its office. They were the real losers of the 'Assets Against Liability Agreement' reached between Shell and the People's Government agency authorized to take them over. Nearly all the men had been with Shell for a very long time, some since the 1920s. During the Japanese occupation of Shanghai, some of them made the long and arduous journey from Shanghai to the company's office in the wartime capital of Chungking, abandoning home and family; others remained in the city and suffered great economic hardship rather than work for the Japanese oil company that had taken over Shell's premises. Most of the men were nearly sixty and approaching retirement. The Agreement specified that they were all to be given jobs in Chinese organizations. What was not mentioned was that they would not be given jobs commensurate with their former positions in Shell but would be employed as clerks or translators at a low rate of pay with much reduced retirement pensions. None of them had dared to oppose the terms of the Agreement since it was what the government wanted them to accept. Both the last general manager and I tried to obtain assurances from the Union chairman, but we were told that every member of our staff was pleased with the terms of the Agreement.

At my last meeting with the Shell Union chairman, he had said to me, 'Everybody is extremely pleased at the prospect of being freed from the anomalous position of working for a foreign firm. They all look forward to making a contribution to socialism as workers of a government organization.' That was the official line in which even the Union chairman himself could not possibly have believed. Senior members of the staff who came to my office during those last days would shake their heads and murmur sadly, '*Mei you fa tze!*' a very common Chinese phrase meaning, 'Nothing can be done', or 'It's hopeless', or 'No way out', or 'There's no solution'.

From nine o'clock to lunch-time, when the meeting might be adjourned, was more than three hours. The room was bound to get a great deal hotter as time went on. I knew I had to conserve energy while waiting for events to speak for themselves. The narrow wooden bench was just as uncomfortable as the one I had sat on during the war in a cave in Chungking while the Japanese planes rained incendiary bombs on the city. Perspiration was running down my face. To get a handkerchief, I opened my bag. I saw that Chen Mah had put in it a small folding fan made of sandalwood with a painting of a peony on silk done by my painting teacher. I took it out and fanned myself to clear the air of the unpleasant odour of packed humanity.

Suddenly there was a commotion at the rear. Several men dressed in short-sleeved shirts and baggy cotton trousers came through the door at the back and mounted the low platform. One of them came forward to a small table covered with a white cloth while the others sat down on the row of chairs behind him. One could no longer assess a man's station in life by his clothes in China because everybody tried to dress like a proletarian, a word the Chinese translated into *wu chan cheh* which meant 'a man with no property'. To look poor was both safe and fashionable for the Chinese people. So, while I could not tell the approximate rank or position of the man in charge of the meeting, I thought he must be an official of the Shanghai Labour Union.

'Comrades!' he said, 'our Great Leader Chairman Mao has initiated and is now personally directing the Great Proletarian Cultural Revolution. With our Great Helmsman to guide us, we shall proceed to victory without hindrance. The situation is excellent for us, the proletariat!

'The Great Proletarian Cultural Revolution is an opportunity for all of us to study the Thought of Mao Tze-tung more thoroughly and diligently than ever before so that our political awareness is sharpened. Only then can we truly differentiate between those who are within the ranks of the People and those who are on the side of the Enemy.

'The enemies of socialism are cunning. Some of them raise the red flag to oppose the red flag, while others present us with smiling faces to cover up their dirty scheme. They cooperate with the imperialists abroad and the capitalist class within to try to sabotage socialism and lead the Chinese people backwards to the misery and suffering of the old days. Should we allow them to succeed? Of course not! No! A hundred times no!

'It's seventeen years since the people of Shanghai were liberated. Yet, until recently, foreign firms remained in our city. Their offices occupied prominent locations and their cars sped through our streets. The foreigners and the few Chinese who forgot their national identity and worked with them swaggered around with insolence. We all know these firms were agents of the imperialists, who hoped to continue their exploitation of the Chinese people. We could not tolerate this state of affairs so we have closed their doors and thrown out the foreigners. Most of the Chinese on their staffs have been contaminated and their way of thinking is confused. But we must also recognize the fact that some of them are downright reactionaries. It's our job to implement our Great Leader Chairman Mao's policy of educating and reforming them. For several months we have conducted political indoctrination classes for them. But no one can be reformed if he himself does not come face to face with reality and recognize and admit the facts of his own mistakes. Self-criticism and confession are the first steps towards reform. In order to make a real effort at self-criticism, a man must be helped by the criticism of others. Today's meeting is called to criticize Tao Fung and to hear his self-criticism.

'You all know who Tao Fung is. For nearly thirty-five years he was a faithful running dog of Shell Petroleum Company, which is an international corporation of gigantic size with tendrils reaching into every corner of the world to suck up profit. This, according to Lenin, is the worst form of capitalist enterprise.

'Capitalism and socialism are like fire and water. They are diametrically opposed. Tao Fung could not have served the interests of the British firm and remain a good Chinese citizen under socialism. For a long time we have tried to help him see the light ...'

I was surprised to learn that Tao Fung, the former chief accountant of our office was the target of the meeting, because I had always thought the Party looked upon him with favour. His eldest son had been sent to both the Soviet Union and Czechoslovakia for advanced studies at the government's expense in the fifties and the young man had later joined the Party. I knew that when a student was selected to go abroad the Party always made a thorough investigation of his background, including his father's character, occupation and political viewpoint. Tao Fung must have passed this test at the time his son was sent abroad. I could not understand why he had now been singled out for criticism.

Since the very beginning of the Communist regime, I had carefully studied books on Marxism and pronouncements by Chinese

Communist Party leaders. It seemed to me that socialism in China was still very much an experiment and no fixed course of development for the country had yet been decided upon. This, I thought, was why the government's policy was always changing, like a pendulum swinging from left to right and back again. When things went to the extreme and problems emerged, Peking would take corrective measures. Then these very corrective measures went too far and had to be corrected. The real difficulty was, of course, that a State-controlled economy stifled productivity, and economic planning from Peking ignored local conditions and killed incentive.

When a policy changed from above, the standard of values changed with it. What was right yesterday became wrong today and vice versa. Thus the words and actions of a Communist Party official at the lower level were valid for a limited time only. So I decided the meeting I was attending was not very important and that the speaker was just a minor Party official assigned to conduct the Cultural Revolution for the former staff of Shell. The Cultural Revolution seemed to me to be a swing to the left. Sooner or later, when it had gone too far, corrective measures would be taken. The people would have a few months or a few years of respite until the next political campaign. Mao Tze-tung believed that political campaigns were the motivating force for progress. So I thought the Proletarian Cultural Revolution was just one of an endless series of upheavals the Chinese people must learn to put up with.

I looked round the room while listening with one ear to the speaker's tirade. It was then that I noticed the banner on the wall that said, 'Down with the running dog of imperialism Tao Fung'. The two characters of his name were crossed with red Xs to indicate he was being denounced as an enemy. This banner had escaped my notice when I entered the room because there were so many banners with slogans of the Cultural Revolution covering the walls. Slogans were an integral part of life in China. They exalted Mao Tze-tung, the Party, socialism and anything else the Party wanted the people to believe in; they exhorted the people to work hard, to study Mao Tze-tung Thought and to obey the Party. When there was a political campaign, the slogans denounced the enemies. Since the beginning of the Cultural Revolution, the number of slogans everywhere had multiplied by the thousand. It was impossible to read all that one encountered. It was very easy to look at them without really seeing what was written.

The man was now talking about Tao's decadent way of life resulting from long association with capitalism. It seemed he was

guilty of having extra-marital relations, drinking wine and spirits in
excess and enjoying elaborate meals, all acts of self-indulgence
frowned upon by the Party. These accusations did not surprise me
because I knew that when a man was denounced, he was depicted as
totally bad, and any errant behaviour was attributed to the influence
of capitalism.

When the man had thoroughly dissected Tao's private life and
exposed the corrosive effect of capitalism on him, his tone and manner
became more serious. He turned to the subject of imperialism and
aggression against China by foreign powers. To him Tao's mistakes
were made not because he was a greedy man with little self-control
but because he had worked for a firm that belonged to a nation guilty
of acts of aggression against the Chinese people more than a hundred
years ago. He was talking about the opium war of 1845 as if it had
taken place only the year before.

Though he used the strong language of denunciation and often
raised his voice to shout, he delivered his speech in a leisurely manner,
pausing frequently either to drink water or to consult his notes. He
knew he had a captive audience, since no one would dare to leave
while the meeting was going on. A Party official, no matter how lowly
his rank, was a representative of the Party. When he spoke, it was the
Party speaking. It was unthinkable not to appear attentive. However,
he had been speaking for a long time. The room had become
unbearably hot and the audience was getting restive. I looked at my
watch and found it was nearly twelve o'clock. Perhaps the speaker was
also tired and hungry, for he suddenly stopped and told us the meeting
was adjourned until 1.30. Everybody was up and heading for the exits
even before he had quite finished speaking.

Outside, the midday sun beat relentlessly down on the hot
pavement. In the distance, I saw a pedicab parked in the shade of a
tree. I ran to it and gave the driver my address, promising him double
fare to encourage him to move away quickly.

The man who had led me into the building in the morning dashed
out of the building, shouting for me to stop. He wanted me to remain
there and eat something from the school kitchen so that I would not be
late again. So anxious was he to detain me that he grabbed the side of
the pedicab. I had to promise him repeatedly that I would be back on
time before he let go.

My little house, shaded with awnings on the windows and green
bamboo screens on the verandah, was a haven after that hot, airless
meeting hall. The back of my shirt was wet through and I was

arched. I had a quick shower, drank a glass of iced tea and enjoyed the delicious meal my excellent cook had prepared for me. Then I lay down on my bed for half an hour's rest before setting out again in the pedicab, which I had asked to wait for me.

When I arrived at the meeting hall I was a little late, but by no means the last to arrive. I found a seat on the second row next to a pillar so that I could lean against it when I got too tired and needed support. I had brought along a large shopping bag in which I had put a bottle of water and a glass, as well as two bars of chocolate. Secure in the knowledge that I had come well prepared, I settled down to wait, wondering what the speaker was leading up to.

The hall gradually filled. At two o'clock, the same number of men mounted the platform and took up their positions. The speaker beckoned to someone at the back. I was astonished to see Tao Fung being led into the room wearing a tall dunce's hat made of white paper with 'cow's demon and snake spirit' written on it. If it were not for the extremely troubled expression on his face, he would have looked comical.

'Cow's demon and snake spirit' are evil spirits in Chinese mythology who can assume human forms to do mischief, but when recognized by real humans as devils they revert to their original shapes. Mao Tze-tung first used this expression to describe the intellectuals during the Anti-Rightist Campaign of 1957. He had said that the intellectuals were like evil spirits in human form when they pretended to support the Communist Party. When they criticized the Party's policy, they reverted to their original shapes and were exposed as evil spirits. Since that time, quick to adopt the language of Mao, Party officials used the phrase for anyone considered politically deceitful. During the Cultural Revolution it was applied to all the so-called nine categories of enemies: the former landlords denounced in the Land Reform Movement of 1950-2; rich peasants denounced in the Formation of Rural Cooperatives Movement of 1955; counter-revolutionaries denounced in the Suppression of Counter-revolutionaries Campaign of 1950 and Elimination of Counter-revolutionaries Campaign of 1955; 'bad elements' arrested from time to time since the Communist Party came to power; rightists denounced in the Anti-Rightist Campaign of 1957; traitors (Party officials suspected of having betrayed Party secrets to the Kuomintang during imprisonment by the Kuomintang); spies (men and women with foreign connections); 'capitalist-roaders' (Party officials not following the strict leftist policy of Mao, and taking the 'capitalist road') and intellectuals with bourgeois family origins.

Often the phrase was shortened to just 'cows' and the places in which these political outcasts were confined during the Cultural Revolution were generally referred to as the 'cowsheds'. As the scale of persecution expanded, every organization in China had rooms set aside for 'cowsheds' and the Revolutionaries of each organization had full power to deal with the 'cows' confined therein. Inhuman treatment and cruel methods were employed to force the 'cows' to confess. In many instances, they fared worse than those incarcerated in regular prisons.

How changed Tao Fung looked! When we were working in the same office, he was always full of self-assurance. Now he looked nervous and thoroughly beaten. He had lost a great deal of weight and seemed years older than only a few months ago. The young people behind me sniggered. When Tao was brought to the platform, the crowd at the back stood up to have a better view and knocked over some benches. So a man pushed a chair forward on the platform and told Tao Fung to stand on it. When Tao climbed onto the chair and stood there in a posture of subservience in his tall paper hat, the sniggers became uncontrolled laughter.

Someone in a corner of the room, obviously planted there for the purpose, stood up. Holding the Little Red Book of Mao Tze-tung's quotations (so-called because of its red plastic cover), which everybody had to have by his side, and raising it high in the air, he led the assembly to shout slogans.

'Down with Tao Fung!'
'Down with the running dog of the imperialists, Tao Fung!'
'Down with the imperialists!'
'Down with the capitalist class!'
'Long live the Great Proletarian Cultural Revolution!'
'Long live our Great Leader Chairman Mao!'

The sound of laughter was now drowned in the thunder of voices. Everybody got to his feet shouting and waving the Little Red Book of Mao's quotations. I had not brought along my copy. Embarrassed by my oversight, I was slow to get to my feet. Besides, I was shocked and surprised to see Tao Fung raising his fist and shouting with gusto the same slogans, including those against himself. By the time I had collected my fan, my bag, my bottle of water and the glass from my lap, placed them on the bench and stood up, the others had already finished and had sat down. So I had to pick up my things again and resume my seat. The man sitting next to me was glaring at me with disapproval. He shifted sideways away from me as if he feared contamination by my bad behaviour.

When the crowd had demonstrated its anger at and disapproval of the culprit, he was allowed to come down from the chair. As he bent his head to step down, the paper hat fell off. There was renewed laughter from the young students. Tao stared at the man in charge of the meeting with fear in his eyes, obviously afraid of being accused of deliberately dropping the hat. He heaved a sigh of relief when another man picked it up and placed it on the table.

The man in charge of the meeting called upon other members of the company's staff, including the two men who had come to my house in the morning and junior clerks in Tao Fung's accounts department, to come forward to speak. One by one they marched to the platform and expressed anger and indignation, repeating the same accusations against Tao Fung made by the man in charge of the meeting in the morning session. The scope and degree of criticism was, I knew, always set by the Party official. It was just as ill-advised to try to be original and say something different as not to criticize enough. The Chinese people had learned by experience that the Party trusted them more and liked them better if they didn't think for themselves but just repeated what the Party told them. The criticism of Tao Fung by other members of our former staff went on for a long time. All those who were allowed to speak were workers or junior clerks. None of the senior members of our former staff participated. They sat silently with heads bowed.

Finally the man in charge of the meeting took over again. He told the audience that after several weeks of re-education and 'help' by activists, Tao had finally recognized the fact that he was a victim of capitalism and imperialism. Turning to Tao, the man asked in a voice a stern schoolteacher might have used to address a pupil caught in an act of mischief, 'Isn't it so? It was the high salary paid you by the foreign imperialists that turned you into their slave! You sold yourself to them and were ready to do any dirty work for them because of the high salary you received and the money they promised you. Isn't this the case?'

There was a hush in the room as everyone waited for Tao's reaction. But there was no dramatic, tearful declaration of repentance. He merely nodded his head, looking more dejected than ever.

I thought Tao Fung very stupid to agree that he had sold himself for money because this admission could open the way to all sorts of more serious accusations from which he might find it difficult to disentangle himself. It seemed to me it would have been much better and certainly more truthful to explain that Shell paid its Shanghai staff the same salary after the Communist Party took over the city as it had done before. Since the government did not intervene, naturally the question of reducing the pay of the staff did not arise. What he could also have said tactfully (which the Party officials would find difficult to refute) was that working for a foreign firm did not carry with it the personal prestige of serving the people that workers in government organizations enjoyed.

'Tao Fung will now make his self-criticism,' the man announced.

Still in a posture of obsequiousness and without once lifting his eyes to look at the audience, Tao took a few sheets of paper from his pocket and started to read a prepared statement in a low voice devoid of any emotion. He admitted humbly all the 'crimes' listed by the speakers and accepted the verdict that his downfall was due to the fact that he did not have sufficient socialist awareness. He expressed regret for having worked for a foreign firm for more than thirty-five years and said that he had wasted his life. He declared that he was ashamed that he had been blinded by capitalist propaganda and enslaved by the good treatment Shell had given him. He begged the proletariat to forgive him and give him a chance to repent. He mentioned the fact that his son was a Party member and had been educated abroad at government expense. His own life of depravity, he said, was an act of gross ingratitude to the People's Government. He assured the assembly that he now recognized the dastardly schemes of the foreign capitalists and imperialists against Communist China and would do his best to lay bare their dirty game in order to show his true repentance. He said he was in the process of writing a detailed confession of criminal deeds he had committed for Shell, which he would present to the officials 'helping' him with his re-education.

It was a long statement full of phrases of self-abuse and exaggeration. At times his voice trembled and sometimes he opened his mouth but no words came. When he turned the pages, his hands shook. I did not believe his nervousness was entirely due to fear, since he must have known that he was not guilty of any real crime. After all, Shell was in China because the People's Government allowed, even wanted, it to be there. And I knew that the company had been scrupulously correct in observing Chinese government regulations. Tao must have known this too. I thought his chief problem was mental and physical exhaustion. To bring him to his knees and to make sure that he submitted readily, I was sure those who 'helped' him must have spent days, if not weeks, constantly questioning him, taking turns to exert pressure on him without allowing him to sleep. It was common knowledge that in these circumstances, the victim broke down and submitted when he was on the verge of physical collapse and mental confusion. The Maoists named these inhuman tactics 'exhaustive bombardment'. Many people I knew, including my own brother, had experienced it during the Anti-Rightist Campaign of 1957. The Party officials remained in the background while the activists carried out their orders. When there was excessive cruelty that resulted in death, the officials would disown responsibility but claim it was an accident resulting from 'mass enthusiasm'.

When Tao had finished, the speaker told the audience that he was to be watched to see if his words were spoken in true sincerity. He added that his was only the first meeting of its kind to be held. There were many others like Tao to be dealt with and Tao himself might speak again. Here he paused momentarily and swept the audience with his eyes. Did I merely imagine that his gaze seemed to linger for a fraction of a moment longer in my direction? He concluded that it was the duty of the proletariat to cleanse socialist China of all residue of imperialist influence and punish the enemies of the people. Again I thought he directed his gaze in my direction.

I certainly did not think I was important enough for this whole show to have been put on solely for my benefit. But if it was, it failed to frighten me. The emotion my first experience of a 'struggle meeting' generated in me was one of disgust and shame that such an act of barbarism against a fellow human being could have taken place in my beloved native land, with a history of five thousand years of civilization. As a Chinese, I felt degraded.

There was more shouting of slogans, but everybody was already on his feet moving towards the door.

The same man who tried to keep me from going home for lunch was waiting in the passage. He said to me, 'Will you come this way for a moment? Some comrades would like to have a word with you.'

I followed him to one of the classrooms where the students' seats and tables were piled up in one corner. The man in charge of the meeting and another one who had been on the platform were seated by the teacher's desk. There was a vacant chair. They motioned me to sit in it.

'Did you hear everything at the meeting?' the man in charge of the meeting asked me.

I nodded.

'What did you think of the meeting? I believe this is the first time you have attended one of this kind.'

Obviously I couldn't say what I really thought of the meeting, nor did I want to lie and flatter him. So I asked, 'May I ask you some questions that have been in my mind the whole day?'

He looked annoyed, but said, 'Go ahead.'

'What organization do you represent? What authority do you have to call a meeting like this? Besides the ex-staff of Shell, who were the others present?'

Clearly he resented my questioning his authority. Making a visible effort to control himself, he said, 'We represent the proletarian class. The meeting was authorized by the Committee in charge of the conduct of the Proletarian Cultural Revolution in Shanghai.'

I asked him to explain the purpose of the Proletarian Cultural Revolution. He said that it was a revolution to cleanse Chinese society of factors that hindered the growth of socialism. He repeated an often-quoted line of Mao Tze-tung, 'If poisonous weeds are not removed, scented flowers cannot grow.' He told me that everybody in China without exception had to take part in the Great Proletarian Cultural Revolution.

'You must assume a more sincere attitude and make a determined effort to emulate Tao Fung and do your best to reform,' he said.

'I'm not aware of any wrong-doing on my part,' I said, my voice registering surprise.

'Perhaps you'll change your attitude when you have had time to think things over,' said the second man. 'If you try to cover up for the imperialists, the consequences will be serious.'

'What is there to cover up? Every act of the imperialists is clearly recorded in our history books,' I answered.

The man raised his voice, 'What are you talking about? We are not concerned with what happened in the past. We are talking about now, about the firm you worked for. Tao had already confessed everything. We know the Shell office in Shanghai "hung up a sheep's head to sell dog's meat" [a Chinese expression to mean the outward appearance of something was not the same as the reality]. We are also clear in our mind about the important role you played in their dirty game. You must not take us for fools.'

'I'm completely at a loss to know what you refer to,' I said. 'As far as I know, the company I worked for never did anything either illegal or immoral. The People's Government has an excellent police force. Surely if anything had been wrong it would have been discovered long ago.'

Both men glared at me. Almost simultaneously they shouted, 'You are trying to cover up for the imperialists!'

I said indignantly, 'You misunderstand me. I'm merely stating the facts as I know them. Why should I cover up for anybody? Shell's Shanghai office is closed and the British general manager has left. No one needs my protection.'

'Yes, yes, the British general manager has gone but you are still here. You know just as much as he did. Your husband held the post of general manager for many years. After he died you joined the firm. You certainly know everything about it.'

'It's precisely because I know everything about the Shanghai office of Shell that I know it never did anything wrong,' I said.

The other man intervened. 'I suggest you go home now and think things over. We'll call you when we want to speak to you again. What's your telephone number?'

I gave them my telephone number and left the room.

Outside, it was already dusk. There was a pleasant breeze. I decided to walk home on the tree-lined pavement by a roundabout route to get some exercise and to think things over.

When I passed the No.1 Medical College, I saw my friend Winnie emerging from the half-closed gate, followed by a number of her colleagues. We waved to each other and she joined me to walk home, as she lived in the vicinity of my house.

'Why are you out walking at this time of the evening?' Winnie asked me.

'I've just attended a struggle meeting. I've been told to take part in the Proletarian Cultural Revolution.'

'Is that because Shell has closed its Shanghai office? Tell me about it.'

'I will. Can you join me for dinner?' I asked her. It would be good to hear what Winnie had to say about my experience. She had been through quite a number of political movements and was more experienced than I was in dealing with the situation, I thought.

'All right. I'll phone home from your house. Henry comes home very late these days. He has to pay a price for being a professor whenever there is a political campaign. Professors always seem to become the targets,' Winnie said. Henry was her husband who taught architecture at Tung Chi University.

'Is Henry in trouble?' I inquired anxiously.

'No, not so far, thank God,' Winnie replied, while taking a comb out of her bag to smooth her hair. 'Your servants will have a fit if they see me coming to dinner looking so dishevelled.'

Though she was over forty-five and had three sons, Winnie had kept

her slim figure and managed to look attractive in the ill-fitting Mao
jacket and baggy trousers she was obliged to wear as a teacher of
English and Latin at the Medical College. After getting a degree in
English literature at a New England women's college, she and her
husband, a graduate of Britain's Cambridge University, returned to
China at the end of the Sino-Japanese War. Henry was appointed
professor of architecture at Tung Chi University and soon became
Dean of the department. But in those days of galloping inflation, the
salary of a professor could not keep pace with rising prices. To
supplement the family income, Winnie used to give Chinese lessons to
Europeans living in Shanghai. Disillusioned by the inability of the
Kuomintang Government to cope with pressing post-war economic
problems and institute reform, they welcomed the Communist
takeover in 1949 as an opportunity for peace and stability.

In those days, because of the Kuomintang blackout of all news
about the Communist area, very few Chinese living in Shanghai had
any real understanding of Marxism, the Chinese Communist Party or
Mao Tze-tung. Almost no one knew about the persecution of
intellectuals carried out in Yenan in 1942 or the periodical
witch-hunts for 'spies of the Kuomintang and the imperialists' in the
Communist Party and Army. The only source of information for
Chinese intellectuals about the Chinese Communist Party before
1949 had been the glowing accounts written by some western
journalists and writers who made fleeting visits to the Communist-
held area of China. Most of these men were liberal idealists. They
were impressed by the austerity, discipline and singleness of purpose of
the Communist leaders but they did not have a deep understanding of
either the character of these men or the philosophy that motivated
them. When the Communist Party intensified its propaganda effort,
through its underground in Kuomintang-governed cities, prior to the
final military push to take over the country, its promises of peaceful
national reconstruction, of a united front including all sections of the
Chinese society and of a democratic form of government sounded an
attractive alternative to the corrupt and ineffectual rule of the
Kuomintang. And the Chinese intellectuals accepted the propaganda
effort as a sincere and honest declaration of policy by the Chinese
Communist Party.

After the Communist Army took over Shanghai, women were
encouraged to take jobs. Winnie became a teacher at the Medical
College in 1950. In the following year, Mao Tze-tung, anxious to put
all universities under Party control, initiated the Thought Reform

Movement. Winnie and Henry had their first rude awakening. Although they both survived this campaign more or less unscathed, they suffered the humiliating experience of having to make self-criticism of their family background, their education abroad and their outlook on life as reflected in the architectural designs Henry made and in their teaching methods. Repeatedly they had to write their life histories critically; each time, the Party representative demanded a more self-searching effort. At the end of their gruelling and humiliating experience, Henry was judged unfit to continue as Dean of the architectural department, which was now to use exclusively Soviet materials for teaching. Both Chinese traditional work and architectural designs from the West were scorned as feudalistic and decadent.

After the Thought Reform Movement was concluded in 1951, Party Secretaries were appointed to every level of university administration. They controlled every aspect of the life and work of the teaching staff, even though the majority of them had little education and had never been teachers. Henry and Winnie lived in premises assigned to them, accepted the salary given to them, did their work in the way the Party Secretaries wanted. These two well-educated, lively and imaginative young people, full of good will towards the Communist regime, were reduced by Mao Tze-tung's suspicion and abuse of the intellectuals to teaching machines. But they were the fortunate ones. Many others from universities all over China did not fare as well. Some were sent to labour camps while others were thrown out of the universities altogether.

When the Korean War ended, Mao Tze-tung's witch-hunt for dissidents temporarily relaxed. Prime Minister Chou En-lai, aware of the plight of the Chinese intellectuals, tried then to improve their condition. As a result of a more lenient policy, Henry and Winnie were given a more spacious apartment near my home. There were also fewer constraints placed on their professional activities. Winnie often dropped in to see me either to read the books and magazines I was able to get from Hong Kong and England sent through the office or to listen to my stereo records.

In 1956 Mao Tze-tung launched the campaign of 'Let a Hundred Flowers Bloom and Let a Hundred Schools of Thought Contend'. The Party Secretaries in every organization, and even Mao himself, urged the people to give frank and constructive criticism of the work of the Communist Party. Believing the Party sincere in wishing to improve its work, tens of thousands of intellectuals and more than a million Chinese in every walk of life poured out their grievances and suggestions. But Winnie and Henry refrained from speaking out. They escaped persecution when Mao Tze-tung swung his policy round in 1957 and initiated the Anti-Rightist Campaign. He labelled all those who had offered criticism 'Rightists'. Many of them lost their jobs, became non-persons and were sent to labour camps; others had their pay reduced and were demoted in rank. The treachery of Mao Tze-tung in repeatedly inviting frank and constructive criticism and then harshly punishing those who gave it completely cowed the Chinese intellectuals so that China's cultural life came to a virtual standstill.

When Winnie and I reached my house, the front gate swung open before I pressed the bell. Lao Chao was standing there anxiously waiting for my return. He told me my daughter had telephoned to say that she was not coming home for dinner.

'Please tell Cook Mrs Huang is staying for dinner,' I said to Lao Chao and took Winnie upstairs to my bathroom.

Lao Chao laid the table for two for a European meal with white embroidered linen table mats. A bowl of white carnations was in the centre of the dining table.

'Cook said it's steamed Mandarin fish with a green salad. Is it all right?' Lao Chao asked me. I was usually served either Chinese or European style cooking depending on what my cook was able to obtain at the market.

I looked at Winnie inquiringly and she said, 'That's fine. I love Mandarin fish.'

After we had sat down, Winnie looked up at the large painting of a female figure in pale blue by the famous painter Ling Fong-min who was once the head of the Hangchow Academy of Art. This painting was the centrepiece of decoration of my blue-and-white dining room. It went well in colour and style with the blue-and-white Huan Têh plate and K'ang Hsi vase displayed on the blackwood sideboard.

'Have you heard? Ling Fong-min is in serious trouble,' Winnie told me.

I was surprised. I knew the painter was earning large sums of foreign exchange for the People's Government, which bought his paintings for a paltry sum but sold them in Hong Kong for twenty or thirty times the amount.

'He is accused of promoting the decadent art form of the West. But a more serious charge is that he has maintained contact with people outside China and has given information to captains of foreign ships calling at Shanghai. The foreigners were observed coming to his home by his neighbourhood activists.'

'Well, his wife and daughter are in Brazil. Actually I know for a fact the ships' captains came to buy his pictures,' I said.

'Many other painters are in trouble too. Your old teacher, Miss Pong, is also being criticized. It's said she once painted a branch of the Mei Hua tree (a flowering tree that blooms in late winter or early spring) hanging down rather than upright to symbolize the downfall of the Communist Party.'

I laid down my fork and said to Winnie, 'They are mad. In the paintings by old masters the Mei Hua tree is often depicted hanging over a cliff. It isn't anything she has invented.'

'Well, you know how it is. The Party officials in her organization have probably never seen any paintings by the old masters. Party officials in charge of artists are not required to know the difference between water-colours and lithographs. And most of them don't know.'

Our conversation was so disheartening that it depressed our appetites. We couldn't do justice to the delicious meal my cook gave us.

When we were drinking tea in the drawing room, I told Winnie about the struggle meeting I had just attended. After thinking it over, she said, 'It seems you are going to be treated just like us now that Shell has closed its Shanghai office. No one outside China will know what happens to you.'

'What do you think is the purpose of their getting me to attend the meeting?' I asked her.

'To frighten you, of course.'

'I'm not easily frightened.'

'That, I think, they don't know. All they know is that you are a rich woman who has led an easy life and who has never been involved in any political campaign before. They probably think you are easily frightened. As a rule they underestimate our courage.'

'Why do you think they want to frighten me? What for?'

'That's very hard to say at this juncture. Whatever it is, be prepared for unpleasantness. Be alert and keep your mouth shut. Don't say anything inadvertent, whatever the provocation.'

'What about yourself? How are you getting on?' I asked her.

'I'm worn out. We spend all our time at meetings or writing Big Character Posters. Classes have been suspended. Several professors and medical experts have already been denounced. The situation seems even more serious than in 1957 at the beginning of the Anti-Rightist Campaign.'

'Are you likely to become an object of criticism?' I asked her.

'Of course one can't be sure. But I don't think I'm important enough. I've been a junior lecturer for sixteen years, without promotion or a rise in pay. I always humbly ask my Party Secretary for instructions and never indulge in the luxury of taking the initiative. I carry out his instructions even when I know he is wrong. At indoctrination meetings I never speak unless told to do so. Then I simply repeat whatever was said by our Group Leader or the Party Secretary. I think my behaviour can be considered impeccable. Anyway, in the last analysis, the more senior you are the more likely you are to get into trouble. "A big tree catches the wind" is a true saying.'

'What about Henry?'

'I'm worried about Henry. I think he will be denounced as a "Cow's demon and Snake Spirit" like all the other professors and will be struggled against,' Winnie said helplessly. Then she closed her eyes and sighed.

'I thought he never does anything apart from teaching or says a word outside the classroom any more,' I said.

'It's true. He has learned a lesson from all his friends who had been named Rightists. But he's a full professor, for one thing. Moreover, his family used to be very rich. And his sister is in Taiwan.'

'But you have no contact with his sister. You don't write to her.'

'That doesn't matter. She is there and she is Henry's sister. If the Party wants to make an issue of it, we can't stop them.'

Lao Chao came in to fill our teacups.

'Cook would like to have a word with you before he goes home,' Lao Chao said.

'All right. Ask him to come in,' I told him.

Both Cook and Lao Chao came in.

'The Vice-Chairman of the Shell Labour Union Chi came again tonight just before you returned. He asked us to give you a message,' the cook said.

'What did he say?' I asked him.

'He told us to tell you to be careful when you talk to the Party officials. He said that after you left the meeting, they complained that you were rude to them. Chi wants you to know that the Party officials were annoyed,' the cook said.

'Chi is a good man,' Lao Chao chipped in.

'A good man? You should have seen him denouncing Tao Fung at the struggle meeting!' His ugly performance was still in my mind.

'He can't help it. He had to do it when he was told to. If he weren't a good man he wouldn't have bothered to come to give you this warning,' Lao Chao defended Chi.

'You are right, Lao Chao. I'll remember to be careful. It's good of Chi to have bothered to come. Thank you both for telling me this,' I said to Lao Chao and the cook.

After the servants had withdrawn, Winnie said, 'They are right. You must be careful. It doesn't pay to offend the men directly in charge of you during a political campaign. They have absolute power to decide your fate. If they send you to a labour camp, you will have to go.'

'How can they send me to a labour camp? Winnie,' I said, 'I don't even work for the government. Besides, I haven't broken the law!'

'Don't be naive! They can, if they want to. You live here. You can't get out of the country. The only good thing about not working for the government is that they can't cut your pay.'

Winnie got up to leave. I accompanied her to the front gate.

'Why didn't you go to Hong Kong when Shell applied to close the office last year?' Winnie asked me.

'How could I ask for such a thing? The general manager needed me during the negotiations. He didn't know the language. The whole thing was conducted in Chinese. I couldn't leave him holding the fort alone. Shell has treated me well. I couldn't let them down when they needed me,' I said.

'I hope they appreciate your sense of duty. They can't help you now. You should have gone,' Winnie said.

'I hope you and Henry will both come through this as well as you did the Anti-Rightist Campaign,' I said to her.

'I sometimes feel a real premonition of disaster,' Winnie said sadly. 'Think of all the years we spent just trying to survive!'

We stood outside my front gate to bid each other goodbye. After taking a few steps, Winnie turned and said to me, 'I may not be able to come again until things clarify. Ring me if you need me.'

'I understand. Take care of yourself!' I said.

'You too!' she said and waved.

After closing the front gate, I walked towards the house under a cloudless sky. A thousand stars were sparkling in space. It was a beautiful summer night.

Feeling tired and depressed, I went to my bedroom to get ready for bed. My daughter came home while I was lying on my bed unable to sleep, with scenes of the day's events passing in front of my eyes.

'Mummy, Mummy!' she called as she mounted the stairs two steps at a time just as she did as a teenager. I called out to say that I was in my bedroom. Chen Mah followed her into my room with a glass of milk and a plate of sandwiches on a tray.

'Goodness! I'm famished! I've had nothing to eat since breakfast.' She picked up the glass and drank the milk. I saw that her fingers were stained with ink.

'Look at those fingers! Are you going to eat your sandwiches with inky fingers? You are already a twenty-three-year-old young lady but you behave like a ten-year-old. In the old days, girls of your age were married and had two or three children already,' scolded Chen Mah. As Chen Mah had been with us since my daughter was a small girl, she could scold her as an old servant would.

'Well, this isn't the old days any more, dear Chen Mah, old-fashioned lady!' Meiping protested and went into my bathroom to wash her hands.

Chen Mah placed the sandwiches on the table and turned to leave the room. She said to me, 'You don't have to worry about Lao Chao, Cook and me. We'll always stand by you.'

'Thank you, Chen Mah, for your concern for me. Please tell Lao Chao and Cook not to worry,' I answered, deeply touched by her remark.

'We worry about you because you are alone. I wish the master were still with us,' she murmured and shut the door behind her.

Chen Mah was really old-fashioned. In time of crisis she believed firmly in the superior ability of the male sex. In fact, I had been thinking of my husband as I lay on my bed in the darkened room before my daughter came back. For the first time since he died, I did not regret his death. I was thankful that he was to be spared the insults and persecution that would surely be directed against him if he were still alive.

With the bathroom door closed and the water running, my daughter did not hear our conversation. She was apparently having a shower.

My daughter Meiping was an attractive and intelligent young woman. In the course of growing up in Communist China, she had seen the disappearance of the society in which children of the educated and affluent like herself had enjoyed many advantages. In its place was formed not an egalitarian society in which everyone enjoyed equal opportunity and status, but a new system of discrimination against children like herself and their families. In each stage of her young life, she had been handicapped by her family background. For instance, to be admitted into a good middle school, she had to pass the entrance examination with marks of 80 per cent, while children of workers and peasants got in with a pass mark of 60.

'This is unfair!' I had exclaimed at the time, indignant that my child was being discriminated against. 'What is the reason given for such an unfair regulation?'

'Don't worry, Mummy! I can do it! I can get 80! It isn't hard,' piped the twelve-year-old.

'It isn't fair!' I was still fuming.

'But, Mummy, the teacher told us the children of workers and peasants have to do housework or cook the evening meal after school. And their parents can't help them with homework. The treatment I get is fair, if you consider all that.' She had learned to be philosophical at a young age.

This kind of discrimination followed her in everything she tried to do. Whenever she encountered it, she was made to feel guilty and ashamed of her family background. She, and other children like her, just had to try harder than the children of workers and peasants. They learned from an early age that the classless society of Communism had a more rigid class system than the despised capitalist society, where a man could move from the lower to the upper class by his own effort. Because my daughter had to try harder, she did well. In the prestigious No. 2 Municipal Girls' Middle School, she was a student leader and won honours and prizes. She seemed happily adjusted and had many friends, among them several children from working-class families. Although she was by nature loving and generous, I thought it was mainly the feeling of guilt instilled in her by Communist propaganda about the rich exploiting the poor that created in her the desire to help these children. She would bring them home to share her food, help them with their studies and even went to their homes sometimes to assist them with their chores. While I thought her activities rather commendable, Chen Mah disapproved heartily, especially when she lent her clothes to other girls and then brought home the dirty laundry for Chen Mah to wash.

From early childhood, she had shown an interest in music. We bought her a piano and arranged for her to have private lessons after school. When she was ten years old she became a member of the Children's Palace in Shanghai, a sort of club for specially selected schoolchildren who earned good marks in studies and behaviour. There she acted in plays and took part in musical activities. Being bilingual, she became one of the young interpreters whenever the

Children's Palace had English-speaking visitors from abroad. Having learned to swim as a toddler in Australia, she was the unofficial swimming instructor of her class. When she was fifteen and in middle school, she was selected by the Shanghai Athletics Association for training with the Shanghai Rowing Club during the holidays and became cox for the first Women's Rowing Team of Shanghai.

Although we lived in the midst of periodical political turmoil and the personal tragedy of some of our friends and neighbours saddened us, I never had to worry about my daughter. I took it for granted that she would go to one of the better universities, be given a fairly good job upon graduation because of her good marks, and marry a nice young man. Her pay at work would be insignificant, but I could supplement her income with an allowance, as many other parents were doing in China.

I had hoped that after graduation she would be assigned a job in Shanghai so that she could live at home. But I couldn't be sure of that. I knew that young people with family backgrounds like hers were often deliberately sent to distant regions of China, where living conditions were backward and extremely poor. This had happened to some of my friends' children. As I watched my daughter grow from a lanky teenager into a beautiful young woman, I wondered what was in store for her. However, when I felt optimistic, I would dream of converting the third floor of the house into a self-contained apartment for her and her family. The prospect of nursing a grandchild was immensely comforting to me. I gazed happily into the rosy future of my dream and could almost feel the warmth of the little creature in my arms.

It had been somewhat of a surprise when my daughter told me that two well-known film actresses, concurrently teachers of the newly established Film School of Shanghai, had approached her to suggest that she try for the entrance examination as a specially selected 'talent' to enrol in the school. I could see she was flattered that she had been chosen. But I had hoped for something different for her, some work in which her intellectual power rather than her physical attributes would be an asset.

'The Film School is on Hong Chiao Road near the old golf club. I can come home from it easily for weekends. And the two teachers told me all graduates will be given jobs in the Shanghai Film Studio. Actually the school is a subsidiary of the Film Studio. It has sent talent scouts all over the country to select students for the entrance examination. There is bound to be a big response because everyone wants to live in Shanghai,' Meiping said.

'But do you really want to be a film actress?' I asked her.

'I don't mind. I can do it. It isn't hard.' This was her standard response to any problem.

'I'm sure you can do it. But do you want to?' I believed this to be an important point. To be happy one should do the job one wants to do.

'Well, I never think of what I really want to do. It's no use thinking that way when I know the government is going to assign me a job. Thinking about what I really want to do only leads to disappointment. None of my friends thinks that way either,' she said. 'I'll just enjoy doing whatever the government wants me to do. If I try hard enough to do a job well, I generally end up liking it.'

I suppose my daughter's attitude was sound in the circumstances. But could a man assigned to carry night soil as his lifelong occupation make himself like the job by working hard at it?

'So you have decided to try for the entrance examination?' I asked her.

'Yes, if you agree. The teachers spoke to me officially. It would be hard to say no without appearing unappreciative. Besides, I like the idea of working in Shanghai. I should hate leaving you alone here and coming home only once a year for a few days at Chinese New Year,' my daughter said.

'Yes, yes, darling, that's certainly an important point to consider. I would hate you to go into the interior to work.' I agreed with her whole-heartedly.

So she went to the Film School. Three years later she graduated and was given a job with the Shanghai Film Studio, which was run by the Bureau of Films of the Ministry of Culture.

The acting profession was somewhat glamorous even in Communist China, but those who worked in it did not receive higher pay or enjoy better working conditions than factory workers or teachers of the same age group. The function of an actress was primarily to bring entertainment to the masses, so besides taking part in films, she often gave performances in factories, rural communes, coal-mines and oilfields, travelling far and wide with her unit all over China. It was an arduous life. But she thought her experience enriched her understanding and knowledge of her own country and its people, and believed she was rendering service to them by giving them entertainment. For her, that was a meaningful way of life.

As she munched her sandwiches, she told me about the day's events at her Film Studio.

'I spent the whole day writing Big Character Posters for the Great

Proletarian Cultural Revolution. We were told that the more Big
Character Posters one writes, the more revolutionary enthusiasm one
demonstrates, so everybody wrote and wrote until the notice board
and all the wall space in our section were completely covered.'

'Was that why you didn't come home for dinner?'

'We gave up having lunch and dinner to show our revolutionary
zeal. Actually everyone was hungry but nobody wanted to be the first
to leave.'

'What did you write about?'

'Oh, slogans and denunciations against those who had been labelled
"Cow's Demon and Snake Spirit", and all China's enemies such as
Taiwan, Japan, Britain, the United States and the Soviet Union.'

'How do you know what to write? Do you make things up?'

'Some people do. But I think that's too dangerous. Most of us get
materials from our Section Leader. I concentrate on enemy countries.
The Section Leader allows me to because she thinks I know more
about other countries since I was born abroad. I don't want to write
about individuals. I don't know much about the life of any of the
denounced people and I don't want to lie and insinuate. The older
actresses, actors, directors and scriptwriters have to write their own
self-criticism. A lot of them are being denounced. From time to time,
they are led out by the activists to be struggled against at struggle
meetings or just to stand or kneel in the sun with their heads bowed.'

'How terrible!' I exclaimed.

'Yes, it's terrible. I'm sorry for them. I heard that most of them are
Chiang Ching's enemies from the old days. I heard that Chairman
Mao has given his wife Chiang Ching full power to deal with
everybody in the field of art,' my daughter said.

'Hasn't she been putting on modern Peking operas?'

'Yes, it seems she has been in disagreement with the leaders in the
Cultural Department for some time. In any case, I heard that the old
actresses who got better parts than she did in the old days when she
was an actress in Shanghai have all packed their bags in preparation
for going to labour camps. It's said she is very cruel and jealous. But
it's best not to talk about her at all.'

'Surely that's farfetched. She is the number one lady of China now.
Why should she care about a few old actresses?'

'Perhaps they know too much about her past life. They say that
before she went to Yenan and married Chairman Mao, she had a lot of
lovers and even several husbands.'

'Chairman Mao had several wives too. Why shouldn't she have had

several husbands? She sounds like a proper Hollywood film star,' I
laughed. 'You have been brought up in China, so you have a
puritanical outlook on such matters. Tell me, how about yourself? Are
you likely to get criticized?'

'Mummy, don't be silly. I'm not important enough. I'm just one of
the masses. Of course, my family background and my birth abroad
might get criticized. Wasn't it lucky I was born in Australia rather than
in the United States or Britain?'

'Certainly no one can say Australia is an imperialist country.'

'No, most people at the Film Studio think it's still a British colony
where the people are oppressed. They don't know the Australians are
really British and only the kangaroos are the natives.' My daughter
laughed heartily.

She finished her sandwiches and got up to go to her own room.
Casually she asked, 'What did you do all day, Mummy?'

'I was called to attend a struggle meeting against the former chief
accountant of our office. It seems I also must take part in the Cultural
Revolution. I might even become a target of attack,' I told her.

'Oh, my goodness! This is extremely serious. Why didn't you tell me
before?' Meiping was shocked by my news. She sat down again and
urged me to tell her everything. After I had described my experience of
the day, she became very worried. She asked, 'Was your office all right?
Has it ever done anything wrong?'

'No, of course not,' I told her.

'Why did they single out the chief accountant? Perhaps he infringed
the foreign-exchange regulations on behalf of the firm? Or perhaps
you didn't pay your taxes?'

'We paid our taxes all right. Certainly we were most meticulous in
observing the foreign-exchange regulations.'

We were both puzzled but agreed it was useless to speculate. I urged
her to go to bed. After remaining in silence for a while longer, she said
good night and left the room. She seemed a changed girl, much older
than when she came in.

I switched off the light but remained wide awake. I was thinking
that the Proletarian Cultural Revolution was also my daughter's first
experience of a political movement. I wondered how it was going to
affect her future. After some time, my bedroom door was gently
pushed open. I switched on the light.

'Mummy, I can't go to sleep. Do you mind if I go down and play the
piano for a while?' Meiping asked, standing in her pyjamas in the open
doorway.

'I'll come with you,' I said, getting out of bed and following her downstairs.

Fluffy, Meiping's large Persian cat, was on the terrace outside. When he saw us, he mewed to get in. I opened the screen door. Meiping stepped out and picked him up to carry him into her study. She put Fluffy down, opened the lid of the piano and proceeded to strike a few chords. Turning to me, she asked, 'What shall I play?'

'Anything at all, but not revolutionary songs.'

She started to play one of Chopin's nocturnes and murmured to me, 'All right?'

I made an affirmative noise. Fluffy was stretched out at Meiping's feet under the piano. It was a scene of domestic peace and tranquillity but for an invisible threat hanging in the air.

CHAPTER 2

Interval before the Storm

IN THE WEEKS FOLLOWING that first meeting, I was called by the same men for several interviews. Our conversations varied very little from the first occasion. Once they asked me to provide them with a list of all the Americans and Europeans I had known together with their occupations and the place and circumstance in which I had met each one. Another time they asked me to write about the activities of our office. But when I handed to them the pages I had written, they barely glanced at them. While exhorting me to denounce my former employer, they did not ask me any concrete questions about the company. They never went beyond insinuating that Shell had done something wrong and that I was a part of whatever the crime was.

Indeed I had the impression that the men were marking time, waiting for instructions from above before going any further. Actually, unbeknownst to me and to other Chinese people, the delay in activating the movement was due to a fierce struggle going on amongst the leaders of the Chinese Communist Party. The point of contention was who should conduct the Cultural Revolution: the established Party apparatus or a special committee of Maoists appointed by Mao Tze-tung as Chairman of the Central Committee.

It was later revealed that early in August, at a Central Committee meeting, Mao Tze-tung had written a Big Character Poster entitled: 'Fire Cannon Balls at the Headquarters'. In it he made the extraordinary accusation that the government administration (headed by Liu Shao-chi as Chairman of the People's Republic) and the Party Secretariat (headed by Deng Hsiao-ping as Chief Party Secretary) were the headquarters of China's capitalist class, because, he said, their policies protected and served the interests of the capitalist class. This was a very serious and shocking charge against the entire Party apparatus and the administrative organization of Communist China. Mao was able to make the accusation against Liu and Deng because he controlled the armed forces through his protégé Lin Piao, who was the Defence Minister. Attempting to salvage his own position under the circumstances, Liu Shao-chi made a pro forma statement of self-criticism, saying that his economic policy of allowing private plots for the peasants and free markets to meet the need of the people in the cities had encouraged the revival of capitalism in China and represented a retreat from the road of socialism. Perhaps Liu Shao-chi believed he could save Mao's face by such an admission. The fact remained that Liu Shao-chi's economic policy rescued China from economic collapse after the disastrous failure of Mao Tze-tung's Great Leap Forward Campaign in 1958-60. However, Liu's admission of guilt was to prove a tactical mistake. It placed him at a great disadvantage and opened the way for the Maoists to escalate their attack against him and his followers in the government.

Mao's victory at the Central Committee meeting enabled a special committee of left-wing Maoists to be appointed to conduct the Cultural Revolution. As time went on and the Party and government apparatus became paralysed under the attack by the Red Guards and the Revolutionaries, this committee became the highest organ of government and its members, including Mao's wife Chiang Ching, enjoyed extraordinary power and were all elected to the Party Politburo. Throughout the years of the Cultural Revolution, Chiang Ching made use of her position as Mao's wife to become his spokeswoman and representative, supposedly transmitting Mao's orders and wishes but in fact interpreting them to suit herself. A ruthlessly ambitious woman who had been kept out of Chinese political life for decades, she now was to tolerate no opposition, imaginary or otherwise. Tens of thousands of Party officials, artists, writers, scientists and common people who fell under the shadow of her suspicion were cruelly persecuted. Scores of them died at the hands of her trusted 'Revolutionaries'.

At this August Central Committee meeting, the Defence Minister Lin Piao emerged as Mao's most ardent supporter. His eulogy of Mao was embodied in the meeting's final communiqué published in the newspapers. Lin claimed that Mao was 'the greatest living Marxist of our age', with one stroke placing Mao ahead of the Soviet leaders, including Stalin, as the true successor of Lenin. During the entire ten years of the Cultural Revolution, even after Lin Piao was disgraced, this claim was maintained by the Maoists.

One day, soon after the publication of the communiqué of the Central Committee meeting, Mr Hu, a friend of my late husband, called on me. Because in China male friendship usually excluded wives, after my husband's death his friends ceased coming to our house. Only Mr Hu continued to appear on Chinese New Year's Day to pay me the traditional courtesy call. He generally stayed only a short time, inquiring after my daughter and me and wishing us good health and happiness in the new year. He always mentioned my husband and told me how much he had esteemed him as a man and how much he had valued his friendship. Then he would take his leave, placing on the table a red envelope containing a tip for my servants, an old custom observed by only a few conservative people in China after the Communist Party took over. I was amused by his visits and thought Mr Hu rather quaint but charmingly sentimental.

When Lao Chao announced him, I was surprised. But I told Lao Chao to usher him to the drawing room and serve tea.

Mr Hu had been the owner of a factory manufacturing paint. His product was well known in China and was exported to Hong Kong and South-East Asia. After the Communist Army took over Shanghai, he continued to operate under the Communist Government's supervision. In 1956, during the Socialization of Capitalist Enterprises Campaign, his factory was taken over by the government who promised all the capitalists an annual interest of 7 per cent of the assessed value of their enterprises for ten years. While the assessed value of each of their enterprises was only a fraction of its true worth, the capitalists had no alternative but to accept. Because of his technical skill, the government invited Mr Hu to remain with his factory as the chief engineer and assistant manager when Party officials were appointed as Party Secretary and manager to run his factory.

A well-educated Chinese, Mr Hu was quite untouched by western civilization. He wrote excellent calligraphy; his conversation was interspersed with traditional literary allusions. He was not bothered by the anti-foreign attitude of the Communist regime because his own knowledge and interest did not go beyond the borders of China. On the whole he fared better during political campaigns because Party officials were less suspicious of people like Mr Hu who had no foreign contact than they were of those who had been educated abroad. His philosophical attitude towards the loss of his own factory and his ready acceptance of a subordinate position never ceased to amaze me. My husband once told me that while most capitalists found the Party officials assigned to their factories extremely difficult to deal with, Mr Hu managed to establish a friendly relationship with his Party Secretary who had superseded him as head of his factory.

'I heard you are involved in this latest political movement, the Great Proletarian Cultural Revolution. I wonder how you are getting on,' Mr Hu said, explaining the reason for his visit.

'Not very well, I'm afraid. The Shanghai office of Shell is being investigated. I have been questioned and I had to attend a struggle meeting against our former chief accountant,' I told Mr Hu. 'The men who talked to me seemed to imply there were some irregularities in the firm's activities. But they won't say what they mean. I'm really rather puzzled. I have never been involved in a political movement before.'

Lao Chao brought in the silver tea set, my best china and a large plate of small iced cakes as well as thinly cut sandwiches in the best British tradition, something I reserved for my British and Australian friends who understood the finer points of afternoon tea. This was Lao Chao's idea of treating Mr Hu as an honoured guest. As he placed the tray on the coffee table in front of the sofa, the telephone in the hall rang and he went out to answer it. He came back almost immediately and said, 'It's those people again. They want you to go over there straight away for another interview.'

'Tell them I'm busy. I will go tomorrow,' I said.

Lao Chao went out. I could hear him engaged in a heated argument on the telephone. Then he came back and said, 'They insist you must go at once. They say it's very important.'

'May I ask who is calling? If it is important, don't delay going because I'm here,' Mr Hu said to me.

'It's those officials who have been questioning me,' I told him.

'Oh, you must go at once. How can you refuse to go when those people call you! Please make haste. I'll stay here and wait for you. I want to know more about your position. I owe it to your husband, my dear old friend, to give you some advice. It's my duty. You are inexperienced in dealing with those men. They are mean and spiteful. You must not offend them,' Mr Hu said. He appeared really worried.

I was glad that he was going to wait for me because I very much wanted to hear what he had to say about the Cultural Revolution and the recent Central Committee meeting. I left the house just after four. When I returned at eight, Mr Hu was still there. As I walked into the house, he came out of the drawing room to welcome me back and beamed with pleasure and relief.

'I'm sorry I have been so long.'

'Do sit down and rest. Tell me, how did it go?'

Lao Chao brought me a cup of hot tea. While sipping it, I described to Mr Hu my interview with the Party officials.

In addition to the usual two men, there had been a third person present who might have been their superior. Perhaps to impress this new man, they were even more unpleasant than usual. When I entered the room, one of them said sternly, 'Why didn't you want to come?'

'I was busy. You should have telephoned this morning.'

In the past, one of them had always indicated the chair for me to sit down. But today they just let me stand.

'We are not conducting a dinner party. We are conducting an investigation. Whenever we need to talk to you, you just have to come immediately,' he said with a sneer.

I decided to sit down anyway.

'Look at this long list of your foreign friends! How come you have so many foreign friends? You must like them and admire their culture.' He looked at me accusingly. Then he went on, 'You said they were all friendly towards China and the Chinese people and that some of them were born here and spent their childhood years here. You claim some of them admire Chinese culture and speak our language. Yet included here are men whose ancestors made fortunes in the opium trade. They used to own factories, warehouses, ships, everything under the sun, in China. Now they have lost them all. So how could they have friendly feelings towards the People's Government? Yes, they might have liked China when the Kuomintang was here, when they exploited the Chinese people as much as they wanted, and were able to amass huge fortunes. But they definitely cannot like China now. And you talked about the diplomats having friendly feelings for China. That's even more ridiculous! Diplomats are spies sent here by their government to gather information to be used against us. How could they feel friendly towards us? It's no use your pasting gold on their faces to make them look like benevolent Buddhas. They are our enemies. But they are your friends. Now, it is quite clear where you stand, isn't it?'

'I got to know these people not because I went out of my way to seek their acquaintance or friendship. Most of them I met when my late husband was a diplomat or when he was in charge of the Shanghai Office of the Ministry of Foreign Affairs in the old days.'

'The Shanghai Office of the Ministry of Foreign Affairs of the reactionary Kuomintang Government! Your husband was a senior official of the reactionary Kuomintang Government and later he became the general manager of a foreign capitalist firm,' he said sarcastically. 'Your husband's career was nothing to be proud of.'

'He became the general manager of the Shanghai Office of Shell with the approval of the Shanghai Industry and Commerce Department of the People's Government. The department had to accept his Power of Attorney for the appointment. As for being an official of the Kuomintang Government, he stayed in Shanghai in 1949 instead of going with the Kuomintang Government to Taiwan. Doesn't that show he supported the Communist Revolution and was ready to welcome the establishment of the People's Government?'

'There might have been other reasons why he stayed. We will deal with his case later. Now we want you to denounce British imperialism and confess everything you did for Shell as their faithful agent.'

'Everything I did for Shell was in accordance with the law and regulations of the People's Government,' I declared emphatically.

The new man had not spoken but smoked incessantly, filling the room with the smell of bad tobacco. Now he tossed the butt of his cigarette on the floor and crushed it with his foot. He looked at me steadily for a few seconds to intimidate me before saying, 'Have you lived a completely blameless life? All your life you have been associated with foreigners, especially the British. Do you mean to say that you have never done anything or said anything that was not altogether correct?'

'Whether I did or said anything incorrect or not, I know for a certainty that I never did anything against the People's Government,' I said firmly.

'That's for us to judge. At least you now admit the possibility that you might have done or said something that was incorrect,' he said with a smile.

'Nonsense! I admitted no such thing!' I said.

The new man seemed to me more subtle than the other two. Though he spoke in a quiet voice instead of shouting, I was sure he was looking for an opportunity to trick me. Now he changed the subject, saying, 'Give a resumé of the activities of your office.'

I gave a brief account of our work at the office. When I had finished speaking, the man said, 'What you have just told us is almost exactly what you have already written. I believe you took the trouble to memorize what you had written. Why this precaution?'

'What I have told you and what I have written are just the same because facts are the same, no matter how many times you talk about them,' I said. This interview seemed to have gone on a long time already. I thought of Mr Hu waiting for me so I looked at my watch.

'Are you in a hurry to be gone? Perhaps you find this conversation uncomfortable?' The man was enjoying himself, twisting words and situation to suit his purpose.

'I just think you are wasting your time,' I said.

'We are not afraid to waste time. We're patient. It took us, the Communist Party, twenty-two years to overthrow the Kuomintang Government. But we succeeded in the end. When we set out to achieve our goal, we pursue it to the end.'

There was dead silence. We had reached an impasse. Suddenly the man who spoke at the struggle meeting reverted to his former tactics. He shouted, 'We won't let you get away with it! You must provide us with a list of the things you did and said that were wrong, in order to show your sincerity in changing your standpoint. Otherwise, the consequences for you will be serious. We know for a certainty you are a spy for the British!'

This was the first time any of them had actually used the word 'spy'. Hitherto they had merely hinted at it. Perhaps in the heat of the moment the man exceeded their instructions for the other two glanced at him in surprise.

I laughed at his outburst and said calmly, 'You are quite wrong. I am no more a spy for anybody than you are.'

The new man said quickly, 'Perhaps there are things you did or said which you don't remember offhand. Why don't you go home and think about it? Write down everything you did and said, no matter how trivial or insignificant. We will give you plenty of time. What about two weeks?'

'Two years will make no difference. I don't intend to make up any story,' I told them.

'Well, let's say two weeks. It's painful to admit mistakes. But it has to be done. Our Great Leader compared confession to having an operation. The operation is painful, but only after it is done can one become a new man. You want to be a good citizen of our socialist state, don't you? Then you mustn't lag behind the others. We want you to confess, not because we don't know the facts already, but because we wish to give you a chance to show your sincerity.'

I wanted to tell him that he was mad, but I bit my lip and remained silent, hoping not to prolong the senseless dialogue.

He took my silence as a sign that I was ready to do what he wanted so he dismissed me by saying, 'It's getting late. Go home and think about what I have said. We will call you in two weeks' time.'

With anger and indignation boiling inside me, I walked out of the building. There were no pedicabs. After waiting at the bus stop for a long time, I had to walk home.

Mr Hu listened to my story in silence. Lao Chao came in to announce dinner. My cook had prepared an excellent meal of Chinese dishes because he knew Mr Hu did not enjoy European cooking. During the meal we did not talk about the unpleasant subject of the Cultural Revolution but discussed my daughter's and his children's activities. We were both proud and pleased that our children seemed to have done well in Socialist China in spite of the handicap of their family background.

When we were seated again in the drawing room, I asked Mr Hu a question that had been in my mind all the time I was with my inquisitors.

'These men gave me the impression that they wanted a confession from me even if I made it up. Could that be the case?'

'Oh, yes, yes. They don't care whether it's true or not as long as they get a confession. That's what they are after.'

'But what's the point? Won't they themselves get awfully confused if everyone gives a false confession?' I was genuinely puzzled.

'To get a confession is their job. If they fail, they may be accused of not supporting the movement. The result is that whenever a political movement takes place, many people are attacked and many confessions are made. Later, when the turmoil is over, the sorting out will be done. Some of those wrongfully dealt with might get rehabilitated.'

'How long will they have to wait for rehabilitation?' I asked.

'Maybe a couple of years. Maybe it would never happen. In each organization about 3 to 5 per cent of the total must be declared the "enemy" because that is the percentage mentioned by Chairman Mao in one of his speeches.'

'How terrible!' I exclaimed.

'Yes, it's really bad. There isn't really such a high percentage of people who oppose the People's Government. To fill their quota, the Party officials often included people whom they disliked, such as those who were disgruntled and troublesome, in the list of enemies. But no individual should make a false confession, no matter how great the pressure is.' Mr Hu said this with great seriousness. He looked at me steadily as if to make sure I got his message and added, 'That has always been my policy during each political movement.'

I understood that this was the advice he had come to give me. He did not say outright, 'You mustn't give a false confession, no matter how great is the pressure,' because in a Chinese household the well-trained servant always remained within earshot ready to be of service, especially when there was a guest. Mr Hu did not want Lao Chao to hear him telling me not to confess. He was a cautious man and he trusted no one.

'There always comes a time when a man almost reaches the end of his endurance and is tempted to write down something, however untrue, to satisfy his inquisitors and to free himself from intolerable pressure. But one mustn't do it. Party officials will never be satisfied with the confession. Once one starts confessing, they will demand more and more admissions of guilt, however false, and exert increasing pressure to get what they want. In the end, one will get into a tangle of untruths from which one can no longer extract oneself. I have seen it happen to several people.' Mr Hu was still speaking in the third person and did not say, 'You mustn't.'

His advice was timely and valuable. I was grateful to him for taking the trouble to come and moved by his friendship for my late husband, which was his motive for stretching out a helping hand to me. When he thought I understood what he had come to say, he spoke of political movements in general terms. He told me that he was a veteran of many such movements and had learned by bitter experience how to deal with them.

'What do you think of the communiqué of the Central Committee meeting?' I asked him.

Mr Hu shook his head and sighed. After a moment, he said, 'Chairman Mao has won. It's not unexpected.' Then he added, 'The beginning of a political movement is always the worst period. The hurricane loses its momentum after a few months and often fizzles out after about a year.'

'A year! What a long time!' I said.

Mr Hu smiled at my outburst, and said, 'What's a year to us Chinese? It's but the blinking of an eye in our thousands of years of history. Time does not mean the same thing to us as to the Europeans whom you, of course, know well.'

'I'm accused of being a spy because they think I know the British well.'

'Their accusation is only an excuse with which to fool the masses. Sooner or later they will hit at everyone they do not trust and they probably think now is a good time to deal with you.'

Mr Hu got up to leave, asking me to telephone him whenever I wanted to see him to talk things over. As a final piece of advice he said, 'Nearly all lower-ranking Communist Party officials suffer from an inferiority complex. Although they have power over us, somehow they have a deep feeling of inferiority. This is unfortunate because some of them feel they need to reassure themselves by using that power to make our life uncomfortable or to humiliate us. When you are being questioned, be firm but be polite also. Don't offend them. They can be mean and spiteful. They can also be very cruel.'

'It's not in my nature to be obsequious. But thank you for the warning. I shall remember it,' I said.

I was so wrapped up in my own problems that only then did I think of asking him about himself.

Mr Hu said philosophically, with an air of resignation, 'I have joined the ranks of the workers. Another person has been appointed to my old job. When I tendered my letter of resignation to the Party Secretary, I told him that I felt my class status as a former capitalist rendered me unsuitable for a responsible executive position.'

The thought that he was now working as an ordinary worker in his own factory appalled me. But he was without bitterness.

'It's not so bad,' he said. 'In the Soviet Union, when the Communist Party took over, I believe all the capitalists were shot. I'm still alive and I'm able to look after all three generations of my family. I asked the Party Secretary to assign me to the most unskilled menial job. So now I am just a coolie, pushing drums of raw materials or carting coal. No one can be envious or jealous of a man doing work like that. You know, when I asked him for such a job, the Party Secretary seemed to be quite sorry for me. We used to get on well together.'

I recalled that my husband had told me that the reason Mr Hu and his Party Secretary got on well together was that Mr Hu did the work and the Party Secretary got the credit. Their factory won the Red Flag for good management and high production figures year after year.

'Did you not do all the work for him?'

'Yes, yes, I suppose I did most of the work. But I had spent my whole life building up that factory. In 1930, when I started, I had only a few workers. In 1956 when I handed the factory over to the government, there were fifteen hundred of them. And we ran a laboratory as well as a training centre for young technicians.'

'Why do you want to be a coolie? Surely, with your knowledge and experience you could do more useful work even if you must be a worker.'

He made a negative gesture with his hand. 'To be a coolie at times like this is not bad. We coolies work outside the plant and rest in a shed. If anything should go wrong, no one can accuse me of sabotaging the machinery inside the plant. An ex-capitalist is always the first on the list of suspects during a political campaign when everyone is jittery.'

With that sagacious remark he took his leave. When he shook hands with me, he said, 'Keep fit and try to live long. If you live long enough, you might see a change in our country.'

From my servants' attitude and the quality of the meal served to Mr Hu, I knew that they welcomed his visit. When I went upstairs to my bedroom, Chen Mah was there laying out my dressing gown and slippers. She advised me to listen to any advice from Mr Hu, who was, she declared, a good friend and a gentleman.

To have had someone sympathetic to talk to had been comforting. I was now more than ever resolved not to write anything false to satisfy the demand of the Party officials.

A few days without hearing from my persecutors restored my good humour somewhat. My daughter's birthday was on 18 August. I decided we should have a small dinner party to celebrate the event and to dispel some of the gloom that had descended on the household. I asked my daughter to invite a few of her friends and I rang up my old friend Li Chen to ask her to join us.

I first met Li Chen in the autumn of 1935 when I arrived in London as a student. She had just graduated from the Royal College of Music. Shortly afterwards she married a Chinese government official and returned with him to China. She became a professor at her old school, the Shanghai Conservatory of Music, where she was the head of the piano department. Her husband, Su Lei, the son of a rich Chinese merchant in Hong Kong, had received a liberal education in a British school and university. The colonial atmosphere of Hong Kong in which he grew up and hated, and the glowing reports of a new Soviet society from the pens of prominent British writers and educators that flooded British universities in the early thirties combined to produce a profound effect on his character. He became a fiercely patriotic nationalist and at the same time a believer in Marxism.

When the Communist Army was marching towards Shanghai, Su Lei was jubilant, declaring that a new era of national resurgence and honest government was about to dawn in China. He refused to go to Taiwan with the Kuomintang Government, tried to persuade his friends to do the same and welcomed the Communist takeover with enthusiasm. In 1950, during the Thought Reform Movement in the universities, Li Chen, his wife, lost her position as head of the piano department at the Conservatory of Music. Su Lei was surprised to find that the Party member appointed to take her place could not read music. A worse blow came in 1953 when Mao Tze-tung launched the 'Three and Five Antis Movement' against corruption and bribery, aimed at the Shanghai industrialists and officials like Su Lei who had worked for economic agencies of the Kuomintang Government. Although all the evidence pointed to his honesty, Su Lei became a target. He was confined to his office, where the officials took turns questioning him. And struggle meetings were held against him.

A man like Su Lei was beyond the understanding of the average Chinese Communist, who believed the desire for revolutionary change to be the exclusive right of the poor and down-trodden. However, because of the Korean War and the boycott of China by the United States, the People's Government was anxious to develop trade with Hong Kong. Su Lei's wealthy relatives in the British colony used this opportunity to secure his release through negotiating directly with Peking. The Shanghai authorities had no choice but to allow him to leave Shanghai for Hong Kong with his two children when Peking agreed to concede to his family's request.

Frustrated in their attempt to punish severely the rich man's son who had dared to assume the proud mantle of a Marxist, the local Communist officials in Shanghai refused to grant an exit permit to enable Li Chen to accompany her husband and children, using the pretext that her work with the Conservatory of Music required her to remain in Shanghai. She never saw her husband alive again. However, when he died in Hong Kong in 1957, in the more liberal atmosphere generated in China by the Eighth Party Congress held in 1956, Li Chen was given permission to attend his funeral and to see her children in Hong Kong. She remained there until 1960, when she was invited back to Shanghai by the Conservatory of Music to which she had a life-long attachment. In the meantime, her children had been taken to Australia by an uncle.

When Li Chen returned to Shanghai, the city was suffering from a severe food shortage as a result of the catastrophic economic failure of the Great Leap Forward Campaign launched by Mao Tze-tung in 1958. Long queues of people were forming at dawn at Shanghai police stations, waiting to apply for exit permits to leave the country. This was such an embarrassment for the Shanghai authorities that they viewed Li Chen's return from affluent Hong Kong to starving Shanghai as an opportunity for propaganda. I read of her return in the local newspaper, which normally reported only the visits of prominent Party officials or foreign dignitaries. The Shanghai Government hailed her as a true patriot and appointed her a delegate of the Political Consultative Conference, an organization of government-selected artists, writers, religious leaders, prominent industrialists and former Kuomintang officials whose function was to echo and to express support for the government policy of the moment, to set an example for others of similar background and to help project an image of popular support for the Communist Party policy by every section of the community. In return, the government granted members of this organization certain minor privileges, such as better housing and the use of a special restaurant where a supply of scarce food could be obtained without the surrender of ration coupons.

The Communist officials always rewarded a person for his usefulness to them, not for his virtue, though they talked a lot about his virtue. Li Chen had become a member of the Political Consultative Conference six years earlier when China suffered from severe economic difficulties and food shortages. Now that they were a thing of the past, Li Chen's usefulness to the Communist authorities was over. Besides, the Party liked people to show gratitude with a display of servile obedience and verbal glorification of its policies. Li Chen was quite incapable of either. In fact, she told me that she found attending meetings boring and maintained silence when she was expected to pay homage to Mao's policies on music and education. Her lack of enthusiasm for the part allocated to her as a member of the Political Consultative Conference could not have failed to irritate the Party officials.

These thoughts were in my mind when I telephoned her. I was very pleased when she accepted my invitation to dinner with alacrity.

When I got up in the early morning of 18 August, my daughter's birthday, Chen Mah was not in the house. A devout Buddhist, she always went on this day to the temple at Ching-En-Tze to say a special prayer for Meiping – of whom she was very fond. Thinking that I would disapprove of these temple visits because I am a Christian, she generally slipped out of the house early and returned quietly, hoping I would not notice her absence. I pretended to know nothing about it and never mentioned it to her.

While I was in the dining room doing the flowers, she returned. I heard her talking to the cook in the pantry in an unusually agitated voice. When she came into the hall, I saw that she was wiping her eyes with her handkerchief.

'What's happened, Chen Mah?' I called to her.

She was silent but came into the room where I was. 'What's happened at the temple?' I asked her.

She sat down on a dining chair and burst into tears. 'They are dismantling the temple,' she said between sobs.

'Who are dismantling the temple?' I asked her. 'Not the government, surely!'

'Young people. Probably students. They said Chairman Mao told them to stop superstition. They also said the monks are counter-revolutionaries opposed to Chairman Mao.'

'What did the monks do?'

'Nothing. The students rounded them up. Some were beaten. When I got there I saw them prostrate on the ground in the courtyard. There was a large crowd of onlookers. One of them told me that the students were going to dismantle the temple and burn the scriptures as they had done at other places. I actually saw some of the students climbing onto the roof and throwing down the tiles,' Chen Mah said while wiping away her tears.

'Please, Chen Mah, you mustn't be too upset. You can worship at home. The Christian churches have been closed for several years now. The Christians all worship at home. You can do the same, can't you? In any case, you mustn't cry on Meiping's birthday.'

'Yes, yes, I mustn't cry on Meiping's birthday. But I was upset to see such wanton destruction.' She tucked her handkerchief away and went out of the room.

Then the cook came in to complain that several items of food I had asked him to get for the party were unobtainable. He added that at the food market he and other cooks were jeered at for working for wealthy families.

'I suppose they didn't like to see you buying more things than they could afford. Please don't let it bother you. As for the party, please just use whatever you were able to obtain at the market. I'm sure you will be able to put together a good meal for Meiping's birthday,' I tried to reassure him.

While I could understand my cook's experience at the market as the result of class hatred generated by massive propaganda against the capitalist class, which to the general public was simply 'the rich people', I was puzzled by what had happened at the temple, which was operated by the State. The monks there were in fact government employees. If the government had decided to change its policy, it could have closed the temple and transferred the monks to other forms of employment as the government had done earlier during the Great Leap Forward Campaign. Actually the temple at Ching-En-Tze was a showplace for official visitors from South-East Asia to create the impression that China tolerated Buddhism. I remembered reading in the newspaper that the temple was re-opened after the Great Leap Forward Campaign and the monks brought back again. I wondered why the students had been allowed to do what they were doing and whether the Shanghai Municipal Government was aware of what was going on at Ching-En-Tze.

At six o'clock Li Chen arrived. With her snow-white hair and calm smile, she always seemed the epitome of scholarly authority, tranquillity and distinction. Only her old friends like myself knew that behind her serene exterior was such great sensitivity that she could be depressed or elated by events which would have left an ordinary person relatively unmoved.

Li Chen was a great artist and an able teacher. From time immemorial, China's tradition of respect for teachers gave them a special place in society. A good teacher who had devoted his life to education was compared to a fruitful tree, a phrase certainly applicable to Li Chen, whose many former students worked as concert pianists, accompanists and teachers all over China. Several had won international piano contests and received recognition abroad. I was very fond of Li Chen and greatly admired her total devotion to music and her students. Since her return from Hong Kong, we had seen a great deal of each other. She would often bring her music and spend an evening with me listening to my records. I knew she often felt lonely and missed her children. Fortunately, since Liu Shao-chi had become the Chairman of the People's Republic in 1960 and Mao Tze-tung had retired from active administrative work, China had had no large-scale political upheaval until now so that Li Chen had been able to keep in touch with her children in Australia by correspondence.

After Lao Chao had served us with iced tea, I asked Li Chen, 'How is everything with you at the Conservatory?'

'I'm afraid it's not good,' she said sadly. 'All classes have stopped. We are supposed to devote our entire time to the Cultural Revolution. Everybody has to write Big Character Posters. Professors like myself also have to write self-criticisms and read other people's Big Character Posters against us.'

'Are there many against you?' I asked her anxiously.

'More are written against professors than against others. I don't know whether I have more than other professors. I haven't counted them. But so far, no struggle meeting has been arranged against me. My personal history is comparatively simple. I have never done any other work than being a teacher at the Conservatory.'

'Have there been many struggle meetings against other professors at the Conservatory?' I asked her.

'Yes, there have been several. One was against a former member of the Kuomintang and another was against a former Rightist. The others are from other departments so I don't know their personal history. These two are people who had already been denounced in former political movements,' Li Chen explained. 'I hate struggle meetings. Somehow, everybody behaves like savages.'

'Do you think you will be safe?'

'I have never opposed the Communist Party. I am entirely non-political. When I graduated from the Conservatory I went to England to study. When I came back I returned to the Conservatory to teach. There is nothing about me the Party doesn't know. I should be safe, shouldn't I? But I don't know what may happen. There is something about this political campaign which seems different from previous ones.'

'What is different?' I asked her.

'It's the attitude of the Party officials. In other former political campaigns they were cocksure. They went into it boldly, full of confidence. This time, they seem nervous, almost as if they don't really want to do anything. The fact that they have limited their attack to people who have been denounced already seems to indicate they don't want to expand the scope of attack. Perhaps after the failure of Mao's Great Leap Forward Campaign the Party officials are no longer certain Mao is always right to rely on political campaigns for making progress.'

What Li Chen told me was very interesting. At that juncture we did not know, of course, that the Proletarian Cultural Revolution was in fact a struggle for power between the Maoists and the more moderate faction headed by Liu Shao-chi and Deng Hsiao-ping. It later became known that the chief Party Secretary at the Conservatory belonged to Liu Shao-chi's faction. He was murdered by Chiang Ching's Revolutionaries when Chiang Ching decided to install one of her favourite young men as the Conservatory's Party Secretary.

'The writing of Big Character Posters advocated by Mao seems to me a great waste. At the Conservatory, a great deal of paper, thousands of writing brushes and bottles of ink have already been used. Yet when we neded extra lights in the classroom or additional musical instruments there was never any money for them,' said Li Chen.

'What do the Big Character Posters say against you?' I asked her.

'The usual criticism about my education in England, my sending the children to Australia and my teaching method. When we were friendly with the Soviet Union, we were urged to teach western music and train students to take part in international compositions. After we broke with the Soviet Union, Chairman Mao started to make criticisms about western music. We had to use Chinese compositions exclusively for teaching. But there are so few Chinese compositions. Half my time was spent looking for teaching materials. It's hard enough to carry on as a teacher already. Now my students are made to turn against me. Do you know one of them told me quietly that they had to write posters against me to protect themselves?'

'Exactly. You mustn't mind it. Don't let it hurt you! The poor young people have to do it.'

'I feel very sad. It is almost as if my whole life is wasted,' Li Chen sighed.

'Don't be depressed by it! During the Great Leap Forward Campaign of 1958, the students in Meiping's school from capitalist class families all had to criticize their family background. I told her to go ahead and criticize me. She did. The teacher and her fellow students all applauded her. It's only a formality. It's just acting. Don't let it bother you.'

'I'm afraid I can't laugh it off like you do,' Li Chen said. 'It's so unfair!'

'Doesn't your position as a delegate to the Political Consultative Conference give you some protection?' I asked my friend.

'I hear the Maoists want to abolish that organization. They call it an organization of radishes, red on the outside but white inside. They claim that while all the delegates talked as if they supported the Communist Party, in actual fact they oppose the Party,' she said.

'Is that true?'

'Who knows? When the penalty of speaking one's mind is so great, nobody knows what anybody else thinks,' Li Chen said. I had to agree with her. In fact, after living in Communist China for so many years, I realized that one of the advantages enjoyed by a democratic government which allows freedom of speech is that the government knows exactly who supports it and who is against it, while a totalitarian government knows nothing of what the people really think.

When I told her that I too was involved in the Cultural Revolution, her reaction was the same as Winnie's. She said, 'Now that Shell has closed their Shanghai Office, the Party officials probably feel that they should use the opportunity of this political campaign to frighten you so that they can control you more easily in future.' But she did not think the persecution against me would be serious. 'They can't save money by reducing your salary since you get no pay from the government. They can't sack you from your job since you don't work for them. I can't see that there is much they can do to you except to give you a fright.'

'I hope you are right,' I said.

'You know, I feel so discouraged that I sometimes think I can't go on,' Li Chen said.

'Why don't you ask to retire? Lots of people retire before they are sixty and take a cut in pension to avoid politics.'

'I might just do that when the Cultural Revolution is over,' Li Chen said.

My daughter arrived with four of her young friends: Kung, a handsome male actor from her Film Studio whose father was a very famous film director from the thirties; a violinist with the Municipal Orchestra named Chang; Sun Kai, a mathematics teacher at a technical college who was Meiping's special boy friend; and my god-daughter Hean who had been Meiping's childhood friend in Australia. They were all keenly interested in music and often gathered at our house to listen to our stereo records.

The young possess an infinite capacity to be cheerful. Although all of them came from the type of families likely to be adversely affected by the Cultural Revolution, no mention was made of it. They laughed and chatted about music and books throughout the meal. When Meiping took what remained of her large birthday cake into the kitchen to share with the servants, even Chen Mah recovered her usual good humour. I heard her scolding Meiping fondly for licking chocolate from her fingers. When the meal was over, the young people retired to Meiping's study to indulge in their favourite pastime of playing records on her record-player.

Li Chen and I went into the garden. Lao Chao arranged two wicker chairs on the lawn, put cushions on them, lit a coil of mosquito incense, and placed it on a plate between the chairs. Then he brought us chrysanthemum tea in covered cups. Soothing music from a violin concerto came through the window. I settled deeper into the chair and gazed up at the starlit summer sky.

'You really have a comfortable life. You manage to enjoy the best of the western as well as the Chinese worlds, don't you?' Li Chen said. 'I wonder if that's not what irritates the Party officials.'

'Maybe. Those questioning me certainly seem to hate me. Do you think they really believe it is our fault that the workers and peasants in China are poor?'

'I think they are just envious. People can't all live in the same way. I have a big apartment. It's allocated to me by the Conservatory. That shows they don't expect everyone to live in the same way,' said Li Chen. She seemed more relaxed now.

'Of course, you're different. You have done so much for the country. Hundreds of young people have passed through your hands. Each one of them carried with him something you taught him. Isn't that wonderful?' I truly admired my friend Li Chen.

'I don't hear anyone in the Conservatory say that about me. It's always how I taught decadent western music to poison the minds of the young. They don't stop to think I couldn't have done it if the government had forbidden it. All our teaching materials had to be passed by our Party Secretary before we could use them for the students. And they seem to forget that they used to urge me to teach western music in the early fifties when China was friendly with the Soviet Union.' Li Chen was indignant and distraught. I wished I hadn't mentioned her work again. To try to cheer her up, I asked her about her children.

'They seem so remote, especially now they are married,' she said.

'Do you not long to see them?'

'Oh, I do! But what's the use thinking about it now? The government may never give me a passport to travel to Australia. The children certainly won't come here.'

'Perhaps you shouldn't have come back from Hong Kong,' I said.

'At the time it seemed the best thing to do. I am very attached to the Conservatory, you know. I was trained there and I have worked there. It is really the most important thing in my life apart from the children. Many of my colleagues were fellow students when we studied there together. They all wrote to me. My students wrote to me. The Party Secretary wrote to me. Everybody said I was needed at the Conservatory so I came back.'

'What did Su Lei's family say about your wishing to come back?'

'After Su Lei died, they weren't very concerned about me. Most of them have now settled in Australia. They are a close-knit family. The uncles think of Su Lei's children as belonging to the family rather than to me. Of course, if I weren't able to make a living myself they would look after me. But I found the atmosphere a little stifling.'

Li Chen's last few words were drowned in a sudden burst of noise from drums and gongs in the street. Lao Chao came into the garden and said, 'There's a parade of students passing the house.'

The young people also came outside. Standing on the terrace, Kung, the young actor, said, 'It's probably the Red Guards. A few days ago, Chiang Ching received their representatives at the Great Hall of the People in Peking. That means the Chairman approves of the Red Guards Organization.'

'Who organized them in the first place?' I asked him. 'I have never heard of an organization called the Red Guards.'

'It's something new for the Cultural Revolution, encouraged by Chiang Ching, I heard. Someone told me she actually quietly organized some students from Ching Hua Middle School and then pretended it was the spontaneous idea of the students. Since she is the Chairman's wife, the idea caught on. Now, acting as the Chairman's representative, she has given the Red Guards official recognition,' Kung said. Then he laughed and added, 'My father used to say she was a mediocre actress in the old days. She seems to have improved.' (Subsequently, when Chiang Ching dealt with her 'enemies' in the film world, Kung's father had a terrible time and barely survived the ordeal. Kung himself was not given a part to play in any film production for years because of his father.)

Next day, I read in the newspaper that on 18 August Mao Tze-tung had reviewed the first contingent of the Red Guards in Peking. On the front page was a large photograph of Mao wearing the khaki uniform of a People's Liberation Army officer, with a red armband on which the three Chinese characters for 'Red Guard' – Hong Wei Bing – were written in his own handwriting. From the gallery of the Tien An Men Square (the Gate of Heavenly Peace of the Forbidden City), he had smiled and waved as he received a thunderous ovation from the youngsters gathered below. His special message to the Red Guards was to carry the torch of the Cultural Revolution to the far corners of China and to pursue the purpose of the Revolution to the very end. The young people all over China received this message from the man they had been brought up to worship as a call to arms. At that early stage of the Cultural Revolution the declared target was still only the 'capitalist class'. It was on them that the Red Guards focused their attack.

Group after group of young students continued to pass our house that evening, beating drums and gongs and shouting slogans. Meiping and her friends went out to watch the parade; Li Chen and I retired to my study. The noise from the street was so loud that we couldn't talk. While we listened, I seemed to hear 'Protect Chairman Mao' among the slogans shouted by the Red Guards. When Meiping came back alone, she told us that the students carried Mao's portraits and shouted 'Protect Chairman Mao' or 'We shall protect Chairman Mao with our lives.'

'Who is supposed to be threatening him?' I asked. None of us could think of an answer. In his lofty position as a demigod, Mao seemed beyond human reach.

I was thinking of Stalin in the last years of his life when he suspected so many people of attempting to kill him, when Li Chen said, 'One of the symptoms of senile dementia is suspicion and the other is paranoia.'

'Oh, God!' I murmured.

Li Chen, my daughter Meiping and I stood in my study staring at each other speechlessly. We were rather frightened because suddenly the awesome reality that everybody in China, including ourselves, was at the mercy of Mao's whims struck each of us forcibly.

After a while, Li Chen said, 'I must go. No doubt we will know about everything as time goes on.'

'I'll see Auntie Li home,' said Meiping. 'I don't think there are any buses. The streets have been taken over by the paraders.'

I went with them to the front gate. Teams of teenagers holding coloured flags with slogans and carrying portraits of Mao were passing down the street in front of my house. They were preceded by others beating drums and gongs. Every few yards a leader read out slogans written on a piece of paper, echoed loudly by the others. All the young paraders wore armbands of red cotton on which were written 'Red Guard' in an imitation of Mao's style of handwriting. The parade looked to me well organized and carefully directed, not something the young people could have done on their own. There was the hand of authority behind it, I thought.

Li Chen and I said goodbye to each other. She walked away with Meiping who was pushing her bicycle beside her. I stood there watching them until the parading youngsters hid Li Chen's snow-white hair from my view.

That was the last glimpse I ever had of my dear old friend. A month later, when I was under house arrest, she committed suicide after a particularly humiliating experience at a struggle meeting when the Red Guards placed a pole across the gate of the Conservatory less than four feet from the ground and made Li Chen crawl under it to demonstrate that she was 'a running dog of the British imperialists' because of her education in England and then held a struggle meeting afterwards to compel her to confess her 'love for western music'. She was found dead the next day, seated by her piano, with the gas turned on. The note she left behind held one sentence: 'I did my best for my students.'

The servants had already retired so I waited downstairs for my daughter to get back. When she returned, we mounted the stairs together in silence. On the landing, she put her arms around me to hug me good night. There was much I wanted to say to her, some words of love and reassurance, but I felt choked with a deep feeling of sadness and fear that I could not explain.

'Well, this certainly is the one birthday I won't forget,' my daughter said good-humouredly.

After she had gone into her bedroom, I closed the windows to shut out the noise from the street. The sound was muted and seemed further away, but with the cool evening breeze kept out, the house was very hot. Parade after parade passed outside. The resolute footsteps of young men and women fired with revolutionary fervour and their emotional shouting voices continued to penetrate the walls.

I went into my study, took a book from the shelf and tried to read. But I was restless and could not concentrate. Wandering aimlessly from room to room, I rearranged the flowers, throwing away the dead ones and putting water into the vases. I straightened the paintings on the walls and picked up ivory figures to examine the delicate carvings. All the time the parades went on outside. Even when a parade did not pass down the street by my house, I could hear the sound of the drums and gongs. After wandering around in the house, I went finally to Meiping's room to see how she was. There was no answer to my light tap on the door. I opened it gently and found my daughter already asleep. Her black hair was spread on the white pillow and her sweet young face was peaceful in repose. The light from the gap in the door fell on a snapshot of my husband in a small silver frame on her bedside table. I closed the door softly.

These were the two people in the world closest to my heart. One had died. The other was alive and her life was just unfolding.

'Take good care of yourself and look after Meiping. I am sad to have to leave you both so soon.'

I could hear again the weakened voice of my husband speaking these words before he lapsed into a deep coma from which he never awakened. That was nearly nine years ago. He had charged me to look after our daughter. I had done just that and watched her grow with joy in my heart. She was intelligent, beautiful and warm-hearted. I never had to worry about her. But now, with the start of the Cultural Revolution, a dark cloud had come over our lives. As I tried to look into the future, a deep feeling of uncertainty overwhelmed me. For the first time in my life, I felt unable to control the direction of my own life and guide my daughter. That frightened me.

To cope with problems and changes with determination and optimism was the way I had lived. When my husband died in 1957, I was shattered by my loss and, for a time, felt half dead with grief myself. But I found that taking positive action to cope with problems one by one was therapeutic and good for the renewal of courage.

In old China, women who lost their husbands lost their own identity. They became virtually non-persons, subjected to ridicule and gossip by the neighbours. Although the new Marriage Law passed by the People's Government in 1952 protected women in general and forbade discrimination, the old prejudice against widows and unmarried older women persisted. Chinese society seemed to be offended and embarrassed by the sight of a woman trying to stand on her own.

When I started working at the Shell office, members of the senior Chinese staff were dismayed that a woman with no administrative experience was put in charge of them. I had to prove myself over and over again to earn their respect and confidence. There was nothing I enjoyed more than meeting the challenge of life and overcoming difficulties. And I was pleased and proud that I was able to maintain our old life-style in spite of losing my husband. Never in my life had I found myself in a situation so puzzling as the Cultural Revolution. I knew for a fact that whenever a Chinese national was appointed to a senior position in a foreign firm, the Department of Industry and Commerce of the Shanghai Municipal Government must give permission. Since the police kept a dossier of everybody, the government should know everything about me. There seemed no valid reason for the sudden accusation against me. While Winnie, Li Chen and Mr Hu all seemed to think my being the target of persecution not unexpected, I did not know how best to conduct myself in the days ahead except to resist firmly all efforts to make me write a false confession. That would inevitably bring me into confrontation with officials of the Party. What would be the outcome of such confrontation? How would it affect my daughter's life? Standing outside my daughter's bedroom, I was so deeply troubled and felt so helpless that I invoked the guidance of God in a special prayer.

In the days after Mao Tze-tung reviewed the first group of Red Guards in Peking and gave them his blessing, the Red Guards in Shanghai took over the streets. The newspaper announced that the mission of the Red Guards was to rid the country of the 'Four Olds' – old culture, old customs, old habits and old ways of thinking. There was no clear definition of 'old'; it was left to the Red Guards to decide. First of all, they changed street names. The main thoroughfare of Shanghai along the waterfront, the Bund, was renamed Revolutionary Boulevard. Another major street was renamed August the First to commemorate Army Day. The road on which the Soviet Union had its Consulate was renamed Anti-Revisionist Street, while the road in front of the former British Consulate was renamed Anti-Imperialist Street. I found my own home now stood on Oo Yang

Hai Road, named to commemorate a soldier who had given his life trying to save a mule from an oncoming train. The Red Guards debated whether to reverse the system of traffic lights, as they thought Red should mean Go and not Stop. In the meantime, traffic lights stopped operating.

They smashed flower and curio shops because they said only the rich had the money to spend on such frivolities. The other shops were examined and goods they considered offensive or unsuitable for a socialist society they destroyed or confiscated. Their standard was very strict. Because they did not think a socialist man should sit on a sofa, all sofas became taboo. Other things such as inner-spring mattresses, silk, velvet, cosmetics and clothes that reflected fashion trends of the West were all tossed onto the streets waiting to be carted away or burnt. Traditionally, shops in China had borne names that were considered propitious, such as 'Rich and Beautiful' for a fabric shop, 'Delicious Aroma' for a restaurant, 'Good Fortune and Longevity' for a shop that sold hats for older men, 'Comfort' for a shoe shop, 'Happy homes' for a furniture shop etc. When the government took over the shops in 1956, the names had not been changed. Now, condemned by the Red Guards, they had to be changed to something more revolutionary. Uncertain what alternative would be acceptable, managers of a large number of shops chose the name 'East is Red', the title of a song eulogizing Mao Tze-tung which during the Cultural Revolution took the place of the National Anthem. Since the Red Guards had removed the goods displayed in the windows of the shops, Mao's official portraits were put there. A person walking down the streets in the shopping district would not only be confused by rows of shops bearing the same name, but also had the uncanny feeling of being watched by a hundred faces of Mao.

Daily, my servants reported to me all these incredible actions of the Red Guards. I became so curious that I decided to venture out to see for myself.

I had in a bank in the shopping district two fixed deposits that had matured. I decided to cash one of them so that I would have some extra money in the house, since experience told me that shortages of food and everything else always followed political upheavals. To keep alive, one had to resort to the black market where prices were astronomical. I remembered my cook paying 50 yuan for a piece of pork that was 2 or 3 yuan in normal times, after the failure of Mao's Great Leap Forward Campaign.

Both Lao Chao and Chen Mah suggested that I should be suitably dressed for going out, as the lady next door had had an unpleasant encounter with the Red Guards who had confiscated her shoes and cut open the legs of her slacks, when she went out to visit a friend. So before setting out from the house to go to the bank, I put on an old shirt, a pair of loose-fitting trousers borrowed from Chen Mah and my exercise shoes. As the August sun was strong, Chen Mah handed me the wide-brimmed straw hat my daughter had brought back from the country after working in a rural commune in a programme for students to help the peasants.

The streets were in a ferment of activity. Red Guards were everywhere. There were also many idle spectators. At this juncture of the Cultural Revolution, the 'enemy' was the capitalist class so the majority of the population felt quite safe. To them the activities of the Red Guards were spectacular and entertaining. Many of them were strolling through the streets to watch the fun.

Groups of Red Guards were explaining to clusters of onlookers the meaning and purpose of the Cultural Revolution. I listened to one group for a little while and was puzzled and surprised to hear the Red Guard speaker telling the people that they would be 'liberated' by the Cultural Revolution. Hadn't the people been liberated already in 1949 when the Communist Party took over China? Was that liberation not good enough so that the people had to be liberated again? It almost seemed to me that the Communist Party was making self-criticism. But that was unthinkable. I dismissed what I had heard as unimportant, perhaps merely a slip of the tongue by the young speaker. In fact, to liberate the proletariat again became the theme of the Cultural Revolution. Mao was to claim that his opponents in the Party leadership headed by Liu Shao-chi and Deng Hsiao-ping had revived capitalism in China. However, this was not revealed until much later in the year.

Other Red Guards were stopping buses, distributing leaflets, lecturing the passengers and punishing those whose clothes the Red Guards disapproved of. Most bicycles had red cards bearing Mao's quotations on the handlebars; riders of the few without them were stopped and given warning. On the pavement, the Red Guards led the people to shout slogans. Each group of Red Guards was accompanied by large reproductions of Mao's portraits mounted on stands and drums and gongs. At many street corners, loudspeakers were blaring revolutionary songs at intervals. In my proletarian outfit of old shirt and wide trousers, I blended with the scene and attracted no special attention. I walked steadily in the direction of the bank.

Suddenly I was startled to see the group of Red Guards right in front of me seize a pretty young woman. While one Red Guard held her, another removed her shoes and a third one cut the legs of her slacks open. The Red Guards were shouting, 'Why do you wear shoes with pointed toes? Why do you wear slacks with narrow legs?'

'I'm a worker! I'm not a member of the capitalist class! Let me go!' the girl was struggling and protesting.

In the struggle, the Red Guards removed her slacks altogether, much to the amusement of the crowd that surrounded the scene. The onlookers were laughing and jeering. One of the Red Guards slapped the girl's face to stop her from struggling. She sat on the dusty ground and buried her face in her arms. Between sobs she murmured, 'I'm not a member of the capitalist class!'

One of the Red Guards opened her bag and took out her work-pass to examine it. Then he threw the pass and her trousers to her. Hastily she pulled on the trousers. She did not wait for them to give her back her shoes but walked away quickly in her socks. Almost immediately the same Red Guard seized a young man and shouted, 'Why do you have oiled hair?'

I did not wait to see the outcome of this encounter but went straight to the bank. In China, every bank was a branch of the People's Bank which belonged to the State. There was no brass railing or small windows. The tellers sat behind a plain wooden counter to deal with the depositors. I approached one of the women and placed my deposit slip on the counter in front of her.

Before I left the house, I had considered how much cash I should withdraw. The two deposits past the maturing date were for 6,000 yuan (approximately £1,000) and 20,000 yuan (approximately £3,300) respectively. The cost of living in China was low, as were wages and salaries. In 1966, 6,000 yuan was a large sum of money; 20,000 yuan represented a small fortune. The bank was really a department of the government. Those who worked there were charged with the task of encouraging savings so that money could be channelled to the State. During political campaigns the tellers had the power to refuse payment of large sums of money to depositors even when the deposits had matured. Sometimes they would demand a letter of approval from the depositor's place of work to certify the reason for the withdrawal. To avoid a possible rejection of my request to withdraw my money, I decided to cash the lesser sum of 6,000 and to renew the 20,000 for another year. But I had no difficulty whatever. The teller handed me the cash without uttering a single word and before I had finished counting the bank notes, she had already picked up her knitting again. Although the walls of the small bank were covered with Cultural

Revolution slogans and a number of Big Character Posters, the atmosphere inside was a contrast to the tension generated by the Red Guards on the streets.

As I stepped once again onto the sun-baked pavement, I rather regretted that I had been too timid to try to cash the larger sum. At the same time I was glad I had encountered no difficulty. I headed for home, but when I turned the corner, I was almost knocked down by a group of excited Red Guards leading an old man on a length of rope. They were shouting and hitting the poor man with a stick. I quickly stepped back and stood against the wall to let them pass. Suddenly the old man collapsed on the ground as if too tired to go on. He was a pitiful sight with his shirt torn and a few strands of grey hair over his half-shut eyes. The Red Guards pulled the rope. When he still did not get up, they jumped on him. The old man shrieked in pain.

'Dirty capitalist! Exploiter of workers! You deserve to die!' shouted the Red Guards.

My heart was palpitating wildly. The sudden and unexpected encounter with the group of Red Guards and the close proximity of the suffering old man combined to give me a fright and made me think of Mr Hu. I wondered how he was faring. Nearly two weeks had passed since he had visited me. I thought I really ought to telephone him to see if he was all right. I slipped away and hastened towards my house. The streets were now even more crowded than an hour before. The Red Guards were seizing people indiscriminately. There were loud screams of protest and tearful pleading from the victims. When I saw that they were seizing women with permanent waves and cutting their hair off, I was really thankful that Chen Mah had given me the large straw hat to wear to cover my curly hair. There were quite a number of policemen on the streets but they were just watching.

It was a relief to leave the busy shopping area behind me. The residential streets were more peaceful. However, when I turned into my street, I saw a large crowd of people in front of my house. They were looking at a Big Character Poster pasted on the front gate of my neighbour's house across the road. He was the chief engineer of the Shanghai Aluminium Company, formerly a Swiss firm taken over a few years earlier by the Chinese Government. Workers of the plant had put up the poster on his front gate denouncing him as a 'running dog of Swiss imperialism'. Beside the poster was a smaller one written in a childish script. It was signed by my neighbour's two small children who had joined in the denunciation of their father and vowed to sever their relationship with him. This unusual poster from an eleven-year-old and a ten-year-old was the reason for the crowd.

When Lao Chao opened the gate for me, I asked about the poster signed by the children of my neighbour. Lao Chao told me that my neighbour's servant had told him that it was the father's idea to save his children from persecution.

The Red Guards' activities intensified by the hour. The very next day they entered the house of my neighbour across the street. His wife refused to open the front gate and turned the garden hose on the Red Guards to prevent them from entering. They simply smashed the gate down, snatched the hose from her and drenched her with water. Then they knocked her down and beat her for resisting their revolutionary action. Her children tried to defend their mother and got into a fight with the Red Guards. They were denounced as 'Puppies of the running dog of Swiss imperialism', and made to assist the Red Guards in burning their father's books.

Day and night the city resounded with the loud noise of drums and gongs. News of looting and the ransacking of private homes all over the city reached me from different sources. I tried to reach Mr Hu by telephone without success. It was the same with my other friends. The violence of the Red Guards seemed to have escalated. I heard of victims being humiliated, terrorized and often killed when they offered resistance. Articles in the newspapers and talks by leading Maoists encouraged the Red Guards and congratulated them on their vandalism. They were declared to be the true successors to the cause of the proletarian Revolution and exhorted to be fearless and to overcome difficulties in their work of toppling the old world and building a new one based on Mao's teachings.

I felt utterly helpless. There was nothing I could do to prevent the destruction of my home and the loss of all my possessions. My daughter became very worried. More than once, she talked about our not being able to live on her small salary. I decided the time had come to tell her about my bank accounts in Hong Kong and elsewhere which, I told her, would be more than sufficient to cover our living expenses. Actually I myself was more worried about her status after the Cultural Revolution. If a new society was to be formed in which descendants of capitalist-class families were to become a permanently unprivileged class in China, like the Untouchables in India, her life would be unthinkable. To me this was of more importance than the loss of our material possessions.

To take care of the servants, I decided to give them the 6,000 yuan I had obtained from the bank straightaway before the Red Guards came to our house. At first they refused to accept the money, reiterating their wish to remain to look after Meiping and myself. They also offered to hide my jewellery and valuables in their homes. Not wishing to implicate them in my own difficulties, I refused. I called Chen Mah, Lao Chao and Cook to my study and discussed with them how best to divide the money among the three of them. Because the gardener was not a full-time employee and came only occasionally, I decided to give him only 400 yuan. Chen Mah offered to take less than the other two because, she said, 'They have to take care of their wives.' After I had divided the money, I placed the 400 yuan for the gardener in an envelope intending to give it to him the next time he came to work in the garden.

I told my servants that if they were afraid, they could leave any time. When the Cultural Revolution was over, if I was financially able, I would give them additional money, for they had all been with me for a very long time.

After that had been done, I waited for the Red Guards.

CHAPTER 3

The Red Guards

As THE TEMPO OF the Proletarian Cultural Revolution gathered momentum, all-night sessions of political indoctrination were often held in different organizations. On the evening of 30 August when the Red Guards came to loot my house, my daughter was at her Film Studio attending one of these meetings. I was sitting alone in my study reading *The Rise and Fall of the Third Reich*, which had come in the last batch of books from a bookshop in London with which I had an account. Throughout the years I worked for Shell, I managed to receive books from this shop by having the parcels sent to Shell because the Shanghai censors always passed unopened all parcels addressed to organizations. Since the office received an enormous amount of scientific literature for distribution to Chinese research organizations, my small parcel attracted no undue attention.

The house was very quiet. I knew Lao Chao was sitting in the pantry as he had done day after day. Chen Mah was in her room, probably lying in bed wide awake. There was not the slightest sound or movement anywhere, almost as if everything in the house was holding its breath waiting helplessly for its own destruction.

The windows of my study were open. The bitter-sweet perfume of the magnolia in the garden and the damp smell of the cool evening air with a hint of autumn pervaded the atmosphere. From the direction of the street, faint at first but growing louder, came the sound of a heavy motor vehicle slowly approaching. I listened and waited for it to speed up and pass the house. But it slowed down and the motor was cut off. I knew my neighbour on the left was also expecting the Red Guards. Dropping the book on my lap and sitting up tensely, I listened, wondering which house was to be the target.

Suddenly the door bell began to ring incessantly. At the same time, there was furious pounding of many fists on my front gate, accompanied by the confused sound of many hysterical voices shouting slogans. The cacophony told me that the time of waiting was over and that I must face the threat of the Red Guards and the destruction of my home. Lao Chao came up the stairs breathlessly. Although he had known the Red Guards were sure to come eventually and had been waiting night after night just as I had done, his face was ashen.

'They have come!' His unsteady voice was a mixture of awe and fright.

'Please keep calm, Lao Chao! Open the gate but don't say anything. Take Chen Mah with you to your room and stay there,' I told him.

Lao Chao's room was over the garage. I wanted both of them to be out of the way so that they could be prevented from saying anything to offend the Red Guards out of a sense of loyalty to me.

Outside, the sound of voices became louder. 'Open the gate! Open the gate! Are you all dead? Why don't you open the gate?' Some were heard swearing and kicking the wooden gate. The horn of the truck was blasting too.

Lao Chao ran downstairs. I stood up to put the book on the shelf. A copy of the Constitution of the People's Republic caught my eye. Taking it in my hand and picking up the bunch of keys I had ready on my desk, I walked downstairs.

Although in my imagination I had already lived through this moment many times, my heart was pounding. However, lifelong discipline enabled me to maintain a calm appearance. By the time I had reached the bottom of the staircase, I was the epitome of Chinese fatalism.

At the same moment, the Red Guards pushed open the front door and entered the house. There were between thirty and forty senior high school students, aged between fifteen and twenty, led by two men and one woman much older. Although they all wore the armbands of the Red Guards, I thought the three older people were the teachers who generally accompanied the Red Guards when they looted private homes. As they crowded into the hall, one of them knocked over a pot of jasmine on a Fên T'sai porcelain stool. The tiny white blooms scattered on the floor were trampled by their impatient feet.

The leading Red Guard, a gangling youth with angry eyes, stepped forward and said to me, 'We are the Red Guards. We have come to take revolutionary action against you!'

Though I knew I was doing something futile and pointless, I held up the copy of the Constitution and said calmly, 'It's against the Constitution of the People's Republic of China to enter a private house without a search warrant.'

The young man snatched the document out of my hand and threw it on the floor. With his eyes blazing, he said, 'The Constitution is abolished. It was a document written by the Revisionists within the Communist Party. We recognize only the teachings of our Great Leader Chairman Mao.'

'Only the People's Congress has the power to change the Constitution,' I said.

'We have abolished it. What can you do about it?' he said aggressively while assuming a militant stance with his feet apart and shoulders braced.

A girl came within a few inches of where I stood and said, 'What trick are you trying to play? Your only way out is to bow your head in submission. Otherwise you will suffer.' She shook her fist in front of my nose and spat on the floor.

Another young man used a stick to smash the mirror hanging over the blackwood chest facing the front door. A shower of glass fell on the blue and white K'ang Hsi vase on the chest but the carved frame of the mirror remained on the hook. He tore the frame off and hurled it against the banister. Then he took from another Red Guard a small blackboard which he hung up on the hook. On it was written a quotation from Mao Tze-tung. It said, 'When the enemies with guns are annihilated, the enemies without guns still remain. We must not belittle these enemies.'

The Red Guards read the quotation aloud as if taking a solemn oath. Afterwards, they told me to read it. Then one of them shouted to me, 'An enemy without gun! That's what you are. Hand over the keys!'

I placed my bunch of keys on the chest amidst the fragments of glass. One of them picked it up. All the Red Guards dispersed into various parts of the house. A girl pushed me into the dining room and locked the door.

I sat down by the dining table and looked around the room. It was strange to realize that after this night I would never see it again as it was. The room had never looked so beautiful as it did at that moment. The gleam of the polished blackwood table was richer than ever. The white lacquered screen with its inlaid ivory figures stood proudly in one corner, a symbol of fine craftsmanship. The antique porcelain plates and vases on their blackwood stands were placed at just the right angle to show off their beauty. Even the curtains hung completely evenly, not a fraction out of line. In the glass cabinet were white jade figures, a rose quartz incense burner and ornaments of other semi-precious stones that I had lovingly collected over the years. They had been beautifully carved in intricate designs by the hands of skilled artists. Now my eyes caressed them to bid them farewell. Having heard from Winnie that the painter Ling Fong-min was in serious trouble, I knew that his painting of a lady in blue hanging over the sideboard would be ruthlessly destroyed. But what about the other ink and brush painting by Chi Pei Shi? He was a great artist of the traditional style. Because of his having been a carpenter in early life, he was honoured by the Communist Party. Would the Red Guards know the facts of Chi Pei Shi's life and spare this painting? I looked at it carefully, my eyes lingering over each stroke of his masterful brush. It was a picture of the lotus, a favourite subject of Chinese artists because the lotus symbolized purity. The poet Tao Yuan Ming (AD 376-427) used the lotus to represent a man of honour in a famous poem, saying that the lotus rose out of mud but remained unstained.

I recited the poem to myself and wondered whether it was really possible for anyone to remain unstained by his environment? It was an idea contrary to Marxism, which held that the environment moulded the man. Perhaps the poet was too idealistic, I thought as I listened to the laughter of the Red Guards overhead. They seemed to be blissfully happy in their work of destruction because they were sure they were doing something to satisfy their God, Mao Tze-tung. Their behaviour was the result of their upbringing from childhood in Communist China. The propaganda they had absorbed precluded their having a free will of their own.

A heavy thud overhead stopped my speculations. I could hear the sound of many people walking up and down the stairs, glasses being broken and heavy knocking on the wall. The noise intensified. It sounded almost as if the Red Guards were tearing the house down rather than merely looting its contents. I became alarmed and decided to try to secure my release by deception.

I knocked on the door. There was such a din in the house that no one heard me. I knocked harder and harder. When I heard a movement outside the door, I called out, 'Open the door!'

The handle was turned slowly and the door opened a narrow gap. A girl Red Guard in pigtails asked what I wanted. I told her I had to go to the bathroom. She let me out after cautioning me not to interfere with their revolutionary activities.

The Red Guards had taken from the storeroom the crates containing my father's books and papers and were trying to open them with pliers in the hall. Through the open drawing room door, I saw a girl on a ladder removing the curtains. Two bridge tables were in the middle of the room. On them were laid a collection of cameras, watches, clocks, binoculars and silverware which the Red Guards had gathered from all over the house. These were the 'valuables' they intended to present to the State.

Mounting the stairs, I was astonished to see several Red Guards taking pieces of my porcelain collection out of their padded boxes. One young man had arranged a set of four K'ang Hsi winecups in a row on the floor and was stepping on them. I was just in time to hear the crunch of delicate porcelain under the sole of his shoe. The sound pierced my heart. Impulsively I leapt forward and caught his leg just as he raised his foot to crush the next cup. He toppled. We fell in a heap together. My eyes searched for the other winecups to make sure we had not broken them in our fall, and, momentarily distracted, I was not able to move aside when the boy regained his balance and kicked me right in my chest. I cried out in pain. The other Red Guards dropped what they were doing and gathered around us, shouting at me angrily for interfering in their revolutionary activities. One of the teachers pulled me up from the floor. With his face flushed in anger, the young man waved his fist, threatening me with a severe beating. The teacher raised her voice to restore order. She said to me, 'What do you think you are doing? Are you trying to protect your possessions?'

'No, no, you can do whatever you like with my things. But you mustn't break these porcelain treasures. They are old and valuable and cannot be replaced,' I said rather breathlessly. My chest throbbed with pain.

'Shut up! Shut up!' A chorus of voices drowned my voice.

'Our Great Leader said, "Lay out the facts; state the reasons",' I summoned all my strength and yelled at the top of my voice to be heard.

The teacher raised her hand to silence the Red Guards and said, 'We will allow you to lay out the facts and state the reasons.' The Red Guards glared at me.

I picked up one of the remaining winecups and cradled it in my palm. Holding my hand out, I said, 'This winecup is nearly three hundred years old. You seem to value the cameras, watches and binoculars, but better cameras, better watches and more powerful binoculars are being made every year. No one in this world can make another winecup like this one again. This is a part of our cultural heritage. Every Chinese should be proud of it.'

The young man whose revolutionary work of destruction I had interrupted said angrily, 'You shut up! These things belong to the old culture. They are the useless toys of the feudal Emperors and the modern capitalist class and have no significance to us, the proletarian class. They cannot be compared to cameras and binoculars which are useful for our struggle in time of war. Our Great Leader Chairman Mao taught us, "If we do not destroy, we cannot establish." The old culture must be destroyed to make way for the new socialist culture.'

Another Red Guard said, 'The purpose of the Great Proletarian Cultural Revolution is to destroy the old culture. You cannot stop us!'

I was trembling with anxiety and frantically searching my mind for some convincing argument to stop this senseless destruction. But before I could utter another futile word, I saw another young man coming down the stairs from the third floor with my Blanc de Chine Goddess of Mercy, Kwan Yin, in his hand. I turned to him and asked uneasily, 'What are you going to do with that figure?'

He swung his arm holding the Kwan Yin carelessly in the air and declared, 'This is a figure of Buddhist superstition. I'm going to throw it into the dustbin.'

The Kwan Yin was a perfect specimen and a genuine product of the Têh Hua kiln in Fukien province. It was the work of the famous seventeenth-century Ming sculptor Chen Wei and bore his seal on the back of the figure. The beauty of the creamy-white figure was beyond description. The serene expression of the face was so skilfully captured that it seemed to be alive. The folds of the robe flowed so naturally that one forgot it was carved out of hard biscuit. The glaze was so rich and creamy that the whole figure looked as if it were soft to the touch. This figure of Kwan Yin I always kept in its padded box, deeming it too valuable to be displayed. I took it out only when knowledgeable friends interested in porcelain asked to look at it.

'No, no, please! You mustn't do that! I beg you.' I was so agitated that my voice was shrill. The Red Guard just fixed me with a stony stare and continued to swing his arm casually, holding the Kwan Yin now with only two fingers.

Pleading was not going to move the Red Guards. If I wanted to communicate, I must speak their language. The time had come to employ diplomacy, it seemed to me. If the Red Guards thought I opposed them, I would never succeed in saving the treasures. By this time, I no longer thought of them as my own possessions. I did not care to whom they were to belong after tonight as long as they would be saved from destruction.

'Please, Red Guards! Believe me, I'm not opposed to you. You have come here as representatives of our Great Leader. How could I oppose the representatives of Chairman Mao? I understand the purpose of the Cultural Revolution. Did I not surrender the keys willingly when you asked for them?' I said.

'Yes, you did that,' conceded the teacher with a nod. The Red Guards gathered around us seemed to relax a little.

Somewhat encouraged, I went on, 'All these old things belong to the past era. The past is old. It must go to make way for the new culture of socialism. But they could be taken away without immediate destruction. Remember, they were not made by members of the capitalist class. They were made by the hands of the workers of a bygone age. Should you not respect the labour of those workers?'

A Red Guard at the back of the group shouted impatiently, 'Don't listen to her flowery words. She is trying to confuse us. She is trying to protect her possessions.'

I quickly turned to him and said, 'No, no! Your being in my house has already improved my socialist awareness. It was wrong of me to have kept all these beautiful and valuable things to myself. They rightly belong to the people. I beg you to take them to the Shanghai Museum. You can consult their experts. If the experts advise you to destroy them, there will still be time to do so.'

A girl said, 'The Shanghai Museum is closed. The experts there are being investigated. Some of them are also class enemies. In any case, they are intellectuals. Our Great Leader has said, "The capitalist class is the skin; the intellectuals are the hairs that grow on the skin. When the skin dies, there will be no hair." The capitalist class nourishes the intellectuals, so they belong to the same side. Now we are going to destroy the capitalist class. Naturally the intellectuals are to be destroyed too.'

The quotation of Mao she mentioned was new to me, but this was no time to think of that. I pursued my purpose by saying, 'In that case, consult someone you can trust, someone in a position of authority. Perhaps one of the Vice-Mayors of Shanghai. Surely there are many private collections in the city. There must be some sort of policy for dealing with them.'

'No, no! You are a stupid class enemy! You simply do not understand. You are arguing and advising us to consult either other class enemies or the revisionist officials of the government. You talk about official policy. The only valid official policy is in this book.' The young man took his book of Mao's quotations from his pocket and held it up as he continued, 'The teachings of our Great Leader Chairman Mao is the only valid official policy.'

Changing the direction of my argument, I said, 'I saw a placard saying, "Long Live World Revolution." You are going to carry the red flag of our Great Leader Chairman Mao all over the world, aren't you?'

'Of course we are! What has that got to do with you? You are only a class enemy,' a girl sneered. She turned to the others and warned, 'She is a tricky woman. Don't listen to her nonsense!'

Getting really desperate, I said, 'Don't you realize all these things are extremely valuable? They can be sold in Hong Kong for a large sum of money. You will be able to finance your world revolution with that money.'

At last, what I said made an impression. The Red Guards were listening. The wonderful prospect of playing a heroic role on the broad world stage was flattering to their ego, especially now they were getting intoxicated with a sense of power.

I seized the psychological moment and went on. 'Please put all these porcelain pieces back in their boxes and take them to a safe place. You can sell them or give them to the Museum, whatever you consider right, according to the teachings of our Great Leader.'

Perhaps, being an older person, the teacher felt some sense of responsibility. She asked me, 'Are you sure your collection is valuable? How much would you say they are worth?'

'You will find a notebook with the date of purchase and the sum of money I spent on each item. Their price increases every month, especially on the world market. As a rough estimate, I think they are worth at least a million yuan,' I told her.

Although members of the proletarian class did not appreciate value, they understood price. The Red Guards were impressed by the figure 'one million'. The teacher was by now just as anxious as I was to save the treasures, but she was afraid to put herself in the wrong with the Red Guards. However, she found a way for the Red Guards to back down without loss of face.

'Little Revolutionary Generals! Let's have a meeting and talk over this matter.' She was flattering the Red Guards by calling them 'Little Revolutionary Generals', a title coined by the Maoists to encourage the Red Guards to do their bidding. The Red Guards were obviously pleased and readily agreed to her suggestion. She led them down the stairs to the dining room.

I knelt down to pick up the remaining winecups and put them in the box. The Kwan Yin had been left on the table. I took it and carried the pieces upstairs to the large cupboard on the landing of the third floor where I normally kept my collection. I saw that all the boxes had been taken out. On the floor there were fragments of broken pieces of porcelain in colours of oxblood, imperial yellow, celadon green and blue and white. My heart sank at the realization that whatever my desperate effort might now achieve, it was already too late. Many of the boxes were empty.

The third floor rooms resembled a scene after an earthquake except for the absence of corpses. But the red wine spilled out of broken bottles on white sheets and blankets was the same colour as blood.

Because we lived in a permanent state of shortages, every household with enough living space had a store cupboard in which we hoarded such daily necessities as flour, sugar and tins of meat as reserve supplies. Each time I went to Hong Kong I also brought back cases of food and soap to supplement our meagre ration even though the rate of import duty was astronomical. The Red Guards had emptied my store cupboard. Flour, sugar and food from tins they had opened lay on top of heaps of clothing they had taken out of cupboards, trunks and drawers. Some suitcases remained undisturbed, but I could see that they had already dealt with my fur coats and evening dresses with a pair of scissors. The ceiling fan was whirling. Bits of fur, silk and torn sheets of tissue paper were flying around.

Every piece of furniture was pulled out of its place. Tables and chairs were overturned, some placed on top of others to form a ladder. As it was summer, my carpets had been cleaned, sprinkled with camphor powder, rolled up and stored in an empty bedroom on the third floor. Behind the largest roll of carpet, I found a shopping bag in which were stuffed two of my cashmere cardigans and several sets of new underwear. It seemed a thoughtful Red Guard had quietly put them away for personal use.

In the largest guest room where the Red Guards had carried out most of their destructive labour of cutting and smashing, a radio set was left on a local station from which revolutionary songs based on Mao's quotations were being broadcast. A female voice was singing 'Marxism can be summed up in one sentence: Revolution is justifiable.' There was a note of urgency in her voice that compelled the listeners' attention. This song was to become the clarion call to battle not only for the Red Guards but also for the Proletarian Revolutionaries when they were organized later on. I thought of switching off the radio but it was out of my reach unless I climbed over the mountain of debris in the middle of the room.

I looked at what had happened to my things hopelessly but indifferently. They belonged to a period of my life that had abruptly ended when the Red Guards entered my house. Though I could not see into the future, I refused to look back. I supposed the Red Guards had enjoyed themselves. Is it not true that we all possess some destructive tendencies in our nature? The veneer of civilization is very thin. Underneath lurks the animal that is in each of us. If I were young and had belonged to a working-class background; if I had been brought up to worship Mao and taught to believe him infallible, would I not have behaved exactly as the Red Guards had done?

The struggle over the porcelain had exhausted me. My chest throbbed with pain. I wondered whether a rib had been broken. Examining my chest in the mirror of the bathroom, I saw a large bruise on the right side. I went down to the second floor looking for somewhere to lie down and rest. I opened the door of my own bedroom. It was in the same state of disorder as the third floor. Through the open door of my study, I saw my jewellery laid out on the desk. Since the Red Guards were still in the dining room discussing what they were going to do with the porcelain, I quickly withdrew to avoid suspicion that I was attempting to recover anything. I turned the handle of my daughter's bedroom door to find the room as yet undisturbed. The strong breeze from the open window was tossing the gauze curtain. Crossing the room to secure it to the loop, I chanced to look down and was attracted by the sight of bright leaping flames in the garden. I saw that a bonfire had been lit in the middle of the lawn. The Red Guards were standing around the fire carelessly tossing my books on to the flames. My heart tightened with pain. I turned my back to the window and closed my eyes, leaning against the windowsill for support. Hoping to shut out what I had seen and heard during the last few hours, I tried to escape to my inner self for a moment of peace and prayer.

Suddenly, a girl Red Guard appeared in the doorway and switched on the light. 'What are you doing here? Who told you to come here? Are you up to some tricks?' She bombarded me with questions but did not wait for me to answer her before she said, 'Come along! We need you.'

I followed her to my study. Several Red Guards were gathered around my desk. Seated on the chair was a thin girl with bobbed hair in a faded blue cotton blouse that she had outgrown. In a society where food was at a premium, those who had to depend entirely on official rations, without recourse to perks or the black market, generally acquired a pinched look. She was just such a girl. I supposed she came from a working-class family living on a tight budget, without either of her parents being smart enough to become a Party member. She sat there tensely with head bowed and I guessed that the others, who fell silent when I entered the room, had been questioning her. One of the male teachers was standing next to the girl. He said to me, 'Pull up a chair and be seated.'

Several Red Guards brought chairs from my bedroom next door and both the teacher and I sat down. I was directly opposite the girl on the other side of my desk. As I took my seat, she looked up and hastily threw me a nervous glance that was half-frightened and half-appealing. On the desk in front of me was my jewellery case and some of the jewellery was on the blotting pad on the desk.

'Is this all the jewellery you have? Look them over and tell us if everything is here,' the teacher said.

Opening the case, I saw that several rings, bracelets and a diamond watch were missing. The teacher asked again, 'Is it all here, your jewellery? Speak the truth. We are going to check with your servants too. Have you hidden some? Some of the capitalist families have tried to hide their jewellery among flowers in the garden.'

It was a tense moment. The boys at the other end of the room removing records from the record cabinet stopped to wait for my answer too. I understood the situation fully. They all suspected the girl, who had probably been left alone for a short moment, of having secreted some pieces of jewellery. In fact, that was probably exactly what she had done. If I lied to protect the girl and if my servants, who knew what jewellery I had, did not, I would be laying myself open to charges that I had hidden my jewellery. There was no choice for me but to tell the truth. Yet, the girl looked so pitiful that I hated having to incriminate her.

'The main pieces are here. The most valuable ones such as this jade necklace and this diamond brooch are here. A few pieces are missing but they are not the most valuable.' I tried to minimize the girl's predicament.

'What is missing?' the teacher asked impatiently.

'A watch, several rings and gold bracelets.'

'What is the watch like? What make is it? Is it like this one?' The teacher stretched out his wrist and I saw that he had on an imported Swiss watch, a status symbol in Communist China. He thought I had a man's watch like most other Chinese women who tried to achieve equality by being the same as men. But I had never followed the new fashion.

'No, the missing watch is a small one with diamonds and a platinum strap. It's French. The name of the maker is Ebel.'

'I hope you are not lying. How come you had such an unusual watch? Swiss watches are the best, aren't they?' While the teacher was speaking to me, he gestured to a Red Guard to go to the drawing room downstairs to see if such a watch was among the cameras and binoculars. The Red Guard soon came back and shook his head.

'The Ebel watch was bought in Hong Kong when my late husband and I were there in 1957. It was his last gift to me. Please ask Chen Mah. She knows all about it and is familiar with all my things, including my jewellery.'

No one said anything more. The poor girl was almost in tears; her pale face looked so sad and frightened. The teacher asked me about the rings and bracelets. As I described them, an idea occurred to me. The floor of my study, especially around my desk, was knee deep with paper – wrappings, tissue paper wrinkled into balls, old magazines torn to pieces, many old copies of the airmail edition of the London *Times* in shreds, exercise books, note pads, and unused stationery from my desk drawers. Mixed with all these were also stacks of books waiting to be carried to the garden fire. When I finished describing the missing jewellery, I said, looking at the girl in front of me, 'All of you have made such a mess with all these papers and books on the floor. Perhaps the missing watch, rings and bracelets have dropped among the debris.'

The girl's pale face reddened. In an instant, she disappeared under the desk. The other Red Guards followed suit. The teacher remained in his seat, contemplating me with a puzzled frown. It seemed to me he saw through my game but did not understand my motive for covering up for the thief. Confucius said, 'A compassionate heart is possessed by every human being.' This was no longer true in China, where in a society pledged to materialism, men's behaviour was increasingly motivated by self-interest. The teacher probably thought I had hoped to gain favour from the Red Guards.

After searching among the papers, the Red Guards recovered the rings and bracelets. The girl was smiling. But there was no watch. Probably someone else had taken it.

In my bedroom next door, the Red Guards were hammering on the furniture. Right in front of me, they were breaking my records. I stood up and said to the teacher, 'These records are classical music by the great masters of Europe in the eighteenth and nineteenth centuries. They are not the forbidden music of the dance halls and night clubs. Western music of this kind is taught in our music academies. Why not preserve the records and donate them to the Music Society?'

'You live in the past,' he said. 'Don't you know that our Great Leader has said that western music of any kind is decadent? Only certain passages of certain compositions are all right, not the whole of any composition,' he said.

'Isn't every section of any composition an integral part of the whole?' I murmured.

'Shut up! In any case, do the peasants and workers want Chopin, Mozart, Beethoven or Tchaikovsky? Of course not! We are going to compose our own proletarian music. As for the Music Society, it's disbanded.'

The night seemed interminable. I was so tired that I could hardly stand. I asked the teacher for permission to rest for a while.

'You may go to your daughter's room. She is an independent film worker earning a salary of her own. Her room is not included in our revolutionary action.'

I returned to my daughter's room and lay down on her bed. It was still dark but through the window I could see the faint light of dawn on the eastern horizon. I closed my eyes and slowly drifted off to sleep.

When I woke, the sun was streaming into the room. The house was a great deal quieter. There was the sound of a news broadcast from a radio but there was no longer the noise of furniture being dragged about overhead. I had a shower in my daughter's bathroom and dressed in her slacks and shirt. Outside the room, I found the Red Guards sitting on chairs and on the stairs eating hot buns sent to them from their school. There seemed fewer of them and none of the teachers was in sight. I went down the stairs to the kitchen to look for breakfast.

The cook was there removing food from the refrigerator, which, he told me, the Red Guards wanted to take away. I asked him to make some coffee and toast.

I sat down by the kitchen table and the cook placed the coffee percolator, toast, butter and a jar of Cooper's marmalade in front of me.

A pretty girl with a lithe figure and two long plaits over her shoulders came into the kitchen and sat down on the other side of the table watching me. After I had drunk the coffee and put the cup down, she picked it up. There was still some coffee in it. She put the cup to her nose and sniffed.

Making a face of distaste, she asked me, 'What is this?'

'It's coffee,' I said.

'What is coffee?'

I told her that coffee was a beverage rather like tea, only stronger.

'Is it foreign food?' She put the cup down with a clatter.

'I suppose you could call it foreign food.' I picked up another slice of toast and started to butter it.

She looked at the butter and picked up the jar of marmalade with its label in English. Then she leaned forward in her seat and stared at me with her large black eyes blazing. 'Why do you have to drink a foreign beverage? Why do you have to eat foreign food? Why do you have so many foreign books? Why are you so foreign altogether? In every room in this house there are imported things, but there is not a single portrait of our beloved Great Leader. We have been to many homes of the capitalist class. Your house is the worst of all, the most reactionary of all. Are you a Chinese or are you a foreigner?'

I smiled at her outburst. My house must have seemed rather different from the others they had looted. At the beginning of the Cultural Revolution, Lao Chao did suggest that I hang up a portrait of Mao Tze-tung. But so many people had the same idea that we couldn't find a single one in any shop and had to abandon the idea. However, I thought I might try to help this pretty girl see things in their proper perspective.

'Do you eat tomatoes?' I asked her.

'Of course I do!' she said. Tomatoes were common in Shanghai. When the harvest was in, the price dropped to a few cents a catty (a catty being a little over a pound in weight). Every adult and every child in Shanghai ate tomatoes either as fruit or vegetable.

'Well, the tomato is a foreign food. It was introduced into China by foreigners. So was the watermelon, brought from Persia over the silk route. As for foreign books, Karl Marx himself was a German. If people didn't read books by foreigners, there would not have been an international Communist movement. It has never been possible to keep things and ideas locked up within the national boundary of any one country, even in the old days when communication was difficult. Nowadays, it's even more impossible. I'm pretty sure that by now people all over the world have heard that Chinese high school students are organized into Red Guards.'

'Really?' she said, and became thoughtful. It was apparent that I had opened a new horizon for her. After a while, she said, 'You are good at making things clear. Have you been to a university?'

I had a mouthful of toast, so I just nodded. She looked wistful. 'I had hoped to go to a university when I finish high school. But now there won't be any university to go to. All of us young people will have to become soldiers.'

'You are a girl. You won't have to be a soldier.'

'It's much worse for girls!' She sounded depressed.

'In any case, there won't be a war, so you don't have to worry.' I tried to console her.

She turned quickly to look at the door and shot a glance of apprehension at the cook who was bending over the sink washing vegetables. Putting a hand on my arm, she warned in a whisper, 'Don't say that! It's dangerous to say that! Our Great Leader has already told us to prepare for a People's War against the American imperialists, the Soviet revisionists and the reactionary Kuomintang in Taiwan. You must not speak such peace propaganda and oppose what was said by our Great Leader!'

I smiled at her and nodded in agreement.

The kitchen door was opened. A boy poked his head into the room to ask the cook whether the refrigerator was ready. The girl quickly removed her hand from my arm and stood up. Although the boy had already withdrawn, she said in a firm loud voice, 'You are a class enemy. I'm not going to listen to your nonsense.'

She turned to leave. But at the door she looked back and gave me a sweet smile.

At the sink, the cook said, 'Not all of them are young fools!'

Remembering that his youngest son was a high school student, I asked him whether the boy also belonged to the Red Guard organization.

'Oh, yes! How could he not join? He would have been looked upon as a renegade and punished. Besides, young people always want to do exactly what other young people are doing. But when he comes home my wife searches him to make sure he hasn't taken anything that doesn't belong to him.'

'Is there a lot of that kind of thing going on?'

'Yes. The temptation is there. Some parents even encourage the youngsters to take things. But I'm not going to let my son be turned into a habitual thief,' the cook said.

'What about the children from capitalist families?'

'They are having a hard time. They are made to feel like outcasts and required to draw a line between themselves and their parents. Young people can be very cruel to each other, you know. There have been an increasing number of suicides.'

Outside the kitchen, I saw a man who had not been present with the Red Guards the night before. I could tell by his air of self-assurance that he was a Party Official, perhaps a veteran of the Civil War, as he was obviously over forty.

'I'm a liaison officer of the Municipal Government,' he introduced himself to me. 'It's my job to inspect the revolutionary action of the Red Guards. Have you been beaten or ill treated?'

It was a pleasant surprise to learn that the Shanghai Municipal Government was endeavouring to check the excessive behaviour of the Red Guards. This attempt at moderation was to be very quickly curtailed by the Maoists in the Party leadership in Peking. The work of the liaison officer was short-lived. But when he spoke to me he was unaware of his own impending downfall and his manner was authoritative.

'No, not at all,' I said to him. 'These Red Guards carried out their revolutionary action strictly according to the teachings of our Great Leader Chairman Mao. I have been allowed to eat and sleep.' The Red Guards standing around us beamed.

He declared, 'That's good. It's not the purpose of the proletarian class to destroy your body. We want to save your soul by reforming your way of thinking.' Although Mao Tze-tung and his followers were atheists, they were very fond of talking about the 'soul'. In his writing, Mao often referred to the saving of a man's soul. During the Cultural Revolution, 'soul' was mentioned frequently. Several times, Defence Minister Lin Piao stood on the balcony of Tien An Men to speak on behalf of Mao Tze-tung to the Red Guards gathered below about allowing the revolutionary spirit to touch their 'souls' in order to improve themselves. While no one could ask Mao Tze-tung or Lin Piao what exactly they meant when they talked about a man's 'soul', it greatly taxed the ingenuity of the Marxist writers of newspaper articles who had to explain their leader's words to the people.

Then the liaison officer raised his arm and swung it in a circle to embrace the whole house. 'Is it right for you and your daughter to live in a house of nine rooms with four bathrooms when there is such a severe housing shortage in Shanghai? Is it right for you to have each room covered with woollen carpets and filled with rosewood and blackwood furniture when there is a shortage of wood and basic furniture for others? Is it right for you to wear silk and fur and sleep under quilts filled with down? Is it right for you to have three servants to wait on you?'

He looked at me for a moment. When he saw I was not going to argue with him, he went on, 'As I said a moment ago, it is not our objective to destroy your body. You will be allowed enough clothing and basic furniture to carry on a normal life but you won't be allowed to maintain a standard of living above that of the average worker.'

He looked at me again for my reaction. Seeing none, he continued, 'It's now quite warm, but winter will be here soon. The Red Guards will take you upstairs to pack a suitcase of clothing for yourself. Pick a warm padded jacket. You won't have central heating in this house again. Coal is needed for industry. It's not for the luxury of the capitalist class.'

He went into the dining room and closed the door. I followed a Red Guard to the third floor to pick up warm clothes from the debris. A male Red Guard who had been there the night before but had gone away in the morning returned to the house. He came up the stairs two steps at a time and said to the girl helping me, 'Incredible! It's incredible! You know what I found when I went home? They are looting my house! How can they do this? My father and grandfather are both workers.'

Indeed, this was extraordinary. We stopped sorting the clothes and asked him to explain.

'It's my aunt. During the Japanese invasion, she lost everything when the Japanese soldiers burned her area of Nantao city. She borrowed money to have a fruit stall after the war. She did quite well and made a living for herself and her children but she gave it up two years ago when she got too old to manage it. Now they say she is a capitalist because she had a private business of her own. Our home is being looted because she is now living with us since her children are not in Shanghai.'

The young man was full of indignation and almost in tears. The incident was a terrible blow to a self-righteous and proud Red Guard who was the third generation of a working-class family. It was also an eye-opener for me. Apparently, I decided, there were capitalists and capitalists and some were more equal than others. If owners of fruit stalls were included in the category, the Red Guards in Shanghai had a big job to do.

More Red Guards joined us to hear the young man's story. I noticed that a couple of them slipped away quietly afterwards, no doubt going home to investigate.

Thinking of my daughter, I asked the Red Guards for her winter clothes.

'She is not included in our revolutionary action. We did not go to her room,' they replied.

'But her winter clothes are not in her room. They were put away for the summer up here,' I told them.

Evidently mellowed by his own family's experience, the boy whose home was looted volunteered, 'We must pack a couple of suitcases for her too.'

My daughter and I were each allowed a suitcase with clothes and a canvas bag with bedding.

The work of destruction accomplished, the Red Guards were getting things ready for removal. By the afternoon, there were no more than a dozen of them left in the house. One of them called me to the dining room.

The liaison officer and two of the teachers were seated by the dining table which was strewn with old letters my grandfather had written to my father when the latter was a student in a naval college in Japan before the 1911 Revolution when China became a Republic. They were included among the family papers brought to my house after my widowed mother passed away in Nanking in 1962. I had never opened the boxes because they were to be sent to my brother in Peking. Being the eldest son, he was the rightful heir. I could see that the paper as well as the envelopes were yellow with age but the brush and ink handwriting of my grandfather had not faded.

After motioning me to sit down on a vacant chair, the liaison officer pointed to the letters and asked me, 'Have you read these letters from your grandfather to your father?'

'My father showed them to me when I was in my teens a long time ago,' I told him.

'Your grandfather was a patriot even though he was a big landlord. He sent your father, his eldest son, to Japan to learn to become a naval officer because China suffered defeat in the naval battle against Japan in 1895. He also took part in the abortive Constitutional Reform Movement, When that failed, he returned to his native province and devoted himself to academic work. Do you respect your grandfather?'

I thought the liaison officer very brave to say my grandfather was a patriot even though he was a big landlord, because all big landlords were declared enemies of the State and shot during the Land Reform Movement in 1950. No attempt was made to verify whether any of them was a patriot. I remembered my father saying at the time that it was fortunate my second uncle, who managed the family estate, had died some years before the Communist takeover so that my grandfather in heaven was spared the indignity of having one of his sons executed.

All Chinese revered our ancestors. Although I had never seen my grandfather, I loved him. So I said to the liaison officer, 'Of course I respect and love my grandfather.'

'Then why did you choose to work for a foreign firm? Don't you know the foreigners have never had any good intentions towards us? They exploited the Chinese people for economic gains or tried to enslave us politically. Only the scum of China work for foreigners. You should know that. You were offered a job to teach English at the Institute of Foreign Languages. But you preferred to work for Shell. Why?'

I couldn't tell him that I had made the decision to work for Shell because I was afraid to get involved in the new political movement initiated by Mao Tze-tung. In 1957 when I was called upon to make the choice of either going to the Foreign Language Institute to teach or to accept the job with Shell, the Anti-Rightist Campaign was in full swing. It was a campaign primarily aimed at the intellectuals, especially those trained in foreign universities and suspected of harbouring ideas hostile to Communism. Many of my friends and acquaintances had been denounced and persecuted. Some were sent to labour camps; a few went to prison. All the universities and research organizations including the Foreign Language Institute were in a state of turmoil. Under such circumstances, it would have been asking for trouble to join the teaching staff of the Foreign Language Institute. I did not regret accepting the job with Shell even though I was aware that working for a foreign firm carried with it neither honour nor position in Chinese society.

'You were probably attracted by the pay you got from the foreigners?' he asked. I realized at once that I was on dangerous ground. It was the common belief in China, the result of persistent propaganda, that members of the capitalist class would do anything for money, criminal or otherwise.

'No,' I said. 'I already had a great deal of money. It was mainly the working conditions at Shell such as shorter working hours, the use of a car, etc. I suppose I am lazy,' I added, feeling a gesture of self-criticism was called for. Laziness was another characteristic attributed to the capitalist class.

He stood up and looked at his watch. 'There are several more places I have to go to,' he said. 'You had better think over the things you did for the foreigners and be ready to change your standpoint to that of the people. It's not our policy to destroy the physical person of the members of the capitalist class. We want you to reform. Don't you want to join the ranks of the glorious proletariat? You can do so only after being stripped of your surplus belongings and changing your way of life. It's the objective of the Proletarian Revolution to form a classless society in which each individual labours for the common good and enjoys the fruit of that labour and where no one is above any one else.'

It was an attractive and idealistic picture. I used to believe in it too when I was a student. But after living in Communist China for the past seventeen years, I knew that such a society was only a dream because those who seized power would invariably become the new ruling class. They would have the power to control the people's lives and bend the people's will. Because they controlled the production and distribution of goods and services in the name of the State, they would also enjoy material luxuries beyond the reach of the common people. In Communist China, details of the private lives of the leaders were guarded as State secrets. But every Chinese knew that the Party leaders lived in spacious mansions with many servants, obtained their provisions from special shops where luxury goods were made available to their household at nominal prices and sent their children in chauffeur-driven cars to exclusive schools to be taught by specially selected teachers. Even though every Chinese knew how the leaders lived, no one dared to talk about it. If and when we had to pass the street on which a special shop of the military or high officials was located, we carefully looked the other way to avoid giving the impression we knew it was there.

It was common knowledge that Mao Tze-tung himself lived in the former winter palace of the Ching dynasty Emperors and had an entourage of specially selected attractive young women for his personal attendants. He could order the Red Guards to tear up the constitution, beat people up and loot their homes and no one, not even other Party leaders, dared to oppose him. Even this liaison officer, a very junior official in the Party hierarchy, could decide how many jackets I was to be allowed from my own stock of clothes and how I was to live in future. He could make all these arbitrary decisions about my life and lecture me or even accuse me of imaginary crimes simply because he was an official and I was just an ordinary citizen. He had power but I had none. We were not equals by any stretch of the imagination.

After the liaison officer had left my house, the Red Guards learned that no trucks were available that day for them to take away the loot, so they put my jewellery and other valuables in Meiping's study and sealed the door. They also charged my servants to watch me so that I could not take back any of my things.

It was late afternoon when the last Red Guard passed through the front gate and banged it shut. Lao Chao and the cook tried to clear the debris that covered the floor of every room – pieces of broken glass, china, picture frames and a huge amount of torn paper. I told them not to remove anything or throw anything away in case something the Red Guards wanted were lost and we be accused of deliberately taking it away. They just cleared a path in the middle of each room and swept the debris into the corners.

When I went up to my bedroom to inspect the damage, I found Chen Mah already there sitting at my dressing table staring at the mess around her. I told her to help me pick up the torn clothes and put them in one corner so that we might have some space to move about in. The cover of my bed was soiled with the footmarks of the Red Guards. When Chen Mah and I took it off the bed, we saw that they had slashed the mattress. On the wall, over my bed, where a painting of flowers had hung, someone had written in lipstick: 'Down with the running dog of imperialism!' The Red Guards had punched holes in the panels of the lacquered screen. Hanging on the frame of the screen were strips of coloured paper with slogans such as: 'Long Live the Dictatorship of the Proletariat' and 'Down with the Capitalist Class'. I folded the broken screen and put it in the passage outside, slogans and all. Then I picked up the crushed white silk lampshades, while Chen Mah swept up the broken pieces of the porcelain lamps.

In the bathroom, soiled towels lay in a heap. The bath was half full of coloured water because the Red Guards had emptied all the medicines from the medicine cabinet into it. I put my hand into the water to pull the plug to let the water out.

Suddenly the front door bell rang again. Lao Chao rushed up the stairs, shouting, 'Another lot of Red Guards has come!'

Hastily I wiped my stained hands on a towel and came out to the landing. I said to him, 'Keep calm and open the gate.'

'Cook is there,' he said breathlessly.

I walked downstairs. Eight men dressed in the coarse blue of peasants or outdoor workers stood in the hall. Though they were middle-aged, they all wore the armbands of the Red Guards. Their leader, a man with a leather whip in his hand, stood in front of me and said, 'We are the Red Guards! We have come to take revolutionary action against you!'

The situation was so absurd that I couldn't help being amused. 'Indeed, are you the Red Guards? You look to me more like their fathers,' I said, standing on the last step of the staircase.

The leather whip struck me on my bare arm just above my elbow. The sharp pain made me bite my lip. The men seemed nervous; they kept on looking over their shoulders at the front door.

'Hand over the keys! We haven't time to stand here and carry on a conversation with you,' their leader shouted.

'The keys were taken by the Red Guards who came here last night.'

'You are lying!' The man raised his whip as if to strike me again but he only let the tip of the whip touch my shoulder.

Another man asked anxiously, 'Have they taken everything?'

'No, not everything,' I answered.

One of the men pushed me and my servants into the kitchen and locked us inside. He remained outside guarding the door while the others collected a few suitcases of things from the house. They departed so hurriedly that they forgot to unlock the kitchen door to let us out. The cook had to climb out of the kitchen window into the garden in order to get into the house to unlock the kitchen door.

Chen Mah went back to my bedroom to try to make a bed for me for the night. I sat down by the kitchen table to drink a cup of tea the cook had made for me. He sat down on the other side of the table and started to shell peas.

'What's going to happen next?' he asked. 'There is surely going to be lawlessness and disorder. Anybody wearing a red armband and calling himself a Red Guard can enter anybody's home and help himself.'

'The Red Guards have put up a Big Character Poster on the front gate. Shall I go out and see what it says?' Lao Chao asked me.

'Yes, please go and see,' I told him.

Lao Chao came back and told me that I was accused of 'conspiring with foreign nations' which during the Cultural Revolution meant that I was a 'foreign spy'. Strictly translated the four Chinese characters, Li Tung Wai Kuo, meant 'inside communicate foreign countries'. It's probably considered normal and innocuous anywhere else. But in Maoist China communicating with foreign countries other than through official channels was a crime.

I was thinking how the Chinese language lent itself to euphemism when I heard my daughter opening and closing the front gate and pushing her bicycle into the garage.

'Mei-mei has come home! She will be upset!' both Lao Chao and the cook exclaimed. (Old servants in Chinese households often give pet names to the children. Mei-mei was what my servants had called my daughter since she was a little girl.)

I composed myself to appear nonchalant and got up to meet her.

She opened the front door and stood there, stunned by the sight of disorder. When she saw me, she rushed forward and threw her arms round my shoulders and murmured, 'Mummy, oh, Mummy, are you all right?'

'Don't be upset,' I said in as cheerful a voice as I could manage. 'When the Cultural Revolution is over, we will make a new home. It will be just as beautiful, no, more beautiful than it was.'

'No, Mummy, no one will be allowed to have a home like we had again,' she said in a subdued voice.

We mounted the stairs in silence with our arms around each other's waist. I accompanied her to her bedroom. At least there everything was still just as it was. I sat down in the armchair while she went into her bathroom. When we came out, Lao Chao had already cleared a space in my study and laid out a folding bridge table in preparation for dinner. The cook had managed to produce a noodle dish with a delicious meat sauce served with green peas. I did not know how exhausted and hungry I was until I started to eat.

While we were eating, I told my daughter that the liaison officer had said that I would be left basic furniture and utensils necessary for a simple life, the same as that of an ordinary worker. I would ask the government for the second floor of the house to live in and give the rest to the government to house other families. We would have my bedroom and bathroom, Meiping's bedroom and bathroom and the study. It would be enough for us. To be able to plan and look ahead was good. I was already resigned to a lower standard of living. It would be a novelty and probably quite pleasant not to have too many things to look after. The human spirit is resilient and I was by nature optimistic.

I noticed that as I talked about my plan for the future Meiping became visibly more relaxed. She told me that in addition to appointing liaison officers to supervise the Red Guards, the Shanghai Party Secretariat and Municipal Government had passed a Ten-Point Resolution stressing the importance of protecting cultural relics and pointing out it was against the constitution to ransack private homes. Lao Chao stopped what he was doing to listen and Chen Mah came out of my bedroom and clapped. They were comforted by this piece of good news. But the behaviour of the Red Guards who had just left my house and what they said about revisionist officials in the government made me sceptical of the extent to which the Ten-Point Resolution was enforceable.

I knew my daughter was worried about me as she kept on looking at me anxiously. To put her mind at ease, I told her how I had lost all my possessions in Chungking during the Sino-Japanese War.

'It happened in Chungking in the summer of 1941. Daddy and I were about to leave for Canberra with the first group of Chinese diplomats and their families to open the new Chinese Legation there. Two days before we were scheduled to leave, we had a prolonged and severe air raid. A bomb landed on the tennis court right in front of our house. The blast tore off the roof and part of the house collapsed,' I said.

'Goodness! Where were you?' my daughter asked.

'I was in the shelter under the house. Daddy was in the shelter at his office. The shelters in Chungking were deep caves dug into the side of mountains, very deep and quite safe.'

'Did you lose everything in the house?'

'Fortunately we had put the packed suitcases under the stairs when the alarm sounded. The stairs collapsed and buried the suitcases underneath. We managed to dig three of them out. Of course they were in a terrible state. When we got to Hong Kong we had to buy everything all over again. We didn't have time to get the furniture out of the rubble. To this day, I have no idea what happened to it,' I told her. 'So you see, we did in fact lose almost everything we had.'

'You never told me any of this.'

'It happened such a long time ago, before you were born, when I was not much older than you are now. I had actually forgotten all about it. It was the looting by the Red Guards that made me remember it again.'

'Oh, Mummy, how could you have forgotten something terrible like that? You lost everything!'

'Yes, I did forget. But it was wartime. People were being bombed out all over the place. Bad experience is more bearable when you are not the only sufferer.'

'I'll never forget how our house looks today, not in a million years,' my daughter said.

'It's always best to look ahead and not backwards. Possessions are not important. Think of those beautiful porcelain pieces I had. Before they came to me, they had all passed through the hands of many people, surviving wars and natural disasters. I got them only because someone else lost them. While I had them, I enjoyed them; now some other people will enjoy them. Life itself is transitory. Possessions are not important.'

'I'm glad you are so philosophical,' she said, smiling for the first time since she had come home. 'Of course, we must not let our happiness be dependent on possessions. We still have each other. We can be happy together even if we are poor.'

'We won't be poor. I have already told you about the assets abroad. We will always be better off than most others in China. You are worn out. I can see dark shadows under your eyes. You had better try to get some rest.'

Meiping sat on in silence for a while longer, lost in thought. When she stood up she declared, 'Mummy, we will weather the storm together. I still believe in the future of our country. Things will change. They can't always be unfair like this. There are good leaders in the Party, such as Premier Chou, and many others.'

'Well, I wonder what they are doing now, allowing so many innocent people to suffer?'

'Don't lose heart! Surely they will do something when the time comes. I love China! I love my country even though it is not always good or right,' my daughter declared in a firm voice.

Her words brought tears to my eyes. I also had a deep and abiding love for the land of my ancestors, even though, because of my class status, I had become an outcast.

CHAPTER 4

House Arrest

I WOKE TO THE sound of a heavy downpour. After a while the rain settled to a steady drizzle. The wet garden, littered with ashes and half-burned books, was a sorrowful sight. I stood on the terrace contemplating this depressing scene and wondering what to do.

The morning passed slowly. There was no sign of the Red Guards. I wandered around the house aimlessly. There was no book to read. On the bookshelves covering two sides of the walls of my study only the four slim volumes of *The Collected Works of Mao Tze-tung* and the small book of his quotations in the red plastic cover remained. I couldn't do any sewing or knitting; the Red Guards had so messed up everything that I did not know where my knitting wool or needles and thread were. I couldn't write a letter or draw a picture; all the paper and envelopes were torn and I did not know where my pen was. I couldn't listen to the radio as the radio sets in the house were locked up with the 'valuables'. I could only sit there staring at the huge pile of debris in each room that we didn't dare to remove.

In the afternoon the rain stopped and the sun came out. Several parades passed the house but none of the Red Guards came back. Lao Chao brought me the day's issue of the *Shanghai Liberation Daily*, which always came out in the afternoon though it was a morning paper. On its front page, in bold print, was reprinted a leading article from the *People's Daily* in Peking, the official organ of the Central Committee of the Communist Party. Since all Chinese newspapers were government-owned and voiced government policy, especially the *People's Daily*, I recognized the importance of this article and read it carefully. Written in stirring revolutionary language, the article seemed superficially to be aimed at stimulating hatred for the capitalist class and rallying the masses to join in the activities of the Cultural Revolution. But I noticed that the articles also made the claim that officials of the Party and government administration in many parts of China had pursued a capitalist line of policy opposed to Mao Tze-tung's teachings. The writer of this article called these unnamed officials 'capitalist-roaders'. The 'revolutionary masses', the article said, must identify these enemies, because 'our Great Leader Chairman Mao trusted the revolutionary masses and had said their eyes were bright and clear as snow.'

The article warned the 'revolutionary masses' that the capitalist class was cunning and made the allegation that its members hoarded gold and secreted weapons in their homes so that when an attack against China came from abroad they could cooperate with the enemy to become a fifth column. It praised the revolutionary action of the Red Guards, calling them 'little revolutionary generals'. In conclusion, the article mentioned the existence of a 'counter-current' against the Cultural Revolution and the Red Guards. It warned everybody to beware of this counter-current and to avoid being influenced by it. Those 'capitalist-roaders' who had a consistent 'revisionist' outlook and tried to 'protect' the capitalist class would be dealt with by the 'revolutionary masses' and be swept away onto the rubbish heap of history.

The article was frighteningly irresponsible because no clear definition was offered for either the 'revolutionary masses' who were to identify the enemies and to punish them or the 'capitalist-roaders' who were to be the victims. The article left me in no doubt that Mao Tze-tung and his specially selected committee to conduct the Cultural Revolution intended to expand the scope of their attack and increase the degree of violence against those they had listed as victims. The chilling tone of the article could not be ignored. Since a leading article in the *People's Daily* was to be obeyed immediately, the tempo of the Cultural Revolution in Shanghai was sure to escalate. The Party Secretariat and the Municipal Government would be quite unable to implement the Ten-Point Resolution. I expected the Red Guards to come back soon and I expected their attitude to become even more hostile and intransigent. I thought it was only fair to urge my servants to leave my house and go back to their homes.

The cook said that since he did not live in, he could come and go freely until the Red Guards told him to stay away. Lao Chao said, 'I'm not afraid to remain. You need someone to go to the market to buy food. It's not safe for you to go out. I am from a poor peasant family. My son is in the Army and is a Party member. We are the true proletariat. The Red Guards have already smashed and confiscated everything. What else can they do? If they tell me to leave, I must go. Otherwise, I will stay.' Chen Mah wept and said she wanted to stay with my daughter.

At a time like this, the loyalty of my servants was something very noble. I was deeply moved. I did not insist on their leaving immediately because having them in the house was better than waiting for the Red Guards alone. However, I wrote to Chen Mah's daughter who lived in another province when the cook had bought me some paper from the market. I told her to come and fetch her mother home. I felt more responsible for Chen Mah than for the cook and Lao Chao.

When my daughter came home with the news that the Municipal Government building was besieged by the Red Guards demanding the immediate withdrawal of the Ten-Point Resolution, denounced as a document offering protection to the capitalist class, I was not surprised. She also told me that a long-time associate of Chiang Ching, Mao's wife, had been appointed to conduct the Cultural Revolution in Shanghai.

'His name is Chang Chuan-chiao. Someone at our film studio said that he had been a journalist in Shanghai in the thirties when Chiang Ching was an actress. Those in the studio who used to know them both are terrified. Some of them have packed their bags in preparation for going to jail. They seem to believe Chang Chuan-chiao will put them under detention so that they could be prevented from talking about him and Chiang Ching in the thirties. Mummy, do you think those innocent actresses and actors will really go to jail?' My daughter was both puzzled and shocked by what she had heard at her film studio. Not knowing anything about Shanghai in the thirties, I had no idea what Chiang Ching and Chang Chuan-chiao were afraid of nor what the actresses and actors at the film studio knew about them that was so dangerous.

'Can you stay at home tonight?' I asked her as I hoped to spend a quiet evening with her to talk over the situation.

'I'm afraid not, Mummy. I really dashed back to see how you are and whether the Red Guards had come back. The others are all remaining at the studio. An urgent meeting has been called to discuss an important article in the *People's Daily*. I was told it was written by someone close to Chairman Mao so it is very important and represents Chairman Mao's viewpoint,' she said hurriedly and looked at her watch. 'Goodness! I must run!'

Lao Chao brought her a bowl of noodles and said, 'Eat some of it. It has been cooled. You can't go without food.'

My daughter took the chopsticks and put some noodles into her mouth, swallowed and said to Lao Chao, 'Thanks a lot. I really must go.'

She gave me a hug and dashed out of the house. I had much to say to her, but there was no time to say anything.

Lao Chao brought me his transistor radio so that I could listen to the evening news. Every station I could get was broadcasting the leading article of the *People's Daily*. The announcer read it in the excited, high-pitched voice I was to come to know well during the following years. I left the radio on in the hope of hearing some other item of news, but there was nothing else. By the time I fell into an uneasy sleep I had listened to the article so many times that I almost knew it by heart.

The next morning, the cook brought the news that there was very little food at the market as the peasants from the surrounding countryside, who used to bring vegetables, fish and shrimps to the markets, had answered Chairman Mao's call and joined the ranks of 'revolutionary masses' to take part in the Cultural Revolution. They had come into the city in large numbers and occupied several hotels in the business section of Shanghai. Their leaders demanded, and got, from the frightened hotel managers, free food and service. As news of the luxury of hot running water, inner-spring mattresses and carpeted floors filtered back to the communes, women and children accompanied the men to the city to seize the opportunity for a free holiday. In the meantime, Red Guards were arriving at the railway station from Peking and other northern cities to 'exchange revolutionary experiences' with the Shanghai Red Guards. At the same time the Shanghai Red Guards were travelling to Peking in the hope of being reviewed by Chairman Mao. The Red Guards commandeered trains and ships for their transport, leaving normal passengers and goods stranded at stations and wharves. Nobody dared to oppose the Red Guards. Since the mention of 'capitalist-roaders' by the leading article of the *People's Daily*, the officials were paralysed with fear.

The denunciation of its Ten-Point Resolution put the Shanghai Municipal Government on the defensive. To avoid giving any further cause for complaint to the Red Guards, it provided free meals for the incoming and outgoing Red Guards. Food stalls at the railway station and wharves were set up. All the shops making steamed buns and the former White Russian bakeries, now State-owned, were mobilized to produce buns and bread for the Red Guards. Determined to find fault with the Shanghai officials, the Red Guards denounced the western-style bread made by the bakeries as 'foreign food' and refused to eat it. At the same time, factory workers decided to join the 'revolutionary masses' by organizing their own Cultural Revolution groups. To embarrass the Shanghai officials, they made extravagant economic demands. To protect themselves and to win the support of the workers, the officials authorized payments of bonuses and benefits to the workers. After only a few days, the cash reserves of the local banks were exhausted. The workers whose demands were not met became so infuriated that they joined the Red Guards to attack the Municipal Government and its leading officials. Behind all these activities of the Red Guards and the workers against the Municipal Government was the hand of Chang Chuan-chiao, who directed their revolutionary activities from the comfort of a suite of rooms at the Peace Hotel which became the temporary headquarters of the Maoist leaders when they came to Shanghai, until the Shanghai Party Secretariat and Municipal Government were toppled by the Revolutionaries in January of the following year.

A few of my daughter's friends were high school teachers. Because they also wore the red armbands, they could drop in to see us without attracting undue attention. Lao Chao also took the opportunity of the lull of the Red Guards' activities against me to go out to visit his friends and mingle with the crowds on the streets. The cook's son, a factory worker, paid his father a visit and told him the conditions at his place of work. The stories they related were so astonishing and the reluctance of the Shanghai Party and government officials to exercise their power was so unusual that I began to wonder whether there wasn't something more to the Cultural Revolution than its declared purpose of destroying the remnants of the capitalist class and purifying the ranks of officials and intellectuals.

One day, Hsiao Hsu, a schoolteacher friend of Meiping, came to our house to see her when she was away at the film studio. He told me that the Red Guards had dismantled the Catholic Cathedral's twin spires which were a landmark in Shanghai. During the night, he said, the Red Guards had broken into the Shanghai Municipal Library and destroyed a large number of valuable books. When they went to the Historical Museum, they failed to break down the strong iron gate. So they went to the home of its director and dragged the old man from his sickbed to a struggle meeting.

'The old man is now in hospital. Some said he has died already. The Red Guards are getting quite wild. I think you should take Meiping and try to escape to Hong Kong,' he said.

'Do you think Meiping would want to go?' I asked him this question because once when he was in our house, just before I was to make a trip to Hong Kong, both he and my daughter said they would never want to live as second-class citizens in colonial Hong Kong.

'The situation is different now. After the Cultural Revolution, young people from non-working-class family backgrounds will have no future in China at all. In the past, if we worked twice as hard as the young people of the working class and expected no advancement, we could have a reasonably happy private life. In future, we will be like the Untouchables in India, whose children and children's children suffer too. The only way out is to escape. You have many friends abroad. Why don't you take Meiping and go?' he urged me.

'I think it's too late to escape now. You know the penalty of attempting to escape to Hong Kong is very serious, something like ten or twenty years in prison,' I said.

'It's not too late. I have made some investigations. The whole railway system is in a state of confusion. No one buys a ticket or has a travel permit any more. Red Guards are going all over the country by just getting on a train. No one asks any questions. I have been both to the station and the wharf. There are no ticket collectors at either place. No one in authority at all.'

'I think the moment I get on a train, I would be recognized and dragged off or beaten.'

'You can both be disguised as Red Guards. I will get you some red cloth for armbands. And I will write the three characters for "Red Guard" for you. I have done quite a few of these for our students,' he said.

'I think I'm too old to be taken for a Red Guard.'

'All you have to do is to have your hair cut short, take the book of quotations by Chairman Mao in your hand and pretend to be absorbed in it. You can even wear a cap to cover your hair. If anyone should question you, you can say you are a teacher. As for Meiping, she can easily pass for a Red Guard,' he said impatiently.

When I shook my head again, he declared, 'You are foolish not to try. In any case, talk it over with Meiping when she comes home.'

(I saw Hsiao Hsu again in Hong Kong in 1980, when I came out of China. He told me that he was turned back at the border when he tried to reach Hong Kong by train. But later, he swam to Macao. A few years later he got to Hong Kong where he worked hard and saved money. In 1980 he was the part-owner of a toy factory in Kowloon that exports toys to many parts of the world. Since conditions in China had changed for the better after Mao died, he was thinking of making a trip to Shanghai to visit his mother.)

I was in the bathroom when I heard the sound of furious hammering on the front gate again. Halfway down the stairs, I came face to face with a little girl about fifteen years of age. She was dressed in a khaki-coloured uniform with a cap sitting straight on her head. The edge of the cap covered her eyebrows so that her eyes peered from underneath it. Her small waist was gathered in by a wide leather belt with a shiny buckle. In her hand she carried a leather whip.

'Are you the class enemy of this house? How well fed you look! Your cheeks are smooth and your eyes are bold. You have been fattened by the blood and toil of the peasants and workers. But now things are going to be different! You'll have to pay for your criminal deeds! Come with me!' From her accent I knew she was a Red Guard from Peking.

I followed her downstairs. Several boys and girls in similar attire were in the hall by the door of the dining room. She went into the room and I followed her.

'Kneel down!' one of the boys shouted. Simultaneously his stick landed on my back. Another boy hit the glass door of the cabinet. It broke. He swung the stick round and hit the back of my knee. The decision of whether or not I should comply with the kneeling order was taken out of my hands. I collapsed on the floor.

'Where is the cash?' one of them asked.

'The Red Guards who were here before took it.'

'Did they take all of it?'

'No, they left a few hundred yuan for me to live on.'

'Where is it?'

'In a drawer in my desk.'

The boy kicked my leg as he passed me going upstairs with the others. The girl with the whip was left to watch me. She swung her whip in the air back and forth, missing my head by a fraction each time. The others came down again with the drawer and tipped the bank notes onto the dining table. They told me to turn round to face the wall. I could hear them counting the notes.

There was the sound of more people entering the house. I wondered if the front gate had been left open but I heard a man's voice ordering Lao Chao to call Chen Mah and the cook to the hall. Then he said to someone, 'Take them upstairs and question them.'

The Red Guards went into the hall and then they all came into the dining room.

'Here she is,' someone said.

'You may go now. We will deal with her ourselves,' said the same person who had spoken before.

I heard the Red Guards leave the house, hitting the walls and the furniture with their sticks and whips as they went out. They banged the front door so hard that the house shook.

'Stand up! Come over here!' the man yelled.

I stood up and turned to face the new intruders. The man who spoke was of medium height, slightly built, wearing a pair of tinted spectacles. There were two other men and a woman in the room. Although they all wore the cotton trousers and ill-fitting shirts and jackets of the working class, they spoke like people of some education. On their armbands were the three Chinese characters for 'Revolutionaries'.

They all sat down in a half moon facing where I stood. The man said to me, 'You are the class enemy of this house. You are guilty of conspiring with foreign powers. It's written on the Big Character Poster on your front gate. Do you deny it?'

'Of course, I deny it! Who are you anyway? What do you want?'

'We are the Proletarian Revolutionaries.'

'Never heard of such a title,' I said.

'You are going to hear a lot about us. We are the Revolutionaries who represent the working class which is the ruling class in China,' he said with a lift of his chin.

'Isn't the working class in China represented by the Chinese Communist Party?' I asked.

'Shut up! We don't have to justify ourselves to you. You are an arrogant class enemy! You have no right to discuss who represents the working class in China. We are responding to Chairman Mao's call to take part in the Great Proletarian Cultural Revolution. That's quite good enough,' said the woman.

'You are a class enemy and a running dog of the Anglo-American imperialists. You went to an American-endowed university in Peking and then to a British university in London so you were trained from an early age to serve the imperialists,' the man said.

I remained silent as it seemed pointless to talk to them.

'Is it because you are ashamed that you do not speak?' the woman asked me.

'Why should I be ashamed? Many graduates of Yenching University have become leaders of the Communist Party. To have been a student there doesn't mean I am a running dog of anybody. The London School of Economics was a left-wing college founded by the Fabian Socialists of Britain. In fact, it was there that I first read the Communist Party Manifesto by Marx and Engels,' I told her.

'Ha, ha, ha! What a joke! A class enemy and a running dog of the imperialists has read the Communist Party Manifesto! The next thing you are going to say is you want to join the Communist Party,' the man with the tinted glasses said sarcastically.

The woman said, 'Lenin denounced the Fabian Socialists as reformers. They were not true socialists because they did not advocate revolution by violence. Don't try to ingratiate yourself with us. Your only way out is to come clean.'

'I'm a law-abiding citizen,' I declared. 'I worked for a foreign firm and had no access to government secrets. I do not know any foreign governments and they do not know me.'

Another man said, 'You do know and are on friendly terms with a number of foreign government officials.'

'You needn't get so excited. All the senior staff of foreign firms are spies. You are not the only one,' joined another man.

'Why should foreign governments trust us?' I asked them. 'What hold have they got over people like us who live in China?'

'Ah! Nearly all of you have money abroad. You don't deny you yourself have money abroad,' the man said.

'That's a hold on you. They can confiscate your money,' added the woman.

'You don't understand. Governments abroad cannot interfere with the banks. They cannot confiscate the deposit of anybody,' I told them.

'Why do you keep money abroad anyway? Why should an honest Chinese want to keep money abroad?'

'I make trips to Hong Kong and have to pay for my food and hotel bills when I am there. I'm not allowed to take my Chinese money with me, as you know. There is foreign-exchange control. Each time I went out of China, I was allowed only 5 US dollars. Besides, I have to bring money into China to buy coal and other things from the Overseas Chinese Store,' I explained. 'I have some money abroad, but I have a lot more money in Shanghai. I have this house. I have my only child here. She is worth more than anything in the world to me. She is a member of the Communist Youth League. Why should I oppose the Communist Party and the People's Government?'

'You would oppose the Communist Party even if your daughter were a Party member. It's your class instinct,' the man with the tinted glasses, who seemed to be their leader, said.

Several other men and women came into the room, followed by my servants. The man looked at them. The newcomers shook their heads. Evidently they had not got what they wanted from my servants.

The man with the tinted spectacles assumed a severe tone of voice and asked me, 'Where have you hidden your gold and weapons?'

'What gold and weapons?' I was surprised by his question until I remembered the leading article of the *People's Daily*. It had accused members of the capitalist class of secreting gold and weapons in order to form a fifth column when foreign powers invaded China.

'You know what gold and weapons! You had better come clean.'

'I have no gold or weapons. The Red Guards have been here. They went through the entire house. They did not find any gold or weapons.'

'You are clever. You hid them. Our Great Leader told us that the class enemies are secreting gold and weapons. He can't be wrong.'

'We are going to find the gold and weapons, if you don't come clean. Then you will be severely punished,' said their leader. 'Come along! They must be somewhere in this house.'

I wondered whether they really believed the leading article or whether they just had to appear to believe it. The fact was that soon after the Communist takeover in 1949, possession of firearms was declared illegal. Those who had them had to hand them over to the government and were subject to a house search by the police. The former Kuomintang military and police personnel were arrested and 'reformed' in labour camps. Their families all had to move out of their homes. Therefore, it seemed utterly absurd to say some Chinese could still have weapons in their homes in 1966.

However, the Revolutionaries took my servants and me all over the house. They ripped open mattresses, cut the upholstery of the chairs and sofas, removed tiles from the walls of the bathrooms, climbed into the fireplace and poked into the chimney, lifted floorboards, got on to the roof, fished in the water tank under the ceiling and crawled under the floor to examine the pipes. All the while, they watched the facial expression of my servants and myself.

I had lost track of time but darkness had long descended on the city when they decided to dig up the garden. The sky was overcast and it was a dark night. They switched on the lights on the terrace and told Lao Chao to bring his flashlight. When they came to the coalshed, my servants and I were told to move the coal to a corner of the garden they had already searched. The damp ash-covered lawn had been trampled into a sea of mud; all the flowerbeds had been dug up and spades were sunk into the earth around the shrubs. They even pulled plants out of their pots. But they found nothing for nothing was there to be found. The Revolutionaries, my servants and I were all covered with mud, ashes and sweat.

In the end, physical exhaustion got the better of their revolutionary zeal. We were told to go back to the house. They were fuming with rage because they had lost face in not finding anything. I knew that unless I did something to save their face they were going to vent their anger on me. If only I could produce something in the way of gold such as a ring or a bracelet. I remembered my jewellery sealed in Meiping's study.

'The Red Guards put my gold rings and bracelets in the sealed room. Perhaps you could open the room and take them and let the Red Guards know,' I said to the woman.

'Don't pretend to be stupid. We are looking for gold bars,' she said.

We were standing in the hall. The man with the tinted glasses had removed them to reveal bloodshot eyes. He glanced at my servants cowering by the kitchen door and he looked at his fellow Revolutionaries around him. Then he glared at me. Suddenly he shouted 'Where have you hidden the gold and weapons?' and took a step towards me threateningly.

I was so weary that I could hardly stand. Making an effort, I said, 'There simply aren't any. If there were, wouldn't you have found them already?'

The fact he had been proven wrong was intolerable to him. Staring at me with pure hatred, he said, 'Not necessarily. We did not break open the walls.'

He stood very close to me. I could see every detail of his sneering face. Although I found him extremely repulsive and would have liked to step back a pace or two, I did not move for I did not want him to think I was afraid of him. I simply said slowly, in a normal and friendly voice, 'You must be reasonable. If I had hidden anything in the walls, I could not have done it alone. I would have needed a plasterer to put the walls back again. All workmen work for State-controlled businesses. They would have to report to their Party Secretary the sort of work they did.' I was so tired that it was a real effort to speak.

The man was beside himself with rage for I had implied that he was unreasonable. His face turned white and his lips trembled. I could see the bloated veins on his temple. He raised his arm to strike me.

At that very moment, Meiping's cat Fluffy came through the kitchen door, jumped on the man's leg from behind and sank his teeth into the flesh of the man's calf. Screaming with pain, the man hopped wildly on one leg, trying to shake the cat off. The others also tried to grab Fluffy but the agile cat was already out of the house like a streak of lightning through the French windows we had left open when we came in from the garden. We all rushed outside. Fluffy was sitting on his favourite branch of the magnolia tree, out of reach. From this safe perch, Fluffy looked at us and mewed. The wounded man was almost demented. With his trousers torn and blood streaming down the back of his leg, he dashed to the tree and tried to shake it. Fluffy hopped on to a higher branch, turned round to give us all a disdainful glance, ran onto the roof of my neighbour's house and disappeared into the night.

We came in again. In the drawing room, the man sat down on the sofa the Red Guard had broken and he had slashed not long ago. When I asked Chen Mah for some mercurochrome or iodine, she reminded me that the Red Guards had already poured everything away.

The Revolutionaries were greatly embarrassed by the rather unheroic appearance of their leader who was now wiping his leg with a handkerchief, completely deflated. Tactfully my servants withdrew into the kitchen. I was left there to witness his discomfiture. One of the women pushed me out through the connecting door between the drawing room and the dining room, saying, 'We don't need your help or sympathy. You keep a wild animal in the house to attack the Revolutionaries. You will be punished. As for the cat, we will have the neighbourhood committee look for it and put it to death. You are very much mistaken if you think by making your cat bite us we will give up. We are going to look further for the gold and weapons.' She turned the key in the lock and went round to the hall to lock the other door also. Again, I was incarcerated in the dining room.

Do they really believe I have gold and weapons? I wondered. Or, do they merely have to carry out the order of Chairman Mao to search for them? Surely they had done enough, if it were the latter case.

I heard Lao Chao calling me in a low whisper in the garden. I went to the window and saw him standing outside.

'The cook has gone to the Film Studio to tell Mei-mei not to come home tonight. Is it all right?'

'Thank you, Lao Chao. It's very thoughtful of you. It's best she is not here.'

Suddenly there was the sound of hammering on the front gate again. Lao Chao hurried away to open it. He came back to tell me that the Red Guards who had first looted my house had come back.

'Please go to your room and take Chen Mah with you,' I told him, anticipating more trouble.

There was the sound of many people running up and down the stairs and there was loud shouting. Angry arguments seemed to have broken out overhead, followed by fighting. There was nothing I could do. I resigned myself to the possibility of the total destruction of my home.

Pulling three dining chairs together, I lay down on the cushions. I was so exhausted that I dozed despite the loud noise.

After daybreak, several Red Guards and Revolutionaries threw the door open. It seemed that their dispute, whatever it was, was resolved. A girl shouted, 'Get up! Get up!'

A woman Revolutionary told me to get something to eat in the kitchen quickly and then 'come upstairs to do some useful work'. I went into the downstairs cloakroom to wash my hands. Looking into the mirror over the basin, I was shocked to see my dishevelled hair and puffy white face, with smudges of mud on my forehead and cheeks. Stepping back, I saw in the glass that my clothes were spattered with mud. In fact, I looked very much like a female corpse I had seen long ago being dug out of the debris on a Chungking street after an air raid during the Sino-Japanese war. The sight of that dead woman had haunted me for days. She seemed so finished, unable to do anything or even to make the smallest gesture of protest against the unfairness of her own fate. The recollection of her dead body now made me resolve to keep alive. I thought the Cultural Revolution was going to be a fight for me to clear my name. I must not only keep alive but I must be as strong as granite, so that no matter how much I was knocked about, I could remain unbroken. My face was puffy because I had not drunk any water for a long time and my one remaining kidney was not functioning properly. I had to remedy that immediately.

In the kitchen, I drank two glasses of water before eating the bowl of steaming rice and vegetables Lao Chao provided me with. It was amazing how quickly food turned into energy and how encouraging was a resolute attitude of mind. I felt a great deal better already.

A Red Guard opened the kitchen door and yelled, 'Are you having a feast? What a long time you are taking! Hurry up, hurry up!'

Lao Chao and I followed the Red Guards up the stairs. Chen Mah also joined us. We found that the Red Guards and the few remaining Revolutionaries required our help in packing up my belongings so that they could be taken away. Anxious for them to be out of the house, I helped readily. The presence of the Red Guards and the Revolutionaries was more intolerable to me than the loss of my possessions. They seemed to me alien creatures from another world with whom I had no common language.

In the eyes of the Red Guards and the Revolutionaries, Lao Chao was not a class enemy, even though they probably thought him misguided and lacking in socialist awareness to work for me. They chatted with him freely; I could see Lao Chao was doing his best to appear friendly too. While we were sitting on the floor packing up the things that had been scattered everywhere, I heard the Red Guards excitedly discussing their forthcoming journey to Peking to be reviewed by Chairman Mao. The few who had taken part when Mao reviewed the Red Guards from the gallery of the Tien An Men Gate in Peking on 18 August were describing their experience with pride. They spoke of the role of the Army in organizing their reception in Peking, in providing them with accommodation and khaki uniforms and in drilling them for the review. It was the Army officers who had selected the quotations and slogans the youngsters were to shout.

I was interested in what the Red Guards were saying. It seemed the Army was working behind the scenes to support and direct the Red Guards' activities.

When everything was packed, the trucks came. But to my great disappointment the Red Guards did not leave the house when the trucks drove away.

A woman Revolutionary said to me, 'You must remain in the house. You are not allowed to go out of the house. The Red Guards will take turns to be here to watch you.'

I was astonished and angry. I asked her, 'What authority have you to keep me confined in the house?' Disappointment so overwhelmed me that I was trembling.

'I have the authority of the Proletarian Revolutionaries.'

'I want to see the order in writing,' I said, trying to control my trembling voice.

'Why do you want to go out? Where do you want to go to? A woman like you would be beaten to death outside. We are doing you a kindness in putting you under house arrest. Lao Chao will be allowed to stay and do the marketing for you. Do you know what's going on outside? There is a full-scale revolution going on.'

'I don't particularly want to go out. It's the principle of the matter.'

'What principle? Since you don't want to go out, why argue with me? You stay here until we decide what to do with you. That's an order.'

She swept out of the house. I was furious but there was nothing whatever I could do.

I was given the box spring of my own bed placed on the floor to sleep on. A change of clothes and a sweater hung in the empty cupboard. A suitcase containing my winter clothes and the green canvas bag with a quilt and blankets for the colder days were left in a corner of the room. Besides the table and chairs in the kitchen, I was left with two chairs and a small coffee table. The Red Guards detailed to watch me sat on these two chairs outside my room so that I had to sit on the box spring on the floor. Every now and then one of them would open my door to see what I was doing. The only place where I had some privacy was my bathroom.

My daughter was allowed to live in her own room but I was not allowed in there or to speak to her when she came home which was very seldom as she had to spend more and more nights at the Film Studio taking part in the Cultural Revolution. In the evenings, I would gently push the door of my room open hoping to obtain a glimpse of her as she came up the stairs. On the nights when she did come home and we managed to look at each other, I felt comforted and reassured. Generally I would sleep peacefully that night.

Lao Chao went to market to purchase food, but neither he nor my daughter was allowed to eat with me. The Red Guards had a rotation of duty hours so that they went home for their meals. At night, one or two of them slept on the floor outside my bedroom on a makeshift bed.

Two days after I was placed under house arrest, Chen Mah's daughter came to fetch her mother. We had a tearful farewell. Chen Mah wanted to leave me a cardigan she had knitted but the Red Guards scolded her for lack of class consciousness and refused to let her hand it to me. 'She won't have enough clothes for the winter. She isn't very strong, you know,' Chen Mah pleaded with the Red Guards.

'Don't you realize? She is your class enemy. Why should you care whether she has enough clothes or not?' the Red Guard said.

Chen Mah's daughter seemed frightened of the Red Guards and urged Chen Mah to leave. But Chen Mah said, 'I must say goodbye to Mei-mei!' Tears were streaming down her face.

One of the Red Guards became impatient. She faced Chen Mah militantly and said, 'Haven't you stayed in this house long enough? She is the daughter of a class enemy. Why do you have to say goodbye to her?'

When I put my arms round Chen Mah's shoulders to hug her for the last time, she burst into loud crying. The Red Guards pulled my arms away and pushed Chen Mah and her daughter out of the front door. Lao Chao followed them out with Chen Mah's luggage and I heard him getting a pedi-cab for them.

Longing to know what went on outside, I read avidly the newspaper that Lao Chao left on the kitchen table each day. One evening, when I went into the kitchen to have my dinner, I saw a sheet of crudely printed paper entitled *Red Guard News* left on a kitchen chair. The headline of the paper said, 'Hit back without mercy the counter-attack of the class enemies' which intrigued me. I longed to know more. There was no one about so I picked up the small sheet and secreted it in my pocket. Later, in the quiet of my bathroom, I read it. After that, I kept a lookout for any crumpled piece of paper left by the Red Guards. These handbills produced by the Red Guards were mostly full of their usual hyperbole about the capitalist class and the revisionists. However, in the course of denouncing these enemies they revealed facts about certain Party leaders which had hitherto been kept secret from the general public. I was particularly interested in reports that certain officials in the Shanghai Municipal Government and the Party Secretariat were attempting to 'ignore' or 'sabotage' Mao's orders. The extent of conflict caused by policy differences within the Party leadership seemed far greater than I had thought. Being uncensored, these Red Guards publications and handbills inadvertently exposed some of the facts of the power struggle in the Party leadership and contributed to the breakdown of the myth that the Party leaders were a group of dedicated men united for a common purpose.

After a week indoors, I asked the Red Guards how long I was supposed to remain without outdoor exercise, and requested that I be allowed to use the garden. After making a telephone call, they allowed me to go into the garden to walk round or to sit on the steps of the terrace with Fluffy on my lap. The 'sin' of biting a Revolutionary leader did not seem to be regarded as important by the young Red Guards. They would often play with Fluffy too.

Soon, Meiping realized that I was fairly often in the garden, especially in the early morning. Whenever she came home at night, she would throw notes there, rolled into a small ball for me to pick up when I went down for my daily exercise next morning. But when it rained during the night, as it often did in September, the paper got wet and disintegrated when I tried to unroll it. She could not say much on a tiny strip of paper, but her messages of 'I love you, Mum,' 'Take care of yourself,' 'We will be brave and weather the storm together, dear Mummy' ... etc. gave me great comfort and tempered my feeling of isolation.

If Lao Chao happened to be in the kitchen when I went for my meals, a Red Guard would follow me there to make sure we did not converse. But Lao Chao and the Red Guard would chat with one another. After a while I found that much of what Lao Chao said was information for my ears also. For instance, one day he said to a Red Guard, 'Do you beat up your teachers often?'

I was astonished to hear Lao Chao's question because when the Red Guards came to loot my house on the night of 30 August they seemed quite friendly with their teachers. I waited breathlessly for the answer.

The Red Guard said casually, 'We beat them up when they are found to have capitalist ideas or when they insist we study and not have so many revolutionary activities. Some of them do not seem to understand the importance of carrying on with the Cultural Revolution. They still believe in the importance of learning from books. But our Great Leader Chairman Mao told us, 'Learn to swim from swimming.' We should learn from taking part in revolutionary activities and from active labour. We don't need the old type of school any more. Those teachers who still believe in books obviously oppose our Great Leader so we must treat them as enemies.'

Another time, Lao Chao asked the Red Guard, 'Did you go to surround the building of the Municipal Government?'

'Of course! And this wasn't the first time or the last time either. The entire Shanghai Municipal Government is rotten with revisionism.'

It was from Lao Chao's conversations with the Red Guards and from their handbills and publications that I gained the impression that, daily, thousands of new Revolutionaries were flocking to join the Red Guards and workers' organizations that had sprung up like 'bamboo shoots after the spring rain'. Whether hoping for personal gain or merely fearful of being thought politically backward, people felt compelled to become a part of the Proletarian Cultural Revolution.

The ransacking of the homes of members of the capitalist class and the attack on the intellectuals inflated the ego and whetted the appetite of the Red Guards and the Revolutionaries for violence. They were impatient to go further. It seemed to me that the Maoist leaders used this psychological moment to direct their anger and channel their energy towards putting pressure on the Shanghai Party Secretariat and Municipal Government, both of which were accused of protecting the capitalist class and opposing Mao's policies. It was alleged that for years Mao's orders were deliberately ignored. But officials of the Shanghai Party Secretariat and Municipal Government were not novices to the political game. They were experienced Communists who had survived many political storms and purges. And they were not unfamiliar with Mao's tactics. Since Mao used the masses, they decided to use the masses themselves. Speedily they organized their own Red Guards and Revolutionaries to take part in the Cultural

Revolution. They vied with the Maoist Red Guards and Revolutionaries to gain control of the situation in Shanghai. To succeed, each group had to be more red, more revolutionary, more cruel and more left in their slogans and action. Thus, not only was it at times extremely difficult to identify on which side a certain group was until the bloody civil wars broke out but also the so-called capitalist class and the intellectuals were confronted by two contesting groups who competed with each other in dealing the heaviest blow to demonstrate their authenticity.

As the scale of violence escalated and the scope of the Cultural Revolution expanded to include an ever-increasing number of class enemies, a new slogan was coined to emphasize the undesirability of children of capitalist class families. It said, 'A dragon is born of a dragon, a phoenix is born of a phoenix and a mouse is born with the ability to make a hole in the wall.' In short, it meant that since the parents were class enemies, the children would naturally be class enemies too. While I thought it rather astonishing in a country pledged to materialistic Marxism that a slogan should be coined based entirely on the importance of genetics, I had no time or the heart to dwell on it. Soon after its publication, my daughter Meiping was taken from the rank of the 'masses' and placed in the 'cowshed' where all those in the Film Studio denounced as class enemies were concentrated. The 'cowshed' earned its name from the fact that Mao Tze-tung had delineated all class enemies as 'cow's demons and snake spirits'. In the 'cowshed' the victims spent their time writing confessions and self-criticisms over and over again in an effort to purge themselves of heretical thinking contrary to Mao Tze-tung Thought. I was informed of this situation through Lao Chao's conversation with one of the Red Guards. In a loud voice, just outside my bedroom, he asked the Red Guard's permission to take bedding and clothing to my daughter in the so-called 'cowshed' of the Film Studio because she could no longer come home. Later, when I went into the kitchen for my evening meal, which I could not swallow but pretended to eat, in order to find out about my daughter's condition, Lao Chao did not disappoint me. As soon as I sat down, he talked about Meiping to the unsuspecting Red Guard.

'I saw her when I went to the Film Studio to give her the things. She looked quite well and seemed cheerful. She told me she was writing self-criticism about herself and her class origin. She also said all those in the cowshed were very friendly. In fact, she seemed quite all right and is taking everything philosophically. But why should she have to write self-criticism? She is a member of the Communist Youth League and everywhere she went she got citations of merit. She is sympathetic and friendly towards the proletariat. Once she even saved the life of a poor peasant woman by rowing her in a boat through the creeks to the County Hospital when the woman was suddenly taken ill.'

'She was born abroad and from a family like this. Of course she has to write self-criticism,' the Red Guard said to Lao Chao. 'She is probably a radish; red outside but white within. In any case, the Communist Youth League is disbanded. The General Secretary of the Youth League, Hu Yao-bong, is a revisionist.'

Shortly afterwards, a group of Revolutionaries from the Film Studio came to ransack her room and took away what was left of her things. I was desperately unhappy with the new turn of events. I could keep my spirit buoyant when the attack was directed at me alone, but now that she had also become the object of persecution I suffered from deep depression.

In the late afternoon of 27 September, I was taken by a Red Guard and a Revolutionary to the same school building I had gone to in July. A large gathering was already there waiting for us. This time I was the object of the struggle meeting, attended not only by the Red Guards and the Revolutionaries who had come to my house but also by the former staff of Shell and the men in charge of their indoctrination who had questioned me. The man with the tinted spectacles was in charge.

The room was arranged differently. Instead of rows of chairs facing the platform, seats were put in an irregular circle. I was told to stand in the middle, with a Red Guard on each side. The man with the tinted glasses was quite a fluent speaker. He, too, started with the opium war, giving a vivid description of how the invading fleet of Britain bombarded the Chinese coast. His account, full of inaccuracies, aimed at creating hatred for me, made me personally guilty for Britain's action against China over a hundred years ago. He spoke as if it was I who led the British fleet up the Pearl River. Then he declared that Shell was a multinational firm with branches in all parts of the world. He said that Lenin had stated that such companies were the worst enemies of socialism. He told the audience that from time immemorial Shell had sent salesmen deep into the rural areas of China to gather information useful to the imperialists under the pretence of selling kerosene to the peasants. He also gave figures to show the enormous profit the company had made with its China trade and called it the 'commercial exploitation of the Chinese people'. He told the audience that the British imperialists were more subtle than the Americans.

While the United States Government openly opposed the People's Government of China and protected the Kuomintang in Taiwan, the British gave the People's Government diplomatic recognition while voting with the United States at the United Nations to prevent the People's Government from taking China's seat as its representative.

He turned to an account of my family background, telling the audience that I was the descendant of a big landlord family which owned ten thousand *mu* of fertile agricultural land (there are roughly 6 *mus* to an acre). Unlike the liaison officer of the Municipal Government who had said my grandfather was a patriot, he now told the audience that my grandfather was a dirty landlord and an advocate of feudalism because in the history books he wrote he praised several Emperors. Furthermore, he said, evidence had been found among papers left by him that he was a founder and shareholder of the Han Yeh Ping Steel Complex, which included the An Yuan coal-mine where the Great Leader Chairman Mao once personally organized the workers in their struggle against the capitalists. This accusation was supposed to give concrete proof that my grandfather and Chairman Mao were on opposing sides; in fact, the two men belonged to two different generations. He went on to say that my father was a senior official of the Peking Government and spent many years in Japan in his youth. He reminded everyone that Japan had been guilty of aggression against China and in eight years of war and occupation had killed ten million innocent Chinese men, women and children. Carefully he avoided mentioning that my father went to Japan in the early years of this century long before the Japanese invasion of China in 1937; instead he tried to create the impression that my father went to Japan in spite of what Japan did to China. Pointing at me, he said that I went to England when I was twenty years old and was trained by the British to be 'a faithful running dog' in one of their universities. My late husband was described as a 'residue of the decadent Kuomintang regime' who was fortunate to have died so that he escaped judgement by the Revolutionaries.

Throughout his speech, the audience showed their support and agreement by shouting slogans. Added to the usual slogans of the Cultural Revolution there were a number accusing me of being a 'spy' who conspired with foreign powers against China and others simply denouncing me as a 'running dog' of the British.

When he had finished speaking, the Red Guard who had led the other Red Guards into my house shouted into the microphone a description of the 'luxury' of my home. Another Red Guard told how I had tried to 'undermine' their 'revolutionary activities' by fighting with them to preserve 'old culture'. A Revolutionary spoke of my stubborn arrogance and accused me of deliberately keeping a 'wild animal' in the house to wound the Revolutionaries.

Members of the ex-staff of Shell were then called upon to provide further evidence against me. I could easily see how frightened they all were and I wondered what they must have gone through. The men who got up to speak were white and their hands holding the prepared statements shook. None of them looked in my direction. There was very little substance in what they said, but every sentence they uttered contributed to the picture that I enjoyed a warm and friendly relationship with the British residents in Shanghai. A web of suspicion was carefully woven. One of the office lift operators declared that the British manager always stepped aside to let me get into the lift before him. A driver testified that whenever the manager and I shared a car, the manager always allowed me to get in first. This was supposed to demonstrate my value and importance to the 'British imperialists' because in Communist China a senior man would not dream of letting his female assistant get into a car or a lift before him.

Other members of the staff spoke of files kept in a room next to the manager's office, not accessible to anyone but the manager and myself. A senior member of the staff who had been with Shell for many years said that maps of geological formation of areas of China with possible oil deposits were routinely kept at the office because they were of value to the imperialists. Another speaker read out excerpts allegedly taken from reports written by Shell branch managers in other parts of China during the time of the Civil War (1946-9) when the armies of the Kuomintang and the Communists were locked in a bitter struggle. Troop deployments of both sides were mentioned in these reports. This was supposed to repudiate my claim that Shell was interested only in commerce.

My late husband came in for severe criticism too. It was alleged that whenever the interest of Shell clashed with the interest of the State, both my husband and I stood on the side of Shell. All the statements were a mixture of fact and fiction, misrepresentation and exaggeration, calculated to mislead the ignorant minds of the gullible and the uninformed.

The meeting dragged on. Night had long ago descended on the city. But the drama of my misfortune was so absorbing that none of the Red Guards or the Revolutionaries left the room. The majority of them, I thought, were stunned by what they believed to be an exposure of a real international spy. Others simply had to pretend to believe in the allegations. I could see that the men who were running the show were gloating with success.

Years later, I was to learn that the date of this struggle meeting had been postponed several times because the organizers had hoped to get my daughter to take part in my denunciation. Despite enormous pressure, she refused repeatedly. But National Day, October the First, was approaching. The Maoists leaders ordered the Revolutionaries in Shanghai to produce concrete results to celebrate the day in a mood of victory. It was in response to this order that the men in charge of my case decided to hold the meeting without my daughter.

When the man with the tinted glasses judged that sufficient emotion had been generated among those present, he complimented the men and women who took part in my denunciation for their high level of socialist awareness. He also had a good word to say for our former staff members declaring that most of them had emerged from their re-education with clearer heads. But he issued a warning to those whose heads were still foggy, calling upon them to redouble their efforts at self-criticism to shake off the shackles of capitalism.

Turning to me, he said, 'You have listened to the mountain of evidence against you. Your crime against the Chinese people is extremely serious. You can only be reformed by giving a full confession telling us how you conspired with the British imperialists in their scheme to undermine the People's Government. Are you going to confess?'

'I have never done anything against the Chinese people and Government. The Shell office was here because the Chinese Government wanted it to be here. The order to allow Shell to maintain its Shanghai office was issued by the State Council and signed by no less a person than Premier Chou En-lai. Shell is full of goodwill for China and the Chinese people and always observed its laws and regulations scrupulously. It is not Shell's policy to meddle in politics ... ' I said.

Even though I spoke in a loud and clear voice, no one in the room could hear a complete sentence for everything I said was drowned by angry shouts and screams of 'Confess! Confess!' and 'We will not allow a class enemy to argue!' At the same time, the hysterical Red Guards and Revolutionaries crowded round me threateningly, shook their fists in my face, pulled at my clothes and spat on my jacket, while yelling 'dirty spy', 'dirty running dog', 'we will kill you' and so on. Several times I had to brace myself to stand firmly when they pushed me very hard.

While the pandemonium was going on, the men on the platform

were smiling; the man in the tinted glasses seemed particularly pleased to see me suffer at the hands of the mob. What was I to do? It was useless to try to explain and worse than useless to try to resist. If I had made any move at all, the mob would have jumped on me. I could only stand there looking straight ahead, with my eyes fixed on the distant wall, hoping their anger would soon spend itself.

Eventually the noise died down a little. The man said, 'Our patience is exhausted. You are guilty. We could give you the death penalty. But we want to give you a chance to reform yourself. Are you going to confess?'

Everybody stared at me expectantly. I had stood there enduring their abuse for so long, I suppose I should have been filled with hatred for every one of them. Looking back, I remember distinctly that my predominant emotion was one of great sadness. At the same time, I longed to see my daughter. I was sad because I knew I could not reach out to these people around me to make them understand that I was innocent and that they were mistaken. The propaganda on class struggle they had absorbed, not only since the beginning of the Cultural Revolution but also since 1949 when the Communist Army took over Shanghai, had already built an impregnable wall between us. It was not something I could break down in a moment.

After staring at me for a few seconds and finding me silent, the man beckoned to a young man at the back of the mob. The crowd parted to let him through. He carried in his hand a pair of shiny metal handcuffs which he lifted to make sure I saw them. When the young man came to where I stood, the man in charge of the meeting asked again, 'Are you going to confess?'

I answered in a calm voice, 'I've never done anything against the People's Government. I have no connection with any foreign government.'

'Come along!' the young man with the handcuffs said.

I followed him out of the building into the street. The others came behind us. The cool night air was refreshing and I felt my head clearing magically.

Parked in front of the entrance of the school was a black jeep, a vehicle of the Shanghai Police Department. It was a familiar sight to the people of Shanghai. During the height of every political movement, they saw it dashing through the streets with siren screaming taking victims to prison. We stood beside the jeep with the Red Guards, the Revolutionaries, the ex-staff of Shell and a number of pedestrians who stopped to watch.

'Are you going to confess?' the man in the tinted glasses asked again.

I was silently reciting to myself the Twenty-third Psalm, 'The Lord is my shepherd; I shall not want ... '

'Have you gone dumb?'

'Have you lost your voice?'

'Speak!'

'Confess!' They were shouting.

The man with the tinted spectacles and the man from the Police Department were looking at me thoughtfully. They mistook my silence as a sign of weakening. I knew I had to show courage. In fact, I felt much better for having recited the words of the Psalm. I had not been so free of fear that whole evening as I was in that moment standing beside the black jeep, a symbol of repression.

I lifted my head and said in a loud and firm voice, 'I'm not guilty! I've nothing to confess.'

This time there was no more shouting from anybody. The Red Guards, the Revolutionaries as well as the onlookers were perhaps awed by the solemnity of the occasion. After I had spoken, at a signal from the man in the tinted glasses, the young man from the Police pulled my arms behind my back and put the handcuffs on my wrists. There was a deep sigh from an elderly man.

Suddenly, a girl pushed her way to the front and called in an agitated voice, 'Confess! Confess quickly! They are going to take you to prison!' Her clear young voice was like a bell above the hum of the noisy street. It was the girl with the short hair and pale face who had sat by my desk guarding my jewellery when the Red Guards were in my house. Her impulsive effort to save me from going to prison was immediately checked by a woman who pulled her back and took her into the school building.

The driver of the jeep started the engine.

'Get in!' The young man gave me a push.

It was good to sit down. I looked out at the faces of the men and women watching this dramatic scene and saw relief in the eyes of the former staff of Shell. Perhaps they thought that with me out of the way they would be freed from pressure. Others of the crowd looked excited. To them, it was like watching the end of a thrilling drama, only better for their having taken part in it.

The young man from the Police Department got in with the driver and the man with the tinted glasses sat down beside me. The jeep drove off into the dark streets.

PART II
The Detention House

CHAPTER 5

Solitary Confinement

THE STREETS OF SHANGHAI, normally deserted at nine o'clock in the evening, were a sea of humanity. Under the clear autumn sky and in the cool breeze of September, people were out in thousands to watch the intensified activities of the Red Guards. On temporary platforms erected everywhere, the young Revolutionaries were calling upon the people in shrill and fiery rhetoric to join in the Revolution, and conducting small-scale struggle meetings against men and women they seized at random on the street and accused of failing to carry Mao's Little Red Book of quotations or simply wearing the sort of clothes the Red Guards disapproved of. Outside private houses and apartment buildings, smoke rose over the garden walls, permeating the air with the smell of burning as the Red Guards continued to burn books indiscriminately.

Fully-loaded trucks with household goods confiscated from capitalist families by the Red Guards were parked along the pavements ready to be driven away. With crowds jamming the streets and moving in all directions, buses and bicycles could only crawl along. The normal life of the city was making way for the Cultural Revolution, which was rapidly spreading in scope and increasing in intensity.

Loudspeakers at street corners were broadcasting such newly-written revolutionary songs as: 'Marxism is one sentence: revolution is justified', 'To sail the ocean we depend on the Helmsman; to carry out a revolution we depend on the Thought of Mao Tze-tung' and 'The Thought of Mao Tze-tung glitters with golden light'. If one heard only the marching rhythm of the music but not the militant words of the songs, if one saw only the milling crowd but did not see the victims and the Red Guards, one might easily think the scene was some kind of fair held on an autumn night to provide the people with entertainment, rather than a political campaign full of sinister undertones designed to stir up mutual mistrust and class hatred among the populace.

Both my body and my mind were paralysed with fatigue from continued stress and strain, not only from the last few hours of the struggle meeting but also from the events of the preceding two and a half months. I had no idea where I was being taken and I did not speculate. But I was indignant and angry for the way I was being treated because I had never done anything against the People's Government. The accusation that I had committed crimes against my own country was so ludicrous that I thought it was just an excuse for punishing me because I had dared to live well. Clearly I was a victim of class struggle, and, as my friend Winnie had said, since Shell had closed its Shanghai office, the Maoists among the Party officials in Shanghai believed they should bring me down to the level of the masses.

The sight of the police vehicle in which I was being transported was not unfamiliar to the people of the city. Whenever it was forced to halt momentarily, a curious crowd pressed forward to peer at the 'class enemy' inside; some applauded the victory of the proletarian class in exposing yet another enemy while others simply gazed at me with curiosity. A few looked worried and anxious, suddenly turning away from the ominous sight of another human being's ill fortune.

In Mao Tze-tung's China, going to prison did not mean the same thing as it did to people in the democracies. A man was always presumed guilty until he could prove himself innocent. The accused were judged not by their own deeds but by the acreage of land once possessed by their ancestors. A cloud of suspicion was always over the heads of those with wrong class origins. Furthermore, Mao had once declared that 3-5 per cent of the population were enemies of socialism. To prove him correct, during the periodically launched political movements, 3-5 per cent of the members of every organization, whether it was a government department, a factory, a school or a university, must be found guilty of political crimes or heretical thoughts against socialism or Mao Tze-tung Thought. Among those found guilty, a number would be sent either to labour camps or prison. Under such circumstances, a completely innocent person being taken into prison was a frequent occurrence. Going to prison no longer carried with it the stigma of moral degeneration or law infringement. In fact, the people were often sceptical about government claims of anybody's guilt while those unhappy with their lot in Communist China looked on political prisoners with a great deal of sympathy.

From the moment I became involved in the Cultural Revolution in early June and decided not to make a false confession, I had not ruled out the possibility of going to prison. I knew that many people, including seasoned Party members, made ritual confessions of guilt under pressure, hoping to avoid confrontation with the Party or to lessen their immediate suffering by submission. Many others became mentally confused under pressure and made false confessions because they had lost control. When a political campaign ended, some of them were rehabilitated. Many were not. In the Reform through Labour camps that dotted the landscape of China's remote and inhospitable provinces such as Kansu and Chinghai, many innocent men and women were serving harsh sentences simply because they had made false confessions of guilt. It seemed to me that making a false confession of guilt when I was innocent was a foolish thing to do. The more logical and intelligent course was to face persecution no matter what I might have to endure.

As I examined my own position, I realized that the preliminary period of my persecution was drawing to a close. Whatever lay ahead, I would have to redouble my efforts to frustrate my persecutors' attempt to incriminate me. As long as they did not kill me, I would not give up. So, while I sat in the jeep, my mood was not one of fear and defeat but one of resolution.

When the jeep reached the business section of the city, the crowds became so dense that the car made very slow progress and was forced to stop every few blocks. The man in the tinted glasses told the driver to switch on the siren. It was an eerie wail with a pulsating rhythm changing from high to low and back again, rising above the sound of the revolutionary songs and drowning all other noise as well. Everybody turned their heads to watch as the crowd parted to make way for the jeep. The driver speeded up and we proceeded through the streets with no further hindrance. Soon the jeep stopped outside a double black iron gate guarded by two armed sentries with fixed bayonets which glistened under the street lamps. On one side of the gate was a white wooden board with large black characters: The No. 1 Detention House.

The gate swung open and the jeep drove in. It was completely dark inside but, in the beams of the jeep's headlights, I saw willow trees on both sides of the drive, which curved to the right. On one side was a basketball court; on the other side were a number of man-sized dummies lying on their sides near some poles. They looked like human bodies left carelessly about. It was not until several months later, when I was being take to a prison hospital, that I had an opportunity to see the dummies in daylight and discovered that they were for target practice by the soldiers guarding the prison compound.

I knew that the No. 1 Detention House was the foremost detention house in Shanghai for political prisoners; from time to time it had housed Catholic bishops, senior Kuomintang officials, prominent industrialists and well-known writers and artists. The irony of the situation was that it was not a new prison built by the Communist regime but an old establishment used by the former Kuomintang Government before 1949 to house Communist Party members and their sympathizers.

A detention house for political prisoners was an important aspect of any authoritarian regime. Up to now, I had studied Communism in China from the comfort of my home as an observer. Now I was presented with the opportunity to study the situation from an entirely different angle, at close range. In a perverse way, the prospect excited me and made me forget momentarily the dangerous situation in which I found myself.

The jeep followed the drive and went through another iron gate, passing the barracks of soldiers guarding the detention house and stopping in front of the main building of the courtyard. The two men jumped out to disappear inside. A female guard in a khaki cap with its red national emblem at centre front led me into a bare room where another uniformed woman was waiting. She closed the door, unlocked the handcuffs on my wrists, and said, 'Undress!'

I took my clothes off and laid them on the table, the only piece of furniture in the room. The two women searched every article of my clothing extremely thoroughly. In my trouser pocket they found the envelope containing the 400 yuan I had intended to give to my gardener.

'Why have you brought so much money?' asked one of the guards.

'It's for my gardener. I was waiting for him to come to my house to get it. But he didn't come. Perhaps someone could give it to him for me,' I said.

She handed me back my clothes except for the brassière, an article of clothing the Maoists considered represented decadent western influence. When I was dressed, the female guard led me into another room across the dimly lit narrow passage.

A man with the appearance and complexion of a peasant from North China was seated there behind a counter, under an electric light bulb dangling from the ceiling. The female guard indicated a chair facing the counter but a few feet away from it and told me to sit down. She placed the envelope with the money on the counter and said something to the man. He lifted his head to look at me. Then, in a surprisingly mild voice, he asked me for my name, age and address, all of which he entered into a book, writing slowly and laboriously as if not completely at home with a pen and having difficulty remembering the strokes of each character. That he was doubtless barely literate did not surprise me, as I knew the Communist Party assigned jobs to men for their political reliability rather than for their level of education.

When the man had finally finished writing, he said, 'While you are here, you will be known by a number. You'll no longer use your name, not even to the guards. Do you understand?'

I nodded.

We were interrupted by a young man carrying a camera with a flash. He walked into the room and said to me, 'Stand up!' Then he took several photographs of me from different angles and swaggered out of the room. I sat down again, wishing they would hurry up with the proceedings, for I was dead tired.

The man behind the counter resumed in a slow and bored manner, '1806 is your number. You will be known henceforth as 1806. Try to remember it.'

I nodded again.

The female guard pointed to a sheet of paper pasted on the wall and said, 'Read it aloud!'

It was a copy of the prison regulations. The first rule was that all prisoners must study the books of Mao Tze-tung daily to seek reform of their thinking. The second rule was that they must confess their crimes without reservation and denounce others involved in the same crime. The third rule was that they must report to the guards any infringement of prison rules by inmates in the same cell. The rest of the rules dealt with meals, laundry and other matters of daily life in the detention house.

When I had finished reading, the female guard said, 'Try to remember the rules and abide by them.'

The man told me to dip my right thumb in a shallow inkpot filled with sticky red paste and press my thumb to make a print in the registration book. After I had done so, I asked the man for a piece of paper to wipe my thumb.

'Hurry up!' the female guard was getting impatient and shouted from the door. But the man was good-natured. He pulled out a drawer and took out a wrinkled piece of paper which he handed to me. I hastily wiped my thumb and followed the woman out of the room and the building.

My admission into the No. 1 Detention House had been done in a leisurely manner; the attitude of the man and of the female guards was one of casual indifference. To them my arrival was merely routine. For me, crossing the prison threshold was the beginning of a new phase of my life which, through my struggle for survival and for justice, was to make me a spiritually stronger and politically more mature person. The long hours I spent alone re-examining my own life and what had gone on in China since 1949 when the Communist Party took power also enabled me to form a better understanding of myself and the political system under which I was living. Though on the night of 27 September 1966 when I was taken to the detention house I could not look into the future, I was not afraid. I believed in a just and merciful God and I thought he would lead me out of the abyss.

It was pitch dark outside and the ground was unevenly paved. As I followed the female guard, I breathed deeply the sweet night air. We walked round the main building, passed through a peeling and faded red gate with a feeble light and entered a smaller courtyard where I saw a two-storeyed structure. This was where the women prisoners were housed.

From a room near the entrance, another female guard emerged yawning. I was handed over to her in silence.

'Come along,' she said sleepily, leading me through a passage lined with doors locked with bolts and heavy padlocks. My first sight of the prison corridor was something I have never been able to forget. In subsequent years, in my dreams and nightmares, I saw again and again, in the dim light, the long line of doors with sinister looking bolts and padlocks outside and felt again and again the helplessness and frustration of being locked inside.

When we reached the end of the corridor, the guard unlocked a door on the left to reveal an empty cell.

'Get in,' she said. 'Have you any belongings?'

I shook my head.

'We'll notify your family in the morning and get them to send you your belongings. Now, go to sleep!'

I asked her whether I could go to the toilet. She pointed to a cement bucket in the left-hand corner of the room and said, 'I'll lend you some toilet paper.'

She pushed the bolt in place with a loud clang and locked the door. I heard her moving away down the corridor.

I looked around the room and my heart sank. Cobwebs dangled from the ceiling; the once whitewashed walls were yellow with age and streaked with dust. The single naked bulb was coated with grime and extremely dim. Patches of the cement floor were blackened with dampness. A strong musty smell pervaded the air. I hastened to open the only small window with rust-pitted iron bars. To reach it, I had to stand on tiptoes. When I succeeded in pulling the knob and the window swung open, flakes of peeling paint as well as a shower of dust fell to the floor. The only furniture in the room were three narrow beds of rough wooden planks, one against the wall, the other two stacked one on top of the other. Never in my life had I been in or even imagined a place that was so primitive and filthy.

The guard came back with several sheets of toilet paper of the roughest kind, which she handed to me through a small square window in the door of the cell, saying, 'There you are! When you get your supply, you must return to the government the same number of sheets. Now, go to sleep. Lie with your head towards the door. That's the regulation.'

I could not bring myself to touch the dust-covered bed. But I needed to lie down as my legs were badly swollen. I pulled the bed away from the dirty wall and wiped it with the toilet paper. But the dirt was so deeply ingrained that I could only remove the loose dust. Then I lay down anyhow and closed my eyes. The light from the naked bulb hanging from the centre of the ceiling was directly above my head. Though dim, it irritated me. I looked around the cell but could not see a light switch anywhere.

'Please, excuse me!' I called, knocking on the door with my hand.

'Quiet! Quiet!' The guard hurried over and slid open the shutter on the small window.

'I can't find the light switch,' I told her.

'We don't switch off the light at night here. In future, when you want to speak to the guards, just say "report". Don't knock on the door. Don't say anything else.'

'Could you lend me a broom to sweep the room? It's so dirty,' I asked her.

'What nonsense! It's past two o'clock. You just go to sleep!' She closed the shutter but remained outside to watch me through the peephole to make sure I obeyed her orders.

I lay down on the bed again and turn to face the dusty wall to avoid the light. I closed my eyes to shut out the sight of the dirty wall but I had to inhale the unpleasant smell of dampness and dust that surrounded me. In the distance, I heard faintly the crescendo of noise from the crowds on the streets. While it no longer menaced me, I worried about my daughter. I hoped my removal to the detention house would free her from any further pressure to denounce me. If that was indeed the case, and she could be treated as just a member of the masses, I would be prepared to put up with anything.

Suddenly a horde of hungry mosquitoes descended on me. I sat up and tried to ward them off with my arms but they were so stubborn and persistent that I was badly bitten. The itchy welts greatly added to my discomfort and annoyance.

Just before daybreak, the electric light in the cell was switched off. In the darkness, the dirt and ugliness of the room disappeared. I could imagine myself elsewhere. It was a moment of privacy and relief; I felt as if a tight band around me had been loosened. But not for long. Soon the narrow strip of sky turned grey and then white. Daylight slowly poured into the cell, bringing the ugly features of the room into focus again. However, during all the years I spent in that prison cell, the short time of darkness after the light was switched off and before daybreak was always a moment when I recovered the dignity of my being and felt a sense of renewal, simply because I had a precious moment of freedom when I was not under the watchful eyes of the guards.

Footsteps in the passage approached. 'Get up! Get up!' It was the voice of the same guard calling at the door of each cell. I could hear the muted sound of people stirring all over the building and whispering voices and movements in the cell above mine.

The shutter of the small window on the door was pushed open. A young woman called, 'Water,' and pushed the spout of a watering can through the opening.

When I had told her I had no utensil for the water, she withdrew the can but pressed her pale young face against the opening to look at me. When our eyes met, she smiled. A few days later, I caught a glimpse of a square piece of white cloth pinned on her jacket front stating that she was a prisoner serving a sentence of Labour Reform. After that, whenever there was an opportunity, we would smile at each other to acknowledge the painful fate we shared as prisoners of the State. This silent contact I had with her and the flicker of a smile I observed on her pale face came to mean a great deal to me in the years I spent in the detention house. When she disappeared, perhaps having completed her sentence, I experienced a deep sense of loss and felt despondent for days.

The shutter opened again. An oblong aluminium container was placed there. A woman's voice said impatiently, 'Come over, come over!'

When I took the container from her, she said, 'In future, stand here at mealtimes and wait.' She also handed me a pair of bamboo chopsticks that were wet and worn thin with prolonged usage.

The battered container was three-quarters full of luke-warm watery rice porridge with a few strips of pickled vegetables floating on top. I wiped the edge of the container with a piece of toilet paper and took a

tentative sip. The rice tasted smokey for some reason and the saltiness
of the pickled vegetables made it bitter. The food was worse than I
could possibly have imagined, but I made a determined effort to drink
half of it. When the woman opened the small window again, I handed
her back the container and the chopsticks.

In a little while, another female guard came. She said, 'Why didn't
you eat your rice?'

'I did eat some of it. May I see a responsible person?' I asked her.
Chinese Communist officials did not like to be called 'officials' unless
they were addressed by their exact titles such as 'Minister Wang' or
'Director Chang'. Generally speaking, the officials are known as *ganbu*
which the official Chinese-English dictionary translates as 'cadres'.
Minor officials were usually referred to as 'responsible persons', which
could mean cadres or just clerks.

'What's the hurry? You have only just arrived. When the
interrogator is ready, he will call you. What you should do now is to
consider the crime you have committed. When he calls you, you must
show true repentance by making a full confession in order to obtain
lenient treatment. If you denounce others, you'll gain a point of merit
for yourself.'

'I've never committed a crime,' I declared emphatically.

'Ah, a lot of you say this when you first come here. That's a foolish
attitude to assume. Just think, there are ten million people in this city.
Why should you have been brought here rather than someone else?
You have certainly committed a crime.'

It seemed pointless to argue with her. But her words convinced me
that I was going to be there for some time. The dirt in the cell was
intolerable. I simply had to deal with it if I was to live in that cell for
another night. Besides, I had always found physical work soothing for
frayed nerves. Since I was deeply unhappy to find myself in prison and
terribly worried about my daughter, I asked her whether I could
borrow a broom to sweep the floor.

'You are allowed to borrow a broom on Sundays only. But since
you have just come, I'll lend you one today.'

A few moments later she came back with an old worn broom which
she squeezed through the small window to me. I pulled the bed round
the cell to stand on it to reach the ceiling with the broom to get at the
cobwebs. When I brushed the walls, the cell was enveloped in a cloud
of dust.

The shutter was opened again. A sheet of paper was pushed through
to me. Looking out, I saw a male guard standing there.

'The money you brought here last night has been banked for you. This is your receipt. You are allowed to use the money to buy daily necessities such as toilet paper, soap and towels,' he said.

'That's just what I need. Could I buy some now?' I asked him.

'You may buy what you need,' the man said.

'Please get me a washbasin, two enamelled mugs for eating and drinking, some sewing thread, needles, soap, towels, a toothbrush and toothpaste and some toilet paper. Am I allowed to buy some cold cream?'

'No, only necessities.'

Soon he returned with a washbasin decorated with two large roses, six towels with colourful stripes, a stack of toilet paper, six cakes of the cheapest kind of laundry soap, two enamelled mugs with lids, a toothbrush, a tube of toothpaste and two reels of coarse cotton thread. He told me that prisoners were not allowed to have needles in the cell but they could borrow them from the guards on Sundays.

The guard had to open the cell door to hand me the washbasin. While it was still open, another male guard brought me the clothes and bedding left me by the Red Guards in my house, as well as the *Collected Works of Mao Tze-tung* and the Little Red Book of Mao's quotations. After I had signed the receipt for these things, the two guards locked the door and departed.

I looked through everything very carefully, hoping to find a hidden note from my daughter. There was nothing. I sat on the edge of the bed, weary with disappointment and sadness. I longed for a moment with my daughter and prayed for her safety. After some time, I felt more peaceful. I decided to tackle the dirty room. What I needed was some water.

'Report!' I went to the door and called.

It was another female guard who pushed open the shutter and said sternly, 'You don't have to shout! Now, what do you want?'

I knew from her tone of voice that she would probably refuse whatever I might ask for. To forestall such a possibility, I quickly recited a quotation of Mao which said, 'To be hygienic is glorious; to be unhygienic is a shame.' Then I asked her, 'May I have some water to clean the cell?'

She walked away without saying a word. I waited and waited. Eventually the Labour Reform girl came to give me enough water to fill the new washbasin as well as the one brought from my home with my things. First I washed the bed thoroughly; then I climbed onto my rolled-up bedding to reach the window to wipe the dust-smeared windowpanes so that more light could come into the room. After I had washed the cement toilet attached to the corner of the cell, I still had enough cold water left to bathe myself and rinse out my dirty blouse. When hot water for drinking was issued, I sat on the clean bed and drank it with enjoyment. Plain boiled water had never tasted so good.

The midday meal was dry rice and some boiled green cabbage. With a portion of the rice I made a paste which I used to glue sheets of toilet paper onto the wall along the bed so that I and my bed clothes would not touch the dirty wall while I was sleeping. After that I felt much better. When the guard came to tell me to walk about in the cell for exercise, I said, 'May I return the broom, please?'

She opened the small window to accept the broom and saw the toilet paper I had pasted onto the wall.

'It's against regulations to make changes in the cell,' she said. I remained silent, wondering how best to deal with the situation if she should order me to remove the paper. But she only picked up the broom and closed the shutter. A moment later, I heard her upstairs calling from cell to cell, 'Exercise! Exercise!'

I could hear footsteps of many people walking round and round in the room above mine. When the guard called for everybody to sit down at the end of the exercise period, I heard many prisoners flopping down onto the floor. Evidently in the multiple cell upstairs there was no bed; the inmates were sleeping and sitting on the bare floor. The wall between mine and the next-door cell was too thick for me to hear any sound, but I could hear quite clearly every word spoken aloud in the cell above. The sound of movement of the women prisoners overhead and the murmuring of their voices, when the guard was not near, somewhat mitigated my acute feeling of loneliness and isolation.

The contrast of colour and shapes and the blending of different sounds that please the senses in normal life were completely absent in prison. Everywhere I looked I saw ugly shapes and the uniform shade of depressing dirty grey. There was nothing other than the cold and indifferent voice of authority of the guards to break the ominous silence. Sitting in the cell, I found my gaze straying often to the window. I would stare at the narrow strip of sky through the iron bars for hours at a time. It was not only that light and fresh air came in through the window to sustain my life; the window was also the only channel through which I maintained a tenuous link with the world outside. Often, while my body sat in the cell, my spirit would escape through the window to freedom. One of my most vivid memories of prison life was watching the shifting shadow of the window bars on the cement floor. With its slow movement across the floor of the cell, I watched the passage of time, while I waited and waited day after day and year after year, sometimes for the next meal, sometimes for the next interrogation, but above all for some political development that would curb the power of the Maoist Revolutionaries.

Daylight faded and the electric light was switched on. I ate another portion of rice and green cabbage. The guard on night duty was another woman. She handed me the newspaper. Putting her face to the small opening on the door, she shouted, 'What have you done to the cell?'

'I cleaned it according to Chairman Mao's teaching on hygiene,' I answered.

'If you heed the teaching of our Great Leader Chairman Mao, why are you locked in a prison cell?' she yelled. 'Did the Chairman tell you to commit a crime?'·

'I've never committed a crime. There has been a mistake. It can be cleared up by investigation and examination of the facts,' I said.

'You have a glib tongue, that I can see. You're trying to bring your capitalist way of life into this place, aren't you? I advise you to think less of your own personal comfort and more of your criminal deeds. Give the matter serious consideration. When you are called, be sure to give a full confession so that you can earn lenient treatment.' She closed the small window so that I could not answer back.

I was getting very tired of this talk of confession and how it could earn lenient treatment for the prisoner. Perhaps it was true, I thought, that a really guilty person could earn a lighter sentence by confessing voluntarily. But I was not guilty. It was infuriating to be told so often that I had committed a crime when I had not.

I picked up the newspaper and stood directly under the feeble light to read it. Like other newspapers in China, the *Shanghai Liberation Daily* was published, financed and completely controlled by the People's Government. The journalists were officials appointed by the Party's propaganda department; their job was to select and often distort news, especially foreign news, for propaganda purposes and to write articles praising government policies. The newspaper is used in China everywhere, including in the prisons, for the education of the people.

The Chinese people had long ago learned that the only way to read the newspaper was to read between the lines and pay attention to the omissions as well as to the printed items. In fact, the real source of news for the Chinese people was not the newspaper at all, but political gossip passed from one person to another in low whispers, often in the language of symbols and signs with no name mentioned. This was called 'footpath news', meaning that the news did not come openly through the main road; that is, official channels. In the past, before the Communist Party took control of the country, its underground organizations had used 'footpath news' effectively to undermine the Chinese people's confidence in the Kuomintang Government. Now, they themselves were plagued by it. When the people mistrusted the official newspapers and could not obtain news freely, they were naturally more than eager to listen to and believe in whatever they could pick up in the way of political gossip.

In the detention house, the *Shanghai Liberation Daily* was my sole source of information about what went on outside the prison walls. I read it very carefully, sometimes going over the same news item or article twice, in order to follow the development of the Cultural Revolution and evaluate the political development that was taking place. From the way items of news were presented, the subject of special articles, the tone of the editorials and the quotation of Mao Tze-tung selected for use for a certain day, I could often discern what the Maoists hoped to accomplish or what had not gone according to plan. However, my full understanding of much of the details of the struggle for power within the Communist Party came only after my release. I succeeded then in gathering together a collection of uncensored Red Guard publications and had the opportunity to question young people who had taken part in the revolutionary activities.

When Sunday came round, I asked the guard for the loan of a needle. I joined two of the newly purchased towels to make a seat for the cement toilet, sewed together layers of toilet paper to make a cover for one of the washbasins I used for storing water and cut up a handkerchief to make an eyeshade to cover my eyes at night. When I asked to use scissors, the guard stood at the small window to watch me, taking them back as soon as I had finished cutting. Doing something practical to improve my daily life made me feel better. I found sewing, in particular, a soothing occupation.

Several days passed. I made a request every day to see the interrogator, without result. One sunny morning, the prisoners were told to get ready for outdoor exercise. The guard went to each cell calling, 'Fong-fung!' (Out to get air!)

Eager for sunshine and fresh air, I jumped up, laid down Mao's book I had been reading and rushed to stand by the door. But I had to wait for quite some time before being let out. An elaborate system was practised in the No. 1 Detention House to prevent inmates of different cells from meeting one another. I had to wait until the prisoner in the cell next to mine turned the corner and was out of sight before being allowed to leave my cell. Guards were posted along the route to watch the prisoners and to lead them to the exercise yards.

The exercise yard I was locked into was spacious, but in a state of dismal neglect. Broken plaster on the walls exposed the bricks underneath. The ground was covered with dirt and loose gravel. I saw something green in one corner and discovered a cluster of resilient weeds struggling to keep alive. Pleased to see something growing in this inhospitable place, I went over to examine it closely and saw tiny pink flowers at the tip of each stem. Every flower had five perfectly formed petals that were no bigger than a seed. In the midst of dirt and gravel, the plant stood proudly in the sunshine giving a sign of life in this dead place. Gazing at the tiny flowers which seemed incredibly beautiful to me, I felt an uplifting of my spirit.

'Walk about! Walk about with your head bowed! You are not allowed to stop walking!' a guard shouted at me from the raised platform built on top of the walls of the exercise yards. There were two pavilions on the platform, one open and one enclosed with glass windows. As the weather was fine, the guards were watching the prisoners from the open pavilion.

I started to walk around in the exercise yard; gradually the heaviness on my chest loosened and I breathed more easily. The autumn air was cool and dry; the sun was warm on my face. Time passed slowly in prison with each day endlessly long. But not so during outdoor exercise periods. Even in the depths of winter when my clothes could not keep my starved body warm and I shivered incessantly in the bitter north wind, the outdoor exercise period passed altogether too quickly for me.

The male guard who led me back to my cell could not find the right key for the door immediately. While he was trying one key after another, I took the opportunity to make another request to see the interrogator.

'I've been here such a long time already. May I see the interrogator?' I asked him.

'A long time already?' He straightened up and turned to face me, 'You talk nonsense. I know you've been here less than a month. A month is not a long time. There are people who have been here for years and their cases are not yet resolved. Why are you so impatient? You are always asking to see the interrogator. What are you going to say to him when you do see him? Are you ready to make a full confession?'

'I'll ask the interrogator to investigate my case and clarify the misunderstanding.'

'What misunderstanding?' He appeared genuinely puzzled.

'The misunderstanding that brought me here,' I said.

'You are here because you committed a crime against the People's Government. There is no misunderstanding. You mustn't talk in riddles.'

'I've never committed a crime in my whole life,' I said firmly.

'If you have not committed a crime, why are you locked up in prison? Your being here proves you have committed a crime.'

His logic appalled me. It was based on the assumption that the Party and the government could not be mistaken. I could not argue with him without appearing to offend the Party and the People's Government so I merely said, 'Honestly, I have never committed a crime. There has been a mistake.'

'Perhaps there was something you did that you don't remember. Prisoners often need help and guidance from the interrogator to confess.'

'I don't think I could forget if I had committed a crime,' I told him. I recalled cases I had heard of when the interrogator fed the prisoners with things to say while the prisoners were confessing. All of it was written down and held against the prisoners eventually.

'Perhaps you did not realize you were committing a crime at the time. You are probably still quite muddled,' the guard said. He seemed quite sincere.

Could it be possible that what I had considered innocent behaviour had really been interpreted by others as criminal deeds against the State? Although I had followed political and economic developments in China carefully and tried to acquire an intelligent understanding of events, I had never studied the Communist Government's penal code. I decided to make good this omission without further delay. So I said to the guard, 'In that case, I'll study the law books to see if I have indeed committed a crime inadvertently. Will you please lend me your law books?'

'What law books? You talk just like the capitalist intellectuals that are being denounced in this Cultural Revolution. You think in terms of law books, rules and regulations. We are the proletariat, we do not have anything like that.' He seemed highly indignant as if my assumption that they had law books was an insult.

'If you do not have law books, what do you go by? How do you decide whether a man has committed a crime or not?'

'We go by the teachings of our Great Leader Chairman Mao. His words are our criteria. If he says a certain type of person is guilty and you belong to that type, then you are guilty. It's much simpler than depending on a law book,' he said. To him, it was perfectly good and logical to have the fate of men decided arbitrarily by the words of Mao Tze-tung, which varied from time to time depending on his priorities during a particular period and often so vague that local officials could interpret them to suit themselves. The absolute infallibility of Mao's words was a part of his personality cult. But I wondered how the guard would have felt if not I but he had been the victim.

After he had locked me into the cell again, I made no further request to see an interrogator. Instead I settled down to study assiduously and seriously the *Collected Works of Mao Tze-tung*. I wanted to know how his words could be used against me, and I wanted to see if I could not use his words to refute my accusers. I thought I should learn to speak Mao's language and be fluent in using his quotations when the time came for me to face the interrogator.

Many weeks passed. One day merged into another. Prolonged isolation heightened my feeling of depression. I longed for some news of my daughter. I missed her terribly and worried about her constantly. Often I would be choked with emotion so that breathing became difficult. At other times, a heavy lump would settle on my stomach so that I had difficulty swallowing food.

Outside the prison walls, the Cultural Revolution seemed to be increasing in intensity. The loudspeaker of the high school nearby was blaring all day long. Instead of revolutionary songs, angry denunciations of local officials and prominent scholars were pouring out. I strained my ears to listen to them, trying to catch a word here and a phrase there when the wind was in the right direction. Within the gloomy cell, I studied Mao's books many hours a day, reading until my eyesight became blurred by the dim light.

One day, in the early afternoon, when my eyes were too tired to distinguish the printed words, I lifted them from the book to gaze at the window. A small spider crawled into view, climbing up one of the rust-eroded bars of the window. The little creature was no bigger than a good-sized pea; I would not have seen it if the wooden frame nailed to the wall outside to cover the lower half of the window hadn't been painted black. I watched it crawl slowly but steadily to the top of the iron bar, quite a long walk for such a tiny thing, I thought. When it reached the top, suddenly it swung out and descended on a thin silken thread spun from one end of its body. With a leap and swing, it secured the end of the thread to another bar. The small spider then crawled back along the silken thread to where it had started and swung out in another direction on a similar thread. I watched the tiny creature at work with increasing fascination. It seemed to know exactly what to do and where to take the next thread. There was no hesitation, no mistake, and no haste. It knew its job and was carrying it out with confidence. When the frame was made, the spider proceeded to weave a web that was intricately beautiful and absolutely perfect, with all the strands of thread evenly spaced. When the web was completed, the spider went to its centre and settled there.

I had just watched an architectural feat by an extremely skilled artist and my mind was full of questions. Who had taught the spider how to make a web? Could it really have acquired the skill through evolution, or did God create the spider and endow it with the ability to make a web so that it could catch food and perpetuate its species? How big was the brain of such a tiny creature? Did it act simply by instinct or had it somehow learned to store the knowledge of web-making? Perhaps one day I would ask an entomologist. For the moment, I knew I had just witnessed something that was extraordinarily beautiful and uplifting. Whether God had made the spider or not, I thanked Him for what I had just seen. A miracle of life had been shown me. It helped me to see that God was in control. Mao Tze-tung and his Revolutionaries seemed much less menacing. I felt a renewal of hope and confidence.

My cell faced south-west. For a brief moment, the rays of the setting sun turned the newly-made web into a glittering disc of rainbow colours before it shifted further west and sank below the horizon. I did not dare to go up to the window in case I should frighten the spider away. I remained where I was watching it. Soon I discovered it was not merely sitting there waiting for its prey but was forever vigilant. Whenever a corner of the web was ruffled or torn by the breeze, the spider was there in an instant to repair the damage. And as days passed, the spider renewed the web from time to time; sometimes a part of it was remade, sometimes the whole web was remade.

I became very attached to the little creature after watching its activities and gaining an understanding of its habits. First thing in the morning, throughout the day and last thing at night, I would look at it and feel reassured when I saw that it was still there. The tiny spider became my companion. My spirits lightened. The depressing feeling of complete isolation was broken by having another living thing near me, even though it was so tiny and incapable of response.

Soon it was November. The wind shifted to the north-west. With each rainy day the temperature fell further. I watched the spider anxiously, not wishing to close the window to shut it out. It went on repairing the wind-torn web and patiently making new ones. However, one morning, when I woke up, I found the spider gone. Its derelict web was in shreds. I felt sad, but hopefully kept the window open in case it should come back. Then I chanced to look up and saw my small friend sitting in the centre of a newly-made web in a corner of the ceiling inside the cell. I quickly closed the window and felt happy to know that my small friend had not deserted me.

Towards the end of November, one morning, I woke up with a streaming cold and a severe headache. Blowing my nose and feeling miserable, I sat on the edge of the bed wondering whether I should ask for some medicine. When the watery rice was given to me, I made myself drink it up, hoping the warm liquid might give me some relief, but I could not eat the dry rice and boiled cabbage at noon. I returned it to the woman from the kitchen untouched. Throughout the afternoon, the guard on duty came frequently to watch me through the peephole. She made no attempt to speak to me until evening, when she suddenly pushed open the small window and said, 'You have been crying!'

'Oh, no,' I said, 'I've a cold.'

'You are crying. You are crying because you are not used to the living conditions here. You find everything quite intolerable, don't you? We have been watching you trying to improve things. Also you are crying because you miss your daughter. You are wondering what's happening to her,' the guard said.

'No, really, I just have a cold. May I have an aspirin?'

'Aspirin isn't going to help you. What's bothering you is in your mind. Think over your own position. Assume the correct attitude. Be repentant,' she said.

I sat in the cell for the rest of the evening with my face averted from the door and tried not to blow my nose or wipe my eyes. When rice was given to me in the evening, I ate some and tipped the rest into the toilet, pouring water in to wash it away. Nevertheless, so firmly did the guards believe I was crying because I could not endure the hardship of prison life that they seized on what they thought was a psychologically weakened moment and called me for interrogation the next day.

CHAPTER 6

Interrogation

THE MORNING DAWNED BRIGHT and sunny. When I opened the window, frosty fresh air flowed into the cell. Winter was not far off, I thought. The guard was going from cell to cell calling the inmates to take their sheets off their beds for laundering, a routine that took place once a month on a sunny day. Extra cold water was issued to the cells. The inmates soaked their sheets in it, rubbed soap on the wet sheets and then pushed them out of the small windows of the cells, to be collected by the Labour Reform girls who completed washing them in the laundry room.

While I was rubbing soap on my wet sheet, a male guard unlocked the cell door, threw the door open wide and yelled, 'Come out!'

'I'm doing my laundry,' I said.

'Don't argue. When I say come out, just come out.'

The female guard on duty also came to the door. She said, 'You can do your laundry later. Now you must go for interrogation.'

Interrogation! At last it seemed I was to come face to face with my antagonist. I hurriedly wiped my hands on a dry towel.

'Hurry up! Bring your book of Chairman Mao's quotations,' the male guard said impatiently.

I followed him out of the cell, through the courtyard of the women's prison into an area at the back of the prison compound. At the approach to a building there was a large white wooden board on which was written in black characters: 'Lenient treatment to those who confess frankly. Severe punishment to those who remain stubborn. Reward to those who render meritorious service.'

My heart palpitated with excitement; my footsteps were eager with expectancy. The long-awaited opportunity to answer questions and to have my case examined dispassionately was here at last. I believed a government interrogator couldn't possibly behave like a hysterical Red Guard or a Revolutionary. He must be a trained man with a sense of responsibility, able to distinguish a guilty person from an innocent one.

Several guards were lolling on wooden chairs in a small room beside the entrance to the building. I was handed over to one of them who led me through a long corridor with many interrogation rooms ranged on either side. Most of the doors were closed. But I heard the muffled sound of voices and an occasional shout from some of them. The guard stopped in front of one of the rooms, threw open the door, and shouted, 'Go in!'

The room was narrow and long and rather dark, with only a small window, like the one in my cell, high on the back wall. Two men, dressed in the baggy and faded blue cotton Maoist uniform worn by nearly all men in China except senior officials, were seated behind a wooden counter under the window. About two yards away, facing the window, was a heavy wooden chair for the prisoner. The room was very dark but the little light that came through the window was focused on the spot where the prisoner sat. I noticed that the walls were dusty, the cement floor was black with damp and the wooden counter and chair had been rubbed into a neutral colour of grey.

After I entered the room, one of the men said, 'Read the teaching of our Great Leader Chairman Mao from your book of quotations.' The quotation he selected was the same one used by the Red Guards when they came to loot my home.

'When the enemies with guns are annihilated, the enemies without guns still remain. We must not belittle these enemies.' I read the quotation in a firm voice, conscious of the fact the two men were watching me closely. I tried not to show any sign of nervousness lest it should be interpreted as a sign of guilt.

'Sit down,' the man said, pointing to the chair for the prisoner.

As I turned to sit down, I saw a small window rather like the one in the door of my cell, only perhaps a little larger, in the wall behind the chair for the prisoner. I concluded that interrogations carried out in the room were being listened to by someone in the corridor.

I sat down on the heavy wooden chair and looked at the two men behind the counter. They had the pale faces of men who worked indoors with little chance for exercise. Unlike the man who registered my arrival, these two men exuded an air of authority and self-confidence common to men of official position despite their rather shabby appearance. They were quite relaxed, almost casual; of course, interviewing a prisoner was just routine work to them. I assumed the one who spoke to me to be the interrogator while the one with sheets of paper in front of him was the secretary.

After I was seated, the interrogator looked past my shoulder at the small window behind me and gave a barely perceptible nod. It seemed my initial perception was correct; a man was indeed outside listening in to my interrogation. Disappointment overwhelmed me for a moment. It seemed the interrogator was just an intermediary and I was not going to see my real antagonist after all. How I wished I could deal face to face with the man who had treated me so unjustly and have his features carved on my memory never to be forgotten!

In a low voice that was almost bored, the interrogator asked me for my name and other personal particulars. Then he looked up, raised his voice and asked firmly, 'Do you know what this place is?'

'I suppose it's some sort of prison or concentration camp since everybody is locked up.'

'You are quite right. This is the No. 1 Detention House, a prison for political prisoners. This is the place where counter-revolutionaries who have committed crimes against the People's Government are locked up and investigated.'

'In that case, I should not have been brought here,' I declared firmly.

He was not perturbed by my remark but went on calmly, 'You are locked up here precisely because you have committed a crime against the People's Government.'

'There must have been some mistake,' I said.

'The People's Government does not make mistakes.'

'You are not an irresponsible Red Guard. You are a government representative. You can't make wild accusations like that.'

'It's not a wild accusation.'

'You will have to provide some evidence to prove what you are saying.' I was deeply disappointed that the long-awaited interrogation was turning out to be just like the sessions I had had with the Revolutionaries before my imprisonment.

'Of course we have the evidence,' the interrogator bluffed shamelessly.

'Produce it then,' I said sarcastically, calling his bluff. 'Why waste time having an interrogation? Why not just produce the evidence and punish the culprit?'

'You must not underrate the masses. The Red Guards and the Revolutionaries can obtain all the evidence we need. Nothing can be hidden. Those who have made mistakes or committed crimes are making confessions and providing denunciations of others. They want to earn lenient treatment by confessing and to receive rewards by incriminating others.'

'I don't believe you could possibly have any evidence against me, not because I fail to understand the nature of the Proletarian Cultural Revolution or underestimate the power of the masses. It's because I don't think you, or anybody else for that matter, could have something that simply doesn't exist. I have never committed any crime; how could there be any evidence to show that I have done so?' I said. Because he had lied about having evidence, I had gained a moral advantage over him. It reinforced my self-confidence.

'It would be an easy matter to produce the evidence and punish you. But that is not the policy of our Great Leader. The purpose of this interrogation is to help you to change your way of thinking and to give you an opportunity to earn lenient treatment by confessing frankly so that you can make a clean break with your criminal past and become a new person.'

'I'm not a magician. I don't know how to confess to something that did not happen.'

'Perhaps you are not ready yet. We are patient. We can wait.' He fixed his gaze upon me and spoke slowly so that his implied threat of long imprisonment would sink in.

'A million years would make no difference. If something didn't happen, it just didn't happen. You can't change facts no matter how long you wait.' I also spoke slowly and firmly to make him see that he had failed to frighten me.

'Time can change a person's attitude. A woman like you would not last five years in this place. Your health will break down. Eventually you will be begging for a chance to confess. If you don't, you will surely die.'

'I would rather die than tell a lie.'

'Not at all. To want to live is the basic instinct of all living things, humans included.'

'I will obey our Great Leader Chairman Mao's teaching. He said, "Firstly, do not fear hardship, and secondly, do not fear death." '

'That quotation was not for the likes of you. That is for the Liberation Army soldiers,' he said indignantly.

'Marshal Lin Piao said, "The teachings of our Great Leader have universal significance and are applicable in all circumstances." ' A subtle change had taken place in my mood since the interrogator had given me the moral advantage by lying. I was beginning to enjoy this interrogation now. It was a lot better than being left in a dark damp cell with no one to talk to.

There was a moment of silence. The interrogator again looked past my shoulder. Then he said, 'You are audacious. But you can't talk your way out of your difficulties. The only way out for you is to assume a correct attitude of sincerity. It's my duty to help you to come to a full understanding of the policy of the Government and to realize that you have no alternative to showing sincerity of repentance by giving a full confession. Do not belittle the Dictatorship of the Proletariat! This interrogation room is the equivalent of the People's Court. You must take everything said here extremely seriously.'

'Am I not to expect justice from the People's Government?'

'Justice! What is justice? It's a mere word. It's an abstract word with no universal meaning. To different classes of people, justice means different things. The capitalist class considers it perfectly just to exploit the workers, while the workers consider it decidedly unjust to be so exploited. In any case, who are you to demand justice? When you sat in a room of your well-heated house and there were other people shivering in the snow, did you think of justice?'

'You are confusing social justice with legal justice. I can tell you that it was precisely because my late husband and I hoped that the People's Government would improve conditions in China so that there would never be anybody suffering cold and hunger that we remained in China in 1949 rather than follow the Kuomintang to Taiwan,' I told him.

'In any case, we are not concerned with the abstract concept of justice. The army, the police and the court are instruments of repression used by one class against another. They have nothing to do with justice. The cell you now occupy was used to lock up members of the Communist Party during the days of the reactionary Kuomintang Government. Now the Dictatorship of the Proletariat uses the same instruments of repression against its own enemies. The capitalist countries use such attractive words as "justice" and "liberty" to fool the common people and to prevent their revolutionary awakening. To assume a proper attitude you must get all that rubbish out of your head. Otherwise you will get nowhere.'

What he said was not new to me or to anybody who had lived in China and followed events since 1949. It was the accepted Marxist theory of class struggle. 'The army, the police and the court are instruments of repression used by one class against another' was said by Mao Tze-tung in his essay 'On the Dictatorship of the People's Democracy'. In the fifties Mao Tze-tung and his propaganda machinery used 'The Dictatorship of the People's Democracy' to describe the Communist regime in China. The facts of history have demonstrated, however, that the Communist regime in China was a dictatorship by Mao Tze-tung until his death in 1976. Mao's essay 'On the Dictatorship of the People's Democracy' was published on 1 July

1949 to celebrate the anniversary of the founding of the Chinese Communist Party in 1921. That essay had actually heralded and justified a series of political campaigns and large-scale arrests of men and women suspected of being hostile to the new Communist regime.

I saw that the interrogation was getting nowhere. As long as the interrogator did not ask concrete questions, nothing could be clarified. There was no point in my engaging in theoretical arguments over Marxism. One either believed in it or one did not. There was no middle way. My own outlook and my values had been formed long ago. I did not believe in dividing people into rigid classes and I did not believe in class struggle as a means to promote progress. I believed that China needed a peaceful environment and the unity of all sections of society to rebuild the country after so many years of war, not perpetual revolution. I could not change these beliefs. Unfortunately the interrogator would not see that, at least not at that moment. At that moment, he hoped to confuse me, to overcome my resistance with a combination of threats and arguments. The session was going to be long-drawn-out and tedious. My head was throbbing from my cold. I decided to let him talk on and hear him out.

After a moment's silence, the interrogator went on, 'The first requisite to confession is an admission of guilt. You must admit your guilt not only to the People's Government, but also to yourself. The admission of guilt is like the opening of the floodgates. When you admit sincerely that you are indeed guilty, that you were opposed to the People's Government even though you had pretended not to be, your confession will flow out easily.'

He stopped for a moment and looked at me searchingly to see my reaction. He had said 'opposed' to the People's Government. Of course, I had been opposed to some measures of the People's Government such as large-scale arrests of innocent people, to declare a man an enemy just because of his class origin ... etc. But I never talked about any of these things to anybody. And certainly I never tried to do anything about it. I only hoped that when the regime achieved maturity and experience, it would become mellowed. The interrogator was trying to instil in me a feeling of guilt because he knew very well that every citizen in every country opposes some measures of his or her government at one time or another. He hoped to manipulate me psychologically. But I saw through him at once, so I just sat there without any expression on my face. In my mind I thought of all the aspects of the People's Government's work that I fully supported such as the improvement in public hygiene and the resettlement of the homeless ... etc. On the whole, I thought of myself as a supporter of the People's Government. This assessment of my own positive attitude towards the Communist regime bolstered my courage to resist the interrogator's attempt to promote a sense of guilt in my mind. It proved invaluable in all the years I spent in prison.

The interrogator continued, 'The thing for you to do is to look over your own life and examine your family background. Find your correct place in the political and economic structure of our socialist state. Where do you stand? With the working people and the Revolutionaries or with the class enemies? You do not need me to tell you that you came from a feudal family that owned an enormous amount of rich agricultural land. For generations, your family exploited the peasants and lived off the riches they created. Your grandfather, your father and your husband were all senior officials of reactionary regimes that cooperated with foreign imperialism, exploited the people and opposed the Communist Party. You yourself decided to work for a multinational foreign firm though you were offered the opportunity to become a teacher at an educational institution of the people. It's seventeen years since the Communist Army liberated Shanghai. Scores of Chinese with backgrounds like yours have changed their mode of life and fallen in line with us. What have you done? You just went on as if nothing had happened. You carried on arrogantly in your old life-style, wore the same bourgeois clothes and even dared to speak English in public and maintain friendly contact with a large number of foreigners here and abroad.

'Do you think your attitude of intransigence could pass unnoticed? The proletariat has been watching you for years. Our Great Leader said recently, "The eyes of the masses are clear and bright as snow." Do you still think you could hide anything from us?

'You are an intelligent woman. Do you honestly think we would let you out of here without succeeding in completely transforming your way of thinking?

'You have been here nearly two months already. I must admit you surprised us with your adaptability. Nevertheless, no matter how nonchalant you appear, you must find the living conditions in the prison cell extremely trying. Winter is soon to be upon us. I do not believe you have ever passed a single winter in an unheated room in your whole life. That cell is going to be very cold. Then, there is the coarse food you often find difficult to swallow. We have observed that. And what about your daughter? Do you not miss her? Do you not often wonder what is happening to her?'

He paused again. But when I continued to maintain silence, he went on, 'First of all, we want you to write your autobiography. Nearly everyone in the country has done that but we could find nothing like that in your file. Write everything down clearly. Do not try to whitewash yourself. Do not try to hide anything. We will check what you write with the material we already have about you. If you omit anything, we will think you are not sincere. Write in chronological order, starting with your family. We will make an assessment of your political standpoint and your sincerity from what you write.'

The man taking notes got up and handed me a roll of paper. After I had accepted it, the interrogator said, 'If this paper is not enough, the guard on duty will give you more. She will also give you pen and ink. You are not allowed to make a draft. You are not allowed to throw away the paper on which you make a mistake. Hand it in with the rest when you finish.'

He looked at me with great seriousness and said, 'Think over carefully everything I have said today. When you have finished what you have written, give it to the guard on duty. We will call you again.'

The door of the interrogation room opened and a guard appeared. I followed him through the long corridor back to my cell. I had no way of knowing how long I had been gone, but it seemed ages. I was hungry, tired and very disappointed.

My wet sheet was spread on the stacked bed which I used as a table. I picked up the cake of soap to rub on it. When I had finished, I called to the guard on duty, 'Report!'

She came to the small window and handed me a pen and a bottle of ink.

'May I have my sheet washed now?'

'Laundry time is over. You can keep it for the next time.'

'But it's wet, and I have soaped it. It's not hygienic to keep a wet sheet for a whole month,' I said.

She did not wait for me to finish speaking but banged the small window shut and walked away.

During the afternoon, however, she came repeatedly to the peephole to look into the cell. After several trips, she opened the small window and asked me, 'Why are you not writing?'

'How can I write? I'm worried about the wet sheet. It will smell. I haven't another sheet to use.'

Perhaps to ensure my getting on with writing my autobiography as the interrogator wanted, she relented and got the Labour Reform girl to take the sheet to wash. It was returned to me the next day, clean and dry.

The guard continued to come regularly to the peephole to look into the cell. To give the appearance of writing, I laid one of Mao's books on my lap, placed a sheet of paper on it and put the ink bottle beside me. After that, the guard left me alone.

Before writing anything, I had to ascertain what the interrogator hoped to achieve by ordering me to write my autobiography. His excuse that all other Chinese had done it was not a valid one. Although I had never been asked to write an autobiography, I believe the police in my district had a detailed record of my life already, as they had of everybody else who lived there. Obviously the interrogator hoped that through writing the autobiography I would provide him with some material they could twist and use against me.

A point that puzzled me was that I was not the only Chinese woman in Shanghai who had carried on with a comfortable life-style, wore traditional Chinese dress instead of the Mao suit and had foreign friends. But I had been singled out for imprisonment. No doubt the others had suffered in the hands of the Red Guards and probably had their homes looted. Maybe they had been beaten up. But I did not think they could all have been arrested. There was in fact much in the situation that was still a mystery to me. It would be foolish to plunge in and write frankly about myself and my life, revealing my innermost thoughts and standpoint. Besides, I had known cases of men being asked to write autobiographies over and over again. When discrepancies were found, the men were enmeshed in deep suspicion. Obviously the only thing I could do was to write just a simple record of my life giving the bare facts in chronological order. If I were to be asked to write my autobiography again, I would have no difficulty in producing an identical version.

In the evening there was a sudden drop in temperature. By nightfall a strong wind was blowing. The window of the cell was so badly fitted that it rattled. Cold air came through the gaps in sharp gusts. I folded sheets of toilet paper into strips and pushed them into the gaps to stop the wind. By then the web of my small spider friend was already torn. Instead of making a new web promptly as it always had done in the past, the small spider descended from the corner of the ceiling on a long silken thread. When it reached the floor, it crawled across the room very slowly and with difficulty. I crouched down to watch it closely, wondering what it was going to do. My small friend seemed rather weak. It stumbled and stopped every few steps. Could a spider get sick, or was it merely cold? Watching it anxiously, I saw it went from corner to corner, probably looking for a sheltered place away from the wind. Finally it disappeared into the corner where the cement toilet was joined to the wall. There, in the crevice, it made a tiny web, not as well done or beautiful as the ones before, but the layered threads were thicker, forming something rather like a cocoon. I thought my small friend was well protected. When I had to use the toilet, I carefully sat well to one side so that I did not disturb it.

Next morning, I wrote my autobiography rather quickly on a few sheets of paper and finished it in the afternoon. Then I went to the window and called, 'Report!'

The same guard who was on duty the day before came to the window. I handed to her what I had written together with the remaining blank sheets of paper.

'You have finished writing already?' she asked doubtfully, eyes fixed on the five sheets of paper covered with my handwriting.

'Yes, I have finished,' I answered.

'It seems so short. Have you put everything down?'

'Yes.'

'Why is it so short?'

'Oh, is it too short? In any case, I did put everything in.'

She said nothing more and walked away. I half expected some sort of immediate reaction. When nothing happened, I became rather light-hearted. For the whole evening I watched the small spider, for it had abandoned its newly-made home and was again crawling with difficulty across the room, stumbling and stopping frequently. Finally it headed straight in my direction. When it came close to my feet, I wondered if it intended to climb up my leg for warmth. But it continued past my feet and disappeared under the bed. I waited for it to come out again, but hours passed and nothing happened. Perhaps under the bed was in fact the most sheltered place in the cell and my little friend had decided to remain there for the winter.

Next morning, when the guard called me to get up, I looked carefully on the floor to make sure the small spider was not there before putting my feet on the ground. In fact, while I ate my watery breakfast my eyes strayed continuously to the area of the cement floor next to the bed where I hoped to see the small spider emerging with renewed vigour. But nothing happened. Looking up at the ceiling, I found the torn web gone. No trace was left of the life of the small spider at all; I might have imagined the whole thing. Yet, while it was there, it had worked and lived with such serious effort, making and remaking its web. The small spider had obeyed its natural instinct for survival. I should do the same. As long as I was in the No. 1 Detention

House I would fight on resolutely and seriously to the best of my ability.

My thoughts were interrupted by the sound of the cell door being unlocked. A male guard shouted, 'Come out!'

I picked up Mao's book of quotations and followed him, bracing myself for a stormy session with the interrogator, who I guessed would probably share the guard's view and consider my autobiography not up to expectations.

I was led to the door of another interrogation room, identical with the previous one. The same two men were seated just as before except that their uniforms bulged with sweaters which were peeping out over their collars and cuffs. The room was icy and damp. Outside, the strong north-west wind from Siberia lashed the city relentlessly, rattling the window and whistling through the gaps. The interrogator looked at me with knitted brows. When he told me to read the quotation by Mao, he spoke sharply and stared at me sternly to register displeasure. I knew he was deliberately putting on an act to impress and frighten me.

I ignored the attitude of the interrogator which I thought rather childish and amusing but read the quotation in a clear and firm voice just as I had the day before. 'The imperialists and their running dog, the reactionary clique, will not readily accept their defeat in China. They will continue to conspire and use every available means to oppose the Chinese people. For instance, they will send agents into China to make trouble. This is a certainty. They will not forget this kind of work', I read from the Little Red Book of Mao's quotations.

He did not tell me to sit down but asked, 'Do you understand the meaning of this quotation?'

'It seems quite clear to me.'

'Explain what you understand it to mean.'

'This is a quotation familiar to all Chinese people, taken from a speech made by Chairman Mao at the preparatory meeting of the New Political Consultative Conference held on 15 June 1949, in Peking. He warned the Chinese people to be vigilant because he believed the imperialists and the Kuomintang would not accept their failure in China but would send agents into the country to make trouble.'

'Quite right! Events of the past seventeen years have proven that the warning of our Great Leader was both timely and correct.' He stared at me for a moment and asked, 'What do you think?'

Obviously I could not very well say Mao was paranoid and over-suspicious. At the same time, I could not agree with what he said without implying some knowledge of such activities by the regime's enemies. So I answered diplomatically, 'Oh, I just believe every word of our Great Leader Chairman Mao, whatever it is. He's always correct, isn't he?'

The interrogator glared at me. After a moment, he said, 'Sit down!'

I heard the wooden cover of the small window behind me being opened. The interrogator looked at me to observe if I had noticed the slight noise. I simply looked straight ahead at the window behind him as if lost in thought. I did not want him to think I was watchful and alert to every sound. From the behaviour of the interrogator, I realized that they did not want me to know that someone in the corridor was listening to my interrogation.

The autobiography I had written was in front of him. The interrogator picked it up and said, 'Do you call this a serious effort at self-examination?'

Since there was nothing I could say, I remained silent.

'You gave a statistical record of your life like someone writing down an account of daily expenditures. Do you call this writing your autobiography?' He waved the few sheets of paper in the air towards my direction.

'Is it no good? I'm afraid I have never written an autobiography before,' I said innocently.

'You have never written an autobiography but you have read many of them. On your bookshelves there were autobiographies by both Chinese and foreign writers,' the interrogator said.

'Yes. It's true I have read many autobiographies of important people. All of them have achieved a great deal, in one sphere or another. I have done nothing worth speaking of. Except for the last nine years since my husband died, I was just a housewife.'

'A housewife, were you?' the interrogator asked sarcastically. He snorted and went on, 'Did you spend your time sewing, knitting or cooking? No, you studied Marxism, read every sort of magazine and newspaper and copied down speeches by our Party and government leaders and kept a file of resolutions passed at Party Central Committee meetings. When the Red Guards went to your house to take revolutionary action against you, they found your bookshelves full of political books and your desk drawers full of notes in your handwriting. You had a powerful shortwave radio in your bedroom. Your servants said you were in there regularly to listen to foreign broadcasts. What housewife did all that? A housewife's concern is for her family and her home. Your concern was for politics. You were never a simple housewife by any stretch of the imagination.'

'I'm not ashamed that my interest went beyond the house and my family. I thought the People's Government and the Communist Party encouraged women to study Marxism and to take an interest in political affairs. I merely did what I thought was the right thing to do, since women in China were liberated by the Communist Party,' I told him.

'We encourage women to study Marxism under our guidance and direction. If you were so keen to study Marxism to raise your political consciousness, why did you not join an indoctrination class? We were told you never took part in any of the activities organized by the Residents' Committee in your district for the indoctrination of women living there. If your interest in politics was because you wished to be a good citizen, why did you turn up two hours late to cast your vote when there was an election for the Shanghai People's Congress? Was that the behaviour of the woman conscious of her own liberation? Don't smear gold paint on your face to make yourself look like a harmless Buddha. Why not admit that your interest in politics was for an ulterior purpose?'

'I did not take part in the indoctrination classes organized by the Residents' Committee simply because I could study better by myself. Besides, they took place in the afternoons. It was not possible for me to join them after I started working for Shell. As for being late to cast my vote, I admit I simply forgot to go until someone called to remind me. I did not think my vote was important. I didn't know that all Shell staff members had to vote together, so that by being late I was holding everybody up. In any case, there was only one candidate appointed by the Party. He would have been elected whether I voted or not,' I explained.

'You dare despise the election process of the People's Government! You did not think it was important! What was important to you was to do the dirty work of the imperialists!' the interrogator said heatedly.

'That's a wild accusation and an irresponsible one too,' I said, shaking my head at his outburst.

He picked up the five sheets of paper again.

'I told you to write an autobiography. You produced this. Why? Because you have something to hide!'

'Please tell me what you have in mind. I didn't intend to hide anything. If there's something about my life, whatever it is, you want to know, I'll be only too glad to tell you about it.'

'That's good. This is the first time since the interrogation began that you have shown sincerity. I hope you now realize the hopelessness of your situation and will make a full confession.'

'You are again talking in riddles. I said I would be glad to tell you everything about my life because I believe facts are more eloquent than arguments. I believe when you are in full possession of all the facts you will know that I am innocent. I have never done anything to harm the People's Government and the Communist Party.'

'I want a full and frank answer to all my questions. If you want to earn lenient treatment, don't try to hide anything,' he warned.

'I promise you I have nothing to hide. I understand fully the power of the People's Government and the ability of the interrogator to get at the truth. In fact, I count on you to clear me of the unwarranted accusation flung at me and to restore my reputation,' I told him.

'I accept your declaration of sincerity. You may now go back to your cell. This afternoon you can tell me about your dealings with the British agents Scott and Austin, the truth about the company you worked for and who was responsible for introducing the White Russian double agent to your general manager.'

I could hardly believe my ears. I started to speak but the interrogator silenced me with a gesture and stood up.

'Don't say anything now. We will give you ample opportunity to confess this afternoon.'

A guard was already standing at the open doorway waiting to take me back to the cell.

I was so stunned by what the interrogator had said that I did not remember how I got back to the women's prison.

Instead of sitting in her small room at the entrance, the female guard on duty was standing in the cold wind waiting for me to return. She had her hands in her pockets and her shoulders were hunched while she shuffled her feet impatiently. From the moment I came in sight, all the way to the door of the cell, she was constantly throwing glances at me as if watching every expression on my face. After locking me in, she remained at the peephole to observe me. From her behaviour, I understood that she had been instructed to watch me to observe my reaction to what the interrogator had said. That was why the interrogator had terminated the interview and sent me back to the cell. Although I was greatly shocked to hear the interrogator call two of my British friends 'British agents' and refer to the White Russian secretary of the general manager of the Shell office in Shanghai as a 'double agent', I knew that it was vital that I should behave normally. Any sign of agitation on my part would certainly be interpreted as a sign of guilt.

I poured some water into the washbasin and refreshed myself by washing my face and hands. Then I picked up a volume of Mao's books and sat down near the window, bending my head over it and turning its pages from time to time to give the impression of reading with absorption. After standing at the peephole for quite a long time, the guard went away. But a minute later another guard took her place. When it was time for the midday meal, I ate the rice and cabbage rather quickly because I was hungry. After the woman from the kitchen collected the container, I heard her say to the guard, 'All eaten up.' After the prisoners had walked about in the cell for the usual ten minutes' exercise, the guard went from cell to cell to tell everybody to sit down. She came to me last and took up her position at the peephole at once. Although she moved very quietly, I had been in the detention house long enough to identify every kind of noise and could easily sense her presence. But I pretended I did not know she was there. I lay against my rolled-up bedding, closed my eyes and feigned sleep. Sleeping in daytime was strictly against regulations and usually incurred the wrath of the guards. I had often heard the guards scolding prisoners for the offence. So anxious was she that I should not know I was being watched that she did not shout for me to get up.

After an hour or so, I was called again to the interrogation room. I had to read the same quotation I had read in the morning.

'Let's start with MI5 agent Scott. How did you meet him? Did you know him before he came to China? What information did you give to him?' asked the interrogator.

'Before I give you an account of how I met Scott, I think I should point out to you that I knew him only as a British diplomatic officer.'

'You may point out anything you like. Whether we believe it or not is another matter. Proceed with your account.'

'I first met Scott in September 1961 at someone's dinner party. I no longer remember who the host and hostess were,' I said.

'Your host was the Indian Consul-General. We have the guest list. But that's not important. Did you know Scott before you met him at the Indian Consul-General's dinner party?'

'No.'

'You went to Hong Kong shortly afterwards. And while you were in Hong Kong you were in contact with another MI5 agent who was a British air force officer during the Second World War. He was well known in Hong Kong as a British spy though he assumed the cover of a businessman. Did Scott send you to that man to receive instructions?'

'I met many people socially in Hong Kong. I was not aware any one of them was an agent. My trip was arranged before I met Scott. I went to Hong Kong every two years. As you know, everyone needs a travel permit from the police to go to Hong Kong. I made my application to my police station long before I met Scott,' I said.

'You want me to believe your meeting with Scott was accidental, but the facts tell a different story. Scott came to Shanghai just before you went to Hong Kong. He returned to Peking as soon as you left. But he came back again before you returned and stayed several months. When the ship you travelled on was delayed in the river by a typhoon, he came on board to see you several times. That was not the usual behaviour of two people who have just met at a dinner party. Moreover, when he was in Shanghai you went out together a great deal. He always drove the car himself when he went out with you, while he used the chauffeur when he went out with others.

'The gossip of the foreigners in Shanghai was that you were having a decadent love affair, but none of the people assigned to watch you reported anything to indicate that this was the case. We believe your relationship with Scott was a political one. You deliberately created the impression of a liaison to mislead those around you.

'The British are racially arrogant. And the discipline of his organization would not have allowed its agent to form a sentimental attachment to a native woman of the country in which he was operating. In fact, we know that while he was in Shanghai he was having an illicit relationship with the wife of a British bank manager.

'Now that you see how much we know about this odious business, do you still hope to avoid telling the truth? Confess what Scott asked you to do and what you actually did for him!' the interrogator concluded his accusation and sat there glaring at me.

'You are making a perfectly ordinary situation sound suspicious,' I said. 'I did see Scott rather frequently, mainly because he led an active social life and entertained a great deal. Often he showed British films after dinner. That's always an attraction because we did not have the opportunity to see films like that. I remember on several occasions he invited officials from the Foreign Affairs Bureau to those film shows. It's customary to return hospitality. I had a collection of porcelain. I would have a dinner party and invite several friends including Scott to see my newly acquired pieces. And he taped quite a number of my records. The Red Guards must have told you that I had a large collection of records. I think he did drive himself more than other Europeans in Shanghai probably because he speaks Chinese and so was not afraid. As for the fact that he arrived in Shanghai just before I left for Hong Kong and came back again just before I returned, that was pure coincidence. When the ship on which I was travelling was delayed in the river due to a typhoon, he came on board, not to see me, but to see the captain. There was another passenger from Shanghai. I think he was a Danish businessman. They drank and talked together. I did not join them. When foreign vessels are in the river, many soldiers and customs officials remain on board. Why don't you ascertain from them whether he came on board to see the captain or me?' I said.

'Your relationship with Scott was more than that of a casual acquaintance,' the interrogator said.

'Whatever it was, your interpretation of the situation is far-fetched and incorrect.'

The interrogator glared at me and said, 'My advice to you is not to try to get out of your difficulties by claiming you did have a love affair with Scott. A Chinese woman degrading her country by having a love affair with a barbarian from the West deserves incarceration in a camp for "reform through labour".'

Chinese throughout the ages suffered from racial arrogance. Those who had never been out of the country and had no close contact with other nationalities often thought of people in other lands as alien, therefore uncivilized, creatures with strange habits and called them 'foreigners' or even 'foreign devils'. The self-imposed isolation during Mao Tze-tung's reign and Party propaganda on the evils of capitalism had greatly reinforced the Chinese people's unfortunate state of self-delusion. When Deng Hsiao-ping threw open China's door to the rest of the world and a flood of well-meaning and obviously affluent 'foreigners' came to China with money to invest and ideas to share, the Chinese people suffered such a traumatic awakening that they sunk in shame and self-reproach only to emerge with eagerness to jettison everything Chinese in order to become thoroughly 'civilized'.

There was nothing I could say to the interrogator really, though I realized by his stance that sending me to a labour camp was not satisfactory, unless I could be sent as a 'spy'. This was interesting and I asked myself why. Normally when the Party picked a victim to be punished, the Party didn't much care what excuse it used for imposing sentence. Indeed, sometimes the excuses used were extremely vague or none at all. To punish was the aim. In my case, judging from the attitude of the interrogator, it would seem that I had to be punished as a 'spy', not for some other reason. Why? I was not to know until much, much later.

'I see you are not attempting to tell more lies. Now confess what Scott said to you when you were together,' the interrogator said.

'You cannot expect me to remember conversations that took place several years ago. There was nothing of any significance. We talked about books, music, Chinese porcelain, places we both knew and our families and so on.'

'Your conversation never touched politics at all?'

'Well, we probably exchanged views on current affairs sometimes, mostly international affairs. Scott was a diplomat. He would not have wanted to comment on anything that was going on in China to a Chinese.'

To all the Europeans I had met, whether diplomats or businessmen, China under Mao Tze-tung was a fascinating subject mainly because the closed-door policy of the Communist Party shrouded the country in mystery. There were also some who came to China because they were interested in Chinese culture. When they had an opportunity to meet a Chinese with whom they could talk, naturally they asked questions. But these questions had nothing to do with political secrets. As a Chinese I believed that helping people from other lands understand China, her history, her cultural heritage and her aspirations was not a bad thing. But the Communist Party officials of the radical faction did not see things in this light. They assumed that any Chinese not parroting the official propaganda line was hostile to the regime and everybody coming to China was trying to find fault with the Communist system. So they were always suspicious of the Chinese who worked in foreign firms and had contacts with the Europeans.

Before the Cultural Revolution, my feeling of safety had rested on the fact that I knew no Chinese of any significance in the official world and was not in a position to learn of anything that could possibly be considered a state secret. And I took great care never to ask questions on sensitive subjects when I saw my Chinese friends and relatives, especially when they happened to be Party members. (In the end this policy paid off because during the Cultural Revolution, when my friends and relatives were cross-examined, they could honestly say that I never showed any interest in State secrets.)

'Scott was an intelligence officer. It was his duty to find out things. What did he ask you to do? Did he not ask you to find out things for him?' persisted the interrogator.

'Never! How could I find out things for him? I worked for Shell, a foreign firm. I knew nothing more than the foreigners knew.'

'It's not possible for an intelligence officer to refrain from trying to gather information useful to his government.'

'Are you sure he was in fact an intelligence officer?' I asked the interrogator.

'Do not doubt our information.'

'Then why did you not arrest him or declare him *persona non grata* and expel him from China?'

'It was much better he did not know we knew. We put him under close surveillance and we knew everything he did. The British were working not only for their own country but also for the United States, since the Americans could not come here openly. The United States cooperates closely with the Kuomintang, so the British were helping the Kuomintang also.'

Raising his voice and abandoning his matter-of-fact manner, he went on, 'In 1962, when Scott came to Shanghai for the second time, the Kuomintang were preparing for an attack against us. Scott chose to establish contact with you because you were connected with the Kuomintang.'

'Nonsense! I was never connected with the Kuomintang.'

'Your husband was a senior official of the Kuomintang Government. But that's not the whole story. Your class origin dictated that your sympathy would be with the Kuomintang. The teaching of our Great Leader on class struggle is like a telescope as well as a microscope. Armed with Mao Tze-tung Thought, we see through the superficial phenomena and get to the heart of the matter.'

I knew that the official propaganda line of Peking in 1962 was that the Kuomintang were about to launch an attack against the mainland. But none of the newspapers and magazines I got from abroad ever hinted at any sign of military preparation in Taiwan. Besides, I was sure Taiwan would not undertake an attack against the mainland without the consent of the United States and that, in 1962, the United States was unlikely to allow such a venture. In Shanghai, however, I had heard frequently, at that time, of movements of Chinese troops to, and the withdrawal of families of military personnel from, Fukien province facing Taiwan. Many people believed that Mao planned military action against Taiwan, not the reverse. The gossip in Shanghai was that only the economic collapse caused by the failure of Mao's Great Leap Forward campaign and dissension within the Party leadership compelled him to shelve his plan.

As I tried to recall whether anybody in the foreign community, including Scott, had asked me about Taiwan during that time, I became thoughtful. The interrogator, observing me closely, but misunderstanding the reason for my thoughtfulness, seized the moment to say, 'Whether you confess or not, we have a complete record of what you said to Scott.'

'In that case, you would know for a certainty that we never talked politics,' I told him.

'You are obviously not ready to confess straightaway. You need time to think and to recollect. That's perfectly all right with us. We'll give you plenty of time to prepare for a full and frank confession. After today, you should know it's useless for you to try to evade. Now, we will talk about that female agent Austin. Give an account of your dealings with her.'

'As you know, Mrs Austin was the wife of a businessman. My contact with her was purely social. We played bridge together and dined with each other.'

'You brought her into contact with an ex-Kuomintang Army officer!'

'What! Who was that?' I was genuinely shocked and I showed my surprise. The interrogator, watching me, relaxed visibly.

'The Chinese doctor of traditional medicine you took to her apartment was a ranking officer of the Kuomintang Army before he practised medicine.'

'I knew nothing of his background. I knew only he was a very good doctor of Chinese traditional medicine. Mrs Austin confided in me that she was unhappy because she could not have children. She had been to European doctors who could not find anything organically wrong. I was sorry for her, so I asked the doctor if Chinese medicine could do something for her. Since he said that he could not be certain without seeing her, I introduced them to each other. You could easily get confirmation of what happened from the doctor himself.'

'He committed suicide soon after the Red Guards started their revolutionary action against him.'

Had the Red Guards tortured him because he had had contact with a British agent? God, why did I introduce him to her? How stupid I had been not to realize fully the complexity of life under Mao! Since good intentions and sympathy for others often led people into trouble, the Chinese people had invented a new proverb which said, 'The more you do, the more trouble you have; the less you do, the less trouble you have. If you do nothing whatever, you will become a model citizen.' Why did I not heed the experience of others? I felt greatly saddened by the death of this poor man.

'Besides taking the doctor to see her, you also travelled to Peking with her. What did you do there and whom did you see?'

'The tomb of Ming Emperor Wan Li had been newly opened in Peking in 1959. In 1960 we went to see it. Travelling with foreigners I could stay in a good hotel, while as a Chinese citizen, I would only be allowed to stay in a third-rate guesthouse. So I went with Mrs Austin and another British woman friend. For them, it was convenient to have me with them because I knew Peking well, having lived there in my childhood and I speak the language.'

'Did you introduce her to anybody in Peking?'

'No, I don't know many people in Peking myself.'

'What about your brother? He visited you at the hotel, we know.'

'On the day my brother came, the two British ladies went to the Jade Temple without me. My brother did not want to meet them.'

There was a slight noise behind me. The interrogator looked past my shoulder and then at his watch. After a few whispered words with the man taking notes, he stood up and said, 'You may go back to your cell. When I call you again we will talk about the dirty work you did for the company that employed you and the reason your office engaged as secretary the White Russian woman who was also a Soviet agent. I don't think you will find it easy to deny your involvement with the affairs of the firm that employed you.'

After a momentary pause, he went on, 'Think carefully about your relationship with Scott. Remember, we already know he used you to gather information and we have a good idea what you told him.'

'I couldn't have told anybody more than I knew myself. Since I knew nothing, how could I have been of use to him?'

'Well, we think he came to Shanghai to see you, both before you went to Hong Kong and after you came back. He wouldn't have done that if it hadn't been worth his while.'

A guard opened the door of the interrogation room. The interrogator told me to go. I realized that he was not interested in prolonging the session after the man listening at the small window had departed.

Back in the cell, I was continuously watched by the guards. My mind was troubled as I felt responsible for the death of that poor doctor. And I wished I had never met Scott or Austin. Were they really British agents? Even if they were, it still did not explain why I was in prison now. Both the foreign residents in Shanghai and the senior Chinese working in foreign firms were under constant observation by our servants at home and other Chinese staff members at our place of work. In public places, not only were there always policemen and uniformed sentries, but also plainclothes operatives working for the police and zealous activists eager to report any unusual behaviour. Personal privacy did not exist in Shanghai as it does in other cities of the world. If the People's Government had been suspicious of my relationship with Scott and Austin, the Shanghai police should have acted years ago. Indeed there was much in the situation I did not as yet understand. It seemed quite likely that the interrogator would go through the whole list of my foreign friends and declare them all secret agents. Scott and Austin were merely the first two being named to frighten me. I realized that I was being drawn into a quagmire. I would have to watch my steps to avoid sinking into its depths.

Ever since I had been brought to the No. 1 Detention House, I had been wondering why I had been arrested. This was the question that puzzled me most. Who was behind my arrest? Did they really suspect me of having done something criminal or did they merely hope that I would be frightened into providing them with a false confession which they could use against me? Winnie seemed to think that because Shell had closed its Shanghai office, it was my turn to be punished. Was she correct?

As I sat in the cell thinking of my encounter with the interrogator, I couldn't help recalling all the cases of innocent men and women sentenced to terms of imprisonment and hard labour that I had heard of. My spirit of bravado deserted me and I became really frightened, not because I was burdened with a sense of guilt but because I feared that the task of defending myself might be beyond my ability.

In the evening, I composed myself for that quiet moment of daily prayer, but the stern voice of the interrogator intruded. I felt lost and unhappy, almost as if God had turned away from me as well.

That night, I had a nightmare, the first of many during my imprisonment. I dreamt I was standing on the narrow ledge of a sheer rocky cliff by the sea. The roaring waves of the incoming tide were rising higher and higher to engulf me. It was pitch dark, I was utterly alone and I was petrified.

Instinctively, I pulled my quilt over my face to stifle a cry of terror. I opened my eyes to find the electric light glaring down at me. My eyeshade had slipped onto the floor. Remembering the guard standing forever outside the door with her eyes glued to the peephole, ready to interpret any sign of restlessness as a sign of guilt, I froze in fear and apprehension. But the sound of a heavy bolt being driven in place somewhere upstairs told me that she was temporarily elsewhere, putting a newly arrived prisoner into a cell.

CHAPTER 7

The January Revolution and Military Control

I WAITED FOR THE interrogator to call me again. However, several days passed and nothing happened. I felt tension in the atmosphere; the guards looked harassed as they dashed in and out of the corridor. Something was happening in the world outside, I felt sure. Often, I would go to stand by the door, hoping to hear what the guards were talking about in their little room at the other end of the corridor, but all I could discern was an unusually excited, high-pitched intonation in their voices. Sometimes they seemed to be arguing about something, while at other times they lowered their voices to an almost inaudible whisper. Even though the prison was deadly silent, I could not make out what they were talking about. My inability to find out what was actually going on frightened me.

Early in December, not long after my first interrogation, the guards stopped giving me the newspaper. Since the newspaper was considered important material for the prisoners' indoctrination and the guards always told us to read it carefully, this was very strange. After waiting for a few days, I asked for it. At first the guard ignored my request for the paper. When I asked again, the guard simply said impatiently, 'Don't you know there's a revolution going on?'

By the middle of December, winter came in earnest. A penetrating north wind swept the city with icy blasts, lowering the temperature daily until it was hovering around zero centigrade. The window and door of my cell rattled with each strong gust. The folded strips of toilet paper I had pushed into the gaps to stop the wind were often blown onto the floor. I had already put on both my sweaters and a padded jacket but still my teeth chattered as spasms of shivering shook my body. In the icy room, my breath appeared as white cloudy puffs and I had to stamp my feet and rub my hands to bring blood to my toes and fingers. When the guards yelled for the prisoners to get ready for outdoor exercise, I thought they must hate to have to leave their stove on a day like this.

In spite of the wind, it was in fact a little warmer outside than in the damp cell. Besides, walking improved my circulation. But the strong wind whirled the dust and gravel into the air so that I could hardly keep my eyes open.

Suddenly I saw all the guards rushing out of the closed pavilion on the raised platform from where they had been watching us, dashing down the steps and disappearing from view. At the same time, the noise from the street grew louder and louder as if a mob of several thousand were storming into the detention house. In the sentry box overlooking the exercise yards, the soldier holding a rifle stiffly by his side was craning his neck in the direction of the prison entrance but he did not abandon his post. A woman prisoner in a neighbouring exercise yard said in an excited whisper loud enough for all the prisoners to hear, 'It's probably the Red Guards trying to get in to rescue their comrades imprisoned by the Municipal Government!'

Immediately, the voice of a young girl shouted from one of the exercise yards, 'Let me out! Let me out! I'm a Red Guard! Long live our Great Leader Chairman Mao!' Her urgent entreaty for freedom was accompanied by the sound of her fist knocking on the heavy door of the exercise yard.

The commotion at the entrance of the detention house went on until we heard the sound of gunshots, probably fired by the soldiers guarding the detention house. The sound of the mob receded. After a while the guards came back to let the prisoners out of the exercise yards. Obviously the attempt by the Red Guards to break into the detention house had given the guards quite a jolt. When the guard unlocked my exercise yard, he seemed rather subdued, did not shout 'come out' as usual but waited by the door for me to walk out.

In the following days, I observed a marked change in the behaviour of the guards. They neglected their duties and were often absent from their post. Frequently there was no sight or sound of any of them for hours at a time. Fortunately the woman from the kitchen continued to bring the prisoners their food and hot drinking water and the girl doing Labour Reform gave the prisoners cold water for washing as usual. When the guards did come on duty, they gathered in the little room, holding excited discussions. From the occasional word I overheard, I concluded that they were being drawn into the Proletarian Cultural Revolution and were forming their own revolutionary organizations so that they too could join the ever-swelling ranks of the Revolutionaries. For the prisoners, the relaxed interest of the guards was like the lifting of an enormously heavy weight. Sometimes I heard the whispering voices of the inmates rising to the normal sound of conversation and occasionally I even heard giggles.

When the newspaper stopped coming on 2 December, I started to make light scratches on the wall to mark the passing days. By the time I had made twenty-three strokes, I knew it was Christmas Eve. Though the usual hour of bedtime had passed the guards were not yet on duty to tell the prisoners to go to sleep. While I was waiting in the bitter cold, suddenly, from somewhere upstairs, I heard a young soprano voice singing, at first tentatively and then boldly, the Chinese version of 'Silent Night'. The prison walls resounded with her song as her clear and melodious voice floated in and out of the dark corridors. I was enraptured and deeply moved as I listened to her. I knew from the way she rendered the song that she was a professional singer who had incurred the displeasure of the Maoists. No concert I had attended at Christmas in any year had meant more to me than that moment when I sat in my icy cell listening to 'Silent Night' sung by another prisoner whom I could not see. As soon as she was confident that the guards were not there to stop her, the girl sang beautifully without any trace of nervousness. The prison became very quiet. All the inmates listened to her with bated breath.

Just as the last note of her voice trailed into space, the guards' footsteps echoed on the cement floor. They rushed from cell to cell asking, 'Who was that?' 'Who was singing?' 'Who was breaking the rules?' None of the prisoners replied.

A few days after the New Year, the loudspeaker in the corridor was switched on and all the prisoners were told to sit still to listen to an important announcement.

A man's voice read a proclamation by the Shanghai Workers Revolutionary Headquarters. It stated that the Red Guards and the Revolutionaries in the city, acting with the approval of the Cultural Revolution Directorate in Peking, had seized power in Shanghai on 4 January and had overthrown the 'reactionary' Party Secretariat and Municipal Government, which for a long time had 'opposed the correct policy of our Great Leader Chairman Mao and pursued a revisionist line in order to revive capitalism in China'.

It was subsequently revealed in newspaper articles that the 'hero' of this coup was a former security chief of a textile factory, Wang Hong-wen, who had succeeded in forming an affiliation of all mass revolutionary organizations that had sprung up all over the city into one organization called the Shanghai Workers Revolutionary Headquarters with himself as its head. He was backed by Chang Chuan-chiao, the long-time associate of Mao's wife Chiang Ching and the representative of the Peking Cultural Revolution Directorate in

Shanghai. Eventually, Chiang Ching, Chang Chuan-chiao, Wang Hong-wen and a well-known left-wing writer Yao Wen-yuan were to form a tightly knit political faction known as the notorious 'Gang of Four'.

It seemed that while anyone who was not a class enemy could join a revolutionary organization and become a Revolutionary, the leadership of such organizations was now firmly in the hands of approved Maoist activists.

The man also read a document by the State Council, giving approval to the rebels' action but urging the workers not to neglect production. This statement by the State Council, the office of the Prime Minister, gave the unprecedented revolutionary action by the Maoist radicals a semblance of legality. That Prime Minister Chou En-lai should have given the rebels his support and approval shocked me. I simply could not believe he truly agreed with their action. However, I thought his call for the workers not to neglect production was at least a note of sanity in the atmosphere of madness. It wasn't until after my release from prison that I learned of the tremendous pressure Chou En-lai was being kept under by the radicals, who had persistently tried to dislodge him from his position as Prime Minster. It was only by skilful and subtle handling of the situation and by always identifying himself with Mao's designs that Chou En-lai managed to survive the Cultural Revolution and give protection to a few of the old guards in the Party.

A few days after the announcement of the coup, the guards handed me a copy of the *Shanghai Liberation Daily*, which reappeared under new revolutionary publishers. Under banner headlines printed in red ink, it announced that the Red Guard and Revolutionaries had seized the newspaper, after prolonged struggle, on 2 December, as a preliminary to the overthrow of the Municipal Government.

Reading the news items and reports carefully, I learned that final victory for the Revolutionaries was made possible only when two senior officials of the Shanghai Municipal Government were persuaded to switch allegiance to the Revolutionaries. At a public rally to indict the former Chief Secretary of the Party and the Mayor of the city, the two turncoats, anxious for their own acceptance by the Maoists, had demonstrated their firm stand on Mao's side by slapping the faces of their former colleagues to the loud and prolonged cheers of assembled Red Guards and Revolutionaries. (These two officials, Ma Tien-shui and Hsu Ching-hsian, were to rule Shanghai on behalf of the Gang of Four until Mao's death and the Gang's arrest. In 1982, both were sentenced to long terms of imprisonment for crimes, including murder, committed at the order of the Gang of Four. Subsequently Ma Tien-shui went mad.)

The overthrow of the Shanghai Municipal Government by the radicals shattered any hope I had had of a quick solution to my own predicament. I realized that my case would have to wait for the reorganization of all the departments of the new Shanghai Government, including the Public Security Bureau, which held jurisdiction over the No. 1 Detention House. This process would take time, especially if there were overt and covert resistance to the new office-holders. I also thought the viability of the new Shanghai Government and its smooth functioning depended on how quickly the rest of the country could be taken over by the Revolutionaries. From the numerous articles denouncing officials in other cities of China, I could see that the Revolutionaries and the Red Guards were meeting resistance elsewhere stronger than that which they had encountered in Shanghai.

In the spring of 1967, the *Liberation Daily* published Mao Tze-tung's call for the Army to support the Leftists. It included a quotation of Mao stating that the People's Liberation Army was not only a military organization but a political one as well. From the statement, it seemed obvious to me that the Red Guards and the Revolutionaries had been unable to take over many local governments in other parts of China by their effort alone. However, intervention by the military did not immediately produce the desired result. In many instances, the military was quite unable to distinguish right away between the Red Guard and Revolutionary organizations led by Maoist activists and those organized by Party officials whom Mao wished to topple, since both sides claimed to be dedicated to Mao's policy. Furthermore, many military commanders were concurrently local administrators such as those in Tibet and Hsinchiang. They simply declared themselves as the true Leftists and turned their troops on the Red Guards and the Revolutionaries. In the bitter struggle which ensued there was much bloodshed. In many regions, fearful of committing a political error, the military turned a blind eye when different factions of self-styled Leftists raided their arsenals. However, when the dust settled, it appeared that in most parts of the country, the aid given by the military substantially helped one or another group of rebels to seize power.

The prominent part played by the military in assisting the Red Guards and the Revolutionaries to seize power raised the prestige of the Army and its commander-in-chief, Defence Minister Lin Piao.

Numerous photographs of him walking with or standing beside Mao appeared in the press, a sure sign of enhanced status. He was referred to as 'The close comrade-in-arms of our Great Leader Chairman Mao', a phrase elevating his position to the second place in the Party hierarchy, after Mao, and before that of Premier Chou En-lai, who was now caught by the photographer's camera walking behind Lin Piao in third place. Lin Piao lost no time in purging the Army command of his possible opponents and in appointing his cronies to key positions in their place. The newspaper reported the successful exposure of an anti-Mao group of officers in the former Army high command. A list of new names appeared for the post of chief staff officers of the army, navy, air force and logistics. Lin Piao was heartily congratulated by the rebel-controlled press for the change.

In Shanghai, the Red Guards and the Revolutionaries began taking over subsidiary organizations in the city one by one. Daily, the newspaper revealed the fact that not only had they to contend with stiff resistance and sabotage of their efforts by those they wanted to overthrow and replace, but also that they themselves broke into conflicting factions struggling for the spoils of office. Actual fighting took place in every district of the city. Control of organizations changed hands frequently. The city was in a constant state of upheaval. The sound of yelling mobs reached my cell from the streets. In the exercise yards, I could hear the broadcast speeches of denunciation clearly. The sound of mob fury conjured up for me fearful scenes of death and destruction and I greatly feared for the safety of my daughter.

Instead of trying to control the disturbances and bloodshed, the rebel leaders seemed to be encouraging it. One day, I read a newspaper article entitled, 'It's an honour to have our hands stained with the enemy's blood.' On another day, there appeared a statement attributed to Lin Piao: 'There are casualties in all revolutions, so let us not exaggerate the seriousness of this situation. Many people have commited suicide or been killed. But these deaths are fewer than those incurred during the war of resistance against Japan or the Civil War, or even during natural disasters. Thus, our gains are greater than our losses.' These callous words made me sick with apprehension for the safety of my daughter. I could no longer eat or sleep normally.

One evening, after I had again refused the rice, a guard came to the small window and pushed it open.

'What's the matter with you? Are you sick?' she asked.

'I'm worried about my daughter. Could she be brought here to stay in this cell with me?'

'Of course not! She hasn't committed any crime. Why should she be locked up in prison?' the guard replied.

'I haven't committed any crime either, but I'm locked up in prison just the same,' I told her.

'I've no time to argue with you about that. Whether you have committed any crime or not, I don't know. In fact, I don't know any more what's a crime and what's not a crime. But since you are here already, you must just wait. Someone will deal with you one day. You're not so badly off. You get eight hours' sleep every night and have rice to eat. We have to attend meetings after work and don't get eight hours' sleep.' She banged the window shut and walked away.

The behaviour of the guard astonished me. This was the first time a guard had revealed herself as a normal human being to me. She certainly sounded discouraged and grumpy. I concluded that the struggle within the Party leadership was having a demoralizing effect on the guards. To have been selected to work in such sensitive jobs as prison guards, they must have been firm believers in the Party and its leadership. It must be disheartening, if not downright shattering, for them to learn that according to Mao Tze-tung so many of their superior officers were no more devoted to the ideals of Communism than the men in the street and some of them were in fact working to revive capitalism in China. They lost interest in their work. The prison gradually degenerated into a disorderly place, with prisoners shouting, crying, fighting with each other and banging the floor when the guards were not in evidence. One night I was awakened by low hysterical laughter coming from another solitary cell in the dark recess of the long corridor. The guard on duty, if there was one, made no effort to stop the prisoner.

I began to observe the guards more closely and to see them as individuals. I noticed that many guards looked unhappy and subdued while a few younger ones appeared wearing the red armbands of the Revolutionaries. These younger guards swaggered in and out insolently, full of self-importance. They assumed an air of authority, not only shouting orders to the prisoners but also speaking in a commanding voice to the other guards.

During 1967, while anarchy ruled the city of Shanghai, control gradually disintegrated in the No. 1 Detention House. By autumn, the guards, split into rival factions, were fighting among themselves. When the prisoners were allowed outdoor exercise, I saw their civil war slogans scribbled on the walls and the paved walks of the courtyard. From my cell, I would often hear the familiar voices of the guards at the women's prison shouting with other voices in argument and once or twice even the sound of scuffling. The points of contention seemed to be what constituted Mao Tze-tung's policy and who among the officials were 'capitalist-roaders' to be overthrown.

Often guard duty was taken over by prison administrators and interrogators who, because they were considered 'intellectuals', were excluded from revolutionary organizations. During the Cultural Revolution, all intellectuals, whether Party members or not, were denounced as 'the stinking ninth category'. The eight other categories of enemies were: landlords, rich peasants, counter-revolutionaries, bad elements, rightists, traitors, foreign agents and 'capitalist-roaders'. The ninth category were the intellectuals, including not only people with degrees working as professors or research fellows but also school-teachers, technicians and white-collar office workers. The word 'stink' used as a Chinese slang word also meant 'unjustified pride'. Because intellectuals were often thought to be arrogant and proud of their superior knowledge or training and enjoyed positions of honour and respect in traditional Chinese society, the Revolutionaries called them the 'stinking' ninth category to show their contempt for the intellectuals and for the Chinese tradition of honouring them.

At the beginning of my second winter at the detention house, I again developed a bad cold which refused to clear up in spite of aspirin tablets the young prison doctor gave me. When my cold turned to bronchitis, my body shook with fits of coughing, particularly severe during the night when the cell became extremely cold. One night, while I was lying under my quilt almost fully dressed, with two sweaters and a pair of knitted long johns to keep warm, I could not control persistent fits of coughing. It was after midnight. The prison had long ago settled down to complete silence. No matter how I lay on that hard bed in the cold room, I coughed and sneezed continually. To ease the irritation in my throat, I drank some of the water left in my mug. The cold liquid actually made me worse. I covered my head to muffle the sound of coughing and hoped the warmth of the quilt would give me some relief.

I heard the small window being opened. The sound was different from the usual loud bang made by the guards. I then heard a man's voice saying quietly, 'Come over here!'

I got out of bed, pulled on my slacks and threw my padded jacket over my shoulders, wondering what the man wanted of me in the depth of night. When I walked to the small window and looked out, I was astonished to see my former interrogator standing there, holding a thermos flask in his hand.

'Have you a mug? Bring it over,' he said.

I took the mug to the window and he poured some hot water into it.

I had been waiting for over a year for him to continue with the interrogation. This seemed a good opportunity to ask him, so between fits of coughing, I said, 'When are you going to clarify my case?'

After a moment's hesitation, he said, 'When the Revolutionaries are ready, they will call you. More important issues are at stake right now. You must be patient. Now, drink the hot water. That should ease your cough. Tomorrow, report to the doctor. He'll give you some medicine.'

He seemed to be saying that he was no longer dealing with my case. I wondered if he still thought I was guilty or indeed if he had ever really thought I was guilty. Suddenly I thought how perfectly ghastly to have to work as an interrogator in such circumstances, when he knew a person was innocent and yet it was his job to find the person guilty. I drank the hot water quickly but was seized with another fit of coughing and vomited.

'Never mind, never mind! I'll give you some more hot water.' The interrogator opened the small window again. He was joined by another man with dark-rimmed glasses whom he addressed as Director Liang.

'May I borrow a mop to clean the floor?' I asked between coughs.

'You can clean it tomorrow. Is it dirty? Is there anything else besides water?' Director Liang asked.

I looked down on the floor. Indeed there was only water which was already being absorbed by the cement floor. Certainly Director Liang was in an excellent position to know how empty the stomach of a prisoner was. After all, he had been the Director of the No. 1 Detention House before the Red Guards and the Revolutionaries reduced him to guard duty.

They both remained there until I drank more water. Then they closed the small window and went away.

I got back into bed and thought: the Cultural Revolution was certainly producing some strange phenomena. For the Director and interrogator of the detention house to give a prisoner hot drinking water from their own thermos must be one of them. Such humane behaviour had to be in direct contravention of their belief that the No. 1 Detention House was 'an instrument of repression used by one class against another', as I had been told by the interrogator. Perhaps, as the Red Guards and the Revolutionaries expanded the scope of their revolutionary action, they were alienating potential supporters and pushing Party intellectuals into the enemy camp.

Next morning the doctor gave me some sulphadiazine tablets. But I continued to waken during the night with coughing when the cell became unbearably cold. It was in the small hours of one morning that I overheard a whispered conversation outside my door. That night a former female interrogator was on guard duty. She had given me my medicine for the night and told me to go to sleep. Now I heard her voice talking to the woman locked in the cell opposite mine. Though their voices were kept very low, the prison was very silent, and I got the gist of their conversation. I was shocked to discover that the woman in the cell was an official of the Public Security Bureau and a former school friend of the interrogator when they were both at the College for Public Security Officers. They were talking about the violent struggle at the office of the Shanghai Public Security Bureau after Mao's wife Chiang Ching called upon the Red Guards and the Revolutionaries to 'smash the security, prosecution and law-enforcement agencies'. They were saying that this person jumped out of a window, that person was beaten to death and someone else was taken to hospital ... It was obvious that the Public Security Bureau was in disarray and unable to function at all.

After listening to their conversation, I decided that the Cultural Revolution was going to be a long-drawn-out affair, with the Party officials Mao wanted to remove fighting for survival with cunning and desperation. For the time being the radicals seemed to be winning because they enjoyed the support of Mao and the Army. But unless the ousted officials were all to be killed, which was an impossibility, they would be bound to wait for a chance to stage a comeback. In the meantime, they would probably do everything within their power to sabotage every move made by the radicals. I thought the situation was extremely complicated and would surely remain unsettled for a very long time to come.

A few nights later, just before the prisoners' bedtime, the guard on duty came to the cells again to tell the prisoners to sit quietly to listen to a broadcast. Through the loudspeaker, a man's voice announced that the No. 1 Detention House had been placed under military control.

'All of you prisoners listen attentively! The revolutionary situation is excellent! The true supporters of our Great Leader Chairman Mao and the followers of his close comrade-in-arms, Vice-Supreme Commander Lin, have overcome all obstacles and have already overthrown the reactionary Municipal Government of this city! We are now in the process of taking over the whole country and will continue to exterminate all our enemies. The sludge and filth left by the old society have been thrown onto the rubbish heap of history. Our achievement is great, great, great! Our losses are small, small, and small! Some people say we have created chaos. Chaos is an expression of class struggle. Our Great Leader Chairman Mao has said, "A revolution is not a dinner party, or writing an essay, or painting a picture, or doing embroidery; it cannot be so refined, so leisurely and gentle, so temperate, kind, courteous, restrained and magnanimous. A revolution is an insurrection, an act of violence by which one class overthrows another." There is nothing wrong in sowing chaos to confuse the enemy. Some people say we have killed too many. Nonsense! We have killed fewer people than during the war against the Japanese imperialists and the war of liberation. In fact, we have not killed enough. There are still enemies lurking in dark corners. We'll get them. Don't underestimate our determination or belittle our ability to exterminate our enemies. We are Revolutionaries! We are not afraid of chaos and killing. They are the natural outcome of a revolution. They inspire our own side and send terror into the hearts of the enemy. We won't fear even the collapse of heaven. The teachings of our Great Leader Chairman Mao will prop it up again.

'Our dear comrade Chiang Ching told us, "Smash to pieces the security and law-enforcement agencies." We have done it! The Shanghai Security Bureau and all its subsidiary organizations are now under our control. This detention house was run by the revisionists and "capitalist-roaders" of the Security Bureau. It's absurd the prisoners here should have such good treatment. You eat rice three times a day. You live better than the poor peasants. That proves the revisionists at the Security Bureau love the counter-revolutionaries better than the peasants. This is because they themselves are also counter-revolutionaries. From now on your ration will be cut to conserve grain. You do not labour. Two meals a day is ample. And you will eat sweet potatoes and other grains rather than rice. You won't die. But if you do, it is no loss to the Revolution. We have plenty of people in China. We will not miss a few counter-revolutionaries!

'A lot of you have been here a long time already. But some of you have not confessed. You hope to slip through the net. This is sheer wishful thinking. The iron fist of the dictatorship of the proletariat will crush you without mercy if you don't confess. Let that be a warning to you all!

'The policy of our Great Leader Chairman Mao is "Lenient treatment for those who confess, severe punishment for those who remain stubborn, and reward for those who render meritorious service by denouncing others. Tonight we will deal with some of the outstanding cases here to give expression to our Great Leader Chairman Mao's policy.'

After a moment's silence, he called out one name after another of prisoners sentenced to death because they had not confessed to their crimes. He gave such particulars as their age, address, occupation, 'reactionary' family background and described the 'crimes' the prisoners had committed, all of which came under the category of 'revenge against the proletarian class'. Those so-called crimes were in fact no more than statements of opposition to the Cultural Revolution or disparaging remarks against Chiang Ching, Lin Piao or Mao Tze-tung himself. Then the man shouted at the top of his voice, 'Take him out! Immediate execution!'

His voice was an inhuman roar, charged with cruelty. In spite of my rigid control, I shivered involuntarily.

The list of names of people to be executed went on and on. It was followed by a list of those sentenced to life imprisonment or to terms of twenty-five or more years in jail, all examples of 'severe punishment' dealt out to prisoners who had not confessed fully or whose confessions were not considered adequate or sincere. Finally he read out a list of names of cases given 'lenient treatment', because those men and women not only confessed but also rendered meritorious service by providing information to incriminate others. A woman was ordered to be released immediately because she had provided information leading to the arrest of several other people who had plotted to escape to Hong Kong. Others received short sentences of three to five years.

After the loudspeaker was switched off, the threat in that man's voice reverberated in my ears. Never in my life had I heard anything so shocking. The thought that this person was now in charge of the No. 1 Detention House and of my own fate frightened me. The night, already icy, seemed to get even colder. Spasms of shivering ran through my body while I waited for the guard to tell me to go to bed. The other prisoners, I thought, were probably frozen with fear too, as there was not the slightest sound of movement anywhere.

The door at the other end of the corridor banged and I heard the sound of leather boots echoing down the corridor. The small windows of the cells along the corridor were being opened and shut. There were shouts of 'What about you?' 'Have you confessed?' and 'Did you confess everything?' The heavy footsteps drew nearer and nearer. I braced myself for an unpleasant encounter. The footsteps stopped outside my cell. The shutter of the small window was pushed open. I heard the sound of rustling paper and the voice of a male guard saying, 'It's this one.'

'Come over!' The guard sounded even more severe than usual, perhaps to impress the Military Control officer.

Through the opening, I could see only a pair of black leather boots and the lower part of the uniformed body of an air force officer, not his face or head. But I pictured him in my mind's eye as having what we Chinese called a villain's face with 'horizontal flesh'. We believe a man's face reflects the life he has led so a wicked man would end up having an unpleasant face with 'horizontal flesh'. Somehow, thinking of him in these terms encouraged me. I felt that whatever he was going to say, I could cope with it.

'Why haven't you confessed?' It was the voice of the man who had made the broadcast.

'I haven't committed any crime. How can I confess?' I replied.

'Nonsense! You are a spy of the imperialists. Do you want to be shot?'

'I expect the new authority of this detention house to release me after examining the facts and finding me innocent.'

'You are dreaming! Do you think we are fools? You'll never be released if you do not confess! Didn't you hear the other cases of those who did not confess? They are dead,' he shouted vehemently, 'dead! Do you hear?' Then he said something to the guard who took out his bunch of keys and unlocked the door.

'Come out!' the guard shouted.

I stepped out of the cell, uncertain what the man in the air force uniform was going to do to me. He was already halfway down the corridor heading for the entrance. I followed the guard after him but before we had taken more than a couple of steps, there was a heavy thud and commotion overhead. Several voices called, 'Report!' 'Report!' Others were yelling, 'Come quickly! She is bleeding!'

Low hysterical laughter came from another direction, rising to a shrill cry. With the corridor shrouded in shadows under the dim light, the scene took on a sinister aspect. The male guard stopped abruptly, pushed me back into the cell, snapped the lock and hastened upstairs.

I heard footsteps of several guards running to the cell above mine. 'Take her out!' the voice of the air force officer shouted overhead. 'How dare you threaten the dictatorship of the proletariat with suicide! Did you think you could get out of confessing by bashing your head on the cement toilet? Your act proved you are guilty. You will be punished without mercy.'

There was a girl's voice sobbing and mumbling, and the sound of people moving about. Then silence.

After some time, a female guard came to order everybody to bed. When she came to me, she said, 'Why are you standing here?'

'I'm waiting to be called for questioning,' I said.

'No more questioning. Go to bed!' she said.

It seemed that I had been forgotten in the commotion overhead. I wondered what unpleasant fate would have awaited me if the girl upstairs had not chosen just that moment to bash her head on the cement toilet. While the method she used could not have resulted in her total escape from persecution, it demonstrated how desperate her mood was after listening to the broadcast. In fact, attempts at suicide were seldom successful at the No. 1 Detention House. The only person I heard of who actually did succeed was a young and talented surgeon, Dr Sung, the son of a Vice-Mayor of Shanghai. I was told that he painstakingly sharpened the handle of his toothbrush by grinding it on the cement floor and then used it to pierce his artery. It was revealed after Mao's death that the Revolutionaries had put the young doctor in the detention house and tortured him to make him denounce his father.

Next day, the prisoners were not given any food until mid-morning. It was dry rice with boiled cabbage. In the afternoon, a portion of boiled sweet potatoes was pushed through the small window. On subsequent days, this alternated with strips of mouldy dried sweet potato boiled in water. Since I found this impossible to eat or digest, on those days I had to be content with only the mid-morning meal. After some time, hunger became a permanent state so that it was no longer a sensation but an ever-present hollowness. The flesh on my body slowly melted away, my eyesight deteriorated and simple activities such as washing clothes exhausted my strength.

Some of the guards disappeared. New guards came to work wearing the red armbands of the Revolutionaries. Early in the morning, at midday and at night, I would hear them shouting to each other 'Long Live Our Great Leader Chairman Mao' and chanting his quotations. The newspaper reported a new ritual observed by all Chinese people called, 'Ask for instructions in the mornings, check your action with Chairman Mao's teachings at noon and report everything at night.' Apparently everyone went through the formality in front of an official portrait of Mao. To ask for instructions was to read passages from the Little Red Book, to check was to read again from the same book and to report was also to read from the same book. In short, three times a day, every day, every Chinese, except babies, had to read from Mao's book of quotations. The newspaper published articles to discuss whether one should do it when one was alone at home on Sundays. The conclusion was that one should not neglect going through the ritual even when one was lying in bed sick. Fortunately for us, this absurd practice was the privilege of only the approved 'masses' and was not allowed for class enemies locked in prison!

Military control had restored discipline. There was no more fighting or arguing among the guards. And they came on duty promptly. But it also created a frigid atmosphere. The guards no longer chatted with one another as they had done before. If one guard was alone with the prisoners, he or she seemed more relaxed. But whenever two were on duty together, they seemed to be on guard, almost as if each one feared that the other would report his or her behaviour to the Military Control.

There were new schedules for the prisoners besides the changed mealtimes. Every morning, the entire prison listened to news bulletins, first from the Central Broadcasting Service in Peking and immediately afterwards from the Shanghai Broadcasting Station. Frequently, the prisoners were lectured through the loudspeakers. At such times, lists of those getting 'lenient treatment' and 'severe punishment' were read out to encourage the rest of us to confess. Whenever the loudspeaker was switched on, the guards walked from cell to cell, to make sure the prisoners were listening.

One of the loudspeakers was just outside my door. The din was deafening. With the guard watching, I could not put my hands to my ears to shut out the noise. When Sunday came round, I asked for scissors, cut up a tiny piece of cloth, rolled the broken fibres into two small balls and used them as earplugs when there was a broadcast. While they did not stop the noise altogether, the sound was sufficiently muted to be bearable.

From time to time, I was called to the interrogation rooms for special indoctrination and questioning by militant guards who seemed to enjoy the confidence of the Military Control. Only selected prisoners received this treatment, I noticed. Whether we were the most hated class enemies or the most intransigent, I had no way of knowing. The guard used these occasions to abuse me verbally, calling me a 'dirty exploiter of peasants' or a 'running dog of foreign imperialists'. They attacked me for my family background, for my job with Shell and for my 'resistance to re-education' in not confessing to my 'crime' readily. They would bombard me with questions but did not wait for me to give any answers. They would tell me I would be shot soon or that I would be kept at the detention house for the rest of my life.

I soon discovered that there was no need for me to do anything except to listen, as the guards never stopped speaking once I entered the room. After several similar sessions, it dawned on me that their performances were solely for the purpose of establishing themselves as bona fide Revolutionaries. I was placed there merely as a necessary stage prop for their act. I concluded that even the militant guards who appeared so confident felt insecure in the atmosphere of suspicion created by the Cultural Revolution, when long-trusted Party leaders were suddenly condemned as 'hidden enemies of Communism' who had 'raised the red flag to oppose the red flag'.

One day, the prisoners were allowed outdoor exercise. When I stepped out of the door of the women's prison, I saw ex-Director Liang and several other men digging up the flowerbeds. This sight did not surprise me for the day before I had read in the newspaper that Mao had said that flowers and decorative plants were a softening influence which undermined the revolutionary spirit of the masses. The same report also said that in Mao's own garden in the former imperial palace, Chung Nan Hai, only apple trees and sunflowers were grown since they had practical economic value. In fact, during this period of the Cultural Revolution, Mao's personality cult was such that every word of his, no matter how insignificant, was applied and implemented with alacrity. Conversely, nothing could be done if Mao had not pointed the way.

In the distance, I saw other men and women sweeping the drive and carrying buckets of water towards the kitchen. From their appearance and the rather clumsy way they were working, I knew they were the Party intellectuals of the detention house, like ex-Director Liang, being reformed by physical labour. Mao had said that the more knowledge a man had, the more reactionary he would become, unless he purged himself through arduous physical labour.

Years later, I heard that during the Cultural Revolution millions of men and women had been ordered to give up their jobs in the cities to settle in rural areas to receive re-education through physical labour. Those intellectuals allowed to remain in the cities were assigned the work of common labourers in their organizations. It was the practice of that time to have medical doctors emptying bedpans in the hospitals, professors cleaning toilets in the universities and artists and musicians building walls and repairing roads. While they were doing all these things, they had to attend struggle meetings and political indoctrination classes at which they had to abuse themselves by 'confessing' to their 'crimes'. Indeed Mao's abuse of intellectuals reached an unprecedented level of cruelty during the Cultural Revolution. It very nearly destroyed China's tradition of respect for scholarship. During that time, anywhere in China, a man found reading a book other than Mao's four slim volumes ran the risk of being labelled as someone opposed to Mao.

When I reached the exercise yard, the guard told me to pull weeds out of the ground with my bare hands. Since it was winter, only a small patch was growing at the foot of the wall facing the sun. But the ground was frozen hard. It was slow work to get the weeds out without tools. When the guard returned, he kicked the small pile of dead weeds at my feet and yelled, 'Is this all you have done? You didn't dig out the roots.'

'I have nothing to dig the roots with.'

'You have hands. You could get the roots out with your fingers. You are just lazy!' He kicked the pile of weeds again, sending them flying in all directions.

When I stood up, dark shadows blinded my eyes and I felt dizzy. However, I managed to stagger after him back to the cell.

Two soldiers were in the corridor. The door of my cell was open. I saw a militant female guard going through my things. My sheets, quilt and blanket were already on the dusty floor. She was tossing other things out of my canvas bag. When she saw me, she grabbed the front of my padded jacket and pulled me roughly into the cell.

'Unbutton your jacket!' she yelled. When I unbuttoned it, she pulled it off my back and threw it on the floor. Holding my shoulders, she pushed me to a corner of the cell and turned me to face the wall. I stood there shivering and coughing.

'Take off your trousers!' she yelled when she had finished examining my jacket.

'Please let me put on my jacket before I take off my warm trousers. I already have a bad cold.'

'You are still soft and pampered. Prison life hasn't done you any good, has it? You haven't changed one little bit. I don't think you will die of cold if you take off both your jacket and your trousers. Take them off!'

I sneezed and coughed while she looked over my trousers. Then she threw them on the floor too and frisked me. She tore the toilet paper off the wall by my bed and deliberately walked over my bedclothes.

Pushing my eyeshade along the floor with her foot, she kicked it out of the cell and locked the door. I heard her unlocking the door of the cell next to mine and shouting to the inmate, 'Come over!'

I picked up my padded jacket and trousers and put them on. Then I had to sit down on the bed to calm myself and wait for my heartbeat to slow down before collecting my things from the floor and cleaning them as best I could. Next day, when rice was given to me, I used some to make a paste to replace the toilet paper on the wall, quite a sacrifice, now that every grain of rice was precious to me for survival. To make another eyeshade, I had to wait until Sunday to borrow the needle.

To search prisoners' cells became an established routine. It was done at irregular intervals by the militant female guard or others like her. I replaced the toilet paper on the wall many times and made many eyeshades; many a time I counted the grains of rice individually so that I used just enough to paste the paper but not a grain more than was necessary.

After coughing all night and being unable to sleep because of a terrible headache, I could barely get out of bed the next day. I went to the window and called, 'Report!'

It was a mild guard who opened the small window.

'I think I'm sick. May I see the doctor?' I requested.

She brought a thermometer and put it into my mouth. After a few minutes, she took it out, looked at it and said to me, 'You have a fever. It's quite high.' She gave me two aspirin tablets and told me to drink plenty of water. I waited for the doctor but he did not come. Just before the guard went off duty, I asked for the doctor again.

After a moment's hesitation, she said, 'The doctor has gone to the countryside to receive re-education through physical labour. I don't know when he will be allowed to come back. Maybe someone will come to take his place. Report again tomorrow. If you feel unwell, you may go to bed now.' She gave me two more aspirin tablets.

It was good to be allowed to lie down but I had a splitting headache. When my body shook with spasms of cold shivers, I knew my temperature was going up.

I heard the night duty guard arrive and the two guards exchange shouts of 'Long Live Our Great Leader Chairman Mao'. Then the night duty guard walked along the corridor towards my cell to inspect the prisoners in cells along the way. She walked briskly and stopped briefly at the peephole of each cell.

'What? Lying in bed already? You know how to be comfortable, don't you? Get up! It's not bedtime yet,' she shouted when she reached my cell. From her voice, I knew she was the same guard who had searched my cell the previous afternoon.

'I'm ill. The guard who just left told me to go to bed.' Unless I was dragged out of bed, I intended to stay there. She didn't bother to come in. In a moment, I heard her upstairs scolding another prisoner.

Next day, a young man came in response to my request for medical attention. After I told him I had a fever and had been coughing for nearly two months, he declared, 'You probably have hepatitis. There is a lot of it going round in this detention house. I'll examine a specimen of your blood.'

I was astonished. Any ignoramus with no special medical knowledge would know I had bronchitis, possibly verging on pneumonia, not hepatitis, an inflammation of the liver with symptoms entirely different from mine. What sort of 'doctor' was this young man? I bent down to look at him through the opening of the small window. I saw a country lad no more than twenty years of age in a soldier's uniform. I realized he was not a trained doctor at all, but had been given the job because Mao Tze-tung had said, 'We must learn swimming from swimming,' when referring to appointing unskilled workers who were politically reliable to do technical jobs. The young man was simply carrying out Mao's order to 'learn to be a doctor by being one'.

There were many reports in the newspaper during that time of cases when untrained hospital coolies were said to have performed operations successfully after mastering Mao's quotations. During an operation, Revolutionaries anxious to prove the magic of Mao's words remained in the operating room reciting quotations from the Little Red Book while the untrained 'doctor' struggled with the patient. However, when Mao himself or one of the other radical leaders needed medical attention from medical experts other than their own personal doctors, those experts, trained in western universities before the Communist Party took over China, were bundled into special planes and flown to Peking, often hastily removed from the countryside where they had been exiled to perform hard labour.

The young 'doctor' took me to the room reserved for the guards. In the warm room, where a stove was burning, my head cleared and I stopped shivering. After he had unwrapped his instruments and taken out the syringe, he told me to take off my jacket and roll up my sleeve. When he plunged the needle into my arm, he could not locate my vein. After several attempts, a bruise appeared under my skin and my arm became very painful. He was visibly agitated. Beads of sweat appeared on his forehead and his hand trembled.

I felt sorry for this poor creature who had been given a job beyond his ability. I knew that if I did not calm him, he might easily inflict worse damage to my arm.

'I've very small veins. All doctors have trouble taking blood from me,' I said, trying to give him confidence and to steady his hand.

He looked at me with what might be called a grateful glance and tried again while I held my breath. Finally he managed to locate the vein and fill the syringe.

Several days passed; my fever got so high that I no longer felt the cold in the cell. The guard told me to stay in bed. Twice a day, the Labour Reform girl was allowed to come in, under the watchful eyes of the guard standing at the open doorway, to bring me liquid rice and hot drinking water. I slept most of the time, in a state of semi-consciousness, with fantastic dreams of myself floating in and out of the cell through the iron-barred window as if I were an ethereal spirit.

One morning, the young man came back and said, 'You don't have hepatitis. It's probably TB. A lot of prisoners have TB. Get dressed. You may go to the hospital to have a fluoroscope.'

Though I was sure I did not have TB, I welcomed the idea of going to a hospital.

In the afternoon, a female guard unlocked the cell door and took me out. My legs felt wobbly and I was weak but she did not shout or urge me to walk faster. At the entrance of the detention house, a male guard was waiting with a pair of handcuffs. The female guard shook her head and whispered, 'Too ill'. I did not know whether the female guard meant I was too ill to escape en route so that the handcuffs were unnecessary, or that I was so ill that they had to show me consideration. In any case, the male guard put the handcuffs away.

A black jeep was waiting just inside the second gate. The female guard and I got into it.

How changed the drive of the detention house appeared from that night over sixteen months ago when I had been brought there! The place was now ablaze with colour and activities. Red boards mounted on sticks with Mao's quotations dealing with the suppression of class enemies were placed alongside the willow trees that lined the drive. The quotations were written in large characters with yellow paint. The boards were arranged to face the front entrance, probably to create an impact of fear on the prisoners being driven in to the detention house. On a large banner of red cloth suspended over the soldiers' barracks were three slogans written in white paint: 'Down with the US Imperialists', 'Down with the Soviet Revisionists' and 'We must liberate Taiwan'. Dummies dressed in western men's suits with the names of the President of the United States, the General Secretary of the Soviet Communist Party and the leader of the Kuomintang in Taiwan pinned on the front of the jackets were tied to wooden poles. Soldiers were practising bayonet charges on them. As one uniformed figure after another rushed forward to sink his bayonet into the dummies, all soldiers present yelled, 'Kill!'

Under an overcast sky, the streets of Shanghai were almost deserted. On the long drive across the city from the detention house to the prison hospital at Ti Lan Chiao, I saw only a few people bundled up in their padded winter jackets struggling on the pavement against the sharp north wind. I felt very ill but it was so long since I had seen the streets of the city that I made a special effort to observe the changes caused by the Cultural Revolution. Somehow, I had hoped that what I might see would give a hint of my daughter's life under the new circumstances.

There was evidence of destruction everywhere; scorched buildings with blackened windows, uprooted trees and shrubs and abandoned vehicles. Debris whirled in the wind. Grey bent figures were digging hopefully among heaped rubbish. Traffic lights were not operating. Slogans and quotations covered the walls of every building we passed. They were even plastered on the sides of buses and trucks. Some were chalked on the pavements. Instead of policemen, armed soldiers patrolled the streets. We passed several truckloads of helmeted Revolutionaries armed with iron rods and shouting slogans, probably on their way to carry out revolutionary actions against some rival factions. Large portraits of Mao on wooden boards several feet high stood at main street corners. Painted to make the old man look extremely youthful, healthy and fat (a sign of well-being in China), these pictures provided a mocking contrast to the thin, pale-faced pedestrians walking listlessly below them.

Ti Lan Chiao was the name of a district of Shanghai in which the city's main prison was located. In time, Ti Lan Chiao became the three characters used to denote the prison itself. The prison complex was enormous, covering many acres of land. Prisoners who had already passed through the various detention houses of the city and had been sentenced were sent there. There were political prisoners as well as common criminals considered unsuitable for labour camps, either because they were too ill or too old for heavy physical work or because their special skills could be better utilized in the numerous workshops run by the prison. No one knew for certain how many prisoners were kept in the large prison compound, but it was widely believed that over twenty thousand men and women laboured in the various workshops, producing goods that ranged from primitive computers to buttons, some for the export market.

The prison hospital was situated inside the Ti Lan Chiao prison compound. I noticed that security was more strict here than at the No. 1 Detention House. The jeep passed through two checkpoints where its papers were carefully scrutinized before it was allowed to drive through the heavy iron gate guarded by more soldiers. The guards who looked into the jeep had revolvers at their belts.

The prison compound looked extremely bleak, with not a single tree or plant in the entire place. It included many workshops with the sound of motors moving at high speed, a row of houses for interrogation and administration, all marked with written notices, and a lot of brightly coloured slogans denouncing class enemies and urging hard work in production as a means of reform. In the distance, enclosed by a tall steep fence, stood six huge buildings with windows covered by black wooden boards just like mine, so I surmised that those buildings were the living quarters of the prisoners.

The guard led me into the hospital building. The walls inside were covered with slogans, quotations and large posters showing Mao's portrait. Whoever had done the decoration had done a thorough job; even the glass windowpanes were painted with Mao's face. Some had a red heart pierced with an arrow underneath his face while others had the Chinese character for loyalty – Chung – written beside them.

The waiting room of the prison hospital could only be described as a scene of hell, though no one was being devoured by wild beasts, burning in a roaring fire or drowning in boiling sea. This was a hell of poverty and silent suffering, full of emaciated human beings draped in tattered clothes, with pain and agony clearly written on their wasted faces, waiting patiently for the end. Whether ravaged by illness or hunger or both, they appeared to be past the stage where the skill of a medical doctor could make them whole again. I had heard of the high mortality rate at Ti Lan Chiao. Now I was having a glimpse of the cases that would shortly contribute to the next statistic.

Besides the hunched figures on the benches, there were others wrapped in patched quilts lying on dirty canvas stretchers placed on the cement floor. Right in front of where I was told to sit was an old man with a bald head on one of these stretchers. Except for spasms of quick and jerky breathing through his half-open mouth, he seemed already dead, with sunken closed eyes and transparent skin tautly stretched over his waxen face.

With all the windows closed, the air in the room, smelling of a mixture of disinfectant and human decay, was foul and stifling. I closed my eyes to shut out the depressing sight and tried to hold my breath while I waited for my turn to see the doctor.

'1806!' A nurse in a gown that had been white but had become worn and washed into a neutral colour of dingy grey called at the door of the waiting room.

I followed her into the clinic where the female guard who brought me there was talking to a middle-aged woman doctor. In the middle of the large room there was a stove with a kettle boiling on it. Around the stove were small tables behind which sat doctors in the process of examining patients. There was no concession to customary Chinese decorum. Men and women undressed in full view of others in the room, and the questions and answers exchanged by the doctors and patients could be heard by everyone. At the time, I thought this crude practice was due to the fact that prisoners were not generally looked upon as human beings. But after my release, I was to discover that all hospitals in Shanghai had degenerated to a similar low standard during the Cultural Revolution.

While I was busily thinking how best to respond if the doctor should ask me to undress, she handed me a thermometer. I put it into my mouth. Fortunately that was all she wanted to do. When she looked at the thermometer, she said to the female guard, 'She had better stay here for a few days. Her temperature is very high. The ward is on the fifth floor. I don't think she should walk up. She had better be carried on a stretcher.'

'Please let me try to walk,' I pleaded with her. The very thought of lying on that dirty stretcher was unbearable.

The doctor had a deeply lined face with greying hair at her temples. Her soft eyes were kind and full of understanding. Perhaps she realized my reluctance to come into contact with the dirty stretcher, for she said to the guard, 'You may use the lift for the staff. It's quicker than waiting for a stretcher. She is really very ill, probably with pneumonia.'

The female guard went with me to the ward on the fifth floor. After cautioning me not to discuss my case with anybody, she told me that my washbasin and face towel would be brought over from the detention house when the guards came again with other sick prisoners.

Then she handed me over to a young woman with a Labour Reform badge pinned on the front of her jacket. A soldier on duty stood a few feet away watching us.

The ward was a small room with five beds in it. The two near the door were occupied. I was given the innermost one against the wall, separated from the other two women by two empty beds. The Labour Reform girl told me to undress and lie down.

How good it was to rest my feverish aching body on a real bed again! The unbleached calico sheets were rough but quite clean. Though the room was icy cold, the quilt was thick. I took off my jacket and trousers and lay down in my sweaters and long knitted pants. The girl brought another quilt and laid it across the bed. I soon fell asleep.

For the next few days, I drifted in and out of consciousness, sometimes faintly aware of my surroundings but mostly in a dream world of my own. When my mind came into focus again, I found my arm bound to the side of the bed. The needle in my vein was attached to a long rubber tube which led to a bottle held upsidedown on top of a tall stand. I was being fed intravenously by the liquid dripping through the rubber tube into my arm. The Labour Reform girl was pushing a thermometer into my mouth to take my temperature. Then she saw that I was fully awake, she untied my arm, removed the needle and took everything away. Though I seemed to have regained full consciousness, I felt languid and drowsy.

After a while, she brought me a bowl of steaming liquid. 'Drink it!' she said.

Although my arm was stiff, I held the bowl quite steadily. Lifting my head from the pillow, I drank the liquid. It tasted rather strange. Then I realized that it was soya bean milk with quite a lot of sugar. Since I had not had sugar for a long time, I did not immediately recognize its sweet taste.

I seemed much better. The dizziness had gone and my head was clear. I put my hand on my forehead. It felt cool and moist with perspiration. The young woman came back with a small syringe filled with a milky liquid. She told me to turn on my side. I braced myself, remembering the experience with the young medical soldier. But I felt no pain, for she gave the injection swiftly and expertly. She worked like a professional nurse, she held the syringe like a professional nurse and she walked in the pert way that only a professional nurse, confident of her skill, walks. I was sure that in real life she had been a professional nurse. I wondered with a deep feeling of sadness what had brought her to do Labour Reform in the ward of a prison hospital.

For the evening meal, she gave me a bowl of softly cooked rice and a plate of vegetables with a whole yellow fish on top cooked in oil and soya sauce with scallion and garlic. The fish was only a tiny one, no longer than six inches, but it tasted more delicious than anything I remembered. I ate it all up. My toilet things were on a chair beside my bed. On the floor was a bedpan and a chamber pot. I managed to get out of bed and give myself a badly needed wash.

After the young woman had taken away the empty dishes, a soldier locked the heavy steel door of the ward and retired to his room some distance away. One of the women occupying one of the other beds came over to chat to me.

'You were unconscious for six days. They thought you were going to die. Do you feel better now?' She was as thin as a reed, with hollow cheeks, colourless dry skin but burning bright eyes. Her padded jacket was patched and patched again. She looked over sixty but her voice was that of a young woman of thirty. She spoke in low whispers, constantly glancing at the door.

I nodded and smiled at her, glad to have her company but still too weak to enjoy talking. She sat down on the edge of my bed.

'Have you just been transferred to Ti Lan Chiao? When did you receive your sentence?' she asked me.

Remembering the warning of the female guard not to discuss my case with anyone, I said nothing but merely smiled again.

'Don't be afraid. I won't report you. Here we prisoners have to protect each other, you know,' she told me. After a moment's pause, she asked me, 'Have you got TB? This is a TB ward. That's why we get better food. But I go back to the cell tomorrow because I no longer cough blood. When my condition deteriorates and I cough blood again, they will let me come back here to have a rest and receive streptomycin injections. They don't bother to cure us, but they don't let us die either,' she sighed.

'I'm sorry you have TB ...' I felt a surge of sympathy for her.

'Nearly everybody gets it sooner or later at this place. It's inevitable really. We catch it from one another. Twenty people in one cell, sleeping within inches of one another, how can we avoid it? And there is the poor diet and hard work.'

'Do you work? What do you do?' I asked out of curiosity.

'Sewing. Ten hours and more a day and six days a week I sew buttons and make buttonholes on cardigans. They are for export, so the work must be good. It earns me a few yuan a month for soap and toilet paper. My husband cannot afford to send me any money. We have three children.' Talking about herself depressed her. She bowed her head, almost in tears. But she continued to sit by my side. I thought she wanted to have someone to talk to. As for me, after being in solitary confinement for so long, I found her presence by my side strangely comforting.

'I was an accountant in a factory where my husband is a technician. It was a good job, but I carelessly threw it away,' she said.

'Did you do something wrong with the money in your charge?' I asked her.

'No, nothing like that. I criticized our Party Secretary. Someone reported me during the Elimination of Counter-revolutionaries Campaign in 1956. I was denounced but I fought back. Instead of apologizing to the Party Secretary, I said more. I was so inexperienced! The Party Secretary got angry and included me in the list of counter-revolutionaries he was drawing up for our factory. I was arrested and sentenced to twelve years.'

'Could you not appeal to a higher court? To criticize your Party Secretary is not so serious a mistake. Twelve years is a long sentence.'

'What's the use? A higher court would only refer the case to my Party Secretary again. The Security Bureau always cooperates with Party Secretaries. You know the Chinese saying, "An official is always on the side of another official." '

'Well, you have been here a long time already. The worst is behind you. You will soon be reunited with your family.' I tried to comfort her.

'It won't be long now. I hope when I see them again my children will still recognize me and my husband hasn't got involved with another woman.'

'Don't they come to see you on visiting days?' I knew that once a prisoner was sentenced and sent to Ti Lan Chiao, he or she was allowed a monthly visit by a family member. In fact prisoners left for a long time in various detention houses often made false confessions to get sentenced so that they could see members of their families.

'No, I asked them to sever their relationship with me, as soon as I was sentenced. That was the only way to make sure my husband retained his job and to protect the children. You know how badly treated are the families of counter-revolutionaries. My husband and I were very much in love. Ours wasn't an arranged marriage. When I told him to divorce me and never come to see me again, he cried bitterly and told me that he would pretend to divorce me but in fact wait for me.'

I felt terribly sad for her but I could find nothing to say to her that might lighten her burden. She was again lost in thought. After some time, she changed the subject.

'You are lucky to have that nice doctor. She is highly qualified, a graduate from a world-famous medical college in the United States, I heard. She's very kind and considerate of others. When I first came here, she was still a prisoner like us. After her release, she came back to work here. I heard she volunteered to come. It's very hard to go back to the outside world after being here. People outside don't want to associate with ex-prisoners. Your superior doesn't dare to assign you to a decent job and there is no hope of promotion. You are a marked person, always singled out for insults and criticism. Once a counter-revolutionary, always a counter-revolutionary. You suffer for it in prison and you suffer for it afterwards. Your family suffers for it too. I have seen others in our factory treated like that. Now, I'm one of them. Sometimes I dread going out of here back into the world again.'

I was shocked to the core to hear that the woman doctor had been a prisoner at Ti Lan Chiao. It never occurred to me that behind her kind face there was a sad story, but then, she did have a very special expression in her eyes, not just kindness and understanding. It was almost as if she had some special knowledge of life that made her extremely wise and tolerant.

'She came back to China from abroad in response to the People's Government's call for patriotic Chinese from the United States to come back and serve the people. I understand she had a good job there. But she gave it up and returned. Even when I first met her, she was always speaking frankly, like a foreigner. Of course, she got into trouble.'

In the early 1950s, the Chinese People's Government mounted a quiet propaganda campaign through their agents and sympathizers among overseas Chinese to persuade Chinese intellectuals living in the United States to return to China and 'help with national reconstruction'. The real purpose of the campaign was to attract physicists who could help China to build the atomic bomb, but the campaign was conducted in general terms to avoid attracting attention to Peking's real purpose. Strong appeals were made to the patriotic feelings of all Chinese intellectuals living abroad everywhere, but especially in the United States. Quite a number in different professions responded. They abandoned good jobs and comfortable living standards to answer the call of the motherland and returned to China, only to find that they were not really wanted. The Communist Party officials' deep suspicion of anyone with what they called 'foreign connections' and their prejudice against all intellectuals added to the difficulties of the returnees. Since the strained relationship between Washington and Peking made it impossible for them to return to the United States, they had to put up with the conditions in China as best they could. A few lucky ones made their way to Hong Kong. But the majority remained inside China and accepted whatever jobs the Party was willing to give them. Many suffered persecution during one political campaign after another, especially the Anti-Rightists Campaign of 1957. Those who survived to 1966 were virtually all caught up in the net of the Proletarian Cultural Revolution. Only the physicists working on China's nuclear arms programme were protected by Prime Minister Chou En-lai. It was a sad story of callous disregard for human rights and another instance of the readiness of the Chinese Communist Party to sacrifice individuals for political purposes.

We sat in silence in the hospital ward, each with her own thoughts. The patient in the other bed began to groan and cough. At the sound of a door opening in the distance, the prisoner sitting on my bed became nervous. She said goodnight to me and slipped into her own bed.

I lay there wide awake. My thoughts were with my daughter. Where was she at that moment? Was she well and managing to cope with the complicated situation of the Cultural Revolution? I prayed to God to guide and protect her.

Next morning, I got out of bed just to put my feet on the floor. I was still very weak and my heart palpitated wildly when I moved about. Afterwards, I took a few steps each day until I could walk round the ward easily. With nutritious food and medication, I gradually became stronger.

There were now only two of us in the room. The other woman was very ill and never left her bed. Once I walked to her side, but she did not open her eyes and seemed unaware of my presence. Beside her pillow was a container half full of sputum and blood. Her face was like old parchment and she lay there without moving except when she coughed. At mealtimes, the Labour Reform girl fed her with a spoon.

I never asked the Labour Reform girl any questions and she did not venture to speak. But we smiled at each other to convey our friendly feelings. Although she brought nutritious food to me, I noticed that she herself had only the usual rice with cabbage or boiled sweet potatoes. She was poorly dressed and seemed always cold, with her lips blue and her shoulders hunched. I tried to give her one of the sweaters I was wearing. I took it off when she wasn't in the room, and when she came in, I tried to give it to her without speaking because of the soldier outside. However, she was too frightened to accept. She looked at the prostrate form of the woman at the other end of the room nervously and pushed the sweater back to me.

A year later, when I was ill and back in the hospital again, she was no longer there. I liked to think she was now working on the ward of an ordinary hospital in Shanghai, walking pertly, syringe in hand, ministering to the sick.

After another week, when my temperature was normal, the doctor told me I could return to the No. 1 Detention House. She spoke softly and her eyes were full of kindness as if she saw something good and lovable in me that I was not aware of myself. There was something saintly about this woman, I thought. I did not believe she came back to work at the prison hospital because she could not cope with the outside world after imprisonment. I believed she came back because she knew the prisoners needed her. She had found a mission to which she could devote her life even though her position was not honourable or rewarding in the eyes of the world. She seemed to possess great spiritual strength. She had obviously become a finer person because of her suffering.

A few days later, when a guard brought other prisoners to the hospital, he took me back to the No. 1 Detention House.

CHAPTER 8
Party Factions

THE BOUT OF PNEUMONIA I suffered in the winter of 1967 marked the beginning of rapid physical deterioration. The prolonged lack of nutritious food, sunshine and fresh air made full recovery impossible and caused the body's ageing process to be speeded up. It also reduced my mental powers to such an extent that I often found it difficult to concentrate on one subject for long. To think logically and analytically required a great deal of conscious effort. I was beginning to understand why abject poverty produces a vacant stare and lethargic movements. In fact, I knew I was experiencing all the symptoms of mental and physical exhaustion that could lead to a breakdown. The prospect of losing my ability to think clearly frightened me more than the fact that my hair was falling out by the handful, my gums bled and I had lost a great deal of weight. The psychological effect of total isolation was also taking its toll. Often my mood was one of despair. Sometimes I had difficulty swallowing the meagre food I was given, even though I was desperately hungry.

Outside the prison walls, the general situation remained confused. In spite of military control, violence and factional wars by the Red Guards and the Revolutionaries continued well into 1968. It seemed that after unleashing the Red Guards and the Revolutionaries to serve his political purposes, Mao Tze-tung was no longer able to control them. The detention house could not resume normal working order as long as the political situation remained unsettled. No one would be in a position to deal seriously with my case and I would be left in the cell waiting. The fear that I might die before my case could be clarified became a real one.

One day, after the Labour Reform girl had given me cold water, I could hardly carry the filled basin from the small window to place it on the usual spot only a couple of feet away. My hands shook and my heart palpitated wildly. My legs were so wobbly that I had to place the basin on the floor and sit down.

While I sat on the bed panting to catch my breath, I thought that if I was going to survive the Cultural Revolution, I must discipline myself with physical and mental exercise. Inspired by my own resolution, I stood up rather abruptly. Dark shadows almost blinded me and I had to sit down again. But from that day onwards, I devised a series of exercises that moved every part of my body from my head to my toes and did them twice a day. At first, the exercise exhausted me and I had to interrupt it with frequent periods of rest. Also I had to avoid the prying eyes of the guards, as exercise other than the few minutes of walking in the cell after meals was forbidden. Nevertheless, I managed to exercise each day and after a few months recovered my physical strength somewhat as well as my feeling of well-being.

For mental exercise, I first tried to memorize some of Mao's essays which I thought would enable me better to understand his mentality and to use his quotations more fluently when I had to face an interrogator again. I liked best of all his essay on guerrilla warfare in which he advocated the importance of seizing the initiative whenever and wherever possible so that a small band of poorly equipped guerrillas could cause havoc and defeat a well equipped army. Although Mao was a hateful dictator who had killed millions of Chinese people and imprisoned more with his political campaigns and had several times brought the nation's economy to the brink of ruin with his disastrous economic policy, I had to concede that he was a brilliant strategist in guerrilla warfare. While his essays on Marxist principles were often half-baked, his essay on guerrilla warfare was, I thought, a masterpiece of clear thinking based on the experience of the Communist Army. But in the last analysis, to study Mao's books for many hours a day was in itself a depressing occupation for me, his victim, because it constantly reminded me of his evil power prevailing on my own fate and my own impotence to overcome it.

I turned instead to the T'ang dynasty poetry I had learned as a schoolgirl. It really amazed me that I was able to dig out verses from the deep recesses of my brain that had lain dormant for decades. Trying to remember poems I thought I had forgotten was a joyful occupation. Whenever I managed to piece together a whole poem, I felt a sense of happy accomplishment. The immortal words of the great T'ang poets not only helped to improve my memory but also transported me from the grim reality of the prison cell to a world of beauty and freedom.

My persistent efforts to maintain sanity had a measure of success. But there were still moments when I was so burdened with hunger and misery that I was tempted to let go my tenuous grip on the lifeline of survival. At those times, I had to depend on conflict with the guards to stimulate my fighting spirit.

'Report!' I would walk to the door of the cell and call out with all my strength.

'What do you want?' Shuffling footsteps approached my cell as the guard spoke lazily. 'How many times do I have to tell you not to shout?'

'How long do I have to wait for the government to investigate my case? It's illegal to lock up an innocent person in prison. It's against Chairman Mao's teachings.' In fact no mention was ever made in his four volumes of such practice, but I was pretty sure that the semi-literate guard had not read Mao's books thoroughly.

'Hush! Don't shout! The government will deal with your case in due course. You are not the only one.'

'But I have been here such a long time already. I want to see the interrogator!' I would raise my voice deliberately.

'Lower your voice! You mustn't shout! The interrogator is busy.' I knew very well that there was no interrogator working at that time. She knew I knew it, but we kept up the pretence.

The prison was exceptionally silent. Our voices carried to the four corners of the building. I knew the other prisoners were listening, as they had nothing else to do. I also knew that they probably enjoyed hearing another prisoner being defiant, just as I felt encouraged whenever I heard another prisoner brave enough to answer the guards back. The knowledge of the other prisoners listening to my exchange with the guard forged a link between them and me. I no longer felt alone. Encouraged by what I was sure was their silent approval, I acted with renewed effort, though I was already fatigued by my own shouting.

'I'm innocent. I've never committed any crime. I've never done anything to oppose the People's Government. You have no right to lock up a law-abiding citizen! I demand rehabilitation and an apology!' I yelled at the top of my voice.

'Have you gone mad? Keep quiet!' The guard was now shouting in anger.

'I'm not mad. The person who ordered my imprisonment was mad.'

'Do you want to be punished for creating a disturbance?'

I heard urgent footsteps. Another guard had come to join her. The second guard said, 'You are committing a crime at this moment by creating a disturbance.'

'Our Great Leader Chairman Mao taught us, "Lay out the facts; speak with reason." I'm merely following his instructions. I'm innocent. I've not committed a crime. I should say so.' I argued in a loud voice.

'Come out!'

The guard would unlock the door of the cell and lead me into a room in a remote corner of the prison compound where we could continue to shout at each other without being heard by the other prisoners. I would give in and stop talking when I became utterly exhausted. Sometimes my endurance outlasted the guards' patience. When that happened, they resorted to physical violence to silence me, either hitting my body or kicking my legs. They called me a 'hysterical old woman' and often deplored my 'mad fits', but they never knew my real purpose in provoking them. During my six and a half years of solitary confinement, I deliberately caused scenes such as this many times. Whenever deep depression overwhelmed me to the extent that I could no longer sleep or swallow food, I would intentionally seek an encounter with the guards.

Though my arms became bruised and my legs bear to this day scars inflicted by their heavy leather boots, I always enjoyed a period of good humour and calm spirits after fighting with the guards. Then tension would gradually build up in me again. I believed that what I needed was human contact; even encounters with the guards was better than complete isolation. Besides, fighting was a positive action much more encouraging to the human spirit than merely enduring hardship with patience, known as a virtue of the Chinese race. Many of my friends and acquaintances survived their ordeal during the Cultural Revolution by that virtue. But for me, only the positive stimulant of fighting buoyed up my spirits.

On 6 August, a particularly stifling hot summer's day, the newspaper came very late. I overheard the male guard who brought copies of the newspaper to the women's prison saying to the female guard on duty, 'Very important news!' I wondered what it was. But I had to wait until nearly bedtime for the newspaper to reach my cell.

I saw that on the paper's front page in large characters, with banner headlines printed in red, was the news item that the day before Mao Tze-tung had sent a basket of mangoes to the workers and peasants engaged in indoctrinating the students at the famous Tsinghua University in Peking. The mangoes had been originally a gift to Mao from Pakistan's foreign minister when he came for an official visit. The newspaper reported the jubilation and excitement of the workers when Mao's gift was brought to them. According to the report, the workers and peasants cheered with joy and wept with gratitude. Chanting Mao's quotations, they pledged their loyalty to the Leader.

Although I did not know that Mao had disowned the Red Guards when he called together their leaders in Peking and criticized their violence a few days before, I recognized immediately that Mao's well-publicized action had important political significance. Undoubtedly the workers and peasants had been sent to Tsinghua, one of China's leading universities where the Red Guards' organization had been especially militant and unruly, to restrain the young Revolutionaries. To make a present to the workers and peasants there rather than to the Red Guards in Tsinghua was a clear and eloquent warning to the Tsinghua Red Guards not to resist the disciplinary actions of the workers sent to tame them.

For the next few days, the newspaper reported the organization of 'Mao Tze-tung Thought Propaganda Teams' all over the country. Photographs of these men marching into universities and schools appeared daily. Although named 'Workers' and Peasants' Propaganda Teams for Mao Tze-tung Thought', the teams included no peasants and few workers. They were composed mainly of military men in civilian clothes and Party officials considered to be loyal by the Maoist leaders such as Mao's wife Chiang Ching and the Defence Minister Lin Piao.

Although Communist totalitarianism in China was in essence military dictatorship, from the inception of its power in 1949 Mao and the Chinese Communist Party were always careful to keep the gun in the background and to create an impression of civilian rule by persuasion rather than by military coercion. Political indoctrination was the preferred method used to bend the will of the populace. Only in extreme cases of mass armed uprising in remote areas inhabited by minority races had troops been called out. To use the Workers' and Peasants' Propaganda Teams to overcome the resistance of the Red Guards and restore order by non-military means rather than to use the speedier method of sending in contingents of soldiers illustrated once more how anxious Mao was to preserve this carefully cultivated image of a benign government.

While the Red Guards were being dealt with, the Maoist leadership in Peking continued in their efforts to organize provincial and municipal Revolutionary Committees, a new name for the provincial and municipal governments, and to form new Party Secretariats. The newspaper frequently published leading articles expressing the hope that this process should be speeded up so that conditions would become felicitous for the convening of the Ninth Party Congress. I concluded that the Maoists who had seized power were anxious to give themselves official status by being elected to the Central Committee and the Politburo of the Party and to have the old officials they had ousted from office expelled from the Party so as to remove any possible future threat to their own power.

Time dragged on and it was again autumn. With each rainy day, the temperature dropped a few degrees. I had thought that by adhering to a

regimen of mental and physical exercise I had stalled the rapid
deterioration of my health. So it was quite a shock when something new
and alarming happened. I had been losing an unusually large amount of
blood at each menstrual period. When the interval between
haemorrhages shortened and the amount of blood lost increased to the
extent that every ten days or so blood dripped out of my body for several
days, I became very frightened. Yet remembering my experience with
the untrained medical orderly, I did not dare to ask for medical
attention. Depression once again overtook me; I often had nightmares
from which I would waken sweating and panting for breath.

One night in October, while I was still struggling with my own
physical problems, the guard went again from cell to cell to order the
prisoners to sit quietly to listen to a broadcast. A man's voice came
through the loudspeaker to make the startling announcement that at a
Central Committee meeting presided over by Mao, a resolution was
passed to expel Liu Shao-chi, the Chairman of the Chinese People's
Republic, from the Chinese Communist Party and to strip him of all
his official positions.

Liu Shao-chi, a long-time Communist Party leader, was second only
to Mao Tze-tung in the Party hierarchy. When Mao was leading the
armed struggle from the Chinese Soviet in Ching Gang Shan in the
early thirties, Liu was directing the Communist underground in
Kuomintang-held areas. After 1949, when Mao occupied the twin
positions of Chairman of the Central Committee of the Communist
Party and Chairman of the Chinese People's Republic, Liu Shao-chi
was the General Secretary of the Communist Party. The two men
worked in close collaboration and there was no sign that Liu was trying
to usurp power from Mao. Indeed, the term 'Mao Tze-tung Thought'
was coined by Liu Shao-chi in his report as Party Secretary at the
Seventh Party Congress held in 1945. However, in 1960, after the
failure of Mao's Great Leap Forward Campaign when China's fragile
economy was pushed to the brink of ruin, Mao Tze-tung relinquished
the position of Chairman of the People's Republic in favour of Liu
Shao-chi. The rumour that reached the Chinese people was that there
had been fierce debates within the Party leadership and Mao had been
obliged to make a humiliating gesture of self-criticism in front of a
meeting of seven thousand leading Party officials.

Liu Shao-chi immediately adopted a series of policy reversals to save
the rapidly deteriorating economic situation. When his economic
policy succeeded where Mao's had failed and Liu Shao-chi was seen to
become an increasingly popular leader by Party members and the

Chinese people, eclipsing Mao Tze-tung in influence and importance, Mao became alarmed. He carefully plotted to destroy the man who threatened his position for he feared losing not only everything he had believed in and worked for but also his place in history.

While the Great Proletarian Cultural Revolution was different things to different people, the gigantic struggle lasting ten full years was essentially a contest of two conflicting Party policies personified by Mao Tze-tung and Liu Shao-chi. The irony of the situation was that although Mao Tze-tung had Liu Shao-chi persecuted to death and seemed to have won during the Cultural Revolution, after his death, Deng Hsiao-ping led China along the route of economic liberalization first tried by Liu Shao-chi twenty years earlier, and went much further than anybody in China or the rest of the world could possibly have imagined during the days of the Cultural Revolution.

In the resolution passed by the Central Committee, Liu was declared 'a traitor, a hidden agent and a scab'. However, no evidence was offered to substantiate the accusation, and, as was customary in Communist China, the victim was not allowed to defend himself. Furthermore, for the meeting of the Central Committee rather than a meeting of the Party Congress to expel Liu Shao-chi was not strictly legal. But at the zenith of his power, Mao could afford to ignore this fine point.

After the announcement of the Central Committee resolution against Liu Shao-chi, the nation's propaganda machinery was mobilized to denounce him. Day after day, the newspaper was filled with articles listing Liu Shao-chi's 'crimes', the foremost of which always seemed to be that he 'opposed the policies of the Great Leader'. The newspaper also described mass meetings held all over the country for the people to voice their 'strong and unanimous support' for the resolution and to express their deep hatred of Liu. I concluded that the primary objective of the radical-controlled press was to frighten those who might sympathize with Liu Shao-chi and to silence them. Therefore, while the newspaper gave the impression that the whole nation hated Liu Shao-chi, I knew it was not true, because long ago I had learned how to read the Communist press like so many of my fellow compatriots. Having lived in China since the Communist Party assumed power, I knew that probably most of the non-Party members of the country were indifferent because they had no special feelings for either Mao Tze-tung or Liu Shao-chi, while the Party members, except for a small group of Maoists, were doubtless embarrassed by this development, because it exposed the ugly nature of Party politics.

When the cold wind again swept down from the north and frosty nights left the iron bars on the window glistening with moisture in the mornings, a 'Workers' and Peasants' Propaganda Team for Mao Tze-tung Thought' came to the No. 1 Detention House to assist the Military Control Commission in conducting the Cultural Revolution. There was no formal announcement of their arrival on the loudspeaker as there had been when the detention house was placed under military control. However, when the prisoners were given outdoor exercise, I saw strips of coloured paper with slogans of welcome to the team pasted on the walls of the prison compound. 'The working class must exercise leadership in everything' – a Marxist slogan used to herald the arrival of a 'Workers' and Peasants' Propaganda Team' to every organization – was in prominent display.

A few weeks later, prisoners were being called for interrogation again. With hope and expectation I heard the familiar sound of loud clangs when the heavy bolts on the doors were being driven into place. I asked the guard's permission to write a letter to the Workers' and Peasants' Propaganda Team for Mao Tze-tung Thought, half expecting her to refuse. But to my surprise she handed me a sheet of paper, a pen and a bottle of ink. I wrote a polite letter requesting investigation of my case, using quotations from Mao's Little Red Book, now the usual practice to demonstrate a writer's correct political standpoint. Every article in the newspaper was sprinkled with them. After I had handed the letter to the guard, I waited for the resumption of my long-interrupted interrogation.

One day, I had another haemorrhage which stained my underclothes. I was washing them when a female guard came to the peephole.

She opened the small window and said to me, 'What's happened to you? How did your trousers get stained with blood?'

'It's just my period.'

'There's such a lot of blood. Is this normal?' She unlocked the door and came into the cell. The toilet was full of bloody toilet paper I was going to wash down with the water I was using to wash my underclothes.

'Why did you not report your condition?' She stood there staring at me for a while before leaving the cell and locking the door behind her.

Later, she brought the young doctor, who seemed to have got his job back again.

After asking me my age, the doctor said, 'You are probably having your menopause. But you might also have a growth. You should be examined by a gynaecologist but there isn't one at the prison hospital.

I'll give you some injections to stop the bleeding.'

The injections he gave me were effective. But I was left with the nagging fear that I might have a growth and that the growth might be malignant. More than ever, I was anxious to leave the No. 1 Detention House.

It was a bitterly cold January day in 1969, over two years after my last interrogation at the end of 1966, when things finally started moving for me again.

I was seated on the bed in my usual posture with a volume of Mao's books on my lap when the door of the cell was unlocked and two Labour Reform girls came in. Behind them, the militant female guard who had searched my cell positioned herself in the open doorway, with her hands on her wide hips, watching. Another guard was hovering behind her in the shadows. The Labour Reform girls removed my things from the top of the two stacked beds I was using as a table and placed them on the floor. Then they carried the top bed to the window.

'Pick up your things! Do you think your old servants will come here to pick them up for you?' the militant female guard shouted sarcastically.

While I was putting my things back on the remaining bed, the Labour Reform girls brought in a bedroll and a washbasin. A female prisoner in her early thirties followed them into the cell. She walked in slowly with her head bowed in the manner required of all prisoners and carried in her hands a few articles of clothing.

After the Labour Reform girls withdrew from the cell, the guard locked the door.

After living in isolation for so long, I was as thirsty for human contact and companionship as a man lost in the desert is thirsty for water. My first reaction to the arrival of another prisoner in my cell was a lightening of spirit and a readiness to show her welcome. But my awareness of the Maoists' fondness for devious practices warned me not to accept the situation at its face value. I returned to my seat and again bent my head over my book while I tried to assess this rather unexpected development. Since military control had been imposed and the Cultural Revolution had entered a new phase, the work of the detention house seemed to have slackened. There was no large influx of new prisoners. In fact, I detected a thinning down of the prison population when I noticed fewer footsteps in the cell overhead during exercise periods. The arrival of another prisoner in my cell did not appear to be due to overcrowding. I waited for events to enlighten me.

The new arrival was arranging her things on the bed but from time to time she stole glances in my direction, as if hoping to catch my eye.

'How long have you been here already? Is it very bad? Do they beat people?' Finally she came over to sit beside me while she whispered.

I was surprised at the implication of her remarks. She did not look like a newly arrested person fresh from freedom and a full rice bowl. Her face had that unhealthy pallor tinged with grey peculiar to prisoners who have been locked up for quite some time. Her hair was thin, brownish and dry as straw from lack of protein in her diet, and her clothing hung on her starved body in the same way as mine did. She looked at me with lacklustre eyes that were desperate and frightened.

'We mustn't talk. It's not allowed,' I told her. I shot a glance at the peephole and caught sight of a black eye before it hastily disappeared from view. It was strange that the guard did not open the small window to scold her when she moved over to sit beside me on my bed, I thought.

When we were given our evening meal, she ate her portion of sweet potatoes very quickly. Seeing that I took only a few pieces to put into my mug to eat, she grabbed the container and tipped the rest into her own. While she was eating, she muttered, 'We mustn't waste food.'

While I did not object to her having what was left of my portion of sweet potatoes, the episode proved beyond doubt to me that she had been lying when she implied by her initial question that she had just been arrested. She was much too hungry.

If I had been familiar with prison practice, I would have suspected her role immediately. But it was years later that I learned that it was a rule of the Security Bureau never to put two prisoners in one cell. The minimum number for multiple cells was three because the prison authorities believed that it was more difficult for three prisoners to conspire together than for two.

I sat on my bed waiting to see what she was going to do next. But apart from using my soap and toilet paper, she made no further attempt to speak to me.

Next morning, after the news broadcasts, she again came to sit next to me.

'I just hate this terrible Cultural Revolution, don't you? My home was looted by the detestable Red Guard. Was your home looted too?'

I had heard so frequently from the loudspeaker that people were sentenced to long terms of imprisonment just for criticising the Cultural Revolution and the action of the Red Guards that I knew such criticism was regarded as an extremely serious offence. It was extraordinary for her to express her feelings so freely, unless, of course, she had been told to do so by the guards as a means to prompt me to agree with her. So I just answered, 'You shouldn't complain. Why don't you read Chairman Mao's books rather than just sitting here chatting? If the guard sees us talking to each other, we will be punished.'

I looked around the cell and discovered that she did not have a set of Mao's books. Since the beginning of the Cultural Revolution, Mao's books had become an essential part of every Chinese, as important as his shirt or trousers and just as necessary for protection, because having or not having Mao's books was taken as a test of a man's political reliability. Besides, I remembered one of the prison rules I had been told to read aloud on the night I arrived at the detention house dealt with the fact every prisoner was required to study Mao's books. How could she have been brought into prison without them? The only explanation seemed to me to be that she had been removed from another cell rather hastily into mine. There hadn't been time to gather up all her things. That was probably why she had been obliged to use my soap and toilet paper the night before.

'Where are your books by Chairman Mao? Did they not make you bring them with you when you were brought to the detention house? How could they have overlooked that?' I exclaimed. Her face went red. I offered to lend her mine but she pushed them away.

'I don't want to read his books. I hate him. He destroyed my home. I think the Kuomintang was a great deal better than the Communist Party, don't you?'

Instinctively my eyes went to the peephole. No one was watching us. It was such a serious offence to praise the Kuomintang that I was more than ever convinced that she had been given a mandate to do so by the militant guard, probably a Maoist activist, anxious to incriminate me. I said, 'You mustn't talk wildly. I may report you, you know.'

But she ignored my caution and continued to try to make me talk. 'Were you not living in Shanghai before 1949? Wasn't the Kuomintang much better?' she persisted.

'I really have no idea what life was like before 1949. I was abroad,' I said.

'How lucky for you to have lived abroad! I hate living in China under the Communist Party! We have no freedom at all. Don't you hate the Communist Party?' she tried again.

'I'm a Christian. A Christian is supposed only to love and never to hate anybody. We even forgive those who have wronged us,' I told her.

I could see she was sceptical that I could forgive those who had wronged me because she smiled in a rather supercilious manner. Then, perhaps to gain my confidence, she suddenly declared, 'I'm also a Christian!'

'That's good! Let's say the Lord's Prayer together. Our Father who art in heaven ...' She did not join in but looked completely lost.

'You shouldn't pretend to be a Christian when you are not,' I said. 'But never mind, I'll teach you the Lord's Prayer.'

She shook her head, missing the opportunity to report me for spreading religious propaganda. I realized she did not have the intelligence to know that the Maoists who sent her would have been just as pleased to catch me teaching her the Lord's Prayer as to catch me saying derogatory things about the Communist Party. While the Communist Party claimed to allow the Chinese people religious freedom, to spread religious propaganda, that is, to talk about religion or to teach religious rites, was strictly forbidden even before the Cultural Revolution. Since the beginning of the Cultural Revolution, the penalty for religious observance in any form was very severe. Almost one of the first acts of the Red Guards was the destruction of all temples and churches and the punishment of nuns and monks.

In the afternoon, the same tough female guard unlocked the door and called my cellmate's number, 'Come out for interrogation!' she yelled.

I waited rather anxiously to see what would happen when they found that she had failed to incriminate me. After a couple of hours, she came back, wiping her eyes as if she had been crying. The sight of a tearful person always upset me; I was sorry she had to suffer because I had refused to fall into their trap. But I refrained from trying to comfort her, for I did not want to give her the opportunity of tricking me into saying something inadvertent. I expected her to try again. But I was surprised to find that she showed no more interest in talking to me.

For the whole of the next day, she did not try to engage me in conversation but looked out of the window as if lost in thought. However, a couple of times when she thought I was absorbed in reading, I caught her looking in my direction.

In the afternoon, she was called for interrogation again, and again she came back wiping her eyes. This went on for three successive days. On the fourth day, she did not come back. When the woman from the kitchen came to give us our evening meal, she gave me only one container of sweet potatoes. When I asked her for another for my roommate, the woman merely shook her head. However, I kept some of my sweet potatoes for her in my mug.

The loudspeaker was switched on. One guard followed by another came to my small window to make sure I was seated there ready to listen to the broadcast. An announcement was made of the sentences passed that afternoon on a number of prisoners. One death sentence was declared 'carried out immediately'. The number of the prisoner given was the same as that of the girl who had shared my cell. The announcer said that she had been a spy for the imperialists and the Kuomintang, 'hidden in our midst' for many years but was uncovered by the Red Guards and the Revolutionaries during the Cultural Revolution. She had been given the opportunity to confess and to earn lenient treatment but she did not confess because she had hoped 'to slip through'. Now she had been punished by 'the iron fist of the Dictatorship of the Proletariat' which had 'crushed her to powder'.

My first reaction was one of shock; the announcement of any death sentence was rather terrifying. I raised my head and caught sight of an eye glued to the peephole observing me. Like lightning, the realization struck me that she was neither a spy for anybody nor had ever been accused of being one. If I should show fear or nervousness at the announcement, the Maoists would interpret it as a sign of guilt. I stared straight at the door as if I were listening carefully to the broadcast while leaning against my bedroll in a relaxed posture.

When the loudspeaker was switched off, the guard opened the small window and called me over.

'Did you hear the announcement of the death sentence?' she asked me.

'Yes.'

'What do you think of the case of your former cellmate?'

'Since she was a spy for the imperialists and the Kuomintang, she deserved to die,' I said casually.

'You should consider her fate in relation to your own position,' the guard pointed out.

'I don't see the connection. She was a real spy. I'm not. I expect the People's Government to clarify my case and give me full rehabilitation in due course,' I answered.

'You are not being realistic,' she said.

'I don't agree. What could be more realistic than to trust the People's Government?' I said.

She closed the small window but remained at the peephole to watch me. I picked up one of Mao's books and sat down at my usual place on the bed, calmly reading.

Just before bedtime, the militant female guard opened the door of the cell. The Labour Reform girls came in and removed my former cellmate's things. They stacked the beds up again and left. This indicated that the girl was indeed alive. It was a bitterly cold night. The girl needed her quilt if she was not to freeze. They had to come to get it for her.

Since the guards had trusted her enough to let her undertake the task of trying to incriminate me, she must have been a prisoner they felt they could control and manipulate at will. She was probably promised some favour if she were successful in getting me to say something wrong. When she failed, they changed their tactics and pretended to sentence her to death in order to frighten me.

After the Labour Reform girls had left the cell, the militant female guard came in.

'Stand up!' she shouted threateningly, standing only a foot or so away from me.

When I stood up, she slapped my cheek with the back of her hand. The sting brought tears to my eyes but I blinked them back. I just stood there looking straight ahead as if nothing had happened and she wasn't there. This seemed to infuriate her further. She slapped me again and kicked my leg with her heavy boot.

'Remain standing! You are being punished. You are smart, aren't you? The imperialists trained you well, didn't they? Well, you won't get away with it. The proletariat is going to destroy you. Remain standing!'

She banged the heavy door shut and locked it before stumping down the corridor to the exit of the women's prison.

After the night duty guard came, she made her routine check of each cell. When she came to me, she asked, 'Why are you standing here?'

'I'm being punished by the other guard.'

'Which guard? The one on day duty?'

'No, another one.'

'You are imagining things. Go to bed!'

She did not seem to be in the picture at all. Perhaps the scheme to trap me was the work of only a few Maoists in the detention house. 'I'll never know the truth,' I said to myself. But I was glad I did not have to stand there all night.

One of the kicks had landed on my ankle, which was unprotected by my padded trousers. The bruise was throbbing and the skin was broken. The woollen socks I was wearing were not very clean; my only other pair hadn't dried in the damp cell. I was afraid the bruise might get infected. 'What to do?' I asked myself, while my eyes searched the

bare cell and my meagre belongings. When I saw the tube of
toothpaste, I decided it might contain some ingredients that were
antiseptic. So I smeared a thin layer of toothpaste over the wound and
laid on it a piece of cloth torn from an old shirt. Then I tied my ankle
up with the only handkerchief I had left.

My ankle was so painful that I had a restless night, waking frequently
from fragments of dreams in which I was either crippled and unable to
move or being kicked again and again by the same female guard.

The misery of hunger and cold, the interminable days of waiting, the
persistent yearning for freedom, the nagging worry for my daughter
and this latest abuse by the female guard produced the cumulative
effect of making me very angry. When I got out of bed next morning, I
was no longer depressed; I felt as if something inside me was about to
explode. I told myself that in my present circumstances such civilized
virtues as tolerance, forgiveness and even a sense of humour were
luxuries I could ill afford. The Maoists were deadly serious in their
design to destroy me. I must be equally serious in my efforts to
frustrate them.

Although I was tired because of lack of sleep, I was wide awake. My
ankle was swollen and painful but I paced the cell restlessly in urgent
strides, impatient to seek an encounter with the Maoists. The more I
thought of what Mao Tze-tung was doing to me, to my friends and a
multitude of other unknown fellow sufferers, the angrier I got. I swore
I would hit back at the Maoists somehow.

Suddenly the cell door was opened. It was almost as if God had
speedily granted me my wish for an encounter with the Maoists. 'Come
out for interrogation!' a male guard shouted.

I picked up Mao's Little Red Book of quotations with alacrity and
followed him down the corridor, limping hurriedly to keep up with
him.

The loudspeaker was broadcasting a leading article from the *People's
Daily* explaining Mao's latest directive: 'Dig deep tunnels, store grain
everywhere and never seek hegemony.' The reverent tone of voice of
the announcer followed me from loudspeaker to loudspeaker as I
followed the guard through the prison compound. While I listened to
his words of homage to Mao, I remembered Mao's awesome power
like a blanket over China threatening to smother whomsoever he
chose. I reminded myself to be careful not to say anything that could
be interpreted as opposition to Mao, the Communist Party or the
People's Government. If I did, I would become a 'counter-revolutionary' and the Maoists would have won a victory over me. My tactics

must be to insist that the officials in charge of my case were mistaken in their understanding of Mao's policy, while the policy itself was correct. If necessary, I would lie and declare that I supported Mao, even revered him, as so many other Chinese were doing daily in order to survive. To fight was not enough, I must fight well and intelligently, I warned myself.

A heavy quilted curtain of blue cotton covered the entrance to the interrogation building. The guards were no longer lolling on chairs in the small room at the entrance. They stood to attention, while armed soldiers patrolled the corridor. Several blue-uniformed men went in and out of the interrogation rooms, which had their doors open. It seemed the day's work had just begun and I was among the first to be called. Remembering what had happened the night before, I knew I was going to have an unpleasant encounter. The Maoists had hoped to trick me into saying something wrong and to frighten me. They had failed. While I cautioned myself to be alert and to be brave, I was eager to hear what they had to say. Whatever it was, they would reveal themselves to me. The more they revealed themselves to me, the more chance I would have of finding out what they really wanted of me and why. There was still much in the situation that was puzzling to me.

The guard opened the door of one of the rooms and shouted, 'Go in!'

The walls of the interrogation room had been whitewashed; it was much brighter and cleaner. On either side of the window were two long banners made of red cloth. Written on them with white paint were two slogans: 'Long Live the Dictatorship of the Proletariat' and 'Long Live Our Great Leader Chairman Mao'. A large reproduction of the official portrait of Mao was on the wall.

Five men, one of them in army uniform, were seated facing the door. I tried to assess their background and status. Since the abolition of military insignia by Defence Minister Lin Piao in 1963, all military personnel wore similar baggy, loose-fitting uniforms in a revival of the old guerrilla tradition. It was difficult to identify the rank of the round-faced young man sitting astride the chair in the gloomy interrogation room, but I saw his uniform had four pockets. This indicated that he was an officer, as soldiers were allowed only two pockets on their jackets. The other four wore the usual faded blue Mao suits. One was much older than the others. His face was deeply lined and his hands resting on top of the table were the calloused hands of an industrial worker. I assumed that the young man in uniform represented the Military Control Commission, the older worker and perhaps one or two of the others represented the Workers' and Peasants' Propaganda Team for Mao Tze-tung Thought while another one might be the representative of the Revolutionaries who had taken over the Public Security Bureau of Shanghai.

As I looked at the five men in the room, I knew that they were all beneficiaries of the Communist Revolution of 1949. Their attitude to Mao Tze-tung and to the Communist Party could not be expected to be the same as mine. I knew also that the old worker probably had only bad memories of the days before the Communist Party came to power and the others were hardly old enough to have any clear memories at all. Therefore, I could expect them to see me, the widow of an official of the former regime and the daughter of an affluent family, as an enemy. Furthermore, because China had closed her doors since 1949 and isolated herself from the western world, I knew that whatever these men knew of the West was simply the repeated criticisms of capitalism and imperialism which was fed them through official propaganda, including virulent attacks against the western nations in general and the United States in particular during the Korean War and the recent fighting in Vietnam. My heart sank at the formidable task of having to break down this iron wall of prejudice and ignorance. If I wanted to walk out of the No. 1 Detention House free and cleared of the accusation against me, I had to try.

After entering the room, I stood beside the prisoner's chair, holding the Little Red Book in my hand, waiting for them to tell me which quotation to read. The interrogator indicated Mao's portrait on the wall with a wave of his arm, 'Bow to our Great Leader Chairman Mao and apologize to him for your crime!' he said.

Apologize to Mao for my crime? I decided to use this opportunity to show resistance and disrupt their procedure. 'I have not committed any crime. I can't apologize for something I haven't done,' I replied while remaining upright.

'What! You have the audacity to refuse to bow to our Great Leader! How dare you! Everybody in China bows to the portrait of our Great Leader morning and night. You dare to refuse?' the interrogator shouted sternly, half rising from his chair. The others glared at me with astonishment and disapproval. For the first time that morning I felt really good.

'You misunderstood me. I merely said that I haven't committed any crime. I can't apologize for something I haven't done. I did not say I would not bow to Chairman Mao's portrait. I can bow to his portrait to show my respect to him, of course.' I spoke in a calm voice as I became more relaxed.

'Do it then! What are you waiting for?' the interrogator shouted and sat down again.

I bowed to the portrait. My resistance was not in vain; at subsequent sessions of interrogation, no one mentioned apologizing for my crime any more. Whenever I entered the interrogation room, the interrogator merely waved his arm in the direction of the portrait without speaking.

The quotation the interrogator chose was the same one I had read before. It was a much-used favourite of the Cultural Revolution. 'When the enemies with guns are annihilated, the enemies without guns still remain. We must not belittle these enemies,' I read. Then he asked me to read one about the Army. It said, 'Without the People's Army, the people would have nothing.' The frequent use of this quotation at this period of the Cultural Revolution reflected the ascendancy of the military and of the Defence Minister Lin Piao in the power structure of the Party.

I sat down in the prisoner's chair. In front of me, a few feet away, was the outside panel of the counter behind which the interrogator sat. It was now painted white. Freshly written on it in large characters was: 'Lenient treatment for those who confess; severe punishment for those who remain stubborn.' On either side of the official portrait on the wall were other messages urging the prisoners to confess.

I heard the small window behind me slide open softly and saw the interrogator looking over my shoulders to the small window and giving a barely perceptible nod before speaking.

'You wrote a letter requesting an interview with the Workers' Propaganda Team. Are you now ready to give a full confession?'

'I requested the Workers' Propaganda Team to investigate my case and clear me of the false accusation against me. I understand that the Workers' Propaganda Teams represent Chairman Mao. I expect you to implement the correct policy of Chairman Mao of distinguishing the innocent from the guilty. I have been held here for over two years already. Isn't that long enough for an innocent person to be incarcerated in a detention house?' I said.

'You have been here more than two years already but your attitude has not improved. You are still hoping to slip away. Don't you realize that a great victory has been won by the Proletarian Revolutionaries? The situation is now very different from the time of your last interrogation. Did you not hear the announcement of the resolution passed by the Central Committee on Liu Shao-chi? Even he could not slip through the net of the Proletarian Revolutionaries. What hope have you of escaping?'

'I've nothing to hide. All I request you to do is to get at the facts,' I said.

'We'll get at the facts about you just as we did about Liu Shao-chi. He was the agent of the imperialists abroad, the Kuomintang in Taiwan and the capitalist class in China. He was the number one "capitalist-roader" and the backstage boss of all of you. Now you should understand fully that the whole intrigue to destroy socialism in China is exposed and defeated.'

'Who wanted to destroy socialism in China? I don't know what you are talking about,' I told him.

'All of you who belong to the capitalist class are actual or potential agents of the imperialists and the Kuomintang. Liu Shao-chi and his clique were hidden agents who infiltrated the leadership of the Communist Party,' the interrogator said.

His argument was so absurd and the accusation against Liu Shao-chi was so ridiculous that I felt disgusted. Mao Tze-tung and the other radical leaders insulted the intelligence of the Chinese people when they expected them to believe the Central Committee resolution against Liu Shao-chi. Furthermore, I looked upon these men seated in front of me with contempt because they were obviously cowardly enough to want to be a part of Mao's despicable scheme against Liu Shao-chi. My one wish at that moment was to irritate them. Pretending to be stupid, I said, 'I always had the greatest respect for Chairman Liu Shao-chi. I'm not at all sure he is really guilty of the charge against him. Perhaps there was some mistake. It's well known that he fought against the imperialists, the Kuomintang and the capitalist class and risked his life doing so.'

I was pleased to see that my seemingly innocent remarks had the effect of a bombshell. All of them stood up and shouted at me, 'How dare you defend a traitor of the Communist Party!' 'How dare you oppose the Central Committee resolution!' 'How dare you oppose our Great Leader Chairman Mao!'

Their behaviour was the correct one required by their position as representatives of the Revolutionaries but, strangely, only the young worker and the military officer appeared really angry. The other three were staring at me with curiosity and amusement, definitely not anger or disapproval. I thought they looked quite pleased to hear me defend Liu Shao-chi and seemed surprised that someone who was supposed to be opposed to the Communist Party could feel so strongly about their deposed leader.

The discovery that among the seemingly ardent supporters of the radicals there were some who harboured sympathy for Liu Shao-chi intrigued me and I decided to prolong this dialogue a bit further. 'I did not oppose the Central Committee resolution and I did not oppose Chairman Mao. Who would dare to do that? I merely suggested that the evidence against Chairman Liu Shao-chi might not be completely reliable,' I said.

'Shut up! You are not allowed to refer to a traitor as "chairman",' the young worker shouted vehemently. The interrogator was gazing at the paper in front of him and so was the man taking notes. The old worker seemed to be enjoying the situation. The ghost of a smile hovered at the corner of his mouth.

'You are not allowed to refer to somebody denounced by a Central Committee as "chairman",' said the interrogator.

'I did it from habit,' I said. 'For sixteen years, in the newspapers, in daily broadcasts and in books published by the government printing press, Chairman Liu ... ' I paused when I caught sight of the interrogator glaring and saw the young worker stand up.

'Liu Shao-chi,' I continued, 'was always presented to the Chinese people as a revolutionary hero who had made a tremendous contribution to many aspects of the work of the Communist Party, including the development of the Party apparatus and the education of its members. I found in Chairman Mao's books several complimentary references to Liu Shao-chi. It's so difficult to turn round now and think of him as totally bad. Perhaps he had just made a mistake. If that is the case, I hope Chairman Mao will forgive him. After all, they were close comrades for many years.'

'You are dreaming! Chairman Mao will never forgive him!' the young worker said.

'Well, the outside world must be laughing at us now. How could such an important man who was Chairman of the Chinese People's Republic suddenly be discovered to have been a traitor all these decades? It's incredible that he could have fooled all the other leaders, including the Great and Wise Leader Chairman Mao himself. It just doesn't make sense. Doesn't this make Chairman Mao lose face too?' I asked them.

'We don't care what the imperialists and capitalists in other countries say. They don't have anything good to say about us anyhow. What happens in China is none of their business,' the young worker continued heatedly. 'To defend Liu Shao-chi is a criminal offence. He's a counter-revolutionary and so are you!'

'I'm not a counter-revolutionary, that I know. I'm a supporter of the People's Government and the Communist Party. I have the greatest respect for our Great Leader Chairman Mao. I challenge you to produce concrete facts to prove that I have ever done anything or said anything against the People's Government or the Communist Party,' I said calmly but firmly.

'You think you can slip away through bluffing. That's the game you are playing. Who do you think you are to challenge the People's Government? Even if you have never committed any crime, you are still just a dirty exploiter who has lived all your life on the blood and sweat of the labouring class. In any case, we have irrefutable evidence that you are a spy of the imperialists,' the interrogator declared, and he banged the table.

I got so angry and disgusted with them that I marched up to him and banged the table right in front of him. All of them stood up, surprised by my action.

The soldier pulled the revolver from its holster. Pointing the gun at me he shouted, 'What do you think you are doing?'

I stood in the middle of the room and faced him squarely. I said, 'You may shoot me if you can prove me guilty with concrete evidence.' There was stunned silence in the room as we confronted each other.

'Quiet! Quiet! You are a hysterical woman given to mad fits, I have heard already. Try to control yourself. Go back to your chair. If you dare to get out of that chair again, I'll have you chained to it.' The interrogator raised his arm to order me back to the prisoner's chair. The soldier pushed his gun into its holster while he continued to glare at me.

During the commotion, the only one who remained calm was the old worker. He looked at me with an expression that was akin to sympathy. Perhaps he was beginning to realize that I could really be innocent.

I returned to the prisoner's chair and sat down. The interrogator assumed an air of gravity and gave me a few words of education.

'To defend someone denounced in a resolution of the Central Committee of the Communist Party is a very serious offence. On that account alone I could sentence you to several years of imprisonment. But in consideration of the extenuating circumstance of your having had no opportunity to follow developments of the Cultural Revolution so that your understanding has not caught up with events, we will overlook your mistake this time.

'The Revolutionaries under the leadership of our Great Helmsman Chairman Mao are determined to expose all hidden enemies of socialism in our midst, no matter how senior their rank or how cleverly they are disguised. You should have no doubt on this point. You must cast away your illusions and realize you cannot escape,' the interrogator said.

'I understand the situation perfectly. And I think it quite right to punish the real enemy. But you should not mistake for enemies innocent people who have not opposed the People's Government. I request you to make a thorough investigation of my case. If you should find real evidence that I have lied and I have indeed committed crimes against the People's Government or the Communist Party, you can give me the death penalty. But if you find that I am indeed innocent, the People's Government must apologize to me and you must have the apology published in the newspaper for everyone to see,' I said with sincerity.

'You want an apology?' the young worker sneered. 'Who do you think you are? You have an inflated idea of your own importance.'

'All men are equal in the eyes of the law. Although I am not an official, I'm a citizen of this country.'

'You have just repeated a statement of the revisionists. No wonder you defended Liu Shao-chi. He was truly your backstage boss. Men are not equal. Men are divided into conflicting classes. The victorious class imposes its will on the vanquished class. As long as there are classes, there cannot be true equality,' the interrogator said.

'Do you mean to say that you will ignore the law and punish an innocent person simply because that person is a member of the bourgeois class?'

'Why not? If it's necessary to punish somebody, we will certainly do so. The bourgeois class is our enemy. We hope to re-educate most of its members and make them labour for their food. Those who resist and oppose us will certainly be eliminated. In any case, the victorious proletarian class makes the law to suit its purpose and to serve its interest.'

'Well, that seems to simplify matters greatly. Since you have already classified me as a member of the bourgeois class and I'm too old and weak to labour for my food, why not just shoot me and be done with it? Why waste time having an interrogation?'

'We want you to confess because others are involved. You yourself are of no importance. We couldn't care less whether you are dead or alive,' the interrogator said with an air of indifference.

He said others were involved. Whom did he mean? I became more than ever puzzled at the situation in which I found myself.

'Who are involved? Do you mean the ex-staff members of the Shanghai office of Shell?'

'No, of course not! They are completely unimportant, like you. We are interested in those who made it possible for you and others like you to undermine the security of China on behalf of the imperialists.'

'Who do you mean? Do you mean Liu Shao-chi? I assure you I have never met him.'

'Liu Shao-chi was one of them. But he doesn't matter any more. There are others who are still "raising the red flag to oppose the red flag". They are yet to be exposed. It's their policy which made it possible for you to carry on your dirty work against China on behalf of the imperialists.'

How incredible! It seemed that their persecution of me and the denunciation of Shell was not simply because of their anti-foreign attitude or their adherence to the principles of class struggle. The problem was much more complicated than I had thought. Their targets I saw were the Party officials whose policy permitted foreign companies to operate in China. If they could make me and others like me confess to being foreign spies, they could claim that allowing foreign firms to operate in China was providing a safe haven for the intelligence activities of foreign agents. Whether I liked it or not, I was a pawn in the struggle between the two irreconcilable policies of the Communist Party. When I argued and fought back, I was defending some officials in the Communist Party whom I did not know and who did not know me. This bizarre situation was too ridiculous! It was like a surrealist painting, understandable only to the initiated.

The voice of the interrogator cut short my speculations. 'Now, cast your mind back to 1949, just before the People's Liberation Army took over Shanghai. Under what circumstance did the Kuomintang order your husband to remain in Shanghai? Did they order him to work his way into the People's Government and undermine it from within?'

'My husband stayed in Shanghai because he hoped the People's Government would rescue China from economic chaos and political confusion after so many years of war and build a strong and prosperous country for all the Chinese people. Both my husband and I were idealistic and ignorant. We knew nothing of class struggle. Essays written by Chairman Mao were being circulated in Shanghai by the Communist Party underground. Our friends who were professors at various universities gave them to us to read. None of these essays

mentioned class struggle. Chairman Mao talked about the formation
of a united front and cooperation with all patriotic Chinese,' I pointed
out.

'That was the correct policy at that time. That policy was for the
purpose of winning the support of the bourgeois class and to undermine
the Kuomintang. After the Kuomintang was successfully overthrown,
naturally that policy was no longer needed. In every circumstance, we
unite the lesser enemies to fight the major enemy. When the major
enemy is overcome, one of the lesser enemies will become the new
major enemy. So the struggle goes on. That's dialectical materialism.'

There was nothing for me to say. The interrogator had put the
philosophy of Mao's regime in a nutshell. It was entirely my own fault
that I had not understood it before. After a moment, the interrogator
asked, 'Did your husband discuss his plan to remain in China with
anyone? Perhaps he discussed it with some of his foreign friends?'

'No, it was entirely his own idea. Early in 1949, my daughter and I
were in Hong Kong. My husband asked us to come back to Shanghai.
After my return, he told me that he had decided to remain in China. It
seemed he was influenced by his old university friends in the
Democratic League. As you know, the Democratic League supported
and cooperated closely with the Communist Party and helped to foster
friendly feelings for the Communist Party among the intellectuals and
Kuomintang officials with a liberal outlook. I knew quite a number of
intellectuals who decided to remain in China at that time because of
the efforts of the leading members of the Democratic League,' I said.

'The Democratic League was an instrument of the American
imperialists. Its leaders wanted to establish parliamentary democracy in
China and share political power with the Communist Party. They were
absurd dreamers with absurd ideas. Without an army, what can
politicians achieve? In 1957, during the Anti-Rightists Campaign, most
of the League's leaders were exposed as rightists. They deserved it.'

'They did render service to the Communist Party in 1949,' I
reminded the interrogator. The fate of the leaders of the Democratic
League was a chilling example of Mao's habit of using people and then
ruthlessly discarding them when they were no longer needed.

'Circumstances changed ...' the interrogator started to explain
dialectical materialism again.

'I understand. It's another case of the application of the theory of
dialectical materialism to real life,' I said hastily to save myself from
another explanation.

'It's our conclusion that your husband remained in Shanghai under orders from the Kuomintang and the imperialists in order to infiltrate the Ministry of Foreign Affairs of the People's Government.'

'Chang Han-fu, who later became Vice-Minister of Foreign Affairs in Peking, was the man who took over my husband's office in Shanghai when the Liberation Army came into the city. When he was about to go to Peking to take up his new appointment as Vice-Minister, he asked my husband to join the People's Government and go with him to Peking to work at the Ministry of Foreign Affairs. My husband refused Chang Han-fu's invitation. If my husband had wanted to infiltrate the Ministry of Foreign Affairs, why did he refuse to go to Peking in 1950?' I asked.

When I was answering him, I was thinking of the few former Kuomintang diplomats who did go to Peking to join the Communist Ministry of Foreign Affairs. A former Ambassador to Burma was imprisoned as a counter-revolutionary. All the others suffered persecution during one political campaign or another. I used to feel deeply thankful that my late husband had refused Chang Han-fu's invitation.

'Chang Han-fu is a member of the dirty Liu Shao-chi clique. When he was arrested before Liberation by the Kuomintang, he betrayed Communist Party secrets. He is now under arrest.' I was shocked by this revelation because I knew Chang Han-fu was a follower of Prime Minister Chou En-lai.

'The fact remains that he was Vice-Minister of Foreign Affairs when he invited my late husband to go to Peking to work at the Ministry of Foreign Affairs of the People's Government. My husband refused. You can check the record. If my husband had wanted to infiltrate the Ministry of Foreign Affairs, would he have refused to join it?'

The point I made was such simple logic that even the interrogator was momentarily lost for words. I took the opportunity to settle the issue once and for all.

'In fact, by remaining in Shanghai and not following the Kuomintang to Taiwan, my late husband demonstrated his goodwill towards the Communist Party. He was an official of the Kuomintang Government. Yet he disobeyed their orders. It's the Kuomintang in Taiwan who should loot our home and put us in prison. They are powerless to do so. You have done it for them. Now, who is acting for the Kuomintang?'

Being accused of acting for the Kuomintang was an intolerable insult to the Revolutionaries. I could see the face of the interrogator turning pale and the veins on his temple stood out as he tried to control his temper. But it was the soldier who stood up and made a gesture of pulling out his revolver again.

'Shut up!' he shouted.

But the old worker said in a conciliatory voice, 'It's all right for you to state your point of view. Our Great Leader said, "Lay out the facts and speak with reason." We permit you to defend yourself. But you mustn't malign the Revolutionaries and accuse them of acting for the Kuomintang.'

The interrogator looked at his watch and whispered something to the others. Then he said to me, 'You may go back to your cell now. We'll resume in the afternoon.'

I had been called for interrogation before the first of the two daily mealtimes for the prisoners. Now I was hungry and exhausted. When I stood up, the room whirled and everything went black in front of my eyes. I had to steady myself by holding on to the arm of the chair for the prisoner. My legs were so wobbly that I did not think I could walk away steadily. But I did not want the others to misinterpret my unsteadiness as a sign of nervousness. So I pointed at my swollen ankle and said, 'I want to lodge a protest against a guard who came into my cell and kicked me last night.'

'Nonsense!' the interrogator said. 'The guards are not allowed to kick or beat prisoners.'

'This one certainly did.' I hobbled out of the room behind a male guard.

I was famished and feared that I had missed the only meal of rice of the day. The evening meal of potatoes always caused me indigestion. But while she led me towards my cell, the female guard on duty at the women's prison told me that my portion of rice was being kept warm for me wrapped in my blanket. 'If you want, I can give you some hot water to drink,' she said.

Even though she was one of the nicer guards whom I always thought of as the 'mild' ones, such humane consideration was unheard of. I found the container of rice and cabbage wrapped in a towel and a blanket. It was not yet completely cold. The guard came to the small window with her thermos of hot water and poured a generous amount into my mug. I sat down on the edge of the bed to eat my rice while trying to sort out the impression of the morning.

The interrogator was definitely the best educated and most intelligent of those five men. Judging by his air of self-confidence, I thought he must be a seasoned Party official. Whether he was a true

Maoist or not I couldn't tell. But he was certainly acceptable to the Maoists because he had been given the job as interrogator. The old worker was not a true Maoist. I thought he had probably been chosen to be a member of the Workers' Propaganda Team because he was an old industrial worker of many years' standing, the sort of man put on the Workers' Propaganda Team for cosmetic purposes. The young man who took notes appeared indifferent. He merely participated as a secretary; that was probably his job. I detected no real annoyance in his voice or in his expression when I spoke up for Liu Shao-chi. The young worker and the military man were the true Maoists. They looked and behaved like Mao Tze-tung era young people from poor family backgrounds who had received so much political indoctrination that they had completely lost the ability to think for themselves.

The behaviour of the guard on duty at the women's prison was the most strange. What had I done that morning to earn her goodwill? That was the question I puzzled over as I chewed the tough cabbage leaves. The only thing I had done that could be considered unusual was speaking my few words in defence of poor Liu Shao-chi. Did she reward me because what I had said was the same as what she thought but could not say because of her position as a prison guard?

Personal relations always were important to the Chinese in a tradition that dated back thousands of years. The Communists were no exception. When a Communist leader fell from grace, all those who had ever worked with him would be disgraced, no matter how remote the connection. Since the entire Public Security Bureau had been denounced by the Maoists, there must exist in the No. 1 Detention House a number of men and women whose fate was linked to that of Liu Shao-chi and who would be sympathetic to him. If my defending Liu Shao-chi was to earn me better treatment and more humane consideration, it would be worth doing. To improve my chance of physical survival must be my primary concern. However, this was a situation I had not anticipated when I impulsively defended Liu Shao-chi because my sense of justice was outraged.

When I was called to the interrogation room again in the afternoon, the interrogator waved his arm towards Mao's portrait. I bowed. Then he selected the following quotation for me to read, 'All reactionaries are paper tigers. Superficially the reactionary clique looks strong, but in actuality the reactionary clique does not have great strength.'

After I had finished, the interrogator said, 'You may go on with your account. Describe the circumstances under which your husband joined the British spy organization.'

'My husband never joined any spy organization. Shell is an international oil company of good repute,' I said.

'Its Shanghai office was a spy organization.'

'It was not.'

The interrogator took out a stack of paper from under the counter and started to read in silence while the two workers watched me closely. Every now and then, when the interrogator turned a page, he would look at me and shake his head disapprovingly as if he had found something about me in the paper he was reading that shocked him. I knew he was acting, and the paper he was pretending to read might be about astrology for all I knew, so I assumed a blank expression and quietly waited for the interrogator to speak again.

After a while he laid the paper down and said, 'The other members of your staff are more enlightened than you are. They know where their interests lie. They have already confessed everything.' He pointed to the paper and continued, 'These are some of their confessions. The ones written by the various heads of departments, including your ex-chief accountant, gave very interesting details of the spy activities of your office.'

'All right, then. Since you have got what you wanted, why bother to press me to make a false confession?' I said.

'Each of you must speak for himself.'

'If you want me to speak, I can tell only the truth. Shell is a trading firm. It has nothing to do with politics. Shell was in China because Shell wanted to develop trade with China. In any case, it was here in Shanghai because the People's Government allowed it to be here. Both my late husband and myself were given the impression by the officials we dealt with that the People's Government encouraged Shell to maintain an office in Shanghai.'

'Exactly. The "capitalist-roaders" in the Communist Party tried to shield a foreign spy organization. It's obvious,' the interrogator said.

'I advise you to be careful about what you are saying. It was the State Council which gave permission for Shell to remain in China.'

What I did not mention was that the order to permit Shell to retain its head office in Shanghai had been signed by Prime Minister Chou En-lai. The interrogator must have been aware of this. I couldn't help wondering whether Prime Minister Chou was one of the leaders the Maoists hoped to topple next. But they would never dare to come out with an accusation openly as long as Chou remained the Prime Minister.

'Shell is a multinational corporation. As such, according to

Marxism, it is the worst form of capitalist enterprise. It exploits the working class of many countries. Politically such companies are invariably the most anti-Communist and reactionary. It should never have been allowed to remain in China after Liberation,' the interrogator said.

'I don't agree with you. I think it was an extremely clever and subtle move to allow a British oil company to remain in China when the United States was imposing an oil embargo against China. It created dissension in the enemy camp. What could be more clever than that? I understand from reading Chairman Mao's books that he advocates creating dissension and friction among the enemies as an effective tactic of class struggle,' I said.

The young worker joined in and said, 'Our Great Leader Chairman Mao taught us to be self-reliant. We do not need foreign companies.'

'Our Great Leader Chairman Mao said, "We do not refuse foreign aid but we rely chiefly on our own strength." He did not rule out accepting aid from friendly sources.'

'You cannot classify doing trade with a company like Shell as aid from a friendly source,' the interrogator said.

'For years Shell did not trade with Taiwan or maintain an office there. What could be more friendly to the People's Government than that?'

'You certainly have a glib tongue. First you defended Liu Shao-chi. Now you defend a reactionary multinational organization. Even if you have never committed any other crime, what you have said in this interrogation room today is enough for us to pass sentence on you,' said the interrogator.

'Everything I have said is the truth. Everything you have said is just wild accusation based on imagination. Yet you are supposed to be an enlightened Revolutionary representing the People's Government and the Communist Party and I'm merely a backward old woman.'

Angered by my remark, the interrogator banged the table again. 'You are forgetting yourself! This is the interrogation room of the Dictatorship of the Proletariat!'

'Stand up! Stand up! Remain standing! You must be punished for showing contempt for the Dictatorship of the Proletariat,' the young worker joined in excitedly.

I stood up.

'Give an account of the circumstances in which your husband joined the British spy organization,' the interrogator said.

'If you put it like that, I simply cannot answer you.'

'You are very careful, aren't you? The imperialists trained you well, didn't they? You do not concede a single point,' said the interrogator.

The old worker said, 'Answer the question the interrogator asked you. We'll leave the matter of spy organization aside for the time being.'

'Exactly! Conclusion should come after investigation. That's what Chairman Mao taught us also. He said, "Without investigation, you have no right to speak",' I told them.

The interrogator banged the table again and shouted, 'Did we ask you to lecture us? You are impertinent. You seem to forget that you are a prisoner and we are the representatives of the People's Government.'

'I expect the representatives of the People's Government to be reasonable, to abide by the law and to get at the truth of my case,' I said.

'That's exactly what we are trying to do. But you refuse to confess.'

'It would be irresponsible of me to make a false confession. I do not believe a false confession serves the interest of the government or anybody else. It would only create confusion. I have never done anything against the law. To help you ascertain the true facts, I will be glad to answer any question you may wish to ask me. I'll speak the truth. If I lie and try to cover up, you may punish me severely. In fact, I'll gladly sign a paper to that effect, if you will give me a sheet of paper,' I said.

After checking with the interrogator, the secretary held out a sheet of paper to me. I walked up to the counter and wrote down the following: 'I am a patriotic Chinese and a law-abiding citizen. I've never done anything against the People's Government. If the investigators of the People's Government should ever find anybody in the whole of China from whom I have tried to obtain information of a confidential nature, I'm prepared to accept the death penalty. At the end of the investigation of my case, when I am found to be completely innocent, the People's Government must give me full rehabilitation, including an apology to be published in the newspaper.'

I signed my name and wrote down the date before handing the paper over to the interrogator. He read it and passed it on to the others. The old worker took out his reading glasses, carefully wiped the lenses and put them on. He read my pledge while nodding with approval. Pointing to the chair for the prisoner, the old worker said to me, 'Sit down, sit down!'

Both the soldier and the young worker refused to read my pledge. The young worker said with a sneer, 'You are just bluffing like a poker player!'

The interrogator handed my pledge to the secretary who stored it in a folder.

'In what circumstances did your husband become the general manager of the Shanghai office of Shell?' the interrogator asked.

'To invite a national of the country in which it operated to be general manager was a policy adopted by Shell after the Second World War,' I told them.

'Was it not because they believed that being a Chinese national your husband would be able to obtain information more easily than a British manager?' he asked.

'The only advantage my husband had over a British manager was the fact that he did not need an interpreter when he talked with a representative of the Import and Export Corporation of the People's Government,' I told them.

'Your husband made trips to Hong Kong several times and both of you went to England and Europe in 1956,' the interrogator said. 'We are especially interested in your trip to Europe because we know you received instructions from the headquarters of the British intelligence organization.'

'You are getting things mixed up. We went to London to visit the head office of Shell. Then we travelled to The Hague for the same purpose because half of Shell's head office was there. My husband held discussions with directors about trade prospects in China. The Import and Export Corporation as well as the Chemicals Corporation in Peking were anxious for him to make the trip. They wanted to purchase many things from Shell. Trade prospects looked promising and British experts were invited to come to China to help Chinese organizations with research. But soon after we came back the Anti-Rightist Movement was launched. This was followed by the Great Leap Forward Campaign. Everything had to stop. The Peking officials who were so enthusiastic could no longer make decisions. Shell experts already on their way to China had to turn back. Nothing further could be done,' I told them.

'How did you obtain your passports? Who gave you permission to go to Europe? Private people are usually not allowed to make trips abroad,' the interrogator said.

'My husband applied for our passports at the Foreign Affairs Bureau in Shanghai. We were given permission to go, I suppose, because the government considered his trip useful to China's interest,' I said.

I remembered accompanying my husband to Peking when he was invited by the Import and Export Corporation to discuss the supply of insecticides and chemical fertilizers to China by Shell. Mao Tze-tung wanted a dramatic increase in China's grain output to prove the superiority of the agricultural cooperatives formed in 1955 in his first step towards the collectivization of agriculture. The day before we were due to return to Shanghai, my husband went to the Import and Export Corporation for a last interview. The man there, with whom he had had pleasant business discussions for a week, informed my husband that our passports were approved and waiting for us at the Foreign Affairs Bureau in Shanghai. Then he added in a confidential manner, 'The Prime Minister personally gave approval to issue you with passports.' Normally Party officials did not give more than the bare minimum of information when dealing with an outsider like my husband. We thought the official mentioned Prime Minister Chou's personal approval of our trip to encourage my husband to obtain from Shell in London all the things the corporation wanted to buy from the company.

The interrogator had alleged that our trip to London was 'to visit the headquarters of the British intelligence organization to receive instructions'. If indeed that had really been the case and I were made to confess to it, the Prime Minister's approval to issue us with passports would have been tantamount to facilitating spy activities, to put it mildly. Was it possible that the Maoists were hoping to cast doubt on Prime Minister Chou En-lai? The whole thing seemed farfetched and absurd. But the allegations against Liu Shao-chi were equally farfetched and absurd. When the interrogator said that he wanted me to confess because others were involved and that there were officials who were still 'raising the red flag to oppose the red flag', could he possibly mean to include Prime Minister Chou En-lai? I could only speculate. I would probably never know, I said to myself. But I did not think it out of character for either Lin Piao or Mao's wife Chiang Ching to wish Chou En-lai out of the way. Every Chinese knew that Chiang Ching hated Chou En-lai. Lin Piao probably considered the Prime Minister an obstacle to his ambition.

The voice of the interrogator brought me back to the interrogation room again. He was saying, 'Your trip was not useful to China's interest.'

'The officials my husband saw in Peking gave him to understand that he would be rendering service to China if he could obtain what China needed from Shell. They also said that trading with foreign countries was beneficial to China,' I told him.

'That was the policy of the "capitalist-roaders" in the Party and against the teachings of our Great Leader Chairman Mao,' the interrogator said.

'You can't expect us outsiders to have known that. To my husband and myself, the People's Government was the government and the officials representing the government were the people we had to listen to and believe in,' I said.

'Give a truthful account of your activities in England and other European countries you visited and confess what information you divulged.'

'My husband visited the offices of Shell in London and in The Hague. He met several directors and others concerned with the Far Eastern area. He also visited factories and installations. We saw some old friends.'

'Did you see any British government officials?'

'Yes, some of our friends were diplomats we used to know.'

'Did they not ask you about conditions in China?' asked the interrogator.

'Conditions in China in 1956 and 1957, before the Anti-Rightist Campaign, were very good. We were very happy to tell them about it. For the first time, after many years of war, inflation was brought under control. The first five-year plan was successfully accomplished. People were contented. There was peace. They all knew it.'

'There must have been something you told them that they did not know already. You must confess everything,' said the interrogator.

'What could we have told them? If you bother to look into who our friends and contacts in China are, you will find we did not know anybody who could possibly tell us anything that was of any importance. Since we obviously could not get into a government office to steal documents, everything we knew must have come from our friends. If we did not know anyone who knew anything important, we couldn't tell our British friends anything important, could we?'

'It's not up to you to judge what is important and what's not important. It's up to us to judge. I want you to write a detailed account of your trip to Europe in 1956-7. Give a list of all the people you saw and put down everything you said to them. We will see if you told them anything that was important.'

'It's an impossible task that would serve no purpose. How can I remember every sentence we ever spoke ten years ago? Besides, I was not with my husband when he went to the office or to oil installations and factories. How am I to tell you what he said? And how are you to check what I have written? You can't carry your inquiry to England.

What you should do is examine our Chinese contacts to see if we had any possible source of secret information inside China. I can assure you we did not know anybody who could possibly tell us anything that could be interpreted as "intelligence".'

'Are you conducting this investigation or am I?' the interrogator asked with irritation.

I knew of course that the interrogator hoped to trip me up. A seemingly innocent account could be made to look suspicious if a word were taken out here and a sentence taken out there. And when one is writing about mundane affairs, one is not on guard. So I merely said, 'Of course, you are the interrogator, and, as you told me yourself, you are the representative of the People's Government. I'll do whatever you say. But it seems a waste of time.'

'We do not mind wasting time if we can expose agents of the imperialists. It's our belief that all foreign firms operating in China have double status. They trade to make money because money is God to the capitalists. But they also gather information for their governments.

'The capitalist countries will never give up trying to subvert China because China is a socialist country. We are now powerful. They cannot hope to destroy us by military means. So they pin their hope on internal dissension. All of you trained in their universities or working in their offices are their potential allies. Britain was the first imperialist power to invade China. She still occupies Hong Kong. While she recognizes the People's Government, she votes with the United States at the United Nations to prevent our taking China's seat in that world organization. While the United States is openly supporting the Kuomintang, the British are playing a two-faced game which is more dangerous because people can be fooled by it,' the interrogator said.

'You exaggerate,' I told him.

'You had better not try to defend the British imperialists. That will put you in a worse position than you are in now,' said the interrogator.

It was obviously futile to engage in a debate on international relations with him. I kept quiet and waited to hear what else he had to say.

'Before you write your confession, you should correct your thinking about Liu Shao-chi. You should realize that the "capitalist-roaders" are finished. Those who are already exposed will never be able to stage a come-back and we are going to get at those who are yet to be exposed. Victory belongs to the policy of our Great Leader. So your only way out is to confess everything and come over to the side of the

Proletarian Revolutionaries. It would be a big mistake for you to think China might go back to pre-Cultural Revolution days and those of you with foreign connections would again be protected by the "capitalist-roaders",' the interrogator said.

I was quite pleased with the day's interrogation because I had been given the opportunity to speak and I thought I had clarified several points. Now I decided to use the opening he had given me to defend Liu Shao-chi further. I needed to see whether I was right in thinking that mixed with the Maoists in the detention house there were also a number of Liuists.

Assuming an air of innocent stupidity, I said, 'Honestly, I still don't understand what Chairman Liu Shao-chi did that was wrong and why Chairman Mao wants to punish him. In his books, Chairman Mao praised Chairman Liu in several places. I counted them when I was studying Chairman Mao's books. I do hope Chairman Mao will forgive Chairman Liu Shao-chi. Don't you think that would be best for China and for the Communist Party? Besides, wasn't it Chairman Liu who first used the term "Mao Tze-tung Thought" and urged the Party members to study Chairman Mao's books? Surely that showed he did respect Chairman Mao.'

'You are not allowed to refer to a traitor as Chairman!'

'You are not allowed to defend Liu Shao-chi!'

They shouted.

When they had quietened down, I said, 'Of course I do not dare to defend Liu Shao-chi if he is really guilty. But I do wonder if the material on which the Central Committee based its judgement was really reliable. You know how people could easily be frightened into making false confessions. I suppose it happens all the time.'

I couldn't resist making this dig at them. It was just a small revenge for the things they were doing to me. Actually what I had said probably touched a sensitive spot. From the traces of fear I saw on each of their faces and from the way they quickly tried to shut me up, I was sure they knew, or at least suspected, that the so-called evidence against Liu Shao-chi was indeed manufactured by the Maoists.

(After Mao's death in September 1976 and the subsequent arrest of his widow Chiang Ching, the people of China were told officially in a Central Committee document just how a special committee set up by Chiang Ching and Defence Minister Lin Piao manufactured the evidence against Liu Shao-chi. The document said that Maoist activists selected by Chiang Ching and Lin Piao rounded up Liu's associates and tortured them to make them provide the necessary false evidence.

To prove to Chiang Ching and Lin Piao that they had carried out their assignment faithfully, the Maoist activists on the special committee dealing with the Liu case taped the tortured cries of their victims and played it for Chiang Ching and Lin Piao to listen to.)

'Shut up! Shut up! You are a mad woman!' the interrogator shouted, seemingly terrified by my candid remark. He quickly added, 'Liu Shao-chi was guilty and you are too!'

'I'm not guilty, that I know for sure. As for Chairman Liu Shao-chi, I have a feeling he is innocent too,' I said.

'Shut up! Shut up! Close your lips. You are not allowed to speak again,' ordered the interrogator.

I heard a loud noise behind me. This time no attempt was made to soften the sound from the small window behind the prisoner's chair. It seemed that the man listening outside was tired of the game. He shut the small window with a loud bang to show his displeasure. The interrogator hurriedly got up and went out of the room.

When he came back, he did not resume his seat, but handed me a roll of writing paper.

'Go back to your cell and write about your trip to England and other European countries. Put down the names of all the people you saw and everything you said to them. Give a full confession.'

A guard was already standing in the open doorway. I followed him out.

Hot drinking water had been issued during my absence. It had been kept warm for me, like the rice earlier in the day. Such kindness and consideration were extraordinary. Was I correct in thinking their kindness to me was due to my defence of Liu Shao-chi? Or did the Maoists think I could be moved by gestures of kindness into doing their bidding? Such thoughts were in my mind as I sat on the edge of the bed drinking the hot water. Hot water may mean very little under normal circumstances, but in that prison cell, in the middle of winter, it tasted very good indeed.

Suddenly the small window in the door of the cell was pushed open. The voice of the young doctor said, 'Come over!'

'What's the matter with your ankle?' he asked.

What a surprise! I had never heard of the doctor coming to a prisoner without his visit being requested. Often I would hear a prisoner's voice, anxious and urgent, when she repeatedly made her requests to see the doctor. The guard was standing outside. After I had explained that I had a bruise on my ankle that seemed to be inflamed, she opened the door of the cell. The doctor stepped in. He examined my ankle and pressed the swollen flesh.

'No bone is broken. It's just superficial inflammation. I'll give you some bandages and ointment.'

Later, the guard on duty handed me a tube of auromycin and a roll of bandages. Before I could recover from my surprise at this change in my treatment, I was handed a container of rice and cabbage instead of the usual sweet potatoes for the evening meal. When I returned the container and chopsticks to the woman from the kitchen, she murmured, 'Doctor's orders for you to have rice.'

Thinking over the day's events and going through the interrogation carefully several times in my mind, I felt quite pleased. The new interrogator was a Party official but not a professional interrogator like the first man. I thought he was not too unreasonable, under the circumstances. At least he listened to what I had to say and everything was recorded. Even though I knew that the Maoists would do everything within their power to make me confess to something I hadn't done, I was now hopeful that at least those who were not diehard Maoists would in time realize I was innocent. When I prepared for bed, I was in a calmer mood than I had been for a long time. However, the exertion and excitement of a full day's interrogation and debate with the interrogator were too much for my weakened body. That night, I had the worst haemorrhage ever. In a short while, all the toilet paper and towels in the cell were used up; there was blood everywhere, even on the cement floor. I was alarmed and called the guard, who quickly summoned the doctor. He gave me an injection and told me to lie perfectly still on a plastic sheet. At daybreak, I was taken to the prison hospital in an ambulance.

CHAPTER 9

Persecution Continued

The antiquated ambulance sped through the streets of Shanghai, accompanied by the loud and continuous clang from the bell hanging on its side. I lay on the stretcher on the floor of the vehicle, while a female guard perched on the folding seat. The interior of the ambulance was by no means clean. I kept my eyes closed, partly to avoid looking at the guard, who hovered over me in the confined space, and partly to be alone with my thoughts.

I was deeply disappointed that I had had another haemorrhage just as the long-awaited interrogation seemed to have begun in earnest. I wondered whether I had a malignant growth. I thought of death. It did not seem frightening. After all, my death was the natural and unavoidable result of my having lived. In any case, being a Chinese, I believed that my own death would be only an interval in the continuity of life, for I would go on living in my child and her children, generation after generation, a flowing stream without end. But thinking of my daughter always caused my heart to contract with pain and worry. How was she living? What sort of future would she have after the Cultural Revolution?

The ambulance jerked to a sudden stop. I heard the loudspeaker in the distance broadcasting Mao's directive, 'Dig deep tunnels, store grain everywhere and never seek hegemony.' When the stretcher was lifted out of the ambulance, I caught sight of a group of young male prisoners with shaven heads being led by a guard in front of the hospital. They all carried spades, shovels and large baskets; their Little Red Books of Mao's quotations were slung over their shoulders on a string. They seemed to be on their way to 'dig deep tunnels' somewhere behind the prison hospital; Mao's directives always had to be obeyed immediately. But they looked so emaciated that I did not know how they could perform heavy physical labour. Their pathetic appearance and dejected air with their heads bowed reminded me forcefully that I was just like them, a non-person without any rights, quite unable to control my own fate. I turned my head to avoid looking at the sad spectacle of human ruin and for the first time I was glad that being in a cell by myself without a mirror, I could continue to entertain an illusion of self-esteem.

I was put into a ward with surgical cases. In the small room, beds were placed next to each other with only a few inches of space between. My bed was by the door, through which a cold draught blew into the room in a vain effort to dispel the odour of blood, urine, disinfectant and unwashed humanity. On the other side of my bed was a woman groaning and muttering in a state of semi-consciousness, obviously just returned from the operating room. I wondered why I was put there among the surgical cases and whether the arrangement meant that the doctors at the prison hospital intended to operate. This prospect was extremely alarming because in a rigidly stratified Communist society, prisoners of the State certainly would get the worst medical service.

However, for several days, I was only given injections. The haemorrhage was brought under control and I felt stronger because of bed rest and better food. One evening a small banana that had gone soft and brown appeared with my supper. I was surprised by my own positive reaction to that sad-looking banana and the pleasure I got from eating it.

A few days after my haemorrhage had stopped, the same woman doctor I had seen when I had pneumonia in the winter of 1967 came to see me in the ward. She took me to a small office and told me that she had been trying to arrange for me to be examined by a gynaecologist in a city hospital. But at that time the hospitals in Shanghai, controlled by the Red Guards and the Revolutionaries, were refusing to give medical treatment to 'class enemies'.

'What do you think I am suffering from?' I asked her.

'It may be a growth or it may be nothing more than the menopause.'

'Could it be a malignant growth?'

'It's hard to say without a biopsy,' she said.

'I'm not afraid to die,' I said. 'But I mustn't die before my case is cleared up. I can't let a cloud of suspicion remain with my daughter for the rest of her life. It would ruin her happiness. Besides, I long to see her again. I've missed her so very much.' My voice quivered and I couldn't go on.

She laid a hand on my arm in a gesture of sympathy. 'In my report to the No. 1 Detention House, I will stress the need for you to have better nourishment.'

'Please, Doctor, tell me what I can do myself to prolong my own life,' I asked her.

'Eat everything that's given to you. Even the most unpalatable food has some nourishment. Try to be optimistic.'

Bitterness had so eaten my heart that I had lost the ability to cry. But the doctor had tears in her eyes when she murmured, 'May God bless you!'

A week later, I was brought back to the No. 1 Detention House. I was then given rice twice a day, and a small piece of pork or fish appeared with the rice and cabbage for the mid-morning meal. Often the pork was mostly fat. Sometimes the skin was not altogether free of half-plucked hairs. And the fish was never really fresh. But remembering what the doctor said, I ate everything.

The young doctor at the detention house gave me written permission to purchase vitamin pills with the money I had deposited with the detention house when I arrived. A male guard came with my banking record and bought for me codliver oil capsules and vitamin B complex tablets. Vitamin C, so vital for my bleeding gums, was unobtainable in Shanghai.

The reaction of the guards to my being given better treatment was by no means the same. The militant Maoists could not conceal their displeasure at the decision of the prison authorities to give me extra food and vitamins. They were always shouting at me or rough-handling me whenever there was an opportunity. When I left the cell for exercise or interrogation, they would give me a hard shove that sent me stumbling, pinch my arms or kick my legs. If I asked them for permission to replenish my supply of vitamin pills, they would refuse and shout, 'Do you eat vitamin pills like rice?' or 'Do you think this place is a health sanatorium?'

The mild guards obeyed the orders of the doctor without question. They bought me vitamin pills whenever I could show them that I had no more. But they bought one or two bottles at a time. The few guards I thought of as the 'Liuists', however, would buy several bottles for me at a time, when they wiuere on duty. Once or twice, they even brought me bags of glucose powder as well as vitamin pills and pushed the lot quickly through the small window into my cell before another guard could see it.

The day after I returned from the prison hospital, the guard on duty handed me a pen and a bottle of ink. She said, 'Get on with writing your confession! The interrogator is waiting for it.'

I picked up the roll of paper the interrogator had given me and saw that instead of the blank sheets I was given in the winter of 1966 when I was told to write my autobiography, page one had a special quotation of Mao. It was enclosed in a red-lined square under the heading, 'Supreme Directive', and it said, 'They are allowed only to be docile and obedient; they are not allowed to speak or act out of turn.' At the bottom of the sheet, where the prisoner usually signed his name, was written: 'signature of criminal'.

My immediate reaction was anger at the insulting word 'criminal', and determination not to sign my name after it. However, after several minutes of consideration, I devised a scheme to exploit the situation and fight back at the Maoists.

Under the printed quotation of Mao, I drew another square over which I also wrote 'Supreme Directive'. Within the square, I wrote another of Mao's quotations: it did not appear in the Little Red Book but I remembered it from his essay, 'On the Internal Contradiction of the People'. The quotation said, 'Where there is counter-revolution, we shall certainly suppress it; when we make a mistake, we shall certainly correct it.'

Then I wrote an account of the trip my late husband and I had made to Europe in 1956, with a list of the countries we visited, the activities I could recall and the names of the people we saw. On the subject of conversations we had, I included general subjects of no political significance. When I had nearly finished writing, I suddenly remembered two important events that had taken place in the world during the time we were in England. They were the Hungarian uprising and the Suez War of 1956. I couldn't very well comment on the first, but I could with impunity include the second as a topic of conversation with friends, as it did not concern China or Communism. At the bottom of the page, following the printed words, 'Signature of criminal', I added 'who did not commit any crime', and signed my name.

I handed the paper to the guard on duty. That very afternoon, I was called for interrogation.

The same men except for the soldier were in the room. A dark scowl was on each face, a fact anticipated by me when I decided to contest their right to assume I was a criminal when I was not. I did not wait for a signal from the interrogator, but bowed to Mao's portrait immediately. The quotation the interrogator chose for me to read was, 'Against the running dogs of the imperialists and those who represent the interests of the landlords and the Kuomintang reactionary clique, we must exercise the power of dictatorship to suppress them. They are allowed only to be docile and obedient. They are not allowed to speak or act out of turn.'

In front of the interrogator was the paper I had written. After I had sat down, he banged the table while glaring at me. Then he banged the table again and shouted, 'What have you done here?' he pointed at the paper. 'Do you think we are playing a game with you?'

I remained silent.

'Your attitude is not serious,' the old worker said.

'If you do not change your attitude, you will never get out of this place,' said the young worker.

Before I could say anything, the interrogator threw my account on the floor, scattering the pages, and stood up. He said, 'Go back to your cell and write it again!'

A guard appeared at the doorway and shouted, 'Come out!'

I followed him back to the cell. The roll of paper I was given was the same as before. I had the same first sheet with the printed quotation at the top enclosed in a red square and 'signature of criminal' at the bottom of the sheet. Since I had embarked on this course of action, I decided I had to carry the fight to the finish. I did not hesitate but wrote the same quotation and again added the words 'who did not commit any crime' before my signature. The account I wrote again could not be exactly the same as the first one. But I have an excellent memory and it was more or less the same. On the third day, I handed the paper to the guard. Again, I was called almost immediately. Again the interrogator threw my account on the floor, scattering all the pages, and told me to write another.

This was repeated once more. Then, the interrogator said to me, 'Are you mad? Perhaps we should send you to the mental hospital and have you locked up with the crazy people.'

'I'm not mad. If you are not satisfied with what I have written, you can point out my mistakes. I would be glad to correct them.'

'Why did you add a quotation under the printed one? Why did you write a qualifying phrase before your signature?' the interrogator asked.

'I was only trying to make the paper reflect the true facts more accurately,' I said. 'I wanted to remind you that our Great Leader Chairman Mao said that we should correct our mistakes. I hope you will carry out Chairman Mao's directive and correct your mistake in my case. As for the added phrase before my signature, it's appropriate. I did not commit any crime. If you must call me a "criminal" then I am the criminal who did not commit any crime.'

'Instead of confessing your crime, you spend your time arguing,' answered the interrogator, no longer shouting.

'I've never committed any crime. If you insist I have, you will have to prove it.'

'We'll certainly prove it. But we want to give you a chance to confess, so that you can earn lenient treatment.'

'Have I not told you over and over again I've never committed any crime? Have I not signed a pledge that you can shoot me if you can prove I've committed a crime?'

'You are bluffing! Don't you worry. We'll shoot you when the time comes,' the young worker said heatedly.

'Go back to your cell and write the account again,' said the interrogator.

The secretary handed me another roll of paper and I followed the guard back to my cell.

When I looked at the paper, I found that this time the first page with the printed quotation and the 'signature of criminal' at the bottom was not included. All the sheets were blank. Again, I wrote down my account. Two days later I gave it to the guard on duty.

To people who have not dealt with such men as the Maoists, my persistent effort to fight back against my persecutors might seem futile and pointless. But the Maoists were essentially bullies. If I had allowed them to insult me at will, they would have been encouraged to go further. My life at the detention house would have become even more intolerable than it was already. Besides, every word I uttered in that interrogation room was recorded. Being an eternal optimist, I hoped that one day a just man would be appointed to investigate my case and that what I had said would help him to arrive at the right conclusion.

Several days passed. Daily I waited for the interrogator to call me and go on with his questioning. But I was never called. Finally, one morning, a militant male guard and the militant female guard who had kicked me came to the door of my cell. 'Come out!' they threw open the door and shouted.

When I bent down to pick up the Little Red Book of Mao's quotations, the female guard stepped into the cell and pushed me roughly. This was so unexpected that I nearly fell down.

'You won't need this where you are going!' She snatched the book out of my hand and tossed it onto the bed. Then she twisted my arms behind my back. The male guard came in and clamped a pair of handcuffs on my wrists. The female guard again gave me a shove. I stumbled. When I regained my balance, she gave me another push.

'Hurry! Hurry!' she shouted.

I followed the guards out of the women's prison and through the main courtyard to the front entrance. The interrogator, the young worker and another man were waiting at the second iron gate. Parked in the drive was a white sedan with a driver. The engine was running.

'Get in! Sit in the middle,' the interrogator said.

I climbed into the back of the car and sat in the middle of the seat. With my hands pinned at my back, I had to sit upright. My first impression was surprise at how soft the seat of the car was. It was a long time since I had sat on a soft seat with springs.

The interrogator and the young worker sat on either side of me. The other man sat with the driver. The car moved slowly along the drive and, gathering speed, drove out of the prison gate.

Where were they taking me? Were they going to carry out their threat and have me confined in a mental hospital? I did not think they were taking me for execution because I thought surely such extreme measures were carried out on the premises of the prison area under cover of darkness. Besides, once they had killed me, they would have no hope of extracting a confession from me. To keep me alive but make my life difficult was their probable aim. I thought a mental hospital was the more likely destination. It would be difficult to continue my fight from a mental hospital. Shrieks and cries of the mentally ill would be depressing. However, I soon discovered that the car was not going towards the road which led out of town where the mental hospital was located.

Through the fluttering silk curtain which covered the window of all official cars, I could see that we were passing through Shanghai's downtown business section and were speeding towards the western suburbs. There were few pedestrians and little traffic. The familiar streets evoked a flood of memories. We crossed an intersection only a block from my house. And there was the No. 1 Medical College. It seemed a lifetime ago that I had met Winnie coming out of its gates in the evening twilight when I first got involved with the Cultural Revolution in the summer of 1966. I wondered how she was faring and whether she had had to go to one of those Cadre Schools which I had read about in the newspaper.

The car slowed down and entered the drive of the technical school where I had attended the first struggle meeting against our former chief accountant, Tao, and from where I was taken to the No. 1 Detention House on the night of 27 September 1966. It was now already early March 1969 and the unwarranted accusation that I had betrayed my country still hung over my head.

Several men were standing in the pale spring sunshine. One of them opened the door of the car and led me into a small room. Another man behind me was pushing my head down, so that all I could see was the pair of legs of the man walking in front of me. I heard the turning of the lock of the door as soon as I entered. I was left there alone.

There was only one solitary wooden bench in the dusty place. Paper pasted on the window prevented me from looking out. The walls were covered with Big Character Posters from ceiling to floor. There were more piled up in one corner of the room. The ones on the walls did not look freshly written. Some were torn; all were stuck on the walls in a haphazard manner, overlapping one another. When the door was opened to admit me, a gust of air blew several onto the floor.

I sat on the bench and let my eyes wander over the posters. Gradually I realized that they had been hastily pasted on the walls entirely for my benefit. They were old Big Character Posters used during the past two and a half years. Now they were on display again to undermine my fighting spirit. Signatures on them were those of Shell's ex-staff members. Some were written by one man, while others were signed by several names. The messages on them denounced Shell, my late husband and myself. The 'crimes' listed were numerous. Some were distortions of facts or misinterpretations of events. Others were pure imagination. Names of our friends and the three British managers who came after my husband died were all listed as 'foreign intelligence officers' with whom I was supposed to have worked in close cooperation. The names of Scott and Austin appeared on several posters. The White Russian woman employed as secretary at our office was denounced as a double agent for Britain and the Soviet Union.

I closed my eyes to shut out the obnoxious lies. After waiting for a long time, I thought I should try to find out what was going on outside. I listened. When I heard footsteps, I knocked on the door.

'What do you want?' the voice of a man asked.

'May I go to the cloakroom?'

The door was unlocked by a woman, who led me to another courtyard at the back. We passed through an area used as a dormitory, with rows of bunk beds jammed into the rooms. Later I learned that the ex-staff members of Shell had been confined there since 1966, undergoing endless indoctrination and writing confessions while doing physical labour. Now, there was no one about. In the distance I could hear the voice of a man addressing a meeting. I thought that whoever lived in the dormitory must be at a meeting.

When I came out of the cloakroom, I was not taken back to the small room with posters, but to the hall where the struggle meetings against Shell's former chief accountant and myself had been held in 1966. Again, a man came behind me and placed his hand on my head to bend it low. Two women held my arms, straining them forward to push me on, so that the handcuffs cut into my wrists painfully. They were behaving in an exaggeratedly militant manner as women trying to appear revolutionary often did in China.

I was taken to the front of the room and half thrown and half dropped onto the floor as if I were a sack. The man kept his hand on my head so that I could not look around. When I sat down on the floor, he sat down right behind me, with his hand firmly exerting pressure.

Just before I sat down, out of the corner of my eye, I saw that the room was filled with people sitting on the floor. This arrangement implied insult, as according to Chinese tradition only slaves, condemned criminals or enemies captured in wars sat on the floor. The people in the room were shouting slogans long familiar to my ears. For a full minute, it seemed, they shouted demands for my downfall and destruction. I heard footsteps coming to the front of the room. When the noise of slogan shouting died down, a young man's voice addressed the meeting.

'Here she is!' he shouted in a loud scream. I imagined him pointing a finger at my bowed head. 'We have brought her here so that she will be exposed for what she is. We'll let her see that we know all her secrets. All of you were involved in the scheme of the imperialists to destroy socialism in China too. To a certain extent, you are also guilty, because you also worked for the firm that exploited the Chinese people from the beginning of this century. It was also a spy organization which gathered information to be used for the imperialists. But the degree of your guilt varies according to the position you held in the firm and the amount of work you did for the imperialists. The more senior you were, the more guilty you are. The more management valued your work, the more guilty you are. We, the Revolutionaries, are very fair-minded. If you are 30 per cent guilty, we do not punish you for 50 per cent. But of course we have our own standard of evaluation. It's the standard set up in accordance with our Great Leader Chairman Mao's teaching.

'During the past two and a half years we have given all of you an intensive course of re-education combined with physical labour. Many of you have made good progress in improving your socialist awareness. You shed your inhibitions and came forth with your exposure of the enemy. That's to be commended. Others of you are still hesitant. You are like a tube of toothpaste. When we squeeze, something comes out. When we squeeze hard, more comes out. When we do not squeeze, nothing comes. Well, if you continue to maintain a negative attitude, naturally we'll squeeze very hard until you are dry.

'Very soon we are going to let some of you return home. This is good news for you. But remember, only those we consider ready will be allowed to go. The others will have to continue with re-education. When or whether you will be allowed to go home and how long you must continue with re-education and physical labour depends entirely on yourselves.'

The speaker was just a voice to me. But it was the voice of an uneducated young man, perhaps a worker who had become a Revolutionary of some standing because of his close adherence to the Maoist doctrine, I thought. These Revolutionaries were the most ardent supporters of the Cultural Revolution because it gave them undreamt-of opportunity for personal advancement. They looked upon the Maoist leaders such as Chiang Ching as redeemers who had elevated them from the mundane existence to which their mediocre intellect and lack of ability had condemned them.

From what the speaker had said, I knew that the people sitting on the floor in the room were mostly ex-staff members of my former office. Now he called on them to 'expose' and 'condemn' me as a means to redeem themselves. They readily complied. But I knew it was all arranged beforehand and that the speakers had been selected and told what to say. And the drafts of their statements had been approved by the Revolutionaries. Even before the Cultural Revolution no one in China could make a public statement without first having it approved by his or her Party Secretary. During the Hundred Flowers Bloom and Hundred Thoughts Contend Campaign of 1956 and the period of the Democracy Wall of 1978-9, the Party ordered the people to speak and write Big Character Posters. In either instance, because the Party did not or could not censor each and every statement and poster and the people exceeded what the Party wanted them to say, the situation quickly got out of hand and the Party had to clamp down again.

The men I used to see daily and worked with for over eight years stood up one after another to repeat what was written on the posters I saw in the small room. Their hesitant and frightened voices were telling lies so outrageous, using words so alien to them that I knew they were suffering shame and anguish. My own emotion was one of deep sorrow that the high-handed Maoist Revolutionaries had degraded all of us to such an extent. But I listened carefully, trying to fathom the intention of the Maoists from the words they had put into these men's mouths.

The floor was hard and my neck was aching from having my head pushed down by the heavy hand of the man behind me. I shifted my position and drew up one leg. Then I rested my head on my knee. In this posture, I could see a corner of the blue jacket of the man seated next to me on the left and nothing more. Since I made no attempt to look up but appeared to be content to bend my head down, the man behind me gradually relaxed his grip.

Statements made by Shell's ex-staff became more and more fantastic by the hour. What they were saying was absurd and unbelievable to anybody who had some knowledge of the world outside China. The sum total of the accusations was an amateurish attempt at a spy drama without a convincing central theme, beginning or end.

I heard the voice of the young man calling on our former chief accountant Tao to speak.

The corner of the blue jacket disappeared from view as the man seated next to me stood up. I wondered why the Maoists had placed Tao next to me on the floor.

Tao was saying in a faltering voice, 'As everybody knows, I was arrested at the beginning of the Cultural Revolution and taken to the No. 2 Detention House. While I was there, the interrogator and the guards most kindly gave me re-education to help me raise my socialist awareness. Gradually I realized the seriousness of my crime against socialism and the Party. A desire to earn lenient treatment was born in my heart. At that juncture, the kind and understanding Revolutionaries brought me back here and allowed my family to visit me ...' He was evidently overcome with emotion and unable to go on.

'My eldest son is a Party member and so is my daughter-in-law. My son received his higher education entirely due to the opportunity given him by the Party and the People's Government. My whole family is eternally grateful to our Great Leader Chairman Mao. I cannot describe the remorse I felt when I saw my wife, my son, my daughter-in-law and my baby grandson ...'

He drew a long breath, broke down and sobbed.

There was dead silence in the room. The pale spring sun cast a shifting shadow of the window on the floor in front of me. I had been watching it move across the floor. Now I wondered how much longer the meeting was going to last. I was getting tired and hungry. But I warned myself not to relax vigilance. Somehow I did not think Tao was called upon merely to set an example for me to follow. After all, I did not have a child specially educated by the Party.

When Tao resumed, he seemed to be making an effort to speak, like a man utterly exhausted. His voice was unsteady as he declared, 'My wife, my son and my daughter-in-law talked to me. The Revolutionaries talked to me. The cadres representing the Party and our Great Leader Chairman Mao talked to me. They showed that I must obey the teachings of Chairman Mao. There is no other way for me to turn. I can't let them down. I'm going to confess and make a clean break with the past. I want to go home and be with my family. To confess fully is the only way.' He again paused for a moment almost as if he were reluctant to go on. Then he plunged in and said in a loud and firm voice, 'I was a spy for the British imperialists. I joined the British spy organization through the introduction of this woman's husband, the late general manager Cheng. After he died, this woman became my boss. At the beginning of the Cultural Revolution, she warned me not to confess and promised me a large sum of money if I would hold out.'

A denial or an argument with Tao would serve no useful purpose. But I must put a stop to this farce. I jerked my head up and laughed uproariously.

My reaction was not what anyone had expected. There was a moment of stunned silence. Then several men rushed to my side. The man behind me pushed my head down again. Another man shouted, 'What are you laughing at?'

Someone else said, 'How dare you laugh!'

The sound of people moving about came from the back of the room. There was even some noise that was like suppressed giggles. The tense atmosphere of a moment ago had collapsed like a burst balloon.

The voice of the young man in charge of the meeting was shouting at me amidst the noise, 'Why did you laugh? Answer me!'

'If you put on a comic play, you must expect the audience to laugh. It's the natural response,' I answered. With my head pressed down, I had to talk to the floor. But I raised my voice and spoke clearly so that every person in the room could hear me. I wanted to show our ex-staff that there was no need to be frightened of the Maoists.

'Take her out! Take her out!' the young man yelled. Then he led the others in the room to shout slogans against me.

I was forcibly dragged out of the room, pulled through the courtyard like a sack and pushed into the waiting car. A woman Revolutionary kept her hand over my mouth to prevent me from speaking, while the man did not relax his pressure on my head. I was pinned on the back seat of the car in an awkward position, with the woman perching on the edge of the seat and the man squatting on the narrow space between the front and back seats. But I was lighthearted. I thoroughly enjoyed breaking up their carefully planned meeting. I wondered what would have happened if I had sat there quietly. I did not rule out the possibility that Tao might have been instructed to talk to me and incriminate me in some way to validate his lies. There must have been a reason, I thought, for the Maoists to have placed me next to him.

It was my bad luck to find the militant female guard on duty when I returned to the cell. Needless to say she had not kept rice for me. She did not take the handcuffs off my wrists. As soon as she unlocked the door, she gave me a hard shove which sent me lurching into the room where I collapsed on the bed. Almost immediately running footsteps could be heard in the corridor. The same male guard who had escorted me from the car came back to call me for interrogation.

The guard was in a great hurry; it was difficult to keep up with him. When I reached the interrogation room, I was out of breath and my heart was beating wildly.

There were no fewer than eight men in the small room; four were seated on chairs placed along the wall opposite Mao's portrait, while others crowded around the interrogator.

The interrogator waved his arm towards the portrait. I bowed and nearly lost my balance. The floor heaved and I closed my eyes.

'Remain standing!' someone said, but his voice seemed to come from very far away.

'Explain yourself! Why did you laugh?' another voice said in the distance.

I tried to say something, but no word came. I must have fainted from hunger. When I opened my eyes, I found myself sitting on the floor supported by a female guard. My arms were freed from the handcuffs. The sleeve of my left arm was pulled up. The young doctor was standing over me, unscrewing the needle from a large syringe. He nodded to the interrogator and left the room. The female guard pulled me up and pushed me into the chair for the prisoner. She also left the room.

My heart was still palpitating and my lips were parched. But I felt better.

'Now, answer my question. Did you not see for yourself that the others are more enlightened than you are? They are coming over to the side of the Proletarian Revolutionaries. They have confessed everything. What are you going to do? Are you going to do the same and admit your guilt?' the interrogator asked.

I was feeling stronger by the minute. What did the doctor give me? Was it just an intravenous injection of glucose or was there something else in the syringe? Perhaps there was a stimulant. I was now wide awake, ready to fight.

Before I could answer the interrogator's question, someone interrupted, "What were you laughing at? Why did you laugh? It's no laughing matter. To be accused of being a spy for the imperialists is a very serious matter.' It was the voice of the young man who had led the meeting at the technical school. I looked at him with curiosity.

To my surprise, he did not look like the young industrial worker I assumed him to have been from his voice and vocabulary. He wore a jacket like that of an Army officer, but without the red patches on the collar that denoted a member of the Liberation Army. His trousers were dark grey, made with good-quality worsted that would cost at least 30 yuan a metre, twenty days' pay for an industrial worker. His hair was plastered down with grease and his black leather shoes were carefully polished. On the wrist of his left hand a gold watch peeped from under the cuff of his shirt sleeve. He was a young man of about twenty-five with an air of self-importance. I was puzzled who he was and how he dared to appear so well dressed during the Cultural Revolution; the clothes he was wearing were denounced as the habitual attire of the capitalist class. Was he not afraid to be mistaken for a class enemy?

Years later, I was to learn that his appearance was typical of the sons of senior Army commanders. The khaki jacket was a hint that the wearer was connected with the armed forces and, therefore, above the law. The status of their fathers gave these young men the privilege of appearing different from the other Revolutionaries they attempted to lead. Direct access to the seat of power through their family connections set them apart. In time they became the Mafia of Communist China as they plundered wealth, raped women and organized black-market and gambling activities.

Those whose fathers were very senior in the military hierarchy became China's biggest 'back door men' and 'fixers'. They could arrange anything, from housing and jobs to import and export trade because they could get things done through their own network of cronies without going through the established bureaucracy. Even merchants from Hong Kong anxious to get a good contract in China had to bribe these swaggering young men, often by giving them 'jobs' to enable them to travel to and from the British colony to smuggle gold, silver and antiques out of China and TV sets, recorders and watches into the country.

'Answer! Answer!' the well-dressed young man shouted. I looked at him and then I looked at the interrogator. But the latter was staring at the paper in front of him, seemingly annoyed that the young man had taken over the job of questioning me.

'I laughed because it was funny,' I told him.

'What was funny?' he asked.

'The whole thing you arranged was funny.'

'Explain yourself.'

'Well, don't you see? Tao was lying, and lying very badly. But you believed him and you were going to let him go home to his family. Isn't that funny?'

'Tao wasn't lying.'

'Wasn't he? Then you mean he was a real spy? In that case, you were going to let a real spy go home instead of punishing him with the death penalty or a stiff sentence? That's even funnier.'

'Never mind what's to happen to Tao. What about yourself? Don't you want to go home?'

'Of course I want to go home. I want full rehabilitation. I want an apology from the People's Government to be published in the *Liberation Daily* in Shanghai and in the *People's Daily* in Peking. But I won't lie. I'll achieve all that by adhering only to the truth,' I said.

I was looking at this well-dressed but rather stupid young man intently, wondering how he could have failed to realize that I laughed merely to break up his carefully arranged meeting. Suddenly he stood up and shouted in an excited voice, 'Bow your head! Bow your head! I won't let a class enemy stare at me with eyes like a pair of searchlights!'

The man seated next to him, obviously a lackey, quickly stood up, walked over to me and stretched out his hand to push my head down.

'It's my habit to look at the person I speak to. If I made you nervous, I apologize. Would you like me to sit with my back to you?' I turned my body to face Mao's portrait on the wall, as the chair for the prisoner was nailed to the ground and could not be moved. From the corner of my eye I caught a glimpse of the interrogator. He was biting his lip to stifle a smile.

'Now, answer my question. Were you or were you not a spy for the British? Are you or are you not going to confess?' asked the young man.

'I'm not a spy for anybody. I have nothing to confess,' I said firmly to the wall from where Mao's portrait looked down on me. As I gazed at Mao's face wearing what was intended as a benign expression but which was in fact a smirk of self-satisfaction, I wondered how one single person could have caused the extent of misery that was prevailing in China. There must be something lacking in our own character, I thought, that had made it possible for his evil genius to dominate.

'You are a spy!' the young man shouted angrily.

'I'm not.' I shook my head.

'We have evidence you are.'

'Produce it then.' I turned to face him once more.

'Didn't you hear your ex-staff members this morning?'

'That was no evidence. Just empty words of accusation made under duress.'

'Don't you worry. We'll show you concrete evidence. One, two, three, four … a very long list of things you said and did. But by then it will be too late for you to win lenient treatment.'

'A real spy shouldn't be given lenient treatment. A real spy should be shot, whether he confesses or not,' I declared.

The interrogator stood up and took over, 'Go back to your cell now and think over everything you heard at the meeting this morning. They were not all lies. Some are serious matters. The situation you are in is no laughing matter.' He got up and walked out of the room. A guard came to lead me back to the cell.

As I approached the women's prison, I saw the woman from the kitchen in her white apron pushing the huge cart with layers and layers of containers of sweet potatoes for the prisoners. She was being helped by two Labour Reform Girls. Apparently another inmate was also being given rice; the two containers of rice and cabbage stood out among the golden brown colour of the potatoes. As soon as I was back in my cell, my portion of rice was pushed through the small window.

My gums were now bleeding almost continuously. I had to rinse my mouth before taking food, or the food tasted of blood. Chewing had become more and more difficult. The cabbage was usually very tough. It took me a very long time to finish a meal. Because I had to return the chopsticks with the container before I could finish eating, I was allowed to purchase a plastic spoon from the prison shop. Now I sat on the edge of the bed, scooped the rice and cabbage into one of the mugs, washed the aluminium container and chopsticks ready to give back to the woman from the kitchen and started to eat my only meal of the day with the plastic spoon. While I ate, I reviewed what had happened during the day.

In spite of being knocked about and handcuffed, I thought that on the whole the day had not been wasted. I had learned what had

happened to the former members of the company's staff and could see
my own predicament in better perspective. I regretted that so many of
them had succumbed to pressure, which must have been great, but I
worried about others whose names I did not see on the Big Character
Posters and who were not among the speakers denouncing me. I
wondered whether they were still in this world.

As for our chief accountant, Tao, I considered his behaviour
dastardly. But I had to forgive him, I believed. The sound of his
sobbing was still in my ears. It was the cry of a tortured soul who had
reached the end of his tether.

The weather was decidedly warmer, and I had stopped shivering
several days earlier. I wondered whether I should wash the warm
woollen sweater I was wearing and put it away. I felt I must take great
care of all my winter clothing, as goods like that were not available in
the prison shop. God knew how long I would have to remain in the
detention house. The struggle between the Maoists and myself was in
fact a war of endurance. I simply must not die.

Soon after I had got into bed, the guard on duty came to the small
window. She pushed open the shutter gently and said in a whisper,
'Would you like to take a hot shower?'

What an unexpected and welcome offer! Prisoners were allowed
one hot shower a month. In the winter months, when it was too cold to
wash in the cell with cold water, I counted the days from one hot
shower to the next. That afternoon, when I came back from
interrogation, I had noticed that the female guards were going to the
shower room one after another throughout the whole evening. Now, it
seemed, they had all finished, so the guard was offering me the chance
to use up the hot water that was left in the pipes.

I jumped out of bed, grabbed my soap box and towels and followed
her to the shower room. While I stood under the spray of warm water,
washing my hair and my body, I marvelled at the changed attitude of
some of the guards since the day I had been bold enough to defend
their former leader, Liu Shao-chi. When I emerged from the shower
room, I slipped into the cell quietly. Soon afterwards, the guards came
and snapped the lock.

It rained the next day, not the chilly drops of winter which
crystallized into ice on the ground nor the angry torrent of summer
thunderstorms. It was the gentle drizzle that softly soaked the earth to
awaken the trees and flowers, warning them of the approach of spring.
I had always loved that wet smell of the earth after a day of spring
rain. It seemed so full of hope and the promise of beautiful scented

flowers and green shady leaves to come. The departure of winter, the relatively better food and vitamin pills and the relaxed attitude of some of the guards combined to make me feel less on edge. I found myself more optimistic about my chances of surviving the ordeal and less worried about the future.

My feeling of euphoria continued to the next day. When I was called again for interrogation, I walked with almost sprightly steps. This time only the well-dressed young man and the young worker were seated behind the counter.

After I had entered the room and the guard had closed the door, the young man raised his arm in the direction of Mao's portrait. I bowed. He told me to read the following quotation: 'A revolution is not a dinner party, or writing an essay, or painting pictures or doing embroidery; it cannot be so refined, so leisurely and so gentle, so temperate, kind, courteous, restrained and magnanimous. A revolution is an act of violence with which one class overthrows another.'

'Do you love England better than you love China?' he asked.

'I'm a Chinese citizen. Of course I love China better,' I answered.

'If we leave out the matter of citizenship, would you still love China more?'

'Chinese blood flows in my veins. Of course I love China more. I have always been a patriotic Chinese.'

'Were you in the United States in 1940?'

'Yes, I was there for a few months.'

'Did you make speeches when you were there?'

'Yes, I made some speeches about the Japanese invasion of China.'

'We have information that you also made speeches in praise of the British war effort. You spoke on a radio programme in New York. You were heard by some of your former Yenching University friends who have now confessed and provided us with this information. Probably you also spoke at other places. In any case, when you returned to Chungking, you made a propaganda broadcast from the Kuomintang radio station. You said the British imperialists were heroic people with great courage who would never give up until they won the final victory. Did the British Government ask you to make propaganda for them? Were you already recruited by the British in 1940? Answer me!'

'I went to New York from England on a British passenger steamer. A number of the passengers were interviewed on a radio programme. The interviewer asked me questions about Britain. Naturally I answered truthfully,' I said.

'You made propaganda for Britain.'

'During the war, Britain and China were on the same side.'

'Not in 1940. The British were helping the Japanese then. What you did proves beyond doubt that you were a British spy as long ago as 1940.'

'Nonsense. I was just a Chinese visitor in Britain who was moved by the courage and resolution of the British people in the face of overwhelming odds when Britain stood alone to resist Hitler's plan to conquer all of Europe.'

'Listen to you! You are at this moment echoing the propaganda line of the British imperialists. We think you love Britain better than China.'

'You can think whatever you want to, but you will have to prove your accusation against me.'

'We will prove it. We will prove that your claim of patriotism is false. It's for the purpose of covering up your evil deeds.'

He took a small brown folder from under the counter and held it up to look at. All I could see was the back of the folder; I wondered what it was that he was looking at with so much assumed concentration. Suddenly he turned the folder round. I saw that enclosed in the folder was a black-and-white photograph of myself dancing with a Swiss friend in the early fifties when the French Club was still in existence in Shanghai. An unemployed photographer snapped pictures of the guests of the club and offered copies to them for a yuan each. To help this man, we all bought the pictures. When the Red Guards came to my house, the photographs were in the store room. They must have taken the lot. My Swiss friend was an excellent dancer who knew many fancy steps. In the picture, he was teaching me something new and we were both laughing.

'Do you call that patriotic?' the young man said severely as if I had been caught doing something terrible.

'What has dancing got to do with patriotism?' I was genuinely puzzled.

'You were dancing with a foreigner. And you looked quite happy dancing with a foreigner. That's decidedly unpatriotic.'

'Is dancing with a foreigner unpatriotic?' I was rather taken aback by his line of attack. But I recovered in a moment and saw how I could turn the argument in my own favour. I went on, 'I didn't know dancing with a foreigner was not patriotic. But I must accept your superior judgement, as you are an enlightened Marxist and a Revolutionary. However, if I were not patriotic, at least I was useful. That's to my credit, don't you think?'

'What do you mean, you were useful?'

'Well, as you have just said, dancing with a foreigner was not patriotic. By dancing with my Swiss friend, I was making him unpatriotic, because to him surely I was the foreigner. If by the simple act of dancing I could make others unpatriotic, isn't that being useful? Think of the possibilities from that point on. You can simply send me to dance with all China's enemies all over the world and let me make them unpatriotic. Then, without firing a single shot, all of them are done for. How could anybody be more useful than that?' I was so overcome with mirth that I had some difficulty speaking the last few words clearly.

But the young man was not amused. His face flushed in anger. Pointing to the door of the interrogation room, he shouted, 'Get out! Get out! I'll have you shot!'

He looked so threatening as he advanced towards me that I fled the room in haste. But in the corridor there was no guard to lead me back to my cell. I waited, trying to stifle my giggles. I did not think it seemly or prudent to break out in laughter in that grim place. They might really think I was mad and consider themselves justified in sending me to the mental hospital.

However, it did not pay to laugh at the expense of someone in authority. This was made amply clear to me the very next day.

I was called to the interrogation room just before the prisoners' mid-morning meal. After the preliminaries, the same young man handed me the fourth volume of the *Collected Works of Mao Tze-tung*, opened at the page where a letter that was broadcast from the headquarters of the Communist Army to a group of Kuomintang generals was printed. The letter was drafted by Mao Tze-tung in December 1948, when Kuomintang troops were encircled by the Communist Army on the north bank of the Yangtze River near Nanking, the capital of the Kuomintang Government. It pointed out the hopelessness of the Kuomintang position and urged the generals to surrender.

'Remain standing and read the letter aloud,' the young man ordered.

I read the text aloud. When I had finished and was about to hand him back the book, he said, 'Read it again! Let the words sink into your stupid mind.'

I read it again. When I had finished it for the second time, he said, 'Did the words sink in? Do you understand the hopelessness of your position? You are surrounded just like those Kuomintang generals. No help is coming! The only way out is to surrender.'

I said nothing. He glared at me for a moment and then yelled, 'Read it again!'

When I had finished reading, we stared at each other. Then he shouted impatiently, 'Read it again! Let the words sink into your granite head!'

There I stood in the interrogation room for hours that day, reading the letter over and over again until I was dizzy, my voice hoarse and my legs badly swollen. By late afternoon, I was so weary that my voice was barely audible and I read the words haltingly. Since by this time I already knew the text by heart, I no longer had to look at the book but spoke the words slowly with my eyes closed. Gradually my arm holding the book dropped to my side. Whenever I stopped or hesitated, the young man yelled, 'Are you going to surrender?' He would wait for me to answer. When I did not answer, he would yell, 'Read it again!'

At first, the young worker stared at me while I read. Now I saw that he had lost interest. With his head on his folded arms, he seemed to be dozing. The two of them took turns to go out to eat. I had to go without food. Hungry and exhausted, I was in a daze. My mouth was so dry that my voice became a low murmur. Still, each time I finished reciting the text the young man yelled, 'Repeat!'

I was allowed to go back to my cell only when it was getting dark. Though I couldn't be sure how long I had stood in the interrogation room reading that letter drafted by Mao, it must have been more than seven hours. No food was kept for me. Throughout the whole day I had only water to drink in the morning before I went to the interrogation room and in the evening after I came back to the cell. To give myself some nourishment, I swallowed a handful of codliver oil capsules and B complex tablets.

This routine went on for three days, except that on the second and third day I was allowed to return to the cell in time for the afternoon meal. The guard on duty at the women's prison cooperated with the young man. She prolonged the evening exercise hour, during which time she took up position outside my cell and saw to it that I walked round and round in the cell for an hour. After I went to bed, the night duty guard came repeatedly to the door of my cell to open and shut the small window with a loud bang or kicked the door with her heavy boot to disturb my sleep. In spite of being awakened by her several times during the night, on the whole I slept soundly.

At the end of the third day, I was again on the verge of collapse. I thought this might have been apparent to the two young men. At the end of the afternoon, they both asked me, 'Are you going to surrender?'

I tried to speak. But I was very weak and my throat was so dry that only a hoarse whisper came.

'Speak clearly! Are you going to surrender?' the well-dressed young man asked.

I made a great effort. With all my strength I managed to say, 'Not guilty!'

'You will surely be shot!'

He left the room in a fit of temper and banged the door. I sat down in the prisoner's chair to rest and to wait for the guard.

The young worker stared at me with a puzzled frown on his brows. After a while, he said, 'What can you be thinking about? What is it you pin your hope on?'

I said nothing. A guard came to lead me out of the room.

Days passed. But I was not called again. Many times a day I thought of the interrogations and exchanges I had had with all the interrogators including the well-dressed young man. Over and over again I went through the questions they had asked me and the answers I had given. Could I have done better? Could I have done otherwise? I came to the conclusion that although sometimes they appeared as if they were trying to find out the actual facts of what had happened, all the interrogations were in fact simply part of the attempt to find me guilty. The questions were asked to elicit answers from me so that they could find something in my answers to be used against me. At the same time, they used the sessions of interrogation to show their power over me so that I would eventually be frightened into submission. Interrogations were not going to help resolve my case. They were used solely to add to my hardship. In fact, there was no point in my hoping for more interrogations.

With the coming of warmer weather my general health seemed to have improved somewhat. One piece at a time, I washed my winter sweaters and socks and laid them out to dry. I cleaned the collar and cuffs of my padded jacket and put it away. Be prepared for a long stay in the detention house, I told myself. As long as I could keep alive, I still had hope. The philosopher Lao-tze once said that when events developed to the extreme, the trend would be reversed. I must wait. I did my daily exercise and spent many hours reciting poetry to myself. Often I would sit there with Mao's book on my lap as if I were absorbed in reading his essays but actually my mind was filled with the stanzas of Li Bai or Tu Fu.

On 1 April 1969, two and a half years after my arrest, the long-awaited Ninth Party Congress opened in Peking. The newspaper reported that Lin Piao delivered the important political report, praising the Cultural Revolution and promising unrelenting efforts at class struggle. Among the fifteen hundred delegates were a large number of his supporters from the Army, Navy and Air Force. In the new Party constitution, Lin Piao was officially named Mao's successor. Both Lin Piao and Chiang Ching succeeded in placing their associates in the new Central Committee of 279 members. Many old well-known Party officials were dropped. Some few like Prime Minister Chou En-lai and Foreign Minister Chen Yi maintained their positions. But as a group the influence of the old guard was greatly diminished. In the final photograph published in the newspaper, Mao stood in the middle. On his left were all the Maoist leaders such as Lin Piao and Chiang Ching. On his right were the few members of the old guard headed by Prime Minister Chou En-lai.

While the Ninth Party Congress was in session, the newspaper reported daily displays of enthusiasm and support by the populace. In the detention house, prisoners were obliged to listen from morning till night to broadcasts of speeches and news bulletins, including long lists of names of delegates. Familiar names disappeared. New names appeared, reflecting the new power realignment that was going on in the Party leadership. On the day Lin Piao gave his political report, all prisoners were roused from sleep, told to get dressed and listen to its recording.

One day, just as I had settled down to eat my rice in the morning, the cell door was unlocked. A male guard yelled, 'Come out!'

I ignored him while I quickly swallowed mouthful after mouthful of rice without chewing.

'Come out!' he yelled again. But he did not come into the cell.

My chopsticks were flying as I swept the rice into my mouth. I was determined to face whatever was in store for me with some food in my stomach. I suspected they always timed the interrogations to make me miss my meals.

'Come out!' he yelled for the third time and came into the cell. Calmly he took from my hand the mug containing food and placed it on the table. 'You can eat it when you come back,' he said.

Quickly I dipped the other mug into the washbasin full of cold water and drank several mouthfuls to wash down the hard rice lingering in my oesophagus.

'Hurry up! You are so slow,' he said.

'Please go outside. I have to use the toilet.'

He had to leave the cell. The female guard on duty came in to watch me. I washed my hands and wiped my mouth. As I was picking up the Little Red Book of Mao's quotations, the mild female guard shook her head and murmured, 'No need to take it.' I put the book back on the bed and followed her out of the cell.

The militant female guard ran into the corridor and shouted breathlessly, 'What are you doing? Why are you so slow?'

I followed her out of the women's prison to the courtyard. Another male guard was waiting with a pair of handcuffs. The female guard twisted my arms back and put the handcuffs on my wrists. Then she gave a hard shove that sent me staggering. As soon as I recovered my balance and started to walk normally, she gave me another hard shove. Thus, by spurts and starts, I reached the front entrance of the detention house. The same white sedan was parked there with the driver in his seat. He had his hand on the horn, emitting intermittent bursts of sound until he saw me coming. The well-dressed young man was pacing to and fro and the old worker was standing nearby.

When they saw me, they both walked over. I knew from the expression on the young man's face that what was going to happen to me this day was a punishment for my intransigence. He said through his clenched teeth, 'You are going to a meeting to celebrate the successful conclusion of the Ninth Party Congress and the election of the new Central Committee. Be sure to behave yourself. Abandon your arrogant manner! Otherwise the Revolutionaries will tear you apart.' He relaxed somewhat, almost as if the prospect of my being torn apart by the Revolutionaries was pleasing to him.

'Here in the No. 1 Detention House, we have rules and regulations about the treatment of prisoners. We have been extremely tolerant and restrained towards you. Outside this gate, the situation is different. The revolutionary masses can do whatever they want. You had better be careful. Don't speak out of turn. In fact, you had better be docile and obedient, otherwise they will kill you. Many people have been killed already in that way,' the old worker said.

Were they really concerned about the preservation of my life? I thought not. They were simply anxious to avoid the criticism that they had failed to tame the prisoner under their control. Possibly senior officials were to be present at this meeting on whom they would want to make a good impression.

'Do you understand the situation?' the young man asked me.

'I will not answer back if I am not provoked,' I told him.

'Perhaps we should really teach you a lesson before we go,' he said, curling his fingers into a fist and waving it in front of my eyes.

'You should know by now I am not to be silenced by physical violence. The more you provoke me, the more I'll answer back.'

'All right then. We shall let the masses teach you a lesson. You had better look out. They will kill you if you answer back.'

'Do you mean to say I must remain silent even if someone asks me a question?' I wanted to get the situation clear.

'Yes, just bow your head and admit your crime.'

'I would rather die than admit something that is not true.'

'Keep silent then. Whatever they say to you, just keep quiet,' said the old worker, who seemed decidedly the better person of the two.

'All right. I'll keep silent, no matter what they say. But that doesn't mean I admit I'm guilty.'

'It's not for the masses to decide whether you are guilty or not,' the old worker assured me.

The young man told me to get into the car. I sat down on the back seat with the old worker and another man. The young man sat beside the driver. As the car emerged from the drive onto the streets, another sedan with all the others who had taken part in my last few interrogations followed.

April was a beautiful month in Shanghai. The polluted air of this industrial city was freshened by the young leaves of plane trees lining the streets. There was a sense of renewal after the rigours of winter. The windows of the car were open; the brown silk curtains fluttered in the breeze so that I could see something of the streets. We were heading north right across town. At road intersections we were frequently held up by parades organized to celebrate the conclusion of the Ninth Party Congress. Red banners, slogans on coloured paper, drums and gongs and the portraits of Mao were the same as had been used in other parades at the beginning of the Cultural Revolution. But I noticed that the people taking part now looked very different from the excited crowd of three years ago. Instead of the animation and excitement I remembered, people looked bored. Their steps were slow and dragging; their voices shouting slogans were weak and flat. Some did not join in at all. They seemed to be suffering from revolutionary fatigue after nearly three years of unremitting enthusiasm for class struggle. Or, perhaps more likely, they were simply disillusioned by the developments of the Cultural Revolution. Many of them probably had children who were Red Guards, to whom they had to send food and clothing in the countryside since nearly all former Red Guards had been dispersed to the rural areas. Others might have found the confusion and shortages created by the Cultural Revolution a heavy burden added to their already straitened living conditions.

Normally streets in Shanghai were filled with loitering people. But on this spring day, apart from the paraders, there were few idle onlookers. I was puzzled because I had not fully realized to what extent the violence by the Red Guards and the Revolutionaries had driven the people off the streets. Stray bullets had claimed many victims during the factional civil wars and the Red Guards and Revolutionaries had beaten up people at random just to keep themselves in a state of readiness for further action.

When the car reached the area of the universities and the military airport on the outskirts of the city, an air force parade came towards us. At the end of the line was a contingent of strikingly beautiful slender young girls in uniform. They looked more like the glamorous females in a film version of the air force than the real thing. Later, after my release, when the Lin Piao affair had officially been made the subject of public criticism, I learned something about these young women. The Chinese people were told that when Lin Piao made his son, Lin Li-guo, second in command of the Chinese air force at the age of twenty-five when he was fresh out of some military college reserved for sons of senior officers, followers of Lin Piao sent Lin Li-guo beautiful girls from all over China to form his 'three thousand beauties in the inner palace', in imitation of the selection of concubines for the Emperor's heir in the old days. The girls were offered jobs in the air force as an enticement. Because membership in the armed forces was a guarantee of higher prestige and better treatment, with special consideration for their families, the girls enrolled eagerly without realizing that they were chosen for Lin Li-guo's pleasure. Then they were brought to Shanghai where Lin Li-guo had a secret and elaborate establishment. The girls were sorted out under the pretext of physical examination. Those who did not catch Lin Li-guo's fancy were assigned jobs in the air force. These were the girls I saw taking part in the parade.

The car turned into the gates of a large compound of red-brick buildings. There was no signboard to indicate the nature of the place and no sentry to guard the entrance, only a solitary man to admit the cars and close the gate after us. He followed the cars inside. The atmosphere was rather mysterious and I decided to observe everything closely. It almost seemed as if they did not want me to know the nature of the place I was being taken to.

After passing between trim lawns and budding willow trees, the car stopped in front of one of the buildings. Two husky-looking women in blue Mao uniforms with the red armbands of the Revolutionaries were waiting. One of them opened the door of the car. The old worker jumped out. I was preparing to alight when the second woman stretched out her hand to pull me out roughly. The two women put their hands under my arms and hoisted me up to take me into the building almost as if they thought I might try to run away. We entered a small room and they pushed me into a corner.

'Face the wall! Don't move!' one of the women yelled.

I heard the women sit down heavily. No one uttered a word. After what seemed a long time, I heard the door being opened; a man's voice mentioned food. After whispered consultation, one of the women left the room. When she came back, the other one went out. All the time I stood with my face to the wall.

More waiting in complete silence. I shifted my weight from one leg to the other for the hundredth time. Suddenly the door opened again. A man's voice said with an air of awe and mystery like a servant in the home of a Chinese high official speaking of his important master, 'Lai-la!' This meant someone had come, or arrived. From the tone of voice of the messenger, it was someone important.

The two women shot out of their chairs like lightning, grabbed my arms again and half-carried and half-dragged me out of the building. We passed beside a deserted basketball court, along a tree-lined path and entered another building. My feet hardly touched the ground; my armpits were bruised by the women's iron fingers.

My curiosity increased by the minute. What could this place be? The layout was like that of a university compound. But the clean buildings and trim lawns seemed to indicate this was no ordinary institution of higher education. The men who came with me were walking a few steps ahead of me. They had an air of restraint and caution. I decided, in spite of the absence of armed sentries at the gate, the place was either the site of a government department of some importance or a military establishment. Chinese people usually tread gingerly in the vicinity of power and firearms.

We entered a meeting hall where about a hundred people were assembled, sitting in two sections facing each other. In the space between, against the wall, was a raised platform. A number of people in civilian clothes were seated in a semi-circle behind the table. The men from No. 1 Detention House joined them. On the walls were the usual Cultural Revolution slogans written with white paint on red cloth. They proclaimed the victory of the Maoists and the utter destruction of the 'capitalist-roaders' in the Party. The 'historical' meeting of the Ninth Party Congress was declared a great success for the promotion of Marxist-Leninist-Mao Tze-tung Thought. I noticed that the portrait of Lin Piao, the official successor to Mao, appeared beside the official portrait of Mao.

Everything in the room was neat and clean, indicating that this building belonged to an organization with a generous budget and a high degree of discipline. This could only mean the military. I looked at the audience. The people seemed to me rather better dressed than the usual crowd on the streets. There were many jackets and trousers made of wool or dacron, not the sea of faded blue cotton at an ordinary Shanghai meeting.

The women dropped me in front of a microphone opposite the platform. One of them pushed my head down so that I was forced to look at the floor. Within my view were tangled wires leading from the microphone. One of the wires must lead to an electricity outlet, I thought. Where did the others lead to? Was it possible that men in another room were listening in on the struggle meeting? Who could they be? Why should they behave in such a mysterious manner? Perhaps they did not want me to see them? Apart from my local policeman and the young woman in charge of the section dealing with foreign firms at the Shanghai Industry and Commerce Department, I knew few government officials by sight. At diplomatic receptions of the few western missions in Shanghai to which I had been invited, I had seen one of the Vice-Mayors and some officials of the Foreign Affairs Department. Surely they must have become victims of the Cultural Revolution when the Shanghai Municipal Government was overthrown. The only possible explanation was that Lin Piao's men had taken over my investigation. The men listening to the struggle meeting were men in uniform. What they did not want me to see was not their faces but their military apparel.

The audience in the room was shouting slogans and waving Little Red Books in the air. After the 'Long Live Our Great Leader Chairman Mao' came 'Good Health to Our Vice-Supreme Commander Lin, Always Good Health!' This seemed to me not only a reflection of the elevated position of Lin Piao after the Ninth Party Congress, but also testimony to the fact that those who organized this meeting were his intimates, anxious to promote Lin Piao's personality cult.

Two legs came into my limited field of vision. A man's voice spoke in front of me. He introduced me to the audience by giving an account of my family background and personal life. I had noticed already that each time my life story was recounted by the Revolutionaries I became richer and my way of life became more decadent and luxurious. Now the farce reached fantastic proportions. Since I had promised not to answer back but to remain mute, I was much more relaxed and detached than at the previous struggle meeting in 1966. However the audience jumped up from their seats when the speaker told them I was a spy for the imperialists. They expressed their anger and indignation by crowding around me to shout abuse.

To be so maligned was intolerable. Instinctively I raised my head to respond. The women suddenly jerked up my handcuffed hands. Such sharp pain tore at my shoulder joints that I had to bend my body forward with my head well down to ease the agony. They kept me in this position during the rest of the man's denunciation of me. Only when the people were again shouting slogans did they allow my arms to drop back. I was to learn later that I had been subjected to the so-called 'jet position' invented by the Revolutionaries to torment their more recalcitrant victims and to force them to bow their heads in servile submission.

Another man took over. He spoke about what he called my 'disobe-dience' to the command of the Revolutionaries, who represented the Communist Party, to confess. I realized for the first time that my failure to provide a confession of guilt was interpreted as an act of defiance against the Party. The audience was now even more angry. Perhaps to disobey the Party was a more serious offence than being a spy? I did not have time to decide on an answer before I was pushed and fell to the floor. However, the female giants by my side pulled me up with their strong arms and I was restored to my previous position behind the microphone.

A third man spoke. He denounced my defence of Liu Shao-chi. After the Central Committee resolution against him and the amount of propaganda which 'proved beyond doubt' that Liu was everything the resolution named him to be, the subject of Liu Shao-chi became one that demanded a strong display of anger from everybody who did not want to get into political trouble. When one tries to show emotion one does not genuinely feel, one tends to exaggerate. This audience was no exception. The women were always prompt and ready to pull me up again. Once or twice they even raised an arm to ward off a blow or two aimed at me.

The people in the audience soon worked themselves into a state of hysteria. Their shouts drowned out the voice of the speaker. Someone pushed me hard from behind. I stumbled and knocked over the microphone. One of the women tried to pick it up, tripped over the wires and fell, dragging me with her. Because my arms were pinned behind me by the handcuffs, I fell in an awkward position. My face was pressed on the floor; many others fell on top of us in the confusion. Everybody seemed to be yelling. There was pandemonium. Several minutes passed. Finally I was pulled up again.

Utterly exhausted, I longed for the meeting to end. But the speeches continued. It seemed everyone sitting round the table on the platform wanted to make a contribution. They had ceased to denounce me; instead they were competing with each other to sing the praises of Lin Piao in the most extravagant flattery the rich Chinese language could provide. Their efforts to register their devotion to Lin Piao could be explained, I thought, only by the probable presence of Lin Piao's loyal lieutenants listening in an adjacent room.

Suddenly the door behind me opened. A man's voice shouted, 'Tso-la!' This meant that somebody had departed. The two simple words produced an effect that was electrical. The speaker stopped in mid-sentence. Since the important person or persons listening in another room had gone, there was no more need to go on with the performance. Some of the audience were already on their feet, while others were collecting their bags and jackets. Hastily the speaker led them to shout slogans. He was largely ignored. Only a few responded while walking out of the room. It seemed the people were no longer angry with me; though they did not smile, the glances directed at me were indifferent. I was just one of the many victims at whose struggle meeting they had been present. They had done what was required of them. Now it was over. Once when a man brushed against me, someone behind him even stretched out a hand to steady me.

The room cleared in a moment. I could hear members of the departing audience chatting as they left the building. 'Getting rather chilly, isn't it?' 'Where are you going for supper?' 'Not raining, is it?' ... etc. etc. They sounded no different from an audience departing after a show in a cinema or theatre.

The tense atmosphere dissipated like the escaping air from a burst balloon. The two women led me to the waiting car. This time they allowed me to walk by myself. For them, also, the show was over.

The 'celebration' of the Ninth Party Congress went on for several weeks. Every few days I was taken to a different struggle meeting, sometimes less well organized than the first one. When the audience was very violent, I suffered very much. Afterwards, I would be called for an interview in the interrogation room and asked whether I was ready to confess. I would either say, 'I have nothing to confess' or 'I'm not guilty' or simply remain silent. Then I would be taken to yet another struggle meeting. This exposure to one struggle meeting after another, called 'rotating struggle', was a mind-numbing experience. Day after day, my ears were filled with the sound of angry accusing voices, my eyes were blurred by images of hostile faces and my body ached from rough handling and physical abuse. I no longer felt like a human being, just an inanimate object. Sometimes my spirit seemed to leave my body to look on the scene with detachment. Though I stopped thinking or observing what went on and withdrew into myself after a certain time, I was never really confused or frightened.

My personal experience of 'rotating struggle', painful though it was at the time, was a comparatively mild one compared to that of many others. After Mao Tze-tung's death in 1976, people became vocal about their experiences in the Cultural Revolution. I met one wizened old man who talked about his experience with a great sense of humour. He told me that he had been struggled against 'more than a hundred times', frequently with a heavy iron chain round his neck, used to punish victims who refused to bow their heads voluntarily. Only when he told me some of his friends and colleagues had died during the struggle meetings did he display emotion. I asked him about the 'jet position', which inflicted so much pain on the victims. He lightly brushed it aside, saying that it was used on all victims.

CHAPTER 10

My Brother's Confession

When the series of rotating struggle meetings was over, summer was upon us. Before the humid heat of July started in earnest, Shanghai had a month of rain which the weather men called the Huangmei, named after the yellow plum which ripened in June. Dampness filled the cell and blackened the cement floor. After a particularly heavy downpour, water overflowed from the drain to seep through the base of the walls, forming dark murky puddles in the corners of the room. The pervading odour of mustiness and decay made each breath an unpleasant experience. Green mould formed on my stored winter jacket, padded trousers and even on the shoes I left overnight on the damp floor.

While I always welcomed the warmer weather with eagerness because I no longer had to shiver in the cold and huddle into all my clothes to keep warm, I was dismayed to find the dampness causing me pain in the joints, which became red and swollen. When cool winds accompanied rainfall, my joints became so stiff that I had difficulty getting out of bed in the mornings. At the same time, the inflammation of my gums became much worse. They bled all the time, not just when I brushed my teeth. I had to rub the gums and press out the blood with a finger and rinse my mouth before eating any food. Even then, the contact of salty food with the inflamed gums sent shivers of pain through my body. I had to wash the vegetables with cold water before eating them in an effort to get rid of the salt. When the pain of my gums became too severe, the young doctor gave me sulpha drugs to reduce inflammation. But he told me there was no dental department at the prison hospital.

My already difficult existence became a constant struggle to keep one step ahead of my body's steady deterioration. Life had never been so demanding or so meaningless. However, despite the physical pain and discomfort, I was in a calmer mood than I had been for some time. This was because I was going through a series of interrogations which again led me to hope for the eventual clarification of my case. Every few days I was called to the interrogation room where the interrogator of the Workers' Propaganda Team questioned me about my relatives and friends, one by one. Between interrogations, I was asked to write lengthy accounts about each one of them and to describe all our contacts. I knew that what I wrote would be checked with what my friends and relatives had written about me and our contacts, such as what they had said to me and what I had said to them, etc. The interrogator and his fellow workers would compare what we had written to find discrepancies which might be used to cast doubts and suspicions about my honesty. Therefore it was important to write accurately, giving all facts but not elaborating on them, in case I contradicted what others had said. Sometimes the interrogation sessions were stormy, with the interrogator voicing threats and dissatisfaction with what I had written or said. At other times, I would be urged to provide incriminating evidence against this one or that one of my relatives and friends. Then I knew the person in question was in serious trouble.

On the whole, to answer questions about my relatives and friends and to write about them gave me the opportunity to speak on their behalf. From what I knew of the nature of their occupations and their past lives, I could generally guess the sort of problems confronting them during the Cultural Revolution. I searched my memory for what they had done and said that might help to improve their standing in the eyes of the Revolutionaries. And I put what I had to say in the language familiar and acceptable to the Maoists.

One of the outstanding characteristics of educated Chinese of my generation was our keen sense of patriotism, born of our knowledge and experience of the outside world and our concern for China's comparative backwardness. We were acutely conscious of the fact that China's recent history was the record of a great civilization which had been in steady decline for a century. In fact, it was the naive belief that the Communist Revolution might provide China with the impetus for progress that led so many of us to remain in, or go back to, China around 1949. Therefore in my accounts I could truthfully speak of my friends' and relatives' deep love for China and their service to the country. But all of it fell on deaf ears. Determined to find fault, the Revolutionaries refused to see virtue. Furthermore, the Maoists confused the concept of nation, which means 'people having common descent', with State, which means 'an organized political community under one government'. If a man had made an important scientific or artistic contribution to China's cultural life before the Communist Party came to power, he was supposed to have served not China, but the Kuomintang regime. Therefore, he was guilty of helping to sustain the rule of the enemy. This point of view was so narrowminded and absurd that I engaged in frequent arguments with the interrogator about it. However, I soon discovered that I was dealing not with the prejudice of the few Maoists in charge of my case but with the accepted view of the Communist Party.

The sessions of interrogation started in the rainy season. Often I arrived in the interrogation room with a wet face, wet matted hair and soaked socks and shoes. I had no raincoat but fortunately it was still cool enough for me to wear several layers of clothing so that I was not drenched through. The interrogations went on into the hot summer months, when dampness and rain gave way to oppressive heat and mosquitoes. Sometimes other men, obviously from the organizations of the persons I was asked to provide material for, joined my interrogator to ask me questions. Then I would know that my friends or relatives were also undergoing investigation just as I was. I would worry about them and watch closely the language and attitude of the strangers. If they looked fairly mild and seemed reasonable, I would be relieved; if they looked particularly stupid and menacing, I would be apprehensive.

In the autumn, I had a gruelling time when a member of the Military Control Commission of the People's Art Theatre came to question me about their director, Huang Tsuo-ling. Huang and his wife, Dan-nee, a beautiful and talented actress, were old friends of my husband and myself from our student days in London. When the Communist Army took over Shanghai, Huang was already a well-known and successful film director. It was believed that the couple had been invited to remain in China by the Communist Party underground in Shanghai. Both of them were accepted by the new regime at once; when the People's Art Theatre was formed, Huang was named its director and became a Party member. Their careers flourished; together they put on the Shanghai stage many first-rate plays, including translations of Shakespeare's comedies and other works by contemporary European and American writers that satirized the capitalist system. It was largely through the efforts of these two that the Chinese audience was made aware of the fact that playwrights of other lands were allowed to present their own societies in a critical light. Huang was considered a first-rate director by the public and the Party leaders in charge of cultural affairs. It was also obvious that he was different from those who followed closely the Maoist line of 'art serving politics' and 'art for the glorification of the workers, the peasants and the soldiers'.

Before I was called to the interrogation room this particular time, I had already read numerous articles in the newspaper criticizing Huang's film, *Fighting for Shanghai*, made in the early fifties to eulogize the

Communist takeover of the city. The film was a very successful propaganda effort carried out with skill; at the time it came out, it was hailed as a great achievement. Now the newspaper devoted several days and many columns to criticizing the film, alleging that Huang had made the Kuomintang defenders of the city 'heroic', thereby slighting the Communist soldiers. The critics also claimed that when he depicted the destruction of the city and the sufferings of the people, he exposed himself as a man opposed to armed struggle in general and the War of Liberation by the Communist Party in particular. It was clear from the avalanche of criticism directed against him in the press that he had been singled out as a victim.

Why had a man like Huang Tsuo-ling, who had served the Communist regime effectively and well, become the target of severe attack? Like many others, he was a victim of the internal power struggle within the Communist Party leadership. The men who gave him his positions and Party membership were old enemies of Chiang Ching in the thirties in Shanghai. At that time, she was a minor film actress struggling for recognition, while they were the leaders of the Left-Wing Cultural Movement in Shanghai that was the rallying point of China's left-wing writers and artists and a part of the Chinese Communist Party underground directed by Liu Shao-chi. Apparently these left-wing intellectuals largely ignored her, thinking of her as a woman of easy virtue and little talent. Chiang Ching had nursed her resentment throughout the years. When she gained the power to deal with the Cultural Department of the Party during the Cultural Revolution, she had all these men arrested and denounced as members of the Liu Shao-chi faction. Since patronage was a part of Chinese political life, the downfall of any official always brought about the downfall of his subordinates.

'Do you know Huang Tsuo-ling, the comprador?' the Military Control representative from the People's Art Theatre, seated beside my interrogator, asked me as soon as I was in the chair for the prisoner after reading one of Mao's quotations selected by my interrogator.

I gathered from his question that since they had failed to find anything wrong in Huang's personal behaviour, they were digging into his background.

A comprador was a man who acted as liaison between foreign firms and Chinese officials. This system had been originally invented by the Ching dynasty at the end of the last century in order to control foreign traders. With the advent of modern business methods, the system died out gradually in the thirties. But big firms like Shell did not sack their compradors. They simply stopped appointing new ones after the death of the old compradors. The Chinese Communist regime regarded former compradors as the most reactionary members of the bourgeois class. After the Communist Army took over Shanghai, those classified as members of the 'comprador-bourgeois class' all suffered imprisonment or heavy fines. Huang's father had been Shell's comprador in Tientsin; he died during the Sino-Japanese war.

'I know Huang Tsuo-ling, the well-known director of films and plays,' I answered.

'He was also a comprador of Shell!' said the man in uniform from the People's Art Theatre. 'We know all about you. You are a diehard reactionary and a spy of the imperialists. We are not surprised you try to evade my questions.

'Huang Tsuo-ling is in serious trouble. He is a class enemy who wormed his way into the Party. If you try to shield him, the consequences will be extremely serious. Your own position will become much worse. If you are clear-headed and cooperative, it will count in your favour as a contribution to the Cultural Revolution,' my interrogator said.

'I'll speak the truth,' I said.

'If you speak the truth, you will say he was a comprador of Shell,' the military man said.

'It was his father who was a comprador of Shell. Huang Tsuo-ling has an unfortunate family origin,' I said.

'He took over the job when his father died,' the man said.

'The position of comprador was abolished long ago. When his father died, it had ceased to exist,' I told him.

'Then what is this?' The man threw a document on the table. The interrogator handed it to me. It was the deed for a piece of land in Tientsin bearing Huang Tsuo-ling's seal as the owner. I saw the serial number on it and recognized it as a document taken from a Shell office file.

'That's an old document,' I said.

'Old or new, it shows that Huang Tsuo-ling was a Shell comprador, a fact he hid from the Party.'

'I can tell you the whole story, if you will listen,' I said.

'Go ahead,' said my interrogator.

'I don't know the date, but it was long before the war that the Kuomintang Government proclaimed a new regulation forbidding foreign ownership of land in China. All the foreign firms owning land transferred their deeds to their compradors' names. Shell did the same. When Huang's father passed away, Huang inherited the family's property holdings. This took place during the war; Tientsin was under Japanese occupation and Huang Tsuo-ling was not there. Shell was not there either. It had ceased operation after Pearl Harbor. I suppose whoever was Huang Tsuo-ling's agent just put his seal on the deeds of all his father's properties, including this piece of land belonging to Shell. That doesn't mean Huang Tsuo-ling was ever employed by Shell as its comprador.'

'He was paid by Shell for his services,' said the military man from the People's Art Theatre.

'I know nothing about that,' I answered.

'Your husband actually made the payment as Shell's general manager.'

'He did not mention the matter to me.' I decided it was best to deny knowledge of the transaction so that they would know I could not help them to incriminate Huang and would leave me alone. Actually my husband did tell me that Shell wanted to give Huang a sum of money to show the Company's appreciation of what his father had done for Shell, even though the land was confiscated during the Land Reform Movement of 1950 by the Communist Government. Such a generous gesture by Shell did not fit the image of foreign exploitation projected by Communist Party propaganda.

'You are lying. Your servants said you and your husband talked about everything together.'

'He did not mention this matter to me. Perhaps he did not consider it was anything important,' I said. 'Certainly we did not discuss everything that took place in his office.'

'We don't believe you.'

'That's as you please. I know nothing about any payment. But that doesn't mean you can't find out. You can look at our office files or you can ask our accounts department.'

'We have already done that. Do you think we would overlook anything like that? I have all the proof that he was paid by your husband.'

'In that case, the fact I do not know anything makes no difference.'

'We want you to admit that Huang Tsuo-ling was a comprador of Shell. He was paid for his services. You are the most senior of Shell's Chinese staff. You can confirm what we know already. Huang Tsuo-ling belongs to the comprador-bourgeois class. The comprador-bourgeois class is the most reactionary of all. He will be expelled from the Party. You and your husband were friends of his. You know him well. You could provide valuable information against him,' the military man said.

To be expelled from the Communist Party was the worst possible fate for a Party member. He could not become again one of the masses. His position in society would be little better than that of a counter-revolutionary; he would be discriminated against at all times. And his family, including his children and their children, would have to suffer with him. For me, it was tragic and unjust that such a future was to await Huang Tsuo-ling, who had devoted his life and talents to serve the Communist cause. The whole situation made me angry. I said firmly, 'As far as I know, Huang Tsuo-ling was a loyal member of the Communist Party. He was never a comprador. When his father died, Shell no longer had any comprador in Tientsin.'

'You are uncooperative,' said my interrogator. 'Don't you want to earn a merit point for yourself?'

'I have to adhere to the truth,' I said.

They became angry. The representative of the Military Commission of the People's Art Theatre went red in the face and stared at me with disappointment and disgust. My interrogator said, 'We want you to write an account of Huang Tsuo-ling, the comprador. Put down everything you know about him. If you try to cover up for him, the consequences will be extremely serious for you. If you provide information that is useful, you will make a contribution to the Cultural Revolution. And you'll get a merit point. Try to remember everything he said to you and your husband and put down what you know of his life and his views. He's a class enemy. You should expose him and denounce him. This is your opportunity to declare your standpoint. If you expose him effectively, we will think you have made an improvement in your own reform.'

'If you want to earn a merit point for yourself, denounce Huang Tsuo-ling,' added the military man from the People's Art Theatre.

What they said was an insult to my integrity. But it was the standard pronouncement made to encourage lying to suit the purpose of the political campaign of the moment. How many people succumbed to such pressure I did not know. In the present instance, it only strengthened my resolve to speak only the truth.

When I had written down everything I knew and remembered of Huang Tsuo-ling's life and views, including his firm belief that the Chinese Communist Party represented progress and enlightenment for China, they threw the account back to me and threatened me with severe punishment because I had failed to state that Huang was a

Shell comprador in Tientsin. I was threatened and warned in stormy
sessions and had to write the account over and over again. But I stuck
to my story and refused to concede to their demands. After a few
weeks, the matter was dropped and the man from the People's Art
Theatre disappeared just as suddenly as he had appeared.

Later, after my release from the detention house, I learned that the
Revolutionaries never succeeded in classifying Huang Tsuo-ling as a
member of the comprador-bourgeois class and expelling him from the
Party. Huang was merely denounced as a member of the Liu Shao-chi
camp. He and his wife spent the years of Cultural Revolution being
struggled against at numerous meetings and worked at various tasks
of heavy physical labour, including carrying loads of earth and bricks
at a building site in severe winter weather and scorching summer
heat. Huang's health was damaged and his beautiful wife became an
old woman.

After Mao's death and the arrest of the Gang of Four in 1976, the
political situation changed in China. Both Huang Tsuo-ling and his
wife were rehabilitated.

One of the most ugly aspects of life in Communist China during the
Mao Tze-tung era was the demand by the Party that people inform
against each other in peacetime and denounce each other during
political campaigns. This practice had a profoundly destructive effect
on human relationships. Husbands and wives became guarded with
each other and parents were alienated from their children. This
practice inhibited all forms of human contact, so that people no longer
wanted to have friends. It also encouraged secretiveness and
hypocrisy. To protect himself, a man had to keep his thoughts to
himself. When he was compelled to speak, often lying was the only way
to protect himself and his family.

While I was being pressured and urged to provide incriminating
material against others, those others were at the same time being
pressured and urged to provide incriminating material against me. I
could usually guess what my relatives and friends had said or written
about me from the questions the interrogator asked. It was not
difficult to discern whether a certain person was still cool-headed and
holding his own or whether he had become panicky and confused.
Towards the end of 1969, I went through a rather difficult time
because of a 'confession' made by my brother in Peking. It illustrated
once again how a perfectly intelligent and well-educated person could
break down under pressure so that he no longer knew the demarcation
line between fact and fiction.

Amid fanfare and celebration, Mao had made another new pronouncement. It appeared in red print in the newspaper and was embodied in a leading article by the joint editors of the *People's Daily* and the *Red Flag Magazine*, both Party organs; and the editors of the *Liberation Army Daily*, which was the Army's newspaper. Mao had declared, 'The Proletarian Cultural Revolution is a great political revolution of the proletarian class against the capitalist class. It is the continuation of the class struggle by the proletarian class against the capitalist class. It is also the continuation of the class struggle by the Communist Party against the Kuomintang.'

After the publication of this piece of wisdom, a campaign was initiated to 'root out the dregs of the Kuomintang'. Daily, the newspaper reported the exposure of undercover Kuomintang agents, hidden Kuomintang military personnel and sympathizers of the Kuomintang regime in Taiwan. So many enemies were unearthed in such a short time that it seemed that China was suddenly full of men and women secretly longing for the Kuomintang. The years of Communist propaganda against the former government seemed a wasted effort. A tense atmosphere of extreme nervousness had been deliberately created. It provided the excuse for another round of witch-hunting and legitimized the escalation of class struggle to create fear in the general public. The only way for a man to prove his innocence was to display exaggerated support for Mao and the Party; to shout slogans louder, to work harder in a spirit of self-sacrifice for no material reward and to be extra cruel to the class enemies. The newspaper urged members of the proletariat to be vigilant and to watch for unusual activities and strange behaviour among their neighbours and fellow workers in the workplace. They were also to increase the surveillance of class enemies not incarcerated in prisons.

The next call for interrogation came as no surprise to me. My persecutor could not afford to leave me out of another round of class struggle if he wished to appear to be following Mao's directives closely. After all, I was the widow of a Kuomintang government official.

The interrogator told me to read the latest directive of Mao as soon as I entered the interrogation room and had bowed to his portrait. When I had finished reading it, he told me to read it again. Then the interrogator said, 'We are to expose the dregs of the Kuomintang. You are one of them.'

Two other men were in the room. Suddenly the younger one of the two shouted, 'Confess!'

'What about?' I asked.

'Don't pretend to be calm and innocent. Confess your relationship with the Kuomintang!'

'I've no relationship with the Kuomintang.'

'You are a loyal supporter of the Kuomintang.'

'I doubt very much the Kuomintang would agree with you,' I said. While I was speaking I observed the two men. From their clothes and their short hair-style, I thought they were from North China. All Chinese are supposed to speak Mandarin, the national spoken language based on the Peking dialect. However, natives of Peking like the young man who had spoken often retained certain recognizable intonations of their original dialect. I wondered why two men from Peking were taking part in my interrogation. In the early stage of this series of interrogations, when I was going through the members of my family, I had already written about my brother and sister-in-law living in Peking, and provided the interrogator with an account of our contacts throughout the years.

'You are a loyal supporter of the Kuomintang. It's useless to deny it.'

'Please prove your accusations,' I said.

'Of course we have proof, otherwise we wouldn't have come such a long way to question you,' said the older of the two men, who seemed to be senior in position. He looked and spoke like an industrial worker with little education, a true member of the proletariat. The younger man looked like a student.

'Have you ever had your photograph taken in front of a Kuomintang flag?' asked my interrogator.

'Maybe I have. I can't remember for sure,' I answered. I thought he was asking me about the days during the Second World War, long before the Communist Party came to power in China, when my late husband was a diplomat at the Chinese Embassy in Canberra, Australia.

'How could you not remember! You can't get out of your difficulty by simply claiming loss of memory,' said the young man from Peking.

'It was so long ago,' I said. 'If there was a photograph the Red Guards who came to my house should have it. They took all my photographs.'

'You must have destroyed the photograph. It's not there,' the older man said.

'Why should I destroy a photograph like that? Everybody knows my late husband was a diplomatic officer of the Kuomintang Government when we lived in Australia.'

'What are you talking about? Who is asking you about those days?' the interrogator said with impatience.

'Aren't you asking me about those days when we lived in Australia?' I asked him.

'Nonsense. We are asking you about the present time, after Liberation. Have you had a photograph taken in front of a Kuomintang flag since Liberation? Answer truthfully. Confess everything!' the young man from Peking leant forward and said to me.

I was astonished that they had thought it possible for anyone in China to have a photograph taken in front of a Kuomintang flag since the Communist Party came to power. I asked, 'How could there be any Kuomintang flag in China after Liberation? Where is it?'

'Never mind about the flag. Just confess why you did it. Was it to show your loyalty to the Kuomintang?' the interrogator asked.

'I never had a photograph taken in front of a Kuomintang flag after Liberation,' I stated categorically, deciding to end this absurd conversation once for all.

'Now don't be so sure. You will regret it. You'll miss the opportunity to earn lenient treatment,' the older man from Peking said.

'You had better assume a serious attitude. Someone else has already confessed, so we know what we are talking about. We are determined to expose all Kuomintang supporters. There is no escape for you,' said the younger man from Peking.

'I don't know what you are talking about. I'm not a supporter of the Kuomintang. If I were, wouldn't I be in Taiwan now?' I asked them.

My interrogator whispered something to the two men and then said to me, 'You had better return to your cell now and think about the whole matter. You have been here long enough to know the policy of the People's Government. You should know it's quite useless to deny something that can be proved.'

I was taken back to my cell, where I continued to puzzle over this extraordinary affair. The men seemed so serious. They must have something on which to base their accusation. Was it someone's malicious plot to incriminate me? I had already been accused of being a spy for the imperialists. Why this sudden diversion?

Three days later, I was called again. I was again pressed to confess; I gave the same answers as I did the first time. Then I was sent back to the cell and told to think it all over again. For three weeks, I went back and forth to the interrogation room every two or three days. The atmosphere became very tense in the interrogation room, but I was quite unable to guess what they had in mind.

During this time, to add pressure, the guards refused to give me the sulpha drug so necessary for keeping the inflammation of my gums in check. The condition rapidly deteriorated. Not only the gums but the lining of my mouth was so inflamed that I could no longer eat the food given to me. I requested the guards to give me liquid rice so that without chewing I could still get some nourishment into my body to keep alive. My gums were now so painful that I was completely preoccupied with them. When I was in the interrogation room, I had difficulty concentrating on the proceedings. I could understand how some prisoners give in under such conditions simply because physical suffering has weakened their will-power. I warned myself to keep a clear head in spite of the pain.

My request for liquid rice gave the Maoists the opportunity to reduce my ration. What was handed to me at mealtimes was no more than a half-container of grey-coloured water with a few grains of rice floating on top. After a few days of this diet, I fainted. It was a mild guard who called the doctor. He gave me an intravenous injection of glucose and sent me with the guard to the prison hospital. I did not know what the guard said to the doctor privately, but the doctor gave her a written order. When I was brought back to the detention house, the regular dosage of sulpha drug was resumed and I was given a thick rice porridge with a piece of steamed bread at mealtimes.

When I was again called to the interrogation room, the interrogator told me to read Mao's latest directive three times. After I had finished and sat down, he asked me, 'Do you fully understand what our Great Leader Chairman Mao has said?'

'I think I do,' I answered.

'Explain.'

'I think Chairman Mao wants everybody to know that the Great Proletarian Cultural Revolution is a political revolution, not simply a revolution limited to the field of culture,' I answered.

'That's correct. What about the two continuations?'

'The Cultural Revolution is the continuation of the class struggle the proletarian class has been carrying on against the capitalist class. It's not a new struggle but the continuation of the same struggle that has been going on,' I explained.

'What about the part concerning the Kuomintang?'

'The Cultural Revolution is also the continuation of the class struggle carried on by the Communist Party against the Kuomintang, which has been going on since 1927.'

'Yes, since you understand that, you should realize the seriousness of the situation. The Kuomintang is our enemy. After its defeat by our army, it took refuge on the island of Taiwan, protected by the United States. Until we have liberated Taiwan and brought the island under the banner of our Great Leader Chairman Mao, the struggle against the Kuomintang will continue. The Kuomintang must be destroyed to complete our Revolution. Our Great Leader is determined to liberate Taiwan and our Vice-Supreme Commander Lin is confident we will succeed. But the "capitalist-roaders" led by Liu Shao-chi opposed them. They said the Taiwan problem is for the next generation. That's a defeatist attitude. Our Great Leader believes the Taiwan issue is for our generation. It must be resolved now while the seasoned military leaders such as our Vice-Supreme Commander Lin, who had had the experience of defeating the Kuomintang before, can still lead our army to victory. The class struggle against the "capitalist-roaders" of the Liu Shao-chi clique is linked to the class struggle against the Kuomintang. Now that we have thoroughly defeated the Liu Shao-chi faction and power is once again concentrated in the hands of our Great Leader, we will deal with the issue of the Kuomintang. That's why we must expose all Kuomintang sympathizers in our midst to prevent the formation of a fifth column for the enemy. The dregs of the Kuomintang must be isolated and watched closely so that they will not be able to do harm,' said the interrogator.

'Your husband was a senior Kuomintang official,' added the older man from Peking.

'Not senior, only middle ranking. But, in any case, he elected to remain here when the Kuomintang went to Taiwan,' I pointed out.

'Yes, yes, many Kuomintang officials did that. Some of them were deliberately planted here by the Kuomintang to do mischief. Each one of them will be closely examined.'

'When my late husband became Shell's general manager in Shanghai, his appointment had to be approved by the Shanghai Municipal Government. Surely the Party had already examined his case thoroughly at that time,' I told them.

'That's not enough. The man who gave approval might have been a "capitalist-roader". We, the Revolutionaries, must examine everybody on behalf of the Party now,' said the interrogator.

'As early as the days of the Chinese Soviet, before the Long March, our Great Leader had already formulated a whole set of effective methods to deal with class enemies before our army started an offensive against the Kuomintang forces. At that time we put the important class enemies in prison, as we have done now during the

Cultural Revolution. The others were given to the revolutionary masses to watch. We have also done that during the Cultural Revolution.' The young man from Peking was obviously a student anxious to display his knowledge of Mao Tze-tung's books. He was referring to Mao's account of the preparations made by the Chinese Communist Party before military engagements against the Kuomintang encirclement campaigns, described in an essay written by Mao in 1936 entitled, 'The Strategy of China's Revolutionary War'.

'You should understand your own position in the struggle between the Communist Party and the Kuomintang. You are on the side of the Kuomintang by virtue of your family background and your husband's association with them,' the older man from Peking said.

'I'm afraid you are quite wrong. I'm not involved in the struggle between the Kuomintang and the Communist Party at all. I regret that the Communist Party and the Kuomintang had to fight each other, killing innocent Chinese people and destroying out national wealth in the process. As a Chinese I hope for peace and unity of the two political parties to work for the common good of the country,' I declared.

'We will achieve unity after we have crushed the Kuomintang,' said the student.

'If you are not a sympathizer of the Kuomintang, if as you say you are not involved in the struggle between the Kuomintang and the Communist Party, why did you have your photograph taken in front of a Kuomintang flag?' asked the interrogator.

'I've no idea what you are talking about. I've tried very hard to guess but I simply can't. Why don't you tell me what it's all about? There must be some misunderstanding,' I said with sincerity.

'Think back to 1962. What happened in 1962?' asked the interrogator.

'I don't know what happened in 1962, except that was the year I lost my mother.'

'That's right!' declared both men from Peking. 'You had better confess and tell the whole story.'

'Do you mean you want to hear about my mother's death?' I asked them incredulously.

'Yes, tell the whole story. Confess everything,' said the interrogator.

I was puzzled. I had no idea what they were driving at. But since they wanted to know, I told them about my mother's death.

'I was called to Nanking by my mother's neighbour, who telephoned me. When I got there, I found my mother unconscious after suffering a heat stroke. It was July and the temperature was persistently at about 35 degrees centigrade. We called an ambulance and rushed her to hospital. At first she got better. But she developed pneumonia and died of heart failure.'

'Did your brothers come to Nanking too?'

'Yes, they came with their wives.'

'What did you do after your mother died?'

'Being the eldest, I arranged her funeral.'

'You indulged in superstition. That's another proof you're a real reactionary,' said the younger man.

'Superstition' is the word habitually used by Communist officials when they refer to any kind of religious practice.

'My mother was a devout Buddhist, so I arranged for her to have a Buddhist funeral,' I said.

'You must have done something illegal. The Buddhist temples were all closed after the Great Leap Forward Campaign and the monks dispersed. Yet you managed to get several monks for your mother's funeral,' said the interrogator.

'I got the monks with the help of the man in charge of the Buddhist Research Institute in Nanking.'

'They are only allowed to perform religious services for foreign visitors from South-East Asia, not for Chinese.'

'The man I saw decided to help me because I begged him,' I said. How well I remembered my prolonged negotiation with the man at the Buddhist Research Institute in Nanking! I obtained the services of the monks by making a large donation, which I was not sure was allowed officially. Finally he agreed to provide me with six monks to recite the sutras at my mother's funeral.

'You are guilty of reviving superstition at your mother's funeral. Your brothers and sisters-in-law are guilty too because they did not stop you. You also put the names of your sisters in the United States on your mother's tombstone. You failed to draw a line between yourself and the traitors who chose to live abroad. All of these things prove beyond doubt you are a reactionary,' the young man said.

'My sisters in the United States are also my mother's daughters. It's a Chinese custom to put all the children's names on the tombstone.'

'We'll talk about all that later on. Now tell me, what did you do after your mother's funeral? After you left the cemetery where did you go?' my interrogator asked. All three of them now seemed to become excited. The two men from Peking were staring at me intently.

'We returned to her house to sort out her things.'

'Before you returned to her house where did you go?'

'Nowhere. We returned to her house directly.'

'Did you not go to the Sun Yat Sen Memorial after your mother's burial?' asked the older man from Peking.

'No, we were all so sad and exhausted.'

'Confess!' the young man suddenly banged the table.

'What do you want me to confess? The funeral of my mother has no political significance.'

'The funeral of your mother has no political significance, but your going to the Sun Yat Sen Memorial with your brothers to have your photograph taken in front of a Kuomintang flag had a great deal of political significance. You wanted to pledge your loyalty to the Kuomintang. At that time, in 1962, the Kuomintang were planning to attack the mainland,' said the young man.

The allegation was so absurd that I wanted to laugh. But I knew the situation was in fact very serious. To talk to these ignorant men was a strenuous effort and I had so little strength because of my poor health and inadequate diet. Throughout each interrogation, I was suffering severe pain in my mouth. Already I was so exhausted that I felt faint. But I had to go on talking to try to clear myself, even though I had no idea how they had formed their absurd suspicion of me in the first place.

'Please be reasonable. First of all, are you sure there was a Kuomintang flag at the Sun Yat Sen Memorial? If there was no flag there after the Kuomintang left Nanking, you will know we couldn't possibly have had a photograph taken in front of one. Secondly, even assuming there was a flag and assuming you are correct in your allegation that I wanted to impress the Kuomintang in case they came back to the mainland, would the Kuomintang accept my declaration of loyalty simply because I could show them such a photograph? The Kuomintang officials are not fools. Wouldn't they become extremely suspicious of my motives, since they knew very well my late husband and I had elected to remain here in 1949 and did not follow them to Taiwan?' I said.

'They would believe you. You are already an agent for the Kuomintang,' the young man declared.

'If indeed I were already an agent of the Kuomintang, I would have no need to prove my loyalty to them. You contradict yourself in your allegation.'

Both the men from Peking shouted, 'You must confess that you did in fact have a photograph taken with your brothers in front of a Kuomintang flag at the Sun Yat Sen Memorial in Nanking.'

'Please ask my brothers and sisters-in-law. They'll tell you it did not happen. We never went to the Sun Yat Sen Memorial in Nanking at all.'

'We did ask your brother at the Foreign Trade Institute in Peking. At first he also tried to deny everything. But when the Revolutionaries made him see the right path to take, he confessed everything. He said it was your idea to go to the Sun Yat Sen Memorial. He also said it was your camera that was used to take the photograph. You had the film developed in Shanghai and sent him a copy of it. Do you still dare to deny it?' the young man shouted.

My heart sank. It was pure fabrication, of course. What had the Maoists done to my poor brother to make him lie like that? I could imagine the agony he must have gone through before he succumbed to their pressure.

To meet this extremely serious situation, I enlisted the help of Mao's Little Red Book. Raising it in my hand, I said, 'Our Great Leader Chairman Mao taught us, "Rice must be eaten one mouthful at a time; a journey must be undertaken a step at a time." I beg you to obey his teaching in this case. Please go to the Sun Yat Sen Memorial in Nanking and see for yourselves. The Sun Yat Sen Memorial is managed by a government department in Nanking and visited by foreign visitors. There simply couldn't have been a Kuomintang flag there so many years after the Kuomintang left Nanking. Please go there and see for yourselves. If you should find a Kuomintang flag, then come back and punish me. I can't run away.'

The two men from Peking simply stared at me, while the interrogator stood up and said, 'You may now go back to your cell and think the matter over.'

Perhaps, I thought, he at last understood the logic of what I had said and decided that the only way to resolve the problem was for the two men to go to Nanking to see for themselves. I hoped they would do just that. When they found no Kuomintang flag at the Sun Yat Sen Memorial, they would return to Peking to report. Perhaps that was what actually happened, for many weeks passed and I was not called again.

During the Cultural Revolution, the Revolutionaries travelled all over China at public expense to 'investigate the crimes of the class enemies' under their charge. They used the opportunity for sightseeing and visiting friends and relatives. Some of them prolonged their trips or took roundabout routes to include famous scenic spots in their itinerary. Since Shanghai was a favourite city for shopping for all Chinese, the Revolutionaries always wanted to come to, or pass through, Shanghai. When the two men from Peking came to Shanghai, they actually passed through Nanking. I thought they had deliberately avoided stopping there to check the matter of the flag at the Sun Yat Sen Memorial because they were afraid they might have had to turn back if they found there was no Kuomintang flag and therefore missed coming to Shanghai. Each session of my interrogation took only a couple of hours at the most. They had the rest of the day free. Since their travel expenses and hotel accommodation were paid for by the Revolutionary Committee of their place of work, they enjoyed a free holiday for over a month. In fact, the opportunity to travel was one of the perks given to the more aggressive Revolutionaries to encourage their loyalty to the Maoist leaders.

Alone in my cell, I could not help thinking over and over again about this strange episode. At first I was indignant that my own brother should have behaved so badly under pressure. But when I thought of his life since the early fifties, the difficulties he had had to endure for so many years and the degree of persecution a man like him must have been subjected to during the Cultural Revolution, my sense of outrage evaporated. A deep feeling of sadness and compassion for this unfortunate man took its place in my heart. I could only assume that some Revolutionaries, over-zealous to unearth as many sympathizers of the Kuomintang as possible, had invented the story and planted it in my brother's mind for him to confess. But before they succeeded in doing that, they must have really damaged his reasoning powers. Normally my brother was neither stupid nor disloyal.

My brother had worked as an economics expert in the Ministry of Foreign Trade in the early fifties, one of a group of young and outstanding economists the Communist Party invited back from British and American universities where they were doing research. His work was to analyse and write reports on world economic conditions. He was given a senior grade and good treatment. However, it soon became apparent that although his work was appreciated by other experts working in a technical capacity in the Foreign Trade Ministry and its agencies abroad, he failed to satisfy the requirements of the Party, which through the Party Secretary of his unit controlled his life and work. The reports he wrote did not bear out the Party propaganda line that predicted impending doom for the capitalist world. Those were unhappy years for my brother. In trying to find a way to compromise between the facts as he knew them and the lies he was required to tell to justify the Party line, he became a very silent man, speaking very little and smiling very seldom. It seemed that no matter how hard he tried to please, unless he fell in with the Party line completely, the Party Secretary was always exasperated with him. Once the man declared bluntly, 'I simply can't afford to allow optimistic reports of the economy of any capitalist country to be sent out from this office. You are subverting the Party if you go on writing like this.'

When the Anti-Rightist Campaign started in 1957, the Party Secretary saw it as an opportunity to get rid of my recalcitrant brother. Much was made of the fact that he had done graduate work in England and for a brief period of time had worked as personal assistant to a senior Kuomintang minister. He was subjected to many gruelling hours of struggle meetings, isolated in his office for several months, not allowed to go home, and questioned continuously by a rally of Party activists day and night without sleep, in what was known as the tactics of 'exhaustive bombardment'. The Party activists did not succeed in making him a 'Rightist' mainly because they could find no evidence that he had criticized the Party, but the ordeal left him a broken man with an ulcer. The last trace of a smile left his face, his hair turned grey and he acquired a faraway look in his eyes. He was then only thirty-seven.

Realizing that he was unwanted at his office, my brother asked to be transferred to another job. Angered at his failure to make my brother a Rightist, the Party Secretary of his unit declared that my brother was too proud and needed a period of time with the peasants to improve his socialist understanding. He was sent to a village outside Peking to raise chickens. Living conditions were primitive; he was allowed to go home only once a month. But he enjoyed being away at last from the Party bureaucrats. He took the job of raising chickens seriously and soon established a reputation for having chickens which were fatter and produced more eggs than anyone else's. Whenever he returned to the village after visiting his family in the city, he would bring back an armful of books and cases of equipment for various experiments to improve his work. The peasants flocked to his dwelling, anxious to get his advice and to talk over their problems with him. This situation offended the Party boss of the village. He urged the Ministry of Foreign Trade to send my brother elsewhere.

This happened at the time the Maoists were retreating after the failure of the Great Leap Forward Campaign and the ensuing acute economic crisis. Generally, at times of real difficulty like this, the Party made some concessions to the intellectuals. The Ministry took the unprecedented step of asking my brother what he wanted to do. My brother requested that he be given a job as an English teacher and he was assigned to the English Language Department of the Foreign Trade Institute as a professor. He gave his new field of work the same serious attention he gave everything else he had undertaken. At the time of the Cultural Revolution he had already become a recognized authority on English language teaching and was conducting training classes for young teachers. He had also published books and articles on the subject.

Later, after my release from prison, I tried to get in touch with my brother. He refused to correspond with me, saying that with my former contacts with the western world I remained a 'dangerous person'. It was not until the winter of 1976, after Mao had died and the Gang of Four had been arrested, that my brother invited me to visit him in Peking. I found him completely broken and shattered by the cruel treatment he had received as a professor during the Cultural Revolution. He and his wife also spent several years doing physical labour in a Cadre School where living conditions were extremely hard. I did not have the heart to ask him what made him say that we had been to the Sun Yat Sen Memorial to have our photograph taken in front of a Kuomintang flag. I did not want him to think I blamed him for succumbing to pressure. He had suffered too much for too long.

After being closed for several years, the Foreign Trade Institute was being reopened. He was busily engaged with other professors in putting the English Language Department together again. He seemed content to be doing something worthwhile after so long. His small apartment was always full of people coming to talk to him. I did not want to remind him of the Cultural Revolution. However, just before my departure, he suddenly mentioned the subject himself.

He said, 'You did send the photograph to me in 1962, didn't you?'

'I sent you a photograph of mother which I had enlarged at Wan Hsiang, the photographic studio in Shanghai,' I told him. 'That was the only photograph I sent you in 1962.'

'Was it simply a photograph of mother? I remembered receiving a photograph from you. The Revolutionaries insisted it was a photograph we had taken at the Sun Yat Sen Memorial in front of a Kuomintang flag. They seemed very sure and were able to tell me exactly what we did. I couldn't remember a thing. But as they repeated it over and over again, I got a picture in my mind. Finally, it seemed to me that what they described did happen.'

'No,' I said angrily, 'it did not happen. We never went to the Sun Yat Sen Memorial at all. The Revolutionaries were liars. They wanted to incriminate us. They wanted to make out we were loyal to the Kuomintang so that they could punish us.'

He laid a hand on my arm and said calmly, with resignation, 'Don't get excited and angry. It's useless to get angry with them. They have the last word always. If they say something happened, it happened. It's useless to resist. I've learned this from my personal experience. I'm sure you learned all that too during your imprisonment.'

'Not at all. I haven't learned a thing. What's more, I do not intend to learn.'

'You will learn to accept. We all have to. I have seen it happen to so many. And it happened to me. It will happen to you too.'

'I won't let it happen to me.'

'I'm sorry to hear you say that. Deeply sorry. You'll get hurt, badly hurt, I'm afraid.'

My sister-in-law came into the room then to tell me that the taxi to take me to the airport was waiting. When I said goodbye to my brother, I was trembling. I did not know whether it was because I was angry at the terrible system under which we had to live or because I was sad that we could not do anything more effective than blind resistance to maintain our dignity. From inside the taxi, I turned to wave to my brother; he had already gone in. I somehow thought he was disappointed in me. I had not behaved like wise Chinese who 'bend with the wind to survive the hurricane'.

I went out to Arizona to see my brother again in March 1984, when he came to the Thunderbird Campus of the American Graduate School of International Management as an exchange professor from the Institute of Foreign Trade in Peking. I found that he was now an old man suffering from emphysema, looking a good ten years older than his age. But the twinkle of humour returned to his eyes when he told me that at last he had been reinstated as a professor of economics and had come to the United States to lecture on China's new economic policy. When I asked him what would happen when the Party's policy swung left again as it had done from left to right and right to left like a pendulum for over thirty years, he took a deep breath and sighed. After a while, he said, 'I'm a very sick man. Each cycle of change takes a number of years to complete. Let's hope that when the time comes for another change, I won't be here to see it.'

CHAPTER 11

A Kind of Torture

After the episode involving my brother, the interrogator continued with his inquiry about all my relatives and friends. This series of interrogations lasted nearly seven months, until the end of 1969. Then I was no longer called to the interrogation room. I waited and waited. A month passed and then another. When there was still no sign of the interrogation being resumed, I spoke to the guard requesting to see the interrogator.

'What do you want to say to the interrogator?' the guard asked me.

'I want to ask him when he is going to clarify my case.'

'He can't clarify your case for you. He just asks the questions and assembles the material. The government will make the decision about your case.'

'When is the government going to do that? I've been here such a long time already. I'm not well, I need medical attention,' I said.

'You are all right. We give you medicine and special food.'

'I'm not all right. My condition gets worse every day. I have had several more haemorrhages recently and my gums are very painful. The sulpha drug I am obliged to take is bad for my kidney. I have only one kidney, you know. When I had my operation, the doctor warned me not to take too much sulpha.'

The guard did not speak for a moment. Then she said, 'The difficulty about your case is really your own doing. You have to stay here because you won't confess.'

'I haven't done anything wrong. What am I supposed to confess? The interrogator has examined my whole life and my contacts with all my relatives and friends. By now the government should know all about me. How can anyone still think I am guilty of anything?' Frustration and disappointment made me raise my voice. But the guard merely closed the window and walked away.

During the past few months when I was going through many sessions of interrogation, I had gained a distinct impression that when my life and activities had been examined, I would be released. Now I could not understand what was holding things up. The guard had said that it was up to the government to make the decision. This made sense to me because it was the usual working method of the Communist

Party. What I did not know was on which level of authority my case was to be decided, and why it was taking so long. If my hopes had not been raised, perhaps my disappointment would not have been so great. As it was, I was plunged into renewed despair and disappointment.

The misery of my life in the winter of 1969-70 was beyond imagination. Looking back on those months of heavy snow storms, intense cold and constant physical pain, I marvel that I could have lived through it all. One day when I asked the guard to buy soap, I was given something that did not lather. The guard told me that soap was rationed and each person was allowed only one cake per month. When I requested permission to buy a little more because I had to wash my underclothes more frequently, the guard became annoyed and shouted, 'When are you going to get rid of your capitalistic way of wanting more than other people? You are lucky to be allowed one cake per month. In many places the people are only allowed one cake per family.'

The toilet paper made of melted-down rice straw was replaced by something even harder, made with old newspaper, string and old cloth; bits of these were clearly visible on the rough grey sheets stiff as a board. This substitute for toilet paper was rationed also. The codliver oil and vitamin pills I was allowed to purchase were often not available. A small lump of fat rather than meat often appeared with my rice. The severe shortages seemed to affect the guards as well. Several of them lost a good deal of weight and even the militant guards who used to stride in and out energetically now looked rather subdued and peaky. It was all too apparent that the country was going through another period of economic crisis that invariably followed each political upheaval.

The newspaper printed reports of peasants 'voluntarily' reducing their already meagre rations and rural Party Secretaries offering to increase the quota of grain which the Communes sent to government purchasing agencies. This was a repetition of the hunger and shortages of the early sixties immediately after the failure of the Great Leap Forward Campaign. In such times of hardship, there were daily stories in the newspaper about heroes who increased production output and decreased their consumption of food and other commodities. However, half a sheet of the *Shanghai Liberation Daily* was still given over to articles of criticism of the 'capitalist-roaders', who were also called 'revisionists'. The subject of contention now was Mao Tze-tung's military theory of the People's War against the capitalistic concept of the importance of military skill and modern weapons. Two ousted and disgraced military leaders, former Defence Minister Peng Teh-huai and former Chief of Staff Lo Jui-ching, were the main culprits. Daily newspaper articles read to us over the broadcasting system accused these two of believing that advanced weapons rather than men armed with Mao Tze-tung Thought were the most important factor in deciding the outcome of war. Since both men had been removed from office several years earlier and handed over to the Red Guards and the Revolutionaries for persecution, the continued campaign to criticize their viewpoint could only mean that their viewpoint was shared by others in the Party and military leadership.

Prolonged hardship and privation were eroding my mental power in a frightening way. The stalling of my investigation produced in me a deep feeling of despondency. Not being able to keep clean because of insufficient soap and toilet paper was demoralizing. Even the evidence in the newspaper of differences of opinion, or perhaps fierce debate, in the Party and military leadership failed to rouse me from lethargy. Every day I sat on the wooden bed, leaning against my rolled-up bedding, too tired and too ill to move.

In early spring, I again became ill with pneumonia and was taken to the prison hospital. There I made a slow recovery. When I returned to the No. 1 Detention House, just before May the First, the weather had become warmer. Even though living conditions continued to be extremely hard, the milder weather made life easier to endure. I felt I had somehow survived another crisis and been mysteriously brought back to life from the brink of death. When I was allowed outdoor exercise on a warm and sunny day and saw the young leaves unfolding on the plane tree over the wall, I thanked God for the miracle of life and the timely renewal of my own.

Since the conclusion of the Ninth Party Congress and the formation of Party Secretariats in each province and municipality, the Party's tight control of every aspect of life was re-established. It became much harder than before for me to find out what was going on outside the prison walls through reading the newspaper. In the turbulent years of the height of the Cultural Revolution, vehement denunciations of the 'capitalist-roaders' often revealed internal struggles in the Party leadership. In explaining Mao's 'correct' policy, the revolutionary writers, often non-Party men, would sometimes inadvertently state facts kept from the Chinese people. Now articles like that had disappeared altogether from the *Shanghai Liberation Daily*. Denunciations continued to appear but I could tell that they were now written by professional Party propagandists. They were using the same stale language and time-worn quotations that were the stock-in-trade of the Party men anxious to say the right thing, but even more anxious not to say it in any way that might bring criticism on themselves.

The first inkling I had of another round of power struggles at the top was when I saw in the newspaper a list of members of the standing committee of the Politburo. Missing was the name of Chen Po-ta, one of the radical leaders who had charted the course of the Cultural Revolution from its very beginning. Soon articles of criticism, without mentioning his name, began to appear. They were directed against a 'fake Marxist' who had declared himself to be a 'humble commoner'. The sudden omission of a prominent man's name without explanation almost always meant he was in disgrace. The criticism against a 'fake Marxist' seemed to me to point to someone renowned as a theorist of Marxism. Chen Po-ta was just such a man.

I was greatly puzzled by this unexpected development because Chen Po-ta was known to the Chinese people as a faithful follower of Mao and his long-time confidential secretary. In fact, it was often whispered in China that many essays purportedly written by Mao Tze-tung were actually from the pen of Chen Po-ta. Though he did not seek the limelight like other radical leaders such as Chiang Ching or Lin Piao, the Chinese people knew him to have been one of the small élite group of Marxist theorists Mao relied upon.

After my release from the No. 1 Detention House a good deal later, I questioned several friends and acquaintances about the downfall of Chen Po-ta. It seemed that at the second plenary session of the Ninth Central Committee held at Lu Shan at the end of August 1970, the new constitution of the Chinese People's Republic was discussed. An important issue for decision was whether to abolish the post of Chairman of the Chinese People's Republic, left vacant by the downfall of Liu Shao-chi. Chen Po-ta proposed that the post be maintained and nominated Lin Piao as the new chairman. Already alarmed by the rapid expansion of Lin Piao's power since the Ninth Party Congress only a year and four months earlier, Mao was not keen to give Lin Piao added power and position. He declared that he favoured the abolition of the post of Chairman of the People's Republic and suggested giving the ceremonial function of the Head of State to the Chairman of the Standing Committee of the People's Congress. In a heated debate, Mao denounced Chen Po-ta's proposal as a counter-revolutionary move designed to re-establish pre-Cultural Revolution conditions.

Others told me that another subject under discussion at the Central Committee meeting was China's relations with the United States after

President Nixon had expressed, through third country intermediaries, the United States' willingness for a rapprochement with Peking. Premier Chou En-lai had convinced Mao that if the United States could be induced to recognize the Chinese People's Republic rather than the Kuomintang Government in Taiwan, Communist China would receive recognition from most other countries in the United Nations. This would not only enable Communist China to take China's seat at the United Nations but it would make the eventual liberation of Taiwan much easier and less costly. Both Lin Piao and Chen Po-ta expressed opposition to any move for a rapprochement with the United States. They argued that as the leader of the capitalist world, the United States was inherently socialist China's main enemy.

But all my informants agreed that the downfall of Chen Po-ta was really Mao's warning to Lin Piao. This was not lost on the military man who correctly concluded that the days of his own usefulness to Mao were numbered. This eventually led to Lin Piao's unsuccessful attempt to wrest power from Mao. In any case, later developments proved that the second plenary session of the Ninth Central Committee was an important one. It ended the brief Lin Piao era and marked a drastic deterioration in Lin Piao's power position relative to that of Prime Minister Chou En-lai.

In 1970, when I was still in my cell in the detention house, I recognized the downfall of Chen Po-ta as something important, and I watched for events which might throw some light on the situation. In the autumn of that year, a photograph of the American writer Edgar Snow standing beside Mao on the balcony above the Gate of Heavenly Peace, Tien An Men, on China's National Day appeared in the newspaper. While Mao had often stood there with other prominent visitors to China, this was the first time an American had been given such an honour. Snow was an old friend of the Communist Party and Mao Tze-tung. His book, *Red Star over China*, published in the thirties, did much to legitimize the Chinese Communist Party in the eyes of the world. Since I had learned that everything Mao did or said had meaning, often a subtle one, I pondered on the significance of his having an American with him on the balcony of the Gate of Heavenly Peace on China's National Day while he reviewed the tens of thousands of enthusiastic men and women carrying his portraits, shouting his slogans and chanting his quotations.

Soon after National Day, the newspaper reported that Peking had reached an agreement with Canada to establish full diplomatic relations based on the five principles of peaceful co-existence: mutual respect for territorial integrity and sovereignty, non-aggression, non-interference in each other's internal affairs, equality and mutual benefit and peaceful co-existence. Canada undertook to sever diplomatic relations with the Kuomintang Government on Taiwan and to recognize Peking as the sole legitimate government of China.

I thought Mao was using the case of Canada to say something to the United States. I believed that his message was that he was ready to be friends if the United States would agree to abandon Taiwan. The establishment of diplomatic relations with Canada was the opportunity for him to declare his conditions for a similar arrangement with the United States. I became quietly excited and hopeful. That Communist China might move closer to the West seemed to be too good to be true.

The north-west wind started to blow again but this time it did not dampen my spirits. For the first time since the Cultural Revolution began, something seemed to be happening in the right direction. When a gust of wind blew a withered leaf of the plane tree into my cell, I picked up the bright yellow leaf and looked at it for a long time, thinking it was a symbol of hope and a good omen.

A calmer mood took the place of anxiety while I waited in my cell for further developments. I thought I had reached the bottom line of suffering and things would get better when they started to move again. I was wrong.

One afternoon in January 1971, I was summoned to the interrogation room. The call was so unexpected that my heart was pounding with excitement as I followed the guard through the courtyard; I hardly noticed that a blizzard was beginning. At the door of the interrogation room, the guard suddenly gave me a hard shove so that I staggered into the room rather unceremoniously. I found several guards in the room. As soon as I entered, they crowded around me, shouting abuse at me.

'You are the running dog of the imperialists,' said one. 'You are a dirty exploiter of workers and peasants,' shouted another. 'You are a counter-revolutionary,' yelled the third.

Their voices mingled and their faces became masks of hatred as they joined one another to go through the list of abuse that I had become familiar with during the Cultural Revolution. While they were shouting, they pushed me to show their impatience. I was passed around from one guard to another like a ball in a ball game. Trying to maintain my balance, I became dizzy and breathless. Before I could gather my wits together, suddenly a young male guard grabbed the lapels of my padded jacket and pulled me towards him. His face was only inches from mine and I could see his eyes glistening with sadistic pleasure. Then he bit his lower lip to show his determination and gave me a hard push. I staggered backwards and hit the wall. But before I collapsed onto the floor like a sack, he grabbed my lapels again and pulled me forward, and again, he bounced me against the wall. He did this several times with lightning speed in a very expert manner. All the time, the other guards continued to shout at me. I became completely disorientated. My ears were ringing, my head was splitting and my body was trembling. Suddenly my stomach heaved and I vomited. Water from my mouth got on the guard's hand and cuffs. He became furious. Pushing me into the prisoner's chair, the guard swore under his breath.

My heart pounded as if it was going to jump out of my throat. My breath came in gasps. I collapsed into the chair and, trying to recover my equilibrium, closed my eyes. Suddenly a stinging blow landed on my cheek. The voice of a female guard shouted, 'Are you going to confess?'

Another sharp blow landed on my other check, while several voices joined in to shout, 'Are you going to confess?'

I remained in the chair with my eyes closed and ignored them. That was my only way to defend myself.

Someone grabbed my hair from behind and jerked my head up. I was forced to look up and found all five of them staring at me expectantly. It seemed that they really expected me to change my mind simply because they had beaten me up. But then I thought, people who resort to brutality must believe in the power of brutality. But it seemed to me that these guards at the detention house were rather stupid not to know me better after watching me day and night for so many years. I knew, however, that they were merely carrying out someone else's orders.

One of the female guards was the militant young woman who had made trouble for me on many previous occasions. Now she said, 'Are you going to confess or do you want more punishment?'

When she saw that I remained silent, she gave my cheek another smart slap, took my arms and draped them on the back of the chair on which I was seated. The young male guard who had pushed me against the wall grabbed my wrists together and clamped a pair of handcuffs on them.

'These handcuffs are to punish you for your intransigence. You will wear them until you are ready to confess. Only then will we take them off. If you confess now, we will take them off now. If you confess tomorrow, we will take them off tomorrow. If you do not confess for a year, you will have to wear them for a year. If you never confess, you will have to wear them to your grave,' said the militant female guard.

'Think about it! Think about the situation you are in!' a male guard shouted.

'If you decide to confess now, we will take off the handcuffs straightaway and you can return to your cell,' another female guard said.

'What about it? Are you ready to confess? Just say yes and we will take the handcuffs off,' another male guard said.

'Speak! Speak!' several of them shouted.

I looked at them all and said in a feeble voice, 'I've done nothing wrong. I've nothing to confess.'

'Louder! Louder! Speak louder!' they yelled.

Though I spoke in a low voice, each one of them inside the room had heard what I had said. Someone must be listening outside in the corridor. They wanted this person to hear my answer. From where I sat I could not see whether the small window behind the prisoner's chair was open. But I did notice the guards glancing in that direction when they were pushing me around.

I pulled myself together with an effort and stated in a clear and loud voice, 'I'm innocent. You have made a mistake. I have nothing to confess.'

I heard the small window behind the prisoner's chair closing with a loud bang. My tormentors waited a little while before opening the door to usher me out, perhaps to make sure the person outside had time to get out of sight. When I stood up, the militant female guard came behind me and put her two hands round the handcuffs to tighten them a few notches so that they fitted snugly round my wrists.

The blizzard was now in full force. Whirling snowflakes were falling from the darkened sky and the strong wind nearly knocked me over when I stepped out of the interrogation building. The guard said, 'Follow me!'

He did not return me to the women's prison but led me in another direction into a small building in a corner of the prison compound. When he opened the door and flipped the switch on the wall to put on the dim light, I saw that the place was in an even worse state of neglect than the rest of the prison compound. A thick layer of dust covered the floor and the walls. When we moved down the corridor, cobwebs floated down from the ceiling. The guard unlocked a small door and said, 'Get in!'

The room was very dark. I waited for him to switch on the light, but he just closed the door after me. Standing outside, he asked, 'Are you going to confess?' When I did not reply, he snapped the lock and went away.

I stood just inside the door in total darkness, trying to make out where I was. An unpleasant odour of staleness and decay assailed my nostrils. Gradually I realized that the tiny room in which I was locked had no window. However, the door fitted badly; a thin thread of light seeped through the gap. When my eyes became accustomed to the darkness, I saw vaguely that there was a wooden board on the dusty floor and a cement toilet in the corner. Actually I was standing on the only space left, for the room was no more than about five feet square. Something soft dropped on my forehead. I was so startled that I experienced a moment of panic. With my hands tied at my back, I could do nothing to brush it away. I shook my head hard and it slid down my face to my jacket. Perhaps not many insects could live in this dark room, I thought. It must have been a cobweb from the ceiling.

My heart was still beating very fast. In spite of the unpleasant smell in the room, I breathed in and out deeply and slowly to try to calm down and slow my heart beat. When I felt better I sat down on the wooden board and tried to look round in the dark. I was relieved not to see anything that suggested blood, excrement or vomited food left by previous prisoners. I was so tired that I put my head on my drawn-up knees and closed my eyes to rest. The only compensation for being locked in a cement box, I thought, was that without the window to admit the cold air and wind, the place was decidedly warmer than my cell.

The handcuffs felt different from the others I had worn before. I examined them with my fingers. Indeed, they were different, much heavier and thicker, with a square edge, not rounded like the others. My hands felt hot and my fingers were stiff. I tried to exercise my hands by moving them as much as the handcuffs allowed.

'Are you going to confess?'

The sudden sound of a voice startled me. Had the guard been outside all the while or had he just come into the building? How was it that I had not heard him?

There was really no point in exhausting what little strength I had, so I did not answer him but remained where I was with my head resting on my knees. I tried to take my mind off the present by recalling beautiful scenes and pleasant experiences in the past. But it was very difficult. The ugly reality was all too real and overpowering.

Other guards came at intervals to ask me the same question. I listened for their footsteps. Some came quite stealthily, while others did not bother to soften their tread. When they opened the door of the building to come inside, I could hear the howling wind and the sound of the guards stamping their feet to get rid of the snow. I supposed they were told to come and see if I had succumbed to their new form of pressure. Some of them lingered for a moment after asking their question; others did not wait for my answer but left almost immediately after delivering their question.

Apart from the guards, there was no sound whatsoever. I must have been the sole occupant of that building on that day. If there were other prisoners, surely I would have heard a sigh or a moan long ago.

I did not know how long I sat there. In a dark room, in complete isolation, time assumed a different meaning or had no meaning at all. I only knew that my legs felt stiff and my head ached. But I refrained from moving as long as the guards continued to come. When a guard switched off the light in the corridor on his departure, I thought they might have decided to retire for the night. But I still waited for a while before standing up. It was not possible to walk because there was simply no space and I was afraid to bump into the dirty wall in the dark. So I shuffled my feet to try to restore circulation to my legs. My arms ached from being held at my back in the same position for so long and my hands felt very hot. I tried to get some relief by moving my shoulders up and down.

After standing for a while, I sat down again. With my head on my knees, I rested. Perhaps I had snatches of real sleep or perhaps I just dozed while murmuring prayers. Then I would stand up again to repeat my newly devised exercise. I felt very weak. My natural inclination was to move as little as possible but I compelled myself to do the simple exercise, for I knew that was the best way to keep going. In the past I had not suffered from claustrophobia, but there were moments during the night when I felt myself getting tense. My breathing became difficult and I had the sensation that the walls were falling on me. To prevent myself from getting into a panic, I would stand up quickly to move my body as much as possible in that confined space. And I would breathe very slowly and deeply until I felt calm again.

The best way for me to snap out of fear was always to take the initiative in doing something positive. Even the simple act of just moving my body around made me feel better immediately. If I had just sat there feeling dejected and let my imagination run wild, I could easily have become terribly confused and unable to cope with the guards. Of course I was hungry and my throat was parched. But when I thought of the cement toilet coated with dust and grime, I was reconciled to not having any food or water that might force me to use it.

The night dragged on very slowly. More and more I felt that I was buried in a cement box deep underground. My hands became very hot and uncomfortable. When I found it difficult to curl my fingers into a fist, I knew they were swollen. My hands became my sole preoccupation and worry. I feared that the brutal and ignorant men, intent on getting what they wanted from me, might inadvertently cripple me. I knew that when a Communist Party official tried to achieve an objective during a political campaign, he went to excess to carry out his orders and ignored all possible complications. Trained to obey promptly by such slogans as 'Wherever Chairman Mao points, there I will run', and fearful of the consequences of appearing hesitant or reluctant, he exaggerated everything he had to do. If the victim suffered more than was intended or was left a cripple, that was just too bad. I had seen this happen again and again. Hands are so important. If my hands were crippled, how would I be able to carry on with my daily life when the Cultural Revolution was over?

I pressed my fingers in turn. At least they were not numb. But I could tell they were badly swollen. I wondered how long I would remain manacled like this and how long I could live without food or water. Vaguely I remembered reading in an article that a human being could live for seven days without sustenance. In my present weakened state, perhaps five days, I thought. In any case, hardly twenty-four hours had passed. At that moment I did not need to think of the threat to my life, only the threat to my hands. What could I do to lessen possible damage to them? It seemed to me the swelling was caused by the tight handcuffs fitted firmly round my wrists which prevented proper circulation. When the militant female guard put her hands round the handcuffs to tighten them, she knew exactly what she was doing. If she had not tightened them but had left them as they were when they were put on, perhaps the state of my hands would not have been so bad now. The guard who first put the handcuffs on had not tightened them, so they were probably just instructed to put the handcuffs on, and no instruction was given to tighten them. In that case, a mild guard might be persuaded to loosen them a little. I decided to show my hands to the guard who would come in the morning, and request the handcuffs to be loosened.

When finally I heard the sound of a guard coming through the outside door and saw the thin line of light appear again around the door, I stood up.

'Are you going to confess? Have you thought over the matter?' It was the voice of a male guard.

'I would like to speak to you for a moment,' I said.

'Good! So, you have decided to confess at last.'

'No, no, it's not about confession. It's about my hands.'

'What about your hands?'

'They are badly swollen. The handcuffs are very tight. Could you loosen them a bit?' I asked.

'You are feeling uncomfortable now, are you? That's good! Why don't you confess? If you confess, the handcuffs will be taken off.'

'Can't you loosen them a bit now?'

'Why don't you just confess like the other prisoners? You have brought this on yourself. It's not the fault of the handcuffs.'

'Please look at my hands. They are badly swollen.'

'I can't do anything about that. If you decide to confess, I will unlock this door and take you out. That's all I can do,' the guard said.

'Could you not report to your superior that my hands are very badly swollen?'

'No. If you decide to confess, I will take you out.'

It seemed useless to go on. I sat down on the wooden board again.

'Are you going to confess?' he asked me once again. I did not answer. He remained there for a moment longer before going away.

The fact that my hands were badly swollen was no surprise to the guard. Of course he knew the effect of the handcuffs. I could not have been the first person they had done this to. He was probably telling his superior at that moment that I was getting worried and agitated about my hands. From that his superior would think I was nearer to doing what he wanted. They would never loosen the handcuffs to prolong what they would regard as the period of waiting for me to confess. I decided it was useless to ask the guards to loosen the handcuffs. I must just trust God to preserve my hands.

'Come here!' the voice of a female guard said.

I stood up. I was already right by the door. She had turned up rather quickly, I thought.

'I've come to give you some advice,' she said in a normal voice, as if she was talking to another guard, not with the harsh tone the guards habitually used to address the prisoners. 'You are not a stupid woman. Why don't you do the intelligent thing and confess? Why punish yourself by being stubborn?'

I didn't say anything.

'You are worried about your hands. That's quite right. Hands are very important to everybody, but especially to an intellectual who must write. You should try to protect your hands and not let them be hurt. You can do that easily by just agreeing to confess.'

I still did not say anything.

'You know when they said they would never take the handcuffs off until you agree to confess, they really meant it. They will do it too. The dictatorship of the proletariat is not something to be trifled with, you know.'

I continued to remain silent.

She waited for quite a long time. Then she said, 'Well, you think carefully about what I have just said. It's good advice I have given you. I'm sorry for you. Think about what I said.'

When I heard her footsteps going away from the door, I sat down again.

I was angry with myself for being so stupid. How could I have thought for one moment that they would loosen the handcuffs? Now that I had shown them my weakness, they would be glad and think I might indeed succumb to their pressure because of concern about my hands. I said to myself, 'I'll forget about my hands. If I have to be crippled, then I'll accept being crippled. In this world there are many worthy people with crippled hands or no hands at all.' I remembered when my late husband and I were in Holland in 1957, we had bought a painting by a veteran of the Second World War who had lost both his hands. He used his toes to hold the paint brush, I was told. I used to treasure this painting as a symbol of human courage and resourcefulness. It was slashed by the Red Guards when they looted my home. But the thought of this artist whom I had never met inspired me with courage and helped me to become reconciled to the possibility of losing the use of my hands after this ordeal.

The female guard was followed by others. All of them lectured me on the advantage of obeying the dictatorship of the proletariat and confessing. Now that they knew I was suffering discomfort and worrying about my hands, they did not dash away but lingered hopefully outside the door waiting for my answer. After being so long without food and water and not having had much sleep at all, I felt very weak and faint. My intestines were grinding in protest and I had spasms of pain in the abdomen. But I just continued sitting on the board with my head on my knees waiting for the guards to go away.

The day seemed interminable. Patiently I waited for their next move. At last the door was unlocked. A female voice called, 'Come out!'

The icy cold fresh air in the courtyard miraculously cleared my head and I felt a surge of life to support my wobbly legs. The guard led me back to the same interrogation room in which they had beaten me up the day before.

The militant female guard and the young male guard who had put the handcuffs on me sat in the place of the interrogator behind the counter. After I had entered the room and bowed to the portrait of Mao, the female guard told me to recite a quotation from memory.

'First, do not fear hardship. Second, do not fear death,' I said. It was the first quotation of Mao that came into my head and, under the circumstances, certainly appropriate.

'That quotation is not for the likes of you! Chairman Mao said that to the revolutionary soldiers,' the female guard said indignantly.

But they let it pass. They did not ask me to recite another quotation, although I had another one about overcoming ten thousand difficulties to strive for final victory ready to recite if they gave me the opportunity to do so.

'What are you thinking about now?' asked the male guard.

'Nothing very much,' I answered.

'Don't pretend to be nonchalant. You are worried about your hands. You would like the handcuffs to be loosened,' he said.

I did not say anything.

'What you should think about is why you have to wear them in the first place. It is entirely your own fault. Do we put handcuffs on all the prisoners kept here? Of course not. If you find the handcuffs uncomfortable, you should think why you have to wear them. They can be taken off if you decide to confess. It's up to you entirely,' he said.

'Are you going to confess?' asked the female guard.

When she saw that I said nothing, she got angry and shouted, 'You deserve all you are getting. You are tired of living, I am sure. I have never seen a prisoner as stubborn and stupid as you!'

'Have you lost all reason? Have you lost the wish to protect yourself? You are being extremely stupid. You are like an egg hitting a rock. You will get smashed,' declared the male guard.

A year or two ago, I would have shouted back at them and taken pleasure from doing that. Now I was too ill and too tired. I no longer cared.

They looked at each other and they looked past my shoulder at the small window behind the prisoner's chair. Then they stood up.

'Take her out! Take her out! Let her go to see God with her granite head!' the male guard shouted.

It might seem surprising that a guard in a Communist prison should have spoken of God, but what he said was in fact a quotation from Mao Tze-tung. Referring to political indoctrination and hard labour in labour camps as a means to change the thinking of intellectuals who were supposed to be opposed to the Communist Party, Mao had declared that the purpose of the Communist Party was reform of the enemy rather than annihilation. Then he added, 'If some still want to go to see God with their granite heads, it will make no difference.' Since the publication of his remark, 'to go to see God with his granite head' was generally used to denote a man refusing to change his mind or accept the point of view of the Party.

A guard flung the door open. Although I felt dizzy, I made an effort to walk steadily and followed him out of the room. The icy air outside was like a knife cutting through my clothes. I shivered violently. The guard led me back to the women's prison and my cell. When I passed the small room used by the female guards, I saw from their clock that I had been locked in the cement box in the other building for almost twenty-four hours.

The guard unlocked the door of my cell and said to me, 'Now you will continue your punishment in here.'

When I had been called to the interrogation room the day before, drinking water had just been issued to the prisoners. The water was still in the green enamelled mug on the edge of the table where I had hastily placed it. Now I bent over the mug, removed the lid by gripping the knob on top of it with my teeth and placed it on the table. Then I caught the edge of the mug with my teeth, gradually lowered my body to a squatting position and tipped the water into my mouth. By this method, I succeeded in drinking quite a bit of the water. After that, I moved over to the cement toilet, stood with my back to it, lowered my body and removed the lid with my imprisoned hands. I strained my hands to unzip my slacks. I was able to sit on the seat I had made with two towels joined together and to relieve myself. But to strain my hands to one side to unfasten the zip made the handcuffs cut severely into my flesh. It was very painful.

I sat down on the edge of the bed. The cell was very cold and seemed to get progressively colder. But the familiar cell was not as dirty and stuffy as the cement box where I had spent the previous twenty-four hours. When the second meal of the day was delivered to the prisoners, the woman from the kitchen pushed the aluminium container through the small window for me in the usual manner. Even though I was famished, I had to refuse it for I simply did not know how I could eat with my hands tightly tied behind my back.

No one came to ask me if I was going to confess. But I knew I was under observation, for I could hear the guards come to the peephole to look into the cell. At bedtime, the guard called at each cell for prisoners to go to bed. She came to my cell as if nothing unusual had happened and said, 'Go to sleep!'

With my back to the bed, I unrolled my quilt and blanket and spread them over the wooden bed. It was slow work and strenuous for one who had not eaten any food for so long. But I managed it. Then I lay down on the bed. First, I lay on one side with my body weight pressing down on one shoulder and arm. It was extremely uncomfortable; my arm ached. Then I tried to lie on my stomach with my face turned to one side. I found this position impossible on the hard wooden bed because my body weight was on my breasts. After lying like this for a little while I had to give up. In any case, I could not cover myself with the blanket. While I was performing these acrobatics with my hands in handcuffs behind my back, I never stopped shivering. The room was bitterly cold. Finally I decided lying down to sleep was out of the question. I should try to get some sleep sitting up. I sat across the bed with my legs up and my back leaning on the toilet-paper-covered wall. Then I closed my eyes, hoping to doze off.

It was a such a cold night that there was ice on the windowpanes and the snow piled against the window did not melt. Inside the cell, the feeble light shone through a haze of cold air. Every breath I took was a puff of white vapour. My body shook with spasms of shivering. My legs and feet were frozen numb. I simply had to get up from time to time to walk around the cell to restore circulation to my limbs. The weight of the handcuffs dragged my hands down so that I had to hold them up with my fingers while walking slowly in the cell. The handcuffs seemed to get tighter and tighter and my hands seemed to be on fire. I tired so easily that after walking round for only a little while I simply had to sit down again. Then I got so cold that I had to walk some more. Perhaps I managed a little sleep from time to time when I sat against the wall with my feet up, but the long night was a night of misery and suffering.

However, it came to an end as everything in life must do, no matter how wonderful or unpleasant. I saw the light of dawn creeping into the room and heard the guard calling outside each cell, 'Get up! Get up!'

Soon afterwards the Labour Reform girl pushed the spout of the watering can through the small window to offer me cold water for washing. When she did not see my washbasin, she looked into the cell through the small window. She looked at me inquiringly. I turned my body a little so that she could see my handcuffs. Quickly she closed the small window and went away.

In the circumstances, being unwashed was the least of my worries. While I could carry the empty mug to the window to receive the drinking water with my back to it and drink the water by gripping the edge of the mug with my teeth and gradually squatting so that the water would pour into my mouth, my empty stomach protested with spasms of gripping pain which refused to be assuaged by the water. My hands were so hot that I was in a constant state of restless agitation.

On the third day, the pain in my abdomen miraculously stopped. But I felt very weak. My eyes could no longer focus and the usual sound of prison activities seemed to grow fainter and fainter.

That night, I again sat on the bed, leaning against the wall with my hands crossed to hold the handcuffs with my fingers in an effort to reduce their weight. Though I shivered with cold, I no longer had the strength to get up and walk around the room.

After the prisoners had settled down to sleep, the small window was pushed open gently. I did not hear any sound until a voice that was almost a whisper said through the opening, 'Come over!'

I wondered whether it was just another guard trying to urge me to confess. But she had spoken softly, almost stealthily, as if she did not want others in the building to hear her.

With an effort I moved to the small window and saw the face of one of the older guards there. She was bending down to watch my faltering steps through the opening.

From the beginning of my imprisonment I had found this guard the most humane. At first she attracted my attention because she walked in that peculiar way of women whose feet had been crippled with foot-bending, an old custom that lingered into the 1930s in some remote rural areas of China. When the feet of these women were unbound, they were already permanently damaged. This guard was not a native of Shanghai because she spoke with the accent of North China peasants. I thought she must have been one of those country women liberated by the Communist troops as they swept down the plains of North China and she had joined their ranks and become a Party member. I observed that she carried out her duty in a matter of fact manner and did not seem to enjoy shouting at the prisoners as the other guards did. When the weather got cold, if she were on night duty, I often heard her offering to lend bedding from the prison stock to prisoners who did not have sufficient covering. The last time I fainted because of lack of food, it was this guard who took me to the hospital and got the doctor to sign a paper ordering more rice to be given to me. Since it was the Maoists who had reduced my ration to give me pressure on that occasion, I thought she couldn't be one of them.

'Why aren't you eating your meals?' she asked me.

I thought, 'What a silly question to ask! Doesn't she know I have got the handcuffs on?'

'They will not remove the handcuffs simply because you won't eat, you know. And if you should starve to death, you would be declared a counter-revolutionary. That's the customary procedure for prisoners who die before their cases are clarified,' she added.

'I don't know how to eat without using my hands,' I said.

'It's not impossible. Think hard. There is a way. You have a spoon.'

She sounded sympathetic and concerned. I decided to ask her to loosen the handcuffs a little, as my tightly imprisoned hands were tormenting me. I was in a constant state of tension because of them. They occupied my mind to the exclusion of all else.

'My hands are swollen and very hot. My whole body feels tormented because of them. Could you please loosen the handcuffs a little bit?' I asked her.

'I haven't got the key to unlock the handcuffs. It is being kept by someone higher up. Just try to eat something tomorrow. You will feel better when you have some food inside you,' she said.

A gust of cold wind from the direction of the entrance at the other end of the corridor indicated that the door of the building was being opened and another guard had just entered. She slid the shutter quietly in place and went away.

I returned to the bed and sat there thinking. The guard was right. I should try to eat. To die was nothing to be frightened of. What really frightened me was the possibility that my mind might get so confused that I might sign something without realizing its significance. But how could I handle the food without my hands? The guard said there was a way and told me to think hard. She also mentioned that I had a spoon. My eyes strayed towards the table. First I saw the plastic spoon and then I saw my clean towels neatly folded in a pile. A plan formulated in my mind and I decided to try it when food was offered to me again.

The guard had said that the key to unlock the handcuffs was not kept by the guards but by 'someone higher up'. There was no hope the handcuffs could be loosened. I must think of some way to reduce the heavy weight of the handcuffs, which were not only dragging my hands down but also pulling my shoulders out of their sockets. With difficulty and very slowly, with my back to the bed, I managed to roll up the quilt. Then I pushed the rolled quilt to the wall. When I sat down in front of the quilt against the wall, I placed my hands on the soft quilt. The weight was lifted and I felt a surge of relief.

To have made plans and thought of some way to overcome difficulty gave me a new lease of life. Although I continued to be cold, hungry and miserable, the long night seemed to pass more quickly.

At daybreak, when the guard called the prisoners to get up, I stood up to stretch my legs. I tried to hold the handcuffs with my fingers, and, to my horror, felt something sticky and wet. Turning to the quilt on which I had rested my hands throughout the night, I saw stains of blood mixed with pus. It seemed the handcuffs had already broken my skin and were cutting into my flesh. I shuddered with a real fear of losing the use of my hands, for I realized I was powerless to prevent disaster.

When the woman from the kitchen offered me the aluminium container of rice through the small window, I went to accept it. I turned my back to the opening and she placed the container in my hands. I took it to the table. With my back to it, I picked up a clean face towel from the pile and spread it on the table. Then I picked up the plastic spoon and tried to loosen the rice from the container with it. The Shanghai rice was glutinous. When it was cooked in the container, it stuck to it. I had to dig hard with the plastic spoon to push the rice and cabbage onto the face towel on the table. With each movement of my hands, the handcuffs dug deeper into my flesh. My whole body was racked with pain and tears came into my eyes. I had to rest and take a deep breath. Nevertheless, I persisted with my effort to get the rice out of the container. When I succeeded in getting quite a bit out, I turned round, bent over the towel and ate the rice like an animal.

I repeated this several times. When the woman came to collect the container, she did not immediately open the small window to demand it back but stood outside watching me struggling to get the rice out. Because of the pain and my fear of infection, I stopped after each scoop to take a deep breath. I was very slow. Still the woman said nothing, though normally she was always in a great hurry. As I blinked back tears of pain, I wondered if eating was really worth the effort. But I continued to try, simply because I had decided to stay alive. When I could not carry on any longer and had already got nearly half of the rice onto the towel, I carried the container behind me and pushed it through to her with my wounded hands.

In the afternoon, when rice was given to me again, I found that the woman from the kitchen had already loosened the rice for me. I had only to tip the container and most of the rice fell out onto the towel and bare table.

My being able to consume food seemed to have infuriated the Maoists, for the guards came to the small window again to threaten me. They never mentioned the word 'handcuffs', probably because they did not want the other prisoners within hearing to know what they were doing to me. But they continued to urge me to confess. Although the rice I managed to eat each day did in fact make me feel stronger, I was having difficulty walking. For some reason I could not explain, the handcuffs were affecting my feet. Like my hands, they felt hot and painful. My shoes became so tight and unbearable that I had to kick them off. Fortunately they were soft cloth shoes so that I was able to press down the back and wear them as slippers. Now I just staggered about, for my feet could not bear even the reduced weight of my emaciated body. The stains of blood and pus on the quilt where I placed my hands became larger and more numerous as the handcuffs cut through more skin on my wrists and more deeply into the wounds. Either the weather suddenly got a lot warmer or I was feverish; I no longer felt the cold but shivered from pain whenever I had to move my hands or stagger across the room.

One day, when I was at the small window getting drinking water, my imprisoned hands holding the mug trembled so much that half of the water spilled down the back of my padded jacket and slacks.

'Your hands are very bad. The higher ups don't know it. Why don't you wail? As long as you don't cry out, they will not know how bad your hands are,' the woman from the kitchen whispered through the opening before hastily closing the shutter.

Though the Chinese people were normally restrained about showing emotion, they did wail to show deep grief at funerals or as a protest against injustice that involved death. The sight of someone wailing had always embarrassed me. It was like seeing someone stripping himself naked. From childhood I had been disciplined never to show emotion. The memory of trying for many years to fight back tears lingered; gradually I came to regard crying as a sign of weakness. Should I wail now just to call attention to the fact that my hands were being crippled? I decided against it. For one thing, I did not think I knew how to emit that prolonged, inarticulate cry that was so primitve and animal-like. For another I did not want to do anything that might be interpreted as asking for mercy. 'The man higher up' had ordered the handcuffs put on my wrists so that I would be tormented by them. He believed my suffering would eventually lead to my willingness to give a false confession to save myself. The best way to counter-attack was certainly not to show that I could no longer endure suffering. So I ignored the kind advice of the woman from the kitchen.

Several more days passed. The handcuffs were now beginning to affect my mind, probably through their effect on my nervous system. I got muddled periodically and forgot where I was. I no longer remembered how many days ago I was first manacled. Life was just an unending road of acute pain and suffering on which I must trudge along as best I could.

During moments of lucidity, I tried to discipline my mind by doing simple arithmetic. I would repeat to myself, 'Two and two makes four, four and four equals eight, eight and eight equals sixteen, sixteen and sixteen equals thirty-two ...' But after only a little while my ability to concentrate would evaporate and I would get confused again. The guards still came to the locked door. But what they said was just a jumble of words that made no sense to me.

After several more days, I became so weak that I no longer had the strength to stagger to the small window to get rice or water. I tried to refuse when they were offered to me, but whether words came out of my mouth or not I did not know. Perhaps the woman from the kitchen was urging me to take the rice or the drinking water; I did not hear her voice, only sensed that she stood there waiting for something. Most of the time I was so far away that I did not know what was happening around me. After drifting in and out of consciousness like that for some time, I passed out altogether.

When I opened my eyes again, I found myself lying on the dusty floor.

'Get up! Get up!' a man's voice was shouting very near me. 'You are feigning death! You won't be allowed to get away with it.'

My arms were still bent to my back but they were no longer held together by the handcuffs.

'Get up! Get up!' a female voice joined in.

I pulled myself together and looked up to find the militant female guard and the young man who had put the handcuffs on me standing over me. The cell door was wide open. Dangling in the hands of the female guard was the pair of heavy brass handcuffs they had removed from my wrists. The handcuffs were covered with congealed blood and pus. Probably the guard considered them repulsive, as she was holding them gingerly by the chain by just two fingers.

'Don't think we are finished with you! There are other ways to bring you to your senses. Those who dare to oppose the dictatorship of the proletariat will not be allowed to get away with it,' said the man.

The female guard gave my prostrate form a hard kick as they left the cell and locked the door behind them.

I remained on the floor, too exhausted to move. Although the handcuffs were removed, my whole body was aching and hot. Slowly I brought my left arm forward and looked at my hand. Quickly I closed my eyes again. My hand was too horrible to contemplate. After a moment, I sat up and looked at both hands. They were swollen to enormous size. The swelling extended to my elbows. Around my wrists where the handcuffs had cut into my flesh, blood and pus continued to ooze out of the wounds. My nails were purple in colour and felt as if they were going to fall off. I touched the back of each hand, only to find the skin and flesh numb. I tried to curl up my fingers but could not because they were the size of carrots. I prayed to God to help me recover the use of my hands.

After a while, I tried to get up. But I had to stifle a cry of pain, as my feet could not support my body. As I was very near the bed, I managed to haul myself up to it. The woollen socks were stuck to my feet with dried sticky pus. When I succeeded in peeling the socks off with my numb and swollen fingers, I saw that my feet were also swollen to enormous size. Under each toe was a large blister. I could not take the socks off because some of the blisters had broken and the pus had dried, gluing the socks to my feet. What was making it impossible for me to walk was the fact that some of the blisters had not broken. Obviously I needed a sterile sharp instrument such as a needle to break the blisters so that I could let the fluid out. Also, to prevent infection, I needed bandages and some antiseptic medicine on the wounds on my wrists. I stood up. I almost sat down again immediately because the burning pain in my feet was unbearable. However, I resisted the impulse to sit down and, shuddering, remained standing. I thought that since I had to move about in the cell, the sooner I practised moving about with my swollen feet the better. I moved one foot forward a couple of inches, shifted my weight onto that foot, and moved the other foot a couple of inches. Eventually I arrived at the door. Leaning against it for support, I called the guard on duty.

'Report!' My voice sounded feeble. But almost immediately the shutter on the small window was pushed open. The guard had been right outside the door, watching me through the peephole all the time without my knowledge.

'What do you want?'

'May I see the doctor, please.'

'What for?'

'My wrists and feet are wounded. I need some medicine and bandages,' I explained.

'The doctor does not give treatment when the prisoner has been punished,' declared the guard.

'In that case, perhaps you could just give me some disinfectant ointment or mercurochrome for the wounds?' I knew the guards kept a supply of these in their little room.

'No, not allowed.'

'The wounds may become infected.'

'That's your business.'

'May I just have a roll of bandages to tie the wounds up?'

I lifted my swollen hands to the window to show her the wounds on my wrists but she turned her head the other way and refused to look at them.

'May I have some bandages?' I asked her again.

'No.'

I got angry. 'So, you do not practise revolutionary humanitarianism in accordance with Chairman Mao's teaching,' I said.

'Revolutionary humanitarianism is not for you,' she said.

'No, it's not for me because I'm not a real enemy of the Communist Party. And I haven't done anything against the People's Government. Revolutionary humanitarianism was allowed to the Japanese invaders. The Communist Party gave the wounded Japanese prisoners of war medicine and bandages during the war, according to Chairman Mao's books,' I said sarcastically.

'Look at you! As argumentative and unrepentant as you were before. You learned nothing from the handcuffs. Perhaps you did not have them on long enough. If you argue any more, I am going to put them on you again.' With that threat she retreated to the guards' room and remained there. I knew she had no authority to decide to put the handcuffs back on my wrists again. It was just bluff. She knew I knew it too.

It seemed there was no alternative to relying on myself to deal with the wounds on my wrists and feet. With the help of God, I thought, I would find some way to prevent infection. Very slowly I shuffled to the table and drank up the water in the mug. I heard the woman from the kitchen entering the building with her heavy trolley on which were two huge buckets of boiled hot drinking water for the prisoners. I waited for her at the small window. When she came to me, she gave me a generous portion, filling the large mug almost three-quarters full. I poured this water into the washbasin and with a clean towel carefully washed the wounds on my wrists and wiped away the dried blood and pus. Then I washed my feet in the same blood-stained water. The feel of hot water on my skin was good. I longed to drink some, but I thought it more important to clean the wounds.

While I sat on the bed drying my feet, I wondered what I could tear up and use as bandages. After so many years, my meagre stock of clothing had become even more depleted because I often had to tear up a garment that was worn to patch those that were just beginning to have holes. While I was searching my mind for an idea, I saw the pillow case hanging on the clothes line. I had washed it the morning I was called to the interrogation room. It looked dry. It was the only pillow case I had left but I thought I could dispense with it; I could put the pillow under the sheet at night. I raised my arm to take it off the clothes line. To my dismay, I found I could not reach the pillow case because my arm refused to be raised higher than the level of my shoulders. I supposed after being tied to my back for so long, the tendons were paralysed. I resolved to restore the function of my arms by exercise. But that would take some time. For the moment, at any rate, I would have to leave the wounds on my wrists uncovered.

The Labour Reform girl came with cold water. She poured the water slowly into the washbasin as I held it up to the small window. As soon as she saw my hands shaking because they could no longer bear the weight, she stopped. The washbasin was hardly half full. I poured some of the water into one of the mugs for drinking. With the rest, I washed my face. Then I tried to comb my hair. Since my right arm holding the comb could not reach the top of my head, I used my left hand to hold up the elbow of my right arm. With my head bent forward and turning first this way and then that way, I managed to smooth out my hair. I wanted very much to give myself a sponge bath and change my underclothes. But I was afraid I would catch cold in the icy room. In any case, I was already exhausted and there was no more clean water.

The woman from the kitchen was again at the small window. She handed me the afternoon meal through the opening. The aluminium container was filled to the brim with rice and boiled cabbage. When I pushed the food into my mug, I discovered two hard boiled eggs buried at the bottom of the container.

To forestall, I am sure, any possibility of my thanking her for the eggs, the woman did not open the window to collect the container as was her habit, but shouted through the door as if she were angry, 'You are always so slow! Hand the container over to the guard on night duty when you have finished! I can't stand here all night waiting for you!'

I sat down on the edge of the bed to eat. With each mouthful I swallowed, I felt a little strength flowing back to me. When I had finished, I washed the mug and stood up to exercise my arms. I was most anxious that I should be able to reach the pillow case on the line as soon as possible so that I could make bandages to cover up the wounds on my wrists. I swung my arms up and down many times, each time raising them a little higher in the air to stretch the tendons. My feet were very painful but I remained standing until I was exhausted. After a short rest, I resumed the exercise.

The guard on night duty came to the small window, handed me the day's newspaper and took away the aluminium container. I looked at the date on the newspaper and discovered that only eleven days had elapsed since I had been called to the interrogation room and manacled. It seemed much longer. The guard came to call the prisoners to go to bed.

This was the first time in eleven days that I was to have the chance of a full night's sleep. But it took me a long time to drop off. Somehow, the tight handcuffs had affected my nervous system. My whole body was aching and hot. No matter on which side I lay, it was painful and uncomfortable. The weight of the blanket and quilt seemed unbearable. Since I did not feel the cold, being feverish, I pulled the blanket off. I tried to arrange my feet and arms in such a way that the blood and pus would not stain the quilt. I soon found this impossible.

To put those special handcuffs tightly on the wrists of a prisoner was a form of torture widely used in Maoist China's prison system. Sometimes additional chains were put around the ankles of the prisoners. At other times, a prisoner might be manacled and then have his handcuffs tied to a bar on the window so that he could not move away from the window to eat, drink or go to the toilet. The purpose was to degrade a man in order to destroy his morale. Before my own imprisonment, victims and their families had simply not told me about such practices. But after my imprisonment, I became a member of that special group, so they did not hesitate to tell me of their experiences. However, since the People's Government claimed to have abolished all forms of torture, the officials simply called such methods 'punishment' or 'persuasion'.

It took me many months of intense effort at exercise to be able to raise my arms above my head; it was a full year before I could stretch them straight above me. The minor wounds left no scar after healing but the deeper wounds where the metal of the handcuffs cut through my flesh almost to the bone left ugly scars which remain with me to this day: a legacy of Mao Tze-tung and his Revolutionaries. While the swelling of my hands and fingers subsided eventually, the backs of both my hands could feel nothing for more than two years. The nerves were so damaged that when I experimentally pricked the back of my hands with a needle to draw blood, I felt nothing whatever. Even now, after more than thirteen years, my hands ache on cold wet days. In winter, even in a warm room, I have to wear gloves in bed. If I use my hands a little too much in cleaning, typing or carrying heavy parcels, sometimes I find my right hand suddenly going limp and useless, unable to grip anything. My right hand sustained a greater degree of damage than my left hand, mainly because the zip on my slacks was on the left side. In straining over to the left of my body to unzip my slacks whenever I had to sit on the toilet, the handcuffs cut deeper into the flesh of my right wrist. The irony of the situation was that normally women's slacks in the clothes stores in China had the zip on the right side. Since my slacks had been specially tailored, I had the zip on the left, because I had worn it that way long before the Communist regime came into being. I suppose the interrogator would have said that this was another instance of my stubborn reluctance to change my old way of life.

Some of my friends exclaimed, 'Why did you bother to zip up your slacks at all, when you had your handcuffs on!' I suppose I could have left my slacks unzipped in those circumstances. But I would have felt terribly demoralized. That wouldn't have been good for my fighting spirit. Looking back on those years, I believe the main reason I was able to survive my ordeal was because the Maoist Revolutionaries failed to break my fighting spirit.

On the whole my feet fared better. Though they remained swollen and painful for many weeks after the handcuffs were taken off, there was no permanent damage. When Sunday came round again, I was able to borrow a needle to open the blisters to let the fluid out. After that, I was able to hobble along slowly without excruciating pain until the blisters gradually healed.

The morning after I was freed from the handcuffs, the guard called the prisoners for outdoor exercise. I went to the door to wait for her to come to my cell so that I could ask to be excused.

'May I be excused today? My feet are swollen. I can't get them into my shoes,' I said when she opened the shutter.

She looked at my feet through the opening and saw that I was wearing cloth shoes with the back pressed down.

'You can go out just as you are,' she answered.

'I'm afraid it will be difficult for me to walk the distance to the exercise yard. My feet are very painful. May I be excused this time?' I requested again.

'No, you will have to go. Today, everybody must go.'

She unlocked the door and stood there watching me. Each step I took was sheer agony. My body trembled and I was very slow.

'Please, may I not go today?' After going a yard or so, I asked again.

'No, you have to go today,' she said.

What did she mean? Why must I go today? What was so special about today? I was thinking while making slow progress. She was patiently following me out of the building of the women's prison. Since my cell was at the end of the corridor, I was always the last prisoner from downstairs to go out.

Suddenly, the militant female guard ran into the courtyard. 'Why are you so slow? Walk faster! We can't wait for you all day!' she shouted.

I continued to shuffle along, trying very hard to bear the pain and walk faster. She gave me a hard push impatiently. I collapsed onto the path. The other guard pulled me up.

'You are acting! Hurry up! Hurry up! Can't you walk faster? Walk faster!' she yelled and then dashed off in the direction of the exercise yards.

'I can't walk any faster. To fall down only delays me,' I said to the other guard.

'Never mind. Do the best you can.' She seemed much more reasonable.

Finally I reached the exercise yard. Instead of being locked into my usual place with the plane tree over the wall, I was put into an exercise yard directly below the pavilion on the raised platform from where the guards watched the prisoners walking about in the exercise yards below. The pavilion seemed to be closed. All the guards were standing in the wind on the platform. As soon as the door of the exercise yard was locked, I leaned against it for support and to take the weight off my feet which were burning with pain. I thought I would remain there until the exercise period was over.

'Start walking!' shouted the voice of the militant female guard standing on the platform above me.

I had reached the end of my tether so I ignored her and remained beneath the platform, leaning against the heavy iron door.

'What are you doing there? Start walking!' she called again.

'I can't walk. My feet are excruciatingly painful. Can't you see my arms and hands? My feet are just the same. They are badly swollen and wounded. Blood and pus are coming out of the wounds.' I was so angry that I shouted back at her. I fully expected her to come down and hit me, as prisoners were not allowed to talk about what happened to them in the hearing of other prisoners. My voice was loud enough for all others in the area of the exercise yards to hear clearly. But she did not rush down the platform to punish me. It almost seemed that what I had just said was exactly what she wanted to hear for she moderated her tone of voice when she said, 'Just stand in the middle of the exercise yard.'

I hobbled to the middle of the exercise yard and stood facing her.

'Turn round! Face the other way!'

Why did she want me to face the other way? It seemed she wanted me to be seen but not for me to see what went on on the platform where she stood. It suddenly dawned on me that someone, probably the so-called 'higher up', was on the platform. But I saw only the guards who were familiar to me. The man could be inside the pavilion. It had glass windows. If he were inside, he could see my wounded arms and hands easily. I supposed he had come in person to verify the damage done me by the handcuffs. What I had said to the militant female guard was tantamount to a description of my condition. That, I decided, was why the militant female guard was pleased to hear it. She probably hoped to impress the 'higher up' with the good job she had done in inflicting damage to my wrists and feet. But why did the 'higher up' not stand with the guards on the platform? Why did he have to hide in the enclosed pavilion? I turned my body slightly so that I could see the entrance of the pavilion from the corner of my eye. After a little while, three men in khaki military top coats came out of the pavilion and disappeared down the steps followed by the female guard. Although I had been outside hardly more than ten minutes, I was now told to go back to my cell. On my way back no one urged me to walk faster.

The same guard who had accompanied me out walked back with me. When she opened the door of the cell, I showed her the wounds on my wrists. They were once more covered with blood and pus.

'Please look at these wounds. I need to bandage them up to prevent infection. Could you please help me to take down that pillow case on the clothes line so that I can tear it up to make bandages?' I asked her.

Without a word she stepped into the cell, pulled the pillow case down and handed it to me.

The pillow case was not new in 1966 when I first came to the detention house. Now it was paper thin and fragile. I had no difficulty tearing it into strips. It made two sets of bandages.

The prison was very quiet. I did not hear the voices of the guards calling prisoners upstairs to go out for outdoor exercise, after I came in. It seemed they had stopped the outdoor exercise; something that had never happened before. I thought probably the whole so-called outdoor exercise in which I had participated was arranged solely for the three military men to see the state I was in. It had not been a routine outdoor exercise at all.

When drinking water was given to me again, I washed the wounds and bandaged them up. Very quickly the blood and pus seeped through the cloth. It was out of the question to change the bandages immediately. In the cold and damp cell, the wet bandage would take a long time to dry. I simply had to find a way to dry the bandages more quickly. Perhaps, I thought, I could use the mug filled with hot water as an iron and dry the bandages by wrapping them on the outside of the mug whenever boiling water was given to me. That would enable me to change the bandages at least twice a day. And if I washed the bandages just before going to sleep and left them to dry after first rolling them in a towel to take out the excess moisture, they would probably be dry by next morning. In this manner, I might manage to change the bandages three times during each twenty-four hours.

When hot drinking water was next given to me, I wound a strip of wet bandage firmly on the outside of the mug. It pleased me to see steam coming from the damp cloth, which quickly turned lighter in colour as it dried.

For the next few months I devoted my whole attention to caring for the wounds and gave the newspaper only a cursory glance. But I gained the impression that there were fewer articles of denunciation of a military nature and many articles demanding that Communist China should take her rightful place at the United Nations. It also seemed that Lin Piao's name was mentioned less frequently while

Premier Chou En-lai seemed to have become more prominent than he had been for years.

Because of my poor physical condition, the wounds were slow to heal. It was many weeks before even the most superficial wounds formed scabs. At the same time, my old trouble of inflamed gums and haemorrhages persisted. It amused me to see the young doctor giving me treatment for these while stringently ignoring the wounds on my wrists.

To add insult to injury, several of the guards came to examine my wounds when they were on duty at the women's prison. While most of them made no comment, a few militant Maoist guards told me I deserved the punishment.

I did not expect to be called for interrogation, as everything about my simple life seemed to have been gone through with a fine-tooth comb. I thought probably the Maoists would come up with some other way to torment me. But I did not try to anticipate what it might be.

CHAPTER 12
Release

While I attended to my numerous physical problems and waited for the next move by the Maoists in 1971, spring and summer had come and gone. The golden autumn days were upon us. The most important event of the year, the National Day of the People's Republic of China, was celebrated in the autumn on October the First. It was a national holiday. The pattern of celebrating the National Day had been adhered to by the People's Government ever since its inception. Everyone received extra food rations, was given the opportunity to enjoy free shows in public parks and allowed to purchase more consumer goods in short supply in the State-owned shops.

The major event, organized by the authorities, was a parade held in each city. It displayed diagrams, figures and pictures of economic and cultural achievements of the previous year on colourful floats. Tens of thousands of workers, peasants, students and even housewives marched in procession to pledge their loyal support for the People's Government by shouting slogans specially composed by the Communist Party Propaganda Department for the occasion. The parades were carefully planned and reviewed by leading Party and municipal officials in each locality.

In Peking the parade was held at Tien An Men Square in front of the old Forbidden City and reviewed by Mao Tze-tung and other Politburo members and leading government officials from the balcony above the Tien An Men. Special stands on either side of the balcony were filled with foreign dignitaries and diplomats. At night there was an elaborate firework display.

The spectacle of hundreds of colourful floats with impressive displays and tens of thousands of men and women on foot marching past the review stand, waving red flags, shouting slogans and holding reproductions of Mao's official portraits over their heads was an affirmation of Mao's power and triumph. It must have been an intoxicating moment for the old man to see the adoring faces turned to gaze at him as the marchers passed and to hear their thundering voices wishing him a long life of ten thousand years (in the same words used for Chinese Emperors in history). The smiling photograph of Mao splashed on the front pages of China's newspapers all over the country on 2 October attested to his genuine happiness on this important occasion.

Everybody in China knew that for Mao Tze-tung, the peasant from Shaoshan, the National Day of the People's Republic of China was a great day of personal satisfaction. Therefore it was most astonishing to find that on October the First 1971 there were no celebrations at all. When the morning broadcast did not mention anything, I was surprised. In the afternoon, I waited eagerly for the newspaper. When it came, I saw only Mao's official portrait on its front page. The date, October the First, and 'Nation Day' were printed in red but there was no mention of any activities by leading officials or any special event. While I was still puzzling over this extraordinary omission, a guard suddenly pushed open the shutter on the small window.

'Hand over your book of quotations!' she demanded.

It seemed such a strange order that for a moment I thought perhaps I had inadvertently done something to damage the book and she was going to use it as an excuse to punish me. Hastily I picked up the book and, with a brief glance to make sure it looked all right, handed it to her. After she had closed the shutter, I heard her going upstairs to demand the book from other cells. Then I knew that she had been instructed to collect the book of quotations from all prisoners.

She did not give the book back to me until she called me to go to bed. I examined it to try to find out why she had demanded it in the first place and was greatly astonished to discover that she had torn out the preface. This book of Mao's quotations was first compiled and published by the People's Liberation Army for its semi-literate soldiers to use in studying Mao Tze-tung Thought, on the orders of Lin Piao after he became Defence Minister.

The preface for this book was written by Lin Piao himself. In it he praised Mao as 'the greatest living Marxist of our time, who developed the doctrine of Marxist-Leninism and successfully applied it to the specific conditions of China'. He exhorted the Liberation Army soldiers to study the quotaions of Mao contained in the book and apply them to their daily tasks so that they could 'blend Mao Tze-tung Thought into their blood stream' and become soldiers who 'study Chairman Mao's books, obey Chairman Mao's orders and become Chairman Mao's good fighters'.

There was nothing in the wording of the preface that could be considered objectionable to Mao. In fact it was such blatant flattery that many people found it embarrassing to have to memorize and recite it, a practice made obligatory during the Cultural Revolution. I felt the only possible explanation for the preface to be torn out was that its author was in disgrace, as it was the practice of the Communist Party to obliterate from all its records the name and writings of a disgraced official as if he had never existed. Obviously the guard was under orders to collect the books from the prisoners and to deal with them. My realization that Lin Piao might be in disgrace was so stupendous that I stood there with the Little Red Book in my hand, lost in thought.

'Why are you not in bed?' the voice of the guard said outside the door.

Not wishing to give her the impression that I was interested in what had happened, I quickly arranged my bedding and lay down. But I did not have much sleep that night.

A few days after the guard had torn the preface out of my copy of the book of quotations, the newspaper came out with articles of denunciations of someone 'sleeping by our bedside'. No name was mentioned. To a westerner, 'sleeping by our bedside' would mean a spouse. To the Chinese, the expression meant someone very close. The same expression had been used for Liu Shao-chi when he was denounced. It implied that Mao did not know that very near him was an enemy who wished him ill. Other articles talked about the duplicity of a man Mao had trusted who had voiced support for Mao while plotting Mao's death. There were also frequent mentions of Party history and military engagements during the War of Resistance against Japan and the War of Liberation against the Kuomintang. The Chinese people, including myself, were familiar with Lin Piao's personal history because it had been so frequently glorified when he was being built up as a suitable successor to Mao Tze-tung, just before the Ninth Party Congress. I had now no doubt that he had been ousted, though at that time I didn't know any details of the struggle between him and Mao Tze-tung. Watching events closely and reading every word in the newspaper with meticulous attention, I noticed with relief that the name of Lin Piao's man in charge of Military Control of the Public Security Bureau in Shanghai had disappeared. Since the No. 1 Detention House was a part of the network of prisons under the jurisdiction of the Shanghai Public Security Bureau, this man was also the officer on the highest level in control of the detention house. If my assumption was correct that the motivating force behind my own persecution was the military representatives of Lin Piao in Shanghai, then I had good reason to hope that the downfall of Lin Piao would benefit me. On the other hand, I warned myself to continue watching developments. I thought it was premature to be jubilant for I had no idea whether the power vacuum created by Lin Piao's downfall would be filled by the radicals headed by Chiang Ching or by the old guard headed by Chou En-lai.

One night, late in October, the guards once again called the prisoners to sit quietly to listen to a special broadcast. The loudspeaker was switched on and a man's voice lectured the prisoners on 'the excellent situation created by the Great Proletarian Cultural Revolution'. The central theme of his speech was the announcement that President Nixon was to visit China in February of the following year. He told us that the Proletarian Cultural Revolution had so raised China's importance in the world that the United States of America, which had hitherto adopted a policy of hostility towards the People's Republic, was now on the point of realizing the futility of that policy.

'What is the significance of the forthcoming visit of Nixon, the head of the strongest capitalist country in the world? Would he have decided to come if China were weak and impotent? Of course not! Nixon has decided to come to China to pay his respects to our Great Leader because he has to face the fact that China under the wise leadership of our Great Leader Chairman Mao, after being purified and strengthened by the Great Proletarian Cultural Revolution, is invincible. Don't forget that the United States is the most reactionary capitalist country in the world and our foremost enemy. The forthcoming visit of the President of the United States is a great victory for the Chinese proletarian class. It's a reflection of the great achievement made by the Cultural Revolution. It bears out the fact that the decadent capitalist system is on the decline while our own socialist system is increasing in vigour and influence in the world.

'At first, when he offered to come, many of our comrades thought we shouldn't welcome a man who represents imperialism against Vietnam, exploitation of the workers in the United States and longstanding hostility against the People's Republic of China. But our Great Leader is magnanimous. He said, "Let him come. Let's receive him with courtesy and hear what he has to say. If he admits past mistakes and sincerely wants to change, we'll welcome it. We are Marxists. We give a man a chance if he is honestly repentant." Our Great Leader is so wise! He is right! We'll receive Nixon. And for the next few months we will educate all our comrades about the new situation and help them to see that by accepting Nixon's visit, we are not surrendering our principles but accepting the surrender of the wrong policy of the United States Government. Nixon's visit is a great victory for us!

'In this connection, I want to give a word of warning to many of the prisoners confined in the No. 1 Detention House. Many of you are here precisely because you worshipped the capitalist world of the imperialists and belittled socialist China. You placed your hope in the capitalist world and believed that one day capitalism would again prevail in China. Let the forthcoming visit of the American President be a lesson to you all. Think carefully. If the reactionary Kuomintang had not been thrown out of China, if the United States troops had not been defeated by the Chinese People's Volunteer Army in Korea, if the United States army were not bogged down in Vietnam, and if we had not become stronger as a result of the Great Proletarian Cultural Revolution, would Nixon have wanted to travel across the world to Peking to pay homage to our Great Leader?'

The speech was long-drawn-out, gloating repeatedly over the proposed visit by the President of the United States. I have given the gist of it. After my release from the detention house, I learned that the same interpretation was given to the visit when it was announced to the general public. Discussions were held in every factory, commune and residents' committee meeting to 'prepare' the people for the forthcoming visit and to use the occasion to create the impression that Mao Tze-tung was now the most important leader in the world.

I was elated by the new turn in China's relations with the United States and believed that it could have a decisive effect on the power balance in the leadership of the Communist Party. At least, I thought Chou En-lai's position would be strengthened for a considerable time to come. Perhaps the moderate forces in the Party leadership would gain the upper hand. If so, the end of my own ordeal might be approaching. However, I knew from experience that everything in China developed slowly. The effect of a major switch of policy in Peking often took months if not years to be felt at the base level where I was. I also knew that the radical faction, headed by Chiang Ching, had a strong hold on Shanghai and that her long-time associate, Chang Chuan-chiao, was the Chief Party Secretary here.

After living for so many years without real hope, I became quietly excited by the new development. For weeks I watched the newspaper and waited. The guards appeared preoccupied, as they were in the days after the Revolutionaries and the Red Guards took over the Shanghai Municipal Government in January 1967. I thought they were probably undergoing intensified political indoctrination about the downfall of Lin Piao.

Winter was again approaching. The holes at the elbows of my

sweaters and at the knees of my knitted long johns were beyond repair. The filling of my padded jacket and quilt had fallen to the bottom leaving patches that were no more than two layers of cloth. The only shirt I had left was so patched that it was no longer possible to tell which piece of cloth was the original shirt. Obviously, if I were to survive another winter at the detention house, I desperately needed some additional clothing. While my past requests for clothing had always fallen on deaf ears, I decided to try once more and see whether the changed circumstances might not bring forth a different response.

'Report!' I called at the door.

'What do you want?' A guard's lethargic footsteps stopped outside my cell and the shutter was pushed open.

I held my sweater out to show her the holes and said, 'The weather is getting cold. My clothes and quilt are so worn that they are no longer warm. Please look at this. It's full of holes. I also need a padded jacket and quilt. And I need another shirt. Please look at my clothes. You will see I do need warm clothes for the winter.'

'How long have you been here already? How many years altogether?'

'This will be the sixth winter I am here. I came in September 1966. The clothes and bedding given me by the Red Guards were not new then. After so many years without the padding being renewed, they are no longer warm,' I said.

Now that I could see a glimmer of light at the end of the dark tunnel in which I had been confined for so long, I was determined to survive to the day when that light might guide me out into daylight. Probably my voice showed my anxiety. This seemed to have annoyed her. She closed the shutter and walked away.

Undaunted by her cold indifference, I repeated my request for warm clothing and bedding to each guard who came on duty for several successive days. Finally one of them said impatiently, 'All right! All right! You need warm clothing. We know about it already. Your request is being considered.'

A week passed and then another. The weather got colder and colder. I decided to try once more.

'Report!' I called.

'What do you want?' a guard asked through the closed door.

'May I see the interrogator?'

'What for?'

'I want to make a request for warm clothes.'

'Haven't you got warm clothes already?' The guard opened the shutter and I saw through the opening that it was the older woman who had urged me to eat when I was manacled. I had not seen her since that night.

'My winter clothes are worn out. Please come into the cell and look at them. I'm so afraid I might get ill again this winter if I do not get some warm clothes,' I said.

She unlocked the cell door, came in and examined my clothes and the quilt. Then she said, 'I'll report to the authorities. Would you like to borrow some prison clothes now?'

The thought of wearing prison clothes filled me with horror, not only because I thought they might have bugs but also because it seemed the final surrender of my dignity and independence.

'No, thank you. I do not want to borrow prison clothes. I want to get permission to buy new winter clothes with my own money that is now in the hands of the government.'

She appeared to be thinking over the problem. So I added, 'My money was taken by the Red Guards when they looted my home. One of their teachers told me the government would keep the money for me if the money had not come from exploitation. I have no shares in any factories or land in the countryside. When I told the teacher the position, he told me that the money would not be confiscated.'

'I'll report to the authorities,' she promised.

A few days later, I was called to the interrogation room. The older guard was nowhere to be seen. In the place of the interrogator sat the militant female guard who had always taken a lead in persecuting me. She was flanked by two other female guards, including one I considered mild. The sight of the militant female guard was both a surprise and a disappointment for me. Had the new situation in Peking brought no change at all in the No. 1 Detention House? With this woman in charge, what hope had I that my request would fall on sympathetic ears?

After I had bowed to Mao's portrait and read a passage from the mutilated book of quotations, I sat down on the chair for the prisoner and waited for her to ridicule my request. I was unprepared for her normal, almost kind tone of voice when she said, 'What is this request of yours about winter clothes? Haven't you got winter clothes already?'

'They are worn out,' I said. To prove my point, I pulled off the blue cotton jacket I had on to reveal the padded jacket underneath with its holes and tufts of cotton escaping through them. I raised my arms to show her the frayed cuffs.

'All right! All right! Put on your jacket,' she said.

'The government is holding my assets. I want to ask permission to use some of my own money to buy some much needed clothes,' I said, laying emphasis on the words 'my own money'.

'Which government department is holding your money?' she asked. 'Have you a receipt?'

'The Red Guards took the money when they looted my house. They didn't give me a receipt.'

'You mustn't use the word "loot" when you refer to the revolutionary action taken by the Red Guards. They were acting on our Great Leader's instruction to rid socialist China of the Four Olds and to deal with the exploiting class,' she said.

'I'm not a member of the exploiting class. According to Marxism, only those who live on the interest of their stocks and shares in factories or on rent collected from the peasants are "members of the exploiting class". My money was mostly my salary which I earned legally and family inheritance which was guaranteed by the constitution,' I said heatedly. If I had spoken like this a year ago, she would have exploded. Now she just ignored me.

'Did the teachers of the Red Guards who came to your house to take revolutionary action against you tell you which government department would be holding your money?'

'No, they merely said the money would be held pending a decision by Chairman Mao.'

'Exactly. All personal assets taken by the Red Guards are frozen and cannot be touched before the Chairman makes a decision,' she said.

'I also have a foreign-exchange account with the Bank of China,' I said.

'Foreign-exchange accounts are frozen too.'

'All right then. Let me borrow an English typewriter. I will write a letter to my bank in Hong Kong and get them to send me some money.'

'That won't be allowed. You are not allowed to communicate with anybody outside China,' she said. 'How do we know what you might write?'

'Before posting the letter, you will naturally read the letter I have written.'

'You might send a coded message out of the country. That wouldn't do at all. What we'll do is to report your request to the senior authorities and see to it that you get some warm clothes when it gets really cold. Now you must go back to your cell and study our Great Leader Chairman Mao's books really diligently.'

I was dismissed and led back to the cell. Throughout the interview, the militant female guard had spoken in a normal voice, almost sympathetically. The change was startling. I supposed she was a typical example of those Party members who 'follow the Party line closely'. The Chinese people call them 'chameleons', as they changed attitude and behaviour according to circumstances just as rapidly as the chameleon changes colour. Such Party members were the survivors and achievers. They never questioned the policy of the Party but followed it promptly and carried it out. They were mindless robots, unburdened with the ability for independent thinking or a human conscience. They made the best cadres for any Party Secretary appointed to an organization, as they were always willing and ready to serve him without question as long as he represented the power of the Party and could give them promotions. But should he fall in disgrace, they were always the first to denounce him. They were the new type of successful people produced by the Communist Revolution in China. Because they seemed to maintain their positions through every twist and turn of the Party's policy, they became the example for the young generation of Chinese to emulate. The result was a fundamental change in the basic values of Chinese society.

A week later, a large bundle was deposited on the floor of my cell by a male guard. After I had signed the receipt, he locked the door and departed. I took the bundle to my bed and untied it. To my great astonishment, I found in the bundle the padded jacket, the fleece-lined winter coat, the two sweaters and a pair of woollen underpants the Red Guards had allowed my daughter to keep for her own use after they looted our home in 1966. Also included was the winter quilt for her bed. Wrapped among the clothes were several towels and a mug she used for tea. One of the towels was a rose-coloured Cannon face towel I had brought back from Hong Kong which she was using when I was taken to the No. 1 Detention House. It looked exactly the same as it had in 1966. I examined the padded jacket in navy-blue woollen material lined with maroon-coloured silk. It was new in 1966 and it looked new now. I picked up the white porcelain mug with trembling hands and found it was stained faintly brown inside. It had not been washed and the tea had dried.

My heart was thumping faster and faster as I examined each article and realized their appearance was an ominous message of disaster. Hateful though the idea was, I could not help thinking that something terrible had happened to my daughter not long after I was arrested. She had probably died. That was why the clothes had hardly been worn and the face towel remained unused and new-looking. Perhaps her death happened rather suddenly and unexpectedly so that she did not have time to wash the mug she had used for tea. My legs were shaking so violently that I had to sit down quickly.

The No. 1 Detention House allowed families of inmates to send them articles of clothing and daily necessities such as soap and towels on the fifth day of each month. It was always the loneliest day of my imprisonment as I listened to the guards carrying parcels to other prisoners but never to me. At first I wondered why my daughter never sent me anything. Later, I believed that because she was a member of the Communist Youth League, she had been compelled to renounce me. While I missed not having this tenuous link to my child through monthly parcels, I was glad she was spared the unpleasant task of coming to the prison gate and queuing up for hours to hand over a parcel. Now, deep in my heart, I knew the reason I had never received any parcels was because she had died.

'Report!' I rushed to the door, hoping to find out the truth from the guard.

'What do you want?' The guard opened the shutter and looked at me through the opening.

'These things you have just given to me. They are my daughter's clothes and quilt,' I said.

'Yes,' answered the guard.

'What's happened to my daughter?'

'Nothing has happened to her,' she replied.

I bent down to look at her face through the small window. She appeared quite normal and calm.

'The clothes look as new as they did in 1966. Has she not used them during the past few years?'

'How do I know? She probably bought new clothes. She works, doesn't she? She has her own salary. She can buy new clothes, can't she?'

'Do you mean to tell me that you know for a fact my daughter is alive and well at this moment?' I hoped so much for reassurance.

'I haven't seen her, if that's what you mean.'

'But you do know, don't you?'

'Why should she be otherwise?' The guard closed the shutter and walked away.

Was I being hysterical? Had prison life made me over-suspicious and sensitive? I examined everything again carefully. As I touched each item of her clothing, I became more and more convinced that she had indeed died. The message came to me clear and strong that she was no longer in this world. Yet I needed concrete proof, because I was accustomed to dealing with facts and was suspicious of feelings I could not understand or explain. There was also a block in my mind that prevented me from accepting such a terrible possibility as her death, which would have rendered my years of struggling to keep alive meaningless. Death came to old people, not to someone young and healthy as she was. I kept on trying to convince myself she was all right in spite of what I saw.

But I could not explain the unusual look of her things spread out in front of my eyes. They seemed to say time had suddenly stood still, not long after my imprisonment. The navy-blue jacket looked new. But when I examined the silk lining I saw it had creases at the armpits and that a handkerchief was in one of the pockets. It seemed to me she had worn that jacket, but certainly not for more than one winter at the most. My mind was racing with speculations and ideas as I tried to imagine what could possibly have happened. What the guard said seemed to indicate she was alive and well. Yet she did not specifically say so. An idea came into my head. I went to the window again.

'Report!' I called.

No one came. I called again and again. Still no one came. Yet I heard the guards talking in their room at the other end of the corridor. When the guard on night duty came to tell me to go to bed, I tried to talk to her. But she did not come near my cell, only called out from a distance her order to go to bed.

I was not able to sleep. I became more and more anxious. The first thing next morning, I called the guard again.

'Report!'

No answer. I decided to wait for the daytime guard to come on duty. When she came, I called again, 'Report!'

She came quite promptly. 'What do you want?' the guard asked.

'These things of my daughter the guard brought me yesterday make me very uneasy. I can't understand why my daughter doesn't seem to have used them. The Red Guards left each of us only one padded jacket. Why hasn't she worn hers during the past few winters? To prove my daughter is alive and well, I request you to ask her to write a few words in her own handwriting for me to see.'

'Prisoners in a detention house are not allowed to communicate with their families,' she said.

'Perhaps she could just write "Long Live Chairman Mao" or one of Chairman Mao's quotations or even just her name,' I pleaded.

'No, that's not allowed. I have told you already, prisoners in a detention house are not allowed to communicate with their families,' she said firmly.

'But I have been here such a long time already,' I said.

'That makes no difference.'

I repeated my request to every guard who came on duty during the next few days. I was more and more convinced that my daughter was really dead, because they were either evasive or simply kept silent. One or two of them looked definitely embarrassed when they refused my request to see my daughter's handwriting. They did not look at me but averted their glance or simply looked at the floor.

My mind was in turmoil and my heart in anguish. I longed to know the truth while I was afraid of it. One moment I was convinced that she had died. The next moment I believed I had become over-sensitive and too pessimistic because of prolonged imprisonment.

After a few weeks of anxiety with little food and hardly any sleep, I became sick once more, with a high fever and delirium. I was again taken to the prison hospital. My body was so resilient that in spite of the fact that I no longer had the will to live, I survived. I was brought back to the No. 1 Detention House just before Christmas.

Throughout the years of my imprisonment, I had turned to God often and felt his presence. In the drab surroundings of the grey cell, I had experienced magic moments of transcendency that I had not experienced in the ease and comfort of my normal life. My belief in the ultimate triumph of truth and goodness had been restored and I had renewed courage to fight on. My faith had sustained me in these the darkest hours of my life and brought me safely through privation, sickness and torture. At the same time, my suffering had strengthened my faith and made me realize that God was always there. It was up to me to come to Him.

Under the watchful eyes of the guards, I could not pray openly in the daytime. The only way I could be certain of being left alone with my prayers was to bend my head over a volume of Mao Tze-tung's books while I prayed to God from my tormented heart. As I spoke of my daughter, I relived the precious years from the time of her birth in Canberra, Australia, in 1942 until our forcible separation on the night of 27 September 1966 when I was taken to the struggle meeting and arrested. I felt again and again the joy she had given me at each stage of her growth and knew I was fortunate to have received from God this very special blessing of a daughter. Day after day I prayed. More and more I was remembering the days of her living and less and less I dwelled on the tragedy of her dying. Gradually peace came to me and with it a measure of acceptance. But there was something more. While I could no longer cling tenaciously to the hope that I would see her alive and well on the day I walked out of the No. 1 Detention House, I knew there was much I still had to do both before and after my release. My battle was by no means over. It was up to me to find out what had happened to my daughter and, if I could, to right the wrong that had been done to her. My life would be bleak without Meiping. But I had to fight on.

In February 1972 President Nixon came to Peking. The newspaper devoted whole sheets to reports of the visit and published large photographs of his arrival, the banquet of welcome and his visit to Mao Tze-tung at the latter's home. As I looked at the smiling face of Mao while he was holding the hand of the American President, I thought the moment was indeed Mao Tze-tung's finest hour. In that moment his years of humiliation, of being denied recognition were wiped away. And I was certain that he relished the meeting with the American President not only for its significance to himself and the Chinese Communist Party but also for what it meant to his lifelong foe, the Kuomintang in Taiwan.

In all the photographs and reports, Chou En-lai figured prominently. The newspaper reported that Prime Minister Chou En-lai accompanied President Nixon to Shanghai from where the American President was to return to the United States. It said the departure of the President was slightly delayed. It hinted that there was some last-minute difficulty about drafting the text of the final communiqué. However, eventually it was signed. The published version included the acknowledgement by the United States that Taiwan was an integral part of China. This commitment would render it impossible for the United States to recognize an independent Taiwan State, an event the Chinese Communist Government feared most. Furthermore, in the communiqué China did not renounce the use of force for future reunification of the two Chinas. This was decidedly a victory for Communist China. It seemed Communist China gained a great deal from the President's visit, while the price she paid was no more than a display of elaborate hospitality. The policy of rapprochement with the United States seemed more than justified. I felt that the personal position of Prime Minister Chou En-lai had been greatly enhanced by what must have been his successful and skilful diplomacy.

Now there was a respite from class struggle; a more peaceful atmosphere prevailed. The tone of the newspaper was no longer belligerent. Even the guards seemed to behave more like normal human beings. In March I was called for interrogation. The

interrogator I had when I first came to the detention house was back at
his job. He started from the beginning as if the intervening years had
not existed and asked me to write another autobiography. Then he
questioned me about my family, my relatives and friends as well as
about my personal life and activities, going once more through
everything I had already gone through with the interrogator from the
Workers' Propaganda Team in 1969. When I became impatient and
pointed out to him that I had already answered all these questions, he
merely said, 'You have to answer them again.' I did not think he was
trying to trap me into saying something different so that he could
charge me with lying. It was more likely that the official interrogator of
the No. 1 Detention House and the interrogator of the Workers'
Propaganda Team served different masters.

This series of interrogations lasted several months. I did not
remember how many times I was called to the interrogation room or
how many quotations I read from the book of Mao's quotations.
There was no more shouting or argument. But I was sick and tired and
found the sessions extremely tedious.

One day in the autumn of 1972, the interrogator produced a letter,
obviously taken from our office file, and asked me whether I had
written it. I saw it bore my name so I said, 'Yes.'

'This is proof of your illegal activity. But at the same time, it may
only be a political mistake,' he said.

I was astonished. 'May I see the letter again?' I asked him.

He handed the letter to me. I saw that it was a letter written soon
after my husband died in October 1957. I had gone to the Shell office
to take charge because the Bank of China had refused to cash the
company's cheques unless someone was made responsible for the
office and had his or her personal seal registered with the Bank. I
remembered the circumstances very well. That morning I had received
a telephone call from the general manager of Shell's Hong Kong
office. He told me that a general manager had been appointed to
succeed my late husband but he could not get to Shanghai until March
of the following year. He said, 'London wants to know if it is all right
with you.' I told him it was all right and I would inform the Industry
and Commerce Department of the Shanghai Municipal Government.
Then he asked me to draw up a list of things the new general manager
and his wife should bring with them. In particular they wanted to know
whether they should bring a supply of wheat flour, as they knew the
Chinese people ate rice.

Because our secretary at that time was a British woman, I thought she would know best what advice to give, so I asked her to draw up the list and write a covering letter which I signed. In her zeal to help her compatriots, she gave rather a long list that included items from buttons to detergents. But from a political point of view, the letter seemed to me completely innocuous.

'I can't see anything political in this letter,' I said.

'Nothing political? You divulged information about the grain supply situation in Shanghai,' he said.

'Really? Let me see the letter again.' By now I already realized that he had been instructed to find some excuse for my imprisonment in order to avoid having to declare, at the time of my release, that I was innocent. I knew the Communist Party loathed admitting mistakes since it had declared itself to be 'the great, glorious and correct Chinese Communist Party'.

He handed me the letter again and said, 'Read the passage about grain rations.'

I read, 'The Shanghai government allows everyone twenty catties of grain per month. One can buy either rice or flour. It is more than enough.' I asked the interrogator, 'What's wrong with that?'

'That's divulging information concerning the grain supply situation,' he said.

'The grain ration is given to everyone, including all the Europeans living in Shanghai. It's not a secret. What's there to divulge when it is a fact known to everyone?'

'Your letter was sent abroad,' he said.

'Do you mean to say the Europeans in Shanghai will not tell people abroad about it when they go back to their own countries? What about all the overseas Chinese who come back for short visits? Don't they know what grain rations their family members get? Do they conveniently forget it when they leave China?'

'That's their business. This letter is your business. Do you or do you not admit you wrote this letter?'

'The letter was not actually written by me. But I accept full responsibility for it as I signed it and it was sent out of the office when I was the responsible person. The point with which I disagree with you is whether stating the fact of a ration of twenty catties of rice or flour per person per month constituted "divulging information".'

'It's illegal to divulge information about the grain supply. But we can consider it only a political mistake since you were ignorant of the regulations,' he said.

'Nonsense! It's not a mistake, political or otherwise. Show me the regulations, if you have any.' I was angry. But he just ignored me and adjourned the interrogation.

When winter came, the prisoners were again given three meals a day; I got fish or meat with my midday meal. But my health had deteriorated to such an extent that these measures made no difference. I had another bad haemorrhage. When the bleeding was brought under control, I was taken by the militant female guard, dressed in civilian clothes, to the Chung Shan Hospital of the No. 1 Medical College for an examination. An appointment was probably made beforehand, as we went straight to the gynaecology department and were admitted into the doctor's office ahead of all the other waiting patients.

I was surprised to find the 'doctor' a young woman in her early twenties, with an armband of the Revolutionaries. She was clumsy during the brief examination and afterwards she told the guard I had cancer of the uterus. I did not believe her because I was sure she was not a qualified doctor. I thought she was one of those who had learned to be a doctor by being one, just like the young medical orderly I had encountered before. But apparently the guards and others at the detention house believed her. My treatment improved. Some of the guards looked at me with pity in their eyes. After my release, I learned that the officials in charge of my case looked for housing for me in earnest after my visit to the hospital. Eventually it was decided to allow me an apartment with two rooms and a bathroom because it was assumed that since I did not have any children to look after me I would need a live-in nurse towards the end of my life.

On 27 March 1973, after the midday meal, while I was walking about in the cell, a guard opened the small window and said, 'Pack up all your things.'

'All my things?' I asked her.

'Yes, all your things. Don't leave anything behind.'

Soon afterwards the door was opened and two Labour Reform Girls came into the cell. They collected all my things and took them away. A guard in the corridor said, 'Come out!'

I looked round the cell, my 'home' for exactly six and a half years. Without my washbasin and towels, it already seemed different. I noticed the sheets of toilet paper I had pasted on the wall by the bed and wondered if I should tear them off so as not to leave any impression of myself behind. But I decided to leave them for the next unfortunate woman who was to occupy the cell. As I stood in the room looking at it for the last time, I felt again the cold metal of the handcuffs on my wrists and remembered the physical suffering and mental anguish I had endured while fighting with all the will-power and intellect God had given me for that rare and elusive thing in a Communist country called justice.

'Come along! What are you doing in there? Haven't you stayed there long enough?' the guard called.

I followed her to the front courtyard into the room where I was registered when I arrived at the detention house in 1966. There was no one inside. I sat down on the chair.

The young doctor followed me into the room. He stood by the counter, half leaning on it in a casual manner, and said, 'I want to tell you the medication I have been giving you so that you can tell your own doctor when you leave here.' He named several medicines.

'Thank you very much,' I said.

'Well, you are going to be released shortly. Are you glad?' the doctor asked me.

'It's high time, isn't it? Six and a half years is a long time to lock up an innocent person,' I said.

He winced but went on as if he had not heard me, 'I want to give you some advice before you leave. It's for your own good. During the time you have been here, you haven't exactly behaved in an exemplary manner. In fact, in all the years of the detention house, we have never had a prisoner like you, so truculent and argumentative. When you leave this place, you must try to control yourself. Be careful not to irritate the masses. Shanghai is no longer the same city it was before the Cultural Revolution. You must show some respect for the proletariat. Otherwise you will suffer. You are a sick woman. You don't want to be brought back here again, do you?'

I did not say anything. He stayed a few more minutes and then departed. Obviously he had been told to talk to me. But why, I could not tell. In fact, I wasn't listening to him very carefully. What occupied my mind was simply whether I would find my daughter alive after all.

My bundle of clothing was thoroughly searched by two male guards. When they had finished, I was escorted to one of the interrogation rooms. There was no more bowing to Mao's photograph or reading quotations. The interrogator merely pointed at the chair for the prisoner. I sat down.

Another man I had never seen before sat beside him. This man said, 'You are going out today. We feel the time has come for you to go out. I will read to you the conclusion arrived at by the People's Government on your case. However, after you have heard it, you are allowed to express an opinion, if you have any.'

He took a couple of sheets of paper out of a folder. Then he said to me, 'Stand up to listen to the conclusion.'

I stood up.

He read out my name and other personal particulars such as age and place of birth. Then he went on, 'The above-named person was brought to the No. 1 Detention House on 27 September 1966, for the following reasons. One, in October 1957, in a letter to England, she divulged the grain supply situation in Shanghai. Two, she defended traitor Liu Shao-chi and opposed the Central Committee resolution passed on Liu Shao-chi. These are serious matters that deserved punishment. However, in view of the fact that she is politically backward and ignorant, we decided to give her a chance to realize her mistakes. After six and a half years of education in the No. 1 Detention House, we observed a certain degree of improvement in her way of thinking and an attitude of repentance. We have, therefore, decided to show her proletarian magnanimity by refraining from pressing charges against her and allowing her to leave the detention house as a free person.' When he had finished reading, he lifted his head and looked at me.

I was livid. Anger and disgust were choking me. While I despised their blatant hypocrisy and shamelessness, I knew deep in my heart that the real culprit was not this man but the evil system under which we all had to live. I would have to fight, whatever the price, I told myself. I stared back at him and sat down.

'Haven't you something to say? Aren't you grateful? Aren't you pleased that you can now leave as a free person?' the man said.

I tried my best to control the rage that made me tremble and said, 'I can't accept your conclusion. I shall remain here in the No. 1 Detention House until a proper conclusion is reached about my case. A proper conclusion must include a declaration that I am innocent of any crime or political mistake, an apology for wrongful arrest and full rehabilitation. Furthermore, the apology must be published in the newspapers in both Shanghai and Peking, because I have friends and relatives in both cities. As for the conclusion you have just read, it's a sham and a fraud. I was brought to the No. 1 Detention House long before Liu Shao-chi was denounced. How could you have anticipated that I would speak on his behalf? As for divulging information about the grain supply situation, it's just your invention to save your face. I never divulged anything and you all know it.'

They looked at each other. Then the interrogator said, 'The No. 1 Detention House isn't an old people's home. You can't stay here all your life.'

'It doesn't have to be all my life. I'll stay here until you give a proper conclusion to my case. If you are ready to give one tomorrow, I could leave tomorrow.'

'We have already heard your opinion. As I have said, we allow you to express your opinion. It's noted down. We'll forward it to the senior authorities. You can leave now,' the other man said.

'No. The moment I leave, you will forget the whole thing. The wrong conclusion will go into my personal dossier. I'll stay here,' I said.

The interrogator stood up. He said, 'I have never seen a prisoner refusing to leave the detention house before. You must be out of your mind. In any case, when the government wants you to go, you have to go. Your family has been waiting for you since early this morning. How much longer do you want to delay your departure?'

Did he mean my daughter was out there waiting? Oh, how I longed to see her! Suddenly two female guards came into the room. One on each side, they dragged me out to the second gate.

In the distance, standing beside a blue taxi was the figure of a young woman. She was shorter than Meiping and I realized with a sinking heart that she was my god-daughter Hean.

PART III

My Struggle for
Justice

CHAPTER 13

Where Is Meiping?

I STOOD STILL AND my eyes searched the driveway. Apart from the armed sentry in the distance, there was only my god-daughter Hean coming towards me with her arms outstretched.

'Meiping is dead! That's why she isn't here to fetch me. Meiping is dead! Meiping is dead ...' My ears buzzed and my eyes misted, blurring the scene before me. Even though in the back of my mind I still hoped for some tangible explanation for my daughter's absence, my whole body was weakened by grief and I could not move my legs. Hean grasped my arm and guided me to the waiting cab.

'Where is Meiping?'

I feared the answer, but I had to ask.

Hean didn't reply but merely tightened her grip on my hand. I could not bring myself to say, 'Is Meiping dead?' Putting it into words would make it real.

We sat in the car in silence as it drove through the familiar Shanghai streets. Release from the No. 1 Detention House was not bringing me a feeling of relief, only a new anxiety in the place of the old one.

The taxi stopped in front of a narrow black wooden gate set in a cement wall. Hean paid the driver and knocked on the gate. A middle-aged woman dressed in a blue cotton tunic and loose-fitting trousers like a servant opened the gate and helped Hean with my things.

What must have been a small garden at one time was now covered with rubble. Except for a single elm tree struggling in the midst of broken tiles, bricks and dirt, there were only clusters of weeds. The house before us looked shabby and neglected, the downstairs rooms unoccupied. A thick layer of dust lay on the terrace. The front door opened into a small hall, and we went up the stairs. The hall and staircase had been swept and washed with a wet mop, but the walls were grey. Hean preceded me into a large room at the top of the stairs. A bed with clean white sheets and a floral quilt, a chest of drawers, a small desk, a table, four chairs and an easy chair were in the room. The furniture was the standard set, mass-produced and identical in design, usually rationed to newly married couples.

'These two rooms up here are allocated to you. The Security Bureau issued me with a certificate to buy these few pieces of furniture for you.' Hean hugged me and exclaimed, 'Oh! It's good to have you back again!'

She put her face against mine and held me for a long moment. I realized that she found it difficult to talk about Meiping. I would have to give her time. The fact that she did not explain Meiping's absence proved beyond doubt to me that Meiping was dead. I felt an overwhelming depression and painful anxiety. But I would have to let her come to the subject in her good time.

'They gave me 5,000 yuan of your money. I did not dare to spend it all. I thought you would need some of it to live on. That's why the walls are dirty and the curtains are so skimpy,' explained Hean. 'Mother was coming with me to fetch you, but at the last moment, while we were waiting for the taxi, she was told to go to a meeting of her study group to listen to an official document about Lin Piao. You know about that, don't you?'

'I suppose he is in disgrace, since his name has disappeared from newspaper reports.'

'He's dead! In a plane crash while escaping to the Soviet Union! Premier Chou is now the man next to Chairman Mao. That's why things are getting better. That's why you are saved! Oh, I'm so happy to see you! If only ...' She didn't finish her sentence and what she was going to say turned into a sob. Tears streamed down her face and she bowed her head.

I thought she was going to tell me about Meiping. But we were interrupted by the maid entering the room with two cups of hot tea.

Hean quickly pulled herself together and blinked back her tears, almost as if she were afraid of the maid.

'This is Ah-yee,' Hean introduced her. 'She is here to look after you. She will sleep in the other room.'

'Thank you, Ah-yee,' I said to the maid while accepting the tea cup from her. She was a wiry little woman of about fifty with coarse skin and sinewy hands. When she handed me the teacup, her eyes were summing me up.

'Shall I boil hot water for a bath?' she asked me.

'No, thank you. Not just yet. I'll tell you when I'm ready for a bath.'

When she had closed the door after leaving the room, I asked Hean, 'Are servants still allowed?'

'Why not? There are so many unemployed people. If someone is ill or there are babies, nobody will say anything. In our case, it was the man from the Security Bureau who suggested that I should find a maid

for you. He said you were ill and would need an operation. He led me
to think you were more ill than you are. Though I must say, you look
terribly thin,' said Hean, looking at my emaciated body with wrinkled
brows.

'Don't worry, it's a matter of food. I'll be all right. How did you find
Ah-yee?' I asked Hean, wondering if the Security Bureau had sent the
maid.

'Mother found her through a friend. But,' Hean lowered her voice,
'she isn't the same as Chen Mah. Be careful what you say to her.'

I nodded.

'I think the government wants to be nice to you now that the
situation in Peking is different. You have been given these two rooms
with your own bathroom. And yesterday when I was here hanging the
curtains a man came from the tree-planting section of the Housing
Bureau to tell me that he was sent to plant trees in the garden for you.
He even asked me what kind of trees you liked.'

Because I was given two rooms with a private bathroom and the
tree-planting section of the Housing Bureau offered to plant trees in
the garden, Hean had come to the conclusion that the People's
Government wanted to be 'nice' to me. Since the government was the
sole arbiter of our fate, the Chinese people were sensitive to every little
sign from government agencies, interpreting them as indications of
our position in the eyes of the authorities.

Hean seemed more relaxed and was smiling. So I decided to ask her
about Meiping. 'Are you now ready to tell me what has happened to
Meiping?'

She looked at me searchingly as if she weren't sure whether I could
take what she was going to tell me. Then she seemed to decide to face
the issue. 'I wasn't in Shanghai at the time. As you know I graduated
from the Conservatory of Music in 1966 just when the Cultural
Revolution started. When I came to Meiping's birthday party in
August, I was waiting to be assigned work by the authorities. In
December of that year, I was sent to Kweiyang. Soon after I got there, I
was told to go to an agricultural commune near Kweiyang to be
"re-educated". In the summer of 1967, Mother wrote to me to say that
Meiping had committed suicide.'

So, Meiping was really dead, just as I had suspected when her clothes
were sent to me in the No. 1 Detention House. Yet how desperately I
had clung to the hope that I would somehow find her alive when I
came out of prison. Now my last spark of hope was snuffed out. Now
there was nothing left. It would have been less painful if I had died in

prison and never known that Meiping had died. My struggle to keep alive and to fight against adversity, so vitally important at the time, suddenly seemed meaningless. I felt that I had fallen into a void and become disorientated. Hean's arms were holding me up. Together we wept for Meiping.

What did they do to Meiping that she had to commit suicide? It was not the sort of thing a healthy young woman would even think of, if she weren't pushed to the point of no return, I thought.

'Her name was included in the list of suicides read at a meeting of the entire Film Studio, I was told. Yesterday, the Security Bureau man told me not to say anything to you. He said the representatives of the Revolutionary Committee of the Film Studio would come to notify you tomorrow,' Hean told me.

'Did they announce why she committed suicide?'

'I have attended meetings when suicides were announced. Usually the announcement would just say the persons concerned were "unable to assume a correct attitude towards the Proletarian Cultural Revolution".'

'That means nothing at all,' I said.

'Exactly. I wonder whether we'll ever know the facts. I'm sure no one will dare talk about it," she added.

I would find out how she died, I told myself. It would take time but I would not rest until I found out. However I would have to be careful because if the authorities found out my intentions they would want to stop me. Nobody must know what I intended to do, not even Hean.

'Are you now working in Shanghai?' I asked Hean.

'Oh, no! I was called back by the Shanghai Security Bureau. They sent a letter to my unit in Kweiyang which gave me a month's leave. That was nearly two weeks ago. At first the Security Bureau man wanted my mother to get things ready for you. But she had a heart attack a year ago and cannot stand in queues at the shops. So the Security Bureau decided to get me back to do it. I'll have to go back to Kweiyang soon. The children need me. I'm married and have a girl and a boy.' Hean smiled happily and took out a snapshot of the family from her bag to show me.

'Congratulations!' I said.

The snapshot showed a pretty girl of five and a fine baby boy with her husband and herself smiling towards the camera.

'His name is Li Tong. He was also sent to Kweiyang to work after graduating from the Peking College of Dramatic Art. The Cultural Department of Kweiyang Municipal Government was in disarray. The senior officials were all denounced as "capitalist-roaders". The Revolutionaries were fighting each other to gain control of the department. Nobody knew what to do with the graduates assigned to them so they just sent us all to the same agricultural commune to receive "re-education" through physical labour. Li Tong and I became friends almost at once. Work in the commune outside Kweiyang was very hard because land is cut from the side of huge mountains and terraced. We had to carry heavy loads of water and fertilizers up and down many hundreds of steps each day. The peasants were crude and unpleasant to us. They resented our being there to eat their meagre ration of grain but they didn't dare to refuse to take us. So they were very unpleasant. No matter how hard I worked, they said I didn't do enough. I was so frightened of them. Sometimes I thought I would die from exhaustion and would never come home again. Li Tong used to help me and protect me from the peasants when they got nasty. He is a scriptwriter so he knows a lot of old Chinese stories. He used to keep me going with his good humour and funny stories.'

I looked at Li Tong in the photograph again and saw a skinny man, not at all strong or distinguished looking, but he had a twinkle in his eyes and a sardonic smile. Standing beside him in the photograph, Hean, softly feminine with her round face and small stature, looked like a child.

'Are you quite happy with Li Tong?'

'Oh, yes! We are very happy together. He looks after me and the children. You know, he is secretly writing a play about the Cultural Revolution. It's called *Madness*, a satire.'

'Goodness! What will happen if the manuscript falls into the hands of the Revolutionaries? I suppose you live in rooms assigned to you by the government.' I was alarmed that he was taking such a risk.

'Li Tong said he had to write; otherwise his head would burst. Besides, the Revolutionaries in our organization are very friendly with him and are not likely to search our rooms. Li Tong is a sort of underground writer for the Revolutionaries who have had very little education and have never read a single book on Marxism. They recite Chairman Mao's quotations but they have not read his books. They ask Li Tong to write their speeches for them so that Li Tong can include quotations from books by Marx and Lenin as well as Chairman Mao. That makes the audience think the Revolutionaries are knowledgeable. Sometimes Li Tong even plans their strategies when they have a factional fight with other Revolutionaries,' Hean told me.

'Why on earth would he want to do that?'

Hean laughed so much that she could hardly get the words out. 'Li Tong said that since he could not very well kill the Revolutionaries himself, the next best thing is to let the Revolutionaries kill each other in their factional wars.'

I was speechless with consternation. Asking Hean about Li Tong's family background, I learned that his bitterness was the result of family suffering. His eldest brother, a middle school teacher who believed in the Communist Party, was denounced as a Rightist in 1957. His sister-in-law committed suicide. His father died of a heart attack after the Red Guards accused him of having been a former landlord, put him in a sack and kicked him around.

'I gather you are no longer at the agricultural commune?'

'No, we were called back to Kweiyang when Chairman Mao invited the American table-tennis team to visit Peking. All of a sudden, the Revolutionaries were very nice to me because I was born in Australia. They thought Australia and the United States were one and the same place.' Hean was laughing heartily. 'Everyone must follow the correct line of Chairman Mao. The Revolutionaries watch Peking closely. The visit of the American table-tennis team told them China wants to be nice to the United States so they decided they must be nice to those born in the United States. Some people say that when the Politburo in Peking takes a deep breath, the rest of the country feels a gust of wind.'

'What work do you do now?'

'I play the piano as an accompanist for the Kweiyang Song and Dance Ensemble.'

Hean's mother arrived. My old friend had aged so much that I could hardly recognize her. An expression of defeat and resignation was written on her deeply lined face. She embraced me and exclaimed, 'You look much better than I imagined. Oh, it's good to see you!'

My memory moved back in time and space to Sydney, Australia, over twenty-six years before. Then we were two happy young mothers walking side by side, following our two little girls in frilly sunsuits, running ahead of us with toy buckets and shovels to look for a spot on the wide expanse of golden sand to build a sandcastle. We did not know that we were living in a sandcastle ourselves and how near collapse it was. Hean's father was working in the Chinese Consulate-General in Sydney. All of us were about to return to China and we were looking forward to it.

Obviously Hean's mother was also thinking of Meiping. She said, 'You must be brave. What's happened has happened. We can't undo that. There's your own life to think about. You are not well. Too much grief is not good for you. You must try to be philosophical.'

Then she told me of their experience during the Cultural Revolution. Her account of their humiliation and persecution had not been very different from the suffering of millions of others who had worked for the previous government or lived abroad. She told me that she had been allowed to retire from her work as a schoolteacher but Hean's father was still working in the bank. Because they had never been classified as members of the capitalist class, they were still living in their own home. The Red Guards merely burned their books and confiscated their 'valuables'.

I thanked her for her help in preparing living quarters for me. She said, 'Things are getting better now with Premier Chou in charge. Quite a lot of people are being released from detention.'

'Were many people put into detention houses?' I asked her.

'Oh, yes. Almost all the senior members of foreign firms were locked up. We know the number one Chinese with the Hong Kong and Shanghai Bank, and our neighbour is a relative of the man with the Chartered Bank. Both these men were locked up at the No. 1 Detention House. One was released at the end of last year and the other man is due to be released soon. One of them lost his wife when the Red Guards looted their home. The poor woman was so scared that she jumped out of the window of their sixth-floor apartment.'

I was thinking of what she had just told me when she said, 'The most important thing is to get medical treatment for you. Most of the doctors now working at the outpatient departments of hospitals aren't really trained doctors at all. You need someone with experience. The man from the Security Bureau told us you have cancer of the uterus.'

'I don't think I have cancer,' I told her. 'I've had a bleeding problem for a long time. It started several years ago. It hasn't worsened. If it were cancer, I should be feeling pain by now.'

'That's good. I hope you don't have cancer. What you need is a good doctor to give you an examination.'

'Is it possible to find such a doctor? I wonder what's happened to my old doctor, Dr Kuo Ching at the Second Medical College Hospital?'

'I'm afraid Dr Kuo is very ill. He suffered a lot during the Cultural Revolution. I'll see what I can do to find someone else. We'll probably have to do it through the "back door".'

'What's a back door?' I asked her.

'That's a new way to get things done. It means making arrangements to see a doctor or to buy something one needs urgently through friends or acquaintances rather than going through the regular channels,' she explained. 'Of course, back doors generally cost more because we have to give presents, not money, to those who make the arrangements. But in many instances, it's the only way to get things done nowadays.'

'Isn't that illegal?' I asked her. I remembered how the Party used to frown on such practices and how fearful the people were of doing anything like that. Before the Cultural Revolution, except for the very privileged, nobody dared to make private arrangements for anything.

'All laws and regulations have been declared tools of the "capitalist-roaders" against the people. No one knows what's legal and what's illegal any more. I suppose, when one gets caught, it's illegal. When one gets away with it, it's legal. People using the "back door" seem to get away with it, so everybody does it.'

Ah-yee came in with food. I went into the bathroom to wash my hands. For the first time in six and a half years, I looked at myself in a mirror. I was shocked to see a colourless face with sunken cheeks framed by dry strands of grey hair and eyes that were over-bright from the need to be constantly on the alert. It was a face very different from what I once had. But, after all, six and a half years was a long time. I should have aged in any case. I looked at myself again. I hoped that in time my cheeks would become rounded and my eyes would look at the world with calm appraisal rather than anxious apprehension.

Hean and her mother were already seated at the table. Ah-yee had prepared a good dinner of chicken soup, sliced pork and tender green cabbage stir-fried in oil. The steaming rice was soft. I had not seen food like that for a long time, but I had no appetite and the pain in my gums precluded chewing. I drank some soup and swallowed a few mouthfuls of rice.

'Perhaps I should see a dentist before I see a gynaecologist,' I said.

'I'll take you to my cousin. She is a dentist at the No. 6 People's Hospital,' Hean offered.

'You had better contact her first and make some arrangements,' Hean's mother reminded her daughter.

'Yes, I'll go to see her tomorrow morning. Then I'll come to tell you what she says,' Hean said to me.

When Hean and her mother left, I helped Ah-yee carry the dishes down the narrow back staircase to the kitchen. Then I went to look at the smaller bedroom where Ah-yee was to sleep. There was only a single bed with her things on it, no other furniture at all and the windows were uncurtained. Obviously Hean didn't have either enough money or furniture to furnish both rooms. I took one of the chairs from my room and placed it next to Ah-yee's bed.

I called down to Ah-yee in the kitchen to heat some hot water for me to have a sponge bath. I had already noticed that the bath was ringed with yellow stains and there was nothing to clean it with. Besides, it was still quite chilly at night and there was no way I could heat the bathroom.

To have even a sponge bath in Shanghai was quite an undertaking, for to get enough hot water, Ah-yee had to boil the kettle many times to fill the thermos flasks first. Then she had to heat water in a large pot. While I waited for the water, I discovered some paper and envelopes Hean had placed in the desk drawer. I wrote a short note to Meiping's friend and old classmate Kung, an actor at the Film Studio. I thought he was the one most likely to throw some light on Meiping's death. I requested him to call on me as soon as possible.

I heard Ah-yee coming up the back staircase. She was staggering under the weight of a large pot of boiling water. I quickly picked up the enamelled washbasin I had brought back from the detention house and told her to put the pot in the washbasin before she spilled hot water on her hands. Then we each took one side of the basin and carried the water into the bathroom.

With no guards to hurry me, I washed myself thoroughly, using up all the water in the large pot and the six thermos flasks bought by Hean. When I came out of the bathroom, I stood on the balcony and looked down on the street bathed in the feeble light of street lamps to get my bearings.

The house I was assigned to was one of many in a large residential compound. It was actually at the end of a row of semi-detached houses, all uniform in design and in need of a coat of paint. I could see a similar row of houses in front of me, separated from my garden fence by a cement road six feet wide. From one end of the balcony I could also look into the garden of my immediate neighbour and see laundry fluttering on bamboo poles. Once these houses were homes of Shanghai's middle class. But since 1949 the population of the city had more than doubled and the government had built very few houses. It was Mao's policy to build up cities in the interior rather than the coastal regions. Now several families had to inhabit each of these houses, sharing kitchen and bathroom and using the same hallway. Never in my life had I lived in conditions like that. I wondered whether there was any way to get my own house back.

Even though there was not a soul on the street, I didn't think it was very late. However, I was physically and emotionally exhausted, so I closed the door and lay down on the neatly made bed. It had been a long day. But sleep eluded me. A heavy weight seemed to be pressing on my chest as I tried to suppress my emotion while Hean and her mother were here. Now, with no guard to watch me and Ah-yee already asleep, in the first really private moment for many years, I let my grief take possession and poured out my sorrow in tears.

Next morning, two men from the Film Studio called on me. They told me they were members of the Revolutionary Committee of the Shanghai Film Studio, sent to inform me of the death of my daughter on 16th June 1967 by suicide.

'We were told by the Security Bureau that you were to be released for health reasons. We understand that shortly you may have to enter a hospital. We decided to come straight away to notify you officially of your daughter's death so that her case can be considered closed,' said one of the men.

For the entire interview, he alone spoke. The other man just sat there.

It was a surprise to hear him say that my release was for health reasons. However, that was not a point I could pursue with them. So I merely said, 'I would like to know the circumstances of my daughter's death.'

'She jumped out of the ninth-floor window of the Shanghai Athletics Association building on Nanking Road in the early morning of 16th June 1967.'

'Why was she in the Shanghai Athletics Association building?'

'She was taken there for questioning by the Revolutionaries.'

'Why was she questioned?' I asked him.

'That's not important,' he said, brushing aside my question.

'Of course it's important. It has a bearing on her death,' I said firmly.

'No, it has no bearing on her death. She committed suicide. Her death was her own responsibility,' the man said in a stony voice. 'In any case, we were sent to work at the Shanghai Film Studio with the Workers' Propaganda Team in 1968 long after your daughter died.'

'Did the Film Studio make an investigation of her death either before or after you went there to work?' I asked. Though I was indignant at the man's bureaucratic attitude, I remained calm and polite.

'How could we do that?' he answered impatiently. 'There had been so many suicides. We have so many problems to deal with that are urgent and pressing right now. In any case, according to our Great Leader Chairman Mao, committing suicide is an attempt to resist re-education and reform. It's a crime against socialism. Those who commit suicide are really counter-revolutionaries, though we do not call them that posthumously.'

'Are you quite sure my daughter did commit suicide?' I asked.

'Her name was on the suicide list when we took over at the Film Studio. Your daughter's ashes are stored at the Crematorium. When you are ready to take possession of them, you must come to the Film Studio to get a letter of authorization.'

'Is it not the law that before the body can be cremated the coroner's doctor must examine it?' Speaking of my daughter like this made me ill but I had to maintain my composure and pursue the subject. 'I would like to see a copy of the coroner's report.'

'Don't you realize that your daughter committed suicide at a time when there were widespread disturbances and law and order had broken down completely?' The man was exasperated with me. 'There were many other cases of suicide, perhaps hundreds in one day at that time.'

'Do you mean to say there was no examination before she was cremated?'

'We don't know whether there was or not. In fact, we know very little of the circumstances of her death except that she committed suicide.'

'I would like to make a formal request to the Revolutionary Committee of the Shanghai Film Studio that the death of my daughter be investigated,' I said to both of them.

They glared at me in silence. Then they got up to leave. The other man took from his bag an envelope and several hardcover note-books which I recognized as belonging to Meiping and laid them on the table.

The spokesman said, 'In the envelope you will find a sum of money the Film Studio normally pays to the family of a deceased worker. And these books are a part of the diaries of your daughter. We were told by the Revolutionary Committee to return them to you.'

I stood there watching them go to the door of the room. He turned back to look at me and said, 'From what we heard at the Film Studio, your daughter was well thought of by her colleagues and fellow workers. We regret that because of her unfortunate family background she could not assume a correct attitude towards the Great Proletarian Cultural Revolution.'

The two men walked downstairs followed by Ah-yee going down to lock the front gate after them.

I stood there staring at the books of Meiping's diary but could not bear to touch them. In time, I would derive real comfort from their pages. But just then, the wound was too raw and my sense of loss was too overwhelming for me to read them. I was thinking of what the man from the Film Studio had told me. He did not say very much but I had learned something of Meiping's death. I was more than ever determined to pursue my inquiry discreetly and I believed that eventually I would get at the truth of the matter. I picked up the letter I had written to Kung and asked Ah-yee to take it to the post office.

Following Ah-yee downstairs to bolt the front gate, I thought I should buy a spring lock for the gate and another one for the door leading into the house. There seemed so many things to be done. The walls needed to be whitewashed, the rubble in the garden should be carried away and additional furniture bought. I wondered if I could get my own house back to live in. The government would probably say it was too large for one person. If I had to live in this place for any length of time, I thought, I would have to move the second bathroom at the end of the corridor downstairs and install a kitchen for my own use in the space. That would prevent whoever eventually came to live downstairs from coming up to use the bathroom. The change would also save Ah-yee from having to carry food and water up and down the back staircase. To ensure my privacy and to avoid contact with people downstairs, I should also put a door on the back stairs and build a wall to divide the front hall into two portions. To do all that I would need material and labour. And I would need a large sum of money. How was I to manage all that?

When I reached the landing upstairs and turned the corner to go into my room, I saw, through the uncurtained windows of the corridor, several of my neighbours in the row of houses behind mine leaning on their windowsills watching me. At night, when the lights were switched on, I would be like a goldfish in a fish bowl whenever I stepped out of my room. In fact one of the windows faced the door of my room. If the door were open, the people leaning out of their windows could look right into my room. I decided to make some curtains for those windows straightaway. That was one sum of money I had to spend.

I heard someone knocking on the front gate. It was too soon for Ah-yee to be back. I ran to the balcony and looked down. A man dressed like a worker said in a loud voice from below, 'I'm from the tree-planting section of the Housing Bureau. I'm to tell you about planting trees in the garden.'

I went down and opened the gate for him.

'Are you the new tenant?' he asked me.

'Yes.'

He walked around the garden and kicked at the rubble. 'You will have to clear away all this rubbish before I can plant trees. They won't grow with all that around.'

'That's a job for the Housing Bureau. I can't be held responsible for the rubble. It was all here already when I arrived,' I told him. 'Besides, I haven't got the strength to cart all that out.'

'What about the young woman I saw the other day? Isn't she your daughter?'

'No, she doesn't live here. My daughter has died.'

There! I had said it, 'My daughter has died.' It was an acknowledgement I would have to make often as long as I lived. Each time I said it, my heart would contract with pain and I would see my beautiful girl lying in a pool of blood in Nanking Road.

In spite of my effort to maintain a calm expression, tears ran down my cheeks. I took out my handkerchief and averted my face to wipe my eyes, feeling very ashamed that I had broken down in front of a total stranger.

The man avoided looking at me, however. With his head bowed, he said in a quiet voice, 'I'll report to my unit and see whether we can't find some young men to carry the rubble away,' and left.

In the afternoon, Hean came to tell me that she had arranged for her dentist cousin to give me an examination at the No. 6 People's Hospital the next morning.

'It's the "back door", and we won't have to go there at dawn to queue up for a number. I've already given her your name and other particulars. She'll fill in the card for you and pay the 20 cents registration fee. When she gets to her clinic, she will put your card on top of the others as if you were the first one registered at the outpatient window. Then when we get there you will be seen straightaway,' Hean told me.

'Is that really legal? I would hate to get your cousin into trouble,' I said, rather worried.

'No, she won't get into trouble. It's done all the time by everybody. Every doctor has a number of "back door" patients. Party members and officials all bring their relatives and friends through the "back door" too.'

It seemed China had changed during the years I was in the detention house and the change was not in the direction the Cultural Revolution was supposed to lead the nation. When I went with Hean the following morning to see her dentist cousin, everything was just as Hean had said. Although the waiting room was packed and a number of patients had no seat, we were taken straightaway into her cousin's clinic. Other 'back door' patients were also called in by other dentists. The most astonishing thing was that no one protested. The others just sat there watching us, seemingly content to let us go in ahead of them although they had already waited for a long time and we had only just arrived.

When I asked Hean why they accepted the unequal treatment with equanimity, Hean said, 'They have other "back doors" even though they don't have one at the Dental Department of the hospital. Under other circumstances, somewhere else, they may enjoy priority treatment while we have to wait our turn.'

'What about those who have no "back door"?'

'They'll just have to create some. As long as you have friends and relatives, you'll have "back doors",' she informed me.

That was my first encounter with the new 'back door' system. In time I also became quite an expert at using it, teaching English without charge in return for the favours. The rapprochement between China and the United States and the importation of scientific and technical materials in the English language created a demand for English teachers. Ambitious young men and women who hoped to find jobs as interpreters with delegates going abroad for government agencies and others who planned to emigrate also wanted to learn. Requests for lessons flooded my post.

When Peking decided to release all frozen foreign-exchange accounts to encourage remittances from overseas Chinese which had dried up, I recovered quite a large sum of money I had brought into China to pay for scarce commodities obtainable only through the Overseas Chinese Shop where purchases could be made only in foreign exchange. I used to buy coal for central heating and wood for house repairs. Since I was only allowed to use less than 20 per cent of the foreign exchange for such purposes, the amount of money I did not use had accumulated over the years. With this large sum returned to me, I had no more financial worries and could reward those who opened the 'back door' for me in a practical manner.

All that happened later. When Hean took me into the clinic of her dentist cousin, I felt acutely uneasy and rather less than honourable as

I walked in ahead of all the others in the waiting room.

Hean's cousin examined my teeth and told me that I had a very serious case of gum infection which had been neglected for so long that it was beyond ordinary treatment. She said, 'Although your teeth are good, they will all have to come out.'

She looked at my wasted body and added, 'You are not strong enough for daily extraction. Come every other day. In the meantime, I'll give you a certificate to enable you to buy milk. Have several eggs each day too, if you can get them. When your general health improves, I can speed up the extractions.'

After we came out of the hospital, Hean and I went to a shop for me to buy a much-needed clock. Outside the shop, there was an old man seated on a low stool with scales before him. For 3 cents, a passer-by could step onto the battered scales and weigh himself. I weighed myself and found that with all my clothes on I weighed only 85 pounds, 30 pounds less than my normal weight. After that I weighed myself reguarly on the old man's scales right up to the time I left China.

As my health improved, the dentist was able to extract one or two teeth every day. When it was all over, she told me that the gums had to be allowed to heal and harden before dentures could be fitted. I was very disappointed because I found it difficult to speak clearly or eat anything other than liquids without teeth. And every time I looked into a mirror, I got very depressed by my appearance. So I took to wearing a gauze mask over my mouth even at home.

Hean told me that since I was now well enough to move about the city alone, she would return to Kweiyang to rejoin her husband and children. I was grateful to her for what she had done for me and sorry to see her go.

Kung came to see me one Sunday morning. We sat on the balcony in the warm sun. He wasn't able to tell me much about what had actually happened to Meiping but he was sceptical about the official version of suicide.

'I've known Meiping for a long time, ever since we were in our teens. She was not the type to commit suicide. Besides, what was she doing at the Athletics Association building and who took her there? It wasn't the Revolutionaries from our Film Studio, that's for sure. They would have questioned her in the Film Studio.'

'Do you think she was taken there because she was once a member of the Women's Rowing Team some years ago?' I asked him.

'No, not at all. The Shanghai Athletics Association was disbanded. The building was taken over by a subsidiary organization of the

Shanghai Militia. I heard a secret court had been set up in there. The place sounds sinister,' Kung said.

He got up from his chair and went to the door leading to Ah-yee's room to make sure she was out of earshot.

When he returned to his seat, I asked him anxiously, 'Do you mean there were torture chambers and things like that?'

He did not speak for quite some time. But after I asked him the same question again, he said, 'Well, Meiping wasn't the only person taken there who died in mysterious circumstances.'

I saw Meiping now in my mind not only lying in a pool of blood on Nanking Road but also with her slim body mutilated as a result of torture. The image was so painful that I shuddered.

'All her friends feel very bad about her death,' Kung said. 'One day we'll get to the bottom of it. For the moment, nothing can be done. The political situation is still so uncertain.'

'Isn't Premier Chou in charge of things now in Peking?' I asked him.

'Since Lin Piao's death, Premier Chou's position has become stronger. But Chiang Ching and her group are still there. They will not rest until they obtain supreme power. When the Lin Piao affair blew up, they had to lie low because of their close association with him during the early days of the Cultural Revolution. Besides, Premier Chou is very ill. People from Peking visiting the Film Studio said the Premier is suffering from cancer.'

'Oh, that's bad,' I said.

'The former Secretary General of the Party, Deng Hsiao-ping, has been rehabilitated. The announcement will be made in a few days. He'll become Premier Chou's assistant. Premier Chou probably wants him to take over as Premier eventually. But Chiang Ching and her group are determined that one of them will succeed Premier Chou.'

'What about Chairman Mao? Won't he have to make the decision?'

'He will have to decide. But will he make the right choice? He's very ill, and Chiang Ching is trying to isolate him from direct contact with other leaders, I hear. This is a time of change and turbulence. I'm supposed to be an actor but I spend all my time attending political indoctrination classes or working in an agricultural commune. I never have a chance to act. I feel my life is being wasted.'

'There are still many aspects of the Cultural Revolution I don't understand. A few days ago, Hean gave me some Red Guards publications to read. I find them very interesting. Have you any that you could also lend me to read?' I asked him.

'I've some at home that you may find interesting. Because they are not censored, they reveal a lot about the power struggle within the Party leadership. Of course the aim of the Red Guards publications was primarily to expose the "capitalist-roaders", but inadvertently they exposed the whole Party leadership. The stories that circulated by mouth were worse than those in the publications. You missed all that. However, the major portion of the content of those Red Guards publications is just revolutionary hyperbole. I'll sort them out and bring you the more interesting ones.'

Kung took his leave. I walked with him to the stairs. A flake of plaster floated down from the ceiling. 'Why didn't Hean get this place whitewashed?' he asked me.

'There wasn't enough money. They gave her only 5,000 yuan of my money to do everything.'

'You should write a petition to ask for more money. This is a good opportunity now things are more relaxed. In a few months the situation may become tense again.'

'Won't the officials holding my money use the opportunity to humiliate me and give me a lecture?' I said. 'I would rather borrow some money from my brothers than get in touch with the Revolutionaries who are holding my money.'

'Well, next weekend I'll come with a couple of friends to give these walls a coat of whitewash,' Kung offered.

'Oh, no! I can't let you do that.'

'We are all Meiping's friends. It's our duty to help you.'

'How am I to thank you, then? And the others. I don't even know them.'

'Perhaps one day you'll be in a position to do something for them. As for me, I've enjoyed the hospitality of your house for so many years that it's only right I should now do something for you in return.'

For the small sum of 15 yuan, which was the cost of the distemper, Kung and two other young men from Meiping's Film Studio spent a whole day whitewashing the two rooms, the balcony and the corridor with tools and a ladder from the Film Studio. They told me it was the standard practice for members of any organization to use the tools of that organization for private projects as long as the tools were put back afterwards. Kung also brought me a stack of old Red Guards publications.

Hean's mother found me a woman doctor, Dr Wu, who had agreed to give me an examination. She told me Dr Wu was a graduate of the former Peking Union Medical College, so she had had a long and good training. She had succeeded my old doctor Kuo Ching as the head of the gynaecology department of the Second Medical College Hospital.

'Dr Wu is a friend of the daughter of a friend of mine. Once a week, on Thursdays, she sees patients whose cases are too complicated for the young doctors at the outpatient department to deal with. She'll see you next Thursday. To avoid having to go through the young doctors at the outpatient department, my friend's daughter will take a day off from her work to accompany you to the hospital and introduce you to Dr Wu.'

'I can't let your friend's daughter take a day off just to take me to see Dr Wu. Can't I go by myself?'

'She wants to meet you. When I told her you had been to a university in England, she was most enthusiastic. She hopes you will give her English lessons when you are stronger.'

I could see I was getting entangled in the 'back door' network step by step. But what else could I do? If I went through the normal procedure, not only would I have to queue outside the hospital from dawn but also I would not be able to see a senior doctor like Dr Wu.

On Thursday, when I went to see her, Dr Wu told me that I did not have cancer at all but was suffering from 'acute hormone disturbance', probably caused by prolonged stress and abnormal living conditions, her polite way of referring to my imprisonment. She suggested that I should have a hysterectomy rather than prolonged treatment, which might be interrupted if the work of the hospital was to be disturbed again by political developments. I saw that, like Kung, she anticipated more political struggle and regarded the relatively calm atmosphere now prevailing only as a lull.

A week later I was successfully operated upon. I stayed three weeks in the hospital in a crowded ward with twenty-five other women, some suffering from cancer. Our beds were only a foot apart. The sight of their emaciated bodies and the sound of their groans were as depressing as anything I had seen or heard in the detention house. In fact, when I awoke from the effect of the anaesthetic, for a moment I thought I was back in the prison hospital.

While I was in hospital I received notification from the Bank of China that all foreign-exchange accounts were unfrozen. Being financially solvent again gave me a wonderful feeling of independence. I sent Hean and her husband a belated wedding present and invited them to come to Shanghai with their children for the Chinese New Year.

When I returned home, I went to the dentist again and was fitted with dentures. As soon as I had them in my mouth, I felt sick. The discomfort was so unbearable that my impulse was to tear the dentures out. I felt as though I had two enormous plates jammed inside my mouth and that I was choking. The dentist told me to take them out at night to get some relief. But I decided to wear them twenty-four hours a day so that I could get used to them sooner and shorten the time of agony. At night, when I couldn't sleep because of the discomfort, I took sleeping pills.

Now that I had sufficient money, I proceeded to carry out the plan to make my portion of the house self-contained. A door was put at the foot of the back stairs and the bathroom fixtures were transferred downstairs to make a bathroom in the pantry. In the space where the former bathroom had been at the end of the corridor, I installed a sink and a gas cooker. The work was carried out by three workers from the local section of the Housing Bureau which charged me a fee for the work. With the help of Kung and his friends, I was able to get the sink, the wood for the back door and tiles to fill in the space left by the bath. All done through the 'back door'.

The workers, regular employees of the Housing Bureau on a fixed monthly wage, were to earn nothing extra for the work they did for me. In such circumstances, the normal attitude of the workers was perfunctory. They would ignore the quality of the work and prolong the time they spent on the job. It was against the law for me to offer them money. I had to encourage them to work well and efficiently with what was called by the Chinese people 'treatment'. It included cartons of the best-quality cigarettes and elaborate meals with wine and beer. Kung, Ah-yee and their friends helped me to obtain the provisions by queuing at various shops and opening 'back doors'. When the job was finished, I gave the three young men each a present. I told them I wanted to build a wall to divide the hall space but was unable to obtain bricks. While none of them knew of a 'back door' for bricks, they offered to build the wall for me in their spare time if and when I could get the bricks.

One afternoon, while I was sitting in my room sewing curtains for Ah-yee's room, three ladies from the Residents' Committee called on me.

'We are from the Residents' Committee of this area. My name is Lu Ying. I'm in charge of your unit,' one of the women introduced herself. Then she pointed to a stout woman and said, 'This is our Party Secretary.'

The third woman said, 'I'm her deputy.'

I stood up to welcome them and invited them to be seated. Ah-yee brought each a cup of tea.

The Residents' Committee of each district is an extension of the police, working under its supervision. Officers of the Residents' Committee deal directly with the people and report to the police. The organization is responsible for the weekly political indoctrination of the residents, running the day-care centres, distributing ration coupons, allocating birth quotas and arbitrating in disputes between neighbours. In some instances, officers of the Residents' Committee even help the police solve crimes and capture criminals, as they have such an intimate knowledge of the life of the people in their charge.

Most of the officers of the Residents' Committee were retired workers on government pensions, receiving no pay for their present work. Only in special cases, when the retirement pension was low, were the officers given an additional allowance. These ladies (and a few men) enjoyed great power over the people. Their reports on each individual were treated as confidential and were written into the dossiers kept by the police. In fact, the system of the Residents' Committee enabled the police to remain in the background while maintaining close and constant surveillance of the entire population.

As we took our seats, the Party Secretary gave a broad smile and said to me, 'We have come to see you because we heard you have recently moved to our area. We also want to invite you to join our study group meetings on Tuesday and Friday afternoons.'

'Thank you very much for taking the trouble to come. I should have come to you to register my arrival. But I've been busy with medical treatments and getting my life in order,' I said politely.

'What was the nature of your illness? Was it ...' The Party Secretary hesitated to finish her sentence.

'Nothing serious. The operation was successful,' I said.

'Didn't you have cancer?' The deputy Party Secretary was less tactful.

'Oh, no! Nothing serious like that,' I said quickly, realizing they had been told by someone connected with the detention house, probably the police, that I had cancer.

They exchanged glances, seemingly surprised. But very quickly they regained their composure and looked impassive.

'Can you join our study group meetings, two afternoons a week?' asked Lu Ying.

'I would like to. But could I have a couple of months' vacation so that I can recover further from my operation? The doctor was very firm that I should rest in the afternoons until I am fully recovered.'

The Party Secretary got up and walked to the balcony. She exclaimed,

'What a wide balcony!' She looked into the bathroom and exclaimed, 'A bathroom to yourself!' She even opened the door of the cupboard and peeped inside while she exclaimed, 'What a spacious cupboard!' Then she sat down again and said to me, 'Two large rooms to one person! You have been given very special consideration, you know,' looking at me in earnest as if inviting me to agree with her.

'Normally a single person doesn't get so much living space,' added her deputy.

She couldn't very well compel me to go to the indoctrination meetings of the study group because they were supposed to be voluntary and yet she was displeased that I asked for a few months' holiday. Making a person feel guilty of ingratitude when they want that person to comply with their wishes is a common practice of Party officials.

'I appreciate what the government has done. I hope you will convey my thanks to the appropriate authorities,' I said.

The Party Secretary and her deputy both nodded approvingly, pleased with my words.

'Of course, one day I hope to live in my own home. Do you know what the government policy is concerning private houses?' I thought I might as well remind her that since the government was using my house, to give me a little more room than others was not much of a consideration.

The smile disappeared from her face. She said rather stiffly, 'I'm afraid I'm not very clear on that point.'

Lu Ying said, 'You must get well quickly and join our study group activities to improve your socialist awareness. We all need to study Marxist-Leninism and Chairman Mao's teachings. Members of the capitalist class need it more than others. I live here in this compound, only three houses away from you. I'll come often to visit you to see how you are getting on.'

'That would be very nice,' I said politely.

'I have one room, which I share with my son and daughter. There are three other families in the same house.' Lu Ying was telling me about her own living conditions to illustrate further how very special was the 'consideration' given to me by the government. I also gathered from her tone of voice and facial expression that she did not quite approve of my being given so much living space. Since she was the head of my unit, I would have to deal with her on a regular basis. I hoped she wouldn't be difficult and create trouble for me.

Chinese society under the Communist Party was stratified according to treatment given to each of us by the Party. Before the

Cultural Revolution, I did not mix with the 'masses'. Lao Chao represented our household in all our dealings with the Residents' Committee ladies. The United Front organization of the Shanghai Party Secretariat took charge of people like me and treated me with courtesy. The special treatment given to me and others like me helped the People's Government project an image of tolerance in the eyes of the outside world for we all had visitors from abroad frequently. But the Cultural Revolution changed all that. I had now become a part of the masses. My life during the period after my release from the No. 1 Detention House to the time of my final departure from Shanghai provided me with the opportunity for a deeper understanding of the life and problems of the average Chinese.

My visitors stood up to leave but the Party Secretary had a few last words to say. 'You must study Chairman Mao's books. They will help you to assume a correct attitude towards your recent experience.'

I didn't say anything. What was there for me to say? Would she believe me if I said I had enjoyed being in the detention house? She seemed to be waiting for some answer. When I continued to be silent, the deputy Party Secretary looked at Lu Ying. Lu Ying said, 'Oh, yes, I have brought you your coupons for cotton cloth, knitting wool, sewing thread and quilt fillings. I already gave your oil, meat and tofu ration coupons to Ah-yee the other day.'

I thanked them and they moved towards the door. Etiquette required that I should see them to the front gate. But they insisted that I remained in my room and called Ah-yee to go with them to lock the front gate. Realizing that they probably wanted a private word with Ah-yee, I didn't insist on going down.

I took the teacups to the kitchen and returned to my sewing.

When Ah-yee came back, she asked me, 'Have you taken away the teacups already?'

'Yes, but I'm afraid I didn't wash them. I really want to finish these curtains so that you can have them on your windows before nightfall,' I told her.

Ah-yee threw her arms in the air and exclaimed, 'You are not a bit like what they told me!'

I didn't know who 'they' might have been but I suspected it was either someone from the police or someone at the Residents' Committee. I thought it best to say nothing, but smile.

'You are really a nice person. You helped me carry hot water on the very day you came back from that awful place, when you were really very ill. You gave me one of your chairs to use when you saw I had no chair. You spent a lot of money moving the kitchen upstairs so that I wouldn't have to go up and down the backstairs. When you got your foreign-exchange account back, you raised my wages and now you are making curtains for me. You are very kind-hearted.'

'Thank you, Ah-yee. I'm afraid I haven't done anything extraordinary at all.'

'Well, I won't let you down. You are a decent person. By the way, how do you feel about the Cultural Revolution?' she asked.

I realized that my answer to the last question was what the Residents' Committee ladies wanted her to find out. They, in turn, probably had been told by the police to report on my attitude.

'Well, from my personal point of view, the Cultural Revolution was a disaster. I was imprisoned and my daughter died. But from the point of view of the whole nation, which is of course more important, perhaps it is good and necessary.' I said diplomatically, knowing exactly what the Residents' Committee ladies would like to hear.

She clapped her hands and exclaimed, 'You are so right! You are so enlightened! Why didn't you tell the Party Secretary all that? She would have thought well of you for assuming such an enlightened attitude.'

'They didn't ask me what I thought of the Cultural Revolution,' I said.

'The Party Secretary did talk about your assuming a correct attitude. Remember? Never mind! I'll tell her what you said when I see her at the market tomorrow morning. She fetches milk for her grandson every morning,' Ah-yee told me. Then she went into the kitchen to get supper.

Ah-yee was a simple soul. She had unwittingly revealed to me where she was to report to the Party Secretary about me. It seemed that although I had been released from detention, I was still under surveillance. Probably as long as I lived in Shanghai I could not relax vigilance.

That night as I sat in the quiet of my room alone, the idea that I should leave China for good came to my mind for the first time. To be freed from the atmosphere of political intrigue and the necessity of being constantly on the alert would be true liberation indeed. With my daughter dead, there was nothing to keep me in Shanghai. Although at the moment the idea of leaving China seemed outlandish and impossible, I knew I had to hold on to it and work towards its realization.

It almost seemed God had lifted my downcast eyes to enable me to see the distant green hills on the horizon.

CHAPTER 14

The Search for the Truth

FREQUENT NIGHTMARES IN WHICH I saw my daughter brutally beaten, tortured and killed in a blood-spattered room left me gasping for breath. My heart would palpitate wildly as I lay in the dark conjuring up still more fearful scenes in my imagination. I decided I should make a trip to Nanking Road to have a close look at the Shanghai Athletics Association building. I believed I must take this painful step as soon as I was physically fit so that I could have a clear picture of the place where Meiping died and if possible make some inquiries. I could not tell Ah-yee my intention because she would probably tell the Residents' Committee ladies. What I could do was to set out at the usual hour of my daily walk but take a bus to Nanking Road instead. So I prolonged the time of my walk gradually until I was often away from the apartment for two hours.

'What long walks you are having these days! You must be getting really strong. Your cheeks are quite flushed. Come and sit down! I'll bring you a cup of tea,' Ah-yee would exclaim upon my return.

When my daily long walk had become an established routine and Ah-yee made no more reference to the length of time I was absent, I thought the time had come for me to carry out my plan.

Nanking Road was the main thoroughfare of Shanghai, running across the city from the downtown section by the river to the western suburb. Before the Communist Army took over the city in May 1949, the Shanghai Athletics Association building was the headquarters of the International YMCA. It stood in the middle section of Nanking Road, facing the People's Park, formerly the race-course. From where I lived it was half an hour's journey on the bus. As was always the case in Shanghai, the bus was packed. Not being able to squeeze myself further inside, I stood by the door with my body flattened by the crowd. At times, the woman next to me was pressing so hard on my chest that I thought she must feel my thumping heart. I was intensely nervous, fearful of what I might discover. While my mind told me I must go, my emotions wanted me to turn back. When finally the bus reached my stop, I hesitated. But so many people were getting off that I was carried out by the pushing passengers and found myself standing on the pavement.

I walked along, mingling with the crowd and forcing my eyes to look at the buildings on the other side of the crowded street. Next to the Athletics Association building was the Park Hotel and the Grand Cinema, both built in the thirties but still landmarks of Shanghai. The buildings were decorated with Cultural Revolution slogans on red banners. 'Politics is in Command', 'Do not forget class struggle', etc., fluttered in the autumn wind. On the roof, neon lights spelled out another message urging the people to 'carry the Revolution to the end'. To the people around me, my upturned face would indicate that I was a visitor from another part of China, admiring the urban wonders of Shanghai. No one paid me any special attention. When my footsteps faltered as my eyes counted the floors and searched for the windows of the Athletics Association building, I was rudely pushed by the thick crowd of pedestrians.

At the gate of the People's Park, men and women with children were queuing to buy entrance tickets, others were waiting for their friends and families. I stopped among them and looked up at the building across the street again, for I had counted up to eight floors and then saw no ninth floor but only the slanting roof. To avoid attracting attention, I paced up and down as if I too were waiting rather impatiently for someone. Then, I looked up again. I simply could not see any ninth-floor window from which, I had been told, Meiping had jumped. While I was absorbing the significance of my discovery, I strolled past the People's Park. It was only when I turned round to go back that I saw the ninth floor and the windows on the side of the building of the Athletics Association Building. They did not face Nanking Road at all but were above an alley with low two-storey dwellings. The windows were very narrow with vertical iron bars. Whether there was enough space between the bars for a person to squeeze past was something I could not tell from street level.

What I had discovered was very different from what I had been told. I wanted time to think it all over, so I bought a ticket for the park and walked in. From a bench in a quiet corner I could see the top floors of the buildings across the street. I stared at those narrow windows with iron bars and wondered what was the truth about my daughter's death. I felt sure there was something more to it than what I had been told. The sun felt warm and a slight breeze was rustling the autumn leaves overhead. I could hear the hum of traffic and the sound of human voices. But in my grief I was utterly alone, as alone as a man isolated on a desert island.

Should I cross the street, knock on the door of the Athletics

Association building and attempt to make inquiries? I asked myself repeatedly, unable to decide. A little girl on a tricycle pedalled into view round the corner on the footpath. Her mother was walking behind her. As she gathered speed, the mother called, 'Go slowly! Be careful!' But the child pedalled faster. Her black eyes were mischievous as she looked back at her mother. They passed in front of me and disappeared behind a cluster of shrubs.

As I left the park and walked towards the bus stop, I saw Meiping everywhere; every young woman and every little girl on the street looked like my daughter. My heart was bursting with pain and I felt more desolate and helpless than I had felt at any time in prison. At the bus stop, a crowd was gathered. A bus passed without stopping. I pulled myself together and boldly turned to the intersection to cross the street. At the entrance of the narrow alley, beside the Athletics Association building, I saw a young woman sitting on a low stool, knitting.

'Do you live here?' I asked her.

She nodded and went on with her knitting. A few people went by on the pavement but no one was looking in my direction. I saw that the houses were lean-tos built against the wall of the Athletics Association building, taking up half the space of the alley.

'Are you looking for someone?' the girl looked up from her knitting and asked.

'I'm from Peking,' I lied. 'I heard a young actress of the Shanghai Film Studio committed suicide by jumping out of a window of this building in 1967. Do you know anything about it?' I pointed at the Athletics Association building behind her.

She looked up and shook her head. 'Not in 1967. That was the year after the Cultural Revolution started, wasn't it? The building was being repaired then. There was scaffolding all round it. I remember it because we moved in here not long before the Cultural Revolution started. And the workers made a mess of this alley here. Then they left without finishing the work.'

'I must have made a mistake,' I said quickly and left. A vital piece of information had just been given to me. It seemed certain my daughter couldn't have committed suicide in the way described to me.

I must have walked in the wrong direction on Nanking Road for, after a while, I found myself further from home than I should have been. A bus came along and I boarded it. After a rough ride, I was back on my street again. When I opened the front gate, I saw two bicycles parked in the garden. There were voices in the downstairs rooms.

Ah-yee met me in the corridor with the news that the downstairs portion of the house had been allocated to a family by the name of Chu. She was telling me about the Chu family but I wasn't listening for I was preoccupied with my discovery on Nanking Road.

The death of my daughter continued to be a mystery and I was no nearer to the facts than before. But that she was questioned by the Revolutionaries and died at their hands seemed certain. If she had been murdered and did not commit suicide, somehow I must find the murderer and see that he was punished. In China, the punishment for murder was the death penalty. I no longer saw Meiping in my mind lying on Nanking Road in the pale light of dawn on a summer morning in June when the busy street was temporarily deserted. But in my dreams, and whenever I was alone, I saw her colourless face and lifeless form. And I heard her cries and groans. I swore to God that I would seek vengeance.

A few days later, the Chus moved in. While I was wondering whether I should go down to greet them and say a few friendly words of welcome, Mrs Chu came up the stairs to see me. She was a woman of about my age, with dyed black hair carefully greased and held in place with a mock tortoiseshell comb. A cigarette was dangling from a corner of her mouth. I invited her to sit down. Ah-yee brought her a cup of tea and an extra saucer for an ashtray.

'My daughter Yeh was in the same school as your daughter Meiping.' She was effusively friendly. 'They were good friends.'

'Is your daughter living here with you in Shanghai?'

'Yeh is my eldest daughter. She's in Peking with the Liberation Army Song and Dance Ensemble. Because my husband was a capitalist, we were thrown out of our home and had to live in a garage when the Red Guards looted the house. Can you imagine seven of us all living in the space of a garage? We had to walk more than two hundred metres to get water and to go to the toilet. The Red Guards made me sweep the streets and my husband was beaten up and struggled against I don't know how many times. We are only a small insignificant capitalist class family. We didn't have a lot of money. My husband had a small workshop making face cream at the time of Liberation. That was all.' She became very tense as she spoke and took repeated sucks on her cigarette.

'Since your daughter was with the Army, you should have been spared all that. Isn't your family considered an "Honoured Household"?' I asked her. The title of 'Honoured Household' was given to every family with sons or daughters in the armed forces. They were given special rations and privileges by the Party.

'The Red Guards ignored all that. But now it's recognized. Our status is restored and we have been allocated these rooms here.'

'I hope you will be happy living here,' I said politely.

She patted my hand and said, 'I mustn't talk about myself all the time. You had a worse time than we did. You had to go to the detention house and your beautiful daughter is dead. As soon as I heard Meiping had committed suicide, I wrote to Yeh in Peking. We were all so sad!'

I did not want to talk to her about Meiping and it would have been unwise to complain about what had happened to me, so I did not say anything.

She smiled, put out her cigarette on the saucer and lit another. After drawing deeply on the cigarette and exhaling the smoke, she said, 'I really have come up for a little discussion about the electricity bill. I always believe in getting everything clarified at the very beginning, don't you? Then there won't be any misunderstanding. My son-in-law is an electrician. He noticed that there is only one electricity meter for this house. Would you agree that we share the electricity bill fifty-fifty since you have half of the house and we have the other half.'

Before I could answer her, Ah-yee, who must have been listening in the corridor, came in and said, 'Oh, no, Mrs Chu. We should pay the electricity bill according to the number of persons in each household. You have seven people and we are just two. We'll divide the bill in nine portions. You pay seven portions and we'll pay two portions.'

'Oh, no, although we have seven persons, we don't have more space. The bill should be divided half and half.' Mrs Chu was very annoyed with Ah-yee.

'Since you have more people, you are bound to have more lights. Half and half is not fair,' argued Ah-yee.

I decided to mediate. 'Why don't we find out how others divide the bills. I'll go to see Lu Ying. She is the leader of our unit. She lives in a house with other families. We'll ask her.'

'That won't be satisfactory at all. Everybody except you has been allocated equal living space. You have been given more space than others. If each of these two rooms is allocated to one family, there would be six or seven of you living here,' Mrs Chu said heatedly.

She crushed her cigarette in the saucer and stood up. 'I'll ask my husband to talk to you.' She left the room and went downstairs muttering to herself, without waiting for me to say whether I wanted to see her husband or not.

I couldn't understand why she was so worried about the electricity bill. In the few months I had lived there, the bill had never been more than a few yuan per month.

I heard footsteps on the stairs. A minute later, the door was pushed open. Mr Chu walked in. He was a florid man with a flabby face; he had probably once been quite fat. Almost immediately Ah-yee came back into the room and stood beside me protectively.

'What's this my wife tells me about your not wanting to shoulder your part of the electricity bill?' Mr Chu said boldly.

Since he had entered the room in a rude manner without knocking, I did not get up to greet him but remained seated by my desk.

'In future, if any of you wishes to see me, you must first knock on the door. You must not barge in without knocking. People with self-respect should behave in a civilized manner,' I told him.

He went red in the face and looked ill at ease. 'Do you want to discuss the arrangement for paying the electricity bills?' he asked.

I said firmly, 'No, I'm tired of discussing the payment of electricity bills. I'll pay half of next month's bill. In the meantime, I'll install a meter so that there won't be any further argument. The sum involved is insignificant. I can't think why you want to make a fuss about it.'

He sat himself down on the chair and blurted out, 'You don't know what the fuss is about? The fuss is about money! The Red Guards have confiscated my bank account. I'm not working. We get only 12 yuan (about £3 at the exchange rate of that time) a month each for my wife and myself to live on. One of my sons is unemployed. The other one makes only 40 yuan a month. We have to look after our grandson. His parents are in the north-east. There is very little food there. We also have to send them food parcels.'

I stood up to indicate the interview was over and said, 'I'm sorry about all that. In consideration of your difficulties, I'll pay half of the next electricity bill.'

Mr Chu made a grimace and muttered, 'I haven't come for charity,' and left the room.

Watching the stooped figure of Mr Chu leave the room, I felt sorry for the Chu family and thought how terribly demoralizing was poverty.

Next day, I applied to the Housing Bureau for a permit to buy a meter. But the bureaucrats there ignored my application. Each time I went there to inquire, I was told my application was under consideration.

One day, I met one of the workers who had moved the bathroom for

me. He said, 'You won't get a permit from them. Your best chance to
get a meter is through the "back door".'

A few days later, as I was going out, I was accosted by Mrs Chu's
son-in-law, the electrician. He seemed to have been waiting for me in
the garden. He offered to get me a meter through the 'back door' and
quoted a price that was several times the official price. We bargained.
Finally we agreed a price double the official rate.

'Is this meter you are offering me from the stock of your place of
work?' I asked him point blank because I felt sure he had stolen it
from his organization. Pilfering was common in Communist China's
state-owned enterprises as the Party Secretaries were slack in guarding
properties that belonged to the government and the poorly paid
workers felt it fair compensation for their low pay. The practice was so
widespread that it was an open secret. The workers joked about it and
called it 'Communism' which in Chinese translation means 'sharing
property'.

'Why should you care where the meter comes from? You want to
buy a meter, don't you?' the young man said impertinently.

I hesitated, wondering if I should really buy a piece of stolen
property.

'I'll install it for you,' he said.

'How much are you going to charge me for the work?' I asked him.

'I really should do it for free because you are so nice to us all. But
I'm very badly paid by the government and I need the extra money.
Would 6 yuan be too much?' he asked me.

I looked at this rather unsavoury individual standing in front of me.
He seemed quite intelligent, though undernourished and ill-clad. I
realized that he was just a victim of the system like all of us. Under
different circumstances, given the opportunity to earn a decent living,
he could have been a young man with self-respect. He was looking at
me imploringly. I said, 'Six yuan is quite all right.'

Ah-yee was furious with the Chus about the whole affair and she was
angry with me for what she called my 'weakness' in dealing with the
Chus. She predicted that the Chus would take advantage of me
henceforth. She declared, 'You don't know people like them.'

The grandson of Mrs Chu was a lively boy of six waiting to enter
primary school. He was very spoiled and had no manners. Several
times a day, he would run up the stairs and slip into my room,
especially when I was not there. He would open my drawers and help
himself to whatever he fancied. Sometimes, when I came home from
my walk, I would find him drawing pictures by my desk with my pen

and paper. At other times, he would bring a ball with him and bounce it against my clean walls. Often he would just run in and out of the room to work off his excess energy while yelling some unintelligible war cry. When Ah-yee was cooking, he would help himself to the food and if Ah-yee left small change on the table, it was sure to disappear after the boy had been in the room. I talked to Mrs Chu about him several times but she would always say, 'I'll tell him not to go up. But it's so difficult for me to watch him. I've got all this housework and cooking to do.'

One morning, I opened my door and heard someone yawning at the foot of the stairs. Looking down, I saw the unemployed son of Mrs Chu getting out of bed. During the night, while I was asleep, the Chus had taken over the hall and converted it into a bedroom. The bed was against the wall on their side but on my side was a small table and a chair, leaving me a passage to the door that was no more than a foot in width. In fact, they had even claimed the last few steps of the staircase by putting several bags on them. I called Ah-yee to come and see what had happened. She wanted to go down at once to have a row with Mrs Chu. I had to restrain her.

After breakfast, I went to the office of the Housing Bureau.

'I'm a resident of No. 1 Tai Yuan Lu,' I told the man sitting behind the desk.

'I know who you are, I recognize you,' he said.

'I'm sorry to bother you with an inquiry. Could you tell me something about the area of space the Housing Bureau has allocated to me?'

'You have the use of the upstairs rooms,' he said.

'What about the entrance hall downstairs?'

'The hall downstairs and the garden is half and half. Your rent covers half of the garden and half of the hall space.'

I thanked him for the information and returned home. Mrs Chu was on the terrace, hanging out her laundry. I said to her, 'I notice your son is now sleeping in the hall.'

'Yes, there is no room inside,' she answered casually and went on hanging the clothes.

'I've just been to the Housing Bureau office to verify the point that half the space of the hall belongs to you. The other half belongs to me. Will you please tell your son to move his things to your side of the hall and not to block the staircase?'

'He did leave space for you to come in and out. You are only a slim person. How much space do you need to come in and out?' She was disgruntled.

'How much space I need is not the point. The point is how much space belongs to me. Please tell him to remove his things from my side of the hall,' I said firmly and went inside.

'There are seven of us. My daughter is coming to pay us a visit. We don't have the space to put another bed inside,' Mrs Chu said.

Ah-yee stood on the balcony to listen to our conversation. When I got into my room, she whispered to me, 'We will just have to build a wall. There is no other way to prevent them from encroaching on your part of the house.'

'But we can't find anywhere to buy bricks,' I said.

'Would you give me a few days off so that I can go home to Soochow to see if I can find someone with old bricks for sale?'

'Of course! You should go home for a visit in any case.' I was pleased that Ah-yee suggested going home for a few days. Although she had a day off every week, she seldom went anywhere.

The morning after Ah-yee went home, I got up early to go to market with her shopping basket. Although it was only five o'clock and the sky was still dark, the street leading to the market place was already full of hurrying people buttoning their jackets as they headed towards the food stalls. It was a scene of milling crowds going in all directions. The sound of voices could be heard from a long way off.

Because Ah-yee and I had already consumed our small ration of pork and eggs, I hoped to get a chicken, which was not rationed, to make some soup. And I had to get vegetables and buy our monthly ration of tofu before the ration ticket expired. Also I had to fetch my bottle of milk. Since chicken was more scarce than vegetables, I queued up at the chicken stall first. There was already a long queue. Apart from the people standing there, there was also a motley collection of old objects such as broken boxes, old hats, stools and tin cans arranged in a line with the shoppers. Whenever the queue moved forward a few steps, the women near the odd objects would move them forward too as if they were a part of the queue. From the conversation of the women around me I realized that placing an object in the queue was as good as being there as long as a friend or acquaintance was ready to move it along for you. With this arrangement, one person could stand in two or three queues at the same time. In fact, it was a mutual assistance scheme like the back door; while I moved your object forward in one queue, you could do the same for me in another queue. When a certain object was nearly at the front of the stall, the friend would shout to the person in the other queue telling her to come at once to make her purchase. The person would quickly put an object down to maintain her position in the second queue, dash across to the first queue to make her purchase. Everybody was obliging because everybody needed to be helped by someone else. Under such conditions shopping became a highly organized operation that was extremely exhausting.

I must have waited for nearly an hour, when at last it was my turn. There were only five chickens left in the huge basket, as far as I could see.

'Where is your ration card?' the man asked me.

'Is chicken rationed?' I asked him in surprise.

'Hurry up! Hurry up! Others are waiting! Show him your ration card!' Voices of the women behind me were shouting impatiently and I was being jostled forward.

I quickly took the ration card from my purse and held it out to the man.

'What? Only two persons in the household? You can buy only a chicken of two catties. All I have left are large ones. Come early tomorrow! The smaller ones go very fast.' The man was already turning his attention to the woman behind me. 'Show me your ration card!'

I decided to go and queue at the vegetable stall. I wasn't too sorry not to be allowed a chicken because I was already tired from standing in the queue and listening to the shrill voices of the women around me. If I did get a chicken I would have had to join another queue to have it killed and cleaned up. Even the best chicken soup did not seem to be worth such a great deal of effort, I thought.

As I walked towards the vegetable stall in the crowd, I heard a man's voice behind me calling, 'Tai-tai! Tai-tai' a form of address used for a woman of the upper class by her servants. I was indeed surprised to hear it after the propaganda of the Cultural Revolution and I wondered who the tai-tai might be. The voice seemed to be following me. In a moment, my old gardener was standing beside me. Tears filled his eyes and his voice broke as he said, 'You are still alive! You are still alive! You look quite well. But Meiping ...'

People were looking at us with curiosity and a few stopped to listen. I quickly gave my gardener my address and told him to come to see me later in the morning.

I lost all interest in obtaining food. I had a loaf of bread and a tin of jam as well as some pickles at home. I thought I could survive on that for one day. So I fetched only my bottle of milk and returned home to wait for my old gardener.

How glad I was to see the old man! I had looked for him ever since I was released! I owed him money. His gratuity had been in my pocket when I was taken to the detention house.

He was equally glad to see me. He had put on a new suit and was beaming when I ushered him into my room.

'I'm so glad to have run into you at the market. I want to pay you the gratuity I owed you all these years,' I told him.

'Oh, that! Meiping gave me the money long ago. She came to see me after you were taken to ...' He couldn't quite bring himself to mention the word 'prison'.

Meiping's salary was small and I knew the Red Guards had left her no more than a few hundred yuan in her savings account. She must have given the gardener all the money she had at the time. I was proud of what she had done.

'Do you know anything about her death?' I asked the old man.

'I heard she committed suicide. Except for the day she brought me the money, I did not see her.' The old man bowed his head. 'But Lao Chao saw her. I met Lao Chao on the street once. He told me he was seeing Meiping regularly.'

'Do you think you could find Lao Chao for me and tell him to come to see me?'

'Certainly! I'll find the cook too. They would be so happy to know you are still alive and well.'

'Do you know if Lao Chao and Cook are working?'

'Yes, they have both been given jobs. I think Cook is at a factory and Lao Chao is working as gateman at a school. You know, the Red Guards beat him up and broke his arm. It was badly set. He is crippled,' my old gardener said.

I was shocked and saddened by the news of Lao Chao. I asked the gardener whether he was working.

'I was unemployed for many years. To plant flowers was supposed to be bad, if not counter-revolutionary. But now things seem to have changed a bit. I sometimes get odd jobs now. Even the local police station asked me to plant some flowers for them. It must be all right again, don't you think?' The old man was obviously puzzled by all these ups and downs in what was all right and what was not.

I was wondering if I could ask him to come and do something to the garden here. It certainly looked empty and deserted, even with the trees planted by the Housing Bureau's tree-planting section. He seemed to be thinking the same thing for he said, 'Would you like me to come every now and then to tidy up the garden down below? I notice the hedge needs clipping and you have nothing except trees.'

'That would be wonderful! Can you get seedlings for some flowers? Is it possible to make a lawn?' I asked him eagerly.

'I'm afraid it's not possible to get grass any more. I grow seedlings in boxes at home. My fingers itch if I don't plant something, you know. When the Red Guards were everywhere, I hid my seedling boxes under the beds,' he chuckled.

When I accompanied him downstairs to show him the garden, Mrs Chu was there. I introduced the gardener to her and told her that he was going to plant some flowers.

'Only on your side. We don't want flowers on our side. Don't you know our Great Leader Chairman Mao is against flowers?'

Mrs Chu was obviously not informed about the changed situation regarding flowers. I did not bother to enlighten her since the situation might easily change again. I just asked her, 'Would you want the hedge on your side of the garden clipped?'

'As long as I don't have to pay your gardener. We have no foreign-exchange account and no foreign connections. We can't afford to pay for a gardener.'

She was making an unkind dig at me when she mentioned 'foreign connections'. She was referring to my imprisonment.

Two days later, Ah-yee came back, carrying a basket in which were a large fish, a fat chicken and some eggs which she had obtained in Soochow through the 'back door'. As was her habit, she entered the house from the back entrance. Mrs Chu was in the kitchen and saw Ah-yee with her basket.

'What have you bought on the black market in Soochow?' Mrs Chu asked Ah-yee.

'Who said I bought anything on the black market? These are presents from my husband and son. In any case, it's none of your business.' Ah-yee was very annoyed to be greeted with an accusation.

I heard her and went out of my room to meet her. Ah-yee went into the kitchen and said to me, 'That old woman is a nuisance. How did you get on at the market? Were you able to get vegetables?' After putting her basket on the kitchen table, Ah-yee went into the bathroom. I took the eggs from the basket and wondered whether I should take a few down to Mrs Chu as a present. To buy things on the black market was illegal. But as long as the purchase was not reported, officials generally ignored it; they knew there was nothing they could do to stop the practice.

I heard footsteps on the stairs and Lu Ying appeared on the landing. I walked over to welcome her.

'It's such a long time since I was here. You must be well enough to join our study group meetings now,' she said as she took a seat in my room.

'Thank you very much for your concern. I'm getting stronger every day.'

'Many people have remarked that you should come. They see you going out and walking fast. They know you are fit.'

'Indeed, I am now quite fit.'

'We are studying the crimes of Lin Piao. It's very important. It helps us to clarify our understanding of this criminal who tried to harm our Great Leader Chairman Mao. You had better join us next week.' She spoke firmly in the voice of authority.

'All right. I'll come with pleasure next week.' I gave in because since I could no longer hedge behind the excuse of ill health, I might as well be pleasant about it.

When Ah-yee came out of the bathroom, Lu Ying said to her, 'I hear you have been away.'

'I went home to visit my old man for a couple of days,' Ah-yee said.

'Did you buy anything on the black market?' Lu Ying asked.

'Of course not! We have a Residents' Committee in Soochow too. The things I brought back are presents from my family. We have cousins in the country. They raise chickens and catch fish in the river. They gave these things to my husband.'

'You know buying things on the black market is illegal. Everybody has a duty to report to us when they see such activities. Be sure you don't buy things on the black market.' Lu Ying was quite rude to Ah-yee because she could not prove Ah-yee had really bought those things on the black market. She had lost face and was angry.

Ah-yee left the room. Turning to me, Lu Ying said, 'Incidentally, I hear many people in this neighbourhood comment on your clothes. They say you pay too much attention to your clothes. Your clothes are not only expensive but they are all new.'

'Indeed, I dislike wearing new clothes. Nothing would please me more than to get my old clothes back again, but unfortunately I don't know how to find the Red Guards who took them when they looted my home. Perhaps you could help me get them back?' I said to Lu Ying.

She was visibly embarrassed that she had forgotten about the Red Guards taking all my clothes away. But she wasn't going to give up criticizing me. 'Next time you buy clothes, buy something ready-made in navy-blue drill such as we all wear. Then you'll look more like one of us and won't appear so different in your grey woollen suits.'

When Lu Ying had gone, Ah-yee and I both realized Mrs Chu had reported Ah-yee to the Residents' Committee and perhaps was also the one who had gossiped about my clothes.

I asked Ah-yee what she had found out about the bricks.

'My old man will make discreet inquiries. When he locates them, he'll let us know.'

The next Sunday, both Lao Chao and Cook came to see me. After asking about their work and the members of their family, I questioned them anxiously about Meiping.

Lao Chao said, 'Soon after the Revolutionaries took you away, they gave her a room in a house that belonged to a Professor Chen of Tung Chi University. The professor was denounced by the Red Guards and made to move with his family to the attic. The rest of his house was allocated to other families. Meiping was given a room there. I used to go to see her every ten days or so. She seemed well but worried about you. After she died, I asked Mrs Chen what had happened. Mrs Chen told me Meiping was abducted from the house by a group of Revolutionaries in the middle of the night. Mrs Chen did not think those men were from the Film Studio. She said when she heard Meiping's voice refusing to go with them, she came to the landing to listen. But in the end, the men made Meiping go.'

'What about the other people who had rooms on the same floor as Meiping?' I asked Lao Chao.

'I made inquiries. No one would say anything. They seemed afraid.'

I asked Lao Chao for the address of this house. He wrote it down for me but warned, 'You mustn't go there. You won't find out anything. I got the impression they had all been told not to talk about it.'

'It's better not to make inquiries yourself. If the police hear of your making inquiries, it won't be good,' the cook said.

'Did you say this professor is at Tung Chi University?' I asked Lao Chao this because I thought Winnie's husband Henry, also a professor at Tung Chi, might introduce me to the Chens.

'Yes, Mrs Chen told me herself. She is a very nice lady. Meiping used to tell me she was good to her.'

'Do you know what's happened to my friends Professor and Mrs Huang?'

'They had a lot of trouble and were locked up by the Red Guards. But they are all right now, except that Mrs Huang is very ill.'

'Do they still live in the same apartment?'

'I think so.'

Lao Chao and Cook also told me dear Chen Mah was dead.

'You can't imagine what Shanghai was like in 1967 and 1968,' said the cook. 'The Red Guards and the Revolutionaries went mad. They ran wild in the city, looting and abducting people at will, torturing them in secret courts and killing them in every cruel way imaginable. It wasn't safe for anyone to go out on the streets. They even used ambulances to abduct people when there weren't enough vehicles for their purposes. There were so many suicides! And many people went to the police stations begging to be taken to prison for protection.'

'Not long before I saw her for the last time, Meiping told me she was going to marry Sun Kai, but they wanted to wait until you were released. She seemed to be confident that you would be released soon because she said she knew you had done nothing wrong. Do you want me to find Sun Kai?' Lao Chao said.

'Do you know his address?' I asked him.

'He gave me his address in 1968 and told me to let him know if I had news of you.'

1968 was five years ago. Would Sun Kai still be concerned for me? Since he was likely to know of Meiping's life during that crucial period just before she was abducted, I was naturally anxious to see him.

'Please try to find him. Just give him my address. If he is married already, don't mention Meiping in front of his wife,' I told Lao Chao.

Then I asked Lao Chao to get a letter of authorization from the Film Studio and go to the Crematorium to bring Meiping's ashes to me.

A few days later, Lu Ying came again to remind me of the Residents' Committee Study Group meeting on Tuesday afternoon and told me I must be there.

'Bring a stool with you. There are not enough benches at the meeting place,' she added.

On Tuesday afernoon, I put on a navy-blue cotton jacket with my grey-flannel trousers. I hoped the jacket would make Lu Ying feel she had gained face because I had taken her advice. But my jacket was specially tailored by my old tailor, quite different from the badly cut ready-made ones worn by most other Chinese women. I wanted Lu Ying to see that I had taken her advice but I didn't want to encourage her to give me advice too often. While I would not do anything to imply disrespect for her authority, I had also to make sure she did not think she could do whatever she liked with me. That was the best way to deal with people like Lu Ying.

The Residents' Committee premises were another house similar to the one I was living in. For the meeting, three downstairs rooms had been opened into one. It was already two-thirds full of blue-clad people with toddlers running under foot while others were coming into the room steadily to join the crowd. I was met with stares of undisguised curiosity, leading me to believe that my reputation of being an ex-inmate of the No. 1 Detention House had preceded me.

Mrs Chu, with whom I walked to the meeting place, led me across the crowded room to a group of women under the window. She gestured me to put my stool down and sit among them. Nobody greeted us. Everybody maintained an impassive face as if afraid to be betrayed by carelessly assumed facial expressions. I was to learn some weeks later that the group of women I was sitting with were all members of the denounced capitalist class and intellectuals, the outcasts of the Cultural Revolution, considered undesirable and suspect by the proletariat. We sat with the others in the same room, yet we were apart from the others. Even when the room was packed, a few inches of space separated our group from the stools of the workers.

This segregation was not ordered by the Party or the police. It was the result of political propaganda on 'classes' that had been fed to the people over the years. Once, several weeks later, I arrived when the speaker had already begun. I hastily placed my stool by the door and sat down among the proletariat. Almost as if an electric shock had hit them, the two workers closest to me immediately moved their stools away from me so that I sat there isolated in the crowded room. Though I was really more amused than embarrassed, I dashed across the room with my stool when the speaker paused to take a sip of water. Mrs Chu and the other ladies, with whom I felt by now an invisible bond, welcomed me with nods and approving glances while their facial expressions remained impassive.

The meeting room was decorated with Cultural Revolution slogans familiar to me and reminded me of my own struggle meetings. But it also had many large posters with messages of a more peaceful nature. These extolled the country's economic achievement since the Cultural Revolution, which was supposed to have liberated the forces of production and increased productivity. Of course, the Cultural Revolution had done just the opposite. Official lies like this, habitually indulged in and frequently displayed by the authorities, served no purpose except to create the impression that truth was unimportant. In fact, the posters were meant to show the Residents' Committee's support of the Cultural Revolution and Mao's policy. It was a display of the political *savoir-faire* of our Party Secretary and her co-workers.

Right in front of us, occupying the most prominent position of the room, were the slogans denouncing Lin Piao, the target of our criticism. Large sheets of paper held cartoons and lists of Lin Piao's crimes against Mao and the Party.

The meeting started with all of us standing up to sing 'The East is Red', a song eulogizing Mao Tze-tung as the rising sun of the East. It had taken the place of the national anthem since the Cultural Revolution. When we sat down, a man, whose name and official status were not revealed to us, made a virulent attack on Lin Piao for his crimes. He started with the days of the Long March, went through Lin Piao's entire career as an army officer and ended with Lin Piao's attempt to kill Mao. He reversed the propaganda we had been fed about Lin Piao during the Cultural Revolution while Lin Piao's star was rising. Everything Lin Piao did that we had been told was good now turned out to be bad after all. All Lin Piao's virtues had been turned into vice. And the vices we weren't told about were now exposed. However, hardly anybody was listening. Many women had brought their knitting and mending while the men were either smoking in a relaxed posture or dozing. The study group meeting was a mere formality. People came to it because they had been told to by officials they could not disobey. It was not a serious effort to indoctrinate the people and the result was nil. Nobody became more pro-Communist or anti-Communist as a result of attending study group meetings.

After the man had finished talking several members of the audience stood up to support the view expressed by the speaker, who, on such occasions, represented the Party, no matter how lowly his official rank or status. Everything had been prearranged. The residents who spoke read from their bits of paper pulled out of their pockets. The text of each had already been approved by the Residents' Committee.

At the end of the meeting, everybody stood up to shout slogans expressing our collective disapproval of Lin Piao. Though to hear him condemned gave me some measure of satisfaction, I did not join in. In fact very little noise came from our corner. Perhaps, like me, the others felt that since we were not considered a part of the people, we were merely spectators. When we trooped out into the fading light of the chilly November evening, we definitely walked a great deal faster towards our homes than we did when we came to the meeting.

In the feeble light of the street lamp outside my front gate, I saw a tall young man standing there. When I came nearer, I recognized him as Winnie's son. He had changed from a husky teenager into a thin and rather delicate-looking young man but his features were recognizable. I led him into my room and asked him about his parents.

'We were very pleased to get your letter and to know you had survived the detention house. Mother is very anxious to see you. I'm afraid she is very ill. It's a strange disorder of the skin that is incurable. My father is also unwell. He has heart trouble and high blood pressure.' The young man spoke quietly and looked sad and troubled.

'Tell me more about your mother's illness. Has she seen a skin specialist?' I asked him.

'It's called scleroderma. The skin becomes hardened and rigid. The internal organs are affected too so that they cannot absorb nutrition,' he said. 'She has been in and out of hospital but none of the doctors seems to be able to do anything more than give her intravenous feeding.'

'I'll come to see her tomorrow,' I told him.

'Be prepared to see a great change in my mother. She doesn't look the same as she used to.'

'What about yourself and your two brothers? Are you all working now?' I asked him.

'I was in college when the Cultural Revolution broke out. I was sent to Szechuan. Because of the famine conditions prevailing there, I got TB and was allowed to come back. My two younger brothers were sent to the countryside to be peasants. But after the Lin Piao affair, they were allowed to come back. One is now a delivery man for a shop. But the youngest is unemployed,'

It rained heavily during the night. The damp cold made my arthritis-ridden joints so painful and stiff that I had difficulty getting out of bed. After breakfast, I set out with a heavy heart to visit my old friend Winnie.

Dressed in raincoat and galoshes and with a large umbrella in my hand, I splashed through the water and mud of the badly drained Shanghai streets to Winnie's apartment building. Preoccupied with thoughts of Winnie, I walked past my old home without seeing it. It was only when I had reached my destination and was folding my umbrella that I realized where I had been.

Even now, after more than ten years, the shock of seeing Winnie's rigid form and the once beautiful face so mercilessly wasted away by this frightening and mysterious disease remain vivid in my memory. She was already dying when I saw her. She could no longer move her frail body without the aid of her son. I had to bend over her for her to see me and for me to hear her faltering words.

Her eyes told me that she was happy to see me. But they clouded over when she murmured, 'Meiping is dead. My boys have no future.

We could have gone away in 1949, couldn't we? We were fools to have stayed here.' She closed her eyes, out of breath with the strain of speaking.

I took her hand in mine. It was just a skeleton hand and icy cold. 'We couldn't have known! Don't think that way, dear friend!' I said to her, bending down to her ear.

She sighed. I put her hand down inside the quilt and stood there fighting back tears that I did not dare to shed for fear of making her more sad than she was already. While I looked down at her shrunken form under the quilt, her son gestured for me to leave. I bent down again and kissed her brow. She opened her eyes and her lips moved. Slowly and hesitantly the words came. 'Try to go abroad! You can still make it!' That was her last advice to me.

Outside her apartment, I could no longer control my tears. In the dark passage, I sobbed for Winnie, for her sons, for Meiping, for myself and for all the thousands and thousands of innocent men and women who were mercilessly persecuted by the Maoists. 'Oh, God! Why this waste of our lives?' I asked.

I wiped my eyes hastily when I heard the sound of someone walking with laboured steps up the stairs. Puffing to catch his breath, an old man stood before me. It was Winnie's husband Henry. His hair was snow white, his face was deeply lined and his expression was one of despair. I greeted him by name. For a moment he did not appear to recognize me. When he did, he didn't smile, only nodded and said, 'It must have been terrible. But you survived it. Wonderful!' I asked him about Winnie's illness. He confirmed what their son had already told me. When I asked him about himself, he shook his head and sighed. Finally he told me that he was allowed to do translation work now because of his heart trouble. Before that he had done manual labour. I asked him whether he knew a Professor Chen of Tung Chi University, in whose house Meiping had spent the last few months of her life.

'I know him well. But don't attempt to see him or his wife now,' he urged. 'Wait until the situation is better. Then they will be able to speak more freely.'

'Is the situation going to get better?' I asked him.

'Oh, yes, it's already better. You must be very strong to have survived your ordeal. You can afford to wait.'

Early in December, Ah-yee's husband came with the good news that he had located some bricks for me. Two peasant brothers agreed to bring the bricks to Shanghai on a wooden boat on the Soochow river and land them at a jetty under a certain bridge where such wooden boats were allowed to anchor. The question was whether I could find a truck to take over the bricks when the boat arrived. I sent Ah-yee to notify Kung, with whom I had already discussed the project. When he came that evening, he told me that he could introduce me to a young man at the Power Company who drove a truck to transport repairmen to repair street lamps.

I sent Ah-yee's husband back with an initial payment for the bricks and asked him to wait for a message from me before shipping the bricks to Shanghai. He had measured the width and height of the hall and made calculations. He assured me that the number of bricks available was ample. But he told me I must locate an iron bar to be placed across the floor to support the weight of the wall to prevent the floor from sinking.

Although I was most anxious to have the wall built as soon as possible, I thought it important to ensure that the Chus would not oppose my plan. And to give it a semblance of legality, I should obtain approval from the Housing Bureau office. The best plan was for me to write a petition to the Housing Bureau, signed by both Mrs Chu and myself.

Ah-yee and I joined in a conspiracy to prepare the Chus. I changed the time of my daily walk from the afternoon to early morning and Ah-yee went to the market not through the back door but through the hall and the front door. We would carelessly leave the door slightly ajar when we passed the sleeping figure of Mrs Chu's son so that a jet of cold air hit the very spot where he was sleeping. Sometimes he would get out of bed to close the door, only to find it left open again half an hour later. Whenever he complained, we would apologize profusely. But we went on leaving the door slightly open morning after morning. Two weeks later, when I thought a sufficiently strong impression had been created, I invited Mrs Chu to come up for a cup of tea.

'What do you think of the idea of building a wall to divide the hall space so that your son would have a small bedroom? Then he would not be sleeping in a draught whenever Ah-yee and I go out in the morning,' I asked her.

'That would be good but it would be very costly,' Mrs Chu said.

'I'll pay for the whole thing: the bricks, the cement and the labour.'

'Would you really? I feel uneasy about letting you do it. But you do have more money than we do.'

'I would like to do it, if you agree.'

'Of course, it's a good idea.'

'I'll write a petition to the Housing Bureau,' I told her. 'We can both sign it and I'll take it to them tomorrow morning.'

She signed the petition I wrote. To prevent my request from falling into the bottomless pit of bureaucracy and getting lost, I sought out the young workers who had moved the bathroom for me. They could smooth the way with the officials at the Housing Bureau, I thought. I asked them if they still wanted to build the wall for me after working hours, to earn extra money. When they showed enthusiasm, I told them I had located the bricks and had written a petition. I requested that they speak to the officials before I presented the petition at the office. I handed them a carton of the best brand of cigarettes and left it to them to decide whether to give it to the officials or keep it for their own use. They said, 'No problem. We'll speak to the man who belonged to the same faction of the Housing Bureau Revolutionary organization as we did. He won't refuse us.'

When they gave me the signal, I took the petition to the Housing Bureau office. The man there put the official seal on it without hesitation. With that I went to a special shop and obtained the cement and the iron bar which Kung's friend Little Fong transported to my house in his Power Company truck.

He came after depositing his repairmen at their destination where the street lamps needed repairs. I was waiting for him outside the front gate and climbed in beside him at once. We were able to get the things back to my house before he was due to pick up his repairmen. I asked him whether the mileage and petrol consumption of the truck were checked. He laughed and told me that all rules and regulations were abolished by the Cultural Revolution. Then he said, 'Don't forget, in a socialist state everything belongs to the people. You and I are a part of the people.' However he accepted a carton of cigarettes from me so that he could distribute them to the repairmen. 'I'm supposed to wait for them at the place of their work,' he explained.

I sent Ah-yee home again to organize the delivery of the bricks. I asked her to send me a letter to tell me the date they could set off on the river. The journey would take two days. I would arrange with Little Fong to go with me in his truck to the designated bridge to wait for the boat.

On the day the boat was expected to arrive, Little Fong took me in his truck early in the morning to wait for the boat, since the exact time of its arrival could not be anticipated. I took some sandwiches for our lunch. While we were munching, I asked Little Fong about the repairmen. He told me that he had arranged with another truck driver to take care of them so that he could have the day off. Of course, I had to thank his colleague as well as his repairmen. Again, no money was given, only presents, so that it was not illegal. I did not think using a truck that belonged to the Power Company in the way I was doing was exactly legal but I didn't ask Little Fong about it. I just assumed that the whole affair landed somewhere in the narrow but ever widening gap between what was legal and what was illegal. When I appeared worried, Little Fong said, 'Don't worry, "politics must lead economics", Chairman Mao has said. Economics is not important at all as long as we think the correct political thoughts.'

'Should we shout "Long Live Our Great Leader Chairman Mao" to show that we are thinking correct political thoughts?' I asked him jokingly.

Taking me seriously, Little Fong shook his head and said, 'No need. My Party Secretary is not within earshot.' Then he looked at me and asked, 'Were you really locked up in the No. 1 Detention House for over six years?'

'Yes, it's true.'

'Do you know why you were locked up?'

'They accused me of being a spy of the imperialists.'

'No, you were locked up because you don't understand China. I think you had better learn quickly. You have so many old-fashioned ideas about what's legal and what's illegal. And you worry unnecessarily.'

'Well, to tell you the truth, I feel uneasy about using this truck for my private purposes. I don't really think it's right.'

'We have public ownership in China. Right? What's public ownership? Everything belongs to the public. Right? Who are the public? We are. Right?' Little Fong said rather impatiently.

I couldn't tell whether he was serious or just joking.

In the afternoon, we sighted Ah-yee standing in the bows of a small wooden junk sculled by two peasants. It was slowly approaching the dilapidated jetty beside the bridge. I waved to Ah-yee. She waved back. Little Fong backed the truck to the landing. When the boat pulled alongside, I saw that the bricks piled on the boat looked very old. As far as my eyes could see, there was not a single piece that wasn't broken. Many had already crumbled into dust during the journey. I wondered if they were any use at all, but as he jumped off the boat Ah-yee's husband whispered to me, 'The good ones are hidden underneath to avoid attracting attention.'

The two peasants, Little Fong, Ah-yee, her husband and I worked frantically to load the bricks onto the truck. When it was done, I paid the two peasants, who immediately set off on their return journey.

The landing by the bridge was crowded with people getting on and off the few wooden junks using the jetty. Most of the people carried more baskets, bundles and cases than they could easily manage. Many had shoulder poles with baskets at each end containing a variety of goods, most of which I was sure would end up on Shanghai's black market. They were so intent on their own neither legal nor illegal business that none of them paid more than casual attention to our activities. Nevertheless, I heaved a sigh of relief when we drove away from the place. Whether warranted or not, I had a guilty conscience and hoped I would never have to come to this jetty again.

When we got home, we unloaded the bricks and stacked them in a corner of the garden. The entire Chu family came out to watch us but not one of them offered to help. Though I was utterly exhausted, I felt I simply had to take Little Fong, Ah-yee and her husband to a restaurant to give them a good dinner. Little Fong was in high spirits and toasted our success repeatedly in many bottles of Shanghai beer and warm Shao-shing wine. When I thanked him for his wonderful help without which we couldn't have managed, he raised his glass to toast himself and said, 'Long live the working class!' and quoted the Marxist slogan, 'The working class must exercise leadership in everything!' Then he laughed uproariously. Little Fong was obviously one of those cynical individuals who took nothing seriously.

I was so tired that I slept soundly. The next morning, when I went to the garden to look at the bricks, I discovered that quite a number were missing. The Chus told me that they had heard noises at night and suggested perhaps someone climbed over the garden wall to steal the bricks. But Ah-yee told me the missing bricks were actually taken by the Chus and hidden in their rooms. Soon after the wall was built, the Chus made a flight of steps at the end of their terrace with them.

I went to the Housing Bureau to look for the young workers. They came in the evening after work to start building the wall. Working from five-thirty to eleven o'clock each night with only half an hour's break for dinner, they completed the job in three nights. Ah-yee had the foresight to bring sufficient provisions from Soochow to enable her to provide them with good meals. I supplied them with coffee, cakes and cigarettes after Ah-yee had gone to bed and sat on the staircase to chat with them and be hospitable. Though they were less articulate, essentially they shared Little Fong's philosophy and casual attitude towards work and government property. The implements they used all belonged to the Housing Bureau. When I offered to pay for them, they laughed at me and called me a 'foreigner who did not understand China'.

The building of the wall ensured my privacy and completed the process of my physical rehabilitation. I spent the morning of Christmas Day in prayers of thanksgiving and meditation. I could neither understand nor be reconciled with the death of my daughter. But each day I lived without her, I was a day nearer to acceptance.

Many people, mostly strangers, had come to my aid to help me regain my good health and establish a home. Although I gave them presents and tried my best to return their kindness, I knew that what I was able to give was no match for what I had received. The demand on their time and service, especially in the case of the doctor and dentist, was great. They did not have to choose me as the beneficiary. Besides, when they opened the back door to help me, they exposed themselves to risks that could have led to serious consequences. Even though the authorities turned a blind eye to the practice for the present, back doors were illegal. Government policies often changed abruptly and the Party officials liked to settle old scores.

In the last analysis, they chose to help me because they had pity for a woman who had suffered injustice and the loss of an only child. My tragic misfortune had touched their hearts. For so many years, the official propaganda machinery had denounced humanitarianism as sentimental trash and advocated human relations based entirely on class allegiance. But my personal experience had shown me that most of the Chinese people remained kind, sensitive and compassionate even though the cruel reality of the system under which they had to live had compelled them to lie and pretend.

The Proletarian Cultural Revolution, ushered in with so much fanfare and promise for the Chinese masses, had not really changed their lives or given them new opportunities for development. The Chinese people continued to struggle against poverty, shortages and lack of choice. The Cultural Revolution had merely created a new set of circumstances to which at least the young workers were adjusting with cynicism and audacity.

CHAPTER 15

A Student Who Was Different

A FEW DAYS AFTER the New Year, I took a long bus ride to Foochow Lu where the major bookshops were located. I first visited the Foreign Language Bookshop hoping to find some English textbooks I could use for teaching my students who were to start their lessons after the New Year. Besides the single clerk and myself, the spacious shop was empty. On the bookshelves lining the walls were displayed only the English, German, French and Russian translations of Mao Tze-tung's four volumes of collected essays and the complete works of Marx, Engels, Lenin, Stalin, Kim Il Sung of North Korea and Enver Hoxha of Albania. There were no other books. Near the entrance, a collection of Communist Party newspapers from other parts of the world were gathering dust on a counter. I looked at a copy of the British *Daily Worker* and found it was nearly two months old.

I went up to the clerk and asked her, 'Is there any way I could get some English textbooks?'

She merely shook her head.

Then I went to the main Hsinhua Bookshop, the government agency for selling all publications, to get a copy of *Three Hundred T'ang Poems*. I wanted to check the poems I used to recite in prison to see if my memory of them was correct.

The Hsinhua Bookshop was more lively. A small crowd stood in front of the counter of the section of technical books, and the clerks were busy. Quite a number of customers were buying children's comics, which, in China, were illustrated propaganda stories about the life of revolutionary heroes, the suppression of bad landlords and the unmasking of Kuomintang counter-revolutionaries. The large middle section of the bookshop was for the display of Mao's books. His collected works, his book of quotations and his slim volume of poetry in cloth or paper binding filled the shelves. I remembered that, when I was in the detention house, I had learned from a newspaper report that as many as one hundred and fifty million copies of his collected works and seven hundred million copies of his book of quotations had been printed to enable each Chinese family to possess one set of the collected works and each individual to have one copy of the quotations. Also, the shelves contained Chinese-language versions of the complete works of Marx, Engels, Lenin, Stalin, Kim Il Sung and Enver Hoxha. Though this female clerk presided over the most fully stocked shelves, she had no customers.

In a corner of the shop, I saw under the label 'literature' a few books lying flat on the shelves. I could not see their titles. I went up to the clerk and asked her, 'Have you a copy of *Three Hundred T'ang Poems*?'

She shook her head and said, 'No, of course not.'

From her tone of voice I understood that the *Three Hundred T'ang Poems* had been banned by the radicals. She probably thought me very stupid even to ask for it.

Pointing to the books lying flat on the shelves behind her, I asked, 'What are those books?'

Without speaking, she picked up a copy and turned it round to let me see the title. It was *The Song of Oo Yang Hai*, the story of a soldier who was killed by a passing train when he tried to save his mule. His courage and spirit of self-sacrifice were attributed to the fact that he had studied Mao's books diligently and therefore was fearless. The story had been approved by the Maoist leaders, especially Chiang Ching. Tens of thousands of copies of the book were printed and the author had been made a Central Committee member of the Ninth Party Congress.

'I've already read that. Have you anything else? What about that?' I pointed to the lower shelf.

She patiently picked up the book and showed it to me. It was just another copy of the same book.

'Have you any other book?'

'There is the *Diary of Lei Fong*,' she said.

Lei Fong was another soldier who died and was declared a national hero and a model of self-sacrifice by the Maoists. He had been eulogized in a nationwide campaign before the Cultural Revolution called 'Learn From Lei Fong', when the indoctrination of all Chinese people with Mao's books was intensified. Passages from Lei Fong's diary such as 'read Chairman Mao's books, obey Chairman Mao's orders and be Chairman Mao's good warriors' were widely quoted by newspaper articles and Party leaders including Lin Piao. The case of Lei Fong was used by the Maoists in the Army to illustrate their assertion that political indoctrination was more important than modern weapons and combat skill which were advocated by military leaders subsequently purged during the Cultural Revolution.

'I've already read that. Have you any other books?' I asked her.

She shook her head again.

I walked out of the Hsinhua Bookshop and boarded a bus to go home. I thought, perhaps the Great Proletarian Cultural Revolution should be more aptly renamed Cultural Annihilation.

Since I could not obtain English textbooks, I could not teach students who were beginners but had to accept only those who had studied English already and were equipped with books. I had six students and gave either a morning or an evening to each from Monday to Saturday. After the lesson, we would chat over a cup of tea. My students brought me news and gossip they had heard but which were not printed in the newspaper. It was largely through my students that I was kept informed of the volatile political situation in China during that time.

My most interesting student and the one who stayed with me for many years was a young man who had been a leader of the Red Guards in the early years of the Cultural Revolution. Da Teh had rather an unfortunate personal background. His father deserted his mother when he was only a few months old and disappeared in Hong Kong, never to be heard of again. There was little money. His mother, his two sisters and he lived in great poverty for many years before his mother obtained a job teaching English at the Shanghai Foreign Language Institute. Her salary was small. Even though they no longer had to sell their belongings to buy food, they remained poor. His mother's youngest sister, however, married a general in the Communist Army in the early fifties when, flush with victory, many Communist Party leaders discarded their peasant wives and married attractive city girls.

His family connection with the élite of the Army and his intense hatred of anybody who was rich catapulted him into leadership position, first in the Red Guards organization of his own school and later in the Red Guards organization of the city. He took part in all the Red Guards activities: plundering the wealthy, torturing class enemies, fighting factional wars and killing innocent people. When we practised English conversation and I asked him to tell me stories in English, he would talk about his exploits during the Cultural Revolution in a matter-of-fact voice as if he were talking about the weather. He was not proud, or ashamed, of what he did. I thought Da Teh was amoral. And I wondered why he wanted to learn English from me when his own mother was an English teacher. Once, I asked him point blank. He merely shrugged his shoulders and said, 'You mustn't ask anyone a direct question like that. In any case, you can't afford to believe the answer, whatever it is.'

Da Teh told me that he had lost his leadership position in the Red Guards organization when his uncle by marriage, the general, was buried alive at the order of Lin Piao. This happened after the Ninth Party Congress when Lin Piao was made the official successor of Mao Tze-tung. His uncle, a long-time Party member and much decorated war hero, had voiced his doubts of Lin Piao's suitability because of Lin Piao's addiction to heroin.

'Can I afford to believe what you have just told me?' I asked him half jokingly.

'Yes, definitely. Because believing it will do you no harm. However, you may foolishly choose to trust me more because I'm no longer a leader of the Red Guards and my uncle has died. But I'm sure you know trusting anybody at all is ill-advised,' he said, blithely dispensing wisdom as if he were an old sage.

His name Da Teh means Great Virtue. I couldn't think of anyone I had ever known who was more indifferent either to virtue or vice. Intelligent and self-taught, he was extremely egotistical. In fact, it was his over-developed ego that prompted him to tell me from time to time what he knew of the power struggle within the Party hierarchy. And he loved conflict of any kind. When he talked about the political intrigues of the Party leaders, he glowed with excitement. He seemed to relish other people's misfortune and despised the victims, simply because they had failed to win. To him, there was glamour in success no matter how it was brought about. It was difficult to know where his loyalty lay. Once I asked him, 'On which side are you?'

Pointing to his chest, he said, 'Of course, here, on my own side,'

One day he saw a copy of a Red Guards publication on my desk. 'Why do you bother reading such childish rubbish?' he asked me disdainfully.

'I want to know what went on during the Cultural Revolution when I was locked up in the detention house.'

'I can tell you everything, from beginning to end, and more,' he boasted.

'Won't you get into trouble for doing that?'

'Why should I if you do not tell anybody? And if you do tell anybody, you'll get into trouble just as fast as I will.'

'What if the authorities get to know it anyhow?' I asked him.

'How can anybody know it if neither of us will talk about it? Your room isn't bugged.'

'Are you sure?'

'Of course I'm sure. You are not important enough for mechanical devices which are in short supply, only for human effort,' he said, laughing uproariously.

Da Teh became my student through what I later realized was an elaborate manoeuvre. When I first started to give lessons, one of Meiping's friends, a violinist with the disbanded Shanghai Municipal Orchestra, became one of my students. His mother was a fellow student when I was at Yenching University. She asked me if I would take on her son because the young man hoped to emigrate to the United States, where his uncle was a tenured professor. Because I was under the impression the young violinist was very anxious to learn English, I was extremely surprised to find he was not attentive during lessons and did no homework. In fact, he often did not come at all at the appointed hour.

One day, I was waiting for him and feeling increasingly exasperated when Da Teh turned up. He introduced himself and said, 'I've come to apologize for Chang. He has just been called to the Police Station to get his passport and can't come today.'

He sat down across the table from me, opened the book he was carrying and said, 'I'm sorry to bother you. I'm trying to study English by myself. Could you explain this passage for me?'

I looked at the book. It was *The Gathering Storm* by Sir Winston Churchill.

'Where did you get this book from?' I asked him.

'I borrowed it,' he said, laying emphasis on the word 'borrow'. 'There was a whole set but I managed to borrow only this one volume.'

'Were you a Red Guard?' I asked him.

'Oh, yes!' He smiled at me and said, 'You are very quick-witted, just as I have heard. I have also heard that your spoken English is the best in Shanghai.'

The book had actually been stolen by him when he went with other Red Guards to loot homes. The other volumes had probably been burned.

A few days later, the violinist came with Da Teh to bid me good-bye and asked me to accept Da Teh as a student in his place.

Ah-yee was always excessively polite to Da Teh when she brought us tea, while her attitude towards my other students was one of indifference. Ah-yee's attitude and Da Teh's manoeuvre to become my student aroused my interest in this lanky young man. Also he seemed anxious for my company. In addition to the mornings designated for his lessons, he took to visiting me almost every day under one pretext or another. He told me that he had plenty of time since he was 'waiting for employment' – an expression used by the People's Government for 'unemployment' which was not supposed to exist in a socialist state. He also said that he wished to render service to me in order to repay me for the free lessons.

He often accompanied me on shopping trips. Then he would stand in queues with me, push through the crowd when it was disorderly, and tell me what commodities were available on the counter because he could see over the heads of the other shoppers. Sometimes he even stretched out his long arm to take something from the shop assistant before the other customers could get it. If we failed to find what I wanted after visiting several shops, he would offer to get it for me through the 'back door'. In the bus, he would shield me from the jostling crowd and push others with his elbow to make room for me to get on and off. When I thanked him after an exhausting day, he would say, 'I enjoy shopping with you. You always buy the best of everything. That makes me feel good.'

Very soon I discovered that he enjoyed good food but could not afford to go to good restaurants. So when he accompanied me on shopping trips, I would treat him to a really good lunch in a restaurant of his choice. On the first occasion, he asked me, 'Do you want to go to one of the best restaurants?'

'I'll take you to whichever restaurant you want to go to,' I told him.

'Never mind the cost?'

'Never mind the cost.'

He ordered enough food for four people and finished everything. That was when I realized that he was thin because of undernourishment. I felt sorry for him even though I was aware of the likelihood that he was an informer planted by those who wished me ill.

I would be a hypocrite if I did not admit that I hoped to make use of Da Teh. If he were indeed planted by someone who wanted me under constant observation so that he could make use of a careless word or an inadvertent action to incriminate me, Da Teh was likely to know the truth about my daughter's death. At an opportune moment, I meant to ask him. That moment had to be at a time when such divulgence would not be detrimental to his own self-interest. In the meantime, I thought I could use him to convey an image of myself I wished his peers to have.

Long before there was any possibility of my leaving China, I tried to create the impression that I could not live without servants. Once, in my hearing, Da Teh told Kung, 'She hates housework of any kind and can't even boil rice!' I was sure he despised me as a parasite and probably told everybody so. In fact, the impression I deliberately created of wishing to live in China because I liked having servants probably contributed in the end to my being given a passport to visit my sisters in the United States. Those who decided to give me the passport probably thought I was sure to return after a few months because I could not manage without servants.

Early in 1974, having recovered from my operation and improved the apartment, I was in euphoric mood. Teaching prevented me from brooding over my daughter's death. I felt more peaceful and relaxed than I had been for a long time.

As the Chinese New Year approached, Ah-yee told me that special rations for the festival, first cut back and then abolished by the Revolutionaries, were being distributed again. Unrationed food items were also more plentiful in the shops. It seemed to me that the effort made by Deng Hsiao-ping and his lieutenants to restore China's economy had been fairly successful, in spite of resistance by the radicals. The political wind in China had certainly veered to the right since the Tenth Party Congress as more and more former senior Party officials, denounced as 'capitalist-roaders', were reinstated.

My students brought me reports of drastic measures, such as arrests, being taken against the more intransigent Revolutionaries. One of them told me that the newly rehabilitated Minister of Railways went to Hsuchow, a vital railway junction linking Canton and Shanghai to Peking, to restore traffic. When the Revolutionaries, who had occupied the railway junction and paralysed its work, refused to obey his order, the Minister of Railways, Wan Li, called a mass meeting. He condemned the leading Revolutionaries in front of their followers and had them taken out and shot. Such decisive action by an old Party official was encouraging to the long-suffering people who cheered him and his action. Unfortunately it also hastened the next round of contest as the Radicals saw their hard-won position being eroded under their feet. However, the old Party officials were careful not to repudiate the Cultural Revolution openly. They found enough quotations from Mao's old writings to justify their efforts to restore order and normal life so as to prevent any accusation that they were against Mao's policies.

The Chinese New Year celebrations were traditionally linked to ancestor worship. When I was a child they lasted a full month with preparations beginning fifteen days before the New Year and lasting until the Lantern Festival on the fifteenth of the first lunar month.

Even though life had become much simpler under socialism and family reunion had taken the place of ancestor worship, the Chinese people still prepared seriously for the Chinese New Year celebrations. On New Year's Day everything in the home had to be clean, so Ah-yee and I spent days cleaning the apartment; taking everything out of the cupboards, waxing the floor, polishing the furniture and washing the windows. There was a time when we wore a completely new set of clothes on New Year's Day. Not everybody could afford a new suit of clothes now, not because of the price of a new suit but because there was rationing of clothes coupons. All I could manage was to get Ah-yee a padded jacket. But it was a more stylish one than she normally wore. We both stood in numerous queues to get the food we were going to serve to our visitors. I expected all my students to come to wish me a happy New Year as it was the custom. For those who might bring children, I prepared good luck money wrapped in red paper. As she watched me getting it ready, Ah-yee became nervous and asked whether the Residents' Committee ladies might accuse me of trying to revive an old custom. I told her I would give the money only to those who were not likely to report to anybody.

Since with my returned foreign-exchange account I was obviously a great deal better off than most people, I decided to be generous to everybody. I even bought a large cream cake and two catties of chocolates for the Chus as a New Year present. Deep in my heart, however, I was very sad because while others were surrounded by members of their family, I was alone. And scenes of past New Years I had spent with my daughter and my husband were always in my mind. But I was determined not to let anyone know how I really felt. I wanted the Revolutionaries to think I had assumed a fatalistic attitude towards my daughter's death.

Two days before the Chinese New Year, Hean came home with her husband and children to spend their holiday with her family. I was very happy to meet her extremely intelligent husband and to hear his version of the power struggle going on in Peking. Their two children were adorable. Being too young to feel the political cloud over all our heads, they were completely carefree and happy.

Hean was fortunate to have her husband and children with her. Many young people in China were sent away from their families to work in other parts of the country, thousands of miles away, and allowed short 'marital leave' only once a year. Children grew up hardly knowing their fathers while women faced the dual reponsibility of bringing up the children single-handed and holding demanding jobs. The Party inflicted this mindless cruelty on China's young people in the name of 'the needs of socialism' and 'serving the people'. The hypocrisy of the claim was exposed by the fact that Party officials and their children were seldom asked to make such sacrifices. Instead, they received 'special consideration' and were given jobs in the same city as their spouses.

The news of my release had spread among Meiping's friends. During the holiday period, many of them came to visit me, including those home on marital leave. Much of their conversation was about job transfer. They were anxious to take advantage of the present rampant use of the 'back door' to get themselves transferred to places near their loved ones. Those who had already started the process of negotiation were anxious to exchange information and experience with one another when they met at my place. From their conversations, I learned of the widespread practice of bribery and corruption in all parts of China among the lower-ranking Party officials.

'How do you account for the collapse of idealism on the part of Party officials when the purpose of the Cultural Revolution was to purify Chinese society and promote socialism?' I asked one of Meiping's friends who was on marital leave from Wuhan and was trying to get herself transferred to somewhere near Shanghai where her husband was.

'The new Party officials promoted during the Cultural Revolution were never idealists in the first place,' she said. 'They saw the Cultural Revolution simply as an opportunity for personal advancement and joined the Revolutionaries to realize their ambition. The old Party officials who have been reinstated might have been idealists when they joined the Party a long time ago, but they are now thoroughly disillusioned by their humiliating experiences during the Cultural Revolution. They feel that they have been treated unfairly by the Party and that their sacrifice during the war years in the past was for nothing. All they are concerned with now is their political survival in future power struggles and a comfortable life for themselves and their children.'

'When you give the officials expensive presents or money in order to get permission for a job transfer, are you not afraid you might get into trouble?' I asked her.

'Of course, there's a risk. But I'm desperate. Anyway, I think such instances are too numerous to be investigated. One day, the Party leadership may clamp down, but at the moment they are too busy fighting each other. We must seize the opportunity.'

Our conversation was interrupted by the arrival of Da Teh who had taken upon himself the task of supplying me with freshly baked pies and cakes for my guests from the bakery. I knew, of course, it was just an excuse for making sure that he could pay me a daily visit to see who was visiting me. While he was putting the cakes away in the kitchen, I accompanied Meiping's friend downstairs carrying her baby's paraphernalia while the baby slept quietly in her arms. While we were at the front gate and she saw that no one was around, she whispered to me, 'Be careful of that student of yours. He seems to me like a plain clothes policeman.'

'He's just an unemployed youth,' I told her.

'Don't believe it! Be careful what you say to him,' were her parting words.

Sun Kai, the young man my daughter was going to marry, found out my address and came to see me on the last day of the Chinese New Year holiday. He told me that he was no longer working as a mathematics teacher since the school had been closed. Instead he was in a research institute designing precision instruments.

'In 1966 when Meiping told me you had been arrested, both my parents and I thought Meiping and I ought to get married straight away so that she could move into our place and not have to live alone. But she wouldn't agree. She insisted on waiting for your release and said that she couldn't get married without your being present. Of course, at that time we all thought the Cultural Revolution would be over in a year,' Sun Kai said.

'Did you see her often before she died?' I asked him. I felt terribly sad to see this handsome young man who might have been my son-in-law if my daughter had not been killed so ruthlessly.

'I saw her two or three times a week. We tried to be together as much as we could manage. You know my father was denounced as a Rightist in 1957. I was labelled "the family member of a class enemy" and since I was a teacher, I also belonged to "the stinking ninth category" of enemies. Meiping had to take part in the Film Studio Cultural Revolution activities. She didn't seem to have any trouble there. Then, out of the blue, some unknown people abducted her.'

'Please tell me about it,' I begged him.

'She was supposed to have dinner at our house on 16th June. When I went to fetch her in the afternoon, Mrs Chen, the wife of the professor whose house Meiping was living in, told me Meiping had committed suicide that very morning. I went immediately to the Film Studio. No one seemed to know anything about it. Then I went to the crematorium. But I was not allowed to see their records because I was not a family member. But when the attendant saw how distraught I was, he told me that the body of a young actress of the Shanghai Film Studio had been brought in for cremation that morning.' Sun Kai broke down and wept.

'Do you believe she committed suicide?' I asked him.

'No, of course not! I went there to see the place where she was supposed to have done it. It's not possible.'

'Are you talking about the scaffolding?'

Sun Kai looked at me in alarm and said, 'How did you know about that? Who told you? You mustn't let anybody know you know.' Then he added, 'If those people responsible for Meiping's death think you do not believe she committed suicide, they may do things to endanger your life. You must be extremely careful. They are completely ruthless and cruel.'

'I understand. I won't talk about it,' I assured him. But I asked him, 'Do you know who was responsible for her abduction?'

'I'm not sure. But I think it had something to do with the men conducting the investigation of your case. Whoever they were, they were acting on the orders of some leaders in Shanghai.'

'How did you find that out?' I asked.

'As you know, the Athletics Association was closed by the Red Guards at the beginning of the Cultural Revolution and the Revolutionaries took over the building. But the defunct Athletics Association retained one floor for storage of documents. It was from one of their men that I learned that the men who abducted Meiping were acting on orders from above.'

'Do you think you could arrange for me to see this man of the Athletics Association?'

'That would be dangerous for you.'

'I'm prepared to take any risk to find out the truth.'

'So many years have passed, I don't even know whether he is still there. Why not wait until the political situation clarifies?' Sun Kai seemed reluctant to concede to my request.

Indeed, many years had passed since Meiping had died. One could not grieve for ever. Sun Kai did not visit me again. In the following year, I heard that he had married the daughter of a senior Party official. The man agreed to his daughter's union with the son of a Rightist because he wanted to take a young wife himself after being widowed. He thought that an unmarried daughter of the same age as his new wife would be an embarrassment. I understood why Sun Kai wanted to marry a girl from an official family. After what had happened, it was natural that he should wish to make sure that the woman he married would never become a victim of political persecution. Besides, married to the daughter of a senior Party official, he would no longer have to suffer the stigma of being the son of a Rightist, a burden he had borne with courage since he was a boy.

Sun Kai's visit made me so sad that I told Ah-yee I would lie down in my room to rest. Ah-yee went to clean up the kitchen. Suddenly I heard the sound of knocking on the front gate. The entire Chu family was out. I called Ah-yee and she went out to the balcony to find out if the visitor had come to see them.

She came back from the balcony and said to me, 'It's an elderly man. He asked me if you lived here. Shall I go down?'

'Please do,' I told her, wondering who this visitor might be. And I quickly pulled the cover on the bed and made the room tidy. Then I went to the landing to see who my visitor was.

'Mrs Cheng! Don't you recognize me? How glad I am to see you!' said the man coming up the stairs.

I realized by his voice and the formal manner with which he addressed me that my visitor was Mr Hu, my husband's old friend, whom I had not seen since he paid me an unexpected visit at the beginning of the Cultural Revolution in the summer of 1966.

The hand he stretched out to me was calloused and his little finger was bandaged. Otherwise he seemed little changed. I greeted him warmly, remembering the kind advice he had given me in 1966.

After ushering him into my room, I invited him to be seated.

'I'm really happy to see you again. And you look very well; perhaps, if I may say so, much better than one has the right to expect, under the circumstances,' Mr Hu said.

'How are you and your family? Are you still living in the same house?' I asked him politely.

'Oh, no! I was thrown out of my home by the Red Guards just like all of us,' Mr Hu told me. 'And I have had my share of misfortune. But we mustn't dwell on the past. We must look ahead and be thankful that we have survived. Many of our loved ones didn't. I know about Meiping, of course. I suffered the loss of my dear wife and my beloved mother. Both died of heart attacks during the most terrifying period of the Cultural Revolution. The hospital refused them treatment because they were the family of a capitalist and I was under investigation.' Mr Hu sighed and seemed for a moment to be almost in tears. But he quickly regained control. Taking a handkerchief out of his pocket, he blew his nose.

'How did you find my address?' I asked him.

'It was sheer luck. I met your old servant Lao Chao on the street this morning and was overjoyed to hear that you were free. I had visitors all afternoon but as soon as the last one departed, I came on my bicycle.'

'Are you still working?'

'Yes. I could retire, but there is no point in sitting at home. It's good to do heavy physical work. At night I am so tired that I sleep soundly. I'm now living in my mother-in-law's home. The Red Guards left her one room. We had it partitioned and I moved in. She is well over eighty. I'm glad to be able to take care of her.'

'What about your children?'

'With a capitalist as a father, they were all sent to work in other parts of the country. My eldest son is married and has a baby girl.'

'When you visited me in the summer of 1966, you very kindly gave me some advice. I'm very grateful to you. When I was in the detention house, I often thought of what you said. What do you think of the political situation now?'

'It's infinitely better, of course, but one can't help wondering how long it's going to last.'

'Do you think there will be more power struggles at the top?'

He looked at the half-open door and nodded. After a while, he asked me, 'Would you care to go with me to Nantao tomorrow? I hear the old flower shop is open again and they have narcissus bulbs.'

'I can't go tomorrow. I have a student in the morning and I must do some laundry in the afternoon. Ah-yee is going home for a few days' holiday. She has worked very hard the last few days.'

'May I come to help you with the laundry tomorrow afternoon? I have an extra day's holiday because I volunteered to work on New Year's Eve,' Mr Hu said. I didn't want him to help me with the laundry but I also knew he wanted to talk. I decided that if I wanted to hear what he had to say, I must go out with him.

'Perhaps the laundry can wait. Let's go to the flower shop. It would be nice to have some narcissus bulbs,' I said.

Mr Hu beamed at me for accepting his invitation. I had forgotten how much Chinese men enjoyed having a woman do exactly what they wanted. It almost seemed that my innocent acceptance of his invitation to go to a flower shop had brought our relationship a step more intimate than at the moment he first crossed the threshold. Not only did he hold my hand a fraction of a moment longer than necessary when he took his leave but he actually felt encouraged enough to offer me money.

Taking a package from his jacket pocket, he said, 'I know how stringent is the living allowance given to people like us. I'm getting regular monthly remittances from my cousin in Japan. May I offer to share it with you?'

I was so taken aback by what he was doing that I was momentarily at a loss for words. He held out the package to me and added, 'Please accept it. I would be so happy if you would accept.'

'Thank you very much for your kindness. It's good of you to offer to help me. But I'm not living on an allowance from the government. My foreign-exchange account has been unfrozen and I have no financial difficulty at all,' I said quickly.

He seemed crestfallen but recovered in a moment. He said, 'I have always had the highest regard for you. You cannot imagine how happy I am to see you again. It's a miracle that you came through your ordeal so well. You are a woman of exceptional courage and fortitude.'

I thanked him for his kind words and followed him down the stairs. While I stood in the garden watching Mr Hu push his bicycle towards the front gate, I was conscious of Mrs Chu watching us through the window. It seemed they had returned from their outing while Mr Hu was upstairs.

'I'll call for you at 2.30 tomorrow afternoon,' Mr Hu said.

'That will be fine,' I said.

So curious was Mrs Chu about my visitor that she questioned Ah-yee closely when Ah-yee went through the back door to take out the rubbish. I supposed Mrs Chu would report to the Residents' Committee ladies in the morning and it would become known that I had had a man visitor during the holidays. The ghost of feudalism lingered in China. Although men and women worked together in the same place, they did not become friends in private life. Mr Hu's visit to me would become the subject of gossip, I was certain.

Nantao was the walled city of Shanghai. The walls had been torn down long ago but the Nine-Twists Bridge over the pond and the pavilion made famous by the Willow Pattern of blue and white English dinner services remained. Nantao was now a market place with narrow winding lanes and hundreds of small shops and stalls selling a great variety of commodities from wigs to live frogs for medicinal purposes. It used to be said that one could get everything one wanted in Nantao except a coffin. There were also numerous restaurants offering special food unobtainable elsewhere. In the middle of the market place, near the pond was a Ming dynasty garden, Yu-yuan, with ornate artificial rockeries and many courtyards surrounded by pavilions and studios. The Red Guards did not destroy Yu-yuan because an anti-imperialist revolutionary organization of 1853 called 'The Little Sword Society' had used the place as its secret headquarters.

The street near Nantao was closed to motor traffic because of the crowd visiting the market place during the holiday period. Mr Hu and I got off the bus several blocks away and walked towards one of the entrances of the market. We were literally carried along by the crowd; there were so many people. When we got to the flower shop, there were no flowers left. But the shop was jammed with men, women and children buying or just looking at the Yee-shing teapots and cups on the shelves. There were also attractive porcelain figures, animals, vases and flower pots at a reasonable price. All these products had only recently reappeared after being destroyed and banned by the Red Guards at the beginning of the Cultural Revolution. I bought a Yee-shing teapot in light brown earthenware decorated with the traditional motif of mountains and trees. And I also bought a celadon flower vase that could be made into a table lamp.

When we got out of the shop, Mr Hu said, 'You must be tired. Maybe we could find somewhere to sit down in the Ming garden.'

But when we approached the entrance of the Ming garden, we found a long queue waiting to purchase entrance tickets and another line of people waiting to enter its enclave with tickets in hand. An officious-looking man wearing a red armband was there to keep order. He allowed the same number of people to enter the garden as those that came out.

'Why don't we take the bus and go to Chung Shan Park? We shall be able to sit down and have a quiet chat. There won't be many people at this time of year,' Mr Hu suggested.

Perhaps it was the effect of my solitary confinement for so many years that I felt nervous and exhausted whenever I was in a crowd for some time, even when the crowd was not hostile. So, the deserted park with its wintry scene of bare tree branches and frozen pond was a welcome sight. Mr Hu paid for our twenty-cent tickets and we walked in.

Even though it was a windless day, the February air was icy and seemed colder now that we were not surrounded by people. Both Mr Hu and I were bundled up in many layers of padded winter garments like everybody else in Shanghai, but the skin of my face tingled in the cold as we walked along the path. A holly bush with a profusion of red berries caught my eye. When we approached it, we found a seat behind an artificial rock formation. It seemed a good spot for Mr Hu to tell me what he wanted to say. But I couldn't help thinking how many people in the world would understand that we had to take such elaborate precautions just to have a perfectly innocent private conversation.

After silently observing me for some time, Mr Hu asked, 'You have had a terrible time. I shouldn't remind you of your unpleasant days in the detention house, but I just wonder whether you found out why you had become the target of persecution?'

'I suppose it was because I worked for Shell. They said the Shanghai office of Shell was a "spy organization" and my late husband and I were British agents. In fact, they never accused me of anything concrete. It was just pressuring me to confess.' Once again I remembered those days of shouting accusations by the interrogators and my efforts to cope with everything.

'From the questions they asked you, did you not discern anything concrete?'

'I thought what had happened to all of us probably had something to do with the so-called "struggle between the two lines within the Party",' I told him.

'That's true. I think you will find what I'm going to tell you interesting,' said Mr Hu. 'When the Red Guards and the Revolutionaries took over our factory after the January Revolution of 1967, the Revolutionaries demoted my Party Secretary to the position of an ordinary worker and accused him of being a "capitalist-roader". He was assigned to my unit. As you know, we used to get along very well together before the Cultural Revolution when I was looking after the technical work of the factory and he was the Party Secretary. Now we were both working as coolies. Often, during lunch breaks, when there was no one around, he would talk to me quite frankly. It was my former Party Secretary who told me that your arrest was due to the so-called "conspiracy of foreign companies and government departments".'

'How did your Party Secretary know about me?'

'Before you were taken in, the Red Guards came to our factory to question me about you. The Party Secretary was in charge then. He was present at the interview. Being a film actress, Meiping was well known. When she died, the tragic news was the talk of the city. Your case was frequently mentioned in connection with her death,' Mr Hu said.

'What else did your Party Secretary tell you?' I asked him.

'It seems one of the departments supposedly involved in the so-called conspiracy was the United Front Department which was accused of shielding class enemies. Its Director, a protégé of Premier Chou, died in mysterious circumstances after a struggle meeting. It was alleged that he committed suicide by putting his face on the gas burner. But when his body was found, the windows were open and there was little gas in the room,' Mr Hu said.

'Perhaps his suicide was faked?' I was thinking of my daughter and wondered when I would find out the truth.

'That's what his family claims. In Peking, Premier Chou's adopted daughter, Sun Wei-shih, the Director of the People's Art Theatre, was put in prison and tortured to death simply because Chiang Ching regarded her as an enemy. Two well-known Peking opera actors, Ma Lien-liang and Chen Yen-chiu, were beaten to death because they refused to confess they were Kuomintang spies. I heard these two actors had been invited back from Hong Kong by Premier Chou who was also their sponsor when they joined the Party. There are many cases of scientists accused of being spies for the imperialists who were invited back to China by the Premier too. Just think, if any one of these people had confessed to being a spy, the radicals could have then cast doubt on the Premier, if not actually accuse him of shielding spies,' Mr Hu said.

'Do you mean to say that your Party Secretary was of the opinion that I and other senior Chinese employees of foreign firms in Shanghai were put in prison and pressed to confess just because someone, either Lin Piao or Chiang Ching, wanted to use our confessions, if we made them, to discredit Premier Chou's policy of allowing foreign firms to operate in China?' I asked him.

'Yes, my Party Secretary implied that much. Lin Piao and Chiang Ching both regarded Premier Chou as the major obstacle to their ambition, after Liu Shao-chi was overthrown. In their eyes Premier Chou was difficult to deal with because, unlike Liu Shao-chi, the Premier had never opposed Chairman Mao. So they had to formulate an outlandish scheme. Premier Chou was not a single person alone. Behind him stood a large group of Party leaders and the senior members of the bureaucracy. It's a formidable force in the power structure.'

'Now that Lin Piao has died, Premier Chou has become the most powerful man after Chairman Mao. Isn't his position strengthened and secure?' I asked Mr Hu.

'Strengthened, but not secure, because Chiang Ching and her associates are ambitious. Premier Chou is ill. The question is who will succeed him.'

'Isn't Deng Hsiao-ping going to succeed Premier Chou?'

'That's by no means certain. Deng Hsiao-ping is not a subtle person like Premier Chou. He wants quick results. The radical leaders will feel threatened. That would hasten the next round of struggle,' said Mr Hu.

It was really getting very cold in the deserted park since the sun had gone down. In the distance, several desultory figures were walking towards the exit. I suggested that we leave too. Mr Hu asked me if I would go with him to a restaurant for an early supper but I was depressed and tired. We took a bus home.

Outside the front gate, Mr Hu said goodbye and told me that he would like to visit me again when he had his day off. 'It's ages since I have enjoyed an excursion as I did today. It's good to see you looking so well. You mustn't stay by yourself and brood. I'll come to try to cheer you up.'

I opened the gate to find Mrs Chu standing in the cold on the terrace. I supposed she came out when she heard us.

Taking her cigarette out of her mouth, she said, 'Had a nice outing?'

She probably hoped I would tell her where I had been so that she could report to the Residents' Committee. Resisting an impulse to be rude, I merely said, 'Don't you find it cold standing there?' and went upstairs.

The next day, my old friend, Hean's mother, arrived while I was still with my student. By the time the lesson ended, she had prepared a simple lunch for both of us. While we were eating, she mentioned the Chinese New Year celebrations several times and kept on bringing the conversation round to the guests I had until I suddenly realized that she was hoping I would tell her about Mr Hu. But how did she know Mr Hu had been to see me? Shocked and disappointed I came to the reluctant conclusion that she had been asked to come to see me by those who were having me watched. I went cold all over. I decided to be candid with her so that no one would think I was trying to hide anything.

'Besides all the young people, an old friend also came to see me. Apparently Lao Chao met him on the street and gave him my address. I went with him to Nantao yesterday and bought a Yee-shing teapot and a vase,' I said.

'Is he married?'

'He is a widower.'

'Have you known him long?'

'He was really my husband's friend.'

'What does he do?'

'He used to have a paint factory.'

'Is he interested in you personally?'

'What do you mean?' I asked her, feeling rather annoyed.

'If you'll forgive me saying so, Chinese gentlemen of our generation don't ask Chinese ladies to go out with them unless they are interested in them personally,' my old friend said.

I said to her, 'You mustn't jump to conclusions. I think it's possible he feels lonely and he enjoys my company.' I was thinking perhaps it was just as well that Mr Hu's visit to me was seen by others in this light rather than as something political. 'I'm an old lady now. I consider him only as an old friend who is trying to be kind,' I told her.

'You are an attractive old lady. It's strange that in spite of your terrible experience, you still look years younger than your age. I have no doubt your gentleman friend will eventually ask you to marry him, if you give him the chance.'

'I really don't know Mr Hu very well. It's premature to think our relationship will develop into anything at all.'

'Speaking as an old friend, I would like to see you married. It's not good to be alone in this society. You need someone to discuss things with and to look after you,' my old friend said with sincerity.

After she had left, I drew the curtains and lay down on my bed. It was depressing to know I was being watched so closely. And it saddened me to have Hean's mother join the rank of informers. When would I be able to live a normal life again? I asked myself. As for Mr Hu, I had no idea what his plans were beyond enjoying my company on his days off. In any case, I would not marry him or anybody else. It was still my intention to leave China for good, when circumstances permitted.

Since President Nixon's visit, the Shanghai police had resumed issuing exit permits for private people to go abroad again. Though the period of waiting remained long and there were many rejections, since my release I had heard of several people actually being granted passports to leave the country. I continued to examine Mao's photograph closely whenever it appeared in the newspaper just as I did in prison and I wished for his death no less ardently than when I was in the detention house. I knew that unless there was a change in the political situation, I had no hope of being allowed to leave. To keep myself fit and well so that I could survive still seemed the sensible thing to do.

I heard heavy footsteps on the cement path that ran the length of the house followed by knocking on my door at the foot of the stairs. Since I was in no mood to see anybody, I didn't get up to open the door. After a while, I heard Da Teh talking to Mrs Chu beneath my window.

'Isn't Ah-yee here?' Da Teh said.

'She has gone to visit her family,' Mrs Chu's voice said.

They stood in the garden talking in low whispers for a little while. Then Da Teh knocked again. Again I didn't get up to open the door.

In the evening, Mrs Chu came up with a plateful of fish she had cooked, followed by her grandson.

'I know you don't like to cook so I prepared something for your supper,' she said. She didn't mention Da Teh's visit so I didn't say anything either. I knew she was using the fish as an excuse to come up to find out if I was really soundly asleep and didn't hear Da Teh or if I didn't wish to see him.

I offered her grandson some sweets and invited them to be seated. He held in his hand an armband of the militia. Jokingly I said to him, 'Have you joined the militia?'

He held the armband out and said, 'This belongs to my uncle. He is training under uncle Da Teh.'

'Is Da Teh in the militia?' I asked him. Though I was surprised, I kept my voice as casual as I could.

In spite of Mrs Chu's effort to divert his attention to the sweets, he said, 'Oh, yes! He's a captain.'

'Isn't that wonderful!' I exclaimed. 'I bet when you grow up you would like to be in the militia just like your uncle and Da Teh!'

The child had obviously said something I was not supposed to know because Mrs Chu was not only embarrassed but frightened as well. She said to the boy, 'You are talking nonsense. Uncle Da Teh isn't in the militia at all.'

The child retorted, 'He is! He is!'

Hastily Mrs Chu stood up and said good night to me. As she went down with her grandson, she was still muttering to him for talking out of turn.

Since the militia was a subsidiary of the army, it used to be under Lin Piao's men in Shanghai. After Lin Piao's death, the control of the militia fell into the hands of Chiang Ching's associates in the city. In 1974 and 1975, the radical leaders did a great deal to expand and strengthen the Shanghai militia, hoping to develop it into their own private army.

If Da Teh was a militia captain, he could not have been an 'unemployed youth' as he claimed because members of the militia were recruited among the activists from factories and government offices. I did not think Da Teh was a factory worker because he was too interested in books and his hands were too clean. He must have been an activist in an office of the Shanghai government. In other words, his masters were Chiang Ching's associates in Shanghai. I was glad to know at last Da Teh's true status. Was he with the police or some other organization? It really made no difference to me or to the situation. I had long suspected that he was more than what he seemed.

Time went on and spring came to Shanghai again. I had been out of the No. 1 Detention House a whole year. But I could hardly say I was free. Certainly my material life had greatly improved. I seemed to have no health problems other than arthritis.

Early in the morning I would stand on the balcony to look down at the garden. The meta-sequoia trees planted by the Housing Bureau had grown very fast. Now tiny buds of delicate green dotted the branches. In the short period of a few days they would burst into clusters of young leaves. My old gardener had made two beds of roses and planted a border of mixed spring flowers. He had also put in rambler roses at the base of the pillar of my balcony and made a latticed frame for them to climb on. An increasing number of sparrows were making the garden their home and in the early mornings I had heard a cuckoo singing in the trees.

As the days got warmer, the balcony became my living room. I would sit there with my students for our English lessons. Often I would have my meals out there, sitting in the sun among pots of jasmine, lilies, ferns and other plants I had collected or my students had given me. A beautiful dwarf tree in an ornamental flat vase with a rock formation and moss-covered earth was the pride of my possessions. I succeeded in borrowing a copy of *Three Hundred T'ang Poems*, and spent many pleasant hours copying the poems into an exercise book and reciting them to improve my memory.

Mr Hu came to visit me from time to time. I noticed that if we sat on the balcony, Mrs Chu would be right there below us on her terrace; if we stayed in the room, Ah-yee would be within earshot.

One day in August, when daylight lingered until evening and the temperature was hot, Mr Hu called on me. He wanted me to go out with him to a restaurant. But since Ah-yee had already prepared dinner, I invited him to stay and share it with me. When dinner was ready, we ate on the balcony in fading daylight in the evening breeze. Mr Hu was in a happy mood, chatting to me about his childhood years in Hangchow. After Ah-yee had cleared the table, Da Teh turned up. He always had a good excuse for coming to see me. This time, it was to bring me a bag full of luscious Wuhsi peaches, which he said would have spoiled if he had waited until the following morning to come with them. I introduced him to Mr Hu. It was getting dark. There was no light on the balcony so Ah-yee took the table lamp from my desk and placed it on the windowsill. She also handed Da Teh a large plate. When Da Teh took the peaches out of the bag and laid them on the plate, I saw that each peach was without blemish and was ripened to exactly the right degree. They were better than any I had ever been able to buy from the shops even before the Cultural Revolution.

'Where did you get the peaches?' I asked him.

'I've many back doors. In fact, though I missed going to college, I'm a Ph D of back doors,' Da Teh joked. Then he went to the kitchen to wash the peaches.

Da Teh's sudden appearance seemed to have disconcerted Mr Hu who became silent. However, he allowed an interval of time to pass and complimented Da Teh on the excellent peaches before he politely took his leave. I walked downstairs with him and saw him to the front gate. The Chus were nowhere to be seen, as was always the case whenever Da Teh was with me. They behaved as if they no longer had to pay attention to me when he was there.

'I'll come tomorrow again, if I may,' said Mr Hu as he shook hands with me.

When I returned to the balcony, Da Teh said to me, 'He is a capitalist, isn't he?'

'How do you know?'

'I can tell by his bearing. Besides, he exudes the bad odour of money, like all capitalists,' said Da Teh with vehemence.

'You are still very much the leader of the Red Guards, I can see.'

'No! When I was a leader of the Red Guards, I was just a hot-headed fanatic. Now I'm a Marxist.'

'Are you a Party member?' I asked him.

'Not yet. I'll join the Party one day in the not too distant future.'

'Since you hate the capitalists so much, why do you want to study English with me? Don't you find me as repugnant as the capitalists? Don't I exude the bad odour of money too?'

'You are different. Actually I don't think you would make a good capitalist, as you are rather careless with money. The trouble with you is you are naive enough to believe in kindness, charity, generosity and all that rubbish preached by the ruling class of the capitalist nations to fool their people and undermine their revolutionary spirit,' Da Teh said.

'What do you know about the capitalist nations anyway? You have never been to one.'

'And, more's the pity, I have no hope of going.'

'Do you want to go, if you have the chance?' I asked him.

'Of course, I would go! In the United States or in a European country I could work hard and create my own life. I would probably do quite well,' he said wistfully.

'You puzzle me. A moment ago you wanted to join the Communist Party. Now you say you would like to go abroad if you have the opportunity. Are you perhaps thinking of starting a revolution in a capitalist country?' I asked him.

'Of course not. I want to join the Communist Party because I have to stay here. If I could go abroad to a capitalist country, I should try to become a capitalist,' he said impatiently, almost as if he thought I was too stupid to see his perfect logic.

'What! I thought you hated the capitalists!'

'I hate them now. But if I were one of them, I wouldn't hate them, would I?'

'Won't you be uncomfortable if you become something you hate?'

'Why should I? Don't you understand dialectical materialism?'

After Da Teh left, I sat there on the balcony for a long time thinking of this rather strange young man. Never in my life had I met anyone quite like him. Marxists believed a man's character was formed by environment. Was he the typical product of the Chinese Communist Revolution? In fact, I felt rather sorry for him. He was extremely intelligent and hard-working. If he had the chance to live and work in a free society, he would probably do well. I did not think he would have much of a future in China, even as a Party member. With his over-developed ego and self-confidence, Da Teh was essentially an individualist. The Communist Party was not very tolerant of individualists. And with his uncle dead, he had lost his entry to the proletarian élite.

Mr Hu came again after work the next day. This time I went with him to a noisy restaurant. After we were seated, Mr Hu said, 'That student of yours seems to have access to food reserved for senior government officials. I don't think anyone less than a deputy Party

Secretary of the Shanghai Revolutionary Committee could get hold of those peaches he brought you.'

'You don't think he got those peaches through the back door?'

'No, definitely not! Peaches like those are not for sale through front or back doors. They are reserved for senior officials, who do not have to pay for them.'

'No wonder he couldn't tell me what I owed him.'

'The question is why he was given those peaches to bring to you.' Mr Hu sounded worried.

'Perhaps it was just an excuse to come to see me straightaway. He had to bring something not easily obtainable and not easily kept fresh without refrigeration.' Actually I thought he came because Mr Hu was there. But I did not want to alarm Mr Hu by telling him that.

'Do you think you are under observation?'

'Yes, I'm pretty sure that is the case.'

'To have you under such close surveillance is anomalous. What did they say to you when you were released?' Mr Hu asked me.

'Nothing very much. No mention that I was found to be innocent. They just said that I had been re-educated and had shown a certain degree of improvement in my thinking.' I was remembering my last interview in the interrogation room of the detention house.

While Mr Hu was thinking over what I had said, I remembered the man from the Film Studio.

'The man from the Shanghai Film Studio said that I was released for health reasons,' I told him.

'Really? Did he say that? Do you think they would have kept you there longer if you had not been ill?' he asked me anxiously.

'They thought I had cancer.'

'Perhaps your case is not closed and no decision has been made about the so-called conspiracy. That would explain why you are being watched so closely,' Mr Hu said.

'If they are looking for an excuse to take me back to the detention house again, they won't succeed,' I said.

'Have you tried to get in touch with Shell in London or Hong Kong?'

'No. I don't think I should try to contact anyone abroad when the political situation here is so uncertain.'

'What if they try to get in touch with you?'

'I have already thought of that. If I receive any letter from anybody abroad, I will take it to the police and ask them whether I should respond.'

'That's wise. The political situation is not good. Chiang Ching is making a comeback. Have you noticed that there are many more reports about her activities in the newspaper lately? I also heard that Chairman Mao is relying on her more than ever,' Mr Hu told me.

'Why do we have to suffer so much just because there is a power struggle in the Party? We are not even Party members!' I exclaimed helplessly.

In spite of the heat, the restaurant was crowded. Mr Hu and I were able to talk freely in the din of voices filling the large room.

The night was hot and oppressive. I suggested that we walk back instead of taking the bus full of passengers. The streets we passed were crowded with people sitting on stools fanning themselves or sleeping on stretchers. Their homes were so hot and overcrowded that they had to go to the streets for a breath of air. The population of Shanghai had increased from under four million to ten million since the Communist Party took over the city. Yet little additional housing had been provided by the government and private individuals had not been allowed to build. The result was several families sharing a house, several generations sharing a room and the rooms being partitioned again and again. In the feeble light of the low voltage street lamps, the street scene of Shanghai was one of depressing poverty, rather like a refugee camp.

Mr Hu was correct when he said that the political situation was deteriorating. In the latter half of 1974, the name of Chiang Ching appeared with increasing frequency in newspaper reports from Peking, a sure sign of increasing power. She received foreign dignitaries on Mao's behalf or in her own capacity as a revolutionary leader and a Politburo member. She played hostess to visitors from abroad, inviting them to special performances of her model plays and held conferences with them to discuss affairs of state. Almost every day there was either her picture or an account of her activities prominently displayed on the front page of the press.

The 'Criticize Lin Piao Campaign' became a campaign to criticize both Lin Piao and Confucius. Chiang Ching personally directed the campaign, through her control of the press and all major publications. Maoist writers were organized by her associate Yao Wen-yuan to supply the newspapers with a steady flow of articles and the entire population was mobilized through their indoctrination study groups to take part in the campaign. Scant attention was paid to Confucius's philosophy. Article after article stressed the little known fact that when Confucius was fifty years of age he was made an official in the

Kingdom of Lu and for a short time undertook the duties of the Prime Minister. It was claimed by the Maoist writers that Confucius was a retrogressive upholder of conservatism and therefore a hindrance to progress.

The Chinese people were left in no doubt that Chiang Ching's campaign to criticize Confucius was in fact a campaign against Prime Minister Chou En-lai. The name of the ancient sage was used as a code name for the ailing Prime Minister. The anti-Confucius articles further claimed that at the time of Confucius there existed in China another school of thought that was progressive; the legalists. The struggle of these two schools of thoughts was compared to the struggle between the Revolutionaries and the 'capitalist-roaders'.

Weary of the power struggle between their leaders, the Chinese people, including the rank-and-file Party members, were on the side of their Prime Minister. Rumours about Chiang Ching abounded, many no doubt invented to discredit her. She was such an unpopular figure that outlandish tales of her private life of self-indulgence and sexual promiscuity became the whispered entertainment of the masses. The more serious-minded worried that Mao Tze-tung seemed to be siding with his wife and the other radical leaders. They thought perhaps he was alarmed by the speed with which Chou En-lai, through Deng Hsiao-ping, was reversing the trend of the Cultural Revolution and feared a total repudiation of himself and what he had advocated during the Cultural Revolution.

With the increased political tension caused by the campaign to criticize Confucius and a revival of the Cultural Revolution hyperbole, several of my students dropped out. They were afraid that learning English was going to be taboo again. The Residents' Committee also stepped up its activities. One hundred per cent attendance rate at study group meetings was required. Knitting was no longer allowed. More and more people were organized to stand up to support the Criticize Confucius Campaign. The Lin Piao part was dropped. Ah-yee reminded me to wear only my cotton jacket when I went out so as not to attract attention. Our daily fare became leaner and leaner as she became more and more reluctant to patronize the peasants who sneaked into the city with their eggs and chickens for sale.

At the beginning of winter, an extraordinary event took place that warned me of the fact that I was again in danger of being incriminated.

Among Meiping's friends who came to visit me during the year was a young woman peasant by the name of Chen Lan. Before she started working at the Shanghai Film Studio, my daughter Meiping had to spend six months at the Malu People's Commune outside Shanghai to 'experience the life of a peasant' in accordance with a decision of the State Council. She lived with Chen Lan's family, sharing their life and work. The two girls became good friends. According to Chen Lan, Meiping taught her to read and write, opened her eyes to the larger world outside her narrow existence and introduced her to such girlish pleasures as cold cream and hair shampoo. Chen Lan told me that Meiping once saved her mother's life when the woman was suddenly taken ill. There was no one else at home. Meiping rowed her mother in a boat borrowed from their production brigade through the creeks to the county hospital in time for an emergency operation. After that Chen Lan's family treated Meiping as a daughter and the two girls became sworn sisters.

When she came to see me, Chen Lan brought me a large photograph of Meiping taken with her and several other peasant girls of the village. Through her tears, Chen Lan said, 'This is my most treasured possession. But since you lost all your photographs, I want you to have it.'

I told her that I would get copies made of it and then return the original to her. But for several months I could not find a photographer's shop willing to do this simple work. I was on the point of going out to try the shops at the other end of the city across the Soochow creek when I heard knocking on the door at the foot of the stairs. Presently Ah-yee went down. Then I heard a man's voice saying. 'I'm her daughter's friend.'

A moment later, Ah-yee came into my room followed by a stocky young man of medium height.

I put down the photograph I was looking at and stood up.

'My name is Liu Hing. I'm Meiping's friend.' The young man introduced himself. Then he held out a gift-wrapped box and continued, 'I heard that you are out of detention so I have come to see you to find out if there is anything I can do for you. This is a box of Chang Bai Shan ginseng. It's unobtainable in Shanghai. I was in the north-east on business, so I got a box for you.'

A box of Chang Bai Shan ginseng was a very expensive gift. It would cost a worker a full month's wage. I wondered what he hoped to get from me in exchange for such an expensive gift. I said, 'It's very kind of you to think of bringing me ginseng. But I never take it. How did you get my address?'

'The Revolutionary Committee of the Shanghai Film Studio gave it to me when I went there to inquire.'

It was an obvious lie because Chinese officials never oblige private individuals like that. Somehow I did not believe he was Meiping's friend. He did not look or speak like the type of young man my daughter made friends with. Why had he called on me? What did he want? I was curious and wanted to find out. Deep in my heart, at the same time, I had the feeling that he was probably sent by those who wished me ill.

'Ah-yee, will you please bring a cup of tea to our guest?' I went to the door and called to Ah-yee in the kitchen. My polite gesture was reassuring to my visitor, who smiled and relaxed. He sat down on the chair I indicated and placed the box on the table.

I sat down too and asked him, 'Did you come to our home before the Cultural Revolution? How is it that I don't recall seeing you? And Meiping never mentioned your name to me. She used to tell me about all her friends.'

'You were very close, mother and daughter, weren't you? You were devoted to each other, everybody knows that. That's why I have come to discuss a very important matter with you.' He leaned forward and said in a confidential manner, 'I know some people who could help you hit back at her murderers. These people do not want any money or reward. They feel sorry for you. They simply want to help you.'

What an extraordinary offer, I thought. The correctness of everything that had taken place during the Cultural Revolution had been repeatedly reaffirmed by official propaganda during the campaign to criticize Confucius. For me to try to do anything at all about my daughter's death was certain to take me right back to the No. 1 Detention House. Quickly I said, 'I'm not interested in hitting back at anybody. I'm very sad my daughter had to die as she did. It was entirely unjustifiable and unnecessary. But she has died. Nothing will bring her back.'

'How can you be so magnanimous! It's your duty as her mother to avenge her death,' he said.

'I believe her death will be avenged. I believe the government will carry out an investigation when the time comes. I have full confidence in the People's Government. You haven't told me where and when you knew Meiping.'

'I met her when she was at the Malu People's Commune. She lived with a peasant family there. I used to visit her and have a chat.'

'Were you at the Malu People's Commune?'

'Yes. I was doing some scientific work there. That's when I met her.'

MY STRUGGLE FOR JUSTICE

Was he really Meiping's friend as he claimed? Did he really meet Meiping at the Malu People's Commune? I thought I could check his claim. I said, 'Since you were at the Malu People's Commune and met Meiping there, you must know Chen Lan, the girl Meiping was very friendly with.'

'Oh, yes, indeed. I used to see them together,' he said hastily.

I picked up the photograph of Meiping with the group of peasant girls and handed it to him. 'Someone gave me this photograph. I have never met Chen Lan. Could you tell me which one of these girls is Chen Lan?'

He examined the photograph and pointed at the girl standing next to my daughter with her arm around my daughter's shoulder. It was a good guess, but the girl he pointed out was not Chen Lan. Chen Lan was standing at the end of the row, not near my daughter at all.

His mistake was proof that he had not known my daughter at the Malu People's Commune, if at all. Why had he come? Was it just to persuade me to attempt to avenge Meiping's death so that I could be induced to do something wrong? Or was there something else he hoped to achieve? Because I did not speak, he thought he had made the correct guess. Emboldened by his success, he said, 'I'll come to see you often and let you get to know me really well. I'm interested in world affairs. I'm sure I can learn a lot from you. You can learn a lot from me too because I'm a scientist. If you do not want to meet those people I told you about face to face, I could be your emissary.'

'Why should you want to do that? Isn't it dangerous to oppose the people involved in my daughter's death? Are they not Revolutionaries backed by powerful people?' I asked him.

'I loved Meiping. Ever since I heard she had died, I couldn't stop thinking of her. I hate her murderers no less intensely than you do. I would be glad to do anything to have her death avenged,' he said with mock sincerity, pretending to be very sad.

'You loved Meiping? You must have known her quite well then. It's strange that she never mentioned you to me.'

He went red in the face. 'I loved her from a distance. She did not know it. It was a case of "one-sided longing".'

'I can see you are a romantic. But I think we should wait for the government to avenge her death. No matter how angry we are, we have no legal right to do anything.'

'The present government will never do anything! They are behind the murderers, can't you see? How can you expect them to do anything?' He raised his voice impatiently, perhaps feeling disappointed that I had not swallowed the bait.

'Please calm down. You mustn't malign the government. To say the government is behind the murderers is counter-revolutionary. I cannot allow my guest to talk like that in my home,' I warned him in a stern voice.

'You are a careful woman. It doesn't matter what we say in private. After what happened to Meiping and to yourself, you must hate the Communist Party and the People's Government, even though you don't say so.'

'You are quite wrong. I do not hate the Communist Party or the People's Government. But I'll think over what you have said. If I change my mind, I'll get in touch with you. Will you please show me your work-pass so that I can verify your identification and copy down your address?' I asked him.

'There is no need for you to see my work-pass. I'll write down my address for you.' He seemed flustered by my request to see his work-pass.

'I must see your work-pass, if you expect me to trust you,' I insisted.

Reluctantly he took out his work-pass and handed it to me. I put on my reading glasses and examined it. The work-pass was issued by a factory identified by a number only. Everyone in China knew that such factories belonged to the Army. And stamped across the work-pass was the word 'confidential'. He seemed to be a technician doing confidential work at a factory manufacturing weapons.

My strongest defence during my imprisonment was the fact I did not know anybody who knew government secrets. To be in contact with someone doing confidential work in an Army factory not only would make it impossible for me to leave China but it would also open the way to all sorts of false accusations against me.

I opened the door of my room and called Ah-yee. When she came, I said, 'I want you to be a witness to what I'm going to say to our guest.'

Turning to the man, I handed his work-pass back to him and said, 'Liu Hing, I forbid you ever to come to see me again. I have "foreign connections" and have been wrongfully accused of being a spy of the imperialists. As a scientist at a factory doing confidential work, you have committed a serious mistake by coming to see me. When you go back to your factory, you must report to your Party Secretary at once and confess your mistake. You must report to him exactly what you said to me and what I said to you.' He just stood there, looking embarrassed.

'Ah-yee! This is a serious matter. You must never open our door to admit this young man to this house.'

Opening the door wide, I said again to Liu Hing, 'I presume you are a Party member since your work is confidential. I'm astonished that you did not know better. I should really denounce you to the police. Now go! Don't ever come back.'

He went without a word. But I discovered he had left the box of ginseng on the table. I sent Ah-yee to give it back to him but he had already disappeared on his bicycle.

I was furious about the whole episode and abandoned my plan of going out. Ah-yee brought me a cup of tea and said, 'Don't be angry. It's not worth it.'

A little while later, Da Teh dashed up the stairs and said rather breathlessly, 'Ah, you are home! That's good!'

'You know very well I'm home,' I said to him.

'What's wrong? Are you angry about something?' He professed surprise.

'You know exactly what's wrong.' I handed him the box of ginseng and said, 'Take it back. And tell them to stop their stupid tricks.'

'I'll take away anything you don't want. But I won't tell anybody to stop their stupid tricks. Why should I? Why not let people play their tricks? Why not have a good laugh? Why should you be afraid of tricks? Aren't you smart enough to see through any trick and make people doing them uncomfortable?' Da Teh said in his cynical way.

'It's so dishonest!' I said.

'Why assume anybody should be honest? After what you have gone through, you should know that to be honest is suicidal. Dishonesty is the best policy nowadays!'

'Please go, Da Teh! I'm not in the mood to listen to your nonsense,' I told him.

'I'm only trying to cheer you up. Well, I'll come when you feel better tomorrow.' He went, taking the box of ginseng with him. I wasn't at all sure he would return it to wherever it came from. I had a sneaking suspicion that he took it home and gave it to his mother as a present. Da Teh was that sort of person.

CHAPTER 16

The Death of Mao

LIU HING'S VISIT WAS not an isolated incident. He was followed by a series of visitors all claiming to be my daughter's friends. A few I knew by name but I had met none of them in our home before the Cultural Revolution. They did not come together, but one at a time. And they sometimes came at night. After talking about Meiping's death for an hour, I was sure to have a sleepless night.

'Ah-yee, do you mind not opening our doors to so many visitors who claim to be my daughter's friends? All they want to talk about is what she must have gone through at the hands of her murderers and how I must try to avenge her death. I'm tired of hearing the same thing day after day.'

'I have to open the doors as long as I'm here. I know you are being harassed by these visitors. After you have talked to them, you always look quite ill. But what can I do? Perhaps you had better discharge me. You can easily manage on your own,' she said, looking distressed.

'Can you find another job?' I asked her.

'Frankly I like being here with you. I'm not likely to get another job with the same pay and working conditions,' she said.

I did not want to discharge her. But she had obviously been told to admit visitors who called on me. As long as she was here, she could not refuse to open the door. I would have to think of some way out.

'If I pay the rent, could you find some other place to live?' I asked her. Housing shortage was an extremely serious problem in Shanghai.

'I've a cousin recently widowed. She might take me in and let me share the rent. Do you want me to sleep out?'

'Good! We'll arrange it this way. You go to live with your cousin and come in the mornings only. I'll pay you the same wage and the rent. How about that?'

'That's a good arrangement. You can have quiet afternoons and evenings. If you don't open the door, no one can blame me for it,' she said happily.

That weekend Ah-yee made the arrangement with her cousin and moved out. I got a piece of cardboard, wrapped it up with a sheet of red paper and secured it with tape. Then I pasted a piece of white paper in the centre, leaving a red border. On the white paper I wrote the following message: 'Because of advanced age and indifferent health, I need rest. Visitors without previous appointment will not be admitted. Representatives of the government on official business are welcome any time.' I signed my name, hung the cardboard notice outside my front door at the foot of the stairs with a red ribbon and locked the door.

Next morning, when I opened the door to go into the garden, I saw that my carefully made cardboard notice had been torn up and was lying on the ground. Mrs Chu was on the terrace. I picked up the pieces and confronted her with it.

'Did somebody in your family tear up my notice?' I asked her.

'Oh, no! Of course not! We never go near that door. As you know, when I come up to see you, I always come up the back stairs.'

Her unemployed son came out to lend his support to his mother and said, 'Somebody must have climbed over the wall again last night. We lost two shirts that were hanging on the clothes line on the terrace.'

'You know there have been several cases of thieving in this neighbourhood. Don't you remember the Party Secretary warning us to be extra careful at our last study group meeting?' Mrs Chu joined in.

I did not believe a thief had climbed over the wall at all, so I asked them, 'Have you reported your loss to the police?'

'No,' Mrs Chu's son threw a glance at his mother and said quickly, 'but we will do so certainly.'

'I'll go to the police now and report it,' I said, glancing at my watch to see that it was after eight o'clock.

'Please don't bother. I'll go later,' Mrs Chu's son said.

'I'll go now,' I said.

With the pieces of cardboard in my hand, I walked to the local station at the end of our street. I thought it would be interesting to find out if the police were behind my harassment. If the police were involved, my local policeman, Lao Li, should know about it. I might discern something by watching his reaction during the interview.

The police station of our district was formerly the private residence of a wealthy Shanghai merchant who had fled to Hong Kong just before the Communist takeover. It was one of the largest houses in the area, with an attractive garden. I walked up the steps and entered the house. The large living room had been partitioned. In the front section, a man and a woman in uniform sat behind a counter. There were a few tables and benches scattered about in the room. An elderly man with his Resident Book in hand was registering the arrival of his son on home leave from another province.

I stood by the counter and waited until the policewoman asked me, 'What's your business?'

'I'm a resident of No. 1 Tai Yuan Lu. I've come to see Comrade Lao Li who is in charge of our street,' I answered.

'Did he tell you to come to see him?'

'No. Something happened last night. I've come to report to him.'

'Everybody is at a study group meeting this morning. Come another time,' she said.

'I'll wait for him.'

'They may be a long time. Sometimes the study group meetings last the whole morning.'

Determined not to be put off, I said, 'I don't mind waiting, if it's all right.'

She didn't say anything so I sat down on one of the benches. Several people came to register birth, death, arrivals and departures. I watched the routine work of the police department and from time to time looked up at the clock on the wall. The hands seemed to move very slowly that morning but I was determined to see Lao Li. Soon after eleven o'clock, the door leading to the inner section opened and a man in uniform came out.

'Tell Lao Li there is someone from Tai Yuan Lu to see him,' the policewoman said to the man.

He went inside. After a while Lao Li came out. He was a burly man with a relaxed manner. Unlike most other policemen, he did not wear a habitual scowl on his face nor did he let me know by his attitude that he thought me an undesirable character. I had rather liked Lao Li and respected him as someone down to earth and fair. Behind his mild appearance, he was rather shrewd and alert. On his few visits to my apartment, he was always polite. But I knew he took in the situation at once just by a casual glance at the room. Certainly he was very different from the young policeman who spat on my carpet as he strode into my living room in the early days of the People's Republic.

When Lao Li entered the room, I stood up to show him respect. He told me to sit down and took a seat opposite me across the table.

'I'm from No. 1 Tai Yuan Lu,' I introduced myself.

'I know who you are,' Lao Li said impatiently with a glance at the clock. 'What is it you want to see me for?'

'I've come to report that a thief climbed over the wall at our place last night.'

'Is anything missing?'

'The Chus downstairs said they lost two shirts. I only had this torn up.' I placed the broken pieces of my cardboard notice on the table. Lao Li put the pieces together and read it. The frown on his brows deepened.

'What's this all about? Why did you write this?' He looked genuinely puzzled, so I knew that he did not know anything about my stream of visitors. The Police Department as a department was not involved in harassing me but I could not rule out the possibility that some individual officials, most likely Maoist Revolutionaries promoted to official positions during the Cultural Revolution, were behind it all. During the entire 1970s, Maoist Revolutionaries and the rehabilitated old officials coexisted side by side in every government department in China. In the atmosphere of hostility and non-cooperation, very little got done. The already clumsy bureaucracy became truly unwieldy. If a project had been formulated by the Revolutionaries promoted to official positions during the Cultural Revolution, the rehabilitated old officials would most likely not know anything about it. At the same time, the Revolutionaries would make sure the rehabilitated officials did not recover all the power they had lost when they lost their jobs during the Cultural Revolution. In most cases, the rehabilitated officials found that though they had been given their old titles back, they had become simply figureheads. The Revolutionaries just carried on as if they were not there.

'So many people who claim to be my daughter's friends call on me at all hours to talk about her death. I am tired of seeing them. I'm an old lady. I've had a serious operation. I need to rest,' I told him. He nodded and looked thoughtful.

'Why should a thief want to tear that up?' Lao Li asked me, pointing to the pieces of cardboard on the table. 'It doesn't look like something a thief would do.'

'The Chus told me the thief did it,' I told him.

'All right. I'll go over there to have a word with the Chus this afternoon.'

I thanked him and went home.

It seemed Lao Li did not know anything about my string of visitors. While I was no wiser as to who was behind the scheme to harass me, I derived some encouragement from the fact Lao Li did not tell me to stop putting up cardboard notices. I decided to make another one and hang it up again.

When I got back, Ah-yee was already there. I told her where I had been and showed her the pieces of my cardboard notice. She said, 'It must have been torn up by the Chus. No thief came over the wall at all. It's just a pack of lies.'

'Why should the Chus want to do that?'

'Someone must have told them to do it,' she replied in a low whisper as if frightened, although no one could possibly overhear us.

'Who could have told them to do it?' I asked her.

'Who knows?' she said. But I thought she did know.

I had a peaceful afternoon. The second cardboard notice I made was not disturbed and no one came to the locked door.

On the following day, after Ah-yee had left, my resolution was put to the test. Hean's mother came to the door. I thought she would go away when she had read my notice. But she did not go away. Instead, she called me and knocked on the door. It was difficult to ignore my old friend. But I had to. She called me again. Then she left.

The day after that, my niece came with her baby. She was the daughter of my sister who had died. When the Cultural Revolution started she was only a teenager. Because of her family background, she was treated very harshly. The result was that she became nervous and timid, fearful of offending the Revolutionaries. Because I had been in the detention house, she had been reluctant to visit me. I had to send Ah-yee to urge her to come at Chinese New Year time. Therefore I was very surprised to hear her calling me outside my door. However, I ignored her. After a while she also went away.

I suspected that Hean's mother and my niece were both sent to test my resolution. But I could not be sure. I decided to visit my old friend.

After I had explained to Hean's mother why I could not open the door to her, I asked her, 'Did you read my notice?'

'Yes, I did. But ...' She hesitated, looking at me intently, unable to put into words what she wanted to tell me.

She could not bring herself to say that she had been told to come. Perhaps she felt ashamed or perhaps she was afraid I might blurt it out to somebody. She bowed her head and seemed deeply embarrassed.

After a while, she said, 'Wouldn't it be better just to put up with the visitors? You can always take a sleeping pill. Why seek a confrontation? Are you not afraid of them?'

'No, strange to say, I'm not afraid. I have to fight back, otherwise I would die of anger and frustration,' I told her. Even as I was speaking, I felt anger welling up in my chest. Because of my daughter's death, I hated the Maoists a million times more than I did when I was in the detention house. To fight back at them at least gave me some consolation.

Hean's mother said to me, 'We are such old friends that you should know I'm very fond of you. I hope you would understand if I had said or done things I would not normally have said or done. Living in the present circumstances, we can't always be our true selves.'

'Oh, yes, don't worry! I understand perfectly,' I told her and took my leave.

She accompanied me to the street. 'Would you approve if I told everybody that I'm too ill to visit you? I do have rather serious heart trouble, as you know.'

'Certainly. I would miss seeing you. But it's for the best. I don't want you to be placed in an awkward situation.'

'I'm glad you understand. Let's hope it won't be for long. Take care of yourself.' She sounded relieved.

I continued to be firm and refused to open my door to people without appointment in the afternoons. Da Teh never talked to me about my cardboard notice but he would carefully make appointments with me when he wanted to visit me in the afternoons. After a couple of weeks, the visitors ceased to come.

But the attempts to harass me did not stop. It only moved from my room to the street. One day, when I came home from my walk, suddenly a small group of schoolchildren yelled at me, 'Spy! Imperialist spy! Running dog of the imperialists!'

I walked on, ignoring them. But two bolder ones blocked my way and continued to yell at me. I could not push the children aside without creating a scene, so I stopped and said to them calmly, 'Come with me. Let's have a little chat.'

They fled. I went to the Residents' Committee to complain. They told me that unless I could tell them the names of the children, they could do nothing.

This happened day after day, almost as if the children were waiting there to perform their act of insulting me. I varied the time of my walk. It made no difference. They were always there. And, in the distance, there was the same man with a bicycle. As soon as the children started yelling, he would mount his bicycle and disappear.

Although the children were a nuisance and I was stared at by the few people who passed on our street, I did not give up my daily walk. I would just ignore the children and walk on as if I did not see or hear them.

A couple of weeks later, Ah-yee discovered that someone had written, with a piece of chalk, on our front gate, 'An arrogant imperialist spy lives here.' She was furious and wanted to wipe it off with a piece of wet cloth.

'Please just ignore it, Ah-yee,' I said to her.

'But it's so insulting,' she said. 'What would the people passing our front gate think?'

'Let them think whatever they wish to think. In any case, they must be used to such messages by now. Weren't a lot of such messages written outside people's homes during the early years of the Cultural Revolution?'

I went out at my usual hour of the afternoon, and saw the same man with his bicycle on the pavement across the street. He was close enough for me to see that he was about thirty with a mop of thick black hair. Also I noticed that his bicycle had a rather bright yellow saddle cover. As soon as he saw me coming out, he mounted his bicycle and rode away. I closed the front gate without looking at the message and went on my walk.

A few days later, a heavy downpour obliterated the chalk writing on my front gate. Not long afterwards, the children also tired of their game. The most interesting part was that although Da Teh could not have missed seeing what was written on my front gate, he made no reference to it at all when he came for his lessons.

I enjoyed a few peaceful days. The date 27 March 1975 was the second anniversary of my release from the No. 1 Detention House. I spent a quiet day sitting on the balcony in the pale spring sun knitting and reading T'ang poetry. In the afternoon, I thought of the years I had spent in my cell, remembering the individual guards, the interrogations and felt once again the cold, the hunger and the pain of torture I had endured. I looked at my wrists and saw the scars which will remain with me until I die. It seemed that although I was no longer confined in a prison cell, my struggle against persecution was by no means over. My enemy hovered on the periphery of my existence and I must continue to be vigilant.

I was too depressed to go out so I missed my afternoon walk. The next two days we had a steady drizzle. When the sun came out again, I was anxious for exercise.

'Are you going for your walk today? The weather is so nice,' Ah-yee asked me as she was leaving.

'Oh, yes, I certainly will go today,' I told her.

'Perhaps you can take the handle of the old wet mop to the co-op and get a new mop made.'

'Do I have to take the old handle?'

'Yes, they are short of handles. They won't make one for you unless you bring the old handle.'

At the usual hour of three o'clock, I set out with the handle of our old mop to go to the little cooperative store where a few housewives in the neighbourhood did odd jobs to make a few extra yuan. If I was being followed, I didn't notice it. When I stepped off the pavement to cross the busy street in front of me, suddenly something hit me hard from behind. I shot out and landed flat on my back right in the path of an on-coming bus. Brakes squealed and a man pulled me to the side. The bus slowly rolled over the handle of my old mop, breaking it. The conductor looked out of the window and shouted at me, 'Why didn't you look where you were going? Do you want to kill yourself?' Then the bus gathered speed and pulled away.

Everything had happened so quickly and so unexpectedly that I was dazed. My heart palpitated wildly and my knees were wobbly.

'A bicycle hit you. The man didn't stop,' my rescuer said.

'You saved my life. How am I to thank you?' My voice was shaky. It sounded to me like someone else speaking.

'No, no. The bus stopped in time. You had better go to a hospital to make sure no bone was broken,' the kind man said.

'I think I'm all right, just a little shaken. Please come with me. I would like to thank you in a concrete way with a present. Maybe you could accompany me to the police station to report the incident,' I said.

'You didn't catch the man on the bicycle. The police won't do a thing. In fact, I have a meeting to attend.'

'Did you see the man who hit me?'

'Not really. But I noticed his bicycle had something bright on the saddle.'

'Was it a bright yellow saddle cover?'

'He was sitting on the saddle. But something bright caught my eye.'

'Was he a man with a mop of thick black hair?'

'Yes, do you know him?' the man asked me. 'Is he a personal enemy?'

'No, I don't know him. But I've seen him before.'

'Well, I have to go to my meeting. You had better be careful. He hit you deliberately. The street was empty. He didn't have to hit you. And he rode away quickly.'

I thanked the man again and he disappeared in the crowd.

When I managed to get home, I took two aspirin tablets and went to bed. It was only a little after four o'clock. I slept for about an hour. When I woke up, I found my whole body stiff as a board and aching so excruciatingly that I could hardly move. With difficulty I rolled out of bed and went to the bathroom. I thought a bath with a lot of hot water might help but I couldn't manage to get the water ready without Ah-yee.

The night was terribly long and I was most uncomfortable. Finally Ah-yee came and served me breakfast in bed. Sh was most distressed to hear of my accident. Perhaps she guessed that I was hit deliberately and felt partly responsible, for she had reported where I was going. During the whole morning, she was on the verge of tears.

While she prepared water for a hot bath for me, I read T'ang dynasty poems in bed. Suddenly I remembered that Mr Hu had said he was going to call on me that very afternoon. Although I would have preferred to remain in bed, I got up and tidied up my room. There was no way I could tell Mr Hu not to come. After the revolutionary action of the Red Guards, no one in China was allowed a private telephone. To make a call one had to go to the public telephone. The attendant took down the number one wanted to call and listened in to every conversation. Often she was not there at all and the phone was locked up.

When Mr Hu came at four o'clock, I served him tea and biscuits which Ah-yee had ready in the kitchen. Then I told him I had been knocked down by a man on a bicycle and had nearly been run over by a bus. I expected him to sympathize with me, to show alarm or maybe just say he was sorry. But he stared at me with great seriousness and said, 'Please let me take care of you! If you would allow me to look after you, I would be so happy.' He seemed to be under emotional strain as his voice was not altogether steady.

Was this meant to be a marriage proposal? I wasn't sure. And because I had been preoccupied with what had been happening around me, he caught me by surprise. He seemed embarrassed by my silence. Hastily he added, 'Do you think marriage is for young people only? Perhaps I shocked you with my blunt proposal?'

'Oh, no, not at all. I think it perfectly all right for older people to marry. And I'm sure many women would be proud and happy to be your wife. As for myself, though I am grateful to you and flattered by your proposal, I am bound by a vow I made to my late husband that I would remain Mrs Cheng to the end of my life.'

His kind face softened into a wistful smile. He took my hand in his and said reluctantly, 'I don't know about other women. I have waited ... But never mind! I must respect your resolution to remain faithful to your husband. I have always had the greatest respect and affection for him. He was a very fine person.' He let go of my hand after giving it a gentle squeeze.

The awkward moment passed. I had not caused Mr Hu to lose face by a flat refusal. That was not the Chinese way.

After that afternoon, Mr Hu continued to visit me from time to time. He was always pleasant and attentive. But the interval between his visits lengthened until he resumed his old practice of calling on me on Chinese New Year's day only. In 1978, he came specially to tell me that he had been rehabilitated and restored to his former position as Assistant Manager and Chief Engineer at his factory. He was busily coping with post-Cultural Revolution problems and trying to resume full production.

'I'm working sixteen hours a day. I wish I were younger and could do more. There is so much to do and so much to learn. I have become rusty,' he said, looking so happy that he seemed suddenly to have shed ten years of his age.

In 1980, when I was given a passport to leave China, I wrote to him to say goodbye. He came to see me at once and told me that he had thought all along that I wished to leave China. But I did not think Mr Hu ever understood why I had chosen the uncertain prospect of starting a new life in my old age in some foreign land rather than settling down quietly with a ready-made family in my native country.

To have received a marriage proposal from a worthy man at the age of sixty was pleasant, if not exhilarating. I was in a good mood in spite of my aching limbs when Da Teh came for his lesson next morning.

I had unlocked the front door and was just finishing breakfast when I heard him bounding up the stairs. I looked at the clock. Da Teh was twenty minutes early.

'You are early today,' I said to him when he appeared at my door.

'I have something exciting to tell you.' He came into the room with a big smile. 'I may be going to Peking in the not too distant future.'

'Indeed. Have you been offered a job?' I asked him.

'Not yet. But I may have a wonderful opportunity.' He sat down across the table from me.

'Would you like a cup of tea and a piece of toast?' I asked, as I knew Da Teh was always hungry.

'Some toast would be nice.' He went into the kitchen and came back with four full slices of toast, which he ate in no time at all. I wondered whether he had eaten breakfast, but I did not ask.

Taking a book from his bag, Da Teh asked me, 'Do you think we could study this today?'

I saw the book was Emily Post's *Etiquette*. 'Why do you want to study that? The contents of this book are of no use to a Chinese.'

'Not unless the Chinese is to become a diplomat stationed abroad,' he said.

'I see,' I said. 'Is that your exciting news? Is that why you are going to Peking? Are you going to the Foreign Affairs Institute to train as a diplomat? If that's the case, congratulations!'

Ah-yee arrived and came to my room right away. 'Are you better today?' she asked anxiously. 'Are you still sore all over?'

'Thank you, Ah-yee! I'm a lot better.'

She cleared the table and left the room. Da Teh asked me, 'Have you been ill?'

'I was knocked down by a man on a bicycle and nearly run over by a bus. I thought you knew already,' I said.

Da Teh went red in the face and said indignantly, 'How could I know? Do you think I'm behind every unpleasant thing that happens to you?'

'No, I don't think you are behind them. That would be giving you too much credit,' I told him. Da Teh winced and looked ashamed for the first time since I had known him. 'But I do think you are in the know; you are usually told. I think that whoever is behind all the unpleasant things happening to me trusts you.'

'You don't understand. You think people are free agents. They are not. And the world isn't divided into good men and bad men. In any case, good people are often compelled to do bad things and bad people can also do good things. You will never know the things I have done for you. It doesn't matter. I'll only say that I'm not a piece of stone. You have been decent to me. Often I think you are kinder to me than anybody I have known except my own mother. Do you think I would allow someone to knock you down with a bicycle and have you run over by a bus?' Da Teh said this in a wounded tone of voice.

'My goodness! You have gone soft! If you weren't told, that's bad. It wouldn't do, would it, if you are no longer trusted,' I said sarcastically.

Da Teh asked, 'Are you sure it wasn't just an accident?'

'The street was empty. He didn't have to hit me. However, the bus passing at that precise moment might have been coincidental.'

'The whole thing could have been an accident,' Da Teh argued.

'No, I have seen the same man before. The man who pulled me up told me the man had a mop of black hair and a bright-coloured bicycle saddle.'

From Da Teh's expression, I thought he knew who the man was. After a moment's hesitation, Da Teh said, 'Would you be angry if I give you a little advice?'

'Fire away!' I said, leaning back in my chair ready to listen to him.

'Do you realize there are some people in positions of power who hate your guts? You make them think you despise them. They want to be looked up to, feared and respected. But they think you laugh at them. Why don't you hide your contempt for them and just take it easy sometimes?'

'How do I "take it easy"?' I asked Da Teh.

'Don't react when something happens. Don't get angry. Look at that notice you put down there outside your door. Nobody in China does a thing like that. A man's home may be his castle in England but it isn't the case in China. When you don't allow people to come to see you freely and you send Ah-yee away in the afternoons, naturally people wonder what you are up to. Do you realize the Housing Bureau could have put another family in your other room when Ah-yee moved out?'

'There is no bathroom. Another family cannot come through my bedroom to go to the bathroom, can they?' I asked Da Teh.

'You simply have no idea how people live in Shanghai,' Da Teh said. 'There are many families in this city living in rooms without bathrooms. The Housing Bureau didn't send another family here. It's a special consideration. You should realize it.'

'You puzzle me. Why should I be harassed and persecuted on the one hand and be given consideration on the other?' I asked him.

'I can't tell you more than to advise you not to look upon the situation in a simplistic way. In every government department, there are many people with power to do things. They don't always agree, especially nowadays. The situation is extremely complicated. Just remember, there are people who feel sorry for you. They know you have been victimized. They very much regret the death of your daughter. Please try to be meek and resigned. The political struggle has reached a crucial stage. Why suffer more than you have to?'

'All right! Wise Da Teh! I'll try to be meek and resigned, as you say. But life will be very dull, won't it?'

'No, life won't be dull. Many things are going to happen,' Da Teh said.

'Such as Da Teh going to the Foreign Affairs Institute to train as a diplomat,' I said, changing the subject.

'I'm not going to the Foreign Affairs Institute for training. Comrade Chiang Ching has said that the Ministry of Foreign Affairs must be reorganized. Young men and women faithful to our beloved Chairman Mao's teaching are going to be sent there. She said, "Mix some sand in the sticky clay to loosen it up". The Ministry of Foreign affairs has been under Chen Yi and Premier Chou for so long that it has become an independent kingdom full of capitalist ideas. The proletariat must now march in.'

'Will you be going abroad straightaway, after getting to Peking?' I asked him. From Da Teh's remark, I thought Chiang Ching wanted to take over the Ministry of Foreign Affairs.

'That I don't know. Comrade Chiang Ching wants some Revolutionaries in every Embassy abroad. There will be resistance. It'll be a struggle. But backed by Chairman Mao she will get her way. My name has been included in the list from Shanghai. I hope I'll be chosen. My English is a lot better than that of others on the list.'

'I hope you will be chosen, Da Teh. It will be a break for you. Better than to stick around with the Revolutionaries you are mixed up with now. They seem to me to be a bunch of rascals.'

Da Teh went red in the face again. But he did not argue with me and defend his comrades.

We spent the morning studying the elementary principles of etiquette. When Da Teh left, he was happy in anticipation of a brighter future. Having served the radicals for so many years, he believed he would be rewarded.

During the year 1975, the campaign of denunciation in the press was like the tidal waves of the sea. When one subject was exhausted, another subject was introduced with a deafening roar. When the people's indignation against the ancient sage Confucius was deemed to have waned, other topics of denunciation were presented to stimulate their interest. In this way, the Maoists built up what they called 'revolutionary momentum' and kept the pot boiling.

One day, the Shanghai Liberation Daily came out with a long article that occupied a full page of the newspaper, which had only four pages, denouncing a film depicting life in China made by a famous Italian film-maker, Antonioni. At our study group meeting, the article was read to us and Antonioni was condemned in no uncertain terms. None of us had ever heard of Antonioni and we did not know that he had come to China and had made a film. Furthermore, the film was never shown in any Chinese cinema so that no Chinese had actually seen it. I studied carefully the long article, reprinted from the People's Daily, the official Party organ, and other articles published subsequently to echo its views. Gradually I realized that the denunciation of Antonioni was aimed at the man who had given him permission to come to China to make the film. The article alleged that every shot taken by Antonioni to show poverty, backwardness and ugliness in China was a reflection of the reactionary thoughts of the man who had made it possible for him to do so. What's more, it seemed the film had been used by several Chinese Embassies abroad to entertain guests. Chinese politics operated with gossip and whispering campaigns. It was not long before I learned that the real target of this attack on Antonioni was Prime Minister Chou En-lai and Vice-Premier Deng Hsiao-ping. It seemed they had given permission for Antonioni to make the film and they were of course responsible for the Embassies abroad.

There were many other instances like the one against Antonioni, too numerous to record here. All of the denunciations were in fact veiled attacks either directed against the Prime Minister or the First Vice-Premier Deng Hsiao-ping, who was working hard to restore production both in the factories and in the rural communes.

One day, I was told by my one remaining student besides Da Teh that Chang Chuan-chiao, the Party boss of Shanghai, a Politburo member and a long-time associate of Chiang Ching, had said, 'We would rather have socialism's lower production figures than capitalism's higher production figures.' The radicals in the rural areas took up his statement and proclaimed, 'We would rather have socialism's poor harvest than capitalism's abundance.' Not to be left behind, other radicals declared, 'We would rather have socialism's trains that are behind schedule than capitalism's trains that are on time.' In such an atmosphere, the workers became fearful of doing too much, the peasants became reluctant to go into the field and drivers of trains, buses, and even mules deliberately slowed down so that they could arrive behind schedule. The already strained economy took another tumble. With their controlled propaganda machinery and widespread network of radical organizations which had been developed during the Cultural Revolution, the Maoist leaders succeeded in sabotaging Deng Hsiao-ping's effort to put China's economy back on its feet.

The newspaper headlines and the voice from loudspeakers screamed daily, 'Hit back at the rightist wind of reversing the verdict of the Cultural Revolution!' What did the radicals mean by 'the verdict of the Cultural Revolution'. They meant that Deng Hsiao-ping was denounced as a 'capitalist-roader' during the Cultural Revolution. This 'verdict of the Cultural Revolution' should not have been reversed by Deng's rehabilitation in 1973. The atmosphere became increasingly tense. Anything that incurred the displeasure of the radicals was interpreted as 'attempting to reverse the verdict of the

Cultural Revolution'. And they used this slogan to block any further attempt to rehabilitate old officials. Once again, the Chinese bowed their heads and walked on tiptoes, fearful of treading on dangerous ground or to appear less than totally submissive.

The programme to modernize industry, agriculture, science and technology and the armed forces popularly known as the Four Modernizations Programme, first proposed by Prime Minister Chou En-lai, had been adopted by the People's Congress. Oblivious of the radicals' propaganda war, Deng Hsiao-ping went on with his efforts to normalize life in China and implement the Four Modernizations Programme. Entrance examinations for universities and colleges were reinstituted. But as a concession to Mao's ideology, the candidates for the examinations had to complete first a period of manual labour in a factory or rural commune. The radicals' answer to Deng's decision to restore entrance examinations was to announce the discovery of a young hero by the name of Chang Tieh-shen in Liaoning province governed by Mao's nephew, Mao Yuan-hsin. Chang Tieh-shen, according to press reports, did not answer any of the questions on the examination paper but wrote an essay on the back of the paper denouncing the effort by the 'former capitalist-roaders' to take China backwards to pre-Cultural Revolution conditions. He declared in conclusion: 'We must hit back at the rightist wind of reversing the verdict of the Cultural Revolution!'

Chang Tieh-shen became a hero the radical leaders urged the Chinese young people to emulate. He was sent on tours of the country to 'warn' the people of the importance of 'hitting back at the rightist wind of reversing the verdict of the Cultural Revolution'. Since the Party Secretary of Liaoning province, Mao Yuan-hsin, Mao's nephew, was a close associate of Chiang Ching, the Chinese people realized at once that the whole business of Chang Tieh-shen was manufactured by the radical leaders and the young man simply acted according to their instructions.

Once again, to read a book or to study any subject at all became taboo just as in the early days of the Cultural Revolution. My only other student beside Da Teh, a disabled girl, became very frightened. I told her to study at home but to come to visit me as a guest from time to time so that I could correct her essays. I also told Da Teh to stop coming regularly for his lessons.

One evening, I was in the garden cutting the last of the roses before the frost. I saw Mrs Chu's working son seeing a man off at the front gate. When he came back he asked me whether he could speak to me. I invited him upstairs.

'Did you see the man I was seeing off? He is a great friend of Vice-Chairman Wang Hong-wen. When Wang Hong-wen organized the Shanghai Workers Revolutionary Headquarters to overthrow the Municipal Government and the Party Secretariat in January 1967, he was Wang's trusted lieutenant. They have remained close friends ever since. Whenever Wang Hong-wen comes to Shanghai, he is always invited to wine and dine with him.' He carefully watched my reaction as he told me this.

Obviously he was leading up to something so I listened but made no comment.

'Well, he is going to Peking in a few days' time at the invitation of Vice-Chairman Wang. He is in a position to help you. A word in the ear of the Vice-Chairman and all your troubles are over,' he said.

'What trouble do you think I'm in?' I asked him.

'For one thing, you haven't been properly rehabilitated. And your daughter died in mysterious circumstances. I suppose you would like to see her death avenged. All of that can be done by a word from Vice-Chairman Wang.'

'Do you mean to say that your friend can enlist the help of Vice-Chairman Wang Hong-wen to "reverse the verdict of the Cultural Revolution" for me?' I asked him.

'To reverse the verdict of the Cultural Revolution is not allowed. It needn't be called that if Vice-Chairman Wang would take a personal interest in the matter. It would be called "clarifying the case" or something like that. Of course, you'll have to pay for it. But not more than you can afford. Your money is in the People's Bank; they will know how much to charge you. And you can even get an exit visa to go to Hong Kong for as little as 10,000 yuan,' the young man said.

While I was astonished to learn that the famous Revolutionary hero of the January Revolution that toppled the Shanghai Municipal Government and Party Secretariat and the present Vice-Chairman of the Chinese Communist Party, Wang Hong-wen, was indulging in large-scale corruption, I also realized the danger I was in if I should fall into this trap. So I smiled to him and said in as friendly a voice as I could muster, 'You are really very kind to offer to help me through your friend. I'm most grateful. But at the moment I have no plans to go to Hong Kong. As for my rehabilitation and the death of my daughter, I expect the People's Government will do whatever needs to be done when the time comes. It would be presumptuous of me to trouble such an important person as Vice-Chairman Wang Hong-wen with such a trivial matter.'

'Don't you realize conditions in China have changed?' He was getting impatient and excited. He raised his voice to a high pitch when he said, 'The government won't do a thing if you don't make arrangements privately with an official.'

I looked at the open door and gestured to him to lower his voice. Then I said, 'I've confidence in the People's Government. That can't be wrong, can it?'

'If you are sincere, you are a fool!'

He stormed out of my room, walking quickly down the stairs and banging my front door as he went out. He was plainly disappointed and annoyed that my refusal prevented him from getting his cut in the deal. I thought what he offered me was a straightforward case of corruption, but I could not rule out entirely that it was a trap to get me to take part in 'attempting to reverse the verdict of the Cultural Revolution' and then be found guilty of counter-revolution.

When Da Teh came a few days later, I said to him, 'It's ages since I took you to a restaurant.'

'We mustn't go to a restaurant now. In any case, all the good dishes have been taken off the menu. They are to be served only to visitors from abroad,' he told me.

'It's too bad we only have cabbage and noodles today. Otherwise I would like to ask you to stay for lunch.' I knew Da Teh's aversion to cabbage and noodles, which he had daily when he lived in poverty as a child.

'Would you like me to cook you a dinner?' he asked me.

'There is hardly anything at the market,' I said.

'I'll get the food through my friends. What would you like to eat?'

'Just get what you like,' I told him and handed him three ten-yuan notes, more than two weeks' wages for a worker.

At five o'clock the following evening, Da Teh came with fish, shrimps and a chicken, as well as a bottle of Shaoshing wine and two bottles of beer. I had asked Ah-yee to stay and help him. Between them they produced a really good dinner of several delicious dishes. Da Teh drank the Shaoshing wine with his meal and started on the beer while relaxing on my only easy chair.

Lazily he said, 'Don't you think I'm a pretty good cook?'

'You are an excellent cook. I congratulate you! Now that you have been fed, may I ask you a few questions?' I said.

'Ah, I must pay for my dinner! Glad to tell you anything, as you know,' Da Teh drawled.

'I need to be educated about the present situation. You needn't tell me anything you shouldn't. But I'd like to hear your analysis of the situation,' I told him.

'I've told you already the struggle has reached a crucial stage. It concerns the future course of the Communist Party and the government. Are we going to preserve the fruit of the Cultural Revolution and proceed from there or are we to go back to Liu Shao-chi's policies without Liu Shao-chi?'

'What are Liu Shao-chi's policies without Liu Shao-chi?'

'What Deng Hsiao-ping is doing.'

'I thought the propaganda attack was aimed at Premier Chou.'

'Deng Hsiao-ping is acting on behalf of Premier Chou, who is ill, as you know. The point of contention is who is to succeed Premier Chou. Is it going to be Deng Hsiao-ping or is it going to be Chang Chuan-chiao? The Premier himself and the old leaders like Chen Yun and Yeh Chien-ying want Deng Hsiao-ping to succeed Premier Chou. The present campaign is to impress upon the nation that if Deng Hsiao-ping becomes Premier, he will reverse the verdict of the Cultural Revolution,' Da Teh told me.

'What about Vice-Chairman Wang Hong-wen? Is he going to succeed Chairman Mao?' I asked Da Teh.

'Oh, no! He is just keeping the seat warm for Comrade Chiang Ching. She couldn't very well be appointed Vice-Chairman while Chairman Mao was still living. But she will become his successor when he dies. What Comrade Chiang Ching wants is for her to be the Chairman of the Central Committee of the Communist Party and for Chang Chuan-chiao to be the Prime Minister.'

I thought, good God, don't let that happen! But to Da Teh I could not express such an opinion. Instead I told him about the offer made to me by Mrs Chu's son.

'Have you agreed to do it?' Da Teh asked me, sitting up.

'No. It's illegal to bribe officials,' I told him.

'If you have agreed to do it, you won't see your money again and you won't get an exit visa for Hong Kong either. A lot of people have fallen into their trap already,' Da Teh said and took another sip of his beer.

'What about the victims? Don't they complain?'

'It's a case of "a mute swallowing bitter herbs". He can't speak out. They are already guilty of bribery.' Da Teh laughed heartily and drained his glass. He took the second bottle and opened it.

'It's a shame such things are going on,' I said.

'Don't be a puritan! As long as money can buy the things people need, they will always want to get money. Of course, leaders in high positions are exempt from punishment. *Hsin bu shang da fu* – punishment does not reach senior officials. That's China's tradition. You know that!'

'Shouldn't a socialist government have changed that?'

'Who would do the changing? The senior officials themselves? What a hope!'

Silently Da Teh drank the second bottle of beer. When he had finished it, he stood up to bid me good night and lumbered to the door.

However, he stopped suddenly and said casually, 'I suppose you know Premier Chou is dying of cancer in the Peking Hospital?'

'Is it really true?'

'Yes, it's true. Since he will be removed from the struggle by dying, a lot of cases ... such as the one about a conspiracy of foreign firms and government departments in Shanghai, you know what I mean? Somebody mentioned it to you, perhaps? And others, of course, there are others ... In any case,' he waved his arm in the air, 'all will be shelved!'

'Why only shelved and not clarified?' I asked him anxiously.

Da Teh seemed to sober up and pull himself together when he said, quite clearly, 'Once an accusation is made by a senior source, it can never be clarified, only shelved. You don't expect the senior source to admit he made a false accusation or a mistake, do you?' He did not wait for my answer but sauntered out of the door and down the stairs.

I stood there staring at his retreating figure, momentarily stunned by his message. Perhaps I should have felt relief that the so-called conspiracy of foreign firms and government departments in Shanghai in which I had become so unjustly involved was to be shelved. It could mean the end of my harassment and the beginning of normal existence. But all I was conscious of was a feeling of emptiness. I thought of the wasted years of my life and the senseless murder of my daughter. At the same time, my determination to leave China for good one day was strengthened by what Da Teh had said. I knew that when a case was 'shelved' and not clarified, it could always be revived again when the political climate demanded it. Just because a senior Maoist Party official had made a false accusation and refused to admit he was mistaken, an innocent person like myself would have to live for the rest of her life under a shadow.

The year 1975 drew to a close amidst rumours impossible to verify. I heard from one person that Mao Tze-tung had visited Chou En-lai in hospital. My informant said that when Chou suggested that Deng Hsiao-ping be appointed Prime Minister to succeed him, Mao pretended not to hear Chou's weakened voice. Another person told me that both Mao and Chou were dying. Chiang Ching and her associates hoped Chou would die first so they withheld medical treatment from Chou to hasten his death. Yet another person said that Chiang Ching and Mao's nephew Mao Yuan-hsin had completely isolated the dying Mao Tze-tung from all Politburo members wishing to see him. All messages were transmitted through them, the story went, including directives to the Politburo which might or might not have originated from Mao.

In January 1976, Chou En-lai died after serving as Prime Minister of the People's Republic of China since its inception in 1949. An enigmatic man, Chou was a Communist leader with a difference. To the Chinese people, he resembled those few traditional Prime Ministers immortalized in history and legends because of their high moral calibre. Even Chou's consistent efforts to mitigate the ill effects of, rather than to oppose openly, Mao's disastrous political campaigns such as the Great Leap Forward Campaign and the Cultural Revolution were considered 'wise' by the long-suffering Chinese people. They were only too glad that Chou En-lai was there to pick up the pieces afterwards. Because Chou appeared reasonable rather than intransigent, subtle rather than bombastic, many people who had met him thought him less than a firm believer in Marxism. In actual fact, a close examination of his life and views as reflected in the decisions he made and the speeches and writings that had been published would reveal that Chou En-lai never wavered from his commitment to realize Communism in China made when he joined the Party as a young man. He differed from the radicals only in his belief that intellectuals trained abroad and foreign capital could be utilized to achieve his ultimate aim.

In China, news travelled faster by word of mouth than through the newspapers where the simplest fact could not be published without the approval of several bureaucrats. It was the sudden return of a heart specialist urgently called to the bedside of the Prime Minister, the gathering of local officials at an unusual hour, the cancellation of a major event and a telephone conversation overheard by a subordinate that told the Chinese people that their Prime Minister had died. When the *Shanghai Liberation Daily* finally came out with the news, in the afternoon, the people read it to learn not what had happened but how the newspaper presented the news which they knew reflected Peking's attitude towards the event.

Ah-yee came breathlessly up the stairs and into my room with the basket of vegetables still in her hand. 'Prime Minister Chou has died!' she exclaimed.

She handed me a piece of black cotton cloth and continued, 'I got this for our armbands of mourning. It's already nearly sold out at the cloth shop at the market place. There is a rumour that the Shanghai Revolutionary Committee would not supply extra black cloth for armbands because they do not want the people to wear mourning for Premier Chou. As soon as the people heard this, they abandoned shopping and mobbed the cloth shops.'

At the demand of Party members living in our district, our Residents' Committee organized a memorial meeting for Prime Minister Chou. The room was decorated with wreaths made by the residents. The flowers on the wreaths were made of coloured handkerchiefs because crêpe paper had been sold out in the shops and the Shanghai Revolutionary Committee refused to sanction additional supplies. Lu Ying's son made the frame for the wreath presented by our small unit with dried rice straw, and Mrs Chu and I provided the green leaves from the evergreen ilex hedge from our garden.

The memorial meeting was well attended. A bedridden woman was carried in on a chair and several old men were assisted by their grandchildren. The people came spontaneously and I thought their emotion was genuine. Many were weeping openly and the words of tribute spoken with trembling voices were sincere. It was a simple but moving ceremony. For the first time, I had attended a meeting where everybody was himself and not acting the part that was expected of him.

Meiping's friend Kung called on me in the evening to tell me how the news of Premier Chou's death had been received at the Film Studio. He said that someone close to the radicals had just returned from Peking in the morning. This man said that upon being informed of Chou En-lai's death, Chiang Ching had exclaimed, 'Hitherto I was locked in a cage. Now I can come out to speak!'

'I thought she had been speaking all the time ever since the beginning of the Cultural Revolution. What do you make of such a remark by Chiang Ching?' I asked him.

'God knows what more she wants to say, unless it's to declare her ambition to become the Chairman of the Central Committee of the Communist Party,' Kung said. 'The country is seething with rumours already ranging from a plot to assassinate Deng Hsiao-ping to civil war.'

'I suppose a successor to Prime Minister Chou will be announced soon?' I asked him.

'The delay in making an announcement could only mean the struggle is still going on. There is a move in Shanghai for the city to send a delegation to the Politburo to demand the appointment of Chang

Chuan-chiao. I heard that those close to Chang Chuan-chiao are already preparing slogans and banners to be brought out the moment his appointment is announced. They seem to expect to win.'

'What about Deng Hsiao-ping? At the moment he is the First Vice-Premier,' I said.

'The old leaders are all for him, of course,' Kung said.

'Isn't the Army an important factor in the struggle?'

'Yes. Yeh Chien-ying is the head of the Military Commission. But I hear a few of the area commanders are leaning towards Chiang Ching and her group.'

On subsequent days, apart from reporting the Central Committee's memorial meeting for Chou En-lai, the *Shanghai Liberation Daily*, controlled by the radicals, cut to the minimum the space devoted to Chou En-lai's death. It wasn't until a documentary film of his funeral reached the city's cinemas that the Shanghai people saw the long queues in the capital waiting to pay their last respects outside the Peking hospital where Chou's body lay in state. And one million people braved the bitter January wind of North China to stand for hours along the route to watch his body being taken to be cremated. Close-up shots showed men and women of all ages, some with toddlers in arms, weeping, watching intently and murmuring words the camera did not record.

The people of Peking defied more than the weather when they stood in the cold waiting for Chou En-lai's cortège to pass; they were sending a message of defiance to the radicals who, they thought, had treated Chou En-lai shabbily. The film ended with a shot of a plane flying over the country. From that the people of Shanghai learned that Chou En-lai had willed that his ashes be scattered over China's rivers and mountains. Chou's wish not to be buried in an elaborate tomb at the Eight Precious Hill Cemetery reserved for top Party leaders gave rise to a host of rumours ranging from the radicals' plan to desecrate his grave to Chou's aversion to sharing the same ground with Kang Shen and Hsieh Fu-chih, both collaborators of Chiang Ching.

After Chou En-lai's death, Chiang Ching became even more active and was constantly in the public eye. While denunciation of the attempt by the 'capitalist-roaders' to 'reverse the verdict of the Cultural Revolution' continued, more and more articles appeared in the radical-controlled press praising China's few female rulers in history. Attention was concentrated on Empress Lu (241–180 BC) of the Han dynasty and Empress Wu (AD 624–705) of the T'ang dynasty, both of whom succeeded their husbands upon the men's death. The reigns of these women were described as prosperous and propitious to prove the virtue of female rulers. The Chinese people watched with dismay her manoeuvre to prepare public opinion for her acceptance as Mao's successor. They showed their contempt by circulating stories about her promiscuity and self-indulgence that defied the most fertile imagination. Once at our Residents' Committee meeting, a police official addressed the meeting and told us that we must not pass on rumours about our leaders and must report to the police if we heard any. Although the man did not mention any leader's name, everybody knew that some of the rumours had got back to Chiang Ching and that she was trying to stop their circulation.

The festival of Ching Ming (bright and clear) in March of the lunar calendar took place generally in early April when the Chinese people traditionally visited the graves of their ancestors to pay their respects. When the Communist Party took over the country in 1949, Ching Ming was designated as Martyrs' Day, when school children were organized to present wreaths at the tombs of the revolutionary martyrs. A couple of days before Ching Ming in 1976, people came to the Monument of Revolutionary heroes in the centre of Tien An Men Square in Peking to place wreaths and floral tributes addressed to Chou En-lai. Children tied single white-paper flowers on the branches of the evergreen hedge around the monument with endearing messages addressed to 'Grandpa Chou'.

Chou En-lai was childless, in China considered the greatest misfortune. Furthermore, it was said, and generally believed by the Chinese people, that when advised to take a younger wife so that he could have an heir, Chou had refused and said, 'All Chinese children are my children.' For this, the Chinese people admired Chou En-lai as a man of impeccable moral principle, the more outstanding because many other Communist Party leaders were discarding their older wives in favour of young women in the cities they had conquered.

The wreaths accumulated. They came by the thousands from factories and people's communes in and around Peking, carried by workers and peasants in mourning in a solemn procession and laid down in a ceremony, with the men and women taking an oath of loyalty to the deceased Premier. Soon the steps and the area surrounding the monument were covered. Those who brought the wreaths lingered and others made special trips to come and watch the scene. The men and women read, sometimes with home-made loudspeakers, the poems and pledges they had written for Chou En-lai while others listened and copied down the poems and messages attached to the wreaths and flowers. So many children had tied single white flowers on the hedge that the hedge was entirely covered. It was estimated that on the day of Ching Ming several hundred thousand people had visited the monument and taken part in one form of ceremony or another, swearing allegiance to Chou En-lai and what he stood for. The young people pledged emotionally to accomplish Chou En-lai's unfinished task to rebuild China through his Four Modernizations Programme. By now, the wreaths had overflowed to cover the stands around the square. Increasingly, the poems for Chou went beyond simple epitaphs in praise of the former Prime Minister. Many of them compared the radical leaders unfavourably with the deceased Prime Minister and expressed concern that the control of China's destiny should fall into their hands.

As news of this astonishing activity spread to other cities, trains departing for the capital carried contributions of wreaths and poetry to Peking. The more militant opponents of the radicals chalked slogans and put up posters against them outside the carriages. The train attendants did not wipe off the slogans but kept them fresh so that each train that arrived at Peking railway station was a living protest against the radical leaders.

This mass display of sentiment for Chou En-lai very quickly developed into a mass demonstration of resentment against the radicals, including Mao Tze-tung himself. No name was mentioned. But veiled comparisons of him were made to the first Emperor of Chin (259–210 BC), generally regarded by Chinese historians as a cruel ruler who had persecuted scholars and destroyed books, setting back China's cultural development. The wording of the poems became less ambiguous and the sarcasm against Chiang Ching and her associates became bolder. To go to Tien An Men Square became a must for the young people of Peking. They not only copied poems down and listened to the writers' recitations, but laughed heartily at the radicals and made speeches against them.

Such behaviour was unheard of in Communist China where every demonstration was organized by the government to express support for government policies. On the few occasions when Chinese people supposedly demonstrated outside foreign Embassies, activists had always been there among them to direct everything. During the Cultural Revolution, except for the short time when things got out of hand, the Red Guards were controlled by Maoist Party activists. The radical leaders watched the scene at Tien An Men Square with increasing alarm and decided to take action. On the fatal night of

5 April, the Mayor of Peking, a Chiang Ching collaborator, ordered the Peking militia to surround the area. The police and the militia, both controlled by Chiang Ching and her associates, went in with clubs and pistols to drive the people away from the monument. As the people dispersed, the militia opened fire. Thousands were killed and tens of thousands were wounded. Those found with poems were taken to the Security Bureau, condemned as counter-revolutionaries and shot without trial. Tien An Men Square was cordoned off. It took the cleaners of Peking two days to hose down the blood and remove everything including the corpses.

I was told long afterwards that Mao Tze-tung, terminally ill at home, heard only the version of the Tien An Men affair given him by Chiang Ching and Mao Yuan-hsin who acted as his liaison with the Politburo. They alleged that Deng Hsiao-ping was behind the Tien An Men affair, hoping to discredit Mao and to repudiate the Cultural Revolution. It was the 'capitalist-roaders', they claimed, hitting back at the Proletarian Revolutionaries. In a fit of temper, Mao dictated a directive to a hastily called Politburo meeting, asking its members to pass a resolution to remove Deng Hsiao-ping from the position of Vice-Premier and to appoint Hua Kuo-feng, a relatively junior member of the Politburo, as acting Prime Minister and First Vice-Chairman of the Central Committee of the Communist Party. In effect, Mao Tze-tung had designated Hua Kuo-feng as his successor. Though a very sick, aged and dying man, Mao Tze-tung was astute enough to know that if he had appointed Chang Chuan-chiao as Premier, there would have been civil war in the country and the Communist Party would have been irrevocably split.

Hua Kuo-feng had joined the Communist Party as a guerrilla fighter during the Sino-Japanese War in his native province Shensi. He was relatively unknown to the Chinese people and his career was undistinguished. Just before the Cultural Revolution, he was appointed Party Secretary of Mao's native province Hunan. At the beginning of the Cultural Revolution, he was denounced as a 'capitalist-roader' but was soon rehabilitated when it was found that he had perpetuated Mao's personality cult and was in the process of building an irrigation system for the county where Mao's relatives lived. Hua was not a controversial personality and seemed to have been acceptable both to the radical leaders and to the old guard. He was a compromise choice. Evidently Mao believed that with Hua in charge, his own position in Chinese history would be secure.

The Politburo resolution was quickly broadcast by the Shanghai

Broadcasting Station and appeared in the newspaper the next day. The people were also notified through their Residents' Committee study group meetings. The Tien An Men affair was officially declared a counter-revolutionary attempt to create disturbance. After that no further mention of it was made in the official press. But horrifying details of the massacre spread fast by word of mouth all over the country. Those who had escaped from Tien An Men Square on the day of the massacre secretly wrote down the poems from memory. Soon handwritten copies were circulating surreptitiously among the people.

The appointment of Hua Kuo-feng to the supreme position of leadership both in the government and in the Party created a temporary lull in the published rhetoric but the struggle for power and position went on nonetheless. Public interest in Deng Hsiao-ping was kept alive by rumours of plots to assassinate him. While his whereabouts were unknown, several people told me that he had been seen in Canton living under the protection of the Army.

'It seems so strange that interest in the fate of Deng Hsiao-ping has not flagged since his removal from office,' I said to Da Teh one day when he was chatting to me about Hua Kuo-feng.

'People expect him to bounce back again just as he did before,' my student told me.

'Is it likely?' I asked him.

'Who knows?' Da Teh said.

My student seemed much more subdued since the Tien An Men affair. Though usually forthcoming with comments and information, he never talked to me about what had happened on 5 April at Tien An Men. Also, the appointment of Hua Kuo-feng seemed to have disconcerted him. While he gave me the facts of Hua Kuo-feng's personal background, he refused to be drawn into a discussion of the appointment itself. His half-smile and air of nonchalance disappeared. In its place was often a thoughtful, if not worried, expression.

We had long ago exhausted the book on etiquette and had gone back to a volume of short stories. As I opened the book, Da Teh suddenly brightened up and said to me, 'Would you like to meet my girl friend?'

'Have you got a girl friend? Why haven't you told me before?' I exclaimed in surprise.

'I thought I should wait until we were engaged.'

'Are you engaged now?'

'More or less. Her father still opposes our marriage. I suppose he thinks I'm too poor,' Da Teh said, looking dejected.

'Is he someone important? Is he a senior official?'

'No, he is an ex-capitalist,' Da Teh said, looking at me straight in the eye as if he dared me to say something unpleasant. In fact, I was so surprised that I was quite speechless.

'Well, as you know, I didn't go to Peking after all. They selected two people from Shanghai; both had connections with someone senior in Peking. These two don't even know any foreign languages. I think the best course for me is to become an English teacher in a middle school, get married and settle down in Shanghai. My mother thinks it's best too.' Being bypassed seemed to have given him a jolt. I thought he was beginning to wonder whether he really had a future with the radicals.

'It would be nice to have you remain in Shanghai. You must love the girl very much to accept the handicap of being united with a capitalist-class family in marriage,' I said.

'It isn't such a handicap. The Politburo has already passed a resolution to return with interest all private bank accounts frozen by the Red Guards ten years ago. Her father will recover quite a large sum of money. He has told the children that he will distribute his fortune to them as soon as he gets it back, and not wait until he dies. Of course, I'm not marrying her for her money, though her father seems to think so.'

A few days later Da Teh brought his girl friend to visit me. She was twenty-eight, two years older than Da Teh, not very bright or very beautiful, but quiet and self-assured, obviously in love with Da Teh, whose sharp intellect and vibrant personality must have seemed exciting to her. I congratulated her and asked when she was going to invite me to her wedding feast. She blushed and said, 'That's rather uncertain. At the moment, my father refuses to give permission for me to marry Da Teh. It's not because he doesn't have money. It's because he is a Revolutionary.'

Da Teh said quickly, 'I'm going to become a teacher. The Foreign Language Institute is conducting tests for recruiting English teachers for the middle schools. My mother has already put my name down for it.'

In July, an earthquake registering eight on the Richter scale hit Tangshan, an industrial and mining city in North China. There was no warning because the State Bureau of Seismology was embroiled in a new round of power struggles and its work was completely paralysed. The city was 80 per cent destroyed and over a million inhabitants died or were severely wounded. The quake area included both Peking and Tientsin where, though casualties were not heavy, houses collapsed and thousands were rendered homeless. As the news of the earthquake spread all over the country, rumours of government ineptitude and inability to cope with the situation spread with it. At the same time, based upon mass effort of observing animal and insect behaviour, new and worse earthquakes in many parts of China were predicted. Frantically, the people in cities built temporary shelters, covering every inch of space available with makeshift huts of every shade and description. Everybody lived in a state of hysteria while waiting helplessly for disaster. In Shanghai, the Residents' Committee organized earthquake drills and everybody was told to sleep with their doors open. There were false alarms when I stood with the Chus in the garden in our pyjamas waiting for earthquakes that never came. It was while the nation's attention was thus preoccupied that Mao Tze-tung died in September.

Da Teh had, in the meantime, passed the test for middle school English teachers and had been assigned to teach twelve-year-olds in a school not far from where I lived. After the exciting life of a leader of the Red Guards and a Revolutionary, Da Teh found his new life tedious and dull. Although our regular lessons had ceased, he continued to drop in for a chat. He found in me a willing listener and he knew that since I knew no one of political consequence, his words would not get back to Party men who mattered to him politically. Soon after Mao died he came to see me.

That afternoon, a memorial meeting for Mao Tze-tung was held at Tien An Men Square, attended by half a million representatives of workers, peasants and soldiers. From the platform Hua Kuo-feng, in his capacity as the First Vice-Chairman of the Central Committee of the Chinese Communist Party, read the memorial speech. Beside him were Vice-Chairman Wang Hong-wen in military uniform and Chiang Ching in dramatic black mourning clothes that covered her from head to toe. Our Residents' Committee organized its members to view the proceedings at the homes of those with television sets. I was told to join the Chus downstairs.

After the TV programme from Peking, we viewed the programme of the Shanghai memorial meeting for Mao conducted by Ma Tien-shui, who was a deputy of Chang Chuan-chiao, the official head of the Shanghai Revolutionary Committee. Before the Cultural Revolution, Ma was a junior Vice-Mayor of Shanghai. He joined the radicals after the so-called January Revolution when the Red Guards and the

Revolutionaries toppled the old Shanghai Municipal Government and Party Secretariat. Over the years, Ma Tien-shui became a trusted servant of the radical leaders, taking over the day-to-day administration of Shanghai while Chang Chuan-chiao remained in Peking. The Shanghai memorial meeting was held at the People's Square and timed to follow the Peking meeting.

Mrs Chu's television set was tiny but she turned up the sound so that everybody in the room could at least hear the speeches. Normally, according to Communist Party tradition, Ma Tien-shui's speech should have been the same as the speech given by Hua Kuo-feng, if not a complete repetition word by word. Therefore, I was surprised to notice that Ma Tien-shui's speech differed from the one made by Hua Kuo-feng in two important aspects. Firstly, Ma said, 'We must carry on with Chairman Mao's already decided policy,' while Hua Kuo-feng made no mention of any 'already decided policy'. Secondly, Hua Kuo-feng had used a well-known quotation Mao Tze-tung had made during the Cultural Revolution which said, 'We want Marxism, not revisionism. We want unity, not dissension. We want to be open and above-board, not scheming and intriguing.' Ma Tien-shui had not mentioned it.

When the programme was over, I thanked Mrs Chu and went upstairs. Soon afterwards, Da Teh came. He had watched the TV programme at his school.

'Why didn't Ma Tien-shui make a speech exactly the same as Chairman Hua?' I asked him. 'What did Ma Tien-shui mean by "already decided policy"?'

'The "already decided policy" is for Comrade Chiang Ching to become Chairman Mao's successor, of course,' Da Teh said.

'Do you mean to say that Chairman Mao had decided that before he died?' I asked him.

He shrugged his shoulders.

'If Chairman Mao had wanted his wife to succeed him, why did he give Hua Kuo-feng the note which said, "With you in charge, my mind is at ease"?' I asked him.

'Did any of us actually see the note?'

'It was reproduced in the newspaper,' I reminded him.

'Can you say for sure it was written by Chairman Mao? Can you say for sure there are no other notes?' Da Teh asked me.

'It can't be a forgery, surely,' I said, remembering the hard-to-decipher script, obviously written by a shaky hand.

'Towards the end of his life Chairman Mao lost the power of speech.

He scribbled many notes, you know,' Da Teh said.

'Goodness! So nothing is really settled,' I exclaimed.

'Thanks to my future father-in-law's insistence that I cease to be a Revolutionary, I am out of all of it,' Da Teh said.

'I have been told you are a captain in the militia. Are you still with that organization?' I asked him.

Da Teh was surprised by my question. For a moment I thought he was going to deny it. But he quickly recovered and said with an embarrassed smirk, 'I suppose the Chus told you. As a teacher, I'm now an intellectual. I don't qualify for the militia any more.'

'How did you qualify when you were an unemployed youth?'

'Well, I wasn't exactly an unemployed youth.'

'You told me you were.'

'It was a lie. I was told to lie to you.'

'Did you have a job with a government organization?'

'Sort of. I was only a messenger. Temporary messenger, you might call it. Didn't you once tell me that unimportant people in unimportant jobs are often called small potatoes? Well, I was just a very small potato.'

'Were you a small potato with the group dealing with the case of the so-called conspiracy of foreign firms and government departments?'

He nodded.

'Did you really believe there was a conspiracy?'

'At first.' Da Teh looked at me beseechingly and said, 'Don't you understand? I was told so by people I trusted. They claimed they had evidence against you and the foreign companies. But as time went on and I got to know you, I realized the whole thing was really a plot. You became a victim of the power struggle within the Communist Party like so many other people, including me. I missed going to college and wasted all these years of my life. I became a sort of tool of those who have power over me.'

'Now, you are out of it all. The case is shelved and you have become a teacher.'

'Correct.'

'Did they let you go with good grace? Were they not annoyed that you wanted to marry a girl from a capitalist family?'

Da Teh laughed and said, 'You haven't a clue what those people are like. They are only too glad that they don't have to find a job for me. My usefulness is over. They were pleased to get rid of me. And some of them actually envy me because I am marrying a girl with the prospect of getting a large sum of money. Why do you think people want to get involved in political struggles? To get better jobs, of course. And better jobs mean better living conditions and more pay. There is no way one can get ahead in China except through taking part in political struggles.'

'Please tell me how my daughter died and who killed her. Did they do it for money?' I tried to keep bitterness out of my voice.

He hesitated for a moment and then said, 'Haven't you been told that she committed suicide?'

'I don't believe it. Do you think I should believe it?'

'Her death was not intended. They overdid it, I was told. It was really an accident,' Da Teh said. After a few minutes, he added, 'I'm sorry. Please believe me, I'm terribly sorry it happened.'

'Do you mean to say the men who abducted her weren't ordered to kill her but they did? Isn't that what you are saying?'

Da Teh nodded.

'Why was she abducted anyway?'

Da Teh was reluctant to tell me at first. But after a long hesitation, he said, 'It's the usual formula. Someone thought she should be made to denounce you since you were so stubborn at the detention house and refused to confess.'

'What has happened to her murderers?'

'They are around.'

'Are they in senior government positions?'

'I can't tell you any more. I have already said too much.'

'I'm going to write a petition to the People's Court to request an investigation of my daughter's death. I want those men brought to justice.'

'It's no use. They will be protected. You'll be ignored. It's really worse than useless. If you should write a petition now, they would know you do not believe the official version of suicide,' he told me.

'Would they suspect you of having told me things you shouldn't?'

'They might.'

'I think you should stop coming to see me.'

'Yes, you are right. Perhaps I should not come any more now that ...' Da Teh did not finish his sentence, but I knew what he was thinking about. Hitherto he came to see me as a part of his job. Now that the case was shelved, he really should have stopped coming.

'I have several eggs. Will you stay for supper? I could make some scrambled eggs.'

'I would like to stay, thank you very much,' Da Teh said.

We had supper together. After helping me with the washing up, Da Teh said goodbye. I took 400 yuan from the drawer and said, 'Da Teh, it has been a pleasure knowing you. You are a very intelligent young man. I hope you will have a happy life. This is my wedding present for you. Perhaps you can buy something useful with it.' I handed him the money.

He didn't say a word, obviously overcome with emotion. After standing there for a moment, he accepted the money from me and left.

CHAPTER 17

Rehabilitation

FOR SO MANY YEARS I had waited for Mao Tze-tung to die. When I was in prison, I was desperate enough to pray for it to happen. Now that he had really died, I did not know how to proceed. The prospect of having the men responsible for my daughter's death brought to justice was just as remote as ever.

While I watched the political scene closely, I resumed regular English lessons for my disabled girl student who came every other day in the mornings. Crippled from childhood by poliomyelitis, she had been barred from regular schools but had learned to read and write from her mother who was a nurse in a large hospital. After our lessons, she would thank me politely, pick up her crutches and slowly make her way down the stairs and out into the street to return home on foot.

As I watched her struggling with her disability, I could not help thinking of the irony of life in China. The misfortune of her illness had insulated her from the mainstream of Chinese life and protected her from the political experiments of Mao Tze-tung. But the healthy and normal young people including my daughter were led by the Great Helmsman on a twisted road of frustration and anguish as they struggled to become a part of Mao's socialist new society. Scores of them, like my daughter, had died while others, including the ex-Red Guards like Da Teh, had been victimized. Being disabled, my student did not go to school and was bypassed in the agonizing search for China's destiny. Consequently she was mercifully forgotten and spared.

My student hoped to become an English teacher at a secondary school as Da Teh had done to earn a living for herself.

'I can't depend on my mother all my life. She'll retire soon. My teacher's salary would be a great help to supplement her pension,' she said to me when she asked me to help her prepare for the teachers' examination.

Teaching her became my main occupation. But I was watching and waiting for an opportunity to petition the People's Government to investigate the death of my daughter. I had long ago made a draft of the petition I wanted to send and had written it in the language of socialist China. Since then I had looked at it many times, changing a word here and adding a sentence there. The question was when and to which organization I should submit the petition.

On the morning of 8 October, I awoke at my usual hour of six o'clock. I opened the door to the balcony and saw that it was a fine crisp autumn morning with a few tufts of white cloud floating in the blue sky. Looking down from the balcony, I saw my disabled student standing outside the front gate. When she saw me, she gestured for me to go down.

Quietly I went down the stairs, walked to the front gate and opened it. My student's visit to me at this early hour was most unusual. I thought it best not to disturb the Chus. When I stepped outside, she came close to me and whispered, 'I've been waiting for you. I don't want the Chus to know I'm here so I didn't knock on the door. My brother in the militia has been called suddenly for emergency muster last night. There is going to be a war. I thought I should warn you to stay at home.'

I looked up and down the street and saw that it was deserted. I asked her, 'War? War with whom?'

'I don't know. Last night several men came and told my brother to go with them immediately. They said to my mother that the militia has been put on the alert. We are not supposed to tell this to anyone. But my mother and I thought I ought to come and warn you, as you are alone.'

I thanked her and watched her hobble away before returning to my apartment.

The news brought me by my student was really extraordinary, I thought. I could not imagine any country attacking China or China initiating an armed conflict against any country at this time. Yet she had told me that the militia had been put on the alert.

I had a Shanghai-made transistor radio. Sometimes, at night, when the weather was good, I could get international news bulletins from either the BBC or the Voice of America, if I pressed my ear right against the set and listened carefully. I took the radio to the bathroom, closed the window and door and flushed the toilet to cover the initial noise of the shortwave and switched on the set. Apart from static, I could not get anything at all. When Ah-yee came, I questioned her about conditions at the market. She made her usual complaint about shortages. I tuned the radio to the local station, hoping that if there were any announcement I should not miss it. Then I took out my note-book and spent the morning copying down and reciting T'ang dynasty poems, a wonderful occupation, I had found, to take myself away from my immediate surroundings.

The day passed uneventfully. After supper, I heard Mrs Chu calling me in the garden. When I went to the balcony, she told me that the Residents' Committee had called a meeting; we were to go over immediately. I hastily picked up my stool and joined her to walk across the street.

The room was packed and the atmosphere was rather tense. It was so unusual for the Residents' Committee to call a meeting at night that people sensed something extraordinary had happened. Everyone waited expectantly for enlightenment. There was none of the usual whispering and yawning; even the smokers were refraining from lighting their cigarettes.

After everybody had arrived, a middle-aged official of the District Party Committee got up and read to us a resolution passed by the Politburo. The gist of it was that 'revolutionary action' had been taken on 6 October by the 8341 troops stationed at the Central South Sea (the Winter Palace of the Manchu Emperors and at present homes and offices of the Politburo members of the Party) to take into custody Chiang Ching and her three close associates, known collectively as 'the Gang of Four'. The document said the decision to take action had been made by the acting Chairman of the Central Committee, Hua Kuo-feng, with the agreement of the Defence Minister and senior statesman of the Communist Party, Yeh Chien-ying. The arrest followed a Politburo meeting at which the decision had been approved unanimously, in order to preserve Party unity and prevent the disruption of the work of building socialism. The statement claimed that when Mao was alive he had already perceived the problem presented by the Gang of Four and had declared that it must be resolved. This part of the resolution seemed to me solely to be for the purpose of forestalling criticism that punitive action was taken against Mao's widow only twenty-six days after his death by men who had cooperated with her while Mao was alive. The wording of the document stopped just short of claiming that Hua Kuo-feng was carrying out Mao's orders when he arrested Mao's widow.

The resolution was not long. As soon as it was read, we were told that since it was late, discussions would take place next time. We could go home. There were no cheers, no boos. Nobody said a word. We trooped out of the room just as we had come in – with passive faces, heads slightly bowed to avoid unwittingly speaking with our eyes and moving slowly so as not to show excitement. We behaved as if we had no feelings one way or another because we were afraid. The news we had just heard was too startling, almost unbelievable. We were accustomed to sudden reverses of policy by the Party but nothing like this had ever happened before. To play safe, it was best not to appear to react. Besides, Shanghai was in the hands of the radicals, as we all knew. Most of the local officials were their followers. Perhaps even the man who read the document to us was a Chiang Ching appointee. Shanghai people were wily; they did not wish to risk trouble by untimely laughter or cheers.

Mrs Chu and I walked home together in silence, each with her own thoughts. When we opened the front gate, we saw her militia son standing on the terrace.

'You are home already?' asked the mother.

'Yes, it's all over,' answered the son.

I entered my part of the house and locked the door. As I walked up the stairs, I started to smile. By the time I entered my room, I was thanking God fervently. But I cautioned myself not to be over-optimistic. Obviously the arrest of the Gang of Four was the result of a power struggle within the Party leadership. It did not necessarily mean that Hua Kuo-feng was going to repudiate the policy of Mao. I very seriously doubted he knew any other way to govern China. Nevertheless I spent a restless night speculating on the future and composing petitions seeking my own rehabilitation and the investigation of my daughter's death.

Next morning, Mrs Chu told me that Lu Ying had called. 'There is going to be a citywide parade in support of the Politburo resolution to arrest the Gang of Four. We are to assemble this afternoon at two o'clock at the Residents' Committee office to pick up flags and slogans,' Mrs Chu informed me.

I had never taken part in a parade before. The very idea of marching in formation carrying little flags and shouting slogans was abhorrent to me. I resented being herded and used in such a manner; I considered it an infringement on my privacy, if not an attempt to compromise my personal dignity. Of course, I had been able to maintain such a lofty stance all these years simply because no one had asked me to take part in a parade. Now that I was told to join one, I suddenly found it difficult to put my objection into language others could understand. While I hesitated, wondering how best to refuse to go, Mrs Chu added rather impatiently, 'You will come of course. Everybody is joining in. No one wants to be taken for a supporter of the Gang of Four, you know.'

'I don't think I can walk non-stop for several hours,' I said rather lamely.

'We old ladies are required only to parade in our own district. It won't be for more than an hour, Lu Ying told me,' Mrs Chu said.

Wouldn't it be a great joke if the radicals in Shanghai who, Da Teh told me, 'hated' my guts were to turn round against the Gang of Four and denounce me as the gang's supporter because I refused to join a parade to demonstrate the Shanghai people's support for their arrest? The nimble-footed Party activists were very good at assuming new stances when the Party suddenly reversed its course. Many of them were known to hop right on to the new bandwagon and become the guiding light for new directions, though of course there were some inevitable casualties. I realized I had no alternative. I had to take part in this parade, my very first, and I hoped, my last.

The Residents' Committee ladies must have worked very hard overnight to get the flags and slogans prepared. When I got to the Residents' Committee premises at two o'clock, they were piled high on the table, ready for paraders to pick up. Lu Ying told me to queue up with the ladies who generally sat in our corner. It was the shortest queue and the quietest. Nearly all of us and our families had been victims of the Cultural Revolution. Perhaps we had more reason to rejoice than the retired workers, the members of their families and the young people waiting for employment. But none of us was even smiling. We had been knocked about, kicked around and told so often that we did not belong, but were merely tolerated, in the shining new society of socialism that we no longer felt a part of what went on around us. We knew that in the eyes of good Communists we were the symbol of ill-omen and the harbingers of dangerous ideas, so that we had to be assigned to permanent isolation. Even in a parade, we had to be organized in a formation of our own. However, under our seemingly wooden exterior of unconcern, there was in fact a heightened sense of alertness born of the need to be watchful for the sake of self-preservation.

The parade started. Our contingent brought up the rear. As we passed through the door to go into the street, each of us accepted a paper slogan attached to a bamboo stick. Mine was a simple message saying, 'Down with Chiang Ching'. In the street, we halted for a moment to be addressed by a young activist. He told us that he was to walk beside our group; whenever he shouted slogans from his sheet of paper, we were to repeat them after him. Then several young people with red banners, flags, drums and gongs took up position at the head of the column. At a signal from the young activist, we started marching four abreast, shouting slogans after him. The contingent of workers and youths soon left us to go on to join other paraders in the centre of the city; we remained circling the area in which I lived.

We met another group similar to ours from a neighbouring Residents' Committee. Otherwise we just walked through the quiet, shabby streets without attracting attention or creating a stir. Perhaps we did not have revolutionary charisma; our demonstration was definitely not a success. The young activist gave us up after a little over an hour and we were allowed to return to the empty Residents' Committee office. There we hastily laid down our slogans and fled home, not waiting for further orders.

'Did you know we were nearly in a civil war?' Mrs Chu asked me after we gained the seclusion of our garden and closed the front gate.

'Really? When?' I asked her.

'The militia was mobilized and issued with weapons. They were to march to Peking to rescue Chiang Ching. But news of a possible uprising leaked out. The regular Army surrounded the city. They had to give up. My son told me it was touch and go.'

'It's lucky he didn't have to fight,' I said.

'Indeed. Wouldn't it have been tragic if our son had died for Chiang Ching after what we had been through during the Cultural Revolution?' she said.

Soon afterwards I heard that the radical leaders in the city had been removed from office. Some people said they were taken into custody, pending investigation; others said they were merely confined in a special place to write confessions which would be used against the Gang of Four at a public trial. Not long after these rumours, new leaders were appointed as heads of the Shanghai Revolutionary Committee and Party Secretariat. These men's fate during the Cultural Revolution had been very similar to that of Hua Kuo-feng. They had suffered denunciation by the Red Guards in the initial sweep, but were soon reinstated and 'came to the side of Chairman Mao's correct policy line'. This phrase meant that they had confessed and denounced Liu Shao-chi and Deng Hsiao-ping. After that, they were given positions as senior officials and collaborated with the radical faction headed by Chiang Ching. These men's appointment was symbolic of Hua Kuo-feng's brief four years in power during which time no real change of policy took place and radicals occupying official positions on the base level were not removed.

The Eleventh Party Congress was held in August 1977, while the entire country was engrossed in a campaign of denunciation against the Gang of Four. At this Party Congress, Hua Kuo-feng reached the zenith of his power. Not only was he elected Chairman of the Party's Central Committee but also he became the Chairman of the Party's Military Commission, the official Commander-in-chief of China's armed forces. His portrait now hung side by side with that of Mao Tze-tung in public places. In the newspaper reports, he was referred to as 'Wise Leader Chairman Hua' to differentiate him from Mao's title of 'Great Leader'. Clearly a new personality cult was in the making, carefully promoted by the remaining radicals in the Party and government, who saw in Hua Kuo-feng a possible protective shield for their survival.

The Party Congress reaffirmed that it would 'hold high the great red flag of Mao Tze-tung Thought', and Hua Kuo-feng pledged that he would carry out 'all Chairman Mao's policies' and obey 'all Chairman Mao's directives'.

At the same time, the Party Congress named the Commander of 8341 contingent responsible for the arrest of the Gang of Four, Wang Tung-hing, a Vice-Chairman of the Central Committee. It was a reward for his contribution to Chiang Ching's downfall. It was said that the three men of the Gang were told to attend an urgent Politburo meeting and were arrested upon their arrival at the meeting hall. But Chiang Ching had refused to attend. Wang Tung-hing had to go to her home and personally put the handcuffs on her.

Wang Tung-hing was a long-time bodyguard of Mao Tze-tung. He was given the command of the ten thousand-man 8341 contingent guarding Mao and other Politburo members' living quarters at Chung Nan Hai (the Central South Sea, formerly the Winter Palace of the Manchu Emperors), because of his loyalty and devotion to Mao. It was said that his most outstanding service to Mao was to bring to his master's attention an exceptionally beautiful woman, Chang Yu-fong (Jade Phoenix), whom he placed on Mao's special train. She had become Mao's concubine and was given the official title of 'Secretary in charge of daily life'.

Chang Yu-fong was the last of a succession of young females who had shared Mao's bed. The Chinese people knew but never dared to talk about the fact that their "Great Leader" was a womanizer. In his dotage, the self-styled successor of Marx and Lenin, and the symbol of progress and enlightenment, believed, as some Chinese Emperors had believed, that sexual liaison with young virgins enhanced the chance of longevity in an old man.

Hua Kuo-feng was not a strong ruler. Relatively junior in the echelons of power, and until recently almost unknown to the public and Party rank and file, he had neither the support from the grassroots nor a group of trusted administrative assistants to be placed in key positions. Without such a power base he could not rule effectively.

During 1977, China was in effect split into pockets of power controlled by local military commanders and Revolutionaries, who interpreted Mao Tze-tung Thought in their own way and ignored directives from Peking. At the same time the country was paralysed by economic stagnation. The people had lost confidence in the Party as they had watched for ten years the infighting among the Party leaders and listened to the official voice of denunciation against one leader after another.

The arrest of the Gang of Four was like the lifting of the tight lid of a boiling cauldron. Very quickly it overflowed. People with grievances came out to demand redress. There were demonstrations and protests by both individuals and groups. Crowds gathered outside government offices, sometimes all night long, waiting to be received by reluctant officials. Buildings were besieged. Angry young people exiled to the rural areas demanded the right to return to the cities. The walls of public buildings were covered with Big Character Posters relating personal tragedies and demanding justice. These were eagerly read by the people who added large posters with stories of their own grievances.

At the second plenum of the Central Committee, Hua Kuo-feng made two concessions. He agreed to the demand made by Yeh Chien-ying and other members of the old guard to rehabilitate Deng Hsiao-ping and appoint him a Vice-Premier. And he promised that the Party and government would review all cases of victims of the Cultural Revolution.

I made many trips and wrote many petitions to the People's Court, the Public Prosecutor's office and the Public Security Bureau. This activity lasted the whole of 1977. While junior officials appointed to receive the public and listen to their petitions at the prosecutor's office did receive me and listened with patience to my story, all they said to me each time was that I must write everything down and send in my report. There was no response from either the People's Court or the Public Security Bureau. In short, I was getting nowhere at all. The crowd I had met waiting outside those places did not fare better than I did.

In March 1978, a man from the Public Security Bureau came to see me, accompanied by Lao Li from my local police station.

After they were seated, the middle-aged man in a faded blue Mao suit leaned forward, looked at me earnestly and, with a frown on his brows, said, 'I'm from the Public Security Bureau. You have sent in many letters and petitions both to the Public Security Bureau and the Prosecutor's Office, haven't you?'

'Yes, I've sent a few petitions,' I said.

'Not a few,' he shook his head, 'A great many!' The frown on his brows deepened as he added, 'Why did you have to write so often? Don't you trust the People's Government? Have you no patience at all?'

The man spoke to me irritably. Lao Li fixed his gaze on the floor. Neither of them touched the tea Ah-yee had brought them.

'It's over eleven years since I was wrongfully arrested and it is over ten years since my daughter was murdered. I think I have been very patient. I don't mind telling you that while I trust the Communist Party and the People's Government, my confidence in some individual officials who claim to represent the government has been severely shaken by my experience during the Cultural Revolution,' I said to him firmly.

'I have come here today to tell you to stop writing petitions. In due course your case will be reviewed since it is the policy of the Party and government to review all cases of the Cultural Revolution.'

'How much longer will I have to wait?' I asked him.

'Do you know how many cases we have to deal with in Shanghai? Ten thousand people died unnaturally in this city. Their deaths were all related directly and indirectly to the Gang of Four and their followers. Many times that number were imprisoned. Many are still detained. Our first priority must be to examine these cases immediately and to release the innocent people. Then we will examine the cases of those who are out of prison and are still living, like yourself. After that we will come to the cases of those who are dead, like your daughter. There are many people working very hard to clarify all the cases. You must wait patiently. We'll get to you and your daughter eventually.'

What he had said seemed reasonable. I had not realized the magnitude of the problem facing the officials charged with reviewing the cases.

'It's good of you to take time off to visit me today. I want to thank you and the government which you represent. I must say your visit has somewhat restored my confidence. You are very different from the officials I have had to deal with during the past ten years.'

'Of course I'm different. I've only recently been rehabilitated myself,' the man said with a twist of his mouth which might have been a bitter smile.

'If you have experienced persecution yourself, you will understand how I feel.'

'Of course I understand. But when you think of your own losses and suffering, try to think of the losses and suffering of others too. Think of the Party leaders who fought and sacrificed for the Revolution all their lives such as Liu Shao-chi, Peng Teh-huai, Ho Lung ... and many others who have died in tragic circumstances. And think of cadres like myself who joined the Party during the War of Resistance against Japan and worked hard for the Party without any consideration of personal gain. Because I did not fall in with the wishes of the Gang of Four, I was accused of having an anti-Party attitude and put in jail. Do you know that Mrs Liu Shao-chi has only recently been released from prison? You must try to look beyond your own problems and see the whole situation and put your own problems in perspective,' he told me.

I looked at this man seated in front of me and wondered what his true feeling for the Party was now. The cuffs of his faded blue cotton jacket were frayed and his black cloth shoes were worn. His face was pale and thin. He had had a hard life; his appearance showed it. Dedicated lower-middle-ranking officials like this man were the foundation of the power of the Communist Party. When their faith in the Party became shaken, the Party could not govern effectively. No matter how correct or timely the policy decided upon by the Politburo in Peking, its success or failure depended on officials like this man who implemented the policy.

'I'm grateful to you for coming. I shall not write any more petitions but will wait patiently for you to get in touch with me again,' I told him.

The man seemed pleased that he had accomplished his mission. When the two took their leave, I followed them to the front gate and saw the man from the Public Security Bureau get on his old rusty bicycle to ride away.

I was reassured by the official's visit. It seemed my petitions had reached their destination and in due course I would get rehabilitation. At the same time, I also realized that I would be granted rehabilitation simply because the policy of the Party had changed. It had nothing to do with redressing injustice. In fact, in newspaper reports and in the documents concerning the reviewing of all cases of the Cultural Revolution, the word 'justice' was never mentioned. When the Gang of Four was accused of committing 'crimes' against the Party, the government and the people, it referred not to their breaking the law but to their perverting the Party's policy to further their own ambition. In Communist China, there was no law independent of Party policy.

A few months later, in the summer of 1978, eleven years after my daughter had been killed by the Revolutionaries, three members of the Shanghai Film Studio called on me.

'We have come on behalf of the newly re-established Party Secretariat of the Film Studio to offer you our condolences for the death of your daughter and our fellow worker Cheng Meiping,' said the middle-aged man who introduced himself as the Head of the Personnel Department.

The retired actress who had been Meiping's teacher at the Film School took my hands in hers and with tears in her eyes said, 'All of us were terribly sad. We want you to know that we feel deeply for you.' The once-famous actress, a graduate of Yenan's Lu Shun Art Institute, looked at me as if a camera were on hand to record the scene. Although I had not met her until that moment, I knew that she was the wife of the Assistant Director of the Shanghai Film Studio.

The third person, a young man, introduced himself, and said, 'I was Meiping's classmate at the Film School. I have come on behalf of her former school friends at the Studio to express our sympathy.'

I invited them to be seated and Ah-yee brought them tea. The Director of Personnel said to me, 'Wang Kun here is on the Committee to review all the cases of the Film Studio. We have had twenty-nine cases of death. Many others, including some of our foremost artists, were denounced as counter-revolutionaries and imprisoned. There is a lot of work to be done to review all these cases.'

'How did my daughter die? Who was responsible for her death? Do you know?' I asked all of them.

The young man named Wang Kun said, 'We hope to get the cooperation of the Public Security Bureau to work on her case because it involved people outside the Film Studio.'

'How long do you think the investigation will take?' I asked him.

'We are working very hard. Government policy is very clear. We must clarify every case and where a mistake was made we must correct it,' Wang Kun said.

'Today we have come to convey to you the condolences of the Film Studio and to tell you that we are concerned for you,' the wife of the Assistant Director said to me. 'If you have financial difficulty, you are entitled to assistance by the Film Studio.'

I thought her offer of assistance so many years after my release from prison rather hypocritical but I realized she had been instructed by the Party Secretary to do so. I said politely, 'Thank you very much. I have no difficulties at all.' Then I addressed all three of them and said, 'I hope it will not be too long before you will be able to bring the killer of my daughter to justice.'

'The real culprit is the Gang of Four. We must direct our anger against them,' said the Personnel Director in the tone of voice all Chinese bureaucrats used when they were embarrassed.

'That's true of course. But the man who actually committed the murder must be brought to justice,' I said.

'According to our records, your daughter committed suicide. Until we find evidence to the contrary, we must not assume her death was due to any other cause.' The Personnel Director obviously did not want to hear me say my daughter was 'murdered'.

Perhaps Wang Kun saw that I was getting angry for he said quickly, 'I would like to come and talk to you again very soon. When would it be convenient?'

'Any afternoon would be all right,' I told him.

They got up to leave. The wife of the Assistant Director again expressed her sadness at my daughter's death. Either her emotion was genuine or she was an extremely good actress; she made me cry with her.

Wang Kun came to see me several times. Gradually I came to realize he was trying to prepare me for acceptance of the rehabilitation document the Film Studio had already prepared. From my point of view, this document was not satisfactory because it failed to state clearly how my daughter had died. While it no longer insisted on the verdict of suicide, it merely said that she 'died as a result of persecution'. I was sure someone somewhere was trying to protect my daughter's murderer. I fought for the clarification of this point with the Film Studio through Wang Kun to no avail. He merely told me that politics were a complicated matter and the time was not yet ripe to get to the bottom of many things.

While I was still arguing with the Shanghai Film Studio, representatives of the Public Security Bureau called on me again in October 1978. There were three of them, including the man who had come with Lao Li to tell me to stop writing petitions.

Pointing to a short man of about fifty, he said to me, 'This is Director Han.' Turning to the young woman, he said, 'This is Hsiao Li.'

'We have come on behalf of the People's Government to apologize to you for the wrongful arrest and imprisonment you suffered during the Cultural Revolution. We also wish to extend to you our condolences for the death of your daughter as a result of persecution,' said Director Han in an official manner.

I invited them to be seated. Hsiao Li took out her note-book to record our conversation as all official visits had to be put on record.

'I appreciate your coming today. There is no need to apologize. I feel no resentment against the People's Government. It was obvious to me that followers of the Gang of Four usurped the power of the government and put many innocent people, including myself, in prison. What I'm really concerned with is the fact that those responsible for my daughter's death have not been brought to justice,' I said.

'You must trust the People's Government and the Security Bureau,' the first man said.

'We have come today mainly to discuss your own rehabilitation,' Director Han said. 'We have read the record of your interrogations at the No. 1 Detention House. You were very brave when you defended the late Chairman of the People's Republic, Liu Shao-chi. You spoke up for him when even veteran Party officials were too timid and afraid to speak up. You will be pleased to know that very soon Chairman Liu Shao-chi's name will be completely cleared by a Politburo resolution.'

'I'm very glad the power to control the affairs of our country has once again returned to leaders who will pursue the correct line of Mao Tze-tung Thought,' I said diplomatically.

The first man took a sheet of paper from his bag and laid it on the table. 'This is the draft of your rehabilitation document. We would like to hear your opinion and suggestions before making it official.'

The document gave my name, age and other particulars before stating that my arrest on 27 September 1966 and subsequent detention was a mistake. Investigation by the committee charged with reviewing all cases of the Cultural Revolution had found me not guilty of any crime. Therefore, I must be rehabilitated according to the policy of the People's Government. I told them that I found the wording satisfactory.

'This document will be made official and given to the Residents' Committee. It will be read at one of their general meetings,' Director Han said.

'Soon you will hear from the committee in charge of frozen bank accounts. Your deposits will be returned to you with interest,' said the first man.

'I'll just accept the original sum. Since the country is having economic difficulties, I would rather not accept the additional sum of interest,' I told them.

'You will have to accept. It's government policy,' Director Han told me. Then he smiled and changed the subject, 'Do you know I was rehabilitated and reinstated to my old job only a few months ago? I was imprisoned for three years. I didn't get the special food you were given in the No. 1 Detention House, you know.'

'As I told you before, I feel no resentment about what happened to me. During the six and a half years I was at the No. 1 Detention House I had much time to study and to think. I have learned a great deal. But I do feel deeply disappointed that greater efforts have not been made by the Public Security Bureau to resolve the crime committed against my daughter and to bring the murderer to justice.'

I addressed the above remarks directly to Director Han. But he refused to be drawn into a discussion of my daughter's case. He went on, 'You were given very special consideration at the detention house, you know. The special food, the medical treatment, etc. If you had remained outside, perhaps you wouldn't have survived the Cultural Revolution.'

It was really incredible, I thought, that this man could be trying to make me say I was grateful to the Party and the People's Government for putting me in prison. All the bureaucrats of the Party seemed to have an insatiable appetite for hearing words of gratitude from the people, even when they knew those words could not have been sincere. It was as if they needed reassurance that even when things went very wrong there was something good about the system after all. Perhaps it would have been diplomatic if I had spoken as he had hoped and agreed with him. But I had been too wounded by my suffering and by the death of my daughter to go that far. I remained silent.

For an awkward moment, he waited for me to speak. Finally they took their leave.

I accompanied them to the front gate. As I opened the gate, I said to them all, 'I would like to thank you again for coming today. I will wait for you to notify me when the document for my rehabilitation is finalized. And I would like to repeat my request that those responsible for my daughter's death be brought to justice.'

In November 1978, twelve years and two months after my arrest, I was officially rehabilitated and declared a victim of wrongful arrest and persecution. The rehabilitation document was read at a meeting of the Residents' Committee. Then I was given back my bank deposits. Soon after that, the Shanghai Film Studio held a series of memorial meetings for the twenty-nine members of their staff who had died from persecution. Except for my daughter, the others were nearly all old artists who had known Chiang Ching during the thirties when she was a struggling actress in Shanghai. Among them were film directors who had refused to cast Chiang Ching in parts she coveted, actresses more talented and successful than she, and men with whom she had had love affairs.

The memorial meeting for Meiping, held at Lunghua Crematorium, was attended by over two hundred of her friends and fellow artists, as well as representatives from the Shanghai Cultural Affairs Department and the Bureau of Motion Pictures. These two organizations and the Film Studio also sent wreaths in the name of the directors and the organizations. Kung and other school friends of Meiping decorated the hall. Although the growing of fresh flowers had only recently been revived in the rural areas around Shanghai, they managed to get enough to fill the front part of the hall, where an enlarged photograph of Meiping in a heavy black frame was placed. The rest of the hall was filled with evergreen and wreaths made of paper flowers.

The ceremony was simple and dignified. Meiping's teacher, the wife of the Assistant Director of the Film Studio, made the memorial speech in which she recounted the story of Meiping's short life of twenty-four years, emphasizing the fact that Meiping had received many citations for outstanding achievement and service to other people. The veteran actress delivered the speech with feeling and sincerity and she moved the audience to tears. The sound of sobbing could be heard throughout the proceedings and at times it drowned the mourning music played on a tape in the background. At the end of her speech, led by the officials, everybody came up to bow to Meiping's photograph and to shake hands with me to express personal regret at Meiping's death.

Soon it was all over. Kung accompanied me home in the same car provided by the Film Studio that had fetched me. Even as we were leaving the auditorium, the organization that was to use the same hall for its memorial meeting after ours was already there unloading their wreaths from a truck. Kung told me that all the auditoriums at the Crematorium had been booked well into 1980. To accommodate as many memorial meetings as possible in the course of one day, two hours were allowed for each organization using the hall. In the following year, with more and more cases being clarified and more and more deceased being rehabilitated, it became necessary to combine memorial meetings when several members of the same organization would have their memorial meetings held together.

Kung carried Meiping's photograph upstairs into my room and took his leave. Ah-yee brought me a cup of tea. I told her to go home, as I wanted to be alone.

That night, I could not sleep. Lying in the darkened room, I remembered the years that had gone by and I saw my daughter in various stages of her growth from a chubby-cheeked baby in Canberra, Australia, to a beautiful young woman in Shanghai. I felt defeated that I could do nothing to overcome the obstacle that prevented the complete clarification of her case. I blamed myself for her death because I had brought her back to Shanghai from Hong Kong in 1949. How could I have failed to see the true nature of the Communist regime when I had read so many books on the Soviet Union under Stalin, I asked myself.

Next morning, the newspaper printed a report of the memorial meetings of the Film Studio. Meiping's name was listed among the dead artists. The news of my own rehabilitation also spread, as a result. During the following month of December and over the New Year holiday period, I had many visitors. Relatives who had kept their distance and avoided my daughter and me when our lives were under a cloud now claimed me as their dearest and nearest. They told me that they had worried about me and cried for Meiping. Some of them offered to live with me so that they could take care of me, while others nominated their children for me to adopt so that I would not be childless. None of them attempted to explain why they had not shown us sympathy or given us help when we needed it. They felt no remorse for neglecting us, partly because some of them had had difficulties of their own and partly because they had behaved in exactly the same manner as millions of other Chinese living under the shadow of Mao Tze-tung had behaved. They thought I would understand.

Even minus the large sum that had somehow got lost after the Red Guards took my money away, the money from bank deposits that was returned to me was more than I could possibly use. Through the Party Secretary of the Residents' Committee I learned that the Federation of Women had started a programme to rebuild nursery schools and day-care centres that had been destroyed by the Red Guards. To help young working couples with small children seemed a worthy cause. I gave the Party Secretary a donation of 60,000 yuan (about 40,000 U S dollars at the exchange rate of 1978). And I distributed cash gifts to my husband's and my own relatives, the young people who had helped me after my release from prison, my old servants and widows of former Shell staff members who had died since the Cultural Revolution. To absorb the large amount of cash that had been returned to the people, the government released on the market such articles of household equipment as refrigerators and television sets imported from Japan and organized a travel agency to offer sightseeing trips to scenic spots. The prices charged were very high. For instance, a twenty-inch Hitachi television set was priced at over 2,000 yuan. But the Shanghai people, starved of consumer goods, eagerly bought them. As for those who had large sums returned, they went on a spending spree.

On New Year's Day 1979, China and the United States established diplomatic relations. This development triggered off a terrific vogue for studying English. When I went to the public park to join a class for Tai Chi Chuan exercise in the mornings, I saw young people on the benches, on the lawn and in the pavilions reading English textbooks or spelling English words aloud. The daily English-language lessons broadcast by the Voice of America became very popular. The young people boldly purchased powerful radio sets and tuned in. The fact that they also listened to the news bulletin in special English following the English lessons was incidental. As the government took no action to stop this trend, even people not learning English began to listen openly to the Voice of America broadcasts. To listen to foreign broadcasts had always been taboo in Communist China. Those of us who listened surreptitiously never dared to talk about what we heard even before the Cultural Revolution. Now, the people not only listened to the Voice of America, but they would discuss what they heard openly. In the schools, English became the first foreign language taught to the students. Even eight-year-olds were given English lessons. Now whenever I met the same schoolchildren who used to yell, 'Spy, imperialist spy!' at me, I was greeted with 'good morning' or 'good afternoon'.

Early in the New Year, the Party Secretary of the English Department of the Foreign Language Institute called on me to offer me a job as a teacher of English.

'I've come to invite you to join our department. There is now a great need to teach our young people foreign languages, especially English. We are expanding the department and hiring new teachers,' he declared with a big smile, happy in the knowledge that he and his department had suddenly acquired prominence.

I had already heard that the former Shell doctor had been invited to teach English at the Foreign Language Institute. But I had no intention of getting myself involved and prejudicing my plan of eventual departure from Shanghai. Unemployed, I had a much better chance of getting a passport, for no one would be able to say I was needed for some kind of work and use it as an excuse to refuse my application to go abroad. Since I was going to refuse his offer, I thought I should be extra polite to put him in a good mood. 'I'm honoured by your visit,' I said. 'You are the Party Secretary of the

MY STRUGGLE FOR JUSTICE

department with a lot of responsibility, yet you have taken the time to come to see me yourself rather than sending a deputy. I'm indeed most honoured. But I'm afraid I am not well enough to take on a fulltime job. I have had rather an unusual experience and a serious operation.'

'I know all about that,' he said. 'I have already checked with the Public Security Bureau.'

'Since you have been in touch with the Public Security Bureau, you would know I have only recently been rehabilitated. I need time to get my personal affairs in order,' I told him.

'Don't you want to serve the people?' he asked me.

'To serve the people' was perhaps the most publicized slogan of the Chinese Communist Party. It was a phrase taken from an essay Mao Tze-tung wrote in 1944 to commemorate the death of a Party member; Chang Si-teh. Whenever the Party wanted someone to do something the person did not want to do, the official would ask the man, 'Don't you want to serve the people?'

It was impossible for me to say that I didn't want to serve the people. I thought a compromise was in order. 'Would you agree to my teaching a few students here at my home?'

'You mean teaching them individually?'

'Yes.'

'I'm afraid we've never had that kind of arrangement before. How are we to calculate your pay if you do not come to teach at the Institute?'

'I would be quite happy to do it without pay. To serve the people, as you have said.'

After thinking over my proposal for a few moments, he said, 'I'll have to discuss your suggestion with my colleagues. I will let you know what we have decided.'

He took his leave.

I never heard from him again. By offering an alternative he could not accept I put the ball in his court and saved his face. Instead of my refusing him, he was refusing me. This was the only way to deal with people who hated to be refused.

The newly opened United States Consulate-General was located on Huai Hai Lu, a few blocks from the small park where I did my daily Tai Chi Chuan exercise. On my way to and from the park in the early hours of the morning, I would see people in long queues outside its gate waiting patiently to apply for visas. And my students would bring me news of relatives and friends being given passports to leave the country. The major subject of discussion among young people was no longer how many lovers Chiang Ching had or how many innocent people had been killed during the Cultural Revolution but which Politburo or Central Committee member was sending his sons and daughters to America on the student exchange programme. Now that China was welcoming visitors from abroad, overseas Chinese flocked into China to visit their relatives. They brought with them consumer goods as presents and offered to help with the education of family members who had missed going to college because of the Cultural Revolution. To go abroad, especially to go to the United States, became the most prestigious thing to do for young and old alike.

The political situation in China in 1979 was also good. Although Hua Kuo-feng continued to be the head of both the Party and the government, Deng Hsiao-ping was expanding his power and more collaborators of the Gang of Four were being ousted from Party leadership. There was an atmosphere of relaxation and hope in the country, reminiscent of the middle fifties, before Mao Tze-tung clamped down on the intellectuals with the Anti-Rightist Campaign.

I thought I must somehow get a passport before the Party tightened up again. The question was what reason should I give to the authorities for my proposed journey abroad. The reason I gave had to be good enough to ensure approval because a refusal recorded in my dossier would prejudice the chance of future applications.

One night, while I tuned in to the Voice of America's programme of international news, I learned that China was applying to the United States for the most favoured nation status. Tucked away somewhere in a corner of my mind was a news item I once saw to the effect that the United States Congress had passed a ruling that the most favoured nation status would not be granted to countries that hindered family reunion. It was aimed at the Soviet Union, where a large number of Russian Jews were waiting to go to Israel. But I knew the Chinese Communist Party would take note of this condition. After I had switched off the radio, I thanked God that on this night the voice of the announcer had come through the atmosphere strong and clear so that I did not miss hearing the news. It was something unlikely to be reported in the Chinese press.

I had two sisters in the United States of America. When the Communist Army took over China, they were students in American universities. Subsequently they married and settled in the United States. The younger of the two sisters was only a small child when I left home in 1935 to go to England. We had not seen each other for over forty years. My other sister, Helen, had accompanied her husband back to Shanghai for a short visit a couple of years ago. Since then, I had maintained a sporadic correspondence with her. Now I sat down immediately and wrote her a letter requesting her to send me a letter of invitation to visit both my sisters in California for 'family reunion'. Helen seemed to understand the situation perfectly. She quickly sent me a suitably worded letter signed by both sisters.

Early in March, when the warm current from the South Pacific began to reach Shanghai and the moisture in the wind reawakened the frozen sycamore trees lining the streets, I walked hopefully to the Hsu Chia Huai District Public Security Bureau where the special office for passport and travel document applications was situated. When I reached my destination, I realized that I should have come an hour earlier.

Though it was only a quarter to seven and the office did not open until eight o'clock, there was already a large crowd waiting. By the time the iron gate was opened at half past seven, I found myself in the first third of a long queue which now wound its way round the block. Slowly the queue moved forward as the people were being let into the waiting room. I was squeezed behind a young woman just inside the door. The rest of the queue waited outside in the courtyard. The large waiting room was packed with people sitting tightly against each other on the narrow benches and standing next to each other in the aisles. Everybody was good-natured. When the door to the office opened at eight, there was no jostling for position. People went in one by one. Some came out with a smile and a blank form in hand. Others came out empty handed and did not look so happy. After some time, the young woman ahead of me got a seat. As she moved on, I sat down beside her.

'Are you hoping to go abroad?' she whispered to me.

I nodded.

'Which country?' she asked.

'The United States,' I said under my breath.

Her face lit up with a grin. 'That's where I'm going too. To join my father whom I have never seen. He left in 1949, a month before I was born.'

'Has he sent for you?'

'Yes, he has a restaurant and he said that he wanted to help me if I were willing to work in his restaurant.'

'Have you a job in Shanghai?' I asked her.

'No, I'm waiting for employment. During the Cultural Revolution we had a hard time because my mother had not divorced my father.

The Red Guards said my mother was an American spy. She died at the Cadre School. But recently she has been rehabilitated,' she said with tears in her eyes.

'I hope you'll be happy in the United States,' I said.

'I'm rather scared because I'm not sure my stepmother will like me. Do you think the government will let me go?' she asked me, rather anxiously.

'Oh, yes. I think you'll have no difficulty.'

'Have you been to the United States?'

'Yes, a long time ago.'

'What do you think I should do to prepare myself for living there?'

'Study English, if you can find a teacher.'

She nodded and said, 'I'm working hard at it now.'

While we were chatting we were shifting our position forward towards the benches nearer to the door of the inner room. After more waiting, the young woman ahead of me went in. She wasn't there very long. When she came out, she was smiling. Bending down, she whispered, 'I got it,' and showed me the application form in her hand.

'Next!' a voice called from the room. I went in.

A rather stout middle-aged woman was seated behind a desk. There was a chair facing her and a blank pad and a pencil on the desk. Otherwise the room was bare. I thought she looked to be in an ill temper. It must have been a tedious way to spend a fine morning, interviewing masses of people eager to leave the country under one pretext or another.

'What is it?' she barked at me.

I sat down on the chair facing her and said, 'I would like to make an application for a trip to the United States of America to visit my sisters, one of whom I have not seen for forty-four years.'

'Why do you want to visit them?' she said.

'Family reunion. We are getting on in years. We would like to have a family reunion.'

'Can't they come to Shanghai to see you? Many visitors are coming from the United States,' she said.

'One of my sisters did come with her husband. But the younger sister I haven't seen for forty-four years is too busy. She can't spare the time to come.'

'Which is your unit?' she asked.

'I have no unit,' I said. 'I'm not working.'

'Which was your unit when you were working?'

'I used to work for a foreign firm before the Cultural Revolution.'

'What's your name? What's the name of the foreign firm?'

I told her and she wrote them down on the pad.

'During the Cultural Revolution I suffered wrongful arrest but I am now rehabilitated,' I told her.

She wrinkled her brows and stared at me, thinking. I knew she was in a quandary as to how best to deal with me; naturally she did not want to make a mistake. To prevent her from refusing, which would have been final and irrevocable, I said quickly, 'I'm known by the senior authority at the Public Security Bureau. Director Han and other officials of the Bureau have been to my home. Why don't you just let me make the application and leave it to them to approve or reject according to the policy of the government?'

After a moment's consideration, she said, 'All right, I'll give you the application form. When you hand it in, you must present the required documents,' she told me.

'I have a letter of invitation from my sisters,' I told her.

'Bring your rehabilitation paper too and your resident book,' she said, continuing to stare at me. Her tone of voice had softened considerably since I mentioned Director Han. She must have been wondering how I knew her superior and whether she had not treated me too harshly. With her eyes fixed on my face, she pulled open one of the drawers, took out a form and handed it to me.

I thanked her and left the room. In the waiting room, everybody watched me eagerly to find out whether I had been given a form. Their concern was later explained to me by one of my students who had been through the same experience. It seemed only a limited number of forms were given out each day. The more people coming out of the interview with forms, the fewer would be left for those waiting.

When I got home, to my surprise, I found the woman had given me an application form for a travel document to Hong Kong by mistake. I had to go back to change it for the correct one for passport application. I quickly walked back. The waiting crowd kindly allowed me to get to the head of the queue after I explained the reason I had to come back.

The woman was rather disconcerted when I told her that she had given me the wrong form. But she changed it for me without saying anything.

Next morning I carefully filled out the application form and handed it in with the required documents. I did not expect to hear from the Public Security Bureau for at least a year, about the length of time for the Bureau to process a passport application during 1979. But I also knew cases of people who had to wait for several years for permission to go only to Hong Kong before the Cultural Revolution. In any case, I was fortunate; the woman official did not refuse to give me the application form. If she had refused, there was absolutely nothing I could have done except to give up the whole idea of applying. Although her position in the bureaucratic structure could not have been very senior, the power she was allowed to exercise seemed frighteningly enormous.

CHAPTER 18

Farewell to Shanghai

A FEW DAYS AFTER I had handed in my application form for the passport to go to the United States, Ah-yee brought me an official-looking letter. It was from 'The Bureau for Sorting Looted Goods', which I thought was a unique title for a government department. The letter invited me to go for an interview. Both Mrs Chu and her husband had received a similar call. She was given back a few pieces of costume jewellery and her husband was told to go to a warehouse to search through the dusty volumes stored there to see if he could find some of his books. After being in the airless warehouse for over ten years, the books were rotting with mildew. When he picked up a volume, it fell apart in his hand and exuded a strong, unhealthy odour. He returned to the Bureau for Sorting Looted Goods empty-handed and agreed to sign a pledge relinquishing all claims to his looted property. Mrs Chu likewise had to sign a receipt for the costume jewellery given back to her. It listed 'three rings, one brooch ... etc' without identifying them as costume jewellery. When she asked the man for her rings of real diamonds and jade, the man asked her to produce evidence to prove she actually had them when the Red Guards looted her home.

It would seem the things taken from the looted homes had not been securely stored away. In the course of the ten years of the Cultural Revolution, many people must have had access to them. Now that the government decreed that looted goods should be returned to their owners, the local officials had to make a show of doing so. Thus they organized this Bureau to put on an act and invited us to take part. When a sufficient number of receipts for worthless objects had been collected and enough pledges made to relinquish claims, the work of returning looted goods to their rightful owners could be considered accomplished successfully.

While I was not hopeful that I would recover anything of value, I could not very well ignore a letter from a government department. Therefore I went there at the time and on the day specified. I was received by a woman official, who asked me straightaway if I would be interested in going to a warehouse to look for books and records.

'I'm pretty certain all my books were burned. As for records, it's possible a few were saved. But I'm not interested in getting them back. I'll sign a paper to that effect,' I told her.

'I have some really good news for you,' she said, laying emphasis on 'good news' and 'you'.

After rummaging through the files on her desk, she took out a sheet of paper and said to me, 'Some of your porcelain pieces have been located because they were in boxes bearing your name. These pieces are at a warehouse. However, the Shanghai Museum is interested in purchasing fifteen pieces from you. These fifteen pieces are at the Museum. You can go to the warehouse and show the man in charge this letter of authorization.'

The letter she handed over to me was a document identifying me as the owner of the pieces of porcelain contained in boxes bearing my name.

'What about the pieces displayed in my house and not put away in boxes when the Red Guards came on 30 August 1966?' I asked her.

'If there was no identification, it would be very difficult to find them.'

'What about my white jade collection?' I asked her.

'Items made of precious stones or semi-precious stones were put away with the jewellery. We are still trying to locate them,' she said rather impatiently. I thought she was displeased that I should have mentioned them. She was probably thinking that I should be satisfied that my porcelain pieces had been found.

'I ask only because there were some in boxes with my name on them,' I explained.

'You may find a few pieces with your porcelain,' she said.

'Thank you very much for locating my porcelain pieces. It must have been hard work,' I said to her.

'The Shanghai Museum helped us. They want to get in touch with you so that they can buy some of your pieces,' she said.

I was overjoyed that some of my porcelain pieces had been saved and when I got home I got in touch with Little Fong, asking him to help me to get them back. It would seem my fight to save them in 1966 when the Red Guards were looting my home had not been in vain.

A few days later, Little Fong drove me in his Power Company truck to the underground warehouse at the other end of the city. After I had presented the letter to the security guard, we were allowed to enter the dark, cavernous interior. The man in charge told us to wait by a long dusty table under a feeble light. Others were already gathered there. We waited with anticipation, moving restlessly in the airless room.

When the items were brought out and laid on the table, we were told to identify our own things. There were scrolls, fans, boxes of various sizes and containers tied together with string. Everything was covered with a thick layer of sooty dust peculiar to coal-burning, industrial Shanghai. A man sighed deeply and uttered a stifled exclamation which sounded rather like a sob when he picked up his antique fan to find that the paper on which was the valuable painting by a famous Ming dynasty painter had rotted away with mildew. A woman standing beside him, perhaps his wife, murmured to him to throw away the now worthless fan. But he carefully took out his handkerchief and folded it lovingly around the fan to take it home.

Back home Little Fong helped me to carry my boxes upstairs to my room and took his leave. The odour from them was overpowering. I opened each box and took the porcelain piece out. Then I took all the dirty and broken boxes out to the fresh air of the balcony. I saw that some of the vases, bowls and plates were chipped or cracked; and a few had been broken and then glued together again. All had identification numbers and other indecipherable writing on the delicate glaze. On a large plate of Ming celadon, some Revolutionary had expressed his hatred against the rich by declaring in writing that collectors were bloodsuckers. I was heartbroken to see the beautiful pieces so carelessly defaced. But I knew that they might easily have all been smashed, if someone somewhere hadn't succeeded in talking the Red Guards into taking them to the underground warehouse.

I filled the bath with lukewarm water, sprinkled a little soap powder in it, laid towels at the bottom of the tub and placed the pieces there to soak. In the water the broken pieces disintegrated. I bent over the bath and washed each piece with a soft cloth to remove the markings. After rinsing, I placed them on a sheet spread on the floor of my room. It was already nightfall when I had finished. I realized that fewer than half of my original collection was left intact, among them my Te Hua Kwan Yin, covered with black ink stain, but not broken. After washing, it appeared as gleaming and beautiful as it ever was. I placed it on my desk and sat down to enjoy looking at it. It was like being reunited with an old friend after a long separation.

I checked the list of the fifteen pieces the Museum wished to buy and saw that it included what was left of all my Hsüan-te blue and white as well as an apple green (Fên Ching) Yung Cheng vase I particularly liked. It had a raised pattern of a lizard with such a fluid line that it looked as if it was ready to slither off the vase. The Shanghai Museum also wanted my Cheng-te chicken-fat-yellow plate and my best piece of

Sung dynasty Ting ware with an incised pattern of waterlilies.

Should I concede to the Museum's request to purchase the fifteen pieces they had selected or should I refuse? Before the Cultural Revolution, when I was writing my last will, I had discussed the matter of my collection with my daughter. It was at her suggestion that I had stated in my will that my collection should go to the Shanghai Museum as a gift. Her death and the careless disregard for cultural relics demonstrated during the Cultural Revolution had cooled my enthusiasm for leaving my collection to the Museum, a bureaucratic organization of the government, subject to pressure of politics. On the other hand, I had already decided to leave China. None of my collection was exportable. Would it not be the same thing whether I left it to the Museum or not? Therefore I decided I would give the Museum the fifteen pieces they wanted rather than accept a token purchase price arbitrarily arrived at by some official who had no knowledge of the true worth of the pieces in question. However, I should get something out of the deal, I thought. All the blackwood stands that went with the pieces had disappeared. If I wished to enjoy looking at my collection until I left Shanghai, I must have stands to display them. I decided to ask the Museum to make a few stands for me in exchange for my fifteen pieces. It was not an equal exchange by any means but I did need the stands and there was no other way to get them.

The Shanghai Museum sent me a message for an interview and I went there to see them. The men received me with excessive politeness. They brought out my fifteen pieces, all beautifully clean and gleaming against the white satin lining of the new boxes in which they lay, and allowed me to take them out to examine each piece. Then we talked about them as if we were disinterested connoisseurs, pointing out a particular colour or design and turning them over to examine the markings. When they deemed that sufficient courtesy had been shown me to establish themselves as civilized individuals and to put me in a receptive mood, they turned to the business in hand. The man who seemed to enjoy deference from the others said to me, 'The Museum has to work within the limits of a budget. We have to be very selective when we make purchases. You have many beautiful pieces in your collection, but we have decided, for the time being, to request you to sell us only these fifteen pieces.'

'Of course. You can have the fifteen pieces you have selected. It's better to have visitors to the Museum enjoying them than leaving them in my cupboard,' I said.

They all beamed and the man who spoke nodded with approval of what I had said.

'I'll make a gift of all these fifteen pieces to the Museum if you meet my conditions,' I added.

'What do you want us to do?' the man asked me.

'Nothing very difficult for the Museum,' I told him. 'I would like the Museum carpenter to make some stands for me so that I can display the pieces that have been returned to me in my room and enjoy looking at them. I'll of course pay for the wood and the labour of your carpenter.'

They looked at each other, surprised at the nature of my condition. Then they all laughed heartily.

'That's easy. I'll send our carpenter to your house to measure the pieces. How many do you want made? Do you want a stand for each piece returned to you?' the man asked me.

'No, of course I can't ask you to make so many stands. I think maybe ten or twelve stands would be all I want,' I said.

'That will be perfectly all right,' he promised readily.

'About your idea of making these fifteen pieces a gift to the Museum, will you furnish us with a formal letter to that effect?' another man said.

'Certainly. I'll give it to the carpenter when he comes. Could he come tomorrow?'

'I'll get the carpenter now and you can discuss the matter with him yourself,' the man said and left the room.

When he came back with the carpenter in tow, the old man seemed unhappy to have this extra job thrust upon him.

'I have got a lot of work on hand just now,' he muttered.

'It doesn't seem right to ask this old comrade to do this extra work for me during working hours for the Museum. It might delay whatever he is doing for the Museum. What about asking him to do my work in his spare time and I will settle with him about payment?' I suggested.

'You can't do that,' the Museum official said firmly. Obviously he couldn't condone such a practice. But he had decided to let me have my stands so he told the old carpenter to put aside whatever he was doing for the Museum for the time being. We arranged that the carpenter would come to my apartment the next day to measure the pieces.

'We are holding an exhibition next week of our recently acquired items. All friends of the Museum who have pieces displayed in the exhibition are invited to a special preview and a banquet afterwards. We hope you will come,' the man said, handing me a gold-embossed invitation card. My name was already written on it. Evidently they had been quite certain I was going to let them have my fifteen pieces. Of course, since the Shanghai Museum was a government organization, their request to purchase was as good as a polite order to sell. Nevertheless, I did know of one doctor who had refused to sell his collection of T'ang porcelain pillows. This was told to me by one of the Shanghai Museum officials with a great deal of regret and indignation.

The special exhibition was held in the hall on the ground floor of the Shanghai Museum. Apart from the private collectors who had contributed the exhibits, and their wives, there were also a large number of government officials, escorted by Museum personnel, strolling among the well-lit cases. With each exhibit was a card giving a description of the piece and the name of the donor. Of my fifteen pieces, four were on display including a large Hsüan-te blue-and-white plate sixteen inches in diameter with a pattern of grapes and the Yung Cheng vase with the raised pattern of a lizard. The Museum official showing me round explained to me that due to the limited space, only token pieces from each collector were shown.

The most senior official present was a Vice-Mayor of the city, Chang Cheng-chung, who was concurrently the Director of the Commission for the Administration and Control of Cultural Relics. He was surrounded by a large entourage and many Museum officials ready to answer his questions. After everybody had looked at the exhibits, we were invited to sit down on the chairs already placed in the centre of the spacious hall. Vice-Mayor Chang made a speech praising the patriotic spirit of the private collectors who had added to the collection of the Shanghai Museum. In particular he welcomed a young couple who had travelled to Shanghai from the United States to attend the ceremony as representatives of their grandfather, who had died during the Cultural Revolution and could not personally witness his own collection being included in this exhibition. After his speech, a representative of the Museum invited each private collector to come forward. As each man came to where Chang Cheng-chung was seated, the Vice-Mayor stood up to present him with a Certificate of Merit in a gold frame and a red envelope containing the purchasing price. While this was going on, an official of the Museum slipped onto the seat next to mine and told me in low whispers that a separate ceremony would be held for me because I had donated my pieces. After everybody had been called, we were taken by special buses to the newly opened tourist hotel on Hua Shan Lu and given an elaborate banquet in the large dining room.

The young couple from the United States and other collectors who had links with businessmen in Hong Kong were given the seats of honour at Vice-Mayor Chang's table. Since the new policy of attracting foreign investment was declared, these individuals' personal importance in the eyes of the People's Government had increased a thousandfold. Until the government succeeded in establishing firm business ties with foreign countries, these men were useful for forging a link with Hong Kong and elsewhere through their former contacts with overseas Chinese. The rest of us sat wherever we happened to find ourselves. At each table, an official of the Shanghai Museum acted as host. I knew no one at my table. We did not introduce ourselves or make conversation. And no one ate very much of the delicious food being put in front of us. We were stiff and formal, patiently waiting for the banquet to end. The Museum people were, however, in high spirits. They went round from table to table, wine glass in hand, to toast each other.

Collectors do not like to part with their collections because they form a sort of sentimental tie with the items they have collected. Throughout the meal, I was thinking of the pieces I had surrendered to the Museum. Though I did not regret having given them away, I felt rather sad. I thought the others were probably in the same frame of mind as myself. It was true they had all been paid a purchase price, but they were not really in need of the money and it was a certainty that the price paid represented only a fraction of the market value of the items bought.

When we saw Chang Cheng-chung about to leave, we quietly laid down our chopsticks too. The moment Chang Cheng-chung disappeared out of the door with his entourage, we stood up to shake hands with the host at our table. Then we filed out to the lifts. Those at other tables behaved in exactly the same manner. It was only when we were on the street and about to mingle with the crowd, far from the aureole of officialdom, that we smiled at one another and said goodbye to those within earshot.

A week later, two Museum officials took me in an official car to the Shanghai Mansions, an apartment hotel for foreign visitors. In the penthouse apartment reserved for official use the ceremony of presenting me with the Certificate of Merit was to be held. In the spacious lobby, an attendant led me to a table on which were an ink slab with ink already prepared and several writing brushes. I signed my name in the brocade-covered guest book. While I was bending over the table to write my name with the writing brush, a cameraman took several photographs of me. The officials signed their names after mine. The attendant then threw open the double door leading to the reception room. Other officials of the Museum, including the Director, were introduced to me. I saw that my neighbours, Dr and Mrs Koo Kai-shih, had been invited to make up the party. Dr Koo was an eminent surgeon and his wife a gynaecologist at the No. 6 People's Hospital. He had given his family bronze collection to the Shanghai Museum.

After a little while, Vice-Mayor Chang Cheng-chung arrived. He sat down in the middle of the long sofa which had been left vacant for him. The attendant served us with green tea while we chatted about the weather and politely inquired after each other's health. When the preliminary polite exchanges were over, one of the junior officials of the Museum brought a framed Certificate of Merit and placed it on the coffee table in front of the Vice-Mayor. Chang made a short speech praising my patriotic act of presenting the Museum with pieces from my collection. Then he stood up, took the Certificate of Merit and held it out to me with both hands. I stood up to accept it and bowed to him. Then he presented me with a scroll and said it was a gift from the Shanghai Museum to show their appreciation of my donation. I accepted and bowed again.

The scroll was taken out of its brocade cover and unrolled. I saw it was a beautiful reproduction of the famous painting, *A Lady with Peony*, by the great Ming dynasty painter T'ang Ying. The original was one of Shanghai Museum's proudest possessions. The scroll is about two yards long and twenty-eight inches wide, so perfectly reproduced that it is the exact replica of the original. It now adorns the wall of my Washington D C condominium and is enjoyed by my friends.

When the presentation was over, Chang Cheng-chung sat down. I made a short speech expressing my pleasure in being able to add to the collection of the Museum. During the proceedings, the man with the camera took several pictures. These and the book containing the signatures of the guests at the presentation were later given to me as souvenirs of the occasion.

The attendant announced that lunch was served. Led by the Vice-Mayor, we went into the adjacent dining room and were seated around the table. A sumptuous meal, the most elaborate I had ever had in socialist China, was served to us, with three kinds of wine, fruit and dessert. The Vice-Mayor and everybody else were extremely polite and pleasant. During the meal, the Vice-Mayor told me that he himself had been incarcerated. When I expressed surprise and indignation, he said, 'You are surprised that an old Revolutionary like myself could be incarcerated by people who claim to be Revolutionaries? Politics is a very complicated thing, you know.'

Encouraged by the example of the Vice-Mayor, others also told me about their imprisonment. It soon transpired that among the ten people seated around the table, only three had escaped imprisonment.

'However, we are all rehabilitated now,' one of the officials declared.

Led by the Vice-Mayor, we all raised our glasses and toasted the Chinese Communist Party which had made our rehabilitation possible.

It seemed the People's Government in Shanghai wanted to put me in the right frame of mind. They could so easily have given me my Certificate of Merit without the envelope containing money when the others received theirs. They did not have to organize a separate ceremony and an elaborate party. I thought their giving me the same treatment usually reserved for foreign government visitors of senior rank was mainly because I had applied to go abroad. They wanted me to leave Shanghai with a good impression of the government after Mao. Even the Vice-Mayor's seemingly casual remark that he himself had suffered imprisonment was intended to make me look upon my own unfortunate experience in its proper perspective. He had tried to make me feel that by suffering imprisonment I had somehow joined the distinguished company of veteran revolutionaries and senior officials of the government.

Next morning, in a corner of the *Shanghai Liberation Daily's* four pages, a news item appeared stating that I had made a donation of porcelain to the Shanghai Museum. The newspaper report called it a patriotic act and added that I had not accepted monetary compensation. Since the *Shanghai Liberation Daily*, like all the other newspapers, was controlled by the government, which decided what was to appear on its pages, I felt that the Shanghai officials were continuing in their efforts to put me in a good mood.

With the publication of this item of news, I became an instant celebrity. My friends and neighbours, including the Party Secretary of my Residents' Committee, called to offer their congratulations and to examine the Certificate of Merit which they told me should be hung up on the wall. People who had avoided me now crossed the street to greet me. Lu Ying, who had criticized my clothes only a few years ago, now complimented me on my neat appearance and asked me where I had bought my clothes. It seemed I had come a long way from the days when I was a non-person suffering insults and persecution. Yet I had not changed one iota. It was the Party's policy that had changed.

When the furore of congratulations had died down, Comrade Ho, a representative of the Shanghai Federation of Women, came to invite me to join their study group for women intellectuals. I readily accepted her invitation because it meant I would no longer have to attend the rather dull sessions of the study group meetings of the Residents' Committee. I hoped the women I was to meet at the Federation of Women would be more interesting and congenial.

According to China's Constitution, women enjoyed equal rights with men. But in practice there was a great deal of discrimination. Although in the cities there was no difference in pay or benefits for women doing the same work as men, the great majority of women remained in specialized occupations that traditionally employed women such as textile workers, shop assistants, hospital nurses and schoolteachers. The Chinese traditional attitude of a woman's position being determined by the position of her husband was still upheld. The widow of Marshal Chu Te was the President of the National Federation of Women. Among its local presidents and vice-presidents were wives and widows of other senior veteran Party officials. However, the women who did the actual work of the Federation such as Comrade Ho were Party bureaucrats. Like other organizations in China, the Federation of Women was a government organization that supervised and organized women's activities.

'We are organizing two study groups,' Comrade Ho said. 'One group consists of female factory owners before Liberation and wives of prominent capitalists who used to have jobs in their husbands' factories. The other group consists of female intellectuals. In this group we also include wives of well-known scientists who have made a special contribution to socialism. After careful consideration, we have decided to put you in the latter group. We think you will find this group congenial.'

'I hope you will convey to the senior authorities of the Federation my appreciation of your invitation. I consider it an honour to be invited. And I look forward to coming to the study group meetings,' I told her politely.

'We are having a joint session of the two groups at an inaugural meeting next week on Wednesday at two in the afternoon. It's going to be at the premises of the Shanghai Political Consultative Conference on Peking Road West. We will be using their premises for our weekly meetings too, and they will invite all of us to their special events. There is also an "internal" shop and restaurant for the convenience of our members,' she added.

'I'll be there at two on Wednesday,' I promised her.

She took her leave and I accompanied her to the front gate. After I had closed the gate after Comrade Ho, I saw Mrs Chu coming out of her room to the garden.

'Was that Comrade Ho of the Federation of Women?' she asked me.

'Yes,' I said.

'Has she come to invite you to join their study group activities?'

'Yes. But how did you know?'

'I've also been invited. But I'm going only to the one on the district level. You are going to the one on the municipal level, I suppose?' she asked me.

'I've no idea what's the level of the one I'm going to,' I told her.

'If you are meeting at the Shanghai Political Consultative Conference premises on Peking Road West, then you are going to the one on the municipal level,' she said.

'Anyway, it's just another study group. It makes no difference on what level it is,' I told her.

'Oh, it makes a lot of difference. On the municipal level you will be invited to many things that are not open to those on the district level. What's more, you can use the "internal" shop and restaurant. You'll be able to get things not available to the general public, such as good cigarettes,' she told me.

I was about to enter my part of the house, when she added, 'The reason you are invited to the municipal level is that your donation to the nursery school programme was the second largest in the city.'

'You seem extremely well informed,' I said dryly.

'You are the subject of gossip in many circles. People are saying you make fine gestures in order to buy a passport to leave the country,' she said, watching my reaction.

'Do you mean to say that you know people who believe the People's Government is an agency for selling passports?' I asked her, trying to appear incredulous. Actually I was rather amused by what she was telling me. The Chinese people are extremely sharp and cynical. They believed fine gestures and noble behaviour are always motivated by selfish designs.

Rather frightened, Mrs Chu said hastily, 'Nobody is saying the People's Government would sell passports.'

'Good! In that case, there is no point in trying to buy one, is there?' I did not wait for her reply but went inside.

I thought Mrs Chu was jealous of me because in her view I had somehow got ahead of her.

The Political Consultative Conference was a United Front organization, a part of the campaign for national unity. The appointed delegates had no real voice in the affairs of state. In theory they were there to be 'consulted'; in practice they were there merely to add an affirmative voice to decisions already taken by the Party. The organization in Shanghai was housed in a large mansion that once was a part of the famous 'Chang Family Garden'. Other palatial mansions in Shanghai were often relics of the days of foreign domination. This particular house, however, enjoyed an aura of revolutionary mystery as it used to be the clandestine meeting place for prominent supporters of Sun Yat Sen before the revolution of 1911 which established the Chinese Republic. The large garden with its lake and many pavilions had long disappeared. Other buildings had been added and the mansion itself had been turned into an assembly hall on the ground floor and conference rooms upstairs. At the entrance to the lobby was the 'internal' shop and in a corner of the garden was the restaurant. Both establishments were non-profit-making organizations run by the State for the convenience of the delegates.

Since I left Shanghai, I have met many Europeans and Americans who thought Communist China was an egalitarian society. This simply is not true. The fact is the Communist Government controls goods, services and opportunities and dispenses them to the people in unequal proportions. The term 'internal' was used for goods and services available to officials of certain rank and a few outsiders on whom for one reason or another the government wished to bestow favour. I have heard the term 'internal internal' used to describe goods and services reserved for the very senior officials, especially in the military who seemed to get the first choice and a lion's share of everything. Though the salary of a member of the Politburo was no more than eight or ten times that of an industrial worker, the goods and services available to him and his family without charge was comparable to those enjoyed by kings and presidents of other lands. And the privileges were extended to their families, including their grandchildren even after their death.

The women of the study group of the Federation of Women were not really important in the eyes of the government. Our being given a little favour by the Shanghai Government was to accommodate the new political trend of national unity including the capitalist class and the 'open door' policy of the Four Modernizations. Nearly all of us had some ties with Chinese living abroad. The government was being kind to us in order to win the support of our relatives and to create an image of tolerance in western democracies. As far as those 'perks' were concerned, what I was to enjoy was a minimum; even so, I became the envy of my friends and relatives. And they did not hesitate to ask me to buy things for them at the shop or to bring special food home for them from the restaurant. Soon I was to discover that every member of our study group had the same problem. It was an embarrassment I was glad to leave behind when I finally departed from Shanghai.

Ah-yee was very proud that I had been invited to join the study group of the Federation of Women. She thought I had at last achieved the ultimate in respectability: not only received back into the ranks of the people but also raised by the government to a select group. On the day of the inaugural meeting, she served lunch to me early and hovered around me to make sure I put on clothes she approved of.

'I think the pale grey. You look so nice in that,' she suggested.

'Not the navy-blue?' I took the navy-blue trouser suit out of the cupboard.

'No, pale grey is better. Much younger looking. I wish you would dye your hair. You would look so much younger if you had black hair.'

I put the navy-blue suit back into the cupboard and took out the pale grey. She smiled with satisfaction and went into the kitchen. 'Tell me all about it tomorrow,' she said.

About seventy women, all middle-aged or older, were present at the inaugural meeting of the study groups. We sat in a large, clean conference room with high windows that admitted ample daylight and sunshine. We were served hot green tea in covered glasses. One of the Vice-Presidents of the Federation welcomed us and spoke to us about the Four Modernizations Programme which, she said, had been first proposed by the late Prime Minister Chou En-lai at the Tenth Party Congress and approved by the late Chairman Mao Tze-tung. Then she praised the Wise Leader Chairman Hua for smashing the Gang of Four and paving the way for the realization of the Four Modernizations Programme. Like all official speakers, she repeated the same ideas, almost in the same language, as those contained in Party resolutions and speeches by leaders in Peking.

After we had duly applauded the Vice-President, a woman in her early fifties, smartly dressed in a black trouser suit, was introduced as the next speaker who would tell us about her recent trip to the United States with her husband, a former capitalist. She apologized for being hoarse and explained that she had lost her voice from making many speeches since her return from abroad. The demand for her as a speaker was explained by the content of her speech. She not only described life in the United States as rather less than desirable with muggings, drugs, drunkenness and a costly medical service, but also told the audience that in spite of being offered a lucrative job in America, her husband had decided to come back to China to continue his work as chief engineer of the factory he had handed over to the State. Her husband's greatest ambition was to serve the Four Modernizations Programme and to do his part in the effort to make China strong, she said. When she had finished, we applauded heartily.

Obviously her speech was a political message the government wanted the people to hear, but I did not think its purpose was to malign the United States. The government was probably embarrassed by the sight of the long queue outside the American Consulate-General waiting to apply for visas. Her speech was useful to discourage would-be emigrants. In fact the newspaper had already published several stories of young people who had gone to the United States as immigrants only to find that they could not find jobs or be assimilated into American society. Disappointed, they returned to Shanghai. To their surprise and joy, they found their old jobs waiting for them and their Party Secretaries gave them a hero's welcome. The story invariably ended with the young people pledging to work hard for the Four Modernizations Programme.

For over a year I was a member of the study group organized by the Federation of Women. We studied the same documents and speeches the Party gave out to all study groups all over the country. We joined the delegates of the Political Consultative Conference to hear speeches given by prominent officials on subjects ranging from cultural affairs to international relations. And we made use of the shop and restaurant under a self-imposed restraint so that we did not appear too eager to take advantage of and abuse the privileges accorded to us.

There were thirty-two women in my study group; the average age was just below sixty. The leader of our study group was the seventy-year-old wife of a Vice-Mayor. Comrade Ho was one of two Party officials from the Federation to oversee our meetings, taking notes of the proceedings and ready to guide the discussion should it stray from its designed course. But the Vice-Mayor's old wife was an experienced chairman and the rest of us intelligent enough to know what was expected of us. Our study group activities went along smoothly, never causing Comrade Ho and the other young officials from the Federation a single moment of embarrassment or anxiety.

While I never once spoke at the study group meetings of the Residents' Committee, I had to say something every week at this study group meeting. The youngest member of our group, a writer of fifty years of age, was called upon to read the government document we were to discuss. Then it was up to us, seated around a large conference table, to respond. To be over-eager to speak was considered just as uncouth as a refusal to talk. If one spoke first, one might say the wrong thing; if one spoke last one might find that all the right remarks had been said already.

The reading of the document was generally followed by a few minutes of silence when we gazed at the pad in front of each of us as if seriously considering what we had just heard. Then our chairman, the Vice-Mayor's wife, would add a few words to give us the necessary hints to guide our discussion. After another moment of silence, one of the bolder ladies would take a sip of tea and raise her head to speak. Others followed. Gradually everybody would have added something. I generally tried to get my banal remarks into the middle of the discussion, but sometimes I did not succeed. Then I would hope I would be overlooked and get away with just listening. However, either Comrade Ho or the other Federation official would always ask me, 'What do you think?' and I would have to make a contribution. To speak at the study group was an art. Obviously one could not afford to be original and there were only a limited number of ways of saying the same thing over and over again. We generally chose to be boring rather than to be different.

As I got to know Comrade Ho better and found her free from the class prejudice that inhibited relationships between Party officials and people like myself, I tried to enlist her help to get Meiping's murderer brought to justice. She was extremely sympathetic and introduced me to a female official from the newly re-established United Front Organization of the Shanghai Party Secretariat. Comrade Ho brought the official, Comrade Ma, to my apartment to see me one evening.

After I had told the whole story, Comrade Ma promised to discuss the matter with her superiors. A few days later, she came again with Comrade Ho.

'I've been instructed to inform you that your daughter's case will be dealt with in due course. There are many cases of mysterious death in Shanghai and many families are appealing to the government for clarification. For instance, the former director of our department was supposed to have committed suicide. Now his family has raised doubts and provided evidence to show he was probably murdered. Cases like that, which happened so many years ago, are very difficult to clarify. Even when you can prove death was not caused by suicide, you still have to locate the person or persons responsible. Who is going to point an accusing finger at another man who might be working in the same organization? And even when someone is ready to step out and denounce someone else, can we really believe him?'

'It does seem difficult,' I conceded. 'But I believe it isn't impossible to find the culprit if the government is determined to do so.'

'You must trust the Party and the government. In the not too distant future, there will be an official verdict on the Cultural Revolution. After that, our work to clarify all residue problems will become easier,' Comrade Ma told me. From what she said I understood that since the Cultural Revolution had not yet been officially repudiated, the Revolutionaries who had committed the crimes could not be denounced, because they committed the crimes in the name of the Cultural Revolution. What Comrade Ma did not say but everybody in Shanghai knew was that many Revolutionaries had joined the Party in the meantime and become officials. It is much harder to confront a Party official than an ordinary person.

The two ladies took their leave and I accompanied them to the front gate. I thanked Comrade Ma for coming and promised her that I would wait patiently.

I did not see Mrs Chu standing in the dark on her terrace. After I had closed the front gate, she stepped off the terrace and came towards me. 'Were you talking about your daughter?' she asked me.

'Yes, as a matter of fact, we were talking about her,' I said.

Since I had been bringing Mrs Chu special cigarettes from the 'internal' shop at the Political Consultative Conference, our relationship had become more cordial.

'Well, my son told me that the man responsible for her death has been taken into custody. It seems he was involved in several other deaths too.'

'How did your son know about it?'

'It seems his friends in the militia told him.'

I was surprised by what she told me and wanted to verify its authenticity so I requested her to ask her son to come up to see me.

He came up later in the evening. But he refused to talk to me about Meiping's murderer and flatly denied having told his mother anything about the case. 'My mother made a mistake. She got things mixed up,' he said.

I did not give much credence to what Mrs Chu had told me, brushing it aside as mere gossip, for I thought if the man were in custody the Security Bureau would have informed me, and Comrade

Ma should have known. In fact, Mrs Chu's son had been correctly informed. A week after I left Shanghai, a public trial of the man was held at the Cultural Square attended by members of the families of his other five victims. *Ta Kung Pao*, the left-wing newspaper in Hong Kong, reported the trial and stated that the man was sentenced to death but the sentence was suspended for two years.

One morning in Hong Kong I opened the newspaper and there glaring at me was this news item, with my daughter's name listed as one of the victims. When the initial shock subsided, I realized that the Security Bureau had deliberately waited for me to get out of the country before holding the trial because they did not want me to be present. The Cultural Square had seating for over a thousand people and representatives from every walk of life were normally invited to attend such trials. Members of the families of the victims would occupy the front row of seats and would be invited to express agreement to the verdict reached and sentence pronounced. China had not abolished the death penalty. According to Chinese law, a confessed murderer should suffer immediate execution after sentencing. The officials at the Security Bureau knew very well a suspended death sentence would not be acceptable to me. In every petition I had sent to the Bureau I had stated as much. They had waited until I was out of the way to hold the trial so that I could not be there to protest against the verdict. Meiping's murderer lives in China today, for a suspended death sentence meant that he could go free after two years.

The year 1979 was an important one for Deng Hsiao-ping and for Communist China. The adoption by the plenary session of the Central Committee held in December 1978 of Deng's favourite Marxist adage that 'practice was the only criterion for determining truth' opened the way for his plan to reform and restructure China's economy. His visit to the United States and the warm reception he received there established him as a leader of world stature. And the war 'to punish Vietnam' for her border incursions rallied Party members and the general public around the Party with a surge of patriotism. It also helped to convince most of the military leaders, hitherto steeped in Mao Tze-tung's concept of People's War, of the need to modernize China's armed forces. Deng's position was further strengthened by the ousting from the Party leadership of four of Hua Kuo-feng's supporters. Although, for the moment, Hua Kuo-feng remained the Chairman of the Central Committee of the Party and the Prime Minister, he had become an isolated figurehead with power slipping out of his grip.

One of the measures of economic reform undertaken by Deng

Hsiao-ping was to open China's doors to foreign firms. British Petroleum was the first oil company to open an office in Shanghai. Then I read in the *Shanghai Liberation Daily* that other oil companies, including Shell International Petroleum, had been invited to take part in off-shore exploration. I became more hopeful that I would be given my passport in the not too distant future. In fact, I was so confident that I stopped giving English lessons. But it was another nine months before I could leave Shanghai.

When it was Chinese New Year again, in February 1980, I decided to have a big celebration for what might be my last Chinese New Year in Shanghai. I invited my students, the young people who had helped me and their children, to eat 'foreign food' and watch fireworks with me. Ah-yee and I made pork hamburgers and cream of tomato soup for over thirty people. For dessert I ordered three enormous cakes topped with fresh cream from a former White Russian bakery now State-owned but still producing the same cakes and pastry. My guests were jammed into my aparment. My bed had to be dismantled to make room and we all sat on the floor to eat our supper. Then we took the large collection of fireworks I had bought into the garden, where for two hours my guests, especially the children, had a wonderful time letting off the noisy fire-crackers and illuminating the night sky with brilliant bursts of colourful stars and sprays. My neighbours opened their windows and leaned on their balconies to watch and share the fun. The entire Chu family also came out to watch. But I thought there must have been complaints too, for when I met Lao Li on the street a couple of days later, my policeman asked me, 'What was this great noise you were making the other night?'

'Only fireworks to celebrate the Chinese New Year,' I told him.

'Was it necessary to have so much of it?'

'Oh, it was a double celebration in fact. We were also celebrating our victory in Vietnam.'

I was with one of my young friends when I met Lao Li. After we had left the policeman, she said to me, 'Have you heard what people are saying about the war in Vietnam?'

'No, what are they saying?'

'They are saying that Deng Hsiao-ping ordered the attack on Vietnam to avenge the defeat of the Americans. It was all arranged quietly between him and the American President Carter when he was in the United States,' she told me in low whispers.

'That sounds like something put out by the remnants of the Gang of Four. Don't believe it and don't talk about it,' I told her. Actually from that time on until the present day, Deng Hsiao-ping has been plagued by such rumours circulated by opponents of his policy in the Party.

My young friend said, 'Yes, you are right. Shanghai is still full of followers of the Gang of Four. But the people are with Deng Hsiao-ping. Have you seen the historical film *Jia Wu Naval Battle?*'

'No, what about it?'

'Well, when the naval commander by the name of Deng appears on the screen, the audience cheers and claps. That's the people's subtle way to say they like what Deng Hsiao-ping is doing,' she said.

I was greatly intrigued by what my young friend had told me and went to the local cinema to see the film for myself a few days later. It was indeed just as she had said. The audience broke out in loud cheers when the naval commander appeared on the screen and was addressed by his subordinate officer as 'Your Excellency Deng'.

Before the Chinese New Year, I had received a large gold-embossed invitation card from the Shanghai Revolutionary Committee, the Maoist name for the Municipal Government, to a Chinese New Year Celebration at the Shanghai Exhibition Hall, the Sino-Soviet Friendship building back in the heyday of China's cooperation and friendship with her northern neighbour. The card admitted two persons so I asked my young friend to accompany me. Since it was a fine day and buses were usually overcrowded during the Chinese New Year holiday period, we walked there in spite of the sub-zero temperature.

When we approached the Exhibition Hall, cars were enveloping us in clouds of dust as they sped past us and we saw that the parking space outside the Hall was full of chauffeur-driven cars. However, masses of other guests were on foot like us. It seemed everybody in Shanghai who was considered somebody during that period of time was invited. I presumed I was on the list submitted by the Federation of Women, since in the crowd I saw several other members of my study group.

We showed our invitation card at the door and were allowed to walk in. The place was terribly hot, with central heating at full blast, the more unbearable because we had no heating at home and were not used to it. The hot air hit us like a tidal wave and perspiration broke out on my forehead. We shed our padded jackets and sweaters as well as our top coats quickly and added them to the mountain of similiar garments discarded by others before us. My young friend was impatient to get to the 'internal' shop at the Exhibition Hall which was well known to the Shanghai public but inaccessible. She told me that she had boasted to her friends and neighbours that she was coming with me to the party; consequently they had all asked her to utilize the opportunity to acquire for them commodities they had long hoped to acquire but had been unable to obtain in the ordinary shops.

I told her that since we had come for the celebration, we should at least make a show of taking part in some of the planned activities before going to the shop. Meekly but impatiently, she followed me through the halls where games were being played, the theatre where artists were performing and the cafeteria where refreshments were being served. Then , because of the crowd everywhere, we were able to slip away and make our way in haste to the shop without attracting too much attention.

Much to my young friend's disappointment, when we got there we found not only that a large crowd had preceded us but also that the staff was regulating admission into the shop. We had to join the queue and wait. When we finally got in, half of the things she wanted were sold out. However, we still managed to buy several thousand yuan-worth of things, from cashmere coat material to steel saucepans. We each had four carrier bags weighed down with her purchases, so that we barely managed to stagger to the front entrance to claim our coats and jackets. We tried to get a taxi without success and there were no pedicabs. Then my young friend telephoned home to enlist the help of her two younger brothers who were asked to come on their bicycles. As we stood in the icy air outside the Exhibition Hall waiting for her brothers, others similarly laden joined us. Those driving away in chauffeur-driven cars could afford to depart in a dignified manner without the encumbrance of parcels because they had their own 'internal' source of supply.

Soon after the holiday, almost overnight, temporary housing sprang up on both sides of the pavement on our street. These were no more than makeshift shacks made of old timber, bamboo poles and broken pieces of brick, built against the walls of the existing houses and gardens. The trees on the pavement were enclosed in the structures or used as poles. Soon the leaves dropped and the trees died. Each shack was allocated to one family of several people. There were no washing facilities and no toilets. The Residents' Committee at first told us to keep our front gate open so that our garden taps would be accessible to the people outside. But after several households reported loss of personal property, taps were installed at each end of the street. A young woman sanitation worker came each morning to collect the night soil from buckets in each shack. The odour this operation created was overpowering.

Mrs Chu told me that the decision to house the people on our particular street was made by an official promoted to the District Government during the Cultural Revolution. The female official had said that she had selected our street to house the displaced people because our street was too full of former class enemies and capitalists, too clean and too quiet. To put a large number of proletariat in our midst would be 'good' for us. I was astonished to hear this and asked Mrs Chu why the other officials did not oppose her. Mrs Chu said, 'Nobody wants to offend the former Revolutionaries promoted to official positions. They are afraid things will change back again.'

We had a shack on each side of our front gate. At first, there was enough space left for us to come in and out. But as time went on, much of the space was gradually taken up by the people living in the shacks for storage of their odds and ends. These were covered with old plastic sheets and smelly straw mats to protect them from the weather. Our passage was reduced to a very narrow lane of no more than two feet in width. Boys urinated against our gate and laundry dripped from a line across our entrance. From morning till night, incessant human voices were mixed with the noise of several radio sets tuned to different stations. Our 'too quiet and too clean' street was certainly no longer quiet and far from being clean. It was impossible to use the garden or sit on the balcony. But it was almost with tacit understanding that the Chus and I put up with the inconveniences without complaint. We were very conscious that the spirit of 'class struggle' still lurked, and the Party officials, steeped in Mao's philosophy, could not change easily. Their old working habits had already become second nature to many of them. They simply did not know any other way to discharge their responsibilities. Besides, without the Party leadership taking the bold step of totally repudiating Mao's philosophy, the diehard believers in Maoism could not be removed from office and new blood brought in. These disgruntled Party officials would inevitably make use of every available opportunity to assert their Maoist point of view and to sabotage Deng Hsiao-ping's new policy which they regarded as a betrayal of socialism and Mao Tze-tung Thought. To this day, even though Deng Hsiao-ping's power has increased significantly as compared to 1980, the problem of the recalcitrant Party officials remains the most thorny he has to face. On the other hand, as long as this problem is not resolved, the situation in China will remain subject to sudden change when Deng Hsiao-ping departs from the scene.

The Chus and I knew that although we were rehabilitated, our position in Chinese society was by no means secure. Therefore, we put up with our new neighbours and even extended all possible help to them to make their life more tolerable. We allowed them to store food in our refrigerators and lent them our mops and brooms. We were only too thankful that the female Revolutionary Party official had not ordered the shacks to be erected right inside the garden. If she had, there was simply nothing we could have done to stop it.

Perhaps other residents living on our street who were not former class enemies or capitalists were not so restrained. Lu Ying called on Mrs Chu and me to have a chat and the Residents' Committee officially informed everybody that a new apartment building was being built for the displaced persons. When that was completed, the people would be moved back and our street would be restored to its old shape and condition again.

Since 1978 I had seen several visitors from abroad including my sister Helen and her husband. As the news that I had survived the Cultural Revolution spread among my friends in Europe and North America, I began to receive letters from them. In July 1980, I received a letter from an old friend, Sir John Addis, telling me that he was coming to China and would be in Shanghai in August. He asked me if I could see him. Sir John Addis was a Sinologist with a deep understanding and appreciation of Chinese culture. My husband and I had known him since the forties. When he was serving at the British Chargé d'Affaires Office in Peking in the fifties, he was a frequent guest in our house. During the years he served as British Ambassador to Laos and the Philippines, we had kept in touch and in 1965, when he came to China on holiday, he came to Shanghai to see me. He was a knowledgeable collector of Chinese porcelain. His collection had been given to the British Museum. I was always interested in hearing his opinion of the pieces I had acquired.

In 1972, while I was in prison, I read about his appointment as the first British Ambassador to Peking. When I was released in 1973, the political situation was such that I could not get in touch with him. Then, in 1974, again from the newspaper, I learned he had left Peking to retire. I certainly would like to see him again; on the other hand, I did not want to do anything that might be misunderstood by the government and so prejudice my chance of getting my passport. I decided to seek the advice of my policeman, Lao Li, before replying to John's letter.

I went to the police station and asked to see Lao Li. When he came out of the inner room and sat down across the table from me, I said, 'I've received a letter from a former British Ambassador to Peking.

He's an old friend. He's coming to Shanghai. In the letter he asks if he may come to see me,' I took the letter out and translated it verbatim into Chinese for Lao Li.

Lao Li listened to my translation but said nothing. I asked him, 'Do you think I ought to see him?'

'That's entirely up to you. It's your private business,' said Lao Li.

'Perhaps I should not see him?' I asked him again.

'Wouldn't he think it rather strange if you refuse to see him?' Lao Li said.

'Do you mean to say you think I ought to see him?' I said, trying, of course, to find out what he really meant.

'I didn't say anything like that. It's entirely your own private business whether you see him or not,' he said rather impatiently.

'I need advice from the government. Sir John Addis was an ambassador, not a schoolteacher or someone like that. He's a political person,' I told Lao Li.

'I can't give you advice on your private life,' Lao Li said.

'All right, in that case, I'll write to him to tell him I can't see him,' I said.

'Did I tell you not to see him?'

'Perhaps I should see him?'

'It's entirely your own private business,' Lao Li said again.

It suddenly dawned on me that I was putting Lao Li into a very awkward position by requesting him to give me advice. I sensed that he was in favour of my seeing Sir John but did not want to be held responsible for saying so outright. I said, 'All right, I'll write and tell him I'll see him.'

Lao Li smiled and said, 'It's entirely your own decision.'

'Do you think I should invite him to dinner?' I asked him.

'Can your Ah-yee cook a dinner suitable for an ambassador? Besides, what about those shacks outside your door? He has been to your home before the Cultural Revolution. What would he think of your living conditions now?' Lao Li became quite animated when he was giving me advice freely.

'All right, I'll take him to a restaurant. Thanks for the advice.' I got up from the bench to leave.

Lao Li stood up also. 'I didn't give you any advice,' he said. 'It's entirely your private business.'

'Anyway, thanks for listening to me. I'll come to tell you when Sir John comes in August,' I said and went home to answer John's letter.

On a hot summer's day in late July, I received a printed letter with my name filled in from the Public Security Bureau, calling me for an interview at the office where I had applied for my passport. When I got there, I found only one other person in the waiting room, a young man. He was obviously agitated, pacing among the benches, brushing past one and knocking against another. When he saw me, he said, 'Have you come for an interview about your passport application?'

I nodded and sat down on a bench. He stood towering over me and said nervously, 'Do you think you will get it or do you think you will be rejected?'

'I'll soon know, I suppose,' I said.

'Can one apply again if one gets rejected?' he asked me.

'Please sit down and wait quietly. I don't know whether one can apply again or not. You can ask when it's your turn to go in,' I told him.

He sat down but fixed his eyes on the door to the inner room. When it opened, he jumped up. But I was called. Obviously he had come much ahead of his appointed time.

After I had closed the door and sat down, I laid the printed form I had received on the desk. The official said to me, 'You have applied for a passport to go to the United States?'

'Yes.'

'What is the purpose of your trip?' he asked.

'To visit my sisters for family reunion,' I said.

'Do you intend to visit other countries?'

'Yes, on my way there, I shall visit friends in Canada and Europe,' I answered.

'Do you know many people abroad?'

'A few friends here and there.'

He pulled open a drawer and took out the passport I had been waiting for and said, 'Your application has been approved. Here is your passport. The People's Government wishes to facilitate family reunion. You may go to see your sisters in the United States. And you may go to visit your friends elsewhere. When you see them, encourage them to come and visit China. Tell them about the new conditions here and how we are building socialism. Tell those in Taiwan to come back and visit. They will be allowed to come and go freely.'

'I don't know anyone in Taiwan,' I said.

'Then tell your friends in Hong Kong to come and invest in joint ventures here. Encourage everybody to come and visit,' he said.

I nodded and picked up the passport, glancing at the photograph to make sure the man had not made a mistake.

'When you arrive in the United States, report to our Embassy and get registered,' the man told me.

'My sisters live in California. The Embassy is not there,' I told him.

'Is there no Chinese office where you are going?' He seemed not to believe me.

'No, my sisters live in the country,' I said and left the room.

In his eagerness to come into the inner office, the young man collided with me in the doorway and nearly knocked me over.

My next job was to get a visa from the United States Consulate-General. To avoid having to join the queue outside its gate at an early hour of the morning, I paid a call to the local Chartered Bank manager, a Britisher interested in birdwatching. To take the initiative to see a foreign resident was a bold move not lightly undertaken by a Chinese not working for a foreign firm. It was after many days of consideration that I ventured to the bank's office on Yuan Ming Yuan Road. My late husband and I had banked with the Chartered Bank since the early forties but we had dealt with their branches in Hong Kong and London. Nevertheless, we were not unknown to the succession of managers who had come to Shanghai. Before the Cultural Revolution, they had been guests at our home. The young British manager received me with surprise and welcome and told me that the bank's officials in Hong Kong and London had been told by someone that I had died during the Cultural Revolution. He also told me that my death had been recorded by the American correspondent Stanley Karnow in his book *Mao and China*, and by my former Yenching schoolmate Han Su-yin in one of her autobiographies.

I asked him to inform the bank in Hong Kong immediately that I was alive and well. And I requested him to make an appointment for me with someone at the American Consulate. He told me that he lived in the same apartment building set aside for foreign residents by the Chinese Government as several American officers of the Consulate and would be glad to speak to them about my case.

Two days later I called at the American Consulate-General and was given a visa.

When Sir John Addis arrived in Shanghai early in August, I was able to tell him that I would definitely leave China in the autumn. We sat on two easy chairs in the middle of the large empty hotel lobby in full view of the man behind the desk at one end of the room. Although he was really too far away to listen in to our conversation, I did not dwell on my imprisonment and my daughter's death; rather I talked to him mainly about my rehabilitation and the memorial meeting for Meiping. When I told him that my collection of porcelain had been returned and I had donated fifteen pieces to the Shanghai Museum, he asked me if he might come to my apartment to see the pieces I had left. Because the official banquet for him next day was to take place at noon, I invited him to dinner at the East Wind Restaurant, formerly the Shanghai Club, a famous British institution with the so-called 'longest bar in the Orient'. I said, 'I will see whether I can arrange for you to come to my apartment after we have had dinner.'

'I would like to see how you have been living during the last few years,' John said.

When I told Lao Li that Sir John had arrived and that I had seen him, Lao Li asked me, 'Did you tell him everything that had happened to you and your daughter?'

'He knows all about the Cultural Revolution already. He was stationed in Peking himself so I wouldn't think it was a surprise to him to learn what had happened to us,' I told him.

'Still, it's somebody he knows personally,' Lao Li said.

'He has many Chinese friends, including Party officials, I believe. I think he knows China very well indeed.'

'Is he friendly to China?'

'Oh, yes, he is most friendly to China. Would he be invited back now if he weren't?'

Lao Li visibly relaxed. To him, the Chinese Government's acceptance of Sir John as a friend made a great deal of difference.

'I've invited him to a dinner party at the East Wind Restaurant this evening. I've also invited the Chartered Bank manager and two Chinese friends to make up a party. Is that all right?' I asked him.

'Sure, sure, there must be a few other guests to show him due respect. He was an ambassador,' said Lao Li.

'I'm afraid he wants to come and see my porcelain after dinner. What shall I say to him?'

Poor Lao Li was taken aback. 'Oh ...' he wrinkled his brows, stroked his chin and looked thoughtful. I knew he was thinking about those shacks.

'You know Sir John was stationed in Nanking and Peking for many years. He must have seen worse sights than those shacks outside my door,' I reminded him.

'Yes, yes, you are right. In any case, you can't very well refuse to let a friend come to your home. Bring him after dinner. What time would you be coming?' Lao Li asked me.

'Maybe nine o'clock, or a little later,' I told him.

When I brought John and the Chartered Bank manager to my apartment by taxi that night, I found the entire street cleared of people. No laundry was hanging outside the shacks and there was no sound of radio broadcasts. The things that blocked our entrance had all been removed and the pavement had been swept clean. When John stood on my balcony to look down at my garden, he commented on how peaceful and quiet the place was and said, 'Your living conditions are much better than I had imagined.' I didn't tell him that Lao Li had probably given orders for the shack people to be indoors and to keep quiet for his benefit.

I have recorded John's visit here mainly because I think Lao Li's behaviour rather interesting. While he controlled my life, he did not want to appear to do so. It was up to me to anticipate his wishes and act accordingly. All Chinese Party officials behave in exactly the same manner towards the people. But of course not all of them are so touchingly human as my policeman who was basically a very kind individual.

After obtaining visas from the different embassies of the countries I wanted to visit during my trip, I rented a house for two weeks on Mokanshan, near Hangchow, from the Shanghai Travel Service and went up the mountain for a retreat. In spite of all that had happened, I was sad to leave China never to return. All Chinese have this feeling of attachment to our native country. No matter how far we travel or how long we are absent, eventually we want to return to die in China. 'The fallen leaves return to the root', we call it. But I had decided already that I would never come back. I would die elsewhere, in some country that would accept me. Now that my departure was imminent, I felt terribly sad. I wanted to sort out the conflicting emotions in my mind through prayers and self-examination before embarking on a new chapter of my life.

When I returned to Shanghai, a farewell tea party was arranged for me by my Federation of Women study group. After our leader announced to the group that I was about to go abroad to visit my sisters, I made a short speech, thanking the Federation of Women for giving me the opportunity of joining such a distinguished group of ladies for my political studies. I praised their intelligence, their patriotism and the high degree of their socialist consciousness and told them that I had greatly benefited from their example. Several other ladies spoke politely too and urged me to tell my relatives and friends abroad about the new situation in China and to encourage them to come and visit. Comrade Ho informed everybody that I had booked a passage to Hong Kong on a steamer of the newly opened shipping line linking Shanghai and Hong Kong and she invited a few ladies from our group to join her to see me off.

On 20 September 1980, I left Shanghai. Because private individuals without official passes were barred from the waterfront, only Comrade Ho and the five ladies from the study group came to see me off in their capacity as representatives of the Federation of Women. They picked me up in a small bus recently imported from Japan. There were very strict rules governing the amount of luggage and money a traveller could take out of the country; I had only one suitcase and one grip. In my handbag was 20 US dollars' worth of Hong Kong dollars, obtained through the Foreign Exchange Department of the Bank of China. My Chinese bank account and everything else, I had to leave behind.

A light rain was falling by the time we reached the wharf. In spite of Comrade Ho's official pass, the ladies were not allowed to go into the waiting room for the passengers. I said goodbye to them in the rain and they returned to the bus. They wished me a pleasant trip and a happy reunion with my sisters, but none of them mentioned anything about my coming back. I think they knew that I was unlikely to return to the city which held for me such tragic memories.

After a long wait, the customs office opened and the passengers filed in. My suitcase and grip were thoroughly searched by two customs officials. They also looked into my handbag and counted the Hong Kong dollar bank notes. When it was done, I followed the others into a bus which took us to the ship anchored some distance downstream.

When the bus stopped alongside the ship, the light rain had become a heavy downpour, accompanied by thunder and lightning. I had neither a raincoat nor an umbrella. Hastily I staggered up the slippery gangway with my luggage dripping with rainwater. The ship was an old steamer of British origin bought by the Chinese Government and refitted for the Hong Kong–Shanghai run. My first-class single cabin had a small shower. I warmed myself with a shower and put on dry clothes. Then I went on deck to have a last look at Shanghai.

The ship had lifted anchor and was sailing upstream in order to turn round. Through the misty curtain of rain, I caught a glimpse of the Shell building and the window of my old office. Already the past was assuming an unreal dreamlike quality. The ship was gathering speed, sailing down the remaining stretch of the Huang-pu River. When we reached the Yangtze Estuary, the storm was over and rays of sunshine were filtering through the thinning cloud.

Many times in my life I had sailed from Shanghai to go abroad, standing just as I did now on the deck of a ship, with the wind whipping my hair while I watched the coastline of China receding. Never had I felt so sad as I did at that moment. It was I who had brought Meiping back from Hong Kong in April 1949, in response to my husband's request. The shocking tragedy of her death, I believed, was a direct consequence of our fatal decision to stay in our own country at that crucial moment of history. Therefore I felt guilty for being the one who was alive. I wished it was Meiping standing on the deck of this ship, going away to make a new life for herself. After all, it was the law of nature that the old should die first and the young should live on, not the other way round. Also I felt sad because I was leaving for ever the country of my birth. It was a break so final that it was shattering. God knows how hard I had tried to remain true to my country. But I had failed utterly through no fault of my own.

Epilogue

MY REINTRODUCTION TO THE Western way of life took place on a jumbo jet when I travelled across the Pacific on a first-class ticket: a gift from Shell, my former employer.

It was early afternoon in Hong Kong when I boarded the plane. After we took off, an attractive air hostess with shining blond hair bent over me and asked, 'Will you have a bloody Mary or a screw driver?'

I must have looked puzzled for the young man standing behind her said, 'Perhaps you would rather have champagne?'

It was then I realized that bloody Mary was merely a drink and a screw driver in this case was not for putting in or loosening nails.

As I stammered a polite refusal, the smiling air hostess handed me a glass of plain orange juice.

I spent nearly a year visiting friends and relatives and trying to find somewhere to live. Canada was the first country to offer me a home. For two years, I lived in Ottawa, its beautiful capital. But the northern climate of long winters and strong winds proved to be severe for my arthritic limbs. In 1983, I moved south to Washington, DC, where the climate is rather like Shanghai. I bought a condominium and settled down. While I adjusted to my new life of freeway driving, supermarket shopping and mechanical banking, I worked on my manuscript.

In Washington, I am free to do whatever I like with each day. I can travel anywhere without having to ask anyone for permission. Goods and services in abundance are available to me. Back doors in America lead only into people's kitchens. When I am with others, I can speak candidly on any subject without having to consider whether my remarks are ideologically correct or to worry that someone might misinterpret what I have said. I have not found the equivalent of either Lu Ying of my Residents' Committee in Shanghai or Lao Li, the policeman, in my new existence. In this atmosphere of freedom and relaxation, I feel a lightening of spirit. What I enjoy more than anything else is the wealth of information available in the form of books, magazine articles and newspaper reports on matters of interest to me and the activities which bring me into the company of others of similar inclinations. I live a full and busy life. Only sometimes, I feel a haunting sadness. At dusk, when the day is fading away and the level of my physical energy is at a low ebb, I may find myself depressed and nostalgic. But next morning I invariably wake up with renewed optimism to welcome the day as another opportunity given me by God for enlightenment and experience.

Writing about the death of my daughter and my own painful experience during the Cultural Revolution was traumatic. Often I had to put the manuscript away and take up other occupations to regain my peace of mind. But I persisted in my effort. I felt a compulsion to speak out and let those who have the good fortune to live in freedom know what my life was like in Communist China. And my many friends in England, Switzerland, France, Australia, Canada and here in the United States encouraged me. I owe a special debt of gratitude to Peggy Durdin, a retired journalist and a dear friend of forty-five years. It was Peggy who first suggested that I put my experience down on paper when I visited her and her husband Tillman in their beautiful home full of oriental treasures in La Jolla, California, in the winter of 1980. And throughout the time I worked on my manuscript, she gave me useful advice and urged me on.

The expiration date of my Chinese passport has passed. I did not have my passport renewed. The United States Immigration and Naturalization Service has issued me with a document to enable me to travel abroad. I hope in due course to become a citizen of this great nation of open spaces and warm-hearted people where I have found a new life. The United States of America is the right place for me. Here are Jewish survivors of the Holocaust, dissidents of repressive regimes who had been imprisoned, the boat people from Vietnam and political refugees from tyranny. Among people like these, I do not feel alone. And I know that if God has a special place in Heaven for victims of persecution, my daughter Meiping is not alone either.

While I have decided to become a citizen of the United States, I continue to be concerned with the situation in China. I am interested in the future of the country of my birth and the fortunes of the Chinese people. Eagerly I read the newspapers and periodicals I receive from China and Hong Kong and I search the columns of American newspapers for dispatches from their China correspondents. I have friends and neighbours collecting clippings from out-of-town newspapers for me. Also, I study carefully the published official documents my friends in Shanghai send me. In December 1984 I made the long journey to Hong Kong to meet relatives who had been allowed to come out for a short visit.

I am heartened by the news from China and rejoice that

unprecedented economic progress has been made since the implementation of the new economic policy. Often I look back on the wasted years of the Mao Tze-tung era and the madness of the Cultural Revolution. I feel deeply saddened that so many lives were needlessly sacrificed. I was glad when the Cultural Revolution was officially declared a national catastrophe but I regret the Communist Party leadership's inability or unwillingness to repudiate Mao's policy in explicit terms.

From the point of view of the Chinese Communist Party, the greatest damage incurred by the Proletarian Cultural Revolution was the loss of the Party's prestige and its ability to govern. When Mao Tze-tung used the masses (the Red Guards and the Revolutionaries) to destroy his opponents in the Party leadership, he allowed the Chinese people to witness and to take part in an ugly drama of power struggle between himself and the so-called capitalist-roaders. The prolonged struggle and the denunciations of one leader after another enabled the Chinese people to stumble on the truth that the emperor had no clothes. When Mao Tze-tung died in 1976, the country was in a state of political disintegration. Obviously if the Party were to continue to govern, it must change course.

To the impoverished and disillusioned Chinese people, the promise of Communist paradise in some distant future has become meaningless, and the time-worn revolutionary slogans seem to be vapid rather than inspiring. To rally the people and re-awaken their enthusiasm, the Party now appeals to their patriotism. They are told to work for the modernization of China so that the country can regain her historical greatness and take her rightful place in the world. As reward, the Party promises the people an improved standard of living and no more political upheavals.

More than five years have passed since Deng Hsiao-ping gathered the supreme power to rule China into his own hands and became the custodian of the fate of a quarter of the earth's population. His new economic policy of 'open door to the outside world and invigorating the economy internally' has been generally successful. Businessmen and tourists from abroad pour into China in a steady stream. Foreign investment in joint ventures has reached several billion US dollars. In most parts of rural China, where over 70 per cent of the people live, the standard of living has improved. Agricultural production has increased dramatically. A small number of hardworking and re-sourceful people have become rich by Chinese standards. Since 1984, reform measures are being implemented in the cities. Party officials claim that in another three years' time a new economic structure will emerge. It would include joint ventures with foreign investment and technology and Chinese labour, State-owned industries relying more on market forces than on rigid planning from Peking and small-scale private enterprises mainly in the service sector such as restaurants and tailors' shops. The new system is what Deng Hsiao-ping and his team proudly call 'socialism in Chinese style'.

The implementation of Deng Hsiao-ping's reforms has not been without opposition. The old guard who had spent their lifetime in the Party viewed Deng's policy as a betrayal of Marxist principles and the Communist Revolution. Others opposed him because the reform measures threatened their position and privileges. At times, the attempts to undermine Deng's efforts went beyond mere criticism. It was in this uncertain climate that Deng Hsiao-ping went on tenaciously to achieve his goal. At the same time, he went about removing the source of serious opposition while he consolidated his power.

Since the Twelfth Party Congress held in September 1982, he has successfully persuaded a million middle-ranking Party officials to retire on attractive terms. And through rectification campaigns within the Party he weeded out the most stubborn of the recalcitrant officials at the base level. Since the beginning of 1985, he has changed the leadership of several ministries of the State Council and appointed younger men as governors and Party Secretaries in twenty-six of the twenty-nine provinces and autonomous regions. In August 1985, he even achieved the difficult task of restructuring the military command and removed from active service the generals who were among the most severe of his critics. During a series of meetings of the Party Congress and Central Committee in September 1985, he brought about the 'voluntary' retirement of aged Party leaders in the top echelon of power and promoted younger Party officials loyal to his reform policy to take their places.

However, though the voices of the pro-Maoist leaders are muted, Deng Hsiao-ping and his team now face criticism from another quarter. These men differ from the pro-Maoists in the fact that they support the idea of economic reform and do not wish to topple Deng Hsiao-ping. But they are alarmed by the numerous problems the reform measures have created. They think China's door has been opened too wide and the relaxation of central planning and control has gone too far. These men would like to see China admitting foreign capital, technical know-how and equipment without admitting Western ideas and customs. They are especially afraid of the influence

EPILOGUE

of such concepts as democracy and sexual freedom which they fear will
threaten the monolithic rule of the Party and undermine the moral
standards of Chinese society. Since these men constitute a formidable
section of the Party hierarchy and are headed by Chen Yun, a member
of the Standing Committee of the Politburo and a veteran Party leader,
Deng Hsiao-ping and his team cannot afford to ignore their warnings.
Already there are signs of retrenchment and retreat in many sectors.
But economic reform and the open-door policy will not be abandoned,
even though its progress will probably be full of twists and turns.

'Socialism in Chinese style' is in fact a phrase coined to save the face
of the Chinese Communist leaders who do not have the courage to
acknowledge openly that socialism has failed in China. They hope to
revitalize the State-owned industries with methods of management
copied from capitalist countries and to use market forces as a
substitute for central planning while retaining State ownership of those
industries. They want the Party-appointed managers, who are
bureaucrats on fixed salaries, to achieve the same degree of expertise
and commitment as the entrepreneurs of private industries in the West.
They want the workers to work much harder and more competitively
for bonuses and small increases in pay but reduced welfare benefits.
And they hope everybody will be motivated by patriotism to achieve
increased productivity and profit for the State but at the same time to
remain honest and incorruptible. Judging from the large number of
seemingly insoluble problems that have emerged, the reform measures
applied to industry have not brought about the same positive results as
have the agricultural reforms. Sooner or later, the Chinese Communist
Party leadership will have to face the hard choice either to renounce
socialism totally and free China's economy from bureaucratic control
or to go back to the old ways.

Constant change is an integral part of the Communist philosophy.
The Chinese leaders expect the people to rush headlong into whatever
experiment they wish to carry out, whether it be liberalization or
collectivization. For the whole thirty-six years of Communist rule, the
Party's policy has swung like a pendulum from left to right and back
again without stop. However, Communist China today is different in
one important aspect. She is no longer isolated and ostracized from
civilized international society. World opinion and the China policy of
major powers who are the source of foreign investment and trade can
and do influence the course of events in China. The abrupt crumbling
of the Anti-Spiritual Pollution Campaign in 1984 was mainly due to
the unfavourable reaction abroad. With increased contacts and better

understanding of the rest of the world, the Chinese leaders are shedding their paranoia. Many of the students returning to China after studying in Western universities will one day occupy positions of influence. China is now much more conscious of her image in the eyes of the world and is anxious to project a good one. Those wishing for progress and stability in China could have their voices heard.

Index

Index

William Dalrymple

In Xanadu

A Quest

'A classic.'   *Sunday Express*

'William Dalrymple's *In Xanadu* carries us breakneck from a pre-dawn glimmer in the Holy Sepulchre right across Asia to a bleak wind in Kubla Khan's palace . . . it is learned and comic, and a most gifted first book touched by the spirits of Kinglake, Robert Byron and E. Waugh.'

Patrick Leigh Fermor, 'Books of the Year', *Spectator*

'*In Xanadu* is, without doubt, one of the best travel books produced in the last 20 years. It is witty and intelligent, brilliantly observed, deftly constructed and extremely entertaining . . . Dalrymple's gift for transforming ordinary, humdrum experience into something extraordinary and timeless suggests that he will go from strength to strength.'

Alexander Maitland, *Scotland on Sunday*

'The new Theroux.'   *Today*

'Exuberant.'   Colin Thubron

'Dalrymple writes beautifully, is amazingly erudite, brave and honest, and can be extremely funny.'

Quentin Crewe, *Sunday Telegraph*

'The delightful, and funny, surprise mystery tour of the year.'

Sir Alec Guinness, *Sunday Times*

'Erudite, adventurous and amusing . . . reminded me of Evelyn Waugh.'   Piers Paul Read

 flamingo

Where the Indus is Young
Walking to Baltistan

Dervla Murphy

'Altogether the most appallingly fascinating travel book I have ever read'   JAN MORRIS, *The Times*

Dervla Murphy and her six-year-old daughter Rachel walked into the Karakoram mountains in the heart of the western Himalayas and along the perilous Indus Gorge. Accompanied only by a gallant polo pony, they endured conditions that tested the limits of their ingenuity, fortitude and courage.

Yet even when beset by crumbling tracks over bottomless chasms, an assault by a lascivious Kashmiri, the unnerving melancholy of the Balts – and Rachel's continual probing questions – this formidable traveller retained her enthusiasm for her surroundings and her sense of humour. Hair-raising, gloriously subjective and with the quirky vitality of fiction, the resulting book is a classic of travel writing.

'The lasting impression left by this book is one of sheer joy'
                                        COLIN THUBRON, *Sunday Telegraph*

'It is her real reverence for natural beauty that gives her writing its special quality . . . Dervla Murphy is a writer one should be profoundly grateful for'   *Daily Telegraph*

'Miss Murphy is a connoisseur of lost Arcadias'
                                                Times Literary Supplement

ISBN: 0 00 654801 6

Christa Paula

The Road to Miran

Travels in the Forbidden Zone of Xinjiang

Christa Paula, an intrepid young student of Central Asian art and archaeology, set off in 1989 to explore an area closed to Westerners as well as to most Chinese, and one which is firmly under military rule. Tall and blonde, she travelled for the most part incognito, disguised in a Pathan cap, old grey jacket and big padded trousers.

Her goal was Miran, the ancient Buddhist site of fabulous second-century wall paintings. (The last Westerner to set foot in Miran was Sir Aurel Stein, in 1914.) In the company of Chang, a maverick taxi-driver, Christa Paula travelled through an area dotted with nuclear testing sites, forced labour camps and mines in which prisoners dig and process asbestos without protective clothing. She discovered that villages which exist on maps are now radiation-contaminated ghost towns, and she witnessed everywhere the seeds of discontent and political unrest.

Combining scholarship with exotic adventure and an unusual love affair, *The Road To Miran* is a travel book of rare distinction – a journey as much through China's past as through its present.

ISBN 0 00 638368 8

Jung Chang

Wild Swans

Three Daughters of China

Winner of the 1992 NCR Book Award

'It is impossible to exaggerate the importance of this book.'   Mary Wesley

'*Wild Swans* is a very unusual masterpiece. Everything about it is extraordinary.'   Minette Marrin, *Sunday Telegraph*

'Mesmerising.'   Antonia Fraser, *The Times*

'Immensely moving and unsettling; an unforgettable portrait of the brain-death of a nation.'   J. G. Ballard, *Sunday Times*

Combining the intimacy of memoir with the epic sweep of a great novel, *Wild Swans* tells the story of three women whose lives mirror the tumultuous history of twentieth-century China. As the years pass in this beautifully detailed family tapestry, we see three lives unfolding one from the other, through love, tragedy and renewal.

Jung Chang's grandmother was born in 1909. Her feet were bound, and at the age of fifteen she was given to a warlord general as a concubine. Her daughter grew up in Manchuria, under Japanese and then Russian occupation. She became active in the Communist underground, and with Mao's triumph she and her husband became senior officials, helping to launch a social revolution unlike any the world has ever seen. Jung Chang, their daughter, grew up within the privileged circles of China's Communist elite, but the savagery and destructiveness of the Cultural Revolution, and the denunciation and persecution of her parents, led her to question Mao himself, an unimaginable step in a country ruled by terror and utterly devoid of information about the outside world.

Breathtaking in its scope, unforgettable in its descriptions of China's long nightmare, *Wild Swans* is both an important work of contemporary history and an extraordinary testimony to the human spirit.

ISBN 0 00 637492 1